MAPPING THE SOCIAL LANDSCAPE

Readings in Sociology

Mapping the Social Landscape

Readings in Sociology

SUSAN J. FERGUSON
Grinnell College

MAYFIELD PUBLISHING COMPANY
Mountain View, California
London • Toronto

Library of Congress Cataloging-in-Publication Data
Mapping the social landscape : readings in sociology / [edited by]
   Susan J. Ferguson.
     p.   cm.
   ISBN 1-55934-551-9
   1. Social institutions.   2. Socialization.   3. Equality.
   4. Social change.   5. Sociology.   I. Ferguson, Susan J.
   HM131.M23   1996
   301—dc20   95-37936
                                              CIP

Manufactured in the United States of America

10 9 8 7 6 5 4 3 2

Mayfield Publishing Company
1280 Villa Street
Mountain View, California 94041

Sponsoring editor, Serina Beauparlant; *production editor,* Merlyn Holmes; *copyeditor,* Patterson Lamb; *text designer,* Linda M. Robertson; *cover designer,* Jeanne M. Schreiber; *cover photographs,* Lori Eanes; *art manager,* Robin Mouat; *illustrator,* Joan Carol; *manufacturing manager,* Amy Folden. The text was set in 10/12 Book Antiqua by G&S Typesetters, Inc. and printed on 45# Glatfelter Ecolocote by Malloy Lithographing Inc.

Text credits appear on a continuation of the copyright page, p. C-1.

 This book was printed on recycled, acid-free paper.

With love to my grandmother, Edna Catherine Clark, who always believed that an education would open the doors of the world to me. She was right.

Contents

PART II   CULTURE

PART III   SOCIALIZATION

PART IV   GROUPS AND SOCIAL STRUCTURE

GENDER

RACE AND ETHNICITY

PART VII   SOCIAL INSTITUTIONS   357

PART VIII   SOCIAL CHANGE

Preface

As the title suggests, *Mapping the Social Landscape* is about exploration and discovery. It means taking a closer look at a complex, ever changing social world in which locations, pathways, and boundaries are not fixed. Because sociology describes and explains our social surroundings, it enables us to understand this shifting landscape. Thus, sociology is about discovering society and discovering ourselves. The purpose of this anthology is to introduce the discipline of sociology and to convey the excitement and the challenge of the sociological enterprise.

Although a number of readers are already available for students in introductory sociology, I have yet to find one that exposes students to the broad diversity of scholarship, perspectives, and authorship within the field of sociology. This diversity goes beyond recognizing gender, racial-ethnic, and social class differences to acknowledging a plurality of voices and views within the discipline. Like other anthologies, this one includes some of the classic works by authors such as Karl Marx, Emile Durkheim, Max Weber, W.E.B. Du Bois, C. Wright Mills, and Talcott Parsons; in addition, however, I have also drawn from a wide range of contemporary scholarship, some of which provides newer treatments of traditional concepts. This diversity of viewpoints and approaches should encourage students to evaluate and analyze the ideas and research findings presented.

In addition, because I find it invaluable in my own teaching to use examples from personal experiences to enable students to see the connection between "private troubles and public issues," as Mills phrased it, I have included a few personal narratives to help students comprehend how social forces affect individual lives. Thus, this anthology includes classic as well as contemporary writings, and the voices of other social scientists who render provocative sociological insights. The readings also exemplify functionalist, conflict, and symbolic interactionist perspectives and different types of research methodology. Each article is preceded by a brief headnote that sets the context within which the reader should seek to understand the sociological work. Thus, the selections communicate an enthusiasm for sociology while illustrating sociological concepts, theories, and methods.

During the last 25 years, sociology has benefited from a rich abundance of creative scholarship, but many of these original works have not been adequately presented in textbooks or readers. I believe an introductory anthology needs to reflect the new questions concerning research and theory within the discipline. Moreover, I find that students enjoy reading the actual research and words of sociologists. This anthology, therefore, includes many "cutting edge" pieces of sociological scholarship and some of the very recent publications by recognized social analysts. Current issues are examined, including men's changing roles within the family, the effects of globalization, the political influence of corporate PACs, the anti-abortion movement, the rise of paramilitary subcultures, and environmental degradation. In essence, I have attempted, not to break new ground, but instead to compile a collection that provides a fresh, innovative look at the discipline.

I have written an accompanying test manual that contains numerous examination and discussion questions for each reading. As the editor of this anthology, I developed these items with the goal of helping instructors test students' understanding of key sociological concepts and themes.

The completion of this book involved the labor and support of many people. Among them are my colleagues in the sociology department at Grinnell College. Thank you, Kent McClelland, Kesho Scott, Sylvia Thorson-Smith, and Camille Zubrinsky, for discussing current sociological research with me. My special gratitude goes to Chris Hunter for allowing me to regularly raid his bookshelves and for listening to the ongoing decisions that needed to be made concerning the book. I am additionally indebted to the Carnegie secretaries, Faun Black, Vicki Bunnell, and Karen Groves, for the time they spent typing and photocopying portions of the manuscript. My student library assistants, Alice Gates and Adrienne van der Valk, are also commended for carrying innumerable pounds of books between my office and the library. Moreover, I appreciate the help of Bertha Camacho, Heather Farber, and Holly Pfitsch in reading the page proofs. I also am grateful to Grinnell College for generous research support.

Many sociologists reviewed earlier drafts of the manuscript and gave me valuable observations. Offering helpful insights at the first-draft stage was Agnes Riedmann who suggested several key pieces for inclusion. Other suggestions for selections were made by Joan Ferrante, Martin Marger, and Michael Messner. I appreciate their interest.

My special thanks go to Arnold Arluke, Northeastern University; Joanne M. Badagliacco, University of Kentucky; Gary L. Brock, Southwest Missouri State University; Tom Gerschick, Illinois State University; Thomas B. Gold, University of California at Berkeley; Jack Harkins, College of DuPage; Paul Kamolnick, East Tennessee State University; Peter Kivisto, Augustana College; Fred Kniss, Loyola University, Chicago; Diane E. Levy, University of North Carolina at Wilmington; Peter Meiksins, Cleveland State University; Roslyn Arlin Mickelson, University of North Carolina at Charlotte; and Carol Ray, San Jose State University. As a team of reviewers, your detailed comments were enormously helpful in tightening and refining the manuscript. More important, your voices reflect your rich and varied experiences gained from teaching introductory sociology.

At Mayfield Publishing, I benefited from the creative and patient efforts of several individuals, including Merlyn Holmes, Jeanne M. Schreiber, Pamela Trainer, and Julie Wildhaber. I also want to acknowledge the detailed work of the copy editor, Patterson Lamb. My highest appreciation goes to Serina Beauparlant, the acquisitions editor. Serina, if I am a clutch hitter, you are the phenomenal batting coach. I could not have asked for a more thoughtful and attentive sociology editor. Thank you.

Last and with much gratitude, I acknowledge my friend and colleague, Gretchen Stiers, who patiently listened via telephone and e-mail while I went on about this project for several months. Thank you, dear friend, for all your insights and support.

About the Contributors

Elijah Anderson (Reading #8) is the Charles and William L. Day Professor of the Social Sciences at the University of Pennsylvania. An expert on the sociology of black America, he is the author of the highly regarded sociological work, *A Place on the Corner: A Study of Black Streetcorner Men* (1978) and numerous articles on the black experience, including "Of Old Heads and Young Boys: Notes on the Urban Black Experience" (1986), commissioned by the National Research Council's Committee on the Streets of Black Americans; "Sex Codes and Family Life among Inner-City Youth" (1989); and "The Code of the Streets," which was the cover story in the May 1994 issue of the *Atlantic Monthly*. For his recently published ethnographic study, *Streetwise: Race, Class, and Change in an Urban Community* (1990), he was honored with the Robert E. Park Award of the American Sociological Association. He has also won the Lindback Award for Distinguished Teaching at the University of Pennsylvania. Anderson is associate director of Penn's Center for Urban Ethnography and associate editor of *Qualitative Sociology*.

John Anderson and *Molly Moore* (Reading #27) met when they were both hired by the *Washington Post* in 1981. They married each other 11 years later and now are one of three husband-wife reporting teams on the *Post*'s Foreign Staff. They were the South Asia correspondents, based in New Delhi, from the summer of 1992 to the summer of 1995, and are scheduled to become the Mexico City correspondents in January, 1996.

Leon Anderson (Reading #42) was a youth worker and journalist in Alaska before entering graduate school at the University of Texas in 1983. In 1984, David Snow and he began a study of the homeless in Austin, Texas that culminated in their book *Down on Their Luck* (1993). Anderson is associate professor and vice chair in the Department of Sociology and Anthropology at Ohio University in Athens, Ohio, where he is doing research on college students who sell blood plasma.

Richard J. Barnet (Reading #38) is the author of *Global Reach* (with Ronald E. Müller) and 10 other books. His articles have appeared in the *New Yorker, Harper's,* the *New York Times,* and numerous other periodicals. He lives in Washington, D.C.

Dallas A. Blanchard (Reading #45) obtained his Ph.D. in the sociology of religion and social ethics from Boston University. Blanchard is a retired United

Methodist minister who pastored churches in racially changing communities in Alabama, Kentucky, Tennessee, and Rhode Island. During his 17 years as a minister, Blanchard experienced the Selma-Montgomery March, the merging of white and black congregations, and numerous Ku Klux Klan confrontations. Blanchard also has served on the Alabama Advisory Committee to the U.S. Commission on Civil Rights. Currently, he is professor and chair of sociology at the University of West Florida.

Kathleen M. Blee (Reading #17) is associate professor of sociology at the University of Kentucky. Blee hopes that her research on the politics of racial hatred and religious bigotry might help in the development of effective strategies to counteract the growth of organized racism in the United States. She is presently studying the involvement of women in modern-day white supremacist movements, including the Ku Klux Klan and neo-Nazi and racist skinhead groups.

Robert D. Bullard (Reading #56) is Ware Professor of Sociology and director of the Environmental Justice Resource Center at Clark Atlanta University. He is the author of *Dumping in Dixie: Race, Class and Environmental Quality* (1990), *Confronting Environmental Racism: Voices from the Grassroots* (1993), *Unequal Protection: Environmental Justice and Communities of Color* (1994), and *Residential Apartheid: The American Legacy* (1994).

Mary Beth Caschetta (Reading #30) is a treatment advocate for low-income HIV-positive women in New York City. A medical sociologist and lesbian feminist, she has published articles concerning women's health in the *Journal of the American Medical Women's Association,* the *Sex Information and Education Council of the U.S. Report,* the *New England Journal of Medicine,* and the *Encyclopedia of Childbirth.*

John Cavanagh (Reading #38) is co-author of seven books on the world economy and is currently a Fellow at the Institute for Policy Studies and the Transnational Institute in Washington, D.C., where he lives.

Kathy Charmaz (Reading #21) is professor and chair of the sociology department at Sonoma State University. Her research interests include the experience of chronic illness, the development and change of self, and the sociology of time. These interests are reflected in her book, *Good Days, Bad Days: The Self in Chronic Illness and Time* (1991), which won the 1992 Charles Horton Cooley Award from the Society for the Study of Symbolic Interaction and the 1992 Distinguished Scholarship Award from the Pacific Sociological Association. Currently, she is engaged in several projects including an empirical study of bodily experience in health and illness, didactic works on qualitative research, and epistemological critiques of postmodernism.

Dan Clawson (Reading #36) began studying campaign finance in the early 1980s in an attempt to figure out why and how politics shifted so decisively to conservatism. Business actions, he feels, are usually politically decisive but are generally neglected by students, the media, and many scholars. Clawson is professor of sociology at the University of Massachusetts at Amherst and editor of *Contemporary Sociology,* the book review journal of the American Sociological Association.

Patricia Hill Collins (Reading #54) received her B.A. and Ph.D. degrees from Brandeis University and an M.A.T. degree from Harvard University. While her specialties in sociology include such diverse areas as sociology of knowledge, organizational theory, social stratification, and work and occupations, her research and scholarship have dealt primarily with issues of gender, race, and social class, specifically relating to African American women. Her first book, *Black Feminist Thought: Knowledge, Consciousness, and the Politics of Empowerment,* published in 1990, has won many awards, including the C. Wright Mills Award. Her second book, *Race, Class, and Gender: An Anthology* (edited with Margaret Andersen) is widely used in undergraduate classrooms throughout the United States.

Randall Collins (Reading #52) became a sociologist during the civil rights and antiwar movements of the 1960s. He switched from psychology to sociology because it seemed more relevant and interesting. Since that time, he has worked on topics in social conflict (such as the downfall of the Soviet Union) and on the nonrational and emotional basis of solidarity (such as love). He is the author of numerous books and articles including *Conflict Sociology* (1975), *The Credential Society* (1979), and *Four Sociological Traditions: Selected Readings* (1994). Collins is professor of sociology at the University of California, Riverside.

Peter W. Cookson, Jr. (Reading #49) is associate provost at Adelphi University. His current work centers on education reform and applying sociological principles to school policy. He is currently writing a book about education policy for Yale University Press.

Mary Crow Dog, née Mary Brave Bird (Reading #48), grew up fatherless in a one-room cabin without plumbing or electricity, on a Sioux reservation in South Dakota. Her autobiography, *Lakota Woman,* records her memories of growing up female and Native American on the impoverished margins of a racist mainstream America; it also celebrates her liberation from this legacy of despair through activist politics, Native American religion, and childbirth during the occupation of Wounded Knee in 1973. Her life history shows her determination against all odds to save herself in a world that has been hostile to America's First Peoples for centuries.

James R. Curtis (Reading #46) received his doctorate from UCLA and has co-authored award-winning books on Cuban Americans and the Mexican border cities. His article in this volume explores the premise that common features in the built environment, such as yard shrines, reflect and can be used to interpret the culture from which they sprang. *Santería,* the Afro-

Cuban cult described in the article, served as the basis for Curtis' crime thriller novel, *Shango* (1996). He teaches geography at California State University, Long Beach.

G. William Domhoff (Reading #24) says he never had any interest in politics or power until he was in his mid-20s, when he already had finished a Ph.D. in psychology with a dissertation on that most subjective and personal of experiences, dreams. He says he became interested in the topic of the ruling upper class in America mostly through a series of little things here and there rather than a major revelation. He thinks studying both dreams and power is a nice counterbalance, and he teaches courses on both subjects at the University of California, Santa Cruz, where he has been since 1965.

W.E.B. Du Bois (1868–1963) (Reading #31) was born in Great Barrington, Massachusetts. He studied at Fisk University before receiving his Ph.D. from Harvard in 1895. Du Bois was a leading social theorist on race issues in the United States, and his study, *The Philadelphia Negro* (1899), is considered to be a classic empirical sociological work. Another of his works, *Souls of Black Folk* (1903), stirred up controversy within the African American community. Du Bois went on to organize the Niagara Movement (1905–1910), which developed into the NAACP, and he also was active in the Pan-African movement. Du Bois moved to Ghana in 1961, where he died on August 27, 1963, the day of the civil rights march on Washington, D.C.

Kathryn Marie Dudley (Reading #40) is assistant professor of American Studies at Yale University. She is a cultural anthropologist who specializes in the ethnographic study of communities and institutions in the contemporary United States. Her research focuses on the cultural consequences of economic change.

Mitchell Duneier (Reading #16) is assistant professor of sociology at the University of California, Santa Barbara, and University of Wisconsin, Madison, where he is also affiliated with the Institute for Research on Poverty. He is the author of *Slim's Table: Race, Respectability, and Masculinity*, which won the 1994 Distinguished Publication Award of the American Sociological Association. Currently, he is working on a movie with Spike Lee based on *Slim's Table*.

Èmile Durkheim (1858–1917) (Reading #43) was born in Lorraine, France. Durkheim studied cultural anthropology before he began teaching pedagogy and social science at the University of Bordeaux in 1887. In 1902, he was appointed to the Sorbonne in Paris. Durkheim designed early courses around the concept of social solidarity, and he founded the *Ánnee Sociologique* and the French school of Durkheimian sociology. His famous works include his dissertation, *The Division of Labor in Society* (1893), *Rules of Sociological Method* (1895), and *Suicide* (1898). An excerpt from Durkheim's last work, *The Elementary Forms of the Religious Life* (1912), appears in this volume. Durkheim's premature death in 1917, at the age of 59, has been attributed to the grief he felt from losing his son two years earlier.

Gwynne Dyer (Reading #14) is a free-lance journalist who is the author and narrator of the PBS National Television Series, *War.* "Anybody's Son Will Do" is an excerpt from the book based on that series.

Friedrich Engels (1820–1895) (Reading #39) was born in Barmen, Germany. During his youth he studied mercantilism, jurisprudence, religion, and history. In 1842, Engels moved to Manchester, where, during the 1840s, he published several articles that criticized social and political conditions in England. It was through his writing that he met Karl Marx; after corresponding, the two met in Paris during the fall of 1844. This meeting was the beginning of a loyal friendship and fruitful scholarly collaboration. Marx and Engels were co-authors of numerous works, including *The German Ideology* (1845–1846) and the *Manifesto of the Communist Party* (1848); an excerpt of the latter work is included in this volume. Engels' most important work, *The Origin of the Family, Private Property and the State* (1884), is a critical examination of the history of private property, the family, and the subjugation of women. As such, it is considered a fundamental work in feminist theory. Before dying of esophageal cancer in 1895, Engels devoted his last years to editing and defending Marx's final works, including *Capital.*

Richard Erdoes (Reading #48) is the co-author of *Lame Deer: Seeker of Visions, American Indian Myths and Legends,* and the author of more than 20 other titles. His most recent work is *A.D. 1000: Living on the Brink of Apocalypse.* He is an Austrian-born historian, ethnographer, and artist, and has contributed illustrations to many periodicals including *Time, Life, Fortune,* the *New York Times, Smithsonian,* and *Saturday Evening Post.* He was a finalist for the 1981 best Western nonfiction award by Western Writers of America for *Saloons of the Old West.* Erdoes has pursued the protection of indigenous people in North America throughout his entire life.

Kai Erikson (Reading #18) is professor of sociology at Yale University and author of *Wayward Puritans* (1966), *Everything in Its Path* (1976), and *A New Species of Trouble* (1994); the excerpt in this book was taken from the last of these.

Joe R. Feagin (Reading #34) (Ph.D., Harvard University, 1966) is professor of sociology at the University of Florida. He does research mainly on gender and racial discrimination. He recently completed a major research project on the discrimination faced by successful black Americans, a major portion of which was published in spring, 1994, as *Living with Racism: The Black Middle Class Experience.* Working with Professor Hernan Vera, he has recently published another book, *White Racism: The Basics* (1995). Feagin also has served as scholar-in-residence at the U.S. Commission on Civil Rights.

Donna Gaines (Reading #2) is a journalist, cultural sociologist, and New York state certified social worker. As a features writer she has published in *Rolling Stone, Long Island Monthly, Spin, Newsday,* and *Contemporaries.* Her first book, *Teenage Wasteland: Suburbia's Dead End Kids,* is internationally acclaimed and required reading for university course lists in several disciplines. *Rolling Stone* declared *Teenage Wasteland* "the best book on youth culture." Gaines received her doctoral degree in sociology at the State University of New York at Stony Brook, December 1990. She is currently a Senior Fellow at the Institute for Cultural Studies in New York City.

Herbert J. Gans (Reading #26) states: "I came to America in 1940 as a refugee from Nazi Germany and for the first few years here, my family and I were very poor: events that help to explain my later work. Being an immigrant evoked my lifelong curiosity about America and made me a sociologist; being a political refugee stimulated my concern with social injustice; and living in poverty helped create my enduring interest in doing something about it. That interest was furthered by the research done for my first book, *The Urban Villagers* (1962), which remains a popular undergraduate text; it is expressed once more in my ninth and latest book *The War on the Poor: The Underclass and Antipoverty Policy* (1995)."

Kathleen Gerson (Reading #28) grew up in Montgomery, Alabama, and San Francisco, California, where her involvement in the civil rights and women's movements fueled her interest in sociology, social policy, and social change. She attended Stanford University as an undergraduate and received her Ph.D. from the University of California at Berkeley in 1981. Since then, she has taught at New York University, where she helped found the Women and Gender Studies Program. She is currently professor and director of undergraduate studies in the sociology department. Her book, *No Man's Land: Men's Changing Commitments to Family and Work* (1993), is a study of how and why men's lives are changing in the wake of the gender revolution at home and at work. It extends the framework developed in her earlier book on how women choose between work and family commitments, *Hard Choices: How Women Decide about Work, Career, and Motherhood* (1985). She lives in Park Slope, Brooklyn, with her husband, John Mollenkopf, and their daughter, Emily.

J. William Gibson (Reading #9) teaches sociology at California State University, Long Beach. He is the author of two books, *The Perfect War: Technowar in Vietnam* (1986) and *Warrior Dreams: Paramilitary Culture in Post-Vietnam America* (1994); he is co-editor of *Making War/Making Peace: Social Foundations of Violent Conflict* (1989).

Robert Granfield (Reading #13) graduated from Northeastern University in 1989 and has been in the Department of Sociology at the University of Denver for six years. He developed an interest in the legal profession while he was in graduate school and initiated research on legal education that led to his dissertation and a book, *Making Elite Lawyers: Visions of Law at Harvard and Beyond.* In addition to this work, he has published articles on the sociology of drugs, the products liability law, and social theory.

Robert Hummer (Reading #22) is assistant professor of sociology at Louisiana State University. His work currently centers on how social inequality influences the health and mortality levels of different populations. Outside of sociology, he loves to travel with his wife and three-year-old daughter, enjoys fishing, and tries to work in an occasional-to-regular dose of ESPN.

Robin Leidner (Reading #41), associate professor of sociology at the University of Pennsylvania, was once a Jeopardy! champion. While researching *Fast Food, Fast Talk,* she not only put in her time at McDonald's, but also found herself chanting, "I feel healthy! I feel happy! I feel TERRIFIC!" with a group of life insurance sales trainees. Before becoming a sociologist, she spent several years acting and writing for RIFT, the Rhode Island Feminist Theatre.

William F. Lewis (Reading #7) received his Ph.D. in anthropology from the New School for Social Research, and had, in addition, graduate degrees in music, theology, and philosophy. His work on the Rastafarian movement and on cultural and legal pluralism was presented in papers at many anthropological meetings and in scholarly journals; he was a Mellon Seminar participant in 1990. Lewis was a member of the Society for Humanistic Anthropology, and as a Franciscan Brother, he strove to bring the perspectives of humanist cultural anthropology to his church community.

Judith Lorber (Reading #11) has taught courses in gender for 25 years at Brooklyn College and the Graduate Center, City University of New York, starting with Courtship and Marriage and ending with Sociology of Gender. She is the author of *Paradoxes of Gender* (1994) and *Women Physicians: Careers, Status and Power* (1984). In 1986, she founded a new journal, *Gender & Society,* which is still going strong.

Martin N. Marger (Reading #37) is associate professor of sociology at Michigan State University. Marger is the author of *Elites and Masses: An Introduction to Political Sociology* (1987), and he co-edited *Power in Modern Societies* (1993) with the late Marvin E. Olsen.

Patricia Yancey Martin (Reading #22) teaches the sociology of gender, organizations, and work at Florida State University. Her interest in undergraduate student culture includes the social, service, and political organizations to which students belong. She has studied services provided for rape victims in 130 organizations in Florida and is currently interviewing men and women about gender and race-ethnicity in Fortune 500 companies that compete for markets, growth, and profits in a global capitalist economy.

Karl Marx (1818–1883) (Reading #39) was born in Trier in the Prussian Rhineland. He was a prodigy, receiving his doctorate in philosophy from the University of Jena at the age of 23. Marx could not obtain a university position in Germany because of his association with the Young Hegelians, who were considered heretics. He left Germany in 1843, and after living in exile in Paris, Brussels, and Cologne, he moved his family to London. Marx devoted his life to the study of law, history, morality, and the political economy. His scholarly work and brief employment as a journalist did not provide much income, so for most of his life, Marx was dependent on the financial help and friendship of Friedrich Engels. Together they collaborated on many works, including the *Manifesto of the Communist Party* (see Reading #39). Marx is known for his contributions to socialist thought, his synthesis of philosophical knowledge, and his theory of society and history. From his early works, such as the *Economic and Philosophic Manuscripts* (1844), to *Capital* (1867–1879), Marx has left a rich legacy of social thought.

Doug McAdam (Reading #4) teaches sociology at the University of Arizona in Tucson. His research on the civil rights movement includes *Political Process and the Development of Black Insurgency* (1982) and *Freedom Summer* (1988). When he is not "pushing back the frontiers of science," he enjoys playing basketball, exploring Anasazi ruins, and backpacking with his wife and two daughters.

Penelope A. McLorg (Reading #20) is a doctoral student in anthropology at Southern Illinois University at Carbondale. She is interested in the interplay between social and biological factors. Her recent publications involve eating disorders, infant feeding practices, and bone anatomy and measurement.

Michael A. Messner (Reading #12) played high school basketball, but then discovered as a college freshman that he was too short to play forward, too slow to play guard, but just the right size to warm the bench as his teammates played. Though today he still shoots some hoops, he spends the majority of his working hours as associate professor in the Department of Sociology and the Program for the Study of Women and Men in Society at the University of Southern California. Messner is the author of *Power at Play: Sports and the Problem of Masculinity* (1992), co-author of *Sex, Violence, and Power in Sports: Rethinking Masculinity* (1994), and co-editor of *Men's Lives* (1995). He is the father of two young sons.

Roslyn Arlin Mickelson (Reading #47) is associate professor of sociology and adjunct associate professor of women's studies at the University of North Carolina at Charlotte. Her scholarly interests include the education of homeless children, educational policy, and the political economy of schooling—in particular, the ways that social class, race, and gender intersect and contribute to educational processes and outcomes. Her current research project is a National Science Foundation-supported investigation of business leaders and school reform.

C. Wright Mills (1916–1962) (Readings #1 and #35) was born in Waco, Texas. He received his Ph.D. in sociology from the University of Wisconsin and was professor of sociology at Columbia University. During his brief academic career, Mills became one of the best known and most controversial American sociologists. He believed that academics should be socially responsible and should speak out against social injustice. He criticized social conditions through his works, the most famous of which are *White Collar: The American Middle Classes* (1951) and *The Power Elite* (1956); Reading #35 is excerpted from the latter of these. A selection from Mills' *The Sociological Imagination* (1959) also appears in this volume. Mills died of a coronary condition at the young age of 45.

Cherríe Moraga (Reading #33) is a poet, essayist, editor, and playwright. She is author of *Loving in the War Years—Lo que nunca paso por sus labios,* a collection of essays and poetry. She co-edited the groundbreaking anthology *This Bridge Called My Back: Writing by Radical Women of Color* and *Cuentos,* the first collection of stories by Latina feminists published in the United States. She has completed three full-length plays: *Giving Up the Ghost,* which premiered at Theatre Rhinoceros in 1989; *Shadow of a Man,* presented by Brava! for Women in the Arts and the Eureka Theatre in 1990; and *Heroes and Saints,* which was commissioned by the Los Angeles Theatre Center and produced by Brava! in 1992.

Alan Neustadtl (Reading #36) is associate professor of sociology at the University of Maryland at College Park. He was drawn to studying campaign finance after reading books as an undergraduate by early researchers like Floyd Hunter (*Community Power Structure*), C. Wright Mills (*The Power Elite*), and G. William Domhoff (*The Powers That Be* and *Bohemian Grove and Other Retreats*). He is co-author of *Money Talks: Corporate PACS and Political Influence* (1992) and has published research articles on political sociology in such journals as *American Sociological Review, American Journal of Sociology, Social Forces, Social Science Research,* and *Social Science Quarterly.*

Katherine S. Newman (Reading #25) is professor of anthropology at Columbia University where she has been teaching since 1981. She has written several books about the ways that national trends in the economy impact people locally: in their family lives and on the job. As an anthropologist, Newman is particularly interested in the ways that culture—values and beliefs—filters these structural trends, causing people to feel responsible for their own problems yet unable to reverse the insecurity they have experienced. She is especially interested in how economic forces shape the cultural expectations of different generations in American society.

Talcott Parsons (1902–1979) (Reading #51) studied economics in the United States and England before discovering the writings of Max Weber in Germany. Parsons translated several of Weber's works, including *The Protestant Ethic and the Spirit of Capitalism.* After returning to the United States in 1927, Parsons began teaching in the economics department at Harvard University before joining the sociology department at the invitation of Pitirim Sorokin, where he remained until his retirement in 1973. Parsons' seminal work *The Structure of Social Action* (1937) renewed attention to sociological theory and research, and during the 1940s and 1950s, Parsonian functionalism dominated

American sociology. An excerpt from his famous functional analysis of the family, "The American Family: Its Relations to Personality and to the Social Structure," is included here as Reading #51. Parsons served as chair of Harvard's Department of Social Relations from 1946 to 1956, and was president of the American Sociological Association in 1949. He died in 1979.

Caroline Hodges Persell (Reading #49) became aware of the profound social inequalities in the United States as a teenager, while riding the train through Harlem and Westchester County, New York. That interest led her to sociology; she is professor of sociology at New York University where she has taught for 24 years. She particularly enjoys the very diverse students who attend NYU. When not teaching or doing sociological research, she enjoys her family, music, sports, and gardening.

George Ritzer (Reading #55) is an acknowledged expert in the field of social theory and the sociology of work and has served as chair of the American Sociological Association's Sections on Theoretical Sociology and Organizations and Occupations. A distinguished scholar-teacher at the University of Maryland, Professor Ritzer has been honored with that institution's Teaching Excellence award. Two of his most recent books include *Metatheorizing in Sociology* and *The McDonaldization of Society.*

Mary Romero (Reading #3) lives in Tempe, Arizona, where she is currently writing a book about the children of private household workers. Her study of Chicana domestics, *Maid in the U.S.A.,* was published in 1992. She is a professor at Arizona State University where she teaches sociology in the Office of Chicana and Chicano Studies.

Wade Clark Roof (Reading #44) is the J. F. Rowny Professor of Religion and Society at the University of California at Santa Barbara. He is currently conducting research in Los Angeles on Generation X and religion and writing a book on Buddhists, Muslims, and Evangelical Christians in Southern California.

David L. Rosenhan (Reading #19) received his Ph.D. in psychology from Columbia University. His books include *Foundations of Abnormal Psychology* (with P. London), *Theory and Research in Abnormal Psychology,* and *Abnormal Psychology* (with Martin E. P. Seligman). He is professor of psychology and law at Stanford University.

Barbara Katz Rothman (Reading #30) is professor of sociology at Baruch College and the Graduate Center of the City University of New York. She is the author of *In Labor: Women and Power in the Birthplace,* a comparison of the medical and midwifery models of childbirth, and of *The Tentative Pregnancy: Prenatal Diagnosis and the Future of Motherhood,* a study of women's experiences with amniocentesis and selective abortion. Her most recent works are *Recreating Motherhood: Ideology and Technology in a Patriarchal Society,* a feminist analysis of changing ideas about motherhood in America, and *Centuries of Solace,* with Wendy Simonds.

Lillian B. Rubin (Reading #32) is an internationally recognized author and social scientist who was born in Philadelphia, grew up in New York City, and moved to California as a young adult. Since receiving her doctorate in 1971, she has authored numerous books, including *Worlds of Pain: Life in the Working Class* (1976), *Intimate Strangers: Men & Women Together* (1983), and *Families on the Fault Line: America's Working Class Speaks about the Family, the Economy, Race, and Ethnicity* (1994). Her new book, *Fall Down Seven Times, Get Up Eight,* presents case histories of people who have transcended very difficult pasts; it will be published in March, 1996. Rubin currently lives in San Francisco where she is a practicing psychotherapist and Senior Research Fellow at the Institute for the Study of Social Change at the University of California, Berkeley.

Gabrielle Sándor (Reading #5) has written numerous feature articles for the journal, *American Demographics.* The topics of her articles range from cleaning products and hearing aids to college costs and intermarriage. She currently lives in Ithaca, New York.

Denise Scott (Reading #36) is a Ph.D. candidate at the University of Massachusetts, Amherst. Committed to the principles and practices of equal opportunity and justice, her current research focuses on class and gender inequality and issues of power. As an outgrowth of a larger project examining the political behavior of business, Scott's dissertation focuses on women's involvement in corporate-government relations.

Melvin P. Sikes (Reading #34) is a clinical psychologist and consultant. He grew up in Gary, Indiana, where he worked in the steel mills until the war, when he served as one of the Tuskegee airmen. After the war, he attended the University of Chicago and earned a degree in clinical psychology. He has worked in private practice, taught at the Department of Educational Psychology at the University of Texas at Austin, was dean of a couple African American colleges, practiced at a Veterans Administration hospital, and did work in drug and alcohol abuse programs as well as in a Houston police training program. Sikes says that his goal for the book *Living with Racism: The Black Middle-Class Experience* was not so much to fight racism but to help people understand how it affects them and to encourage them to uphold this country's principles of equality and justice.

Alan Simmons (Reading #58) is currently involved in research on the forces shaping Guatemalan and Salvadoran refugee repatriation and development efforts. He also is studying the role of ethnicity and racism in the integration of Afro-Caribbean immigrants in North America. These studies reflect his long interest in international inequality, globalization, and the migration of refugees and workers. Simmons is director of the Graduate Programme in Sociology at York University in Toronto.

Stephen Samuel Smith (Reading #47) is assistant professor of political science at Winthrop University in Rock Hill, South Carolina. His interests include the politics of education, urban political economy, social movements, and program evaluation. Prior to completing his Ph.D., he spent 15 years doing factory work and labor organizing.

David A. Snow (Reading #42) is professor and head of sociology at the University of Arizona in Tucson. He received his Ph.D in sociology from the University of California, Los Angeles, and also has taught at Southern Methodist University in Dallas and the University of Texas in Austin. He is the author or co-author of over 50 articles and chapters on a range of topics, including homelessness, social movements, religious cults and conversion, and qualitative methods. He also is author of a number of books, including *Down on Their Luck: A Study of Homeless Street People,* which was co-written with Leon Anderson and has received several scholarly achievement awards.

Diane E. Taub (Reading #20) is associate professor of sociology at Southern Illinois University at Carbondale (SIUC). Her publications primarily concern the sociology of deviance, with a focus on the experiences of women. She has received several teaching awards, including the 1994 SIUC Outstanding Teacher Award.

Haunani-Kay Trask (Reading #10) is descended from the Pi'ilani line of Maui and the Kahakumakaliua line of Kaua'i. Her books include *From a Native Daughter: Colonialism and Sovereignty in Hawai'i* (1993) and *Light in the Crevice Never Seen* (1994). She co-produced the 1993 award-winning film, "Act of War: The Overthrow of the Hawaiian Nation." Trask is currently director of Hawaiian Studies at the University of Hawai'i at Manoa.

Jeffrey S. Victor (Reading #57) is professor of sociology at Jamestown Community College in Jamestown, New York. He received his Ph.D. from the State University of New York at Buffalo. He has previously published a book and articles in the areas of human sexuality and family relationships. His current research is focused on rumors, claims, and allegations about dangerous satanic cults and resultant threats to civil liberties. He is writing a book on this issue, tentatively titled *Witch-Hunt: The Making of a Contemporary Legend.*

Max Weber (1864–1920) (Reading #23) was born in Erfurt, Germany. Weber studied economics, history, and law at the University of Heidelberg before completing a Ph.D. thesis on medieval societies at the University of Berlin. In 1893, he was appointed to a chair in economics at the University of Freiburg, and in 1895, he transferred to the University of Heidelberg where he became a central figure among a group of scholars. Weber's famous work, *The Protestant Ethic and the Spirit of Capitalism* (1905), reveals his concern for rationality in the modern world. Weber also wrote extensively on bureaucracies, politics, power, and authority. An excerpt from his well-known essay "Class, Status, Party" appears in this volume. After years of struggling with mental health problems, Weber died at the age of 58 years.

Rose Weitz (Reading #6) is professor of sociology at Arizona State University. She is the author of *The Sociology of Health, Illness, and Health Care: A Critical Approach* (1995), *Life with AIDS* (1991), and co-author of *Labor Pains: Modern Midwives and Home Birth* (1988). Weitz is a founding member and past chairperson of the Sociologists' AIDS Network and is president-elect of Sociologists' for Women in Society. She has always believed that the personal is political.

Kath Weston (Reading #53) flirted with the prospect of becoming a mechanic before she became a member of the National Writers Union and associate professor of anthropology at Arizona State University West in Phoenix. With the money from the day job (mechanics) or a night-and-day job (academics), she wanted to write about the ways that sexuality is intertwined with race and class. In addition to *Families We Choose,* she has published a range of articles on queer topics, including "Get Thee to a Big City: Sexual Imaginary and the Great Gay Migration" and "Requiem for a Street Fighter." Her forthcoming book is titled, *Render Me, Gender Me: Lesbians Talk Sex, Class, Color, Nation, Studmuffins & Such.*

Christine L. Williams (Reading #29) is associate professor of sociology at the University of Texas. Williams first became interested in the topic of gender discrimination as a first-year college student in the 1970s, when she took a course entitled "The Sociology of Women." Back then, gender was considered something that affected only women. Today, most of her writings are about society's treatment of men and changing cultural definitions of masculinity. Her books include *Gender Differences at Work* (1989) and *"Doing Women's Work": Men in Non-Traditional Occupations* (1993). The article in this volume was expanded into a book, *Still a Man's World,* published in 1995.

Norma Williams (Reading #15) is associate professor of sociology and assistant vice president, director of the Multicultural Affairs Office, and director of the Multicultural Affairs Center at the University of North Texas. She is author of the monograph, *The Mexican American Family: Tradition and Change* (1990) and continues to write on family life and race and ethnic relations.

Wayne S. Wooden (Reading #50) is professor of sociology and coordinator of the Criminal Justice and Corrections Program at California State Polytechnic University, Pomona. His other published books, besides *Renegade Kids, Suburban Outlaws* (1995), include *Men behind Bars* (1982), *Children and Arson* (1984), and *Return to Paradise.*

Beverly H. Wright (Reading #56) is associate professor of sociology at Xavier University of Louisiana and directs the Deep South Center for Environmental Justice. Wright is a leading environmental justice scholar and advocate of university-community partnerships in addressing local environmental problems.

MAPPING THE SOCIAL LANDSCAPE

Readings in Sociology

Tell me the landscape in which you live, and I will tell you who you are.

José Ortega y Gasset

PART I

The Sociological Perspective

1

THE PROMISE

C. WRIGHT MILLS

The initial three selections examine the sociological perspective. The first of these is an excerpt from C. Wright Mills' (1916–1962) acclaimed book, *The Sociological Imagination.* Since its original publication in 1959, this text has been a required reading for most introductory sociology students around the world. Mills' sociological imagination perspective not only compels the best sociological analyses but also enables the sociologist and the individual to distinguish between "personal troubles" and "public issues." By separating these phenomena, we can better comprehend the sources of and solutions to social problems.

Nowadays men often feel that their private lives are a series of traps. They sense that within their everyday worlds, they cannot overcome their troubles, and in this feeling, they are often quite correct: What ordinary men are directly aware of and what they try to do are bounded by the private orbits in which they live; their visions and their powers are limited to the close-up scenes of job, family, neighborhood; in other milieux, they move vicariously and remain spectators. And the more aware they become, however vaguely, of ambitions and of threats which transcend their immediate locales, the more trapped they seem to feel.

Underlying this sense of being trapped are seemingly impersonal changes in the very structure of continent-wide societies. The facts of contemporary history are also facts about the success and the failure of individual men and women. When a society is industrialized, a peasant becomes a worker; a feudal lord is liquidated or becomes a businessman. When classes rise or fall, a man is employed or unemployed; when the rate of investment

---

This article was written in 1959 before scholars were sensitive to gender inclusivity in language. The references to masculine pronouns and men are, therefore, generic to both males and females and should be read as such. Please note that I have left the original author's language in this selection and other readings. —*Editor*

goes up or down, a man takes new heart or goes broke. When wars happen, an insurance salesman becomes a rocket launcher; a store clerk, a radar man; a wife lives alone; a child grows up without a father. Neither the life of an individual nor the history of a society can be understood without understanding both.

Yet men do not usually define the troubles they endure in terms of historical change and institutional contradiction. The well-being they enjoy, they do not usually impute to the big ups and downs of the societies in which they live. Seldom aware of the intricate connection between the patterns of their own lives and the course of world history, ordinary men do not usually know what this connection means for the kinds of men they are becoming and for the kinds of history making in which they might take part. They do not possess the quality of mind essential to grasp the interplay of man and society, of biography and history, of self and world. They cannot cope with their personal troubles in such ways as to control the structural transformations that usually lie behind them.

Surely it is no wonder. In what period have so many men been so totally exposed at so fast a pace to such earthquakes of change? That Americans have not known such catastrophic changes as have the men and women of other societies is due to historical facts that are now quickly becoming "merely history." The history that now affects every man is world history. Within this scene and this period, in the course of a single generation, one-sixth of mankind is transformed from all that is feudal and backward into all that is modern, advanced, and fearful. Political colonies are freed; new and less visible forms of imperialism installed. Revolutions occur; men feel the intimate grip of new kinds of authority. Totalitarian societies rise and are smashed to bits—or succeed fabulously. After two centuries of ascendancy, capitalism is shown up as only one way to make society into an industrial apparatus. After two centuries of hope, even formal democracy is restricted to a quite small portion of mankind. Everywhere in the underdeveloped world, ancient ways of life are broken up and vague expectations become urgent demands. Everywhere in the overdeveloped world, the means of authority and of violence become total in scope and bureaucratic in form. Humanity itself now lies before us, the super-nation at either pole concentrating its most coordinated and massive efforts upon the preparation of World War Three.

The very shaping of history now outpaces the ability of men to orient themselves in accordance with cherished values. And which values? Even when they do not panic, men often sense that older ways of feeling and thinking have collapsed and that newer beginnings are ambiguous to the point of moral stasis. Is it any wonder that ordinary men feel they cannot cope with the larger worlds with which they are so suddenly confronted? That they cannot understand the meaning of their epoch for their own lives? That—in defense of selfhood—they become morally insensible, trying to remain altogether private men? Is it any wonder that they come to be possessed by a sense of the trap?

———

It is not only information that they need—in this Age of Fact, information often dominates their attention and overwhelms their capacities to assimilate it. It is not only the skills of reason that they need—although their struggles to acquire these often exhaust their limited moral energy.

What they need, and what they feel they need, is a quality of mind that will help them to use information and to develop reason in order to achieve lucid summations of what is going on in the world and of what may be happening within themselves. It is this quality, I am going to contend, that journalists and scholars, artists and publics, scientists and editors are coming to expect of what may be called the sociological imagination.

———

The sociological imagination enables its possessor to understand the larger historical scene in terms of its meaning for the inner life and the external career of a variety of individuals. It enables him to take into account how individuals, in the welter of their daily experience, often become falsely conscious of their social positions. Within that welter, the framework of modern society is sought, and within that framework the psychologies of a variety of men and women are formulated. By such means the personal uneasiness of individuals is focused upon explicit troubles and the indifference of publics is transformed into involvement with public issues.

The first fruit of this imagination—and the first lesson of the social science that embodies it—is the idea that the individual can understand his own experience and gauge his own fate only by locating himself within his period, that he can know his own chances in life only by becoming aware of those of all individuals in his circumstances. In many ways it is a terrible lesson; in many ways a magnificent one. We do not know the limits of man's capacities for supreme effort or willing degradation, for agony or glee, for pleasurable brutality or the sweetness of reason. But in our time we have come to know that the limits of "human nature" are frighteningly broad. We have come to know that every individual lives, from one generation to the next, in some society; that he lives out a biography, and that he lives it out within some historical sequence. By the fact of his living he contributes, however minutely, to the shaping of this society and to the course of its history, even as he is made by society and by its historical push and shove.

The sociological imagination enables us to grasp history and biography and the relations between the two within society. That is its task and its promise. To recognize this task and this promise is the mark of the classic social analyst. It is characteristic of Herbert Spencer—turgid, polysyllabic, comprehensive; of E. A. Ross—graceful, muckraking, upright; of Auguste Comte and Emile Durkheim; of the intricate and subtle Karl Mannheim. It is the quality of all that is intellectually excellent in Karl Marx; it is the clue to

Thorstein Veblen's brilliant and ironic insight, to Joseph Schumpeter's many-sided constructions of reality; it is the basis of the psychological sweep of W. E. H. Lecky no less than of the profundity and clarity of Max Weber. And it is the signal of what is best in contemporary studies of man and society.

No social study that does not come back to the problems of biography, of history and of their intersections within a society has completed its intellectual journey. Whatever the specific problems of the classic social analysts, however limited or however broad the features of social reality they have examined, those who have been imaginatively aware of the promise of their work have consistently asked three sorts of questions:

1. What is the structure of this particular society as a whole? What are its essential components, and how are they related to one another? How does it differ from other varieties of social order? Within it, what is the meaning of any particular feature for its continuance and for its change?
2. Where does this society stand in human history? What are the mechanics by which it is changing? What is its place within and its meaning for the development of humanity as a whole? How does any particular feature we are examining affect, and how is it affected by, the historical period in which it moves? And this period—what are its essential features? How does it differ from other periods? What are its characteristic ways of history making?
3. What varieties of men and women now prevail in this society and in this period? And what varieties are coming to prevail? In what ways are they selected and formed, liberated and repressed, made sensitive and blunted? What kinds of "human nature" are revealed in the conduct and character we observe in this society in this period? And what is the meaning for "human nature" of each and every feature of the society we are examining?

Whether the point of interest is a great power state or a minor literary mood, a family, a prison, a creed—these are the kinds of questions the best social analysts have asked. They are the intellectual pivots of classic studies of man in society—and they are the questions inevitably raised by any mind possessing the sociological imagination. For that imagination is the capacity to shift from one perspective to another—from the political to the psychological; from examination of a single family to comparative assessment of the national budgets of the world; from the theological school to the military establishment; from considerations of an oil industry to studies of contemporary poetry. It is the capacity to range from the most impersonal and remote transformations to the most intimate features of the human self—and to see the relations between the two. Back of its use there is always the urge to know the social and historical meaning of the individual in the society and in the period in which he has his quality and his being.

That, in brief, is why it is by means of the sociological imagination that men now hope to grasp what is going on in the world, and to understand what is happening in themselves as minute points of the intersections of biography and history within society. In large part, contemporary man's self-conscious view of himself as at least an outsider, if not a permanent stranger, rests upon an absorbed realization of social relativity and of the transformative power of history. The sociological imagination is the most fruitful form of this self-consciousness. By its use men whose mentalities have swept only a series of limited orbits often come to feel as if suddenly awakened in a house with which they had only supposed themselves to be familiar. Correctly or incorrectly, they often come to feel that they can now provide themselves with adequate summations, cohesive assessments, comprehensive orientations. Older decisions that once appeared sound now seem to them products of a mind unaccountably dense. Their capacity for astonishment is made lively again. They acquire a new way of thinking, they experience a transvaluation of values: in a word, by their reflection and by their sensibility, they realize the cultural meaning of the social sciences.

Perhaps the most fruitful distinction with which the sociological imagination works is between "the personal troubles of milieu" and "the public issues of social structure." This distinction is an essential tool of the sociological imagination and a feature of all classic work in social science.

Troubles occur within the character of the individual and within the range of his immediate relations with others; they have to do with his self and with those limited areas of social life of which he is directly and personally aware. Accordingly, the statement and the resolution of troubles properly lie within the individual as a biographical entity and within the scope of his immediate milieu—the social setting that is directly open to his personal experience and to some extent his willful activity. A trouble is a private matter: Values cherished by an individual are felt by him to be threatened.

Issues have to do with matters that transcend these local environments of the individual and the range of his inner life. They have to do with the organization of many such milieux into the institutions of a historical society as a whole, with the ways in which various milieux overlap and interpenetrate to form the larger structure of social and historical life. An issue is a public matter: Some value cherished by publics is felt to be threatened. Often there is a debate about what that value really is and about what it is that really threatens it. This debate is often without focus if only because it is the very nature of an issue, unlike even widespread trouble, that it cannot very well be defined in terms of the immediate and everyday environments of ordinary men. An issue, in fact, often involves a crisis in institutional arrangements, and often too it involves what Marxists call "contradictions" or "antagonisms."

In these terms, consider unemployment. When, in a city of 100,000, only one man is unemployed, that is his personal trouble, and for its relief we properly look to the character of the man, his skills, and his immediate opportunities. But when in a nation of 50 million employees, 15 million men are unemployed, that is an issue, and we may not hope to find its solution within the range of opportunities open to any one individual. The very structure of opportunities has collapsed. Both the correct statement of the problem and the range of possible solutions require us to consider the economic and political institutions of the society, and not merely the personal situation and character of a scatter of individuals.

Consider war. The personal problem of war, when it occurs, may be how to survive it or how to die in it with honor; how to make money out of it; how to climb into the higher safety of the military apparatus; or how to contribute to the war's termination. In short, according to one's values, to find a set of milieux and within it to survive the war or make one's death in it meaningful. But the structural issues of war have to do with its causes; with what types of men it throws up into command; with its effects upon economic and political, family and religious institutions, with the unorganized irresponsibility of a world of nation-states.

Consider marriage. Inside a marriage a man and a woman may experience personal troubles, but when the divorce rate during the first four years of marriage is 250 out of every 1,000 attempts, this is an indication of a structural issue having to do with the institutions of marriage and the family and other institutions that bear upon them.

Or consider the metropolis—the horrible, beautiful, ugly, magnificent sprawl of the great city. For many upper-class people, the personal solution to "the problem of the city" is to have an apartment with private garage under it in the heart of the city, and forty miles out, a house by Henry Hill, garden by Garrett Eckbo, on a hundred acres of private land. In these two controlled environments—with a small staff at each end and a private helicopter connection—most people could solve many of the problems of personal milieux caused by the facts of the city. But all this, however splendid, does not solve the public issues that the structural fact of the city poses. What should be done with this wonderful monstrosity? Break it all up into scattered units, combining residence and work? Refurbish it as it stands? Or, after evacuation, dynamite it and build new cities according to new plans in new places? What should those plans be? And who is to decide and to accomplish whatever choice is made? These are structural issues; to confront them and to solve them requires us to consider political and economic issues that affect innumerable milieux.

Insofar as an economy is so arranged that slumps occur, the problem of unemployment becomes incapable of personal solution. Insofar as war is inherent in the nation-state system and in the uneven industrialization of the world, the ordinary individual in his restricted milieu will be powerless—with or without psychiatric aid—to solve the troubles this system or lack of system imposes upon him. Insofar as the family as an institution turns women into darling little slaves and men into their chief providers and unweaned dependents, the problem of a satisfactory marriage remains incapable of purely private solution. Insofar as the overdeveloped megalopolis and the overdeveloped automobile are built-in features of the overdeveloped society, the issues of urban living will not be solved by personal ingenuity and private wealth.

———

What we experience in various and specific milieux, I have noted, is often caused by structural changes. Accordingly, to understand the changes of many personal milieux we are required to look beyond them. And the number and variety of such structural changes increase as the institutions within which we live become more embracing and more intricately connected with one another. To be aware of the idea of social structure and to use it with sensibility is to be capable of tracing such linkages among a great variety of milieux. To be able to do that is to possess the sociological imagination.

2

———

TEENAGE WASTELAND
Suburbia's Dead-End Kids

DONNA GAINES

This reading by Donna Gaines is an example of sociological research that employs Mills' sociological imagination and, specifically, his distinction between personal troubles and public issues. As Gaines illustrates, when one teenager commits suicide it is a personal tragedy, but when groups of teenagers form a suicide pact and successfully carry it out, suicide becomes a matter of public concern. In order to explain adequately why this incident occurred, Gaines examines both the history and the biography of suburban teens.

In Bergenfield, New Jersey, on the morning of March 11, 1987, the bodies of four teenagers were discovered inside a 1977 rust-colored Chevrolet Camaro. The car, which belonged to Thomas Olton, was parked in an unused garage in the Foster Village garden apartment complex, behind the Foster Village Shopping Center. Two sisters, Lisa and Cheryl Burress, and their friends, Thomas Rizzo and Thomas Olton, had died of carbon monoxide poisoning.

Lisa was 16, Cheryl was 17, and the boys were 19—they were suburban teens, turnpike kids like the ones in the town I live in. And thinking about them made me remember how it felt being a teenager too. I was horrified that it had come to this. I believed I understood why they did it, although it wasn't a feeling I could have put into words.

You could tell from the newspapers that they were rock and roll kids. The police had found a cassette tape cover of AC/DC's *If You Want Blood, You've Got It* near the bodies. Their friends were described as kids who listened to thrash metal, had shaggy haircuts, wore lots of black and leather. "Dropouts," "druggies," the papers called them. Teenage suburban rockers whose lives revolved around their favorite bands and their friends. Youths who barely got by in school and at home and who did not impress authority figures in any remarkable way. Except as fuck-ups.

My friends, most of whom were born in the 1950s, felt the same way about the kids everyone called "burnouts." On the weekend following the suicides, a friend's band, the Grinders, were playing at My Father's Place, a Long Island club. That night the guys dedicated a song, "The Kids in the Basement," to the four teens from Bergenfield—"This is for the suicide kids." In the weeks following the suicide pact, a number of bands in the tri-state area also dedicated songs to them. Their deaths had hit close to home.

. . .

A week or two after the suicide pact, *The Village Voice* assigned me to go to Bergenfield. Now this was not a story I would've volunteered for. . . .

. . .

But one day my editor at the *Voice* called to ask if I wanted to go to Bergenfield. She knew my background—that I knew suburbia, that I could talk to kids. By now I fully embraced the sociologist's ethical commitment to the "rights of the researched," and the social worker's vow of client confidentiality. As far as suicidal teenagers were concerned, I felt that if I couldn't help them, I didn't want to bother them.

But I was really pissed off at what I kept reading. How people in Bergenfield openly referred to the four kids as "troubled losers." Even after they were dead, nobody cut them any slack. "Burnouts," "druggies," "dropouts." Something was wrong. So I took the opportunity.

From the beginning, I believed that the Bergenfield suicides symbolized a tragic defeat for young people. Something was happening in the larger society that was not yet comprehended. Scholars spoke ominously of "the postmodern condition," "societal upheaval," "decay," "anomie." Meanwhile, American kids kept losing ground, showing all the symptoms of societal neglect. Many were left to fend for themselves, often with little success. The news got worse. Teenage suicides continued, and still nobody seemed to be getting the point.

Now, in trying to understand this event, I might have continued working within the established discourse on teenage suicide. I might have carried on the tradition of obscuring the bigger picture, psychologizing the Bergenfield suicide pact, interviewing the parents of the four youths, hounding their friends for the gory details. I might have spent my time probing school records, tracking down their teachers and shrinks for insights, focusing on their personal histories and intimate relationships. I might have searched out the individual motivations behind the words left in the note written and signed by each youth on the brown paper bag found with their bodies on March 11. But I did not.

Because the world has changed for today's kids. We also engaged in activities that adults called self-destructive. But for my generation, "doing it" meant having sex; for them, it means committing suicide.

"Teenage suicide" was a virtually nonexistent category prior to 1960. But between 1950 and 1980 it nearly tripled, and at the time of the Bergenfield suicide pact it was described as the second leading cause of death among America's young people; "accidents" were the first. The actual suicide rate among people aged 15 to 24—the statistical category for teenage suicide—is estimated to be even higher, underreported because of social stigma. Then there are the murky numbers derived from drug overdoses and car crashes, recorded as accidents. To date, there are more than 5,000 teen suicides annually, accounting for 12 percent of youth mortalities. An estimated 400,000 adolescents attempt suicide each year. While youth suicide rates leveled off by 1980, by mid-decade they began to increase again. Although they remained lower than adult suicide rates, the acceleration at which youth suicide rates increased was alarming. By 1987, we had books and articles detailing "copycat" and "cluster" suicides. Teenage suicide was now described as an epidemic.

Authors, experts, and scholars compiled the lists of kids' names, ages, dates, and possible motives. They generated predictive models: Rural and suburban white kids do it more often. Black kids in America's urban teenage wastelands are more likely to kill each other. Increasingly, alcohol and drugs are involved. In some cases adults have tried to identify the instigating factor as a lyric or a song—Judas Priest, Ozzy Osbourne. Or else a popular film about the subject—the suicide of a celebrity; too much media attention or not enough.

Some kids do it violently: drowning, hanging, slashing, jumping, or crashing. Firearms are still the most popular. Others prefer to go out more peacefully, by gas or drug overdose. Boys do it more than girls, though girls try it more often than boys. And it does not seem to matter if kids are rich or poor.

Throughout the 1980s, teenage suicide clusters appeared across the country—six or seven deaths, sometimes more, in a short period of time in a single community. In the boomtown of Plano, Texas. The fading factory town of Leominster, Massachusetts. At Bryan High School in a white, working-class suburb of Omaha, Nebraska. A series of domino suicides among Arapaho Indian youths at the Wind River Reservation in Wyoming. Six youth suicides in the county of Westchester, New York, in 1984; five in 1985 and seven in 1986.

Sometimes they were close friends who died together in pacts of two. In other cases, one followed shortly after the other, unable to survive apart. Then there were strangers who died alone, in separate incidents timed closely together.

The Bergenfield suicide pact of March 11 was alternately termed a "multiple-death pact," a "quadruple suicide," or simply a "pact," depending on where you read about it. Some people actually called it a *mass* suicide because the Bergenfield case reminded them of Jonestown, Guyana, in 1978, where over 900 followers of Jim Jones poisoned themselves, fearing their community would be destroyed.

As experts speculated over the deaths in Bergenfield, none could recall a teenage suicide pact involving four people dying together; *it was historically unique.*

I wondered, did the "burnouts" see themselves as a community under siege? Like Jim Jones's people, or the 960 Jews at Masada who jumped to their deaths rather than face defeat at the hands of the Romans? Were the "burnouts" of Bergenfield choosing death over surrender? Surrender to what? Were they martyrs? If so, what was their common cause?

Because the suicide pact was a *collective act,* it warrants a social explanation—a portrait of the "burnouts" in Bergenfield as actors within a particular social landscape.

For a long time now, the discourse of teenage suicide has been dominated by atomizing psychological and medical models. And so the larger picture of American youth as members of a distinctive generation with a unique collective biography, emerging at a particular moment in history, has been lost.

The starting-off point for this research, then, is a teenage suicide pact in an "upper-poor" white ethnic suburb in northern New Jersey. But, of course, the story did not begin and will not end in Bergenfield.

Yes, there were specific sociocultural patterns operating in Bergenfield through which a teenage suicide pact became objectively possible. Yes, there were particular conditions which influenced how the town reacted to the event. Yes, there were reasons—that unique constellation of circumstances congealed in the lives of the four youths in the years, weeks, and days prior to March 11—that made suicide seem like their best alternative.

Given the four youths' personal histories, their losses, their failures, their shattered dreams, the motivation to die in this way seems transparent.

Yet, after the suicide pact, in towns across the country, on television and in the press, people asked, "Why did they do it?" But I went to Bergenfield with other questions.

This was a suicide pact that involved close friends who were by no accounts obsessed, star-crossed lovers. What would make four people want to die together? Why would they ask, in their collective suicide note, to be waked and buried together? Were they part of a suicide cult?

If not, what was the nature of the *social* bond that tied them so closely? What could be so intimately binding that in the early morning hours of March 11 not one of them could stop, step back from the pact they had made to say, "Wait, I can't do this"? Who were these kids that everybody called "burnouts"?

"Greasers," "hoods," "beats," "freaks," "hippies," "punks." From the 1950s onward, these groups have signified young people's refusal to cooperate. In the social order of the American high school, teens are expected to do what they are told—make the grade, win the prize, play the game. Kids who refuse have always found something else to do. Sometimes it kills them; sometimes it sets them free.

In the 1980s, as before, high school kids at the top were the "preps," "jocks," or "brains," depending on the region. In white suburban high schools in towns like Bergenfield, the "burnouts" are often the kids near the bottom—academically, economically, and socially.

To outsiders, they look tough, scruffy, poor, wild. Uninvolved in and unimpressed by convention, they create an alternative world, a retreat, a refuge. Some burnouts are proud; they "wave their freak flags high." They call themselves burnouts to flaunt their break with the existing order, as a form of resistance, a statement of refusal.

But the meaning changes when "burnout" is hurled by an outsider. Then it hurts. It's an insult. Everyone knows you don't call somebody a burnout to their face unless you are looking for a fight. At that point, the word becomes synonymous with "troubled loser," "druggie"—all the things the press and some residents of the town called the four kids who died together in Tommy Olton's Camaro.

How did kids in Bergenfield *become* "burnouts," I wondered. At what point were they identified as outcasts? Was this a labeling process or one of self-selection? What kinds of lives did they have? What resources were available for them? What choices did they have? What ties did these kids have to the world outside Bergenfield? Where did their particular subculture come from? Why in the 1980s, the Reagan years, in white, suburban America?

What were their hopes and fears? What did heavy metal, Satan, suicide, and long hair mean to them? Who were their heroes, their gods? What saved them and what betrayed them in the long, cold night?

And what was this "something evil in the air" that people spoke about? Were the kids in Bergenfield "possessed"? Was the suicide pact an act of cowardice by four "losers," or the final refuge of kids helplessly and hope-lessly trapped? How different was Bergenfield from other towns?

Could kids be labeled to death? How much power did these labels have? I wanted to meet other kids in Bergenfield who were identified as "burn-outs" to find out what it felt like to carry these labels. I wanted to understand the existential situation they operated in—not simply as hapless losers, help-less victims, or tragic martyrs, but also as *historical actors* determined in their choices, resistant, defiant.

Because the suicide pact in Bergenfield seemed to be a symptom of something larger, a metaphor for something more universal, I moved on from there to other towns. For almost two years I spent my time reading thrash magazines, seeing shows, and hanging out with "burnouts" and "dirtbags" as well as kids who slip through such labels.

. . .

I started thinking critically about these people, about where I lived and where I came from. At some point in Bergenfield, I had gotten a strong sense of a new and different generation in a very changed world. Even though I had counseled and advocated for teenage clients, taught college students, and had young friends from the hardcore scene, before the Bergenfield sui-cide pact I hadn't really considered these people as a generation—in a col-lective, historical sense. Apparently, I wasn't the only one guilty of ignoring them in this way.

. . .

From the beginning, I decided I didn't want to dwell too much on the negatives. I wanted to understand how alienated kids survived, as well as how they were defeated. How did they maintain their humanity against what I now felt were impossible odds? I wondered. What keeps young people together when the world they are told to trust no longer seems to work? What motivates them to be decent human beings when nobody seems to respect them or take them seriously?

. . .

As I promised the kids I met hanging out on the streets of Bergen County and on Long Island, "No names, no pictures." Names such as "Joe," "Ed-die," and "Doreen" are fictitious, changed to protect their privacy.

. . .

Joe's been up for more than a day already. He's fried, his clothes are get-ting crusty, and he points to his armpits and says he smells (he doesn't). He's broke, he misses his girlfriend. He says he can't make it without someone. His girlfriend dumped him last year. He's gone out with other girls, but it's not the same. And he knows he can't win in this town. He's got a bad name. What's the use. He's tried it at least six times. Once he gashed at his vein with an Army knife he picked up in Times Square. He strokes the scars.

Tonight, he says, he's going to a Bible study class. Some girl he met invited him. Shows me a God pamphlet, inspirational literature. He doesn't want anyone to know about this, though. He thought the Jesus girl was nice. He's meeting her at seven. Bobby comes back in the room with Nicky, looking for cigarettes.

Later in the living room Joe teases Doreen. Poking at her, he gets rough. Bobby monitors him. "Calm down, Joe." We are just sitting around playing music, smoking cigarettes. Fooling around. "Did you see those Jesus freaks down at Cooper's Pond the other day?" Randy laughs. Nicky tells Joe to forget it. Jesus chicks won't just go with you; you have to date them for a long time, pretend you're serious about them. They don't fuck you right away. "It's not worth the bother."

Suicide comes up again. Joan and Susie have razor scars. The guys make Susie show me her freshly bandaged wrists. I look at her. She's such a beautiful girl. She's sitting there with her boyfriend, Randy, just fooling around. I ask her quietly, "Why are you doing this?" She smiles at me seductively. She doesn't say anything. What the fuck is this, erotic? Kicks? Romantic? I feel cold panic.

Nicky slashed his wrists when his old girlfriend moved out of state. His scars are much older. I motion to him about Susie. Discreetly he says, "It's best just to ignore it, don't pay too much attention." Throughout the afternoon I try every trick I know to get Susie to talk to me. She won't. She's shy, quiet; she's all inside herself.

And I really don't want to push too hard. The kids say they're already going nuts from all the suicide-prevention stuff. You can't panic. But I have to figure out if this is a cult, a fad, a hobby, or something I'm supposed to report to the police. I'm afraid to leave.

I wonder, do they know the difference between vertical and horizontal cuts? Don't their parents, their teachers, the cops, and neighbors see this shit going on? Maybe they feel as confused as I do. Maybe this is why they didn't see it coming here, and in the other towns. You can't exactly go around strip-searching teenagers to see if they have slash wounds.

. . .

I am freaked out about the scars. I don't know how to read them. What are these collective razor scars, the martyr's ecstasy? Wrist cuts. The suicide pact signifier? Mutilation and negation as community? The poetics of suicide? Literary and religious themes go through my mind. To live and die in Bergenfield. Burnouts. Nailed. The stigmata.

It was getting heavy. But how real was this? Joe was very intense, a real drama queen, I could tell. But he was also pretty strung out. His life wasn't working. Susie was accessible only indirectly, through her friends. For Nicky, this "suicide stuff" was behind him; he had plans. And it just didn't seem like Randy's style. Bobby also appeared more explosive than self-destructive. That was comforting. Joan had the wrist bandages too. I had looked at her flesh carvings—superficial, but what was she saying? Doreen seemed fine, but that's what people thought about Cheryl Burress. I didn't know what to think.

. . .

After the suicide pact, parents complained that the kids really did need somewhere to go when school let out. The after-school activities were limited to academics, sports, or organized school clubs. Even with part-time after-school jobs, a number of the town's young people did not find the conventional activities offered by the town particularly intriguing.

But according to established adult reasoning, if you didn't get absorbed into the legitimate, established routine of social activity, you'd be left to burn out on street corners, killing time, getting wasted. It was impossible for anyone to imagine any autonomous activity that nonconforming youth en masse might enjoy that would not be self-destructive, potentially criminal, or meaningless.

Parents understood that the lack of "anything to do" often led to drug and alcohol abuse. Such concerns were aired at the volatile meeting in the auditorium of Bergenfield High School. It was agreed that the kids' complaint of "no place to go" had to be taken seriously. Ten years ago, in any suburban town, teenagers' complaints of "nothing to do" would have been met with adult annoyance. But not anymore.

In Bergenfield, teenage boredom could no longer be dismissed as the whining of spoiled suburban kids. Experts now claimed that national rates of teenage suicide were higher in suburbs and rural areas because of teen isolation and boredom. In Bergenfield adults articulated the fact that many local kids did hang out on street corners and in parks looking for drugs because things at home weren't too good.

Youngsters have always been cautioned by adults that the devil would make good use of their idle hands. But now they understood something else: boredom led to drugs, and boredom could kill. Yet it was taken for granted that if you refused to be colonized, if you ventured beyond the boundaries circumscribed by adults, you were "looking for trouble." But in reality, it was adult organization of young people's social reality over the last few hundred years that had *created* this miserable situation: one's youth as wasted years. Being wasted and getting wasted. Adults often wasted kids' time with meaningless activities, warehousing them in school; kids in turn wasted their own time on drugs. Just to have something to do.

So by now whenever kids hang out, congregating in some unstructured setting, adults read *dangerousness*. Even if young people are talking about serious things, working out plans for the future, discussing life, jobs, adults just assume they are getting wasted. They are.

. . .

For the duration of my stay, in almost every encounter, the outcast members of Bergenfield's youth population would tell me these things: The cops are dicks, the school blows, the jocks suck, Billy Milano (lead singer of now defunct S.O.D.—Stormtroopers of Death) was from a nearby town, and Iron Maiden had dedicated "Wasted Years" to the Burress sisters the last time the band played Jersey. These were their cultural badges of honor, unknown to the adults.

Like many suburban towns, Bergenfield is occupationally mixed. Blue-collar aristocrats may make more money than college professors, and so one's local class identity is unclear. Schools claim to track kids in terms of "ability," and cliques are determined by subculture, style, participation, and refusal.

Because the myth of a democratized mass makes class lines in the suburbs of the United States so ambiguous to begin with, differences in status become the critical lines of demarcation. And in the mostly white, mainly Christian town of Bergenfield, where there are neither very rich nor very poor people, this sports thing became an important criterion for determining "who's who" among the young people.

The girls played this out, too, as they always have, deriving their status by involvement in school (as cheerleaders, in clubs, in the classroom). And just as important, by the boys they hung around with. They were defined by who they were, by what they wore, by where they were seen, and with whom.

Like any other "Other," the kids at the bottom, who everybody here simply called burnouts, were actually a conglomerate of several cliques—serious druggies, Deadheads, dirtbags, skinheads, metalheads, thrashers, and punks. Some were good students, from "good" families with money and prestige. In any other setting all of these people might have been bitter rivals, or at least very separate cliques. But here, thanks to the adults and the primacy of sports, they were all lumped together—united by virtue of a common enemy, the jocks.

. . .

For a bored, ignored, lonely kid, drug oblivion may offer immediate comfort; purpose and adventure in the place of everyday ennui. But soon it has a life of its own—at a psychic and a social level, the focus of your life becomes *getting high* (or *well* as some people describe it). Ironically, the whole miserable process often begins as a positive act of self-preservation.

Both the dirts and the burnt may understand how they are being fucked over and by whom. And while partying rituals may actually celebrate the refusal to play the game, neither group has a clue where to take it beyond the parking lot of 7-Eleven.

So they end up stranded in teenage wasteland. They devote their lives to their bands, to their friends, to partying; they live in the moment. They're going down in flames, taking literally the notion that "rust never sleeps," that it is "better to burn out than fade away." While left-leaning adults have valorized the politically minded punks and right-wing groups have engaged some fascistic skins, nobody really thinks too much about organizing dirts or burnouts. Law enforcement officials, special education teachers, and drug treatment facilities are the adults who are concerned with these kids.

Such wasted suburban kids are typically not politically "correct," nor do they constitute an identifiable segment of the industrial working class. They are not members of a specific racial or ethnic minority, and they have few political advocates. Only on the political issues of abortion and the death penalty for minors will wasted teenage girls and boys be likely to find adults in their corner.

Small in numbers, isolated in decaying suburbs, they aren't visible on any national scale until they are involved in something that really horrifies us, like a suicide pact, or parricide, or incest, or "satanic" sacrifice. For the most part, burnouts and dirtbags are anomic small town white boys and girls, just trying to get through the day. Their way of fighting back is to have enough fun to kill themselves before everything else does.

. . .

In the scheme of things average American kids who don't have rich or well-connected parents have had these choices: Play the game and try to get ahead. Do what your parents did—work yourself to death at a menial job and find solace in beer, God, or family. Or take risks, cut deals, or break the law. The Reagan years made it hard for kids to "put their noses to the grindstone" as their parents had. Like everyone, these people hoped for better lives. But they lived in an age of inflated expectations and diminishing returns. Big and fast money was everywhere, and ever out of reach. America now had an economy that worked sort of like a cocaine high—propped up by hot air and big debt. The substance was absent. People's lives were like that too, and at times they were crashing hard.

In the meantime, wherever you were, you could still dream of becoming spectacular. A special talent could be your ticket out. Long Island kids had role models in bands like the Crumbsuckers, Ludichrist, Twisted Sister, Steve Vai, and Pat Benatar. North Jersey was full of sports celebrities and rock millionaires—you grew up hoping you'd end up like Mike Tyson or Jon Bon

Jovi. Or like Keith Richards, whose father worked in a factory; or Ozzy, who also came from a grim English factory town, a hero who escaped the drudge because he was spectacular. This was the hip version of the American dream.

Kids who go for the prize now understand there are only two choices—rise to the top or crash to the bottom. Many openly admit that they would rather end it all now than end up losers. The nine-to-five world, corporate grunt life, working at the same job for 30 years, that's not for them. They'd prefer to hold out until the last possibility and then just piss on it all. The big easy or the bottomless pit, but never the everyday drone. And as long as there are local heroes and stories, you can still believe you have a chance to emerge from the mass as something larger than life. You can still play the great lottery and dream.

Schools urge kids to make these choices as early as possible, in a variety of ways. In the terse words of the San Francisco hardcore band MDC, "There's no such thing as cheating in a loser's game." Many kids who start out as nobody from nowhere with nothing will end up that way. Nevertheless, everyone pretends that everything is possible if you give it your best shot. We actually believe it. While educators hope to be as efficient as possible in figuring out where unspectacular students can plug into the workforce, kids try to play at being one in a million, some way of shining, even if it's just for a while.

. . .

Girls get slightly different choices. They may hope to become spectacular by virtue of their talents and their beauty. Being the girlfriend of a guy in a band means you might get to live in his mansion someday if you stick it out with him during the lean years. You might just end up like Bon Jovi's high school sweetheart, or married to someone like Cinderella's lead singer—he married his hometown girlfriend and helped set her up in her own business. These are suburban fairy tales.

Around here, some girls who are beautiful and talented hope to become stars, too, like Long Island's local products Debbie Gibson and Taylor Dayne. Some hope to be like actress Heather Locklear and marry someone really hot like Motley Crüe's drummer, Tommy Lee. If you could just get to the right place at the right time.

But most people from New Jersey and Long Island or anywhere else in America don't end up rich and famous. They have some fun trying, though, and for a while life isn't bad at all.

Yet, if you are unspectacular—not too book-smart, of average looks and moderate creative ability—there have always been places for you. Much of your teachers' efforts will be devoted to your more promising peers, and so will your nation's resources. But your parents will explain to you that this is the way it is, and early on, you will know to expect very little from school.

There are still a few enclaves, reservations. The shop and crafting culture of your parents' class of origin is one pocket of refuge. In the vocational high school, your interests are rewarded, once you have allowed yourself to be dumped there. And if the skills you gather there don't really lead to anything much, there's always the military.

Even though half the kids in America today will never go to college, the country still acts as if they will. At least, most schools seem to be set up to prepare you for college. And if it's not what you can or want to do, their attitude is tough shit, it's your problem.

And your most devoted teachers at vocational high school will never tell you that the training you will get from them is barely enough to get your foot in the door. You picture yourself getting into something with a future only to find that your skills are obsolete, superficial, and the boss prefers people with more training, more experience, more promise. So you are stuck in dead-end "youth employment jobs," and now what?

According to the William T. Grant Commission on Work, Family and Citizenship, 20 million people between the ages of 16 and 24 are not likely to go to college. The "forgotten half," as youth advocates call them, will find jobs in service and retail. But the money is bad, only half that of typical manufacturing jobs. The good, stable jobs that don't require advanced training have been disappearing rapidly. From 1979 to 1985 the U.S.A. suffered a net loss of 1.7 million manufacturing jobs. What's left?

In my neighborhood, the shipping and warehousing jobs that guys like the Grinders took, hedging their bets against rock stardom, are now seen as "good jobs" by the younger guys at Metal 24. I am regularly asked to . . . "find out if they're hiring" down at [the] shipping company. Dead-end kids around here who aren't working with family are working "shit jobs."

The skills used in a typical "shit job" . . . involve slapping rancid butter on stale hard rolls, mopping the floor, selling Lotto tickets, making sure shelves and refrigerators are clean, sorting and stacking magazines, taking delivery on newspapers, and signing out videos. They are also advised to look out for shoplifters, to protect the register, and to be sure that the surveillance camera is running. Like most kids in shit jobs, they are most skilled at getting over on the boss and in developing strategies to ward off boredom. It is not unusual to see kids at the supermarket cash register or the mall clothing shop standing around with a glazed look in their eyes. And you will often hear them complain of boredom, tiredness, or whine, "I can't wait to get out of here." Usually, in shit jobs this is where it begins and ends. There aren't many alternatives.

Everywhere, such kids find getting into a union or having access to supervisory or managerial tracks hard to come by. Some forms of disinvestment are more obvious than others. In a company town, you will be somewhat clear about what is going on. At the end of the 1980s, the defense industry of Long Island seemed threatened; people feared that their lives would soon be devastated.

But the effect of a changing economic order on most kids only translates into scrambling for a new safety zone. It is mostly expressed as resentment against entrepreneurial foreigners (nonwhites) and as anomie—a vague sense of loss, then confusion about where they might fit in.

Through the 1980s, people articulated their sense of loss in songs. Springsteen's Jersey was a suicide rap, a death trap. The Pretenders' Chrissie Hynde found that her industrial city, her Ohio, was gone, turned into shopping malls. Billy Joel's "Allentown" mourned for the steelworkers of Pennsylvania who had lost their America. To those of us who relate to music nonlyrically, the middle 1980s "industrial noise" bands, the postpunks, and the death-metal merchants were saying the same thing: When old ways die out, before new ones are firmly established, all that remains is a vacuum, a black hole.

For example, on Long Island, the ripple effect of peripheral industries had forced layoffs at Grumman and the death of Fairchild. It opened up questions about the future of jobs with large corporations like Hazeltine and Unisys. The engineering networks set up to support these industries were now on shaky ground. Small-job shops that produced specific parts for highly sophisticated defense contracts began dying out; universities and specialized technical schools would have to reorient themselves or fold. There would be jobs lost, and then declining property values.

Things were changing everywhere, but it was still too soon to determine the final outcome. Meantime, the social chaos kept seeping in. In *Rusted Dreams,* their book about the devastation in Chicago's Southeast Side following the closing of two steel mills in 1980, David Bensman and Roberta Lynch noted the increase in juvenile crime. Local youth workers attributed the delinquency to "the malaise that has afflicted teenagers since the mills began to decline. It has always been taken for granted that there would be jobs waiting for these kids—decent jobs that required little in the way of prior experience, skills, or education." The authors described aimlessness, hopelessness. There had been a lot of "untimely deaths" among youths, drinking, car accidents, violence. The dropout rate had gone up too, since the kids didn't see the point of going to school when it didn't lead to anything.

By the end of the 1980s many of the unaffluent turnpike towns across America had already felt some degree of devastation. Most parents work locally, and so kids understood that something was going on when their parents began talking about relocating from Long Island to Florida or Pennsylvania because Grumman might shut them out and then they couldn't afford to live here anymore.

In such situations, the immediate chaos is metabolized as a profound insecurity, a panic, loss of place. Like animals before an earthquake, the kids sense trouble ahead, feel desperate.

So where are we going? Some people fear we are polarizing into a two-class nation, rich and poor. More precisely, a privileged knowledge-producing class and a low-paid, low-status service class. It is in the public high school that this division of labor for an emergent postindustrial local economy is first articulated. At the top are the kids who will hold jobs in a highly competitive technological economic order, who will advance and be respected if they cooperate and excel.

At the bottom are kids with poor basic skills, short attention spans, limited emotional investment in the future. Also poor housing, poor nutrition, bad schooling, bad lives. And in their bad jobs they will face careers of unsatisfying part-time work, low pay, no benefits, and no opportunity for advancement.

There are the few possibilities offered by a relative—a coveted place in a union, a chance to join a small family business in a service trade, a spot in a small shop. In my neighborhood, kids dream of making a good score on the cop tests, working up from hostess to waitress. Most hang out in limbo hoping to get called for a job in the sheriff's department, or the parks, or sanitation. They're on all the lists, although they know the odds for getting called are slim. The lists are frozen, the screening process is endless.

Meantime they hold jobs for a few months here and there, or they work off the books, or at two bad jobs at once.

. . .

When he gave the eulogy at his godson's funeral, Tommy Olton's uncle Richard was quoted as saying, "When I held you in my arms at your baptism, I wanted it to be a fresh start, for you to be more complete than we had ever been ourselves, but I wonder if we expected too much. In thinking only of ourselves, maybe we passed down too great a burden."

Trans-historically, cross-culturally, humans have placed enormous burdens on their young. Sometimes these burdens have been primarily economic: The child contributes to the economy of the family or tribe. Sometimes the burden has been social—the child is a contribution to the immortality of our creed. Be fruitful and multiply.

But the spiritual burden we pass on to the child may be the most difficult to bear. We do expect them to fulfill an incompleteness in ourselves, in our world. Our children are our vehicle for the realization of unfulfilled human dreams; our class aspirations, our visions of social justice and world peace, of a better life on earth.

Faith in the child, in the next generation, helps get us through this life. Without this hope in the future *through the child* we could not endure slavery, torture, war, genocide, or even the ordinary, everyday grind of a "bad life." The child-as-myth is an empty slate upon which we carve our highest ideals. For human beings, the child is God, utopia, and the future incarnate. The Bergenfield suicide pact ruptured the sacred trust between the generations. It was a negation.

After I had been to Bergenfield people asked me, "Why did they do it?" People want to know in 25 words or less. But it's more complicated than that. I usually just say, "They had bad lives," and try to explain why these lives ended where, when, and how they did. But I still wonder, at what point are people pushed over the line?

On the surface the ending of the four kids' bad lives can be explained away by the "case history" approach. Three of the four had suicidal or self-destructive adult role models: the suicide of Tommy Olton's father, the drug-related death of the Burress sisters' father. Tommy Rizzo, along with his three friends, had experienced the recent loss of a beloved friend, Joe Major. Before Joe, the death of three other local "burnouts." Then there was the chronic drug and alcohol abuse, an acknowledged contributing factor in suicide. Families ruptured by divorce, death, estrangement. Failure at school.

But these explanations alone would not add up to a suicide pact among four kids. If they did, the teenage suicide rate would be much, much higher. The personal problems experienced by the four kids were severe, painful, but by the 1980s, they were no longer remarkable.

For a while I wondered if the excessive labeling process in Bergenfield was killing off the "burnouts." Essentially, their role, their collective identity in their town was that of the "nigger" or "Jew." Us and Them, the One and the Other. And once they were constituted as "burnouts" by the town's hegemonic order, the kids played out their assigned role as self-styled outcasts with irony, style, and verve.

Yes, Bergenfield was guilty of blaming the victim. But only slightly more guilty than any other town. Labeling, blaming the victim, and conferring rewards on more cooperative kids was cruel, but also not remarkable in the eighties.

As I felt from the beginning, the unusually cloying geography of Bergenfield seemed somehow implicated in the suicide pact. The landscape appeared even more circumscribed because of the "burnouts'" lack of legitimate space in the town: they were too old for the [roller skating] Rink, and the Building [an abandoned warehouse taken over by the teens] was available for criminal trespass only. Outcast, socially and spatially, for years the "burnouts" had been chased from corner to parking lot, and finally, to the garage bays of Foster Village. They were nomads, refugees in the town of their birth. *There was no place for them.* They felt unloved, unwanted, devalued, disregarded, and discarded.

But this little town, not even two miles long from north to south, was just a dot on a much larger map. It wasn't the whole world. Hip adults I know, friends who grew up feeling like outcasts in their hometown, were very sympathetic to the plight of the "burnouts." Yet even they often held out one last question, sometimes contemptuously: "Why didn't they *just leave?*" As if the four kids had failed even as outcasts. My friends found this confusing. "No matter how worthless the people who make the rules say you are, you don't have to play their game. You can always walk and not look back," they would argue. People who feel abject and weird in their hometown simply move away.

But that has always been a class privilege. The townies are the poor kids, the wounded street warriors who stay behind. And besides, escape was easier for everyone 20 years ago. American society had safety nets then that don't exist now—it's just not the same anymore.

During the eighties, dead-end kids—kids with personal problems and unspectacular talents living in punitive or indifferent towns with a sense of futility about life—became more common. There were lots of kids with bad lives. They didn't all commit suicide. But I believe that in another decade, Tommy Rizzo, Cheryl Burress, Tommy Olton, and Lisa Burress would not have "done it." They might have had more choices, or choices that really meant something to them. Teenage suicide won't go away until kids' bad lives do. Until there are other ways of moving out of bad lives, suicide will remain attractive.

In a now famous footnote in *Suicide,* written almost a hundred years ago, the French sociologist Emile Durkheim described fatalistic suicide as "the suicide deriving from excessive regulation, that of persons with futures pitilessly blocked and passions violently choked by oppressive discipline." Where there is overregulation, explains Durkheim, "rule against which there is no appeal, we might call it fatalistic suicide."

Sometimes people commit suicide because they have lost the ability to dream. Having lost transcendent vision, they feel fated, doomed. I think this is what happened in Bergenfield; there was a determination among four persons, bound closely together in a shared existential predicament, to *get out.* But they couldn't. As Joe explained to me, "They were beaten down as far as they could go." Lacking confidence in themselves and the world "out there," they felt trapped. Without a sense of truly meaningful choices, the only way out *was suicide.*

But as far as young people are concerned, fatalistic suicide is not the whole story. True, young people are among the most regulated in our society. With the exception of people in total institutions, only the lives of animals are more controlled. Yet most experts attribute youth suicide to anomie—the opposite of fatalistic suicide in Durkheim's thinking.

In an anomic suicide, the individual isn't connected to the society—the glue that holds the person to the group isn't strong enough; social bonds are loose, weak, or absent. To be anomic is to feel disengaged, adrift, alienated. Like you don't fit in anywhere, there is no place for you: in your family, your school, your town—in the social order.

Where fatalistic suicide may result from overregulation, anomic suicide is attributed to nonintegration. Young people are in the peculiar position of being overregulated by adults, yet alienated from them. Many are integrated only into the world shared with their peers—some may be overly integrated into that world, as in gangs or subcults. Young people are always somewhere on a continuum between overregulation and nonintegration. In the eighties, both ends of this continuum grew to extremes.

3
———————

INTERSECTION OF BIOGRAPHY
AND HISTORY
My Intellectual Journey

MARY ROMERO

This selection by sociologist Mary Romero is another example of Mills' sociological imagination. Romero explains how biography and history influenced her investigation of domestic service work done by Chicanas. In
particular, Romero describes her research process, which involved reinter-
preting her own and others' domestic service experiences within the larger
work history of Mexican Americans and the devaluation of housework.
Thus, this selection is an introduction to Romero's study of domestic work
and the social interactions between domestics and their employers.

When I was growing up many of the women whom I knew worked
cleaning other people's houses. Domestic service was part of my
taken-for-granted reality. Later, when I had my own place, I considered housework something you did before company came over. My first
thought that domestic service and housework might be a serious research interest came as a result of a chance encounter with live-in domestics along the
U.S.-Mexican border. Before beginning a teaching position at the University
of Texas at El Paso, I stayed with a colleague while apartment hunting. My
colleague had a live-in domestic to assist with housecleaning and cooking.
Asking around, I learned that live-in maids were common in El Paso, even
among apartment and condominium dwellers. The hiring of maids from
Mexico was so common that locals referred to Monday as the border patrol's
day off because the agents ignored the women crossing the border to return
to their employers' homes after their weekend off. The practice of hiring undocumented Mexican women as domestics, many of whom were no older
than fifteen, seemed strange to me. It was this strangeness that raised the
topic of domestic service as a question and made problematic what had previously been taken for granted.

I must admit that I was shocked at my colleague's treatment of the
16-year-old domestic whom I will call Juanita. Only recently hired, Juanita
was still adjusting to her new environment. She was extremely shy, and her
timidity was made even worse by constant flirting from her employer. As far
as I could see, every attempt Juanita made to converse was met with teasing
so that the conversation could never evolve into a serious discussion. Her

employer's sexist, paternalistic banter effectively silenced the domestic, kept her constantly on guard, and made it impossible for her to feel comfortable at work. For instance, when she informed the employer of a leaky faucet, he shot her a look of disdain, making it clear that she was overstepping her boundaries. I observed other encounters that clearly served to remind Juanita of her subservient place in her employer's home.

Although Juanita was of the same age as my colleague's oldest daughter and but a few years older than his two sons, she was treated differently from the other teenagers in the house. She was expected to share her bedroom with the ironing board, sewing machine, and other spare-room types of objects.[1] More importantly, she was assumed to have different wants and needs. I witnessed the following revealing exchange. Juanita was poor. She had not brought toiletries with her from Mexico. Since she had not yet been paid, she had to depend on her employer for necessities. Yet instead of offering her a small advance in her pay so she could purchase the items herself and giving her a ride to the nearby supermarket to select her own toiletries, the employer handled Juanita's request for toothbrush, toothpaste, shampoo, soap, and the like in the following manner. In the presence of all the family and the house guest, he made a list of the things she needed. Much teasing and joking accompanied the encounter. The employer shopped for her and purchased only generic brand items, which were a far cry from the brand-name products that filled the bathroom of his 16-year-old daughter. Juanita looked at the toothpaste, shampoo, and soap with confusion; she may never have seen generic products before, but she obviously knew that a distinction had been made.

One evening I walked into the kitchen as the employer's young sons were shouting orders at Juanita. They pointed to the dirty dishes on the table and pans in the sink and yelled "WASH!" "CLEAN!" Juanita stood frozen next to the kitchen door, angry and humiliated. Aware of possible repercussions for Juanita if I reprimanded my colleague's sons, I responded awkwardly by reallocating chores to everyone present. I announced that I would wash the dishes and the boys would clear the table. Juanita washed and dried dishes alongside me, and together we finished cleaning the kitchen. My colleague returned from his meeting to find us in the kitchen washing the last pan. The look on his face was more than enough to tell me that he was shocked to find his houseguest—and future colleague—washing dishes with the maid. His embarrassment at my behavior confirmed my suspicion that I had violated the normative expectations of class behavior within the home. He attempted to break the tension with a flirtatious and sexist remark to Juanita which served to excuse her from the kitchen and from any further discussion.

The conversation that followed revealed how my colleague chose to interpret my behavior. Immediately after Juanita's departure from the kitchen, he initiated a discussion about "Chicano radicals" and the Chicano movement. Although he was a foreign-born Latino, he expressed sympathy for *la causa.* Recalling the one Chicano graduate student he had known to obtain a Ph.D. in sociology, he gave several accounts of how the student's political behavior had disrupted the normal flow of university activity. Lowering his voice to a confidential whisper, he confessed to understanding why Marxist theory has become so popular among Chicano students. The tone of his comments and the examples that he chose made me realize that my "outrageous" behavior was explained, and thus excused, on the basis of my being one of those "Chicano radicals." He interpreted my washing dishes with his maid as a symbolic act; that is, I was affiliated with *los de abajo.*

My behavior had been comfortably defined without addressing the specific issue of maids. My colleague then further subsumed the topic under the rubric of "the servant problem" along the border. (His reaction was not unlike the attitude employers have displayed toward domestic service in the United States for the last hundred years.)[2] He began by providing me with chapter and verse about how he had aided Mexican women from Juarez by helping them cross the border and employing them in his home. He took further credit for introducing them to the appliances found in an American middle-class home. He shared several funny accounts about teaching country women from Mexico to use the vacuum cleaner, electric mixer, and microwave (remember the maid scene in the movie *El Norte?*) and implicitly blamed them for their inability to work comfortably around modern conveniences. For this "on-the-job training" and introduction to American culture, he complained, his generosity and goodwill had been rewarded by a high turnover rate. As his account continued, he assured me that most maids were simply working until they found a husband. In his experience they worked for a few months or less and then did not return to work on Monday morning after their first weekend off. Of course it never dawned on him that they may simply have found a job with better working conditions.

The following day, Juanita and I were alone in the house. As I mustered up my best Spanish, we shared information about our homes and families. After a few minutes of laughter about my simple sentence structure, Juanita lowered her head and in a sad, quiet voice told me how isolated and lonely she felt in this middle-class suburb literally within sight of Juarez. Her feelings were not the consequence of the work or of frustrations with modern appliances, nor did she complain about the absence of Mexican people in the neighborhood; her isolation and loneliness were in response to the norms and values surrounding domestic service. She described the situation quite clearly in expressing puzzlement over the social interactions she had with her employer's family: Why didn't her employer's children talk to her or include her in any of their activities when she wasn't working? Her reaction was not unlike that of Lillian Pettengill, who wrote about her two-year experience as a domestic in Philadelphia households at the turn of the century: "I feel my isolation alone in a big house full of people."[3]

Earlier in the day, Juanita had unsuccessfully tried to initiate a conversation with the 16-year-old daughter while she cleaned her room. She was of the same age as the daughter (who at that moment was in bed reading and watching TV because of menstrual cramps—a luxury the maid was not able to claim). She was rebuffed and ignored and felt that she became visible only when an order was given. Unable to live with this social isolation, she had already made up her mind not to return after her day off in Juarez. I observed the total impossibility of communication. The employer would never know why she left, and Juanita would not know that she would be considered simply another ungrateful Mexican whom he had tried to help.

After I returned to Denver, I thought a lot about the situations of Juanita and the other young undocumented Mexican women living in country club areas along the border. They worked long days in the intimacy of American middle-class homes but were starved for respect and positive social interaction. Curiously, the employers did not treat the domestics as "one of the family," nor did they consider themselves employers. Hiring a domestic was likely to be presented within the context of charity and good works; it was considered a matter of helping "these Mexican women" rather than recognized as a work issue.

I was bothered by my encounter along the border, not simply for the obvious humanitarian reasons, but because I too had once worked as a domestic, just as my mother, sister, relatives, and neighbors had. As a teenager, I cleaned houses with my mother on weekends and vacations. My own working experience as a domestic was limited because I had always been accompanied by my mother or sister instead of working alone. Since I was a day worker, my time in the employer's home was limited and I was able to return to my family and community each day. In Juanita's situation as a live-in domestic, there was no distinction between the time on and off work. I wondered whether domestic service had similarly affected my mother, sister, and neighbors. Had they too worked beyond the agreed-upon time? Did they have difficulty managing relationships with employers? I never worked alone and was spared the direct negotiations with employers. Instead, I cooperated with my mother or sister in completing the housecleaning as efficiently and quickly as possible.

I could not recall being yelled at by employers or their children, but I did remember anger, resentment, and the humiliation I had felt at kneeling to scrub other people's toilets while they gave step-by-step cleaning instructions. I remember feeling uncomfortable around employers' children who never acknowledged my presence except to question where I had placed their belongings after I had picked them up off the floor to vacuum. After all, my experience was foreign to them; at the age of 14 I worked as a domestic while they ran off to swimming, tennis, and piano lessons. Unlike Juanita, I preferred to remain invisible as I moved around the employer's house cleaning. Much later, I learned that the invisibility of workers in domestic service is a common characteristic of the occupation. Ruth Schwartz Cowan has commented on the historical aspect of invisibility:

The history of domestic service in the United States is a vast, unresolved puzzle, because the social role "servant" so frequently carries with it the unspoken adjective *invisible*. In diaries and letters, the "invisible" servant becomes visible only when she departs employment ("Mary left today"). In statistical series, she appears only when she is employed full-time, on a live-in basis; or when she is willing to confess the nature of her employment to a census taker, and (especially since the Second World War) there have frequently been good reasons for such confessions to go unmade.[4]

Although I remained invisible to most of the employers' family members, the mothers, curiously enough, seldom let me move around the house invisibly, dusting the woodwork and vacuuming carpets. Instead, I was subjected to constant supervision and condescending observations about "what a good little girl I was, helping my mother clean house." After I had moved and cleaned behind a hide-a-bed and Lazy-boy chair, vacuumed three floors including two sets of stairs, and carried the vacuum cleaner up and downstairs twice because "little Johnny" was napping when I was cleaning the bedrooms—I certainly didn't feel like a "little girl helping mother." I felt like a domestic worker!

There were employers who attempted to draw parallels between my adolescent experience and their teenagers' behavior: they'd point to the messy bedrooms and claim, "Well, you're a teenager, you understand clothes, books, papers, and records on the floor." Even at 14, I knew that being sloppy and not picking up after yourself was a privilege. I had two brothers and three sisters. I didn't have my own bedroom but shared a room with my sisters. Not one of us would think of leaving our panties on the floor for the others to pick up. I didn't bother to set such employers straight but continued to clean in silence, knowing that at the end of the day I would get cash and confident that I would soon be old enough to work elsewhere.

Many years later, while attending graduate school, I returned to domestic service as an "off-the-record" means to supplement my income. Graduate fellowships and teaching assistantships locked me into a fixed income that frequently was not enough to cover my expenses.[5] So once again I worked alongside my mother for seven hours as we cleaned two houses. I earned about 50 dollars for the day. Housecleaning is strenuous work, and I returned home exhausted from climbing up and down stairs, bending over, rubbing, and scrubbing.

Returning to domestic service as a graduate student was awkward. I tried to reduce the status inconsistency in my life by electing to work only in houses from which families were absent during the day. If someone appeared while I worked, I ignored their presence as they did mine. Since working arrangements had been previously negotiated by my mother, I had limited face-to-face interactions with employers. Most of the employers knew I was a graduate student, and fortunately, most seemed reluctant to ask me too many questions. Our mutual silence served as a way to deal with the status inconsistency of a housewife with a B.A. hiring an ABD to clean her house.

I came to El Paso with all of these experiences unquestioned in my memory. My presuppositions about domestic service were called into question only after observing the more obviously exploitative situation in the border town. I saw how vulnerable undocumented women employed as live-in domestics are and what little recourse they have to improve their situation, short of finding another job. Experiencing Juanita's shame and disgust at my colleague's sons' behavior brought back a flood of memories that eventually influenced me to study the paid housework that I had once taken for granted. I began to wonder professionally about the Chicanas employed as domestics that I had known throughout my own life: how vulnerable were they to exploitation, racism, and sexism? Did their day work status and U.S. citizenship provide protection against degradation and humiliation? How did Chicanas go about establishing a labor arrangement within a society that marked them as racial and cultural inferiors? How did they deal with racial slurs and sexist remarks within their employers' homes? How did Chicanas attempt to negotiate social interactions and informal labor arrangements with employers and their families?

An Exploratory Study

The Research Process

Intending to compare my findings with the research on U.S. minority women employed as domestics, I chose to limit my study to Chicanas, that is, women of Mexican descent born and raised in the United States. Although many women born in Mexico and living in the United States consider themselves Chicanas, my sample did not include women born outside the United States. My major concern in making this distinction was to avoid bringing into the analysis immigration issues that increase the vulnerability of the women employed as domestics. I wanted to keep conditions as constant as possible to make comparisons with the experiences Judith Rollins, Bonnie Thornton Dill, and Soraya Moore Coley report among African American women and with Evelyn Glenn's study of Japanese American women.[6] In order to duplicate similar residential and citizenship characteristics of these studies, I restricted my sample to Chicanas living in Denver whose families had migrated from rural areas of New Mexico and Colorado. All of the women interviewed were U.S. citizens and lived in Denver most of their adult lives.

I began the project by soliciting the cooperation of current and former domestics from my own family. I relied on domestics to provide entree into informal networks. These networks turned out to be particularly crucial in gaining access to an occupation that is so much a part of the underground economy. My mother, sister, and sister-in-law agreed to be interviewed and to provide names of relatives, friends, and neighbors. I also identified Chicana domestics in the community with the assistance of outreach workers employed by local churches and social service agencies. The snowball sampling was achieved by asking each interviewee to recommend other Chicana domestics as potential interviewees.

The women were extremely cautious about offering the names of friends and relatives. In most cases, they contacted the person first and only then gave me the name and telephone number. This actually turned out to be quite helpful. Potential interviewees had already heard about my study from someone who had been interviewed. They had a general idea of the questions I was going to ask and in some cases a little background information about who I was. However, on three occasions, I called women to ask for an interview and was confronted with resistance and shame. The women expressed embarrassment at being identified by their work—as a "housekeeper" or "cleaning lady." I responded by sharing my research interests in the occupation and in the relationship between work and family. I also shared my previous experience as a domestic.[7] One woman argued with me for 20 minutes about conducting research on an occupation that was low status, suggesting instead that I study Chicana lawyers or doctors, that is, "another occupation that presents our people in a more positive light." Another woman denied ever having worked as a domestic even though several women, including her sister-in-law, had given me her name as someone currently employed as a domestic.

The stigma of domestic service was a problem during the interviews as well. From the outset, it was very important for each woman to establish herself as someone more than a private household worker. Conducting nonstructured, free-flowing, and open-ended interviews allowed the women to establish multiple identities, particularly diffuse family and community roles.

The interviews were conducted in the women's homes, usually while sitting in the living room or at the dining room table with the radio or television on in the background. Although family members peeked in, for the most part there were few interruptions other than an occasional telephone call. From time to time, the women called to their husbands in the other room to ask the name of a street where they had once lived or the year the oldest son had been born in order to figure out when they had left and returned to work. The average interview lasted two hours, but I often stayed to visit and chat long after the interview was over. They told me about their church activities and plans to remodel the house and asked me for my opinion on current Chicano politics. Some spread out blankets, tablecloths, and pillow covers to exhibit their needlework. They showed me pictures of their children and grandchildren, giving me a walking tour of living rooms and bedrooms where wedding and high school portraits hung. As each one was identified, I learned more about their lives.

I conducted 25 open-ended interviews with Chicanas living and working in the greater Denver metropolitan area. The most visible Chicano communities in Denver are in the low-income neighborhood located in the downtown area or in one of two working-class neighborhoods in the northern and western areas of the city. I interviewed women from each of these communities. I asked them to discuss their overall work histories, with particular emphasis on their experiences as domestics. I probed for detailed information on domestic work, including strategies for finding employers, definitions of appropriate and inappropriate tasks, the negotiation of working conditions, ways of doing housework efficiently, and the pros and cons of domestic service. The accounts included descriptions of the domestics' relationships with white middle-class mistresses and revealed Chicanas' attitudes toward their employers' lifestyles.

All of the interviewees' families of orientation were from northern New Mexico or southern Colorado, where many of them had lived and worked on small farms. Some of the women had arrived in Denver as children with their parents, others as young brides, and still others as single women to join siblings and cousins in Denver's barrios. Several women recalled annual migrations to northern Colorado to pick sugar beets, prior to their permanent relocation to Denver. In some cases, the women's entire families of orientation had migrated to Denver; in others, parents and siblings had either remained behind or migrated to other cities. Many older women had migrated with their husbands after World War II, and several younger women interviewed had arrived at the same time, as children. Women who had migrated as single adults typically had done so in the last 10 or 15 years. Now they were married and permanently living in Denver.

. . .

Historical Background

After the Mexican American War, Mexicans were given the option to maintain their Mexican citizenship and leave the country or become U.S. citizens. Many reluctantly choose the latter in order to keep their homes. Although the Treaty of Guadalupe Hidalgo was supposed to guarantee land grant provisions to those who chose to remain in occupied territory, legal and illegal maneuvers were used to eliminate communal usage of land and natural resources. Between 1854 and 1930, an estimated 2,000,000 acres of private land and 1,700,000 acres of communal land were lost.[8] In the arid Southwest, small plots were insufficient to continue a subsistence-based farming economy, thus the members of the Hispano community were transformed from landowners to wage laborers. Enclosure of the common lands forced Mexicans from their former economic roles, "freed" Mexicans for wage labor, and established a racially stratified labor force in the Southwest.

As early as 1900, the Hispano farming and ranching communities of northern New Mexico and southern Colorado began to lose their population. A combination of push-pull factors conspired to force rural Hispanos off the land and attracted them to urban areas like Denver. Rural northern New Mexico and southern Colorado experienced drastic depopulation as adults left to find jobs. During the Depression, studies conducted in cooperation with the Works Progress Administration (WPA) noted the desperate situation:

> The Tewa Basin Study by the U.S. Department of Agriculture showed that in eleven Spanish-American villages containing 1,202 families, an average of 1,110 men went out of the villages to work for some part of each year prior to 1930. In 1934, only 157 men out of 1,202 families had found outside work.[9]

Migration in search of jobs became a way of life for many families. New Mexicans and southern Coloradans joined the migratory farm labor stream from Texas, California, and Mexico. World War II further depopulated the rural villages as people flocked to the cities in response to job openings in defense plants and related industries. Postwar migration from New Mexico was estimated to be one-fifth of the 1940 rural Chicano population.[10] This pattern continued in the following decades. For instance, Thomas Malone found that during the decade of the 1950s, only one of seven northern counties in New Mexico had not experienced a decrease in its former predominantly Spanish-speaking population.[11] By 1960, 61 percent of the population had been urbanized,[12] and between 1950 and 1960, an additional 24 percent left their rural communities.[13]

Perhaps because research on population movement among Chicanos has been so overwhelmingly concerned with emigration from Mexico, this type of internal population movement among Chicanos has not been well studied. What research is available has focused primarily on male workers and the relationship between urbanization and acculturation.[14] Chicanas have been either ignored or treated simply as family members—mothers, daughters, or wives, accompanying male relatives in search of work—rather than as wage earners in their own right. Nevertheless, for many women migration to an urban area made it necessary that they enter the labor market. Domestic service became a significant occupation in the experience.

Profile of Chicana Household Workers

Only the vaguest statistical data on Chicana private household workers are available; for the most part these workers remain a doubly hidden population. The reasons are themselves instructive. Domestic workers tend to be invisible because paid domestic work has not been one of the occupations recorded in social science surveys, and the U.S. Census Bureau uses a single code lumping together all private household workers, including launderers, cooks, housekeepers, child-care workers, cleaners, and servants. Even when statistics on domestics can be teased out of the census and labor data bases, they are marred by the common practice of underreporting work in the informal sector. Unlike some of the private household workers in the East,

Chicana domestics are not unionized and remain outside the "counted" labor force. Many private household workers are not included in the statistics collected by the Department of Labor. The "job" involves an informal labor arrangement made between two people, and in many cases payment is simply a cash transaction that is never recorded with the Internal Revenue Service (IRS).

Governmental undercounting of Chicanos and Mexican immigrants in the United States further adds to the problem of determining the number of Chicanas and Mexicanas employed as private household workers. For many, domestic service is part of the underground economy, and employing undocumented workers is reported neither to the IRS nor to the Immigration and Naturalization Service (INS), thus making another source of statistical information unreliable. Chicanos continue to be an undercounted and obscure population. Problems with the categorization of domestics have been still further complicated by changing identifiers for the Mexican American population: Mexican, Spanish-speaking, Hispanic, Spanish-surnamed, and the like make it impossible to segment out the Chicano population.

The 25 Chicanas whom I interviewed included welfare recipients as well as working-class women, ranging in age from 29 to 68. Thirteen of the 25 women were between 29 and 45 years old. The remaining 12 were over 52 years old. All the women had children and the older women also had grandchildren. The smallest family consisted of one child, and the largest family had seven children. The average was three children. All but one of the women had been married. Five of the women were single heads of households, two of them were divorced, and the other three were single, separated, or widowed. The married women were currently living with husbands employed in blue-collar positions, such as construction and factory work. At the time of the interview, the women who were single heads of households were financially supporting no more than two children.

Educational backgrounds ranged from no schooling to completion of high school. Six women had completed high school, and seven had no high school experience, including one who had never attended school at all. The remaining 12 had at least a sixth-grade education. Although the least educated were the older women, eight of the women under 42 had not completed high school. The youngest woman with less than an eighth-grade education was 53 years old. The 12 women over 50 averaged eight years of schooling. Three of the high school graduates were in their early thirties, two were in their early forties, and one was 57 years old. Although one woman preferred to be interviewed in Spanish, all the women spoke English.

Work experience as a private household worker ranged from five months to 30 years. Women 50 years and older had worked in the occupation from eight to 30 years, while four of the women between the ages of 33 and 39 had worked as domestics for 12 years. Half of the women had worked for more than 10 years as private household workers. Only three women had worked as domestics prior to marriage; each of these women had worked in live-in situations in rural areas in Colorado. Several years later, after marriage and children, they returned as day workers. All the other women, however, had turned to nonresidential day work in response to a financial crisis; in the majority of cases, it was their first job after marriage and having children. Some of the women remained domestics throughout their lives, but others moved in and out of domestic work. Women who returned to domestic service after having other types of jobs usually did so following a period of unemployment.

The work histories revealed that domestic service was only one of several low-paying, low-status jobs the women had held during their lives. They had been hired as waitresses, laundresses, janitors, farmworkers, nurses aides, fast-food servers, cooks, dishwashers, receptionists, school aides, cashiers, baby-sitters, salesclerks, factory workers, and various types of line workers in poultry farms and car washes. Almost half of the women had worked as janitors in hospitals and office buildings or as hotel maids. About one-fourth of the women had held semiskilled and skilled positions such as beauticians, typists, and medical-record clerks. Six of the women had worked only as domestics.

Paid and Unpaid Domestic Work

In describing their daily routine activities, these Chicanas drew my attention to the interrelationship between paid and unpaid housework. As working women, Chicana private household workers face the "double day" or "second shift," but in their case both days consisted of the same types of tasks. Paid housework done for an employer was qualitatively different from housework done for their own families.

In the interviews, Chicanas described many complexities of domestic service. They explained how they used informal networks to find new employers for themselves and for relatives and friends. As they elaborated on the advantages and disadvantages of particular work arrangements and their reasons for refusing certain household tasks, I soon realized that these women not only knew a great deal about cleaning and maintaining homes, but they understood the influence of social relationships on household tasks. Analysis of the extensive planning and negotiation involved in the informal and underground arrangements of domestic service highlighted the significance of the social relationships surrounding housework.

Their work histories included detailed explanations of beginning, returning to, and continuing in domestic service. In the discussions, I began to understand the paradox of domestic service: On the one hand, cleaning houses is degrading and embarrassing; on the other, domestic service can be higher paying, more autonomous, and less dehumanizing than other low-status, low-skilled occupations. Previous jobs in the beet fields, fast-food restaurants, car washes, and turkey farms did not offer annual raises, vacations, or sick leave. Furthermore, these jobs forced employees to work long

hours and to keep rigid time schedules, and they frequently occurred outside or in an unsafe work environment. Unlike the other options available,
domestic service did have the potential for offering flexible work schedules
and autonomy. In most cases, domestic service also paid much more. Although annual raises, vacation, and social security were not the norm for
most Chicanas in domestic service, there remained the possibility that such
benefits could be negotiated with employers. Furthermore, as former farmworkers, laundresses, and line workers, the women found freedom in domestic work from exposure to dangerous pesticides, poor ventilation, and
other health risks. This paradox foreshadowed a critical theoretical issue, the
importance of understanding the social process that constructs domestic service as a low-status occupation.

Stigma as a perceived occupational hazard of domestic service emerged
during the initial contact and throughout most of the interviews. The stigma
attached to domestic service punctuated the interviews. I knew that many
women hid their paid household labor from the government, but I did not
realize that this secrecy encompassed neighbors, friends, and even extended
family members. Several women gave accounts that revealed their families'
efforts to conceal their employment as domestics. Children frequently stated
that their mothers "just did housework," which was ambiguous enough to
define them as full-time homemakers and not necessarily as domestics.

Faced with limited job opportunities, Chicanas selected domestic service
and actively sought to make the most of the situation. In comparison with
other jobs they had held, domestic service usually paid more and offered
greater flexibility in arranging the length of the workday and workweek. Although other jobs did not carry the stigma of servitude, workers were under
constant supervision, and the work was similarly low status. Therefore, the
women who chose domestic service over other low-paying, low-status jobs
based their selection on the occupation that offered some possibility of control. Their challenge was to structure the work so as to reap the most benefits: pay, work hours, labor, and autonomy. Throughout the interviews, the
women emphasized job flexibility as the major advantage of domestic service over previous jobs. Nonrigid work schedules allowed time to do their
own housework and fulfill family obligations, such as caring for sick children or attending school functions. By stressing the benefits gained by doing
day work, Chicanas diffused the low status in their work identities and emphasized their family and community identities. The ways in which they
arranged both work and family revealed coping strategies used to deal with
the stigma, and this drew me to analyze housework as a form of labor having
both paid and unpaid manifestations.

The conventional social science separation of work and family is an analytical construct and is not found in the lived reality of Chicana domestics.
Invariably the interviewees mixed and intertwined discussions of work and
family. Moreover, the actual and practical relationships between work and

family were explicit in their descriptions of daily activities: The reasons for seeking employment included the family's financial situation and the desire to raise its standard of living; earning extra money for the household was viewed as an extension of these women's roles as mothers and wives; arranging day work involved planning work hours around the children's school attendance, dentist and doctor appointments, and community and church activities; in some cases, young mothers even took their preschool-age children with them to work. The worlds of paid and unpaid housework were not disconnected in the lives of these women.

Attending to the importance of the relationship between paid and unpaid domestic work led me to ponder new questions about the dynamics of buying and selling household labor. How does housework differ when it is paid work? How does the housewife role change when part of her work is allocated to another woman? What is the range of employer-employee relationship in domestic service today? And is there a difference in the type of relationships developed by employed and unemployed women buying household labor?

The importance of attending to both paid and unpaid housework in researching domestic service became more apparent as I began presenting my research to academic audiences. When I read papers on the informal labor market or on family and community networks used to find work, some of my colleagues responded as women who employed domestics. Frequently question-and-answer sessions turned into a defense of such practices as hiring undocumented workers, not filing income taxes, or gift giving in lieu of raises and benefits. Although I was aware that as working women, many academics employed someone to clean their houses, I was not prepared for scholars and feminists to respond to my scholarly work as housewives or employers. I was also surprised to discover that many of the maternalistic practices traditionally found in domestic service were common practices in their homes. The recurring responses made me realize that my feminist colleagues had never considered their relationships with the "cleaning woman" on the same plane as those with secretaries, waitresses, or janitors; that is, they thought of the former more or less in terms of the mistress-maid relationship. When, through my research, I pointed out the contradiction, many still had difficulty thinking of their homes—the haven from the cruel academic world—as someone's workplace. Their overwhelming feelings of discomfort, guilt, and resentment, which sometimes came out as hostility, alerted me to the fact that something more was going on.

Although written over a decade ago, Margaret Mead's depiction of the middle-class woman's dilemma still seems to capture the contradictory feelings and attitudes that I hear among feminists today.

Traveling around the country, I meet a great many young wives and mothers who are struggling with the problem that seems to have no solu-

tion—how to hold down two full-time jobs at once. . . . As I listen I realize how many of them—guiltily but wistfully—yearn for the bygone
days of servants. . . . They are guilty because they don't quite approve of
anyone's working as a servant in someone else's home.[15]

In a society that espouses egalitarian values, we can expect yearnings "for
the bygone days of servants" to be experienced as a contradiction. A century
ago, Jane Addams discussed the awkward feelings and apprehensiveness
academic women feel:

> I should consider myself an unpardonable snob if, because a woman did
> my cooking, I should not hold myself ready to have her for my best
> friend, to drive, to read, to attend receptions with her, but that friendship
> might or might not come about, according to her nature and mine, just as
> it might or might not come about between me and my college colleague.
> On the other hand, I would consider myself very stupid if merely be-
> cause a woman cooked my food and lived in my house I should insist
> upon having a friendship with her, whether her nature and mine re-
> sponded to it or not. It would be folly to force the companionship of my-
> self or my family upon her when doubtless she would vastly prefer the
> companionship of her own friends and her own family.[16]

In her book on black domestics and white employers in the South, Susan
Tucker addresses the deeper psychological and class factors involved in hiring servants.

> Most studies of domestic work maintain that the prime motivation for
> hiring a servant is the enhancement of the employer's image as a supe-
> rior being. Yet, many women certainly must feel some discomfort, even
> when paying a decent wage, about the possibility of such a motivation.
> . . . There are many conflicting principles and traditions surrounding the
> employment of a socially and economically disadvantaged woman who
> goes daily into a wealthy home. One might feel discomfort if one were
> aware of any number of different types of ideas—feminist, egalitarian,
> religious.[17]

Domestic service must be studied because it raises a challenge to any
feminist notion of "sisterhood." A growing number of employed middle-
and upper-middle-class women escape the double-day syndrome by hiring poor women of color to do housework and child care. David Katzman
underscored the class contradiction:

> Middle-class women, the employers, gained freedom from family roles
> and household chores and assumed or confirmed social status by the
> employment of a servant. . . . The greater liberty of these middle-class
> women, however, was achieved at the expense of working-class women,
> who, forced to work, assumed the tasks beneath, distasteful to, or too
> demanding for the family members.[18]

Housework is ascribed on the basis of gender, and it is further divided along class lines and, in most cases, by race and ethnicity. Domestic service accentuates the contradiction of race and class in feminism, with privileged women of one class using the labor of another woman to escape aspects of sexism.

. . .

I argue that private household workers are struggling to control the work process and alter the employee-employer relationship to a client-tradesperson relationship in which labor services rather than labor power are sold. The struggle over the work process is aimed at developing new interactions with employers that eliminate aspects of hierarchy along the lines of gender, race, and class.

NOTES

1. The conditions I observed in El Paso were not much different from those described by D. Thompson in her 1960 article, "Are Women Bad Employers of Other Women," *Ladies Home Journal:* "Quarters for domestic help are usually ill placed for quiet. Almost invariably they open from pantry or kitchen, so that if a member of the family goes to get a snack at night he wakes up the occupant. And the live-in maid has nowhere to receive a caller except in the kitchen or one [of] those tiny rooms." "As a general rule anything was good enough for a maid's room. It became a catchall for furniture discarded from other parts of the house. One room was a cubicle too small for a regular-sized bed." Cited in Linda Martin and Kerry Segrave, *The Servant Problem: Domestic Workers in North America* (Jefferson, NC: McFarland, 1985), p. 25.

2. David Katzman addresses the "servant problem" in his historical study of domestic service, *Seven Days a Week, Women and Domestic Service in Industrializing America* (Chicago: University of Illinois Press, 1981). Defined by middle-class housewives, the problem includes both the shortage of servants available and the competency of women willing to enter domestic service. Employer's attitudes about domestics have been well documented in women's magazines. Katzman described the topic as "the bread and butter of women's magazines between the Civil War and World War I"; moreover, Martin and Segrave, *The Servant Problem*, illustrate the continuing presence of articles on the servant problem in women's magazines today.

3. Lillian Pettengill's account *Toilers of the Home: The Record of a College Woman's Experience as a Domestic Servant* (New York: Doubleday, 1903) is based on two years of employment in Philadelphia households.

4. Ruth Schwartz Cowan, *More Work for Mother: The Ironies of Household Technology from the Open Hearth to the Microwave* (New York: Basic Books, 1983), p. 228.

5. Earning money as domestic workers to pay college expenses not covered by scholarships is not that uncommon among other women of color in the United States. Trudier Harris interviewed several African American women public school and university college teachers about their college day experiences in domestic service. See *From Mammies to Militants: Domestics in Black American Literature* (Philadelphia: Temple University Press, 1982), pp. 5–6.

6. Judith Rollins, *Between Women: Domestics and Their Employers* (Philadelphia: Temple University Press, 1985); Bonnie Thornton Dill, "Across the Boundaries of Race and Class: An Exploration of the Relationship between Work and Family among Black Female Domestic Servants" (Ph.D. dissertation, New York University, 1979): Judith Rollins, "'Making Your Job Good Yourself': Domestic Service and the Construction of Personal Dignity," in *Women and the Politics of Empowerment,* ed. Ann Bookman and Sandra Morgen (Philadelphia: Temple University Press, 1988), pp. 33–52; Soraya Moore Coley, "'And Still I Rise': An Exploratory Study of Contemporary Black Private Household Workers" (Ph.D. dissertation, Bryn Mawr College, 1981); Evelyn Nakano Glenn, *Issei, Nisei, War Brides: Three Generations of Japanese American Women in Domestic Service* (Philadelphia: Temple University Press, 1986).

7. In some cases, it was important to let women know that my own background had involved paid housework and that my mother and sister were currently employed full-time as private household workers. Sharing this information conveyed that my life had similarities to theirs and that I respected them. This sharing of information is similar to the concept of "reciprocity" (R. Wax, "Reciprocity in Field Work," in *Human Organization Research: Field Relationships and Techniques,* ed. R. N. Adams and J. J. Preiss [New York: Dorsey, 1960], pp. 90–98).

8. Clark Knowlton, "Changing Spanish-American Villages of Northern New Mexico," *Sociology and Social Research* 53 (1969): 455–75.

9. Nancie Gonzalez, *The Spanish-Americans of New Mexico* (Albuquerque: University of New Mexico Press, 1967), p. 123.

10. William W. Winnie, "The Hispanic People of New Mexico" (Master's thesis, University of Florida, 1955).

11. Thomas J. Malone, "Recent Demographic and Economic Changes in Northern New Mexico," *New Mexico Business* 17 (1964): 4–14.

12. Donald N. Barrett and Julian Samora, *The Movement of Spanish Youth from Rural to Urban Settings* (Washington, DC: National Committee for Children and Youth, 1963).

13. Clark Knowlton, "The Spanish Americans in New Mexico," *Sociology and Social Research* 45 (1961): 448–54.

14. See Paul A. Walter, "The Spanish-Speaking Community in New Mexico," *Sociology and Social Research* 24 (1939): 150–57; Thomas Weaver, "Social Structure, Change and Conflict in a New Mexico Village" (Ph.D. dissertation, University of California, 1965); Florence R. Kluckhohn and Fred L. Stodtbeck, *Variations in Value Orientations* (Evanston, IL: Row, Peterson, 1961); Frank Moore, "San Jose, 1946: A Study in Urbanization" (Master's thesis, University of New Mexico, 1947); Donald N. Barrett and Julian Samora, *The Movement of Spanish Youth* (Washington, DC: National Committee for Children and Youth, 1963).

15. Margaret Mead, "Household Help," *Redbook Magazine* (October 1976), pp. 42, 45, 47.

16. See page 545 of Jane Addams, "A Belated Industry," *American Journal of Sociology* 1 (1896): 536–50.

17. Susan Tucker, *Telling Memories among Southern Women: Domestic Workers and Their Employers in the Segregated South* (Baton Rouge: Louisiana State University Press, 1988), p. 231.

18. David Katzman, *Seven Days a Week* (Chicago: University of Illinois Press, 1981), pp. 269–70.

4

FREEDOM SUMMER
In Search of the Volunteers

DOUG McADAM

Most sociologists agree that the best way to learn about research is through the hands-on experience gained by conducting a study. The research process, examined in the next three readings, often turns up new questions and challenges for the researcher. In this selection, Doug McAdam reveals why and how he conducted his research on the volunteers of the Freedom Summer project. Specifically, McAdam discusses the circuitous shifts and accommodations that mark the early part of a research project as the project defines itself, often in ways unplanned and unexpected by the researcher.

[E]very single thing that happened each day was new to me. I was being bombarded with information, bombarded with experiences . . . and my little psyche just almost cracked.[1]

You felt you were a part of a kind of historic moment; that something very profound about the whole way of life in a region was about to change; that . . . you were . . . making . . . history and that you were in some way utterly selfless and yet [you] found yourself.[2]

In terms of the kind of goals that I have in my life for social change, it was the highest possible experience I'll ever have. . . . In terms of participating in history, it was the best I'll ever do, but it . . . [took] its toll on me; . . . [emotionally] it set me back. . . . [Luckily] I didn't come out with any physical disabilities so, at least, physically, I . . . survived.[3]

[It] was very inspirational. I mean, I think the whole thing about . . . beginning to think about what I was going to be doing as a woman and . . . what I was going to do with my life. Was I going to be a professional? Was I going to go to law school? . . . So much of what I'm in now goes back to it. So much of the work I do now goes back to my memory of that time.[4]

It totally flipped me out . . . for the first time the pieces fit . . . this felt like me . . . besides the good I think we did, it was my personal salvation as well.[5]

It was the longest nightmare I have ever had: three months—June, July and August of 1964. (Sellers, 1973: p. 94).

What is the "it" to which all these speakers are referring? What shared experiences produced such varied, yet intense, reactions in so many people? The event in question is the 1964 Mississippi Freedom Summer campaign, or, as it was simply known at the time, the Summer Project.

Spearheaded by the Student Non-Violent Coordinating Committee (SNCC), the project lasted less than three months, from early June until late August. During that time, better than 1,000 people, the vast majority of them white, Northern college students, journeyed south to work in one of the 44 local projects that comprised the overall campaign. While in Mississippi, the volunteers lived in communal "Freedom Houses" or were housed by local black families who refused to be intimidated by segregationist threats of violence. Their days were taken up with a variety of tasks, principally registering black voters and teaching in so-called Freedom Schools.

What this capsule summary misses is the unrelieved fear, grinding poverty, and intermittent violence that beset the project. These elements combined to make the summer a searing experience for nearly all who took part. Just 10 days into the project, three participants—James Chaney, Andrew Goodman, and Michael Schwerner—were kidnapped and beaten to death by a group of segregationists led by Mississippi law enforcement officers. The subsequent search for their bodies brought scores of FBI agents and hundreds of journalists to the state. Despite their presence, the violence continued. One other volunteer died before summer's end and hundreds more endured bombings, beatings, and arrest. Just as significantly, the volunteers experienced the sense of liberation that came with exposure to new lifestyles—interracial relationships, communal living, a more open sexuality—new political ideologies and a radically new and critical perspective on the United States. By all accounts, it was a remarkable summer for a remarkable group of young people. And one that would have enduring consequences for both the volunteers and the country as a whole.

At the outset, the Summer Project reflected the liberal idealism so characteristic of America in the early sixties. Though not without tensions and contradictions, the project *did* embody the ideals of interracialism, nonviolence, and liberal/left coalition that were so much a part of the progressive vision of the era. And so it was with the volunteers themselves.

Poised on the eve of the summer campaign, project workers represented the "best and the brightest" of early sixties youthful idealism. Overwhelmingly drawn from elite colleges and universities, the volunteers tended to be extraordinarily bright, academically successful, politically active, and passionately committed to the full realization of the idealistic values on which they had been taught America was based. For the most part, they were liberals, not radicals; reformers rather than revolutionaries.

In short order, however, both the volunteers and the country were to be dramatically transformed. As a nation we would descend in a matter of years from the euphoric heights of the New Frontier to the domestic unrest of the late sixties. If Freedom Summer was a kind of high-water mark of early sixties liberalism, the foundations on which it rested crumbled soon afterward. Interracialism died amid the calls for black power and black separatism less than a year later. Nonviolence was widely repudiated, at least rhetorically, in the wake of Watts in 1965. The liberal/left coalition failed to survive the summer. The end came in August at the Democratic National Convention when party regulars elected to seat the lily-white Mississippi delegation rather than the challenge delegation that had grown out of the summer campaign.

The volunteers were no less affected by the turbulence of the era than was the nation as a whole. The vast majority were radicalized by the events of the mid to late sixties. Many of them played prominent roles in those events. Virtually none were unaffected by them.

The central theme of this writing is that to fully understand the dramatic changes experienced by the volunteers and America during this era requires a serious reappraisal of the Freedom Summer campaign. For Freedom Summer marked a critical turning point both in the lives of those who participated in the campaign and the New Left as a whole. Its significance lies both in the events of the summer and the cultural and political consequences that flowed from it. The events of the summer effectively resocialized and radicalized the volunteers while the ties they established with other volunteers laid the groundwork for a nationwide activist network out of which the other major movements of the era—women's, antiwar, student—were to emerge. In short, Freedom Summer served both as the organizational basis for much of the activism of the sixties as well as an important impetus for the development of the broader counterculture that emerged during the era. This article represents a retrospective account of the Freedom Summer project and an assessment of its impact on both the volunteers and American society as a whole.

As straightforward as this focus is, it is quite different from the intent with which I began the project some seven years ago. At that time, my interest centered less on the Freedom Summer campaign or those who participated in it, and more on the links between those participants and the later social movements of the sixties and seventies. A series of fortuitous events in the early 1980s prompted me to broaden the focus of my research. . . .

Before embarking on the project, . . . I spent six years researching and writing a book on the origins of the modern civil rights movement (*Political Process and the Development of Black Insurgency, 1930–1970,* University of Chicago Press, 1982). In the course of that research I was struck by the number of

references to whites trained in civil rights organizing who went on to prominent roles in the other major movements of the sixties. I had been aware of
the debt those later movements owed to the black struggle, but having myself come of (activist) age only in the late sixties and early seventies, I had experienced the debt as primarily one of tactics and ideology rather than of
personnel. Certainly, few of the activists I knew in the early seventies had
participated in southern civil rights organizing. But then the number of persons engaged in social action had multiplied so rapidly between 1964 and
1970 that one could hardly have expected the ranks of latter-day activists to
have been dominated by the relatively small number of pioneers who had
been active in the early sixties.

If the personnel debt was not numerical, how was it to be characterized?
My sense of things was that the importance of these early white civil rights
activists lay in the political and cultural bridge they had provided between
the southern black struggle and the college campuses of the North and West.
They were pioneers in an important diffusion process by which the ideologies, tactics, and cultural symbols of the southern civil rights movement
were introduced to the population—northern white college students—that
was to dominate activist politics for the remainder of the era. In this view,
there had not been three or four discrete movements in the sixties, but a
single, broad, activist community with its roots firmly in the southern civil
rights movement and separate branches extending into various forms of activism (principally the black power, antiwar, student, and women's liberation movements).

Asserting this view was easy. Systematically studying the extent and
significance of these ties was quite another matter. Nonetheless, that was the
research project I was determined to tackle once the book on the civil rights
movement had been completed.

Such a project, I reasoned, had to proceed from a systematic base. It
would not do merely to amass anecdotal evidence of the involvement of individual activists in both the civil rights and some other movements of the
period. Knowing that Tom Hayden participated in southern civil rights activities long before his rise to bona fide movement "stardom" in the late sixties
tells us nothing about the frequency of this phenomenon. What proportion
of white civil rights activists went on to pioneering roles in the antiwar
movement? Student protest activity? Women's liberation? And what was it
about their early civil rights experiences that disposed them to do so? These
were the types of questions I hoped to answer. But to do so required systematic access to a large number of individuals who had been active in early civil
rights organizing. Freedom Summer seemed to offer that access. What recommended the project as the starting point for my study was the fact that it
marked the first widespread entrance of young whites into the movement.
Whites, of course, had long been involved in the civil rights struggle. With
but a few notable exceptions, most of the leading figures in the abolition
movement had been white. During the 1930s, the white-dominated Ameri-

can Communist Party had sought to champion the cause of black civil rights in cases such as the one that involved the "Scottsboro boys."[6] Others, such as Anne and Carl Braden, fought the good fight through the lean years of the forties and fifties. A few whites, most notably Glenn Smiley of the Fellowship of Reconciliation (FOR), had been active in the Montgomery Bus Boycott. A minority of the Freedom Riders were white. But in all of these cases, the number of white participants was small. By contrast, the 1,000 or so whites who came to Mississippi for Freedom Summer represented a deluge. The sheer size of the project guaranteed me access to large numbers of white activists, *provided* I could find a list of all the summer volunteers that also included the name of the college or university (if any) each was attending at the time of the project; the only way I could think to track the volunteers in the present was to go through the alumni associations of their respective alma maters.

The search for this list came to resemble a quest for a (not so) holy grail. Fortunately my continuing work on the civil rights book occasioned numerous visits to libraries and archives throughout the South. These trips gave me the chance to inquire into the existence and whereabouts of *the* list. The bad news was that I was repeatedly told by librarians and archivists that they did not have, nor had they ever heard of, any such list. The story was the same at the Martin Luther King, Jr. Center in Atlanta. There, the head librarian, Louise Cook, said she too had never heard of any such list. She did, though, have a variety of other materials on the Summer Project that I was welcome to go through. True to her word, the list I hoped to find was not among these materials. Given what *was* there, however, the absence of the list hardly mattered. For there, nicely organized and catalogued, were the original five-page applications filled out by the volunteers in advance of the summer. Better still, the applications included those filled out, not only by the volunteers, but by an additional 300 persons who had applied to the project, been accepted, but for whatever reason had failed to go to Mississippi. I had serendipitously stumbled onto the makings of a kind of naturalistic experiment. Here were two groups—volunteers and no-shows—that presumably looked fairly similar going into the summer. One had the experience of Freedom Summer. The other did not.

The unexpected discovery of data on the no-shows enabled me to add two other questions to the original focus on links between movements with which I had begun the project. The first was simply the question of differences between the volunteers and no-shows *before* the summer. Were they really similar going into the summer? Or were the volunteers so different from the no-shows as to make any subsequent comparison of the two groups meaningless? The second question depended on a negative answer to the first. Assuming the no-shows *were* a defensible comparison group, *how* did the broad contours of their lives post-summer differ from the biographies of those who had participated in the project? Finally, as the study progressed, I came to regard one additional question as of equal importance to the previous three. It wasn't merely the comparison of participants and nonparticipants that was intriguing, but differences between the male and female volunteers as well. Given the clear differences in the ways men and women were raised in the early sixties, it was simply impossible to view their participation in the project as having meant the same thing either to themselves or to others. Hence a fourth question: How did the experience of the Summer Project and the consequences that flowed from it differ for the male and female volunteers?

I have spent the past six years trying, in a variety of ways, to answer these four basic questions. To do so, however, required that I first be able to locate as many of the applicants as I possibly could. Here the original project applications came in very handy. One piece of information that had been asked of the applicants was the college or university in which they were presently enrolled. This enabled me to assemble lists of applicants to be sent to some 269 alumni associations around the country. As expected, they proved to be my single richest source of addresses.[7] There were others, however. Those applying to the project had also been asked to list the names and addresses of their parents on the application form. Notwithstanding the fact that the United States is a highly mobile society, approximately 20 percent of the parents were still at the same addresses in 1982–1983 as they had been in 1964. In turn, they supplied current addresses for 101 sons or daughters who had applied to the project. Academic directories were also searched for names that matched those who had applied to the project. Lists of applicants sharing the same undergraduate majors—another item asked of those applying—provided the basis for this search. Still other addresses were produced in a variety of idiosyncratic ways. Once contacted, many of the applicants were willing and able to supply addresses of others with whom they had stayed in touch. Friends and friends of friends put me in touch with still more applicants. So too did the publishers of at least two applicants-turned-authors. Others contacted me after hearing about my project. One even turned up as a guest at a party where I happened to be talking about my research.

The result of these varied efforts were verified current addresses for 556 of the 959 applicants for whom I had applications. Of these, 382 (of a total 720) had been participants in the project while another 174 (of 239) had withdrawn in advance of the summer. Foreshadowing a major difference between the two groups, the percentage of no-shows I was able to obtain addresses for—73 percent—was considerably higher than the 53 percent figure for the actual volunteers. Exactly what this difference meant was to become clear only after I had started contacting the applicants.

Contact with the applicants took two forms. First, all of the applicants were mailed questionnaires . . . asking them about their experiences during Freedom Summer, their activist histories, and the broad contours of their lives, personal as well as political, post-Freedom Summer.[8] This was the only way I could compare data on the large number of applicants with whom I was dealing.

However, I also realized that any real understanding of the complex issues I was addressing required that I talk at length to at least some of the applicants in both groups. Between August 1984 and July 1985 I did just that, interviewing 40 volunteers and another 40 no-shows, selected at random from among all of the applicants in each group.[9] More than half of these interviews were conducted in a hectic three-month period during the spring of 1985, during which I camped my way around the country, interviewing applicants as I went. All told, I logged 22,000 miles and interviewed 48 people in the course of the trip. The "sessions" lasted anywhere from two hours to two days and took place under an equally wide range of circumstances. Along the way I took part in a Native American sweat in Colorado, a bar mitzvah in Buffalo, an anti-apartheid demonstration in Washington, D.C., and a formal Japanese tea ceremony at a commune in California. By turns, I felt confused, exhilarated, depressed, and enriched by my contact with the applicants.

The end result, though, was that the trip "worked" in the way I had hoped it would. I came away with a much clearer sense of what Freedom Summer had meant to the volunteers and how it had shaped their lives in ways that clearly distinguished them from the no-shows. The somewhat superficial differences between the two groups that had been apparent in their questionnaire responses came alive in conversation. The two groups may have been similar before the summer, but they emerged from it clearly very different. Just as important, these differences were to *make* a difference, not just in the lives of the volunteers, but in the evolution of the New Left and what would come to be known as the "60s experience." Caught up in a unique confluence of biography and history, the volunteers were among the first white students to sense the possibilities inherent in the moment. Many of them climbed aboard a political and cultural wave just as it was forming and beginning to wash forward. . . . And what of Freedom Summer? If it didn't exactly produce the wave, it certainly gave it momentum and helped fashion many of the specific political and cultural elements we associate with it. Perhaps most important, Freedom Summer created one of the major means by which this emergent sixties culture was made available to its ultimate consumers: white, northern college students. The Freedom Summer volunteers served as influential carriers of the new culture.

NOTES

1. Interview with an anonymous Freedom Summer volunteer, August 14, 1984.
2. Interview with an anonymous Freedom Summer volunteer, April 22, 1985.
3. Interview with Len Edwards, August 17, 1984.
4. Interview with Linda Davis, April 18, 1984.
5. Interview with Marion Davidson, March 21, 1985.
6. The "Scottsboro boys" were nine black teenagers brought to trial in 1931 and convicted on trumped up rape charges in a case involving a white woman. The

name "Scottsboro boys" comes from the small town in northern Alabama where the trial took place. Eventually the convictions were reversed due to the legal efforts of lawyers representing the American Communist Party and the national attention they succeeded in focusing on the case.

7. Of the 556 addresses I know to be current, 465 were supplied by college and university alumni associations.

8. Two questionnaires were actually produced during this phase of the project: one tailored to the experiences of the volunteers, and the other geared to the lives of the no-shows.

9. By the strictest methodological canons, only 90 percent of the interviews were truly random. What enabled me to travel around the country interviewing the former applicants was receipt of a Guggenheim Fellowship. Before learning of this award, I had been content simply to interview any volunteer I came in contact with. In July of 1984 I was lucky enough to attend a reunion of Bay Area volunteers held in Oakland. While there, I arranged to interview 10 of those in attendance on a return trip in August. Upon receipt of the Guggenheim award, I drew the names of 40 volunteers at random. Reflecting their disproportionate concentration in the Bay Area, 15 of the names drawn were those of volunteers who lived in and around San Francisco. Two of these were volunteers I had already interviewed. Rather than discard the other eight interviews I had already done, I merely substituted them for eight of the names I had drawn. So strictly speaking, eight of the 80 interviews conducted were not random.

REFERENCES

Sellers, Cleveland, with Robert Terrell. 1973. *The River of No Return: The Autobiography of a Black Militant*. New York: William Morrow.

5

THE "OTHER" AMERICANS

GABRIELLE SÁNDOR

Social research is concerned with the definition and assessment of social phenomena. Many social concepts, such as racial identification, are difficult to study because of measurement problems. For example, this selection by Gabrielle Sándor illustrates how inaccurate the four racial categories of "white, black, Asian, and American Indian" are in the U.S. census. In 1990, over 10 million people refused to categorize themselves in one of those four categories. The implications of this situation are enormous because the government relies on census data to determine the efficacy of public policies, such as affirmative action and the Voting Rights Act. Thus, survey researchers are in a quandary because even though more detailed data on

racial-ethnic differences are needed, race and ethnicity are social constructions and, therefore, difficult to measure.

Ada Nurie Pagán is a blonde, green-eyed, pale-skinned "person of
color." When asked by affirmative action officers, she says that her
race is Hispanic, Latina, or Puerto Rican. The Census Bureau would
say that Hispanic origin is an ethnicity, not a race, so it classifies Ada as
white. But Ada doesn't want to give that answer.

"I can't check a circle that labels me black, white, Asian, or American Indian, because I'm not any of those things," she says. "My sister and I have
the same parents, but she's much darker than me. If it came down to choosing black or white, I'd have to choose white and she couldn't. That wouldn't
make any sense."

Ada's confusion stems from the ambiguity in current definitions of race
and ethnicity. The Census Bureau sees race and ethnicity as two different demographic characteristics and has separate questions on census forms and
surveys. But the people who fill out the forms sometimes find the two concepts impossible to separate.

The result is much more than a problem for census takers. Ada's misgiv-
ings are part of a significant generation gap in attitudes toward race. The
rules that govern government statistics on race and ethnicity are based on a
16-year-old definition, and young people like Ada live in a world where that
definition seems arbitrary or even offensive.

People in their twenties today never saw sanctioned segregation. They
read about the civil rights movement in history books, and they were taught
in public schools that discrimination is wrong. Small wonder, then, that
young adults are much more likely than older adults to object to racial categories or not to fit within them. In 1990, members of the "other race" category
had a median age of about 24 years, compared with a national median of 33.

Some "other race" Americans are mixed-race children. Though relatively
rare, they are often born to middle-class families that vote and organize. A
larger share are recent immigrants to the U.S. They are likely to be young
adults, and birth rates for most minority groups are higher than they are for
non-Hispanic whites. As a result, younger Americans are more likely to be
minorities.

Mixed-race children are also increasingly common, because the penalties
once attached to interracial dating and marriage are slowly fading away. In
1991, 74 percent of Americans said that interracial marriage was acceptable
for themselves or others, according to the Roper Organization, up from 70
percent who found it acceptable in 1986.

Nonwhite and Hispanic Americans will claim 28 percent of the total U.S.
population in 2000, according to the Census Bureau. But at the same time,
the share of minorities will be 36 percent among children under age 18 and
33 percent among young adults aged 18 to 34. If current trends continue,

Interracial Marriages

The number of black and white interracial married couples has increased 78 percent since 1980. (number of marriages in thousands by type, percent of total married couples, 1980 and 1992; and percent change, 1980–92)

Race	1992 number	percent	1980 number	percent	percent change 1980–92
Total Married Couples	53,512	100.0%	49,714	100.0%	7.6%
Total Black and White Interracial Couples	1,161	2.2	651	1.3	78.3
Black/White Couples	246	0.5	167	0.3	47.3
White wife, black husband	163	0.3	122	0.2	33.6
Black wife, white husband	83	0.2	45	0.1	84.4
White Wife/Other-Race Husband (excluding black)	883	1.7	450	0.9	96.2
Black Wife/Other-Race Husband (excluding white)	32	0.1	34	0.1	−5.9

Source: Bureau of the Census, Marital Status and Living Arrangements; March 1992, *Current Population Reports,* Series P20–468.

minorities will be approaching half of the total U.S. population as early as 2050. Today's children will be the first to see that society.

Four Categories

The conflict over racial statistics worries researchers. "The demand [for detailed data] is going in one direction, and the quality and consistency in counting is going the other way," says Greg Robinson, chief of population and analysis for the Census Bureau. "The quality of the race and ethnic data is deteriorating."

Young adults' attitudes toward race also raise important issues for businesses, because they clash with older rules. "Tolerance and diversity is absolutely the number-one shared value" of young adults, says Gwen Lipsky, MTV's senior vice president of research and planning. "They are much more [tolerant] than any previous generation."

But while young adults embrace tolerance and racial ambiguity, a rule requires federal agencies like the Census Bureau to fit all of their racial data into separate categories. The rule, known as Statistical Directive 15, was adopted in 1978 by the Office of Management and Budget (OMB). It creates four official racial categories—American Indian or Alaskan Native, Asian or Pacific Islander, black, and white. It also defines Hispanic origin as an ethnic category separate from race. The rule helps federal and state agencies share racial data, which are vital to affirmative action and other government programs.

The 1990 census questionnaire asked respondents to put themselves into a racial category and to indicate their ethnicity and ancestry elsewhere. Respondents who felt that they didn't fit into one of the four categories checked a box marked "other race." The number of people who checked that box increased 45 percent between the 1980 and 1990 censuses, to 9.8 million. That's about 1 in 25 Americans.

Most of the people who check "other race" probably have a clear racial identity, because 98 percent claim Hispanic origin on the ethnicity question. In other words, over 40 percent of the nation's 22 million Hispanics aren't willing to identify themselves as black or white.

"Most of them are probably indicating some version of multiracial," says Carlos Fernández, president of the Association of Multi-Ethnic Americans (AMEA) in San Francisco. "Mexicans, especially, regard themselves as mestizo—part Spanish, part indigenous. The large majority of Mexico is multiracial. It's almost the official culture. Mexico hasn't asked a race question on its census since 1921. So on the U.S. census, people who put Mexican for race know full well what it means. It's mestizo, and that is a racial designation, not a nationality."

Many Latin Americans trace the greatest part of their ancestry to native Indians, followed by Europeans and perhaps Africans. But the category on the U.S. census applies only to North American Indians, so a Hispanic person's choices usually come down to black or white. Ada Pagán, whose great-great-grandmother was black, passes as white. But she knows exactly what her dark-skinned sister is. She's "trigueña," which Ada translates as "brown."

Statistical Headache

In 1990, about 400,000 people who marked "other race" were not Hispanic. Though their numbers are small, they are the ones raising their voices the loudest against the census's race question. Many of the protestors may be parents in racially mixed marriages who confront an obvious problem when answering the race question for their children.

The statistical headaches over race get worse every year, as the number of interracial marriages continues to rise. Interracial marriages were illegal in some states until 1967, when the Supreme Court struck down antimiscegenation laws in the aptly titled case *Loving vs. Virginia*. Since 1980, the number of black and white interracial married couples has increased from 651,000 to 1.2 million, according to the Census Bureau. Children born to parents of different races were more than 3 percent of births in 1990, according to the National Center for Health Statistics, up from 1 percent in 1968.

Unfortunately for survey designers, the race problem can't be solved simply by adding new categories for mestizos and multiracials. The reasons are a pair of statistical bugaboos called "primacy" and "recency" effects. Studies show that when respondents see a long list of choices on a written survey,

Multiracial Babies

Forty percent of multiracial babies born in 1990 were black and white, up from 32 percent in 1970. (total live births to parents of different races and percent of all interracial live births, 1970–90)

Race	1990		1980		1970	
	number	*percent*	*number*	*percent*	*number*	*percent*
Total Interracial Births	124,468	100.0%	73,596	100.0%	39,012	100.0%
Total Black/White Births	49,479	39.8	25,289	34.4	12,556	32.2
White mother/ black father	37,661	30.3	19,757	26.8	9,636	24.7
Black mother/ white father	11,818	9.5	5,532	7.5	2,920	7.5
White mother/other-race father (excluding black)	27,269	21.9	17,568	23.9	9,044	23.2
Black mother/other-race father (excluding white)	1,206	1.0	698	0.9	432	1.1
Other Interracial Births	46,514	37.4	30,041	40.8	16,980	43.5

Note: Does not include births for which the race of the mother or father is unknown.

Source: National Center for Health Statistics

they are likely to pick the first choice that might apply to them instead of reading through the whole list. The reverse is true of telephone surveys, when people tend to pick the last choice. The more categories on the list, the more these effects complicate the results.

"We couldn't possibly get every person's idea of their race into the question," says Robert Tortora, associate director for statistical design, methodology and standards at the Census Bureau. "There would be all kinds of methodological effects, and the logistics of it are daunting." Tortora agrees that there are problems with the ways race and ethnicity are currently measured, and he does see changes coming. "Basically, what you're asking is a person's judgment of their race or ethnicity. And since we don't have precise definitions of every possible category, people's perceptions of themselves and their answers can change from census to census."

Race statistics can become muddled in many ways. In 1970, for example, about 1 million residents of midwestern and southern states mistakenly identified themselves as Central or South Americans because they were confused by the census form. Such goofs are relatively easy to correct. When someone writes "German" for their race, for example, they are automatically reassigned to the "white" category by a census computer.

When "other race" is what the person meant to write, the result is a quiet tug-of-war between the respondent's preferences and Statistical Directive 15. If a person won't fit themselves into one of the four racial categories designated by the OMB, a census computer does it for them. Usually, computers scan other answers on the same form and assign the person to the category that seems best. The stubborn few who check "other race," write in "biracial," and give two races are assigned the first race they report.

If someone checks "other race" and writes "Latino," the census's computers will check to see if any other household members designated a race. If no one in the household did, the bureau will check the forms of neighboring households who wrote their race as "Latino" and assign a race on that basis. This process, called "hot-decking," is considered fairly accurate on a nationwide basis. But it may be responsible for serious inaccuracies in neighborhood-level census data.

The Census Bureau says that the number of blacks of Hispanic origin in Los Angeles increased from 17,000 in 1980 to nearly 60,000 in 1990. But two local experts can find no evidence of the change, and they suspect computer error. Latinos in the city's South Central neighborhood may have ignored the race question, says James P. Allen, a geographer at Cal State Northridge. The nonrespondents were probably assigned a race based on the skin color of their neighbors, who are likely to be black, says sociologist David Heer of the University of Southern California. The overcount of blacks may have affected government funds and redistricting plans in L.A., and it doesn't stop there.

"This is a terribly important error," Allen told *Buzz* magazine. "I strongly believe it has happened in Miami, Houston, Chicago, and all cities where Latinos are migrating into black neighborhoods."

Young and Proud

With all of the confusion and the possibility of taking offense, some observers have wondered if collecting any racial statistics is a good idea. "As long as we differentiate, we will discriminate," writes Michael E. Tomlin, a professor of education at the University of Idaho, in a letter to *American Demographics* magazine. Tomlin describes himself as a native-born American of Scotch-Irish descent, but he refuses to answer any federal questions concerning ethnicity or race. "For our nation to truly earn its place as the land of the free," he continues, "we must free ourselves from placing others—and ourselves—in boxes."

Tomlin's objections might seem noble. But if he got his way, the federal government would have no way to fight racial discrimination. Racial data are used to enforce the Voting Rights Act, equal employment regulations, and affirmative action plans, to name just a few. These programs depend on a steady flow of data that conform to Statistical Directive 15, so they can be easily compared with data from other sources. State or federal agencies can ask for more detailed information on race, but the data must ultimately break down into the same four categories.

The 'OMB and Census Bureau are now reviewing Directive 15. Seven months of hearings in 1993 revealed three truths about racial statistics, according to Congressman Tom Sawyer, chairman of the House Subcommittee on Census. First, many people agree on the need to continue collecting ethnic and racial data. Second, the data must be uniform across the government. Third, racial categories must be relevant to the public, or the public won't cooperate.

Groups such as the Association of Multi-Ethnic Americans say that the way to restore relevance to racial data is to add a new multiracial category to Directive 15. "People ask, 'Why don't we eliminate all categories?'" says the AMEA's Carlos Fernández. "I say, that's nice, but you can't erase differences between people by ignoring them. When we get people from different communities intermarrying at a rate we would expect if there were no differences between them, then the categories will become irrelevant. Eventually it will happen."

6

PERSONAL REFLECTIONS ON RESEARCHING HIV DISEASE

ROSE WEITZ

Ethical questions concerning social research are a rather recent discussion in the history of social science. It wasn't until the 1960s and early 1970s that we began to question research protocols and the effects of social experiments on humans. This last reading in the social research section by Rose Weitz takes us inside the research world of one sociologist and reveals her ethical and legal concerns about studying persons with HIV/AIDS.

During my "apprenticeship" as a sociologist, both during and after graduate school, I was taught how to review the literature, conduct interviews, analyze data, and the like. By the time I began this book, I had been out of graduate school and working as a sociologist for eight years. Nevertheless, in all those years, nothing I had read and no one I had studied with had taught me how to deal with the personal, legal, and ethical dilemmas I encountered while interviewing persons with HIV [human immunodeficiency virus] disease.

Personal Dilemmas

When I began this research, I expected it to be psychologically draining. In retrospect, however, I was terribly naive about the stresses I would encounter.

My most serious problem has been the unusually burdensome sense of responsibility this research created. Probably all researchers struggle with doubts about their abilities to do justice to their topics, particularly when others have provided financial support. However, the nature of my work has heightened this sense of responsibility enormously. If my research becomes widely read, it may affect health care policy and hence significantly affect many individuals' lives. Already, for example, I have testified to our Governor's Task Force on AIDS [acquired immune deficiency syndrome], and have learned that my testimony was influential in convincing the task force to oppose mandatory reporting of persons who test positive for HIV. More crucially, in terms of its personal emotional impact, many people I spoke with explicitly referred to their interviews as legacies. They participated in this project despite the emotional and sometimes physical pain it caused them because they believed I would use their stories to help others. Thus they gave me the responsibility of giving meaning to their lives and to their deaths.

I also have encountered personal difficulties in doing this research because it has made the inevitability of death and the possibility of disability far more salient for me. Early in the research, I realized that at each interview I automatically compared my age with that of the person I was interviewing. I was frequently disturbed to find that they were much younger than they looked and often younger than I. (I was 34 when I began this research.) Having to witness the pain of their lives was far more difficult than coping with the knowledge that they were dying, especially because the dying occurred out of my sight.

In addition to teaching me some truths about death and disability, the interviews also forced me to recognize the irrational nature of my own and others' response to potential contagion. To control my fears during interviews with those who have HIV disease, I often found myself repeating silently a calming litany about how HIV is and isn't transmitted. Meanwhile, I had to calm the fears of friends and acquaintances who wondered whether I had become a source of contagion. All I could do was to provide information about HIV, which they might or might not choose to assimilate. Fortunately, no one proved irrationally fearful.

Legal Dilemmas

I initially became involved in research on HIV disease after hearing a lecture about how the government is restricting the civil liberties of persons with this illness. These restrictions include deporting noncitizens and quarantining those judged a danger to themselves or others. I was therefore sensitized to the potential legal problems before I began this research. This was an issue from the start because Arizona law requires all health care workers to report to the state any person who has HIV disease at any stage. According to the state department of health services, I could legally be required to report anyone I interviewed (several of whom told me they had not been reported by their doctors). Moreover, an important recent case had confirmed that sociologists' rights to protect their data against subpoenas is not as strong as the right granted to physicians or lawyers.[1] Consequently, and recognizing that reporting someone could jeopardize their civil rights, I was unusually concerned about protecting the confidentiality of my records.

The need for confidentiality produced some unexpected difficulties. I wanted to make it easy for persons with HIV disease who were considering participating in this research to reach me, because I assumed that any difficulty might diminish their willingness to do so. However, I could not give out my home phone number because my housemate might listen to our answering machine and unintentionally hear a message meant only for me. Similarly, I could not write names, addresses, or phone numbers in the pocket calendar that I use to organize my life because I could not risk having the calendar subpoenaed and losing all my other daily records.

Ironically, my chief worry was protecting the signed "informed consent forms" that my university's research ethics committee required me to obtain from each person I interviewed. When I initially raised this issue with the committee, we were unable to reach an agreement on an alternative that would not require individuals to sign their names. (When, in 1989, I began interviewing persons with HIV disease again, however, we agreed that instead of having each sign a consent form, I would begin each interview by reading a statement about informed consent and would tape both my statement and their response.)

Ethical Dilemmas

Early in my training as a sociologist, I learned the value of informed consent. Translating this principle into action, however, requires more than simply presenting potential interviewees with a description of one's purposes and research methods. While interviewing persons with HIV disease, I soon discovered that many assumed that I was a counselor, worked for one of the community organizations that helps persons with HIV disease, or was a lesbian. I then had to decide how much responsibility I had to correct their assumptions, particularly when they were not explicit. Should I have assumed that they understood what a sociologist was, or should I have carefully differentiated sociology from social work? If an individual commented that I did not wear a wedding ring, should I have assumed that they were searching for a polite way of asking if I was a lesbian? How many times should I have stopped a given interview to explain that I did not work for a community organization, if the person I was interviewing did not understand the first time I explained?

Truly informed consent was even more rare among those who felt they could not afford to refuse to participate. Despite my disclaimers, many individuals obviously believed I worked for either the state or a community organization for persons with HIV disease. As a result, they may have feared that they would jeopardize their access to services if they did not participate. Even if they believed they would not be punished for lack of cooperation, they may still have believed they would be rewarded for helping. Several, for example, mentioned that they wanted their physicians to consider them exemplary patients so that the physicians would remember them when choosing patients for experimental treatment programs.

Truly free consent was even less likely in interviewing individuals who were in jail or prison. Because of the connection between HIV and drug use, many persons with HIV disease are imprisoned. As a result, I initially pursued the possibility of contacting persons with HIV disease through the health department of the state prison system. My first contacts with prison officials seemed promising. Even more than other persons with HIV disease, however, prisoners might have felt that they would be punished if they refused to participate. Moreover, I would have had no way to keep the administration from knowing who had refused, because I would have had to arrange the interviews through prison officials. Consequently, I was relieved when negotiations fell through.

Finally, I faced a broad range of ethical dilemmas when either the persons I interviewed or I myself viewed me as an information or counseling source. Often persons I interviewed asked me questions about the disease, drugs, or doctors. Similarly, I frequently encountered persons with HIV disease whose knowledge of their illness was clearly deficient. I then had to decide whether to answer their questions even if doing so might jeopardize my relationship with influential physicians (who, for example, had not provided information about the side effects of certain drugs). Similarly, I had to decide whether to correct individuals' information if not asked. These questions posed minimal problems compared to those generated by implicit or explicit pleas for counseling. I had no answer for the individual who asked me how to convince her uninfected husband to use condoms. Nor was it clear to me how to respond when individuals told me that their disease was punishment for sins, or that they felt suicidal, or that their greatest grief was losing their children but they would not contact them for fear of infecting them. Saying nothing did not feel ethical to me. Yet saying something required me to break professional norms for sociological research.

Searching for Solutions

The legal dilemmas posed by this research presented the fewest difficulties, because the problems and solutions were purely practical. To avoid writing confidential information in my usual daily calendar, I began carrying a small notepad with me. As is typical in this sort of research, all my records and tapes were number-coded, and all identifying information was removed from the transcripts and resulting publications. I recorded data on individuals' age, marital status, occupation, and the like separately from the taped interviews, so that persons who transcribed the tapes would not have that information. I hoped that this would make it more difficult for the transcriptionist to recognize the person I was interviewing, should the transcriptionist happen to know him or her. All papers with names or addresses were kept in one less-than-obvious location and have now been destroyed. In addition, I decided that if I were subpoenaed, I would refuse to turn over the information. (Of course, such a decision is easy to make in the abstract and I cannot predict what I might have done if actually faced with a jail sentence for contempt of court.) Finally, when some individuals, far from desiring confidentiality, told me that they would like me to use their real names in this "legacy" we were creating, I decided not to do so because the potential "stigma fallout" seemed an unfair burden to thrust on unsuspecting friends and relatives.

The remaining problems had no easy answers. I tried to answer all questions, whether direct or indirect, asked by those I interviewed. I also tried to clarify their understanding of such things as sociology versus social work and working *with* versus working *for* a community organization. If someone still seemed not to understand after two or three attempts at explaining, I did not pursue the matter.

When it came to a choice between being ethical and being "sociological," I went with ethical every time. I felt a strong moral obligation to answer any question I was asked and to provide needed information even when not asked directly. I did try to wait until after the individual had finished stating his views before interjecting any information. And I occasionally requested that individuals not tell their doctors that I was their source.

Similarly, I believe it is wrong to listen to a person's feelings of guilt and self-deprecation without attempting to alleviate those feelings. Thus if a person told me he felt horribly stupid for not using "safe sex" until a couple of years ago, I heard him out and then gently suggested that until recently no one knew how HIV was transmitted. I also volunteered suggestions about sources of information and social support when it seemed warranted. I realize that these tactics may have diminished my credibility as a researcher, but I thought that was less important than diminishing my credibility as a person.

Finally, I did whatever I could to maintain my own mental health, because I realized I would be of little use to anyone if I allowed myself to burn out. So

I tried to restrict my contacts with those who have HIV disease to interviews. This tactic proved insufficient on two notable occasions—once when the family of someone I interviewed, recognizing that the interview had been an important experience for their relative, asked me if I would visit him on his deathbed, and the second time when students asked me to speak at a memorial vigil for an alumnus who had recently died of HIV disease. Finishing this research, especially given my fairly pessimistic predictions for the future, has been made much more difficult because I now have one good friend with HIV disease.

For my sanity's sake, I was grateful that at the time I was conducting most of these interviews I had no friends in high-risk groups (so far as I knew), that I did not know what any of the people I interviewed were like before their illness, and that I did not have to see them as their health deteriorated. For this reason I was very reluctant to do follow-up interviews, even though I knew they would provide invaluable data; it took many months of soul searching before I felt able to do so. Similarly, for a long time I avoided taking any steps that would have committed me to continuing this research for more than a year at a time. Knowing that my commitment was finite made it far more manageable psychologically.

I also learned the hard way that it was much more difficult emotionally for me to interview women than to interview men, because I identified so much more strongly with the women. The summer I began interviewing women was the summer I began having nightmares about contracting HIV disease. Fortunately for my mental health, although not for my research project, few women with HIV disease were available for interviews in Arizona.

To protect my mental and physical health, I tried always to schedule my interviews so that I would have time for exercise afterward, and tried to satisfy my worries with popcorn rather than chocolate. I calmed other new anxieties by updating my will, obtaining disability insurance, and giving a friend a medical power of attorney. I also soon lost most of my inhibitions about discussing the research and my attendant emotions, for I learned that it helped to share the burden. I remember vividly one afternoon when I stopped a casual acquaintance in a supermarket and harangued him for about 40 minutes with my troubles. He felt worse afterward, but I felt much better.

Undoubtedly many other researchers have coped with similar problems over the years. Unfortunately, norms for professional conduct do not allow easy and open discussion with colleagues about either psychological or ethical problems, while the rarity of lawsuits leave few of us sensitized to legal issues. As a result, many universities provide excellent technical training in research skills, but few prepare students for dealing with these nontechnical but equally crucial difficulties. I am sure that I reinvented the wheel in my attempts to deal with these dilemmas, but I found few good places to read about—let alone discuss—my concerns. In the long run, the usual stresses of research on HIV disease may have at least one serendipitous effect, if they pressure scholars to begin tackling these issues openly.

NOTE

1. I subsequently learned, however, that sociologists' rights are greater in circum-stances such as my own where the researcher consistently has emphasized to sub-jects that the data will be kept confidential and has established procedures to ensure this. See Ronald Bayer, Carol Levine, and Thomas H. Murray, "Guidelines for Confidentiality in Research on AIDS," *IRB: A Review of Human Subjects Research* 6 (1984): 1–7.

PART II
Culture

7

THE RASTAFARI
Emergence of a Subculture

WILLIAM F. LEWIS

Culture is defined as the shared ways of a human social group. This definition includes the ways of thinking, understanding, and feeling that have
been gained through common experience in social groups and are passed
on from one generation to another. Thus, culture reflects the social patterns
of thought, emotions, and practices that arise from social interaction within
a given society. In this reading, the first of four to explore culture, William F.
Lewis illustrates cultural variation by exploring the social meanings of the
"dreads" and other aspects of Rastafari culture.

The Rastafari community emerged on the Caribbean island of Jamaica
in the 1930s. Since that time, the Rastafari have spread throughout the
islands of the Caribbean, into parts of the African states of Kenya and
Ethiopia and the urban centers of the United States, England, and Canada.
As part of a larger society, the Rastafari can be called a subculture (a term
they would probably reject) and present an interesting example of a group
specifically in resistance to the culture that surrounds it.

The Rastafari as a group has a value system that emphasizes economic
communalism, solidarity within the group, and a rejection of the economic
values of the culture that surrounds it. Also, Rastafari adherents value the
beliefs and visible markers of identity, such as clothing, hair style, and special linguistic usages, that set it apart from the larger society. In addition, the
Rastafari are often in trouble with the law, particularly because of their use
and distribution of marijuana, and this negatively affects the way in which
they are viewed by the outside world.

The Rastas emerged from the Jamaican peasantry at a time when much
of the peasantry had been incorporated as wage labor into a modernizing,
capitalist economy. Subsequent to the dissolution of slavery in Jamaica, in
1834, a peasant economy had developed, organized around a system of localized and small-scale exchanges involving interpersonal networks of extended
kin. By the 1920s, capitalism had considerably undermined the peasant econ-

omy, which was considered backward and unproductive by the government and elite business class. In spite of the dominance of the capitalist market, there remained a conservative peasantry at the periphery who refused to participate in the modern economy and retained their own self-reliant economic systems. Although the limited trade and small opportunities for capital gain meant there was no large generation of profits, these peasants, in fact, were more immune to the difficulties of economic depression that occurred in the 1930s than were those peasants who participated in wage labor on the plantations.

It was out of this milieu that the Rastafari arose. Unlike the Marcus Garvey movement, occurring somewhat earlier, which tried to connect black identity to successful participation in the capitalist economy, the Rastas emphasized the positive identity of the black peasant as a nonparticipant in the modern economy and growing Jamaican nationalism. The emerging Rasta culture coalesced around the symbol of Ras (Prince) Tafari, who was crowned king of Ethiopia in 1930 and took the name Haile Selassie I. Through a belief in the divinity of Haile Selassie, the rejection of competitive markets and capitalism, their desire to repatriate to Africa, their use of marijuana, and the creation of a special language, the Rastas resolutely clung to the black cultural experience of the Jamaican peasantry.

Rejecting the aspirations of social mobility and participation in wage labor, the Rastas fashion a livelihood by forming networks of cooperation. In Jamaica they engage in fishing, handicrafts, and hustling in the cities, and, in the rural areas, in a family-based subsistence agriculture with minimal involvement in the market economy. The small group of Rastas living in Shashemane, Ethiopia, rely on their agricultural produce and financial donations from abroad. In urban England, Canada, and the United States, Rasta economic activities tend to be small-scale cooperative businesses such as eateries, craft shops, small clothing stores, and the illegal sale of marijuana. All of these enterprises are based on the productivity and input of extended familylike networks. No Rasta enterprise is a lone venture.

In addition to their support of each other's businesses, they circulate their wealth through the community in the form of gifts, loans, and especially parties. The economic exchange among Rastas is ideally a highly personal event between community members. Even money from their ganja (marijuana) trade is distributed equitably within the community.

The central symbol of the Rastas that affirmed blackness and African roots, and disproved the stereotypical Jamaican image of the black peasant as poor and backward, was Haile Selassie, the king of Ethiopia from 1930 to 1974. Haile Selassie was the symbol from which the Rastas derived their name and their affirmation in blackness over and above any connection of black identity to social mobility. Haile Selassie embodied blackness, cooperative efforts, and conservatism. The Rastas ground their belief in their interpretations of biblical prophecies borne out by the coronation of Haile Selassie I, when he was proclaimed "King of Kings and Lion of Judah." This orientation to Ethiopia was to some extent a continuity of the Jamaican peasant's continuing connection to African cultural patterns, modified by European culture and Christianity, which had been part of the slave culture.

In addition to "Ethiopianism" (the importance of Haile Selassie and the orientation to African cultural patterns), repatriation to Africa is another central theme in Rasta philosophy. While some Rastas actually did repatriate to Africa, repatriation (like all symbols) has several meanings: For the Rastas it vacillates between a literal passage to the African homeland and a retribalization of the Rastas in whichever country they find themselves. Ethiopianism and repatriation are the two key symbols of the Rastas' alienation from modern notions of progress, social mobility, and the status of propertyless wage labor.

Two other important symbols of their culture are the use of marijuana and their creation of special linguistic usages. Through their use of marijuana, and through their creation of a philosophy around that use, Rastas weaken their psychological disposition for participation in the dominant economy. The Rasta use of marijuana does not serve as a narcotic tool to create a future utopia for the Rastas. Rather, ganja sustains them in their own independent enterprises as craftspeople, fishermen, and hustlers, and it helps them assert their communal bonds against the world around them, giving them "an entire nontraditional and alternative system of power and control, influence, and prestige."

In addition, the illegal sale of marijuana is part of the underground economy of many Rastas groups. The networks for growing it, preparing it for sale, and its distribution are all based on friendship, alliances, and reciprocity. Although the Rastas have encountered difficulties with law enforcement in connection with their use and sale of marijuana, the drug has provided the Rastas with a livelihood that allows them independence and freedom from the capitalist system, a position they value highly. Ultimately, many Rastas hope that their world will become more and more based on reciprocity and redistribution where each member's work supports every other member's and money as a medium of exchange will disappear from their community.

Rastafari linguistic usages include the invention of "I"-centered words, phrases, and suffixes, such as "ital" for vital, and the substitution of such diminutives as "under" and "sub" with their opposites, such as coining the word *overstand* for understand. (This suggests that the use of the term *subculture* to characterize Rasta relations to the larger society would not be acceptable to them. . . .) In disavowing diminutives, the Rastas appear to be disavowing the hierarchical nature of relations in the marketplace. Rasta language contradicts the submissiveness that an employer expects of an employee through language that includes subtle forms of subordination. The Rastas have devised their language as an assertion of their black self-worth, and this, too, keeps them separate from the world of the boss and the worker.

The Rastas draw boundaries around themselves to exclude the outside world from participation in their economic and social relationships. They do this at the same time they participate in economic opportunities that extend beyond the group. Although there is jealousy, tension, and conflict within the group, occasionally resulting in violence, there is also strong solidarity against outsiders, particularly those in positions of authority. Rastas have rejected much of the social and psychological orientation of modern society, or Babylon, as the Rastas call it. They are a small group movement that deviates from the modern state and persists in a peasantlike identity. While much of their culture is a continuation of the milieu out of which they emerged, they have also created a new culture and adaptive strategies that allow them to survive in a manner consistent with their own view of the world.

8

THE CODE OF THE STREETS

ELIJAH ANDERSON

In this selection, Elijah Anderson demonstrates how cultural values create new standards for behavior. Anderson analyzes the social norms governing street behavior and violence in the inner city. The resulting "code" is a complex system of norms, dress, rituals, and expected behavior. In order to survive within the subculture of the inner city, children and adults must learn the code and adapt their lives accordingly.

Of all the problems besetting the poor inner-city black community, none is more pressing than that of interpersonal violence and aggression. It wreaks havoc daily with the lives of community residents and increasingly spills over into downtown and residential middle-class areas. Muggings, burglaries, carjackings, and drug-related shootings, all of which may leave their victims or innocent bystanders dead, are now common enough to concern all urban and many suburban residents. The inclination to violence springs from the circumstances of life among the ghetto poor—the lack of jobs that pay a living wage, the stigma of race, the fallout from rampant drug use and drug trafficking, and the resulting alienation and lack of hope for the future.

Simply living in such an environment places young people at special risk of falling victim to aggressive behavior. Although there are often forces in the community which can counteract the negative influences, by far the most powerful being a strong, loving, "decent" (as inner-city residents put it) family committed to middle-class values, the despair is pervasive enough to have spawned an oppositional culture, that of "the streets," whose norms are often consciously opposed to those of mainstream society. These two orientations—decent and street—socially organize the community, and their co-existence has important consequences for residents, particularly children growing up in the inner city. Above all, this environment means that even youngsters whose home lives reflect mainstream values—and the majority of homes in the community do—must be able to handle themselves in a street-oriented environment.

This is because the street culture has evolved what may be called a code of the streets, which amounts to a set of informal rules governing interpersonal public behavior, including violence. The rules prescribe both a proper comportment and a proper way to respond if challenged. They regulate the use of violence and so allow those who are inclined to aggression to precipitate violent encounters in an approved way. The rules have been established and are enforced mainly by the street-oriented, but on the streets the distinction between street and decent is often irrelevant; everybody knows that if the rules are violated, there are penalties. Knowledge of the code is thus largely defensive; it is literally necessary for operating in public. Therefore, even though families with a decency orientation are usually opposed to the values of the code, they often reluctantly encourage their children's familiarity with it to enable them to negotiate the inner-city environment.

At the heart of the code is the issue of respect—loosely defined as being treated "right," or granted the deference one deserves. However, in the troublesome public environment of the inner city, as people increasingly feel buffeted by forces beyond their control, what one deserves in the way of respect becomes more and more problematic and uncertain. This in turn further opens the issue of respect to sometimes intense interpersonal negotiation. In the street culture, especially among young people, respect is viewed as almost an external entity that is hard-won but easily lost, and so must constantly be guarded. The rules of the code in fact provide a framework for negotiating respect. The person whose very appearance—including his clothing, demeanor, and way of moving—deters transgressions feels that he possesses, and may be considered by others to possess, a measure of respect. With the right amount of respect, for instance, he can avoid "being bothered" in public. If he is bothered, not only may he be in physical danger but he has been disgraced or "dissed" (disrespected). Many of the forms that dissing can take might seem petty to middle-class people (maintaining eye contact for too long, for example), but to those invested in the street code, these actions become serious indications of the other person's intentions. Consequently, such people become very sensitive to advances and slights, which could well serve as warnings of imminent physical confrontation.

This hard reality can be traced to the profound sense of alienation from mainstream society and its institutions felt by many poor inner-city black people, particularly the young. The code of the streets is actually a cultural adaptation to a profound lack of faith in the police and the judicial system. The police are most often seen as representing the dominant white society and not caring to protect inner-city residents. When called, they may not respond, which is one reason many residents feel they must be prepared to take extraordinary measures to defend themselves and their loved ones against those who are inclined to aggression. Lack of police accountability has in fact been incorporated into the status system: The person who is believed capable of "taking care of himself" is accorded a certain deference, which translates into a sense of physical and psychological control. Thus the street code emerges where the influence of the police ends and personal responsibility for one's safety is felt to begin. Exacerbated by the proliferation of drugs and easy access to guns, this volatile situation results in the ability of the street-oriented minority (or those who effectively "go for bad") to dominate the public spaces.

Decent and Street Families

Although almost everyone in poor inner-city neighborhoods is struggling financially and therefore feels a certain distance from the rest of America, the decent and the street family in a real sense represent two poles of value orientation, two contrasting conceptual categories. The labels "decent" and "street," which the residents themselves use, amount to evaluative judgments that confer status on local residents. The labeling is often the result of a social contest among individuals and families of the neighborhood. Individuals of the two orientations often coexist in the same extended family. Decent residents judge themselves to be so while judging others to be of the street, and street individuals often present themselves as decent, drawing distinctions between themselves and other people. In addition, there is quite a bit of circumstantial behavior—that is, one person may at different times exhibit both decent and street orientations, depending on the circumstances. Although these designations result from so much social jockeying, there do exist concrete features that define each conceptual category.

Generally, so-called decent families tend to accept mainstream values more fully and attempt to instill them in their children. Whether married couples with children or single-parent (usually female) households, they are generally "working poor" and so tend to be better off financially than their street-oriented neighbors. They value hard work and self-reliance and are willing to sacrifice for their children. Because they have a certain amount of faith in mainstream society, they harbor hopes for a better future for their children, if not for themselves. Many of them go to church and take a strong interest in their children's schooling. Rather than dwelling on the real hardships and inequities facing them, many such decent people, particularly the increasing number of grandmothers raising grandchildren, see their difficult situation as a test from God and derive great support from their faith and from the church community.

Extremely aware of the problematic and often dangerous environment in which they reside, decent parents tend to be strict in their child-rearing practices, encouraging children to respect authority and walk a straight moral line. They have an almost obsessive concern about trouble of any kind and remind their children to be on the lookout for people and situations that might lead to it. At the same time, they are themselves polite and considerate of others, and teach their children to be the same way. At home, at work, and in church, they strive hard to maintain a positive mental attitude and a spirit of cooperation.

So-called street parents, in contrast, often show a lack of consideration for other people and have a rather superficial sense of family and community. Though they may love their children, many of them are unable to cope with the physical and emotional demands of parenthood and find it difficult to reconcile their needs with those of their children. These families, who are more fully invested in the code of the streets than the decent people are, may aggressively socialize their children into it in a normative way. They believe in the code and judge themselves and others according to its values.

. . .

Campaigning for Respect

[The] realities of inner-city life are largely absorbed on the streets. At an early age, often even before they start school, children from street-oriented homes gravitate to the streets, where they "hang"—socialize with their peers. Children from these generally permissive homes have a great deal of latitude and are allowed to "rip and run" up and down the street. They often come home from school, put their books down, and go right back out the door. On school nights eight- and nine-year-olds remain out until nine or ten o'clock (and teenagers typically come in whenever they want to). On the streets they play in groups that often become the source of their primary social bonds. Children from decent homes tend to be more carefully supervised and are thus likely to have curfews and to be taught how to stay out of trouble.

When decent and street kids come together, a kind of social shuffle occurs in which children have a chance to go either way. Tension builds as a child comes to realize that he must choose an orientation. The kind of home he comes from influences but does not determine the way he will ultimately turn out—although it is unlikely that a child from a thoroughly street-oriented family will easily absorb decent values on the streets. Youths who emerge from street-oriented families but develop a decency orientation almost always learn those values in another setting—in school, in a youth group, in church. Often it is the result of their involvement with a caring "old head" (adult role model).

In the street, through their play, children pour their individual life experiences into a common knowledge pool, affirming, confirming, and elaborating on what they have observed in the home and matching their skills against those of others. And they learn to fight. Even small children test one another, pushing and shoving, and are ready to hit other children over circumstances not to their liking. In turn, they are readily hit by other children, and the child who is toughest prevails. Thus the violent resolution of disputes, the hitting and cursing, gains social reinforcement. The child in effect is initiated into a system that is really a way of campaigning for respect.

In addition, younger children witness the disputes of older children, which are often resolved through cursing and abusive talk, if not aggression or outright violence. They see that one child succumbs to the greater physical and mental abilities of the other. They are also alert and attentive witnesses to the verbal and physical fights of adults, after which they compare notes and share their interpretations of the event. In almost every case the victor is the person who physically won the altercation, and this person often enjoys the esteem and respect of onlookers. These experiences reinforce the lessons the children have learned at home: Might makes right, and toughness is a virtue, while humility is not. In effect they learn the social meaning of fighting. When it is left virtually unchallenged, this understanding becomes an ever more important part of the child's working conception of the world. Over time the code of the streets becomes refined.

Those street-oriented adults with whom children come in contact—including mothers, fathers, brothers, sisters, boyfriends, cousins, neighbors, and friends—help them along in forming this understanding by verbalizing the messages they are getting through experience: "Watch your back." "Protect yourself." "Don't punk out." "If somebody messes with you, you got to pay them back." "If someone disses you, you got to straighten them out." Many parents actually impose sanctions if a child is not sufficiently aggressive. For example, if a child loses a fight and comes home upset, the parent might respond, "Don't you come in here crying that somebody beat you up; you better get back out there and whup his ass. I didn't raise no punks! Get back out there and whup his ass. If you don't whup his ass, I'll whup your ass when you come home." Thus the child obtains reinforcement for being tough and showing nerve.

While fighting, some children cry as though they are doing something they are ambivalent about. The fight may be against their wishes, yet they may feel constrained to fight or face the consequences—not just from peers but also from caretakers or parents, who may administer another beating if they back down. Some adults recall receiving such lessons from their own parents and justify repeating them to their children as a way to toughen them up. Looking capable of taking care of oneself as a form of self-defense is a dominant theme among both street-oriented and decent adults who worry about the safety of their children. There is thus at times a convergence in their child-rearing practices, although the rationales behind them may differ.

Self-Image Based on "Juice"

By the time they are teenagers, most youths have either internalized the code of the streets or at least learned the need to comport themselves in accordance with its rules, which chiefly have to do with interpersonal communication. The code revolves around the presentation of self. Its basic requirement is the display of a certain predisposition to violence. Accordingly, one's bearing must send the unmistakable if sometimes subtle message to "the next person" in public that one is capable of violence and mayhem when the situation requires it, that one can take care of oneself. The nature of this communication is largely determined by the demands of the circumstances but can include facial expressions, gait, and verbal expressions—all of which are geared mainly to deterring aggression. Physical appearance, including clothes, jewelry, and grooming, also plays an important part in how a person is viewed; to be respected, it is important to have the right look.

Even so, there are no guarantees against challenges because there are always people around looking for a fight to increase their share of respect—or "juice," as it is sometimes called on the street. Moreover, if a person is assaulted, it is important, not only in the eyes of his opponent but also in the eyes of his "running buddies," for him to avenge himself. Otherwise he risks being "tried" (challenged) or "moved on" by any number of others. To maintain his honor he must show he is not someone to be "messed with" or "dissed." In general, the person must "keep himself straight" by managing his position of respect among others; this involves in part his self-image, which is shaped by what he thinks others are thinking of him in relation to his peers.

Objects play an important and complicated role in establishing self-image. Jackets, sneakers, gold jewelry, reflect not just a person's taste, which tends to be tightly regulated among adolescents of all social classes, but also a willingness to possess things that may require defending. A boy wearing a fashionable, expensive jacket, for example, is vulnerable to attack by another who covets the jacket and either cannot afford to buy one or wants the added satisfaction of depriving someone else of his. However, if the boy forgoes the desirable jacket and wears one that isn't "hip," he runs the risk of being teased and possibly even assaulted as an unworthy person. To be allowed to hang with certain prestigious crowds, a boy must wear a different set of expensive clothes—sneakers and athletic suit—every day. Not to be able to do so might make him appear socially deficient. The youth comes to covet such items—especially when he sees easy prey wearing them.

In acquiring valued things, therefore, a person shores up his identity—but since it is an identity based on having things, it is highly precarious. This very precariousness gives a heightened sense of urgency to staying even with peers, with whom the person is actually competing. Young men and women who are able to command respect through their presentation of self—by allowing their possessions and their body language to speak for them—

may not have to campaign for regard but may, rather, gain it by the force of their manner. Those who are unable to command respect in this way must actively campaign for it—and are thus particularly alive to slights.

One way of campaigning for status is by taking the possessions of others. In this context, seemingly ordinary objects can become trophies imbued with symbolic value that far exceeds their monetary worth. Possession of the trophy can symbolize the ability to violate somebody—to "get in his face," to take something of value from him, to "dis" him, and thus to enhance one's own worth by stealing someone else's. The trophy does not have to be something material. It can be another person's sense of honor, snatched away with a derogatory remark. It can be the outcome of a fight. It can be the imposition of a certain standard, such as a girl's getting herself recognized as the most beautiful. Material things, however, fit easily into the pattern. Sneakers, a pistol, even somebody else's girlfriend, can become a trophy. When a person can take something from another and then flaunt it, he gains a certain regard by being the owner, or the controller, of that thing. But this display of ownership can then provoke other people to challenge him. This game of who controls what is thus constantly being played out on inner-city streets, and the trophy—extrinsic or intrinsic, tangible or intangible—identifies the current winner.

An important aspect of this often violent give-and-take is its zero-sum quality. That is, the extent to which one person can raise himself up depends on his ability to put another person down. This underscores the alienation that permeates the inner-city ghetto community. There is a generalized sense that very little respect is to be had, and therefore everyone competes to get what affirmation he can of the little that is available. The craving for respect that results gives people thin skins. Shows of deference by others can be highly soothing, contributing to a sense of security, comfort, self-confidence, and self-respect. Transgressions by others which go unanswered diminish these feelings and are believed to encourage further transgressions. Hence one must be ever vigilant against the transgressions of others or even *appearing* as if transgressions will be tolerated. Among young people, whose sense of self-esteem is particularly vulnerable, there is an especially heightened concern with being disrespected. Many inner-city young men in particular crave respect to such a degree that they will risk their lives to attain and maintain it.

The issue of respect is thus closely tied to whether a person has an inclination to be violent, even as a victim. In the wider society people may not feel required to retaliate physically after an attack, even though they are aware that they have been degraded or taken advantage of. They may feel a great need to defend themselves *during* an attack, or to behave in such a way as to deter aggression (middle-class people certainly can and do become victims of street-oriented youths), but they are much more likely than street-oriented people to feel that they can walk away from a possible altercation with their self-esteem intact. Some people may even have the strength of character to flee, without any thought that their self-respect or esteem will be diminished.

In impoverished inner-city black communities, however, particularly among young males and perhaps increasingly among females, such flight would be extremely difficult. To run away would likely leave one's self-esteem in tatters. Hence people often feel constrained not only to stand up and at least attempt to resist during an assault but also to "pay back"—to seek revenge—after a successful assault on their person. This may include going to get a weapon or even getting relatives involved. Their very identity and self-respect, their honor, is often intricately tied up with the way they perform on the streets during and after such encounters. This outlook reflects the circumscribed opportunities of the inner-city poor. Generally people outside the ghetto have other ways of gaining status and regard, and thus do not feel so dependent on such physical displays.

By Trial of Manhood

On the street, among males these concerns about things and identity have come to be expressed in the concept of "manhood." Manhood in the inner city means taking the prerogatives of men with respect to strangers, other men, and women—being distinguished as a man. It implies physicality and a certain ruthlessness. Regard and respect are associated with this concept in large part because of its practical application: If others have little or no regard for a person's manhood, his very life and those of his loved ones could be in jeopardy. But there is a chicken-and-egg aspect to this situation: One's physical safety is more likely to be jeopardized in public *because* manhood is associated with respect. In other words, an existential link has been created between the idea of manhood and one's self-esteem, so that it has become hard to say which is primary. For many inner-city youths, manhood and respect are flip sides of the same coin; physical and psychological well-being are inseparable, and both require a sense of control, of being in charge.

The operating assumption is that a man, especially a real man, knows what other men know—the code of the streets. And if one is not a real man, one is somehow diminished as a person, and there are certain valued things one simply does not deserve. There is thus believed to be a certain justice to the code, since it is considered that everyone has the opportunity to know it. Implicit in this is that everybody is held responsible for being familiar with the code. If the victim of a mugging, for example, does not know the code and so responds "wrong," the perpetrator may feel justified even in killing him and may feel no remorse. He may think, "Too bad, but it's his fault. He should have known better."

So when a person ventures outside, he must adopt the code—a kind of shield, really—to prevent others from "messing with" him. In these circumstances it is easy for people to think they are being tried or tested by others even when this is not the case. For it is sensed that something extremely valuable is at stake in every interaction, and people are encouraged to rise to the occasion, particularly with strangers. For people who are unfamiliar with the code—generally people who live outside the inner city—the concern with respect in the most ordinary interactions can be frightening and incomprehensible. But for those who are invested in the code, the clear object of their demeanor is to discourage strangers from even thinking about testing their manhood. And the sense of power that attends the ability to deter others can be alluring even to those who know the code without being heavily invested in it—the decent inner-city youths. Thus a boy who has been leading a basically decent life can, in trying circumstances, suddenly resort to deadly force.

Central to the issue of manhood is the widespread belief that one of the most effective ways of gaining respect is to manifest "nerve." Nerve is shown when one takes another person's possessions (the more valuable the better), "messes with" someone's woman, throws the first punch, "gets in someone's face," or pulls a trigger. Its proper display helps on the spot to check others who would violate one's person and also helps to build a reputation that works to prevent future challenges. But since such a show of nerve is a forceful expression of disrespect toward the person on the receiving end, the victim may be greatly offended and seek to retaliate with equal or greater force. A display of nerve, therefore, can easily provoke a life-threatening response, and the background knowledge of that possibility has often been incorporated into the concept of nerve.

True nerve exposes a lack of fear of dying. Many feel that it is acceptable to risk dying over the principle of respect. In fact, among the hard-core street-oriented, the clear risk of violent death may be preferable to being "dissed" by another. The youths who have internalized this attitude and convincingly display it in their public bearing are among the most threatening people of all, for it is commonly assumed that they fear no man. As the people of the community say, "They are the baddest dudes on the street." They often lead an existential life that may acquire meaning only when they are faced with the possibility of imminent death. Not to be afraid to die is by implication to have few compunctions about taking another's life. Not to be afraid to die is the quid pro quo of being able to take somebody else's life— for the right reasons, if the situation demands it. When others believe this is one's position, it gives one a real sense of power on the streets. Such credibility is what many inner-city youths strive to achieve, whether they are decent or street-oriented, both because of its practical defensive value and because of the positive way it makes them feel about themselves. The difference between the decent and the street-oriented youth is often that the decent youth makes a conscious decision to appear tough and manly; in another setting— with teachers, say, or at his part-time job—he can be polite and deferential. The street-oriented youth, on the other hand, has made the concept of manhood a part of his very identity; he has difficulty manipulating it—it often controls him.

Girls and Boys

Increasingly, teenage girls are mimicking the boys and trying to have their own version of "manhood." Their goal is the same—to get respect, to be recognized as capable of setting or maintaining a certain standard. They try to achieve this end in the ways that have been established by the boys, including posturing, abusive language, and the use of violence to resolve disputes, but the issues for the girls are different. Although conflicts over turf and status exist among the girls, the majority of disputes seem rooted in assessments of beauty (which girl in a group is "the cutest"), competition over boyfriends, and attempts to regulate other people's knowledge of and opinions about a girl's behavior or that of someone close to her, especially her mother.

A major cause of conflicts among girls is "he say, she say." This practice begins in the early school years and continues through high school. It occurs when "people," particularly girls, talk about others, thus putting their "business in the streets." Usually one girl will say something negative about another in the group, most often behind the person's back. The remark will then get back to the person talked about. She may retaliate or her friends may feel required to "take up for" her. In essence this is a form of group gossiping in which individuals are negatively assessed and evaluated. As with much gossip, the things said may or may not be true, but the point is that such imputations can cast aspersions on a person's good name. The accused is required to defend herself against the slander, which can result in arguments and fights, often over little of real substance. Here again is the problem of low self-esteem, which encourages youngsters to be highly sensitive to slights and to be vulnerable to feeling easily "dissed." To avenge the dissing, a fight is usually necessary.

Because boys are believed to control violence, girls tend to defer to them in situations of conflict. Often if a girl is attacked or feels slighted, she will get a brother, uncle, or cousin to do her fighting for her. Increasingly, however, girls are doing their own fighting and are even asking their male relatives to teach them how to fight. Some girls form groups that attack other girls or take things from them. A hard-core segment of inner-city girls inclined toward violence seems to be developing. As one 13-year-old girl in a detention center for youths who have committed violent acts told me, "To get people to leave you alone, you gotta fight. Talking don't always get you out of stuff." One major difference between girls and boys: Girls rarely use guns. Their fights are therefore not life-or-death struggles. Girls are not often willing to put their lives on the line for "manhood." The ultimate form of respect on the male-dominated inner-city street is thus reserved for men.

"Going for Bad"

In the most fearsome youths such a cavalier attitude toward death grows out of a very limited view of life. Many are uncertain about how long they are going to live and believe they could die violently at any time. They accept this fate; they live on the edge. Their manner conveys the message that nothing intimidates them; whatever turn the encounter takes, they maintain their attack—rather like a pit bull, whose spirit many such boys admire. The demonstration of such tenacity "shows heart" and earns their respect.

This fearlessness has implications for law enforcement. Many street-oriented boys are much more concerned about the threat of "justice" at the hands of a peer than at the hands of the police. Moreover, many feel not only that they have little to lose by going to prison but that they have something to gain. The toughening-up one experiences in prison can actually enhance one's reputation on the streets. Hence the system loses influence over the hard core who are without jobs, with little perceptible stake in the system. If mainstream society has done nothing *for* them, they counter by making sure it can do nothing *to* them.

At the same time, however, a competing view maintains that the true nerve consists in backing down, walking away from a fight, and going on with one's business. One fights only in self-defense. This view emerges from the decent philosophy that life is precious, and it is an important part of the socialization process common in decent homes. It discourages violence as the primary means of resolving disputes and encourages youngsters to accept nonviolence and talk as confrontational strategies. But "if the deal goes down," self-defense is greatly encouraged. When there is enough positive support for this orientation, either in the home or among one's peers, then nonviolence has a chance to prevail. But it prevails at the cost of relinquishing a claim to being bad and tough, and therefore sets a young person up as at the very least alienated from street-oriented peers and quite possibly a target of derision or even violence.

Although the nonviolent orientation rarely overcomes the impulse to strike back in an encounter, it does introduce a certain confusion and so can prompt a measure of soul-searching, or even profound ambivalence. Did the person back down with his respect intact or did he back down only to be judged a "punk"—a person lacking manhood? Should he or she have acted? Should he or she have hit the other person in the mouth? These questions beset many young men and women during public confrontations. What is the "right" thing to do? In the quest for honor, respect, and local status—which few young people are uninterested in—common sense most often prevails, which leads many to opt for the tough approach, enacting their own particular versions of the display of nerve. The presentation of oneself as rough and tough is very often quite acceptable until one is tested. And then that presentation may help the person pass the test, because it will cause fewer questions to be asked about what he did and why. It is hard for a person to explain why he lost the fight or why he backed down. Hence many will strive to appear to "go for bad," while hoping they will never be tested. But when they are tested, the outcome of the situation may quickly be out of their hands, as they become wrapped up in the circumstances of the moment.

An Oppositional Culture

The attitudes of the wider society are deeply implicated in the code of the streets. Most people in inner-city communities are not totally invested in the code, but the significant minority of hard-core street youths who are have to maintain the code in order to establish reputations, because they have— or feel they have—few other ways to assert themselves. For these young people the standards of the street code are the only game in town. The extent to which some children—particularly those who through upbringing have become most alienated and those lacking in strong and conventional social support—experience, feel, and internalize racist rejection and contempt from mainstream society may strongly encourage them to express contempt for the more conventional society in turn. In dealing with this contempt and rejection, some youngsters will consciously invest themselves and their considerable mental resources in what amounts to an oppositional culture to preserve themselves and their self-respect. Once they do, any respect they might be able to garner in the wider system pales in comparison with the respect available in the local system; thus they often lose interest in even attempting to negotiate the mainstream system.

At the same time, many less alienated young blacks have assumed a street-oriented demeanor as a way of expressing their blackness while really embracing a much more moderate way of life; they, too want a nonviolent setting in which to live and raise a family. These decent people are trying hard to be part of the mainstream culture, but the racism, real and perceived, that they encounter helps to legitimate the oppositional culture. And so on occasion they adopt street behavior. In fact, depending on the demands of the situation, many people in the community slip back and forth between decent and street behavior.

A vicious cycle has thus been formed. The hopelessness and alienation many young inner-city black men and women feel, largely as a result of endemic joblessness and persistent racism, fuels the violence they engage in. This violence serves to confirm the negative feelings many whites and some middle-class blacks harbor toward the ghetto poor, further legitimating the oppositional culture and the code of the streets in the eyes of many poor young blacks. Unless this cycle is broken, attitudes on both sides will become increasingly entrenched, and the violence, which claims victims black and white, poor and affluent, will only escalate.

9

WARRIOR DREAMS
Violence and Manhood in Post-Vietnam America

J. WILLIAM GIBSON

Sociologists are interested in how culture limits our free choice and shapes social interaction. Because each of us is born into a particular culture that has certain norms and values, our personal values and life expectations are profoundly influenced by our culture. For example, what are the values of American culture? Many scholars agree that dominant U.S. values are achievement, Judeo-Christian morals, material comfort, patriotism, and individualism. Contrast these dominant culture values with those expressed by men who are active in the paramilitary culture. What are the values and expected behaviors of men involved in paramilitary groups? The following reading by J. William Gibson takes us inside this subculture to reveal the beliefs, practices, and rituals of men who join paramilitary groups.

We couldn't see them, but we could hear their bugles sound the call. The Communist battalions were organizing for a predawn assault. Captain Kokalis smiled wickedly; he'd been through this before. A "human wave" assault composed of thousands of enemy soldiers was headed our way. The captain ordered the remaining soldiers in his command to check their .30- and .50-caliber machine guns. Earlier in the night, the demolitions squad attached to our unit had planted mines and explosive charges for hundreds of meters in front of our position.

And then it began. At a thousand meters, the soldiers emerged screaming from the gray-blue fog. "Fire!" yelled Captain Kokalis. The gun crews opened up with short bursts of three to seven rounds; their bullets struck meat. Everywhere I could see, clusters of Communist troops were falling by the second. But the wave still surged forward. At 500 meters, Kokalis passed the word to his gunners to increase their rate of fire to longer strings of 10 to 20 rounds. Sergeant Donovan, the demolitions squad leader, began to reap the harvest from the night's planting. Massive explosions ripped through the Communist troops. Fire and smoke blasted into the dawn sky. It was as if the human wave had hit a submerged reef; as the dying fell, wide gaps appeared in the line where casualties could no longer be replaced.

But still they kept coming, hundreds of men, each and every one bent on taking the American position and wiping us out. As the Communists reached 100 meters, Kokalis gave one more command. Every machine gun in our platoon went to its maximum rate of sustained full-automatic frenzy, sounding like chain saws that just keep cutting and cutting.

And then it was over. The attack subsided into a flat sea of Communist dead. No Americans had been killed or wounded. We were happy to be alive, proud of our victory. We only wondered if our ears would ever stop ringing and if we would ever again smell anything other than the bitter-sweet aroma of burning gunpowder. . . .

Although an astonishing triumph was achieved that day, no historian will ever find a record of this battle in the hundreds of volumes and thousands of official reports written about the Korean or Vietnam war. Nor was the blood spilt part of a covert operation in Afghanistan or some unnamed country in Africa, Asia, or Latin America.

No, this battle was fought inside the United States, a few miles north of Las Vegas, in September 1986. It was a purely *imaginary* battle, a dream of victory staged as part of the *Soldier of Fortune* [*SOF*] magazine's annual convention. The audience of several hundred men, women, and children, together with reporters and a camera crew from CBS News, sat in bleachers behind half a dozen medium and heavy machine guns owned by civilians. Peter G. Kokalis, *SOF*'s firearms editor, set the scene for the audience and asked them to imagine that the sandy brushland of the Desert Sportsman Rifle and Pistol Club was really a killing zone for incoming Communist troops. Kokalis was a seasoned storyteller; he'd given this performance before. When the fantasy battle was over, the fans went wild with applause. Kokalis picked up a microphone, praised Donovan (another *SOF* staff member)—"He was responsible for that whole damn Communist bunker that went up"—and told the parents in the audience to buy "claymores [anti-personnel land mines] and other good shit for the kids." A marvelous actor who knew what his audience wanted, Kokalis sneered, "Did you get that, CBS, on your videocam? Screw you knee-jerk liberals."[1]

The shoot-out and victory over Communist forces conducted at the Desert Sportsman Rifle and Pistol Club was but one battle in a cultural or imaginary "New War" that had been going on since the late 1960s and early 1970s. The bitter controversies surrounding the Vietnam War had discredited the old American ideal of the masculine warrior hero for much of the public. But in 1971, when Clint Eastwood made the transition from playing cowboys in old *Rawhide* reruns and spaghetti westerns to portraying San Francisco police detective Harry Callahan in *Dirty Harry*, the warrior hero returned in full force. His backup arrived in 1974 when Charles Bronson appeared in *Death Wish*, the story of a mild-mannered, middle-aged architect in New York City who, after his wife is murdered and his daughter is raped and driven insane, finds new meaning in life through an endless war of revenge against street punks.

In the 1980s, Rambo and his friends made their assault. The experience of John Rambo, a former Green Beret, was the paradigmatic story of the decade. In *First Blood* (1982), he burns down a small Oregon town while suffering hallucinatory flashbacks to his service in Vietnam. Three years later, in *Rambo: First Blood, Part 2*, he is taken off a prison chain gang by his former commanding officer in Vietnam and asked to perform a special reconnaissance mission to find suspected American POWs in Laos, in exchange for a presidential pardon. His only question: "Do we get to win this time?" And indeed, Rambo does win. Betrayed by the CIA bureaucrat in charge of the mission, Rambo fights the Russians and Vietnamese by himself and brings the POWs back home.

Hundreds of similar films celebrating the victory of good men over bad through armed combat were made during the late 1970s and 1980s. Many were directed by major Hollywood directors and starred well-known actors. Elaborate special effects and exotic film locations added tens of millions to production costs. And for every large-budget film, there were scores of cheaper formula films employing lesser-known actors and production crews. Often these "action-adventure" films had only brief theatrical releases in major markets. Instead, they made their money in smaller cities and towns, in sales to Europe and the Third World, and most of all, in the sale of video-cassettes to rental stores. Movie producers could even turn a profit on "video-only" releases; action-adventure films were the largest category of video rentals in the 1980s.

At the same time, Tom Clancy became a star in the publishing world. His book *The Hunt for Red October* (1984) told the story of the Soviet Navy's most erudite submarine commander, Captain Markus Ramius, and his effort to defect to the United States with the Soviets' premier missile-firing submarine. *Red Storm Rising* (1986) followed, an epic of World War III framed as a high-tech conventional war against the Soviet Union. Clancy's novels all featured Jack Ryan, Ph.D., a former Marine captain in Vietnam turned academic naval historian who returns to duty as a CIA analyst and repeatedly stumbles into life-and-death struggles in which the fate of the world rests on his prowess. All were best-sellers.

President Reagan, Secretary of the Navy John Lehman, and many other high officials applauded Clancy and his hero. Soon the author had a multi-million-dollar contract for a whole series of novels, movie deals with Paramount, and a new part-time job as a foreign-policy expert writing op-ed pieces for the *Washington Post,* the *Los Angeles Times,* and other influential newspapers around the country. His success motivated dozens of authors, mostly active-duty or retired military men, to take up the genre. The "techno-thriller" was born.

At a slightly lower level in the literary establishment, the same publishing houses that marketed women's romance novels on grocery and drug-store paperback racks rapidly expanded their collections of pulp fiction for men. Most were written like hard-core pornography, except that inch-by-inch descriptions of penises entering vaginas were replaced by equally graphic portrayals of bullets, grenade fragments, and knives shredding flesh: "He tried to grab the handle of the commando knife, but the terrorist pushed down on the butt, raised the point and yanked the knife upward through the muscle tissue and guts. It ripped intestines, spilling blood and gore."[2] A minimum of 20 but sometimes as many as 120 such graphically described killings occurred in each 200-to-250-page paperback. Most series came out four times a year with domestic print runs of 60,000 to 250,000 copies. More than a dozen different comic books with titles like *Punisher, Vigilante,* and *Scout* followed suit with clones of the novels.

Along with the novels and comics came a new kind of periodical which replaced the older adventure magazines for men, such as *True* and *Argosy,* that had folded in the 1960s. Robert K. Brown, a former captain in the U.S. Army Special Forces during the Vietnam War, founded *Soldier of Fortune: The Journal of Professional Adventurers* in the spring of 1975, just before the fall of Saigon. *SOF*'s position was explicit from the start: The independent warrior must step in to fill the dangerous void created by the American failure in Vietnam. By the mid-1980s *SOF* was reaching 35,000 subscribers, had newsstand sales of another 150,000, and was being passed around to at least twice as many readers.[3]

Half a dozen new warrior magazines soon entered the market. Some, like *Eagle, New Breed,* and *Gung-Ho,* tried to copy the *SOF* editorial package— a strategy that ultimately failed. But most developed their own particular pitch. *Combat Handguns* focused on pistols for would-be gunfighters. *American Survival Guide* advertised and reviewed everything needed for "the good life" after the end of civilization (except birth control devices—too many Mormon subscribers, the editor said), while *S.W.A.T.* found its way to men who idealized these elite police teams and who were worried about home defense against "multiple intruders."

During the same period, sales of military weapons took off. Colt offered two semiautomatic versions of the M16 used by U.S. soldiers in Vietnam (a full-size rifle and a shorter-barreled carbine with collapsible stock). European armories exported their latest products, accompanied by sophisticated advertising campaigns in *SOF* and the more mainstream gun magazines. Israeli Defense Industries put a longer, 16-inch barrel on the Uzi submachine gun (to make it legal) and sold it as a semiautomatic carbine. And the Communist countries of Eastern Europe, together with the People's Republic of China, jumped into the market with the devil's own favorite hardware, the infamous AK47. The AK sold in the United States was the semiautomatic version of the assault rifle used by the victorious Communists in Vietnam and by all kinds of radical movements and terrorist organizations around the world. It retailed for $300 to $400, half the price of an Uzi or an AR-15; complete with three 30-round magazines, cleaning kit, and bayonet, it was truly a bargain.

To feed these hungry guns, munitions manufacturing packaged new "generic" brands of military ammo at discount prices, often selling them in cases of 500 or 1,000 rounds. New lines of aftermarket accessories offered parts for full-automatic conversions, improved flash-hiders, scopes, folding stocks, and scores of other goodies. In 1989, the U.S. Bureau of Alcohol, Tobacco and Firearms (ATF) estimated that two to three million military-style

rifles had been sold in this country since the Vietnam War. The Bureau released these figures in response to the public outcry over a series of mass
murders committed by psychotics armed with assault rifles.

But the Bureau's statistics tell only part of the story. In less than two
decades, millions of American men had purchased combat rifles, pistols, and
shotguns and began training to fight their own personal wars. Elite combat
shooting schools teaching the most modern techniques and often costing
$500 to over $1,000 in tuition alone were attended not only by soldiers and
police but by increasing numbers of civilians as well. Hundreds of new indoor pistol-shooting ranges opened for business in old warehouses and
shopping malls around the country, locations ideal for city dwellers and suburbanites.

A new game of "tag" blurred the line between play and actual violence:
men got the opportunity to hunt and shoot other men without killing them
or risking death themselves. The National Survival Game was invented in
1981 by two old friends, one a screenwriter for the weight-lifting sagas that
gave Arnold Schwarzenegger his first starring roles, and the other a former
member of the Army's Long Range Reconnaissance Patrol (LRRP) in Vietnam.[4] Later called paintball because it utilized guns firing balls of watercolor
paint, by 1987 the game was being played by at least fifty thousand people
(mostly men) each weekend on both outdoor and indoor battlefields scattered across the nation. Players wore hard-plastic face masks intended to resemble those of ancient tribal warriors and dressed from head to toe in
camouflage clothes imported by specialty stores from military outfitters
around the world. The object of the game was to capture the opposing team's
flag, inflicting the highest possible body count along the way.

One major park out in the Mojave Desert 70 miles southeast of Los Angeles was named Sat Cong Village. *Sat Cong* is a slang Vietnamese phrase
meaning "Kill Communists" that had been popularized by the CIA as part of
it psychological-warfare program. Sat Cong Village employed an attractive
Asian woman to rent the guns, sell the paintballs, and collect the $20 en-
trance fee. Players had their choice of playing fields: Vietnam, Cambodia, or
Nicaragua. On the Nicaragua field, the owner built a full-size facsimile of the
crashed C-47 cargo plane contracted by Lieutenant Colonel Oliver North to
supply the contras. The scene even had three parachutes hanging from trees;
the only thing missing was the sole survivor of the crash, Eugene Hasenfus.

The 1980s, then, saw the emergence of a highly energized culture of war and
the warrior. For all its varied manifestations, a few common features stood
out. The New War culture was not so much military as paramilitary. The new
warrior hero was only occasionally portrayed as a member of a conventional
military or law enforcement unit; typically, he fought alone or with a small,
elite group of fellow warriors. Moreover, by separating the warrior from his
traditional state-sanctioned occupations—policeman or soldier—the New
War culture presented the warrior role as the ideal identity for *all* men. Bank-

ers, professors, factory workers, and postal clerks could all transcend their regular stations in life and prepare for heroic battle against the enemies of society.

To many people, this new fascination with warriors and weapons seemed a terribly bad joke. The major newspapers and magazines that arbitrate what is to be taken seriously in American society scoffed at the attempts to resurrect the warrior hero. Movie critics were particularly disdainful of Stallone's Rambo films. *Rambo: First Blood, Part 2* was called "narcissistic jingoism" by *The New Yorker* and "hare-brained" by the *Wall Street Journal.* The *Washington Post* even intoned that "Sly's body looks fine. Now can't you come up with a workout for his soul?"

But in dismissing Rambo so quickly and contemptuously, commentators failed to notice the true significance of the emerging paramilitary culture. They missed the fact that quite a few people were not writing Rambo off as a complete joke; behind the Indian bandanna, necklace, and bulging muscles, a new culture hero affirmed such traditional American values as self-reliance, honesty, courage, and concern for fellow citizens. Rambo was a worker and a former enlisted man, not a smooth-talking professional. That so many seemingly well-to-do, sophisticated liberals hated him for both his politics and his uncouthness only added to his glory. Further, in their emphasis on Stallone's clownishness the commentators failed to see not only how widespread paramilitary culture had become but also its relation to the historical moment in which it arose.

Indeed, paramilitary culture can be understood only when it is placed in relation to the Vietnam War. America's failure to win that war was a truly profound blow. The nation's long, proud tradition of military victories, from the Revolutionary War through the century-long battles against the Indians to World Wars I and II, had finally come to an end. Politically, the defeat in Vietnam meant that the post–World War II era of overwhelming American political and military power in international affairs, the era that in 1945 *Time* magazine publisher Henry Luce had prophesied would be the "American Century," was over after only 30 years. No longer could U.S. diplomacy wield the big stick of military intervention as a ready threat—a significant part of the American public would no longer support such interventions, and the rest of the world knew it.

Moreover, besides eroding U.S. influence internationally, the defeat had subtle but serious effects on the American psyche. America has always celebrated war and the warrior. Our long, unbroken record of military victories has been crucially important both to the national identity and to the personal identity of many Americans—particularly men. The historian Richard Slotkin locates a primary "cultural archetype" of the nation in the story of a heroic warrior whose victories over the enemy symbolically affirm the country's fundamental goodness and power; we win our wars because, morally, we deserve to win. Clearly, the archetypical pattern Slotkin calls "regeneration through violence" was broken with the defeat in Vietnam.[5] The result was a massive disjunction in American culture, a crisis of self-image: If Americans were no longer winners, then who were they?

This disruption of cultural identity was amplified by other social trans-formations. During the 1960s, the civil rights and ethnic pride movements won many victories in their challenges to racial oppression. Also, during the 1970s and 1980s, the United States experienced massive waves of immigra-tion from Mexico, Central America, Vietnam, Cambodia, Korea, and Taiwan. Whites, no longer secure in their power abroad, also lost their unquestion-able dominance at home; for the first time, many began to feel that they too were just another hyphenated ethnic group, the Anglo-Americans.

Extraordinary economic changes also marked the 1970s and 1980s. U.S. manufacturing strength declined substantially; staggering trade deficits with other countries and the chronic federal budget deficits shifted the United States from creditor to debtor nation. The post–World War II Ameri-can Dream—which promised a combination of technological progress and social reforms, together with high employment rates, rising wages, wide-spread home ownership, and ever increasing consumer options—no longer seemed a likely prospect for the great majority. At the same time, the rise in crime rates, particularly because of drug abuse and its accompanying vio-lence, made people feel more powerless than ever.

While the public world dominated by men seemed to come apart, the private world of family life also felt the shocks. The feminist movement chal-lenged formerly exclusive male domains, not only in the labor market and in many areas of political and social life but in the home as well. Customary male behavior was no longer acceptable in either private relationships or public policy. Feminism was widely experienced by men as a profound threat to their identity. Men had to change, but to what? No one knew for sure what a "good man" was anymore.

It is hardly surprising, then, that American men—lacking confidence in the government and the economy, troubled by the changing relations be-tween the sexes, uncertain of their identity or their future—began to *dream*, to fantasize about the powers and features of another kind of man who could retake and reorder the world. And the hero of all these dreams was the paramilitary warrior. In the New War he fights the battles of Vietnam a thou-sand times, each time winning decisively. Terrorists and drug dealers are blasted into oblivion. Illegal aliens inside the United States and the hordes of nonwhites in the Third World are returned by force to their proper place. Women are revealed as dangerous temptresses who have to be mastered, avoided, or terminated.

Obviously these dreams represented a flight from the present and a re-jection and denial of events of the preceding 20 years. But they also indicated a more profound and severe distress. The whole modern world was damned as unacceptable. Unable to find a rational way to face the tasks of rebuilding society and reinventing themselves, men instead sought refuge in myths from both America's frontier past and ancient times. Indeed, the fundamental narratives that shape paramilitary culture and its New War fantasies are often nothing but reinterpretations or reworkings of archaic warrior myths.

In ancient societies, the most important stories a people told about themselves concerned how the physical universe came into existence, how their ancestors first came to live in this universe, and how the gods, the universe, and society were related to one another. These cosmogonic, or creation, myths frequently posit a violent conflict between the good forces of order and the evil forces dedicated to the perpetuation of primordial chaos.[6] After the war in which the gods defeat the evil ones, they establish the "sacred order," in which all of the society's most important values are fully embodied. Some creation myths focus primarily on the sacred order and on the deeds of the gods and goddesses in paradise. Other myths, however, focus on the battles between the heroes and villains that lead up to the founding.[7] In these myths it is war and the warrior that are most sacred. American paramilitary culture borrows from both kinds of stories, but mostly from this second, more violent, type.

In either case, the presence, if not the outright predominance, of archaic male myths at the moment of crisis indicates just how far American men jumped psychically when faced with the declining power of their identities and organizations. The always-precarious balance in modern society between secular institutions and ways of thinking on the one hand and older patterns of belief informed by myth and ritual on the other tilted decisively in the direction of myth. The crisis revealed that at some deep, unconscious level these ancient male creation myths live on in the psyche of many men and that the images and tales from this mythic world of warriors and war still shape men's fantasies about who they are as men, their commitments to each other and to women, and their relationships to society and the state.

The imaginary New War that men created is a coherent mythical universe, formed by the repetition of key features in thousands of novels, magazines, films, and advertisements. As the sociologist Will Wright points out, the component elements of myth work to create a common "theoretical idea of a social order."[8] These New War stories about heroic warriors and their evil adversaries are ways of arguing about what is wrong with the modern world and what needs to be done to make society well again. . . .

War games took these fantasies one step further and allowed men to act on their desires in paramilitary games and theme parks that one would-be warrior described as "better than Disneyland." Here, away from the ordinary routines of world and family life, men could meet, mingle, and share their warrior dreams. Three major types of imaginary war zones developed: the National Survival Game, or paintball; the annual *Soldier of Fortune* convention in Las Vegas; and combat shooting schools and firing ranges. In these special environments, the gods of war could be summoned for games played along the edges of violence.

Finally, the imaginary New War turned into the real nightmares of "War

Zone America." Since the 1970s, a number of racist groups, religious sects, mercenaries, and madmen have literally lived their own versions of the New War. At the same time, as hundreds of thousands of military-style rifles have entered the domestic gun market and become the weapon of choice for some killers, the gun-control debate has escalated to a new level. And not surprisingly, the myths of the New War have profoundly influenced several presidential administrations, affecting both those leaders who make military policy decisions and the lower-ranking personnel who carry out covert and overt operations.

Only at the surface level, then, has paramilitary culture been merely a matter of the "stupid" movies and novels consumed by the great unwashed lower-middle and working classes, or of the murderous actions of a few demented, "deviant" men. In truth, there is nothing superficial or marginal about the New War that has been fought in American popular culture since the 1970s. It is a war about basics: power, sex, race, and alienation. Contrary to the *Washington Post* review, Rambo was no shallow muscle man but the emblem of a movement that at the very least wanted to reverse the previous 20 years of American history and take back all the symbolic territory that had been lost. The vast proliferation of warrior fantasies represented an attempt to reaffirm the national identity. But it was also a larger volcanic upheaval of archaic myths, an outcropping whose entire structural formation plunges into deep historical, cultural, and psychological territories. These territories have kept us chained to war as a way of life; they have infused individual men, national political and military leaders, and society with a deep attraction to both imaginary and real violence. This terrain must be explored, mapped, and understood if it is ever to be transformed.

NOTES

1. Peter G. Kokalis, speaking at the *Soldier of Fortune* firepower demonstration at the Desert Sportsman Rifle and Pistol Club, Las Vegas, Nevada, September 20, 1986.
2. Gar Wilson, *The Fury Bombs,* vol. 5 of *Phoenix Force* (Toronto: Worldwide Library, 1983), p. 30.
3. *SOF* regularly hired the firm of Starch, Inra, Hopper to study their readership. A condensed version of their 1986 report, from which these figures were taken, was made available to the press at the September 1986 *SOF* convention in Las Vegas.
4. Lionel Atwill, *Survival Game: Airgun National Manual* (New London, NH: The National Survival Game, Inc., 1987), pp. 22–30.
5. Richard Slotkin, *Regeneration through Violence: The Mythology of the American Frontier, 1660–1860* (Middletown, CT: Wesleyan University Press, 1973).
6. Mircea Eliade, *Myth and Reality,* trans. Willard R. Trask (New York: Harper & Row, 1963).
7. Richard Stivers, *Evil in Modern Myth and Ritual* (Athens: University of Georgia Press, 1982).
8. Will Wright, *Sixguns and Society: A Structural Study of the Western* (Berkeley: University of California Press, 1975), p. 20.

10
───────

LOVELY HULA HANDS
Corporate Tourism and the Prostitution
of Hawaiian Culture

HAUNANI-KAY TRASK

Many U.S. racial-ethnic groups, including Native Americans, Latinos, and African Americans, have experienced cultural exploitation. Exploitation occurs when aspects of a subculture, such as its beliefs, rituals, and social customs, are commodified and marketed without the cultural group's permission. This selection by Haunani-Kay Trask explores the cultural commodification and exploitation of Hawaiian culture. Trask argues that several aspects of Polynesian and Hawaiian cultures, including their language, dress, and dance forms, have been marketed as products for the mass consumption of tourists.

I am certain that most, if not all, Americans have heard of Hawai'i and have wished, at some time in their lives, to visit my native land. But I doubt that the history of how Hawai'i came to be territorially incorporated, and economically, politically, and culturally subordinated to the United States is known to most Americans. Nor is it common knowledge that Hawaiians have been struggling for over 20 years to achieve a land base and some form of political sovereignty on the same level as American Indians. Finally, I would imagine the most Americans could not place Hawai'i or any other Pacific island on a map of the Pacific. But despite all this appalling ignorance, five million Americans will vacation in my homeland this year *and* the next, and so on into the foreseeable capitalist future. Such are the intended privileges of the so-called American standard of living: ignorance of, and yet power over, one's relations to native peoples.

Thanks to postwar American imperialism, the ideology that the United States has no overseas colonies and is, in fact, the champion of self-determination the world over holds no greater sway than in the United States itself. To most Americans, then, Hawai'i is *theirs:* to use, to take, and, above all, to fantasize about long after the experience.

Just five hours away by plane from California, Hawai'i is a thousand light years away in fantasy. Mostly a state of mind, Hawai'i is the image of escape from the rawness and violence of daily American life. Hawai'i— the word, the vision, the sound in the mind—is the fragrance and feel of soft kindness. Above all, Hawai'i is "she," the Western image of the native "female" in her magical allure. And if luck prevails, some of "her" will rub off on you, the visitor.

This fictional Hawai'i comes out of the depths of Western sexual sickness which demands a dark, sin-free native for instant gratification between imperialist wars. The attraction of Hawai'i is stimulated by slick Hollywood movies, saccharine Andy Williams music, and the constant psychological deprivations of maniacal American life. Tourists flock to my native land for escape, but they are escaping into a state of mind while participating in the destruction of a host people in a native place.

To Hawaiians, daily life is neither soft nor kind. In fact, the political, economic, and cultural reality for most Hawaiians is hard, ugly, and cruel.

In Hawai'i, the destruction of our land and the prostitution of our culture is planned and executed by multinational corporations (both foreign-based and Hawai'i-based), by huge landowners (like the missionary-descended Castle and Cook—of Dole Pineapple fame—and others) and by collaborationist state and county governments. The ideological gloss that claims tourism to be our economic savior and the "natural " result of Hawaiian culture is manufactured by ad agencies (like the state supported Hawai'i Visitors' Bureau) and tour companies (many of which are owned by the airlines), and spewed out to the public through complicitous cultural engines like film, television and radio, and the daily newspapers. As for the local labor unions, both rank and file and management clamor for more tourists while the construction industry lobbies incessantly for larger resorts.

. . .

My use of the word *tourism* in the Hawai'i context refers to a mass-based, corporately controlled industry that is both vertically and horizontally integrated such that one multinational corporation owns an airline, the tour buses that transport tourists to the corporation-owned hotel where they eat in a corporation-owned restaurant, play golf and "experience" Hawai'i on corporation-owned recreation areas, and eventually consider buying a second home built on corporation land. Profits, in this case, are mostly repatriated back to the home country. In Hawai'i, these "home" countries are Japan, Taiwan, Hong Kong, Canada, Australia, and the United States. . . .

. . .

With this as a background on tourism, I want to move now into the area of cultural prostitution. "Prostitution" in this context refers to the entire institution which defines a woman (and by extension the "female") as an object of degraded and victimized sexual value for use and exchange through the medium of money. The "prostitute" is then a woman who sells her sexual capacities and is seen, thereby, to possess and reproduce them at will, that is, by her very "nature." The prostitute and the institution which creates and maintains her are, of course, of patriarchal origin. The pimp is the conduit of exchange, managing the commodity that is the prostitute while acting as the guard at the entry and exit gates, making sure the prostitute behaves as a prostitute by fulfilling her sexual-economic functions. The victims participate in their victimization with enormous ranges of feeling, including resistance and complicity, but the force and continuity of the institution are shaped by men.

There is much more to prostitution than my sketch reveals but this must suffice for I am interested in using the largest sense of this term as a metaphor in understanding what has happened to Hawaiian culture. My purpose is not to exact detail or fashion a model but to convey the utter degradation of our culture and our people under corporate tourism by employing "prostitution" as an analytic category.

Finally, I have chosen four areas of Hawaiian culture to examine: our homeland, or *one hānau* that is Hawai'i, our lands and fisheries, the outlying seas and the heavens; our language and dance; our familial relationships; and our women.

Nā Mea Hawai'i—Things Hawaiian

The *mo'ōlelo*, or history of Hawaiians, is to be found in our genealogies. From our great cosmogonic genealogy, the *Kumulipo*, derives the Hawaiian identity. The "essential lesson" of this genealogy is "the interrelatedness of the Hawaiian world, and the inseparability of its constituent parts." Thus, "the genealogy of the land, the gods, chiefs, and people intertwine one with the other, and with all aspects of the universe."[1]

In the *mo'ōlelo* of Papa and Wākea, earth-mother and sky-father, our islands are born; Hawai'i, Maui, O'ahu, Kaua'i, and Ni'ihau. From their human offspring came the *taro* plant and from the taro came the Hawaiian people. The lessons of our genealogy are that human beings have a familial relationship to land and to the *taro*, our elder siblings or *kua'ana*.

In Hawai'i, as in all of Polynesia, younger siblings must serve and honor elder siblings who, in turn, must feed and care for their younger siblings. Therefore, Hawaiians must cultivate and husband the land which will feed and provide for the Hawaiian people. This relationship of people to land is called *mālama 'āina* or *aloha 'āina*, care and love of the land.

When people and land work together harmoniously, the balance that results is called *pono*. In Hawaiian society, the *ali'i* or chiefs were required to maintain order, abundance of food, and good government. The *maka'āinana* or common people worked the land and fed the chiefs; the *ali'i* organized production and appeased the gods.

Today, *mālama 'āina* is called stewardship by some, although that word does not convey spiritual and genealogical connections. Nevertheless, to love and make the land flourish is a Hawaiian value. *'Āina*, one of the words for land, means *that which feeds. Kama'āina,* a term for native-born people, means *child of the land.* Thus is the Hawaiian relationship to land both familial and reciprocal.

Our deities are also of the land: Pele is our volcano, Kāne and Lono our fertile valleys and plains, Kanaloa our ocean and all that lives within it, and so on with the 40,000 and 400,000 gods of Hawai'i. Our whole universe, physical and metaphysical, is divine.

Within this world, the older people or *kūpuna* are to cherish those who are younger, the *mo'opuna.* Unstinting generosity is a value and of high status. Social connections between our people are through *aloha,* simply translated as love but carrying with it a profoundly Hawaiian sense that is, again, familial and genealogical. Hawaiians feel *aloha* for Hawai'i whence they come and for their Hawaiian kin upon whom they depend. It is nearly impossible to feel or practice *aloha* for something that is not familial. This is why we extend familial relations to those few non-natives whom we feel understand and can reciprocate our *aloha.* But *aloha* is freely given and freely returned, it is not and cannot be demanded, or commanded. Above all, *aloha* is a cultural feeling and practice that works among the people and between the people and their land.

The significance and meaning of *aloha* underscores the centrality of the Hawaiian language or *'ōlelo* to the culture. *'Ōlelo* means both language and tongue; *mo'ōlelo,* or history, is that which comes from the tongue, that is, a story. *Haole* or white people say we have oral history, but what we have are stories passed on through the generations. These are different from the *haole* sense of history. To Hawaiians in traditional society, language had tremendous power, thus the phrase, *i ka 'ōlelo ke ola; i ka 'ōlelo ka make*—in language is life, in language is death.

After nearly 2,000 years of speaking Hawaiian, our people suffered the near extinction of our language through its banning by the American-imposed government in 1896. In 1900, Hawai'i became a territory of the United States. All schools, government operations and official transactions were thereafter conducted in English, despite the fact that most people, including non-natives, still spoke Hawaiian at the turn of the century.

Since 1970, *'ōlelo Hawai'i,* or the Hawaiian language, has undergone a tremendous revival, including the rise of language immersion schools. The state of Hawai'i now has two official languages, Hawaiian and English, and the call for Hawaiian language speakers and teachers grows louder by the day.[2]

Along with the flowering of Hawaiian language has come a flowering of Hawaiian dance, especially in its ancient form, called *hula kahiko.* Dance academies, known as *hālau,* have proliferated throughout Hawai'i as have *kumu hula,* or dance masters, and formal competitions where all-night presentations continue for three or four days to throngs of appreciative listeners. Indeed, among Pacific Islanders, Hawaiian dance is considered one of the finest Polynesian art forms today.

Of course, the cultural revitalization that Hawaiians are now experiencing and transmitting to their children is as much a *repudiation* of colonization by so-called Western civilization in its American form as it is a *reclamation* of our past and our own ways of life. This is why cultural revitalization is often resisted and disparaged by anthropologists and others: they see very clearly that its political effect is de-colonization of the mind. Thus our rejection of the nuclear family as the basic unit of society and of individualism as the best form of human expression infuriates social workers, the churches, the legal system, and educators. Hawaiians continue to have allegedly "illegitimate" children, to *hānai* or adopt both children and adults outside of sanctioned Western legal concepts, to hold and use land and water in a collective form rather than a private property form, and to proscribe the notion and the value that one person should strive to surpass and therefore outshine all others.

All these Hawaiian values can be grouped under the idea of *'ohana,* loosely translated as family, but more accurately imagined as a group of both closely and distantly related people who share nearly everything, from land and food to children and status. Sharing is central to this value since it prevents individual decline. Of course, poverty is not thereby avoided, it is only shared with everyone in the unit. The *'ohana* works effectively when the *kua'ana* relationship (elder sibling/younger sibling reciprocity) is practiced.

Finally, within the *'ohana,* our women are considered the lifegivers of the nation, and are accorded the respect and honor this status conveys. Our young women, like our young people in general, are the *pua,* or flower of our *lāhui,* or our nation. The renowned beauty of our women, especially their sexual beauty, is not considered a commodity to be hoarded by fathers and brothers but an attribute of our people. Culturally, Hawaiians are very open and free about sexual relationships, although Christianity and organized religion have done much to damage these traditional sexual values.

With this understanding of what it means to be Hawaiian, I want to move now to the prostitution of our culture by tourism.

Hawai'i itself is the female object of degraded and victimized sexual value. Our *'āina,* or lands, are not any longer the source of food and shelter, but the source of money. Land is now called real estate; rather than our mother, *Papa.* The American relationship of people to land is that of exploiter to exploited. Beautiful areas, once sacred to my people, are now expensive resorts; shorelines where net fishing, seaweed gathering, and crabbing occurred are more and more the exclusive domain of recreational activities: sunbathing, windsurfing, jet skiing. Now, even access to beaches near hotels is strictly regulated or denied to the local public altogether.

The phrase, *mālama 'āina*—to care for the land—is used by government officials to sell new projects and to convince the locals that hotels can be built with a concern for "ecology." Hotel historians, like hotel doctors, are stationed in-house to soothe the visitors' stay with the pablum of invented myths and tales of the "primitive."

High schools and hotels adopt each other and funnel teenagers through major resorts for guided tours from kitchens to gardens to honeymoon suites in preparation for postsecondary jobs in the lowest-paid industry in the state. In the meantime, tourist appreciation kits and movies are distributed through the state department of education to all elementary schools. One film, unashamedly titled "What's in it for Me?," was devised to convince locals that tourism is, as the newspapers never tire of saying, "the only game in town."

Of course, all this hype is necessary to hide the truth about tourism, the awful exploitative truth that the industry is the major cause of environmental degradation, low wages, land dispossession, and the highest cost of living in the United States.

While this propaganda is churned out to local residents, the commercialization of Hawaiian culture proceeds with calls for more sensitive marketing of our native values and practices. After all, a prostitute is only as good as her income-producing talents. These talents, in Hawaiian terms, are the *hula;* the generosity, or *aloha,* of our people; the *u´i* or youthful beauty of our women and men; and the continuing allure of our lands and waters, that is, of our place, Hawai´i.

The selling of these talents must produce income. And the function of tourism and the state of Hawai´i is to convert these attributes into profits.

The first requirement is the transformation of the product, or the cultural attribute, much as a woman must be transformed to look like a prostitute, that is, someone who is complicitous in her own commodification. Thus *hula* dancers wear clownlike make-up, don costumes from a mix of Polynesian cultures, and behave in a manner that is smutty and salacious rather than powerfully erotic. The distance between the smutty and the erotic is precisely the distance between Western culture and Hawaiian culture. In the hotel version of the *hula,* the sacredness of the dance has completely evaporated while the athleticism and sexual expression have been packaged like ornaments. The purpose is entertainment for profit rather than a joyful and truly Hawaiian celebration of human and divine nature.

But let us look at an example that is representative of literally hundreds of images that litter the pages of scores of tourist publications. From an Aloha Airlines booklet—shamelessly called the "Spirit of Aloha"—there is a characteristic portrayal of commodified *hula* dancers, one male and one female. The costuming of the female is more South Pacific—the Cook Islands and Tahiti—while that of the male is more Hawaiian. (He wears a Hawaiian loincloth called a *malo.*) The ad smugly asserts the hotel dinner service as a *lū´au,* a Hawaiian feast (which is misspelled) with a continuously open bar, lavish "island" buffet, and "thrilling" Polynesian revue. Needless to say, Hawaiians did not drink alcohol, eat "island" buffets, or participate in "thrilling" revues before the advent of white people in our islands.

But back to the advertisement. Lahaina, the location of the resort and once the capital of Hawai´i, is called "royal" because of its past association with our *ali'i,* or chiefs. Far from being royal today, Lahaina is sadly inundated by California yuppies, drug addicts, and valley girls.

The male figure in the background is muscular, partially clothed, and unsmiling. Apparently, he is supposed to convey an image of Polynesian sexuality that is both enticing and threatening. The white women in the audience can marvel at this physique and still remain safely distant. Like the black American male, this Polynesian man is a fantasy animal. He casts a slightly malevolent glance at our costumed maiden whose body posture and barely covered breasts contradict the innocent smile on her face.

Finally, the "wondrous allure" referred to in the ad applies to more than just the dancers in their performances; the physical beauty of Hawai'i "alive under the stars" is the larger reference.

In this little grotesquerie, the falseness and commercialism fairly scream out from the page. Our language, our dance, our young people, even our customs of eating are used to ensnare tourists. And the price is only a paltry $39.95, not much for two thousand years of culture. Of course, the hotel will rake in tens of thousands of dollars on just the *lū'au* alone. And our young couple will make a pittance.

The rest of the magazine, like most tourist propaganda, commodifies virtually every part of Hawai'i: mountains, beaches, coastlines, rivers, flowers, our volcano goddess, Pele, reefs and fish, rural Hawaiian communities, even Hawaiian activists.

The point, of course, is that everything in Hawai'i can be yours, that is, you the tourist, the non-native, the visitor. The place, the people, the culture, even our identity as a "native" people is for sale. Thus, the magazine, like the airline that prints it, is called Aloha. The use of this word in a capitalist context is so far removed from any Hawaiian cultural sense that it is, literally, meaningless.

Thus, Hawai'i, like a lovely woman, is there for the taking. Those with only a little money get a brief encounter; those with a lot of money, like the Japanese, get more. The state and counties will give tax breaks, build infrastructure, and have the governor personally welcome tourists to ensure they keep coming. Just as the pimp regulates prices and guards the commodity of the prostitute, so the state bargains with developers for access to Hawaiian land and culture. Who builds the biggest resorts to attract the most affluent tourists gets the best deal: more hotel rooms, golf courses, and restaurants approved. Permits are fast-tracked, height and density limits are suspended, new groundwater sources are miraculously found.

Hawaiians, meanwhile, have little choice in all this. We can fill up the unemployment lines, enter the military, work in the tourist industry, or leave Hawai'i. Increasingly, Hawaiians are leaving, not by choice but out of economic necessity.

Our people who work in the industry—dancers, waiters, singers, valets, gardeners, housekeepers, bartenders, and even a few managers—make between $10,000 and $25,000 a year, an impossible salary for a family in Hawai'i.

Psychologically, our young people have begun to think of tourism as the only employment opportunity, trapped as they are by the lack of alternatives. For our young women, modeling is a "cleaner" job when compared to waiting on tables, or dancing in a weekly revue, but modeling feeds on tourism and the commodification of Hawaiian women. In the end, the entire employment scene is shaped by tourism.

Despite their exploitation, Hawaiians' participation in tourism raises the problem of complicity. Because wages are so low and advancement so rare, whatever complicity exists is secondary to the economic hopelessness that drives Hawaiians into the industry. Refusing to contribute to the commercialization of one's culture becomes a peripheral concern when unemployment looms.

Of course, many Hawaiians do not see tourism as part of their colonization. Thus tourism is viewed as providing jobs, not as a form of cultural prostitution. Even those who have some glimmer of critical consciousness don't generally agree that the tourist industry prostitutes Hawaiian culture. To me, this is a measure of the depth of our mental oppression: We can't understand our own cultural degradation because we are living it. As colonized people, we are colonized to the extent that we are unaware of our oppression. When awareness begins, then so too does de-colonization. Judging by the growing resistance to new hotels, to geothermal energy and manganese nodule mining which would supplement the tourist industry, and to increases in the sheer number of tourists, I would say that de-colonization has begun, but we have many more stages to negotiate on our path to sovereignty.

My brief excursion into the prostitution of Hawaiian culture has done no more than give an overview. Now that you have heard a native view, let me just leave this thought behind. If you are thinking of visiting my homeland, please don't. We don't want or need any more tourists, and we certainly don't like them. If you want to help our cause, pass this message on to your friends.

NOTES

Author's Note: "Lovely Hula Hands" is the title of a famous and very saccharine song written by a *haole* who fell in love with Hawai'i in the pre-statehood era. It embodies the worst romanticized views of *hula* dancers and Hawaiian culture in general.

1. Lilikalā Kame'eleihiwa, *Native Land and Foreign Desires* (Honolulu: Bishop Museum, Press, 1992), p. 2.
2. See Larry Kimura, 1983. "Native Hawaiian Culture," in *Native Hawaiians Study Commission Report,* Vol. 1 (Washington, DC: U.S. Department of the Interior), pp. 173–97.

PART III

Socialization

11

"NIGHT TO HIS DAY"
The Social Construction of Gender

JUDITH LORBER

In this and the following three selections, we examine the process of learning cultural values and norms called socialization. *Socialization* refers to those social processes through which an individual becomes integrated into a social group by learning the group's culture and his or her roles in that group. It is largely through this process that an individual's concept of self is formed. Thus, socialization teaches us the cultural norms, values, and skills necessary to survive in society. Socialization also enables us to form social identities and an awareness about ourselves as individuals. The following reading by Judith Lorber examines socialization and how we learn our gender identities following birth.

[Gethenians] do not see each other as men or women. This is almost impossible for our imagination to accept. What is the first question we ask about a newborn baby?

—URSULA LE GUIN

Talking about gender for most people is the equivalent of fish talking about water. Gender is so much the routine ground of everyday activities that questioning its taken-for-granted assumptions and presuppositions is like thinking about whether the sun will come up.[1] Gender is so pervasive that in our society we assume it is bred into our genes. Most people find it hard to believe that gender is constantly created and re-created out of human interaction, out of social life, and is the texture and order of that social life. Yet gender, like culture, is a human production that depends on everyone constantly "doing gender" (West and Zimmerman 1987).

And everyone "does gender" without thinking about it. Today, on the subway, I saw a well-dressed man with a year-old child in a stroller. Yesterday, on a bus, I saw a man with a tiny baby in a carrier on his chest. Seeing men taking care of small children in public is increasingly common—at least in New York City. But both men were quite obviously stared at—and smiled at, approvingly. Everyone was doing gender—the men who were changing the role of fathers and the other passengers, who were applauding them silently. But there was more gendering going on that probably fewer people noticed. The baby was wearing a white crocheted cap and white clothes. You couldn't tell if it was a boy or a girl. The child in the stroller was wearing a dark blue T-shirt and dark print pants. As they started to leave the train, the father put a Yankee baseball cap on the child's head. Ah, a boy, I thought. Then I noticed the gleam of tiny earrings in the child's ears, and as they got off, I saw the little flowered sneakers and lace-trimmed socks. Not a boy after all. Gender done.

Gender is such a familiar part of daily life that it usually takes a deliberate disruption of our expectations of how women and men are supposed to act to pay attention to how it is produced. Gender signs and signals are so ubiquitous that we usually fail to note them—unless they are missing or ambiguous. Then we are uncomfortable until we have successfully placed the other person in a gender status; otherwise, we feel socially dislocated. In our society, in addition to man and woman, the status can be *transvestite* (a person who dresses in opposite-gender clothes) and *transsexual* (a person who has had sex-change surgery). Transvestites and transsexuals carefully construct their gender status by dressing, speaking, walking, gesturing in the ways prescribed for women or men—whichever they want to be taken for— and so does any "normal" person.

For the individual, gender construction starts with assignment to a sex category on the basis of what the genitalia look like at birth.[2] Then babies are dressed or adorned in a way that displays the category because parents don't want to be constantly asked whether their baby is a girl or a boy. A sex category becomes a gender status through naming, dress, and the use of other gender markers. Once a child's gender is evident, others treat those in one gender differently from those in the other, and the children respond to the different treatment by feeling different and behaving differently. As soon as they can talk, they start to refer to themselves as members of their gender. Sex doesn't come into play again until puberty, but by that time, sexual feelings and desires and practices have been shaped by gendered norms and expectations. Adolescent boys and girls approach and avoid each other in an elaborately scripted and gendered mating dance. Parenting is gendered, with different expectations for mothers and for fathers, and people of different genders work at different kinds of jobs. The work adults do as mothers and fathers and as low-level workers and high-level bosses, shapes women's and men's life experiences, and these experiences produce different feelings, consciousness, relationships, skills—ways of being that we call feminine or masculine.[3] All of these processes constitute the social construction of gender.

Gendered roles change—today fathers are taking care of little children, girls and boys are wearing unisex clothing and getting the same education, women and men are working at the same jobs. Although many traditional so-

cial groups are quite strict about maintaining gender differences, in other social groups they seem to be blurring. Then why the one-year-old's earrings?
Why is it still so important to mark a child as a girl or a boy, to make sure she
is not taken for a boy or he for a girl? What would happen if they were? They
would, quite literally, have changed places in their social world.

To explain why gendering is done from birth, constantly and by everyone, we have to look not only at the way individuals experience gender but
at gender as a social institution. As a social institution, gender is one of the
major ways that human beings organize their lives. Human society depends
on a predictable division of labor, a designated allocation of scarce goods,
assigned responsibility for children and others who cannot care for themselves, common values and their systematic transmission to new members,
legitimate leadership, music, art, stories, games, and other symbolic productions. One way of choosing people for the different tasks of society is on
the basis of their talents, motivations, and competence—their demonstrated
achievements. The other way is on the basis of gender, race, ethnicity—ascribed membership in a category of people. Although societies vary in the
extent to which they use one or the other of these ways of allocating people
to work and to carry out other responsibilities, every society uses gender
and age grades. Every society classifies people as "girl and boy children,"
"girls and boys ready to be married," and "fully adult women and men," constructs similarities among them and differences between them, and assigns
them to different roles and responsibilities. Personality characteristics, feelings, motivations, and ambitions flow from these different life experiences so
that the members of these different groups become different kinds of people.
The process of gendering and its outcome are legitimated by religion, law,
science, and the society's entire set of values.

. . .

Western society's values legitimate gendering by claiming that it all
comes from physiology—female and male procreative differences. But gender and sex are not equivalent, and gender as a social construction does not
flow automatically from genitalia and reproductive organs, the main physiological differences of females and males. In the construction of ascribed social statuses, physiological differences such as sex, stage of development,
color of skin, and size are crude markers. They are not the source of the social statuses of gender, age grade, and race. Social statuses are carefully constructed through prescribed processes of teaching, learning, emulation, and
enforcement. Whatever genes, hormones, and biological evolution contribute
to human social institutions is materially as well as qualitatively transformed by social practices. Every social institution has a material base, but
culture and social practices transform that base into something with qualitatively different patterns and constraints. The economy is much more than

producing food and goods and distributing them to eaters and users; family and kinship are not the equivalent of having sex and procreating; morals and religions cannot be equated with the fears and ecstasies of the brain; language goes far beyond the sounds produced by tongue and larynx. No one eats "money" or "credit"; the concepts of "god" and "angels" are the subjects of theological disquisitions; not only words but objects, such as their flag, "speak" to the citizens of a country.

Similarly, gender cannot be equated with biological and physiological differences between human females and males. The building blocks of gender are *socially constructed statuses*. Western societies have only two genders, "man" and "woman." Some societies have three genders—men, women, and *berdaches* or *hijras* or *xaniths*. Berdaches, hijras, and xaniths are biological males who behave, dress, work, and are treated in most respects as social women; they are therefore not men, nor are they female women; they are, in our language, "male women." [4] There are African and American Indian societies that have a gender status called *manly hearted women*—biological females who work, marry, and parent as men; their social status is "female men" (Amadiume 1987; Blackwood 1984). They do not have to behave or dress as men to have the social responsibilities and prerogatives of husbands and fathers; what makes them men is enough wealth to buy a wife.

Modern Western societies' *transsexuals* and *transvestites* are the nearest equivalent of these crossover genders, but they are not institutionalized as third genders (Bolin 1987). Transsexuals are biological males and females who have sex-change operations to alter their genitalia. They do so in order to bring their physical anatomy in congruence with the way they want to live and with their own sense of gender identity. They do not become a third gender; they change genders. Transvestites are males who live as women and females who live as men but do not intend to have sex-change surgery. Their dress, appearance, and mannerisms fall within the range of what is expected from members of the opposite gender, so that they "pass." They also change genders, sometimes temporarily, some for most of their lives. Transvestite women have fought in wars as men soldiers as recently as the nineteenth century; some married women, and others went back to being women and married men once the war was over.[5] Some were discovered when their wounds were treated; others not until they died. In order to work as a jazz musician, a man's occupation, Billy Tipton, a woman, lived most of her life as a man. She died recently at 74, leaving a wife and three adopted sons for whom she was husband and father, and musicians with whom she had played and traveled, for whom she was "one of the boys" (*New York Times* 1989).[6] There have been many other such occurrences of women passing as men to do more prestigious or lucrative men's work (Matthaei 1982, pp. 192–93).[7]

Genders, therefore, are not attached to a biological substratum. Gender boundaries are breachable, and individual and socially organized shifts from one gender to another call attention to "cultural, social, or aesthetic dissonances" (Garber 1992, p. 16). These odd or deviant or third genders show us what we ordinarily take for granted—that people have to learn to be women and men. Men who cross-dress for performances or for pleasure often learn from women's magazines how to "do femininity" convincingly (Garber 1992, pp. 41–51). Because transvestism is direct evidence of how gender is constructed, Marjorie Garber claims it has "extraordinary power . . . to disrupt, expose, and challenge, putting in question the very notion of the 'original' and of stable identity" (1992, p. 16).

Gender Bending

It is difficult to see how gender is constructed because we take it for granted that it's all biology, or hormones, or human nature. The differences between women and men seem to be self-evident, and we think they would occur no matter what society did. But in actuality, human females and males are physiologically more similar in appearance than are the two sexes of many species of animals and are more alike than different in traits and behavior (Epstein 1988). Without the deliberate use of gendered clothing, hairstyles, jewelry, and cosmetics, women and men would look far more alike.[8] Even societies that do not cover women's breasts have gender-identifying clothing, scarification, jewelry, and hairstyles.

The ease with which many transvestite women pass as men and transvestite men as women is corroborated by the common gender misidentification in Westernized societies of people in jeans, T-shirts, and sneakers. Men with long hair may be addressed as "miss," and women with short hair are often taken for men unless they offset the potential ambiguity with deliberate gender markers (Devor 1987, 1989). Jan Morris, in *Conundrum*, an autobiographical account of events just before and just after a sex-change operation, described how easy it was to shift back and forth from being a man to being a woman when testing how it would feel to change gender status. During this time, Morris still had a penis and wore more or less unisex clothing; the context alone made the man and the woman:

> Sometimes the arena of my ambivalence was uncomfortably small. At the Travellers' Club, for example, I was obviously known as a man of sorts—women were only allowed on the premises at all during a few hours of the day, and even then were hidden away as far as possible in lesser rooms or alcoves. But I had another club, only a few hundred yards away, where I was known only as a woman, and often I went directly from one to the other, imperceptibly changing roles on the way—"Cheerio, sir," the porter would say at one club, and "Hello, madam," the porter would greet me at the other. (1975, p. 132)

Gender shifts are actually a common phenomenon in public roles as well. Queen Elizabeth II of England bore children, but when she went to Saudi Arabia on a state visit, she was considered an honorary man so that she could confer and dine with the men who were heads of a state that forbids un-related men and women to have face-to-unveiled face contact. In contemporary Egypt, lower-class women who run restaurants or shops dress in men's clothing and engage in unfeminine aggressive behavior, and middle-class educated women of professional or managerial status can take positions of authority (Rugh 1986, p. 131). In these situations, there is an important status change: These women are treated by the others in the situation as if they are men. From their own point of view, they are still women. From the social perspective, however, they are men.[9]

In many cultures, gender bending is prevalent in theater or dance—the Japanese kabuki are men actors who play both women and men; in Shakespeare's theater company, there were no actresses—Juliet and Lady Macbeth were played by boys. Shakespeare's comedies are full of witty comments on gender shifts. Women characters frequently masquerade as young men, and other women characters fall in love with them; the boys playing these masquerading women, meanwhile, are acting out pining for the love of men characters.[10] . . .

. . .

But despite the ease with which gender boundaries can be traversed in work, in social relationships, and in cultural productions, gender statuses remain. Transvestites and transsexuals do not challenge the social construction of gender. Their goal is to be feminine women and masculine men (Kando 1973). Those who do not want to change their anatomy but do want to change their gender behavior fare less well in establishing their social identity. . . .

. . .

Paradoxically, then, bending gender rules and passing between genders does not erode but rather preserves gender boundaries. In societies with only two genders, the gender dichotomy is not disturbed by transvestites, because others feel that a transvestite is only transitorily ambiguous—is "really a man or woman underneath." After sex-change surgery, transsexuals end up in a conventional gender status—a "man" or a "woman" with the appropriate genitals (Eichler 1989). When women dress as men for business reasons, they are indicating that in that situation, they want to be treated the way men are treated; when they dress as women, they want to be treated as women:

> By their male dress, female entrepreneurs signal their desire to suspend the expectations of accepted feminine conduct without losing respect and reputation. By wearing what is "unattractive" they signify that they are not intending to display their physical charms while engaging in public activity. Their loud, aggressive banter contrasts with the modest de-

meanor that attracts men. . . . Overt signalling of a suspension of the rules preserves normal conduct from eroding expectations. (Rugh 1986, p. 131)

For Individuals, Gender Means Sameness

Although the possible combinations of genitalia, body shapes, clothing, mannerisms, sexuality, and roles could produce infinite varieties in human beings, the social institution of gender depends on the production and maintenance of a limited number of gender statuses and of making the members of these statuses similar to each other. Individuals are born sexed but not gendered, and they have to be taught to be masculine or feminine.[11] As Simone de Beauvoir said: "One is not born, but rather becomes, a woman . . . ; it is civilization as a whole that produces this creature . . . which is described as feminine" ([1949] 1953, p. 267).

Children learn to walk, talk, and gesture the way their social group says girls and boys should. Ray Birdwhistell, in his analysis of body motion as human communication, calls these learned gender displays *tertiary* sex characteristics and argues that they are needed to distinguish genders because humans are a weakly dimorphic species—their only sex markers are genitalia (1970, pp. 39–46). Clothing, paradoxically, often hides the sex but displays the gender.

In early childhood, humans develop gendered personality structures and sexual orientations through their interactions with parents of the same and opposite gender. As adolescents, they conduct their sexual behavior according to gendered scripts. Schools, parents, peers, and the mass media guide young people into gendered work and family roles. As adults, they take on a gendered social status in their society's stratification system. Gender is thus both ascribed and achieved (West and Zimmerman 1987).

The achievement of gender was most dramatically revealed in a case of an accidental transsexual—a baby boy whose penis was destroyed in the course of a botched circumcision when he was seven months old (Money and Ehrhardt 1972, pp. 118–23). The child's sex category was changed to "female," and a vagina was surgically constructed when the child was 17 months old. The parents were advised that they could successfully raise the child, one of identical twins, as a girl. Physicians assured them that the child was too young to have formed a gender identity. Children's sense of which gender they belong to usually develops around the age of three, at the time that they start to group objects and recognize that the people around them also fit into categories—big, little; pink-skinned, brown-skinned; boys, girls. Three has also been the age when children's appearance is ritually gendered, usually by cutting a boy's hair or dressing him in distinctively masculine clothing. In Victorian times, English boys wore dresses up to the age of three, when they were put into short pants (Garber 1992, pp. 1–2).

The parents of the accidental transsexual bent over backward to feminize the child—and succeeded. Frilly dresses, hair ribbons, and jewelry created a pride in looks, neatness, and "daintiness." More significant, the child's dominance was also feminized:

> The girl had many tomboyish traits, such as abundant physical energy, a high level of activity, stubbornness, and being often the dominant one in a girls' group. Her mother tried to modify her tomboyishness: "...I teach her to be more polite and quiet. I always wanted those virtues. I never did manage, but I'm going to try to manage them to—my daughter— to be more quiet and ladylike." From the beginning the girl had been the dominant twin. By age of three, her dominance over her brother was, as her mother described it, that of a mother hen. The boy in turn took up for his sister, if anyone threatened her. (Money and Ehrhardt 1972, p. 122)

This child was not a tomboy because of male genes or hormones; according to her mother, she herself had also been a tomboy. What the mother had learned poorly while growing up as a "natural" female she insisted that her physically reconstructed son-daughter learn well. For both mother and child, the social construction of gender overrode any possibly inborn traits.

People go along with the imposition of gender norms because the weight of morality as well as immediate social pressure enforces them. Consider how many instructions for properly gendered behavior are packed into this mother's admonition to her daughter: "This is how to hem a dress when you see the hem coming down and so to prevent yourself from looking like the slut I know you are so bent on becoming" (Kincaid 1978).

Gender norms are inscribed in the way people move, gesture, and even eat. In one African society, men were supposed to eat with their "whole mouth, wholeheartedly, and not, like women, just with the lips, that is half-heartedly, with reservation and restraint" (Bourdieu [1980] 1990, p. 70). Men and women in this society learned to walk in ways that proclaimed their different positions in the society:

> The manly man ... stands up straight into the face of the person he approaches, or wishes to welcome. Ever on the alert, because ever threatened, he misses nothing of what happens around him. ... Conversely, a well brought-up woman ... is expected to walk with a slight stoop, avoiding every misplaced movement of her body, her head or her arms, looking down, keeping her eyes on the spot where she will next put her foot, especially if she happens to have to walk past the men's assembly. (p. 70)

Many cultures go beyond clothing, gestures, and demeanor in gendering children. They inscribe gender directly into bodies. In traditional Chinese society, mothers bound their daughters' feet into three-inch stumps to enhance their sexual attractiveness. Jewish fathers circumcise their infant sons to show their covenant with God. Women in African societies remove the clitoris of

prepubescent girls, scrape their labia, and make the lips grow together to preserve their chastity and ensure their marriageability. In Western societies,
women augment their breast size with silicone and reconstruct their faces
with cosmetic surgery to conform to cultural ideals of feminine beauty. . . .

. . .

Most parents create a gendered world for their newborn by naming, birth
announcements, and dress. Children's relationships with same-gendered and
different-gendered caretakers structure their self-identifications and personalities. Through cognitive development, children extract and apply to their
own actions the appropriate behavior for those who belong in their own gender, as well as race, religion, ethnic group, and social class, rejecting what is
not appropriate. If their social categories are highly valued, they value themselves highly; if their social categories are low status, they lose self-esteem
(Chodorow 1974). Many feminist parents who want to raise androgynous
children soon lose their children to the pull of gendered norms (Gordon 1990,
pp. 87–90). My son attended a carefully nonsexist elementary school, which
didn't even have girls' and boys' bathrooms. When he was seven or eight
years old, I attended a class play about "squares" and "circles" and their need
for each other and noticed that all the girl squares and circles wore makeup,
but none of the boy squares and circles did. I asked the teacher about it after
the play, and she said, "Bobby said he was not going to wear makeup, and he
is a powerful child, so none of the boys would either." In a long discussion
about conformity, my son confronted me with the question of who the conformists were, the boys who followed their leader or the girls who listened to
the woman teacher. In actuality, they both were, because they both followed
same-gender leaders and acted in gender-appropriate ways. (Actors may
wear makeup, but real boys don't.)

For human beings there is no essential femaleness and maleness, femininity or masculinity, womanhood or manhood, but once gender is ascribed,
the social order constructs and holds individuals to strongly gendered norms
and expectations. Individuals may vary on many of the components of gender and may shift genders temporarily or permanently, but they must fit into
the limited number of gender statuses their society recognizes. In the process,
they re-create their society's version of women and men: "If we do gender
appropriately, we simultaneously sustain, reproduce, and render legitimate
the institutional arrangements. . . . If we fail to do gender appropriately, we
as individuals—not the institutional arrangements—may be called to account (for our character, motives, and predispositions)" (West and Zimmerman 1987, p. 146).

The gendered practices of everyday life reproduce a society's view of
how women and men should act (Bourdieu [1980] 1990). Gendered social
arrangements are justified by religion and cultural productions and backed
by law, but the most powerful means of sustaining the moral hegemony of

the dominant gender ideology is that the process is made invisible; any possible alternatives are virtually unthinkable (Foucault 1972; Gramsci 1971).[12]

For Society, Gender Means Difference

The pervasiveness of gender as a way of structuring social life demands that gender statuses be clearly differentiated. Varied talents, sexual preferences, identities, personalities, interests, and ways of interacting fragment the individual's bodily and social experiences. Nonetheless, these are organized in Western cultures into two and only two socially and legally recognized gender statuses, "man" and "woman."[13] In the social construction of gender, it does not matter what men and women actually do; it does not even matter if they do exactly the same thing. The social institution of gender insists only that what they do is *perceived* as different.

If men and women are doing the same tasks, they are usually spatially segregated to maintain gender separation, and often the tasks are given different job titles as well, such as executive secretary and administrative assistant (Reskin 1988). If the differences between women and men begin to blur, society's "sameness taboo" goes into action (Rubin 1975, p. 178). At a rock and roll dance at West Point in 1976, the year women were admitted to the prestigious military academy for the first time, the school's administrators "were reportedly perturbed by the sight of mirror-image couples dancing in short hair and dress gray trousers," and a rule was established that women cadets could dance at these events only if they wore skirts (Barkalow and Raab 1990, p. 53).[14] Women recruits in the U.S. Marine Corps are required to wear makeup—at a minimum, lipstick and eye shadow—and they have to take classes in makeup, hair care, poise, and etiquette. This feminization is part of a deliberate policy of making them clearly distinguishable from men Marines. Christine Williams quotes a 25-year-old woman drill instructor as saying: "A lot of the recruits who come here don't wear makeup; they're tomboyish or athletic. A lot of them have the preconceived idea that going into the military means they can still be a tomboy. They don't realize that you are a *Woman* Marine" (1989, pp. 76–77).[15]

If gender differences were genetic, physiological, or hormonal, gender bending and gender ambiguity would occur only in hermaphrodites, who are born with chromosomes and genitalia that are not clearly female or male. Since gender differences are socially constructed, all men and all women can enact the behavior of the other, because they know the other's social script: "'Man' and 'woman' are at once empty and overflowing categories. Empty because they have no ultimate, transcendental meaning. Overflowing because even when they appear to be fixed, they still contain within them alternative, denied, or suppressed definitions" (Scott 1988, p. 49). Nonetheless, though individuals may be able to shift gender statuses, the gender boundaries have to hold, or the whole gendered social order will come crashing down.

Paradoxically, it is the social importance of gender statuses and their external markers—clothing, mannerisms, and spatial segregation—that makes gender bending or gender crossing possible—or even necessary. The social viability of differentiated gender statuses produces the need or desire to shift statuses. Without gender differentiation, transvestism and transsexuality would be meaningless. You couldn't dress in the opposite gender's clothing if all clothing were unisex. There would be no need to reconstruct genitalia to match identity if interests and lifestyles were not gendered. There would be no need for women to pass as men to do certain kinds of work if jobs were not typed as "women's work" and "men's work." Women would not have to dress as men in public life in order to give orders or aggressively bargain with customers.

Gender boundaries are preserved when transsexuals create congruous autobiographies of always having felt like what they are now. The transvestite's story also "recuperates social and sexual norms" (Garber 1992, p. 69). In the transvestite's normalized narrative, he or she "is 'compelled' by social and economic forces to disguise himself or herself in order to get a job, escape repression, or gain artistic or political 'freedom'" (Garber 1992, p. 70). The "true identity," when revealed, causes amazement over how easily and successfully the person passed as a member of the opposite gender, not a suspicion that gender itself is something of a put-on.

NOTES

1. Gender is, in Erving Goffman's words, an aspect of *Felicity's Condition:* "any arrangement which leads us to judge an individual's . . . acts not to be a manifestation of strangeness. Behind Felicity's Condition is our sense of what it is to be sane" (1983, p. 27). Also see Bem 1993; Frye 1983, pp. 17–40; Goffman 1977.
2. In cases of ambiguity in countries with modern medicine, surgery is usually performed to make the genitalia more clearly male or female.
3. See J. Butler 1990 for an analysis of how doing gender *is* gender identity.
4. On the hijras of India, see Nanda 1990; on the xaniths of Oman, Wikan 1982, pp. 168–86; on the American Indian berdaches, W. L. Williams 1986. Other societies that have similar institutionalized third-gender men are the Koniag of Alaska, the Tanala of Madagascar, the Mesakin of Nuba, and the Chukchee of Siberia (Wikan 1982, p. 170).
5. Durova 1989; Freeman and Bond 1992; Wheelwright 1989.
6. Gender segregation of work in popular music still has not changed very much, according to Groce and Cooper 1990, despite considerable androgyny in some very popular figures. See Garber 1992 on the androgyny. She discusses Tipton on pp. 67–70.
7. In the nineteenth century, not only did these women get men's wages, but they also "had male privileges and could do all manner of things other women could not: open a bank account, write checks, own property, go anywhere unaccompanied, vote in elections" (Faderman 1991, p. 44).
8. When unisex clothing and men wearing long hair came into vogue in the United States in the mid-1960s, beards and mustaches for men also came into style again as gender identifications.

9. For other accounts of women being treated as men in Islamic countries, as well as accounts of women and men cross-dressing in these countries, see Garber 1992, pp. 304–52.

10. Dollimore 1986; Garber 1992, pp. 32–40; Greenblatt 1987, pp. 66–93; Howard 1988. For Renaissance accounts of sexual relations with women and men of ambiguous sex, see Laqueur 1990, pp. 134–39. For modern accounts of women passing as men that other women find sexually attractive, see Devor 1989, pp. 136–37; Wheelwright 1989, pp. 53–59.

11. For an account of how a potential man-to-woman transsexual learned to be feminine, see Garfinkel 1967, pp. 116–85, 285–88. For a gloss on this account that points out how, throughout his encounters with Agnes, Garfinkel failed to see how he himself was constructing his own masculinity, see Rogers 1992.

12. The concepts of moral hegemony, the effects of everyday activities (praxis) on thought and personality, and the necessity of consciousness of these processes before political change can occur are all based on Marx's analysis of class relations.

13. Other societies recognize more than two categories, but usually no more than three or four (Jacobs and Roberts 1989).

14. Carol Barkalow's book has a photograph of 11 first-year West Pointers in a math class, who are dressed in regulation pants, shirts, and sweaters, with short haircuts. The caption challenges the reader to locate the only woman in the room.

15. The taboo on males and females looking alike reflects the U.S. military's homophobia (Bérubé 1989). If you can't tell those with a penis from those with a vagina, how are you going to determine whether their sexual interest is heterosexual or homosexual unless you watch them having sexual relations?

REFERENCES

Amadiume, Ifi. 1987. *Male Daughters, Female Husbands: Gender and Sex in an African Society.* London: Zed Books.

Barkalow, Carol, with Andrea Raab. 1990. *In the Men's House.* New York: Poseidon Press.

Beauvoir, Simone de. [1949] 1953. *The Second Sex,* translated by H. M. Parshley. New York: Knopf.

Bem, Sandra Lipsitz. 1993. *The Lenses of Gender: Transforming the Debate on Sexual Inequality.* New Haven, CT: Yale University Press.

Bérubé, Allan. 1989. "Marching to a Different Drummer: Gay and Lesbian GIs in World War II." In *Hidden From History: Reclaiming the Gay and Lesbian Past,* edited by Martin Bauml Duberman, Martha Vicinus, and George Chauncey, Jr. New York: New American Library.

Birdwhistell, Ray L. 1970. *Kinesics and Context: Essays on Body Motion Communication.* Philadelphia: University of Pennsylvania Press.

Blackwood, Evelyn. 1984. "Sexuality and Gender in Certain Native American Tribes: The Case of Cross-Gender Females." *Signs* 10:27–42.

Bolin, Anne. 1987. "Transsexualism and the Limits of Traditional Analysis." *American Behavior Scientist* 31:41–65.

Bourdieu, Pierre. [1980] 1990. *The Logic of Practice.* Stanford, CA: Stanford University Press.

———— and Jean-Claude Passeron. [1970] 1977. *Reproduction in Education, Society and Culture,* translated by Richard Nice. Newbury Park, CA: Sage.

Butler, Judith. 1990. *Gender Trouble: Feminism and the Subversion of Identity.* New York: Routledge.

Chodorow, Nancy. 1974. "Family Structure and Feminine Personality." In *Woman, Culture and Society*, edited by Michelle Zimbalist Rosaldo and Louise Lamphere. Stanford, CA: Stanford University Press.

Devor, Holly. 1987. "Gender Blending Females: Women and Sometimes Men." *American Behavior Scientists* 31:12–40.

———. 1989. *Gender Blending: Confronting the Limits of Duality*. Bloomington: University of Indiana Press.

Dollimore, Jonathan. 1986. "Subjectivity, Sexuality, and Transgression: The Jacobean Connection." *Renaissance Drama*, n.s. 17:53–81.

Durova, Nadezhda. 1989. *The Cavalry Maiden: Journals of a Russian Officer in the Napoleonic Wars*, translated by Mary Fleming Zirin. Bloomington: Indiana University Press.

Eichler, Margrit. 1989. "Sex Change Operations: The Last Bulwark of the Double Standard." In *Feminist Frontiers II*, edited by Laurel Richardson and Verta Taylor. New York: Random House.

Epstein, C. F. 1988. *Deceptive Distinctions: Sex, Gender and the Social Order*. New Haven: Yale University Press.

Faderman, Lillian. 1991. *Odd Girls and Twilight Lovers: A History of Lesbian Life in Twentieth-Century America*. New York: Columbia University Press.

Foucault, Michel. 1972. *The Archeology of Knowledge and the Discourse on Language*, translated by A. M. Sheridan Smith. New York: Pantheon.

Freeman, Lucy and Alma Halbert Bond. 1992. *America's First Woman Warrior: The Courage of Deborah Sampson*. New York: Paragon.

Frye, Marilyn. 1983. *The Politics of Reality: Essays in Feminist Theory*. Trumansburg, NY: Crossing Press.

Garber, Marjorie. 1992. *Vested Interests: Cross-Dressing and Cultural Anxiety*. New York: Routledge.

Garfinkel, Harold. 1967. *Studies in Ethnomethodology*. Englewood Cliffs, NJ: Prentice-Hall.

Goffman, Erving. 1977. "The Arrangement between the Sexes." *Theory and Society* 4:301–33.

———. 1983. "Felicity's Condition." *American Journal of Sociology* 89:1–53.

Gordon, Tuula. 1990. *Feminist Mothers*. New York: New York University Press.

Gramsci, Antonio. 1971. *Selections from the Prison Notebooks*, translated and edited by Quintin Hoare and Geoffrey Nowell Smith. New York: International Publishers.

Greenblatt, Stephen. 1987. *Shakespearean Negotiations: The Circulation of Social Energy in Renaissance England*. Berkeley: University of California Press.

Groce, Stephen B. and Margaret Cooper. 1990. "Just Me and the Boys? Women in Local-level Rock and Roll." *Gender & Society* 4:220–29.

Howard, Jean E. 1988. "Crossdressing, the Theater, and Gender Struggle in Early Modern England." *Shakespeare Quarterly* 39:418–41.

Jacobs, Sue-Ellen and Christine Roberts. 1989. "Sex, Sexuality, Gender, and Gender Variance." In *Gender and Anthropology*, edited by Sandra Morgen. Washington, DC: American Anthropological Association.

Kando, Thomas. 1973. *Sex Change: The Achievement of Gender Identity among Feminized Transsexuals*. Springfield, IL: Charles C. Thomas.

Kincaid, Jamaica. June 26, 1978. "Girl." *The New Yorker*.

Lacqueur, Thomas. 1990. *Making Sex: Body and Gender from the Greeks to Freud*. Cambridge, MA: Harvard University Press.

Matthaei, Julie A. 1982. *An Economic History of Woman's Work in America*. New York: Schocken.

Money, John and Anke A. Ehrhardt. 1972. *Man and Woman, Boy and Girl*. Baltimore, MD: Johns Hopkins University Press.

Morris, Jan. 1975. *Conundrum.* New York: Signet.

Nanda, Serena. 1990. *Neither Man nor Woman: The Hijiras of India.* Belmont, CA: Wadsworth.

New York Times. February 2, 1989. "Musician's Death at 74 Reveals He Was a Woman."

Reskin, Barbara F. 1988. "Bringing the Men Back In: Sex Differentiation and the Devaluation of Women's Work." *Gender & Society* 2:58–81.

Rogers, Mary R. 1992. "They Were All Passing: Agnes, Garfinkel, and Company." *Gender & Society* 6:169–91.

Rubin, Gayle. 1975. "The Traffic in Women: Notes on the Political Economy of Sex." In *Toward an Anthropology of Women,* edited by Rayna Rapp Reiter. New York: Monthly Review Press.

Rugh, Andrea B. 1986. *Reveal and Conceal: Dress in Contemporary Egypt.* Syracuse, NY: Syracuse University Press.

Scott, Joan Wallach. 1988. *Gender and the Politics of History.* New York: Columbia University Press.

West, Candace and Don Zimmerman. 1987. "Doing Gender." *Gender & Society* 1: 125–51.

Wheelwright, Julie. 1989. *Amazons and Military Maids: Women Who Cross-Dressed in Pursuit of Life, Liberty and Happiness.* London: Pandora Press.

Wikan, Unni. 1982. *Behind the Veil in Arabia: Women in Oman.* Baltimore, MD: Johns Hopkins University Press.

Williams, Christine L. 1989. *Gender Differences at Work: Women and Men in Nontraditional Occupations.* Berkeley: University of California Press.

Williams, Walter L. 1986. *The Spirit and the Flesh: Sexual Diversity in American Indian Culture.* Boston: Beacon Press.

12

BOYHOOD, ORGANIZED SPORTS, AND THE CONSTRUCTION OF MASCULINITIES

MICHAEL MESSNER

An important point about socialization is that societal values, identities, and social roles are learned and *not* instinctual. We have to learn the expected social norms and behaviors of our society. In this reading, Michael Messner challenges the notion that gender identity formation is biological or natural. Instead, Messner examines how masculinity is learned through socialization, especially through the participation of boys and men in organized sports.

I view gender identity not as a "thing" that people "have," but rather as a *process of construction* that develops, comes into crisis, and changes as a person interacts with the social world. Through this perspective, it becomes possible to speak of "gendering" identities rather than "masculinity" or "femininity" as relatively fixed identities or statuses.

There is an agency in this construction: people are not passively shaped by their social environment. As recent feminist analyses of the construction of feminine gender identity have pointed out, girls and women are implicated in the construction of their own identities and personalities, both in terms of the ways that they participate in their own subordination and the ways that they resist subordination (Benjamin 1988; Haug 1987). Yet this self-construction is not a fully conscious process. There are also deeply woven, unconscious motivations, fears, and anxieties at work here. So, too, in the construction of masculinity. Levinson et al. (1978) have argued that masculine identity is neither fully "formed" by the social context, nor is it "caused" by some internal dynamic put into place during infancy. Instead, it is shaped and constructed through the interaction between the internal and the social. The internal gendering identity may set developmental "tasks," may create thresholds of anxiety and ambivalence, yet it is only through a concrete examination of people's interactions with others within social institutions that we can begin to understand both the similarities and differences in the construction of gender identities.

In this study I explore and interpret the meanings that males themselves attribute to their boyhood participation in organized sport. In what ways do males construct masculine identities within the institution of organized sports? In what ways do class and racial differences mediate this relationship and perhaps lead to the construction of different meanings, and perhaps different masculinities? And what are some of the problems and contradictions within these constructions of masculinity?

Description of Research

Between 1983 and 1985, I conducted interviews with 30 male former athletes. Most of the men I interviewed had played the (U.S.) "major sports"— football, basketball, baseball, track. At the time of the interview, each had been retired from playing organized sports for at least five years. Their ages ranged from 21 to 48, with the median, 33; 14 were black, 14 were white, and two were Hispanic; 15 of the 16 black and Hispanic men had come from poor or working-class families, while the majority (9 of 14) of the white men had come from middle-class or professional families. All had at some time in their lives based their identities largely on their roles as athletes and could therefore be said to have had "athletic careers." Twelve had played organized sports through high school, 11 through college, and seven had been professional athletes. Though the sample was not randomly selected, an effort was made to see that the sample had a range of difference in terms of race and social class backgrounds, and that there was some variety in terms of age, types of sports played, and levels of success in athletic careers. Without exception, each man contacted agreed to be interviewed.

The tape-recorded interviews were semistructured and took from one and one-half to six hours, with most taking about three hours. I asked each man to talk about four broad eras in his life: (1) his earliest experiences with sports in boyhood, (2) his athletic career, (3) retirement or disengagement from the athletic career, and (4) life after the athletic career. In each era, I focused the interview on the meanings of "success and failure," and on the boy's/man's relationships with family, with other males, with women, and with his own body.

In collecting what amounted to life histories of these men, my overarching purpose was to use feminist theories of masculine gender identity to explore how masculinity develops and changes as boys and men interact within the socially constructed world of organized sports. In addition to using the data to move toward some generalizations about the relationship between "masculinity and sport," I was also concerned with sorting out some of the variations among boys, based on class and racial inequalities, that led them to relate differently to athletic careers. I divided my sample into two comparison groups. The first group was made up of 10 men from higher-status backgrounds, primarily white, middle-class, and professional families. The second group was made up of 20 men from lower-status backgrounds, primarily minority, poor, and working-class families.

Boyhood and the Promise of Sports

Zane Grey once said, "All boys love baseball. If they don't they're not real boys" (as cited in Kimmel 1990). This is, of course, an ideological statement: In fact, some boys do *not* love baseball, or any other sports, for that matter. There are millions of males who at an early age are rejected by, become alienated from, or lose interest in organized sports. Yet all boys are, to a greater or lesser extent, judged according to their ability, or lack of ability, in competitive sports (Eitzen 1975; Sabo 1985). In this study I focus on those males who did become athletes—males who eventually poured thousands of hours into the development of specific physical skills. It is in boyhood that we can discover the roots of their commitment to athletic careers.

How did organized sports come to play such a central role in these boy's lives? When asked to recall how and why they initially got into playing sports, many of the men interviewed for this study seemed a bit puzzled: After all, playing sports was "just the thing to do." A 42-year-old black man who had played college basketball put it this way:

> *It was just what you did. It's kind of like, you went to school, you played athletics, and if you didn't, there was something wrong with you. It was just like brushing your teeth: It's just what you did. It's part of your existence.*

Spending one's time playing sports with other boys seemed as natural as the cycle of the seasons: baseball in the spring and summer, football in the fall, basketball in the winter—and then it was time to get out the old baseball glove and begin again. As a black 35-year-old former professional football star said:

> *I'd say when I wasn't in school, 95 percent of the time was spent in the park playing. It was the only thing to do. It just came as natural.*

And a black, 34-year-old professional basketball player explained his early experiences in sports:

> *My principal and teacher said, "Now if you work at this you might be pretty damned good." So it was more or less a community thing—everybody in the community said, "Boy, if you work hard and keep your nose clean, you gonna be good." Cause it was natural instinct.*

"It was natural instinct." "I was a natural." Several athletes used words such as these to explain their early attraction to sports. But certainly there is nothing "natural" about throwing a ball through a hoop, hitting a ball with a bat, or jumping over hurdles. A boy, for instance, may have amazingly dexterous inborn hand-eye coordination, but this does not predispose him to a career of hitting baseballs any more than it predisposes him to a life as a brain surgeon. When one listens closely to what these men said about their early experiences in sports, it becomes clear that their adoption of the self-definition of "natural athlete" was the result of what Connell (1990) has called "a collective practice" that constructs masculinities. The boyhood development of masculine identity and status—truly problematic in a society that offers no official rite of passage into adulthood—results from a process of interaction with people and social institutions. Thus, in discussing early motivations in sports, men commonly talk of the importance of relationships with family members, peers, and the broader community.

Family Influences

Though most of the men in this study spoke of their mothers with love, respect, even reverence, their descriptions of their earliest experiences in sports are stories of an exclusively male world. The existence of older brothers or uncles who served as teachers and athletic role models—as well as sources of competition for attention and status within the family—was very common. An older brother, uncle, or even close friend of the family who was a successful athlete appears to have acted as a sort of standard of achievement against whom to measure oneself. A 34-year-old black man who had been a three-sport star in high school said:

> *My uncles—my Uncle Harold went to the Detroit Tigers, played pro ball—all of 'em, everybody played sports, so I wanted to be better than anybody else. I*

knew that everybody in this town knew them—their names were something. I wanted my name to be just like theirs.

Similarly, a black 41-year-old former professional football player recalled:

I was the younger of three brothers and everybody played sports, so consequently I was more or less forced into it. 'Cause one brother was always better than the next brother and then I came along and had to show them that I was just as good as them. My oldest brother was an all-city ballplayer, then my other brother comes along he's all-city and all-state, and then I have to come along.

For some, attempting to emulate or surpass the athletic accomplishments of older male family members created pressures that were difficult to deal with. A 33-year-old white man explained that he was a good athlete during boyhood, but the constant awareness that his two older brothers had been better made it difficult for him to feel good about himself, or to have fun in sports:

I had this sort of reputation that I followed from the playgrounds through grade school, and through high school. I followed these guys who were all-conference and all-state.

Most of these men, however, saw their relationship with their athletic older brothers and uncles in a positive light; it was within these relationships that they gained experience and developed motivations that gave them a competitive "edge" within their same-aged peer group. As a 33-year-old black man describes his earliest athletic experiences:

My brothers were role models. I wanted to prove—especially to my brothers—that I had heart, you know, that I was a man.

When asked, "What did it mean to you to be 'a man' at that age?" he replied:

Well, it meant that I didn't want to be a so-called scaredy-cat. You want to hit a guy even though he's bigger than you to show that, you know, you've got this macho image. I remember that at that young an age, that feeling was exciting to me. And that carried over, and as I got older, I got better and I began to look around me and see, well hey! I'm competitive with these guys, even though I'm younger, you know? And then of course all the compliments come—and I began to notice a change, even in my parents—especially in my father—he was proud of that, and that was very important to me. He was extremely important . . . he showed me more affection, now that I think of it.

As this man's words suggest, if men talk of their older brothers and uncles mostly as role models, teachers, and "names" to emulate, their talk of their relationships with their fathers is more deeply layered and complex. Athletic skills and competition for status may often be learned from older brothers, but it is in boys' relationships with fathers that we find many of the keys to the emotional salience of sports in the development of masculine identity.

Relationships with Fathers

The fact that boys' introductions to organized sports are often made by fathers who might otherwise be absent or emotionally distant adds a powerful emotional charge to these early experiences (Osherson 1986). Although playing organized sports eventually came to feel "natural" for all of the men interviewed in this study, many needed to be "exposed" to sports, or even gently "pushed" by their fathers to become involved in activities like Little League baseball. A white, 33-year-old man explained:

> I still remember it like it was yesterday—Dad and I driving up in his truck, and I had my glove and my hat and all that—and I said, "Dad, I don't want to do it." He says, "What?" I says, "I don't want to do it." I was nervous. That I might fail. And he says, "Don't be silly. Lookit: There's Joey and Petey and all your friends out there." And so Dad says, "You're gonna do it, come on." And in my memory he's never said that about anything else; he just knew I needed a little kick in the pants and I'd do it. And once you're out there and you see all the other kids making errors and stuff, and you know you're better than those guys, you know: Maybe I do belong here. As it turned out, Little League was a good experience.

Some who were similarly "pushed" by their fathers were not so successful as the aforementioned man had been in Little League baseball, and thus the experience was not altogether a joyous affair. One 34-year-old white man, for instance, said he "inherited" his interest in sports from his father, who started playing catch with him at the age of four. Once he got into Little League, he felt pressured by his father, one of the coaches, who expected him to be the star of the team:

> I'd go O-for-four sometimes, strike out three times in a Little League game, and I'd dread the ride home. I'd come home and he'd say, "Go in the bathroom and swing the bat in the mirror for an hour," to get my swing level. . . . It didn't help much, though, I'd go out and strike out three or four times again the next game too [laughs ironically].

When asked if he had been concerned with having his father's approval, he responded:

> Failure in his eyes? Yeah, I always thought that he wanted me to get some kind of [athletic] scholarship. I guess I was afraid of him when I was a kid. He didn't hit that much, but he had a rage about him—he'd rage, and that voice would just rattle you.

Similarly, a 24-year-old black man described his awe of his father's physical power and presence, and his sense of inadequacy in attempting to emulate him:

> My father had a voice that sounded like rolling thunder. Whether it was intentional on his part or not, I don't know, but my father gave me a sense, an image

of him being the most powerful being on earth, and that no matter what I ever did I would never come close to him. . . . There were definite feelings of physical inadequacy that I couldn't work around.

It is interesting to note how these feelings of physical inadequacy relative to the father lived on as part of this young man's permanent internalized image. He eventually became a "feared" high school football player and broke school records in weight-lifting, yet,

As I grew older, my mother and friends told me that I had actually grown to be a larger man than my father. Even though in time I required larger clothes than he, which should have been a very concrete indication, neither my brother nor I could ever bring ourselves to say that I was bigger. We simply couldn't conceive of it.

Using sports activities as a means of identifying with and "living up to" the power and status of one's father was not always such a painful and difficult task for the men I interviewed. Most did not describe fathers who "pushed" them to become sports stars. The relationship between their athletic strivings and their identification with their fathers was more subtle. A 48-year-old black man, for instance, explained that he was not pushed into sports by his father, but was aware from an early age of the community status his father had gained through sports. He saw his own athletic accomplishments as a way to connect with and emulate his father:

I wanted to play baseball because my father had been quite a good baseball player in the Negro leagues before baseball was integrated, and so he was kind of a model for me. I remember, quite young, going to a baseball game he was in— this was before the war and all—I remember being in the stands with my mother and seeing him on first base, and being aware of the crowd. . . . I was aware of people's confidence in him as a serious baseball player. I don't think my father ever said anything to me like "play sports" . . . [But] I knew he would like it if I did well. . . . His admiration was important . . . he mattered.

Similarly, a 24-year-old white man described his father as a somewhat distant "role model" whose approval mattered:

My father was more of an example . . . he definitely was very much in touch with and still had very fond memories of being an athlete and talked about it, bragged about it. . . . But he really didn't do that much to teach me skills, and he didn't always go to every game I played like some parents. But he approved and that was important, you know. That was important to get his approval. I always knew that playing sports was important to him, so I knew implicitly that it was good and there was definitely a value on it.

First experiences in sports might often come through relationships with brothers or other male relatives, and the early emotional salience of sports was often directly related to a boy's relationship with his father. The sense of commitment that these young boys eventually made to the development of athletic careers is best explained as a process of development of masculine gender identity and status in relation to same-sex peers.

Masculine Identity and Early Commitment to Sports

When many of the men in this study said that during childhood they played sports because "it's just what everybody did," they of course meant that it was just what *boys* did. They were introduced to organized sports by older brothers and fathers, and once involved, found themselves playing within an exclusively male world. Though the separate (and unequal) gendered worlds of boys and girls came to appear as "natural," they were in fact socially constructed. Thorne's observations of children's activities in schools indicated that rather than "naturally" constituting "separate gendered cultures," there is considerable interaction between boys and girls in classrooms and on playgrounds. When adults set up legitimate contact between boys and girls, Thorne observed, this usually results in "relaxed interactions." But when activities in the classroom or on the playground are presented to children as sex-segregated activities and gender is marked by teachers and other adults ("boys line up here, girls over there"), "gender boundaries are heightened, and mixed-sex interaction becomes an explicit arena of risk" (Thorne 1986, p. 70). Thus sex-segregated activities such as organized sports as structured by adults, provide the context in which gendered identities and separate "gendered cultures" develop and come to appear natural. For the boys in this study, it became "natural" to equate masculinity with competition, physical strength, and skills. Girls simply did not (could not, it was believed) participate in these activities.

Yet it is not simply the separation of children, by adults, into separate activities that explains why many boys came to feel such a strong connection with sports activities, while so few girls did. As I listened to men recall their earliest experiences in organized sports, I heard them talk of insecurity, loneliness, and especially a need to connect with other people as a primary motivation in their early sports strivings. As a 42-year-old white man stated, "The most important thing was just being out there with the rest of the guys—being friends." Another 32-year-old interviewee was born in Mexico and moved to the United States at a fairly young age. He never knew his father, and his mother died when he was only nine years old. Suddenly he felt rootless, and threw himself into sports. His initial motivations, however, do not appear to be based on a need to compete and win:

> *Actually, what I think sports did for me is it brought me into kind of an instant family. By being on a Little League team, or even just playing with all kinds of different kids in the neighborhood, it brought what I really wanted, which was some kind of closeness. It was just being there, and being friends.*

Clearly, what these boys needed and craved was that which was most problematic for them: connection and unity with other people. But why do these young males find *organized sports* such an attractive context in which to establish "a kind of closeness" with others? Comparative observations of young boys' and girls' game-playing behaviors yield important insights into this question. Piaget (1965) and Lever (1976) both observed that girls tend to have more "pragmatic" and "flexible" orientations to the rules of games; they are more prone to make exceptions and innovations in the middle of a game in order to make the game more "fair." Boys, on the other hand, tend to have a more firm, even [in]flexible orientation to the rules of a game; to them, the rules are what protects any fairness. This difference, according to Gilligan (1982), is based on the fact that early developmental experiences have yielded deeply rooted differences between males' and females' developmental tasks, needs, and moral reasoning. Girls, who tend to define themselves primarily through connection with others, experience highly competitive situations (whether in organized sports or in other hierarchical institutions) as threats to relationships, and thus to their identities. For boys, the development of gender identity involves the construction of positional identities, where a sense of self is solidified through separation from others (Chodorow 1978). Yet feminist psychoanalytic theory has tended to oversimplify the internal lives of men (Lichterman 1986). Males do appear to develop positional identities, yet despite their fears of intimacy, they also retain a human need for closeness and unity with others. This ambivalence toward intimate relationships is a major thread running through masculine development throughout the life course. Here we can conceptualize what Craib (1987) calls the "elective affinity" between personality and social structure: For the boy who both seeks and fears attachment with others, the rule-bound structure of organized sports can promise to be a safe place in which to seek nonintimate attachment with others within a context that maintains clear boundaries, distance, and separation.

Competitive Structures and Conditional Self-Worth

Young boys may initially find that sports gives them the opportunity to experience "some kind of closeness" with others, but the structure of sports and athletic careers often undermines the possibility of boys learning to transcend their fears of intimacy, thus becoming able to develop truly close and intimate relationships with others (Kidd 1990; Messner 1987). The sports world is extremely hierarchical, and an incredible amount of importance is placed on winning, on "being number one." For instance, a few years ago I observed a basketball camp put on for boys by a professional basketball coach and his staff. The youngest boys, about eight years old (who could barely reach the basket with their shots) played a brief scrimmage. Afterwards, the coaches lined them up in a row in front of the older boys who were sitting in the grandstands. One by one, the coach would stand behind each boy, put his hand on the boy's head (much in the manner of a priestly benediction), and the older boys in the stands would applaud and cheer, louder or softer, depending on how well or poorly the young boy was judged to have performed. The two or three boys who were clearly the exceptional players looked confident that they would receive the praise they were due. Most of the boys, though, had expressions ranging from puzzlement to thinly disguised terror on their faces as they awaited the judgments of the older boys.

This kind of experience teaches boys that it is not "just being out there with the guys—being friends," that ensures the kind of attention and connection that they crave; it is being *better* than the other guys—*beating* them—that is the key to acceptance. Most of the boys in this study did have some early successes in sports, and thus their ambivalent need for connection with others was met, at least for a time. But the institution of sport tends to encourage the development of what Schafer (1975) has called "conditional self-worth" in boys. As boys become aware that acceptance by others is contingent upon being good—a "winner"—narrow definitions of success, based upon performance and winning become increasingly important to them. A 33-year-old black man said that by the time he was in his early teens

> *it was expected of me to do well in all my contests—I mean by my coaches, my peers, and my family. So I in turn expected to do well, and if I didn't do well, then I'd be very disappointed.*

The man from Mexico, discussed above, who said that he had sought "some kind of closeness" in his early sports experiences began to notice in his early teens that if he played well, was a *winner*, he would get attention from others:

> *It got to the point where I started realizing, noticing that people were always there for me, backing me all the time—sports got to be really fun because I always had some people there backing me. Finally my oldest brother started going to all my games, even though I had never really seen who he was [laughs]—after the game, you know, we never really saw each other, but he was at all my baseball games, and it seemed like we shared a kind of closeness there, but only in those situations. Off the field, when I wasn't in uniform, he was never around.*

By high school, he said, he felt "up against the wall." Sports hadn't delivered what he had hoped it would, but he thought if he just tried harder, won one more championship trophy, he would get the attention he truly craved. Despite his efforts, this attention was not forthcoming. And, sadly, the pressures he had put on himself to excel in sports had taken most of the fun out of playing.

For many of the men in this study, throughout boyhood and into adolescence, this conscious striving for successful achievement became the primary means through which they sought connection with other people (Messner 1987). But it is important to recognize that young males' internalized ambivalences about intimacy do not fully determine the contours and directions of their lives. Masculinity continues to develop through interaction with the social world—and because boys from different backgrounds are interacting with substantially different familial, educational, and other institutions, these differences will lead them to make different choices and define situations in different ways. Next, I examine the differences in the ways that boys from higher- and lower-status families and communities related to organized sports.

Status Differences and Commitments to Sports

In discussing early attractions to sports, the experiences of boys from higher- and lower-status backgrounds are quite similar. Both groups indicate the importance of fathers and older brothers in introducing them to sports. Both groups speak of the joys of receiving attention and acceptance among family and peers for early successes in sports. Note the similarities, for instance, in the following descriptions of boyhood athletic experiences of two men. First, a man born in a white, middle-class family:

> *I loved playing sports so much from a very early age because of early exposure. A lot of the sports came easy at an early age, and because they did, and because you were successful at something, I think that you're inclined to strive for that gratification. It's like, if you're good, you like it, because it's instant gratification. I'm doing something that I'm good at and I'm gonna keep doing it.*

Second, a black man from a poor family:

> *Fortunately I had some athletic ability, and, quite naturally, once you start doing good in whatever it is—I don't care if it's jacks—you show off what you do. That's your ability, that's your blessing, so you show it off as much as you can.*

For boys from both groups, early exposure to sports, the discovery that they had some "ability," shortly followed by some sort of family, peer, and community recognition, all eventually led to the commitment of hundreds and thousands of hours playing, practicing, and dreaming of future stardom. Despite these similarities, there are also some identifiable differences that begin to explain the tendency of males from lower-status backgrounds to develop higher levels of commitment to sports careers. The most clear-cut difference was that while men from higher-status backgrounds are likely to describe their earliest athletic experiences and motivations almost exclusively in terms of immediate family, men from lower-status backgrounds more commonly describe the importance of a broader community context.

For instance, a 46-year-old man who grew up in a "poor working class" black family in a small town in Arkansas explained:

> *In that community, at the age of third or fourth grade, if you're a male, they expect you to show some kind of inclination, some kind of skill in football or basketball. It was an expected thing, you know? My mom and my dad, they didn't push at all. It was the general environment.*

A 48-year-old man describes sports activities as a survival strategy in his poor black community:

> *Sports protected me from having to compete in gang stuff, or having to be good with my fists. If you were an athlete and got into the fist world, that was your business, and that was okay—but you didn't have to if you didn't want to. People would generally defer to you, give you your space away from trouble.*

A 35-year-old man who grew up in "a poor black ghetto" described his boyhood relationship to sports similarly:

> *Where I came from, either you were one of two things: You were in sports or you were out on the streets being a drug addict, or breaking into places. The guys who were in sports, we had it a little easier, because we were accepted by both groups. . . . So it worked out to my advantage, cause I didn't get into a lot of trouble— some trouble, but not a lot.*

The fact that boys in lower-status communities faced these kinds of realities gave salience to their developing athletic identities. In contrast, sports were important to boys from higher-status backgrounds, yet the middle-class environment seemed more secure, less threatening, and offered far more options. By the time most of these boys got into junior high or high school, many had made conscious decisions to shift their attentions away from athletic careers to educational and (nonathletic) career goals. A 32-year-old white college athletic director told me that he had seen his chance to pursue a pro baseball career as "pissing in the wind," and instead, focused on education. Similarly, a 33-year-old white dentist who was a three-sport star in high school, decided not to play sports in college so he could focus on getting into dental school. As he put it,

> *I think I kind of downgraded the stardom thing. I thought it was small potatoes. And sure, that's nice in high school and all that, but on a broad scale, I didn't think it amounted to all that much.*

This statement offers an important key to understanding the construction of masculine identity within a middle-class context. The status that this boy got through sports had been *very* important to him, yet he could see that "on a broad scale," this sort of status was "small potatoes." This sort of early recognition is more than a result of the oft-noted middle-class tendency to raise "future-oriented" children (Rubin 1976; Sennett and Cobb 1973). Perhaps more important, it is that the *kinds* of future orientations developed by boys from higher-status backgrounds are consistent with the middle-class context. These men's descriptions of their boyhoods reveal that they grew up immersed in a wide range of institutional frameworks, of which organized sports was just one. And—importantly—they could see that the status of adult males around them was clearly linked to their positions within various professions, public institutions, and bureaucratic organizations. It was clear that access to this sort of institutional status came through educational achievement, not athletic prowess. A 32-year-old black man who grew up in a professional-class family recalled that he had idolized Wilt Chamberlain and dreamed of being a pro basketball player, yet his father discouraged his athletic strivings:

> He knew I liked the game. I loved the game. But basketball was not recommended; my dad would say, "That's a stereotyped image for black youth. . . . When your basketball is gone and finished, what are you gonna do? One day, you might get injured. What are you gonna look forward to?" He stressed education.

Similarly, a 32-year-old man who was raised in a white, middle-class family, had found in sports a key means of gaining acceptance and connection in his peer group. Yet he was simultaneously developing an image of himself as a "smart student," and becoming aware of a wide range of nonsports life options:

> My mother was constantly telling me how smart I was, how good I was, what a nice person I was, and giving me all sorts of positive strokes, and those positive strokes became a self-motivating kind of thing. I had this image of myself as smart, and I lived up to that image.

It is not that parents of boys in lower-status families did not also encourage their boys to work hard in school. Several reported that their parents "stressed books first, sports second." It's just that the broader social context— education, economy, and community—was more likely to *narrow* lower-status boys' perceptions of real-life options, while boys from higher-status backgrounds faced an expanding world of options. For instance, with a different socioeconomic background, one 35-year-old black man might have become a great musician instead of a star professional football running back. But he did not. When he was a child, he said, he was most interested in music:

> I wanted to be a drummer. But we couldn't afford drums. My dad couldn't go out and buy me a drum set or a guitar even—it was just one of those things; he was just trying to make ends meet.

But he *could* afford, as could so many in his socioeconomic condition, to spend countless hours at the local park, where he was told by the park supervisor *that I was a natural—not only in gymnastics or baseball—whatever I did, I was a natural. He told me I shouldn't waste this talent, and so I immediately started watching the big guys then.*

In retrospect, this man had potential to be a musician or any number of things, but his environment limited his options to sports, and he made the best of it. Even within sports, he, like most boys in the ghetto, was limited:

We didn't have any tennis courts in the ghetto—we used to have a lot of tennis balls, but no racquets. I wonder today how good I might be in tennis if I had gotten a racquet in my hands at an early age.

It is within this limited structure of opportunity that many lower-status young boys found sports to be *the* place, rather than *a* place, within which to construct masculine identity, status, the relationships. A 36-year-old white man explained that his father left the family when he was very young and his mother faced a very difficult struggle to make ends meet. As his words suggest, the more limited a boy's options, and the more insecure his family situation, the more likely he is to make an early commitment to an athletic career:

I used to ride my bicycle to Little League practice—if I'd waited for someone to pick me up and take me to the ball park I'd have never played. I'd get to the ball park and all the other kids would have their dad bring them to practice or games. But I'd park my bike to the side and when it was over I'd get on it and go home. Sports was the way for me to move everything to the side—family problems, just all the embarrassments—and think about one thing, and that was sports. . . . In the third grade, when the teacher went around the classroom and asked everybody, "What do you want to be when you grow up?," I said, "I want to be a major league baseball player," and everybody laughed their heads off.

This man eventually did enjoy a major league baseball career. Most boys from lower-status backgrounds who make similar early commitments to athletic careers are not so successful. As stated earlier, the career structure of organized sports is highly competitive and hierarchical. In fact, the chances of attaining professional status in sports are approximately 4:100,000 for a white man, 2:100,000 for a black man, and 3:1 million for a Hispanic man in the United States (Leonard and Reyman 1988). Nevertheless, the immediate rewards (fun, status, attention), along with the constricted (nonsports) structure of opportunity, attract disproportionately large numbers of boys from lower-status backgrounds to athletic careers as their major means of constructing a masculine identity. These are the boys who later, as young men, had to struggle with "conditional self-worth," and, more often than not, occupational dead ends. Boys from higher-status backgrounds, on the other hand, bolstered their boyhood, adolescent, and early adult status through their athletic accomplishments. Their wider range of experiences and life chances led to an early shift away from sports careers as the major basis of identity (Messner 1989).

Conclusion

The conception of the masculinity-sports relationship developed here begins to illustrate the idea of an "elective affinity" between social structure and personality. Organized sports is a "gendered institution"—an institution constructed by gender relations. As such, its structure and values (rules, formal organization, sex composition, etc.), reflect dominant conceptions of masculinity and femininity. Organized sports is also a "gendering institution"—an institution that helps to construct the current gender order. Part of this construction of gender is accomplished through the "masculinizing" of male bodies and minds.

Yet boys do not come to their first experiences in organized sports as "blank slates," but arrive with already "gendering" identities due to early developmental experiences and previous socialization. I have suggested here that an important thread running through the development of masculine identity is males' ambivalence toward intimate unity with others. Those boys who experience early athletic successes find in the structure of organized sport an affinity with this masculine ambivalence toward intimacy: The rule-bound, competitive, hierarchical world of sport offers boys an attractive means of establishing an emotionally distant (and thus "safe") connection with others. Yet as boys begin to define themselves as "athletes," they must learn that in order to be accepted (to have connection) through sports, they must be winners. And in order to be winners, they must construct relationships with others (and with themselves) that are consistent with the competitive and hierarchical values and structure of the sports world. As a result, they often develop a "conditional self-worth" that leads them to construct more instrumental relationships with themselves and others. This ultimately exacerbates their difficulties in constructing intimate relationships with others. In effect, the interaction between the young male's preexisting internalized ambivalence toward intimacy with the competitive, hierarchical institution of sport has resulted in the construction of a masculine personality that is characterized by instrumental rationality, goal-orientation, and difficulties with intimate connection and expression (Messner 1987).

This theoretical line of inquiry invites us not simply to examine how social institutions "socialize" boys, but also to explore the ways that boys' already-gendering identities interact with social institutions (which, like organized sport, are themselves the product of gender relations). This study has also suggested that it is not some singular "masculinity" that is being constructed through athletic careers. It may be correct, from a psychoanalytic perspective, to suggest that all males bring ambivalences toward intimacy to their interactions with the world, but "the world" is a very different place for males from different racial and socioeconomic backgrounds. Because males have substantially different interactions with the world, based on class, race, and other differences and inequalities, we might expect the construction of masculinity to take on different meanings for boys and men from differing backgrounds (Messner 1989). Indeed, this study has suggested that boys from higher-status backgrounds face a much broader range of options than do their lower-status counterparts. As a result, athletic careers take on different meanings for these boys. Lower-status boys are likely to see athletic careers as *the* institutional context for the construction of their masculine status and identities, while higher-status males make an early shift away from athletic careers toward other institutions (usually education and nonsports careers). A key line of inquiry for future studies might begin by exploring this irony of sports careers: Despite the fact that "the athlete" is currently an example of an exemplary form of masculinity in public ideology, the vast majority of boys who become most committed to athletic careers are never well rewarded for their efforts. The fact that class and racial dynamics lead boys from higher-status backgrounds, unlike their lower-status counterparts, to move into nonsports careers illustrates how the construction of different kinds of masculinities is a key component of the overall construction of the gender order.

REFERENCES

Benjamin, J. 1988. *The Bonds of Love: Psychoanalysis, Feminism and the Problem of Domination.* New York: Pantheon.

Chodorow, N. 1978. *The Reproduction of Mothering.* Berkeley: University of California Press.

Connell, R. W. 1990. "An Iron Man: The Body and Some Contradictions of Hegemonic Masculinity." In *Sport, Men and the Gender Order: Critical Feminist Perspectives,* edited by M. A. Messner and D. F. Sabo. Champaign, IL: Human Kinetics.

Craib, I. 1987. "Masculinity and Male Dominance." *Sociological Review* 38:721–43.

Eitzen, D. S. 1975. "Athletics in the Status System of Male Adolescents: A Replication of Coleman's *The Adolescent Society.*" *Adolescence* 10:268–76.

Gilligan, C. 1982. *In a Different Voice: Psychological Theory and Women's Development.* Cambridge, MA: Harvard University Press.

Haug, F. 1987. *Female Sexualization.* London: Verso.

Kidd, B. 1990. "The Men's Cultural Centre: Sports and the Dynamic of Women's Oppression/Men's Repression." In *Sport, Men and the Gender Order: Critical Feminist Perspectives,* edited by M. A. Messner and D. F. Sabo. Champaign, IL: Human Kinetics.

Kimmel, M. S. 1990. "Baseball and the Reconstitution of American Masculinity: 1880–1920." In *Sport, Men and the Gender Order: Critical Feminist Perspectives,* edited by M. A. Messner and D. F. Sabo. Champaign, IL: Human Kinetics.

Leonard, W. M., II, and J. M. Reyman. 1988. "The Odds of Attaining Professional Athlete Status: Refining the Computations." *Sociology of Sport Journal* 5:162–69.

Lever, J. 1976. "Sex Differences in the Games Children Play." *Social Problems* 23:478–87.

Levinson, D. J. et al. 1978. *The Seasons of a Man's Life.* New York: Ballantine.

Lichterman, P. 1986. "Chodorow's Psychoanalytic Sociology: A Project Half-Completed." *California Sociologist* 9:147–66.

Messner, M. 1987. "The Meaning of Success: The Athletic Experience and the Devel-
    opment of Male Identity." Pp. 193–210 in *The Making of Masculinities: The New
    Men's Studies*, edited by H. Brod. Boston: Allyn & Unwin.
————. 1989. "Masculinities and Athletic Careers." *Gender and Society* 3:71–88.
Osherson, S. 1986. *Finding Our Fathers: How a Man's Life is Shaped by His Relationship
    with His Father*. New York: Fawcett Columbine.
Piaget, J. H. 1965. *The Moral Judgement of the Child*. New York: Free Press.
Rubin, L. B. 1976. *Worlds of Pain: Life in the Working Class Family*. New York: Basic Books.
Sabo, D. 1985. "Sport, Patriarchy and Male Identity: New Questions about Men and
    Sport." *Arena Review* 9:2.
Schafer, W. E. 1975. "Sport and Male Sex Role Socialization." *Sport Sociology Bulletin*
    4:47–54.
Sennett, R., and J. Cobb. 1973. *The Hidden Injuries of Class*. New York: Random House.
Thorne, B. 1986. "Girls and Boys Together . . . but Mostly Apart: Gender Arrange-
    ments in Elementary Schools." Pp. 167–84 in *Relationships and Development*, edited
    by W. W. Hartup and Z. Rubin. Hillsdale, NJ: Erlbaum.

13

MAKING IT BY FAKING IT
Working-Class Students in an Elite Academic
Environment

ROBERT GRANFIELD

Learning an occupation is a common form of adult socialization. Occupational socialization occurs during formal education, during job training, and
during time spent on the job. Every profession has a set of values that it
wants its colleagues to embrace. For example, to become a doctor one needs
to learn the skills and knowledge of practicing medicine as well as the attitudes and values of the medical profession. Medical students experience an
intense period of professional socialization during the years, almost a decade, they spend in medical school and residency. Law students are socialized as well, and the following reading by Robert Granfield discusses how
working-class students are socialized into elite law schools and into the legal profession.

Research on stigma has generated significant insights into the complex
relationship between self and society. The legacy of Goffman's (1963)
seminal work on the subject can be found in studies on alcoholism, mental illness, homosexuality, physical deformities, and juvenile delinquency.
Even the literature on gender and racial inequality has benefited from an em-

phasis on stigma. Goffman's attention to the social processes of devaluation and the emerging self-concepts of discredited individuals not only created research opportunities for generations of sociologists but contributed to a humanistic ideology that viewed stigma assignment and its effects as unjust.

One of the most vibrant research programs that emerged from Goffman's classic work has been in the area of stigma management. A host of conceptual terms have been employed to describe the process through which discreditable individuals control information about themselves so as to manage their social identity. Concepts such as passing, deviance disavowal, accounts, disclaimers, and covering have often been used in analyzing accommodations and adjustments to deviance, as Pfuhl's (1986) review shows. These tactics, while offering rewards associated with being seen as normal, frequently contribute to psychological stress. Possessing what Goffman (1963) referred to as "undesired differentness" (p. 5) often has significant consequences for one's personal identity as well as for available life chances.

. . .

In this article, I focus on class stigma by examining a group of highly successful, upwardly mobile, working-class students who gained admission to a prestigious Ivy League law school in the East. While upward mobility from the working class occurs far less often within elite branches of the legal profession (Heinz and Laumann 1982; Smigel 1969) or corporate management (Useem and Karabel 1986), a certain amount of this type of mobility does take place. Working-class aspirants to the social elite, however, must accumulate cultural capital (Bourdieu and Passeron 1990; Cookson and Persell 1985) before they are able to transcend their status boundaries.

First, this article examines the ways in which working-class students experience a sense of differentness and marginality within the law school's elite environment. Next, I explore how these students react to their emerging class stigma by managing information about their backgrounds. I then demonstrate that the management strategies contribute to identity ambivalence and consider the secondary forms of adjustment students use to resolve this tension. Finally, I discuss why an analysis of social class can benefit from the insights forged by Goffman's work on stigma.

Setting and Methodology

The data analyzed for this article were collected as part of a much larger project associated with law school socialization (Granfield 1989). The subjects consist of students attending a prestigious, national law school in the eastern part of the United States. The school has had a long reputation of training lawyers who have become partners in major Wall Street law firms, Supreme Court judges, United States presidents and other politicians, heads of foundations, and . . . [have assumed many] other eminent leadership positions. Throughout the school's history, it has drawn mostly on the talents of high-status males. It was not until the second half of the twentieth century that women, minorities, and members of the lower classes were allowed admission into this esteemed institution (Abel 1989).

Most of the students attending the university at the time the study was being conducted were white and middle class.[1] The overwhelming majority are the sons and daughters of the professional-managerial class. Over 70 percent of those returning questionnaires had Ivy League or other highly prestigious educational credentials. As one would expect, fewer working-class students possessed such credentials.

A triangulated research design (Fielding and Fielding 1986) was used to collect the data. The first phase consisted of extensive fieldwork at the law school from 1985 to 1988, during which time I became a "peripheral member" (Adler and Adler 1987) in selected student groups. My activities while in the field consisted of attending classes with students, participating in their Moot Court[2] preparations, studying with students on campus, and at times, in their apartments, lunching with them, becoming involved in student demonstrations over job recruiting and faculty hiring, attending extracurricular lectures presented on campus, and participating in orientation exercises for first-year students. Throughout the entire fieldwork phase, I assumed both overt and covert roles. During the observation periods in classrooms, I recorded teacher-student interactions that occurred.

To supplement these observations, I conducted in-depth interviews with 103 law students at various stages in their training. Both personal interviews and small-group interviews with three or four students were recorded. The interviews lasted approximately two hours each and sought to identify the lived process through which law students experience legal training.

Finally, I administered a survey to 50 percent of the 1,540 students attending the law school. The survey examined their backgrounds, motives for attending law school, subjective perceptions of personal change, expectations about future practice, and evaluations of various substantive areas of practice. Over half (391) of the questionnaires were returned—a high rate of response for a survey of six pages requiring approximately 30 minutes of the respondent's time.

For this article, a subset of working-class students was selected for extensive analysis. Of the 103 students interviewed for the larger study, 23 came from working-class backgrounds, none of these from either the labor aristocracy or the unstable sectors of the working class. Typical parental occupations include postal worker, house painter, factory worker, fireman, dock worker, and carpenter. Many of these students were interviewed several times during their law school career. Many of the students selected for interviews were identified through questionnaires, while others were selected through the process of snowball sampling (Chadwick, Bahr, and Albrecht 1984).

Feeling Out of Place

Working-class students entered this elite educational institution with a great deal of class pride. This sense of class pride is reflected in the fact that a significantly larger proportion of working-class students reported entering law school for the purposes of contributing to social change than their non-working-class counterparts (see Granfield and Koenig 1990). That these students entered law school with the desire to help the downtrodden suggests that they identified with their working-class kin. In fact, students often credited their class background as being a motivating factor in their decision to pursue a career in social justice. One third-year student, whose father worked as a postal worker, recalled her parental influence:

> *I wanted a career in social justice. It seemed to me to be a good value for someone who wanted to leave this world a little better than they found it. My parents raised me with a sense that there are right things and wrong things and that maybe you ought to try to do some right things with your life.*

A second-year student said that he was influenced by the oppressive experiences that his father endured as a factory laborer. Coming to law school to pursue a career in a labor union, this student explained, "I was affected by my father who had a job as a machinist. My father believes that corporations have no decency. I would term it differently but we're talking about the same thing." Identifying with their working-class heritage produced not only a sense of pride but a system of values and ideals that greatly influenced their initial career objectives.

However, identification with the working class began to diminish soon after these students entered law school. Not long after arriving, most working-class students encountered an entirely new moral career. Although initially proud of their accomplishments, they soon came to define themselves as different and their backgrounds a burden. Lacking the appropriate cultural capital (Bourdieu 1984) associated with their more privileged counterparts, working-class students began to experience a crisis in competency. Phrases such as "the first semester makes you feel extremely incompetent," "the first year is like eating humble pie," and "I felt very small, powerless, and dumb" were almost universal among these working-class students. Some students felt embarrassed by their difficulty in using the elaborated speech codes (Bernstein 1977) associated with the middle class. One working-class woman said that she was very aware of using "proper" English, adding that "it makes me self-conscious when I use the wrong word or tense. I feel that if I had grown up in the middle class, I wouldn't have lapses. I have difficulty expressing thoughts while most other people here don't."

The recognition of their apparent differentness is perhaps best noted by examining the students' perception of stress associated with the first year of studies. Incoming working-class students reported significantly higher levels of personal stress than did their counterparts with more elite backgrounds. Much of this anxiety came from fears of academic inadequacy. Despite generally excellent college grades and their success in gaining admission to a nationally ranked law school, these students often worried that they did not measure up to the school's high standards. Nearly 62 percent of the first-year working-class students reported experiencing excessive grade pressure, compared to only 35 percent of those students from higher social class backgrounds.

In the words of Sennett and Cobb (1973), this lack of confidence is a "hidden injury of class," a psychological burden that working-class students experienced as they came to acquire the "identity beliefs" associated with middle-class society. While most students experience some degree of uncertainty and competency crisis during their first year, working-class students face the additional pressure of being cultural outsiders. Lacking manners of speech, attire, values, and experiences associated with their more privileged counterparts, even the most capable working-class student felt out of place:

> I had a real problem my first year because law and legal education are based on upper-middle-class values. The class debates had to do with profit maximization, law and economics, atomistic individualism. I remember in class we were talking about landlords' responsibility to maintain decent housing in rental apartments. Some people were saying that there were good reasons not to do this. Well, I think that's bullshit because I grew up with people who lived in apartments with rats, leaks, and roaches. I feel really different because I didn't grow up in suburbia.

Another student, a third-year working-class woman, felt marginalized because even her teachers assumed class homogeneity:

> I get sensitive about what professors have to say in class. I remember in a business class the professor seemed to assume that we all had fathers that worked in business and that we all understood about family investments. He said, "You're all pretty much familiar with this because of your family background." I remember thinking, doesn't he think there's any people in this law school who come from a working-class background?

Such experiences contributed to a student's sense of living in an alien world. The social distance these students experienced early in their law school career produced considerable discomfort.

This discomfort grew more intense as they became increasingly immersed into this new elite world. Within a short span of time, these students began to experience a credential gap vis-à-vis other students who possessed more prestigious academic credentials. A first-year male student who attended a state school in the Midwest explained:

> I'm not like most people here. I didn't go to prestigious schools. I'm a bit of a minority here because of that. When I got here I was really intimidated by the fact of how many Yale and Harvard people there were here.

At times, working-class law students were even embarrassed by their spouse's lower status. One first-year student described how her husband's credential gap caused her some anxiety:

> *People would ask me what my husband did and I would say he works for Radio Shack. People would be surprised. That was hard. Lately, we haven't done as much with [law school] people.*

Thus students sometimes pruned contacts that would potentially result in stigma disclosure. In general, then, as working-class students progressed through law school, they began to adopt a view of themselves as different. The recognition of this difference subsequently led them to develop techniques of adjusting to their perceived secondary status.

Faking It

The management of identity has critical strategic importance not only for group affiliation and acceptance but for life chances. Stigma limits one's opportunities to participate in social life as a complete citizen, particularly so for those possessing gender or racial stigmas. However, because of the visibility of these stigmas, a person's adjustment to second-class citizenship is accomplished typically through either role engulfment in which a person accepts a spoiled identity (Schur 1971) or through direct confrontation where assignment of secondary status is itself challenged (Schur 1980). Rarely are these groups able to employ the concealment tactics typical among those groups whose stigma is not overtly visible.

Unlike gender or racial stigma, however, individuals often adjust to class stigma by learning to conceal their uniqueness. The practice of concealing one's class background, for instance, is not unusual. Certainly, members of the elite frequently learn that it is in "bad taste" to flaunt their privileged background and that it is more gracious to conceal their eminent social status (Baltzell 1958). Similarly, individuals who experience downward mobility often attempt to maintain their predecline image by concealing loss of status. Camouflaging unemployment in the world of management by using such terms as "consultant" and by doctoring resumés are ways that downwardly mobile executives "cover" their spoiled status (Newman 1988). Concealing one's social class circumstances and the stigma that may be associated with it assist individuals in dealing with any rejection and ostracism that may be forthcoming were the person's actual status known.

Initially, students who took pride in having accomplished upward mobility openly displayed a working-class presentation of self. Many went out of their way to maintain this presentation. One first-year student who grew up in a labor union family in New York explained that "I have consciously maintained my working class image. I wear work shirts or old flannel shirts and blue jeans every day." During his first year, this student flaunted his working-class background, frequently also donning an old army jacket, hiking boots, and a wool hat. Identifying himself as part of the "proletarian left," he tried to remain isolated from what he referred to as the "elitist" law school community.

This attempt to remain situated in the working class, however, not only separated these students from the entire law school community but alienated them from groups that shared their ideological convictions. While much of the clothing worn by non-working-class students suggests resistance to being identified as a member of the elite, working-class students become increasingly aware of their differentness. Although these students identify with the working class, others, despite their appearance, possess traits and lifestyles that are often associated with more privileged groups (see Lurie 1983; Stone 1970). One first-year woman who described herself as "radical" complained that the other law school radicals were really "a bunch of upper-class white men." Subsequently, working-class students must disengage from their backgrounds if they desire to escape feeling discredited.

Working-class students disengaged from their previous identity by concealing their class backgrounds. Just as deviants seek to manage their identity by "passing" as nondeviants (Goffman 1963), these working-class law students often adopted identities that were associated with the more elite social classes.[3] Concealment allowed students to better participate in the culture of eminence that exists within the law school and reap available rewards.

This concealment meant, for instance, that students needed to acquire new dress codes. As Stone (1970) illustrated, appearance signifies identity and exercises a regulatory function over the responses of others. Such cultural codes pertaining to appearance often are used to exclude individuals from elite social positions (Bourdieu 1984; Jackell 1988; Lamont and Lareau 1988). Although working-class students lacked the cultural capital of higher social classes, they began to realize that they could successfully mimic their more privileged counterparts. Like undistinguished prep school students (Cookson and Persell 1985), working-class law students learned how to behave in an upper-class world, including how to dress for a new audience whose favorable appraisal they must cultivate. One second-year male discussed this process:

> *I remember going to buy suits here. I went to Brooks Brothers for two reasons. One, I don't own a suit. My father owns one suit, and it's not that good. Second, I think it's important to look good. A lot of my friends went to Brooks Brothers, and I feel it's worth it to do it right and not to have another hurdle to walk in and have the wrong thing on. It's all a big play act. . . . During my first year, I had no luck with interviews. I was in my own little world when I came here. I wished I had paid more attention to the dressing habits of second- and third-year students.*

Being in their own "working-class world" forced these students to begin recognizing the importance of different interpersonal skills. A second-year woman commented that

I have really begun to see the value of having good social skills. I think that is one of the ways that law firms weed out people. In order to get jobs you have to have those social skills. I'm real conscious of that when I go out on interviews now.

The recognition among working-class students that they were able to imitate upper-class students increasingly encouraged them to conceal their backgrounds. One second-year student, whose father worked as a house painter, boasted of his mastery of "passing":

I generally don't tell people what my father does or what my mother does. I notice that I'm different, but it's not something other people here notice because I can fake it. They don't notice that I come from a blue-collar background.

Paying attention to the impression that one presents becomes extremely important for the upwardly mobile working-class student.

These students were sometimes assisted in their performances by professional career counselors employed by the law school. These professionals gave students instructions on how to present themselves as full-fledged members of this elite community. Students were taught that unless they downplayed their social class background, the most lucrative opportunities would be denied them. A third-year woman from a working-class area in Boston recalled learning this new norm of presentation:

I'm sort of proud that I'm from South Boston and come from a working-class background. During my second year, however, I wasn't having much luck with my first interviews. I went to talk with my adviser about how to change my resumé a bit or how to present myself better. I told my adviser that on the interviews I was presenting myself as a slightly unusual person with a different background. We talked about that, and he told me that it probably wasn't a good idea to present myself as being a little unusual. I decided that he was right and began to play up that I was just like them. After that, the interviews and offers began rolling in. I began to realize that they [interviewers] really like people who are like themselves.

Recognizing that job recruiters seek homogeneity is an important lesson that upwardly mobile working-class students must learn if they are to gain admission into high status and financially rewarding occupations.[4] Kanter (1977) demonstrated, for instance, that managers come to reward those who resemble themselves. More recently, Jackell (1988) documented how the failure of managers to "fit in" resulted in suspicion and subsequent exclusion from advancement. Fitting in is particularly important in prestigious law firms which tend to resemble the high-status clients they represent (Abel 1989). During interviews, however, working-class law students faced a distinct disadvantage, as the interviewers who actively pursued new recruits rarely posed questions about the student's knowledge of law.[5] Most seemed intent on finding students who fit into the law firm's corporate structure. The entire recruitment process itself, from the initial interview to "fly out," represents ceremonial affirmation of these students' elite status in which they need only demonstrate their "social" competence. Working-class students typically found such interactions stressful. One third-year student explained her experiences:

> *They [the recruiters] didn't test my knowledge of law. They were interested in finding out what kind of person I was and what my background was. I tried to avoid talking about that and instead stressed the kind of work I was interested in. I think that most firms want a person who they can mold, that fits into their firm.*

Some of the most successful working-class students enjoyed the accolades bestowed on them because of their hard work and natural abilities. In speaking of her success, a third-year student on law review said that when she entered law school, it never occurred to her that she would clerk for the Supreme Court and then work for a major Wall Street law firm, adding that "once you begin doing well and move up the ladder and gain a whole new set of peers, then you begin to think about the possibilities." However, such success comes at a price, particularly for working-class students of color. Although having achieved success, many of these students continued to feel like outsiders. One such student, a third-year black male, reflected on what he considered the unfortunate aspects of affirmative action programs:

> *I have mixed feelings about the law review because of its affirmative action policies. On the one hand, I think it's good that minorities are represented on the law review. On the other hand, there's a real stigma attached to it. Before law school, I achieved by my own abilities. On law review, I don't feel I get respect. I find myself working very hard and getting no respect. Other students don't work as hard. I spend a lot of time at the review because I don't want to turn in a bad assignment. I don't want them [other law review members] to think that I don't have what it takes.*

Students who perceived themselves as outsiders frequently overcompensated for their failings because they felt judged by the "master status" associated with their social identity. This reaction to class stigma is typical among working-class students in educational institutions. In addition to developing their educational skills, working-class students are confronted with learning social skills as well. This makes succeeding particularly difficult for these students and is a task fraught with the fear of being discovered as incompetent (Sennett and Cobb 1973).

Ambivalence

Despite their maneuvers, these working-class students had difficulty transcending their previous identity. The attempt by these students to manage their stigma resulted in what Goffman (1963) termed "identity ambivalence" (p. 107). Working-class students who sought to exit their class background could neither embrace their group nor let it go. This ambivalence is often felt by working-class individuals who attain upward mobility into the professional-managerial class (Steinitz and Solomon 1986). Many experience the "stranger in paradise" syndrome, in which working-class individuals feel like virtual outsiders in middle-class occupations (Ryan and Sackrey 1984). Such experiences frequently lead to considerable identity conflict among working-class individuals who attempt to align themselves with the middle class.

The working-class law students in my sample typically experienced identity conflicts on their upward climb. Not only did they feel deceptive in their adjustment strategies, but many felt the additional burden of believing they had "sold out" their own class and were letting their group down. Like other stigmatized individuals who gain acceptance among dominant groups (Goffman 1963), these students often felt they were letting down their own group by representing elite interests. One third-year female student ruefully explained:

> My brother keeps asking me whether I'm a Republican yet. He thought that af-ter I finished law school I would go to work to help people, not work for one of those firms that do business. In a way, he's my conscience. Maybe he's right. I've got a conflict with what I'm doing. I came from the working class and wanted to do public interest law. I have decided not to do that. It's been a difficult decision for me. I'm not completely comfortable about working at a large firm.

Another student, who grew up on welfare, expressed similar reservations about his impending career in law:

> I'm not real happy about going to a large firm. I make lots of apologies. I'm still upset about the fact that my clients are real wealthy people, and it's not clear as to what the social utility of that will be.

Like the previous example, this student experienced a form of self-alienation as a result of his identity ambivalence. Students often experience a sense of guilt as they transcend their working-class backgrounds. Such guilt, however, needs to be abated if these students are to successfully adjust to their new reference group and reduce the status conflict they experience. For these working-class students, making the primary adjustment to upward mobility required strategies of accommodation in personal attitudes regarding their relationship to members of less privileged social classes. Secondary identity adjustments were therefore critical in helping students mitigate the ambivalence they experienced over their own success and subsequent separation from the working class.

Resolving Ambivalence

Although accommodation strategies were typical throughout the entire student body,[6] working-class students at this law school were more likely to employ particular types of strategies to help manage their identity. Students sought to manage their ambivalence by remaining "ideologically" distanced from the very social class their elite law school credential had facilitated alignment with. Many of these students became deliberate role models, unreservedly immersing themselves in higher social classes for that specific purpose. Such adjustments might be thought of as political since they were intended to directly challenge the domination of social elites. A black working-class student described how his actions would benefit the less fortunate:

> *I get slammed for being a corporate tool. People feel that I have sold out. I'm irritated by that. For years, blacks have been treated as slaves, sharecroppers, or porters. So I think that whether I want to be a partner at Cravath or to be a NAACP defense attorney, either of these positions are politically correct. We need black people with money and power. I think that I can make significant contributions to black causes.*

For many students who experienced ambivalence, working in elite law firms was seen as the best way to help those they left behind. Other students redefined the value of large corporate law firms for the opportunities that such positions offered in contributing to social change. One third-year student suggested:

> *I used to think that social change would come about by being an activist. That's why I originally wanted to do public interest law. But you really can't accomplish much by doing this. The hiring partner at [a major New York law firm] convinced me that this is the only way to get things done. He served as the under secretary of state in the [former president's] administration. He made sense when he told me that if I wanted to contribute to social change I had to become an important person.*

Students became less convinced that directly serving the less-privileged social classes would effectively resolve the problems that concerned them. A third-year student explained how disenchanted she had become with public interest law:

> *I used to think that you could do good things for people. . . . I don't think that anymore. I'm no longer troubled by the idea of being a corporate lawyer as opposed to a public interest one. I'm still concerned about social problems like poverty or poor housing, but I'm not sure that being a public interest attorney is the way to resolve those things. The needs of the people that public interest lawyers serve are just beyond what I can do as an attorney. I think I can do more good for people if I commit myself to working with community groups or activities in the bar during my spare time.*

The offering of such accounts helps students resolve the contradiction they experience by choosing a large law firm practice, as does the practical planning to use one's spare time (e.g., to do community activities). Unfortunately, given the structure of contemporary large law firms, spare time is a rarity (Nelson 1988; Spangler 1986). Adopting these new definitions regarding the pursuit of effective social change means that working-class students need not feel penitent over their upward mobility. Such strategies, of course, are attractive, as they suggest that the student is becoming elite not solely because he or she is striving for personal reward and success but as a means to best pursue the noble ideals of public service and social activism.

A more drastic accommodation involved avoidance of those who reminded working-class students of their social obligations toward helping the less fortunate. Just associating with individuals whose career path was geared toward helping the downtrodden caused considerable uneasiness in working-class students who had decided to enter large law firms. One third-year student said that he had begun to avoid law students who had retained their commitment to work with the poor:

> It's taken for granted here that you can work for a large firm and still be a good person. The people who don't reinforce that message make me uncomfortable now. Frankly, that's why I'm not hanging out with the public interest people. They remind me of my own guilt.

In some cases, avoidance turned into open hostility. Another third-year student described how she now saw other students who remained committed to their ideals of helping the less fortunate: "They're so single-minded at times and I think a little naive. They've really pushed me away from wanting to do public interest work as a full-time occupation." Condemning her condemners helped this student neutralize the guilt she felt over working for a corporate law firm.

Conclusion

. . .

Upwardly mobile working-class students in this study, as well as in others, interpret and experience their social class from the perspective of stigma. However, since the stigma of being a member of the lower classes is thought to be just, upwardly mobile working-class students frequently construct identities in which they seek to escape the taint associated with their affiliation. Overcoming this stigma is therefore considered an individual rather than a collective effort. As was demonstrated in this study, such efforts often involve managing one's identity in the ways that Goffman outlined. Research that explores identity struggles as they relate to class could offer further extensions of Goffman's comments on stigma. Such research also has potential value in contributing to our understanding of working-class movements in the United States. Indeed, exploring the experience of class from the perspective of stigma and its management could offer great insight into the social psychology of working-class disempowerment.

NOTES

Author's Note: Partial funding for this research was provided by the Woodrow Wilson Foundation.

1. The following are the percentage distributions of social class background on the random sample of questionnaire returnees I collected for the larger project: upper

class (2.8), upper-middle (44.6), middle (30.0), lower-middle (8.0), working (13.1), and lower (0.5).

2. This is a first-year exercise in which students select a case to argue in front of a three-person panel consisting of a law professor, a third-year student, and an invited guest from the legal community. First-year students prepare their cases for several months in advance before formally presenting their oral argument.

3. Similar findings were reported by Domhoff and Zweigenhaft (1991) in which they described the experiences of black students who were enrolled in elite prep schools as a result of affirmative action.

4. Students are actively pursued. During the 1987 recruitment seasons at the law school, an average of 44 recruiters from commercial law firms conducted interviews with students each day. This represents nearly one law firm for each law student eligible to interview. In most cases, law firms are looking to hire more than one student.

5. A recent study of hiring policies among large law firms found that "personal characteristics" ranked second among the criteria for selecting new lawyers (see Buller and Beck-Dudley 1990).

6. Many students are confronted with identity conflicts that stem from the separation of personal values from professional roles. This is felt most among those students who entered law school with social activist ideals (for further discussion of this, see Granfield 1986, 1989, forthcoming).

REFERENCES

Abel, R. 1989. *American Lawyers*. New York: Oxford University Press.
Adler, P., and P. Adler. 1987. *Membership Roles in Field Research*. Newbury Park, CA: Sage.
Baltzell, E. D. 1958. *Philadelphia Gentlemen*. New York: Free Press.
Bernstein, B. 1977. *Class Codes and Control. Vol. 3: Towards a Theory of Educational Transmission*. London: Routledge & Kegan Paul.
Bourdieu, P. 1984. *Distinction: A Social Critique of the Judgment of Taste*. Cambridge, MA: Harvard University Press.
Bourdieu, P., and J. C. Passeron. 1990. *Reproduction in Education, Society and Culture*. London: Routledge & Kegan Paul.
Buller, P., and C. Beck-Dudley. 1990. "Performance, Policies and Personnel." *American Bar Association Journal* 76:94.
Chadwick, B., H. Bahr, and S. Albrecht. 1984. *Social Science Research Methods*. Englewood Cliffs, NJ: Prentice-Hall.
Cookson, P., and C. Persell. 1985. *Preparing for Power: America's Elite Boarding Schools*. New York: Basic Books.
Domhoff, G. W., and R. Zweigenhaft. 1991. *Blacks in the White Establishment: A Study of Race and Class in America*. New Haven, CT: Yale University Press.
Fielding, N., and J. Fielding. 1986. *Linking Data*. Beverly Hills, CA: Sage.
Goffman, E. 1963. *Stigma: Notes on the Management of Spoiled Identity*. Englewood Cliffs, NJ: Prentice-Hall.
Granfield, R. 1986. "Legal Education as Corporate Ideology: Student Adjustment to the Law School Experience." *Sociological Forum* 1:514–23.
———. 1989. "Making the Elite Lawyer: Culture and Ideology in Legal Education." Ph.D. dissertation, Northeastern University, Boston.
———. Forthcoming. *Making Elite Lawyers*. New York: Routledge, Chapman & Hall.
Granfield, R., and T. Koenig. 1990. "From Activism to Pro Bono: The Redirection of Working Class Altruism at Harvard Law School." *Critical Sociology* 17:57–80.
Heinz, J., and E. Laumann. 1982. *Chicago Lawyers: The Social Structure of the Bar*. New York: Russell Sage.

Jackell, R. 1988. *Moral Mazes: The World of the Corporate Manager.* New York: Oxford University Press.

Kanter, R. 1977. *Men and Women of the Corporation.* New York: Basic Books.

Lamont, M., and A. Lareau. 1988. "Cultural Capital: Allusions, Gaps and Glissandos in Recent Theoretical Development." *Sociological Theory* 6:153–68.

Lurie, A. 1983. *The Language of Clothes.* New York: Vintage.

Nelson, R. 1988. *Partners with Power: The Social Transformation of the Large Law Firm.* Berkeley: University of California Press.

Newman, K. 1988. *Falling from Grace: The Experience of Downward Mobility in the American Middle Class.* New York: Free Press.

Pfuhl, E. 1986. *The Deviance Process.* Belmont, CA: Wadsworth.

Ryan, J., and C. Sackrey. 1984. *Strangers in Paradise: Academics from the Working Class.* Boston: South End Press.

Schur, E. 1971. *Labeling Deviant Behavior.* New York: Harper & Row.

———. 1980. *The Politics of Deviance.* Englewood Cliffs, NJ: Prentice-Hall.

Sennett, R., and R. Cobb. 1973. *The Hidden Injuries of Class.* New York: Random House.

Smigel, E. 1969. *The Wall Street Lawyer.* Bloomington: Indiana University Press.

Spangler, E. 1986. *Lawyers for Hire: Salaried Professionals at Work.* New Haven, CT: Yale University Press.

Steinitz, V., and E. Solomon. 1986. *Starting Out: Class and Community in the Lives of Working Class Youth.* Philadelphia: Temple University Press.

Stone, G. 1970. "Appearance and the Self." Pp. 394–414 in *Social Psychology through Symbolic Interaction,* edited by G. Stone and H. Farberman. New York: Wiley.

Useem, M., and J. Karabel. 1986. "Paths to Corporate Management." *American Sociological Review* 51:184–200.

14

ANYBODY'S SON WILL DO

GWYNNE DYER

An important point about socialization is that if culture is learned, it also can be unlearned. Sociologists call this process *resocialization*. This situation occurs when an individual gives up one way of life and one set of values for another. Examples of resocialization include the experience of new immigrants, of a person changing careers, of someone joining a feminist consciousness raising group, or of an individual undergoing a religious conversion, such as a nun entering a convent or a person being initiated into a cult. The following reading by Gwynne Dyer focuses on the resocialization civilians experience during military basic training.

You think about it and you know you're going to have to kill but you don't understand the implications of that, because in the society in which you've lived murder is the most heinous of crimes . . . and you are in a situation in which it's turned the other way round. . . . When you do actually kill someone the experience, my experience, was one of revulsion and disgust.

. . .

I was utterly terrified—petrified—but I knew there had to be a Japanese sniper in a small fishing shack near the shore. He was firing in the other direction at Marines in another battalion, but I knew as soon as he picked off the people there—there was a window on our side—that he would start picking us off. And there was nobody else to go . . . and so I ran towards the shack and broke in and found myself in an empty room.

. . .

There was a door which meant there was another room and the sniper was in that—and I just broke that down. I was just absolutely gripped by the fear that this man would expect me and would shoot me. But as it turned out he was in a sniper harness and he couldn't turn around fast enough. He was entangled in the harness so I shot him with a .45 and I felt remorse and shame. I can remember whispering foolishly, "I'm sorry" and then just throwing up. . . . I threw up all over myself. It was a betrayal of what I'd been taught since a child.

—William Manchester

Yet he did kill the Japanese soldier, just as he had been trained to—the revulsion only came afterward. And even after Manchester knew what it was like to kill another human being, a young man like himself, he went on trying to kill his "enemies" until the war was over. Like all the other tens of millions of soldiers who had been taught from infancy that killing was wrong, and had then been sent off to kill for their countries, he was almost helpless to disobey, for he had fallen into the hands of an institution so powerful and so subtle that it could quickly reverse the moral training of a lifetime.

The whole vast edifice of the military institution rests on its ability to obtain obedience from its members even unto death—and the killing of others. It has enormous powers of compulsion at its command, of course, but all authority must be based ultimately on consent. The task of extracting that consent from its members has probably grown harder in recent times, for the gulf between the military and the civilian worlds has undoubtedly widened: Civilians no longer perceive the threat of violent death as an everyday hazard of existence, and the categories of people whom it is not morally permissible to kill have broadened to include (in peacetime) the entire human race. Yet the armed forces of every country can still take almost any young male civilian and turn him into a soldier with all the right reflexes and attitudes in only a few weeks. Their recruits usually have no more than twenty years' experience of the world, most of it as children, while the armies have had all of history to practice and perfect their techniques.

> *Just think of how the soldier is treated. While still a child he is shut up in the barracks. During his training he is always being knocked about. If he makes the least mistake he is beaten, a burning blow on his body, another on his eye, perhaps his head is laid open with a wound. He is battered and bruised with flogging. On the march . . . they hang heavy loads round his neck like that of an ass.*
> —Egyptian, ca. 1500 B.C.[1]

> *The moment I talk to the new conscripts about the homeland I strike a land mine. So I kept quiet. Instead I try to make soldiers of them. I give them hell from morning to sunset. They begin to curse me, curse the army, curse the state. Then they begin to curse together, and become a truly cohesive group, a unit, a fighting unit.*
> —Israeli, ca. A.D. 1970[2]

All soldiers belong to the same profession, no matter what country they serve, and it makes them different from everybody else. They have to be different, for their job is ultimately about killing and dying, and those things are not a natural vocation for any human being. Yet all soldiers are born civilians. The method for turning young men into soldiers—people who kill other people and expose themselves to death—is basic training. It's essentially the same all over the world, and it always has been, because young men everywhere are pretty much alike.

Human beings are fairly malleable, especially when they are young, and in every young man there are attitudes for any army to work with: the inherited values and postures, more or less dimly recalled, of the tribal warriors who were once the model for every young boy to emulate. Civilization did not involve a sudden clean break in the way people behave, but merely the progressive distortion and redirection of all the ways in which people in the old tribal societies used to behave, and modern definitions of maleness still contain a great deal of the old warrior ethic. The anarchic machismo of the primitive warrior is not what modern armies really need in their soldiers, but it does provide them with promising raw material for the transformation they must work in their recruits.

Just how this transformation is wrought varies from time to time and from country to country. In totally militarized societies—ancient Sparta, the samurai class of medieval Japan, the areas controlled by organizations like the Eritrean People's Liberation Front today—it begins at puberty or before, when the young boy is immersed in a disciplined society in which only the military values are allowed to penetrate. In more sophisticated modern societies, the process is briefer and more concentrated, and the way it works is much more visible. It is, essentially, a conversion process in an almost religious sense—and as in all conversion phenomena, the emotions are far more important than the specific ideas.

. . .

Armies know this. It is their business to get men to fight, and they have had a long time to work out the best way of doing it. All of them pay lip service to the symbols and slogans of their political masters, though the amount of time they must devote to this activity varies from country to country. . . . Nor should it be thought that the armies are hypocritical—most of their members really do believe in their particular national symbols and slogans. But their secret is that they know these are not the things that sustain men in combat.

What really enables men to fight is their own self-respect, and a special kind of love that has nothing to do with sex or idealism. Very few men have died in battle, when the moment actually arrived, for the United States of America or for the sacred cause of Communism, or even for their homes and families; if they had any choice in the matter at all, they chose to die for each other and for their own vision of themselves.

. . .

The way armies produce this sense of brotherhood in a peacetime environment is basic training: a feat of psychological manipulation on the grand scale which has been so consistently successful and so universal that we fail to notice it as remarkable. In countries where the army must extract its recruits in their late teens, whether voluntarily or by conscription, from a civilian environment that does not share the military values, basic training involves a brief but intense period of indoctrination whose purpose is not really to teach the recruits basic military skills, but rather to change their values and their loyalties. "I guess you could say we brainwash them a little bit," admitted a U.S. Marine drill instructor, "but you know they're good people."

The duration and intensity of basic training, and even its major emphases, depend on what kind of society the recruits are coming from, and on what sort of military organization they are going to. It is obviously quicker to train men from a martial culture than from one in which the dominant values are civilian and commercial, and easier to deal with volunteers than with reluctant conscripts. Conscripts are not always unwilling, however; there are many instances in which the army is popular for economic reasons.

. . .

It's easier if you catch them young. You can train older men to be soldiers; it's done in every major war. But you can never get them to believe that they like it, which is the major reason armies try to get their recruits before they are 20. There are other reasons too, of course, like the physical fitness, lack of dependents, and economic dispensability of teenagers, that make armies prefer them, but the most important qualities teenagers bring to basic training are enthusiasm and naiveté. Many of them actively want the discipline and the closely structured environment that the armed forces will provide, so there is no need for the recruiters to deceive the kids about what will happen to them after they join.

> *There is discipline. There is drill. . . . When you are relying on your mates and they are relying on you, there's no room for slackness or sloppiness. If you're not prepared to accept the rules, you're better off where you are.*
> —British army recruiting advertisement, 1976

> *People are not born soldiers, they become soldiers. . . . And it should not begin at the moment a new recruit is enlisted into the ranks, but rather much earlier, at the time of the first signs of maturity, during the time of adolescent dreams.*
> —*Red Star* (Soviet army newspaper), 1973

Young civilians who have volunteered and have been accepted by the Marine Corps arrive at Parris Island, the Corps's East Coast facility for basic training, in a state of considerable excitement and apprehension: Most are aware that they are about to undergo an extraordinary and very difficult experience. But they do not make their own way to the base; rather they trickle in to Charleston airport on various flights throughout the day on which their training platoon is due to form, and are held there, in a state of suppressed but mounting nervous tension, until late in the evening. When the buses finally come to carry them the 76 miles to Parris Island, it is often after midnight—and this is not an administrative oversight. The shock treatment they are about to receive will work most efficiently if they are worn out and somewhat disoriented when they arrive.

The basic training organization is a machine, processing several thousand young men every month, and every facet and gear of it has been designed with the sole purpose of turning civilians into Marines as efficiently as possible. Provided it can have total control over their bodies and their environment for approximately three months, it can practically guarantee converts. Parris Island provides that controlled environment, and the recruits do not set foot outside it again until they graduate as Marine privates 11 weeks later.

> *They're allowed to call home, so long as it doesn't get out of hand—every three weeks or so they can call home and make sure everything's all right, if they haven't gotten a letter or there's a particular set of circumstances. If it's a case of an emergency call coming in, then they're allowed to accept that call; if not, one of my staff will take the message.*

> . . .

> *In some cases I'll get calls from parents who haven't quite gotten adjusted to the idea that their son had cut the strings—and in a lot of cases that's what they're*

doing. The military provides them with an opportunity to leave home but they're still in a rather secure environment.

—Captain Brassington, USMC

For the young recruits, basic training is the closest thing their society can offer to a formal rite of passage, and the institution probably stands in an unbroken line of descent from the lengthy ordeals by which young males in precivilized groups were initiated into the adult community of warriors. But in civilized societies it is a highly functional institution whose product is not anarchic warriors, but trained soldiers.

Basic training is not really about teaching people skills; it's about changing them, so that they can do things they wouldn't have dreamt of otherwise. It works by applying enormous physical and mental pressure to men who have been isolated from their normal civilian environment and placed in one where the only right way to think and behave is the way the Marine Corps wants them to. The key word the men who run the machine use to describe this process is *motivation.*

I can motivate a recruit and in third phase, if I tell him to jump off the third deck, he'll jump off the third deck. Like I said before, it's a captive audience and I can train that guy; I can get him to do anything I want him to do. . . . They're good kids and they're out to do the right thing. We get some bad kids, but you know, we weed those out. But as far as motivation—here, we can motivate them to do anything you want, in recruit training.

—USMC drill instructor, Parris Island

The first three days the raw recruits spend at Parris Island are actually relatively easy, though they are hustled and shouted at continuously. It is during this time that they are documented and inoculated, receive uniforms, and learn the basic orders of drill that will enable young Americans (who are not very accustomed to this aspect of life) to do everything simultaneously in large groups. But the most important thing that happens in "forming" is the surrender of the recruits' own clothes, their hair—all the physical evidence of their individual civilian identities.

During a period of only 72 hours, in which they are allowed little sleep, recruits lay aside their former lives in a series of hasty rituals (like being shaven to the scalp) whose symbolic significance is quite clear to them even though they are quite deliberately given absolutely no time for reflection, or any hint that they might have the option of turning back from their commitment. The men in charge of them know how delicate a tightrope they are walking, though, because at this stage the recruits are still newly caught civilians who have not yet made their ultimate inward submission to the discipline of the Corps.

Forming Day One makes me nervous. You've got a whole new mob of recruits, you know, 60 or 70 depending, and they don't know anything. You don't know what kind of a reaction you're going to get from the stress you're going to lay on them, and it just worries me the first day.

. . .

Things could happen, I'm not going to lie to you. Something might happen. A recruit might decide he doesn't want any part of this stuff and maybe take a poke at you or something like that. In a situation like that it's going to be a spur-of-the-moment thing and that worries me.

—USMC drill instructor

But it rarely happens. The frantic bustle of forming is designed to give the recruit no time to think about resisting what is happening to him. And so the recruits emerge from their initiation into the system, stripped of their civilian clothes, shorn of their hair, and deprived of whatever confidence in their own identity they may previously have had as 18-year-olds, like so many blanks ready to have the Marine identity impressed upon them.

The first stage in any conversion process is the destruction of an individual's former beliefs and confidence, and his reduction to a position of helplessness and need. It isn't really as drastic as all that, of course, for three days cannot cancel out 18 years; the inner thoughts and the basic character are not erased. But the recruits have already learned that the only acceptable behavior is to repress any unorthodox thoughts and to mimic the character the Marine Corps wants. Nor are they, on the whole, reluctant to do so, for they *want* to be Marines. From the moment they arrive at Parris Island, the vague notion that has been passed down for a thousand generations that masculinity means being a warrior becomes an explicit article of faith, relentlessly preached: to be a man means to be a Marine.

There are very few 18-year-old boys who do not have highly romanticized ideas of what it means to be a man, so the Marine Corps has plenty of buttons to push. And it starts pushing them on the first day of real training: The officer in charge of the formation appears before them for the first time, in full dress uniform with medals, and tells them how to become men.

The United States Marine Corps has 205 years of illustrious history to speak for itself. You have made the most important decision in your life . . . by signing your name, your life, your pledge to the Government of the United States, and even more importantly, to the United States Marine Corps—a brotherhood, an elite unit. In 10.3 weeks you are going to become a member of that history, those traditions, this organization—if you have what it takes.

. . .

All of you want to do that by virtue of your signing your name as a man. The Marine Corps says that we build men. Well, I'll go a little bit further. We develop the tools that you have—and everybody has those tools to a certain extent right now. We're going to give you the blueprints, and we are go-ing to show you how to build a Marine. You've got to build a Marine—*you understand?*

—Captain Pingree, USMC

The recruits, gazing at him in awe and adoration, shout in unison, "Yes, sir!" just as they have been taught. They do it willingly, because they are volunteers—but even conscripts tend to have the romantic fervor of volun-teers if they are only 18 years old. Basic training, whatever its hardships, is a quick way to become a man among men, with an undeniable status, and be-yond the initial consent to undergo it, it doesn't even require any decisions.

I had just dropped out of high school and I wasn't doing much on the street ex-cept hanging out, as most teenagers would be doing. So they gave me an oppor-tunity—a recruiter picked me up, gave me a good line, and said that I could make it in the Marines, that I have a future ahead of me. And since I was living with my parents, I figured that I could start my own life here and grow up a little.

—USMC recruit, 1982

I like the hand-to-hand combat and . . . things like that. It's a little rough going on me, and since I have a small frame I would like to become deadly, as I would put it. I like to have them words, especially the way they've been teaching me here.

—USMC recruit (from Brooklyn), Parris Island, 1982

The training, when it starts, seems impossibly demanding physically for most of the recruits—and then it gets harder week by week. There is a con-stant barrage of abuse and insults aimed at the recruits, with the deliberate purpose of breaking down their pride and so destroying their ability to resist the transformation of values and attitudes that the Corps intends them to undergo. At the same time the demands for constant alertness and for instant obedience are continuously stepped up, and the standards by which the dress and behavior of the recruits are judged become steadily more unforgiving. But it is all carefully calculated by the men who run the machine, who think and talk in terms of the stress they are placing on the recruits: "We take so many c.c.'s of stress and we administer it to each man—they should be a little bit scared and they should be unsure, but they're adjusting." The aim is to keep the training arduous but just within most of the recruits' capability to withstand. One of the most striking achievements of the drill instructors is to create and maintain the illusion that basic training is an extraordinary chal-lenge, one that will set those who graduate apart from others, when in fact almost everyone can succeed.

There has been some preliminary weeding out of potential recruits even before they begin basic training, to eliminate the obviously unsuitable minor-ity, and some people do "fail" basic training and get sent home, at least in peacetime. The standards of acceptable performance in the U.S. armed forces, for example, tend to rise and fall in inverse proportion to the number and quality of recruits available to fill the forces to the authorized manpower levels. (In 1980, about 15% of Marine recruits did not graduate from basic training.) But there are very few young men who cannot be turned into passable soldiers if the forces are willing to invest enough effort in it.

Not even physical violence is necessary to effect the transformation, though it has been used by most armies at most times.

> *It's not what it was 15 years ago down here. The Marine Corps still occupies the position of a tool which the society uses when it feels like that is a resort that they have to fall to. Our society changes as all societies do, and our society felt that through enlightened training methods we could still produce the same product—and when you examine it, they're right. . . . Our 100 c.c.'s of stress is really all we need, not two gallons of it, which is what used to be. . . . In some cases with some of the younger drill instructors it was more an initiation than it was an acute test, and so we introduced extra officers and we select our drill instructors to "fine-tune" it.*
>
> —Captain Brassington, USMC

There is, indeed, a good deal of fine-tuning in the roles that the men in charge of training any specific group of recruits assume. At the simplest level, there is a sort of "good cop–bad cop" manipulation of recruits' attitudes toward those applying the stress. The three younger drill instructors with a particular serial are quite close to them in age and unremittingly harsh in their demands for ever higher performance, but the senior drill instructor, a man almost old enough to be their father, plays a more benevolent and understanding part and is available for individual counseling. And generally offstage, but always looming in the background, is the company commander, an impossibly austere and almost godlike personage.

At least these are the images conveyed to the recruits, although of course all these men cooperate closely with an identical goal in view. It works: In the end they become not just role models and authority figures, but the focus of the recruits' developing loyalty to the organization.

> *I imagine there's some fear, especially in the beginning, because they don't know what to expect. . . . I think they hate you at first, at least for a week or two, but it turns to respect. . . . They're seeking discipline, they're seeking someone to take charge, 'cause at home they never got it. . . . They're looking to be told what to do and then someone is standing there enforcing what they tell them to do, and it's kind of like the father-and-son game, all the way through. They form a fatherly image of the DI whether they want to or not.*
>
> —Sergeant Carrington, USMC

Just the sheer physical exercise, administered in massive doses, soon has recruits feeling stronger and more competent than ever before. Inspections, often several times daily, quickly build up their ability to wear the uniform and carry themselves like real Marines, which is a considerable source of pride. The inspections also help to set up the pattern in the recruits of unquestioning submission to military authority: Standing stock-still, staring straight ahead, while somebody else examines you closely for faults is about as extreme a ritual act of submission as you can make with your clothes on.

But they are not submitting themselves merely to the abusive sergeant making unpleasant remarks about the hair in their nostrils. All around them are deliberate reminders—the flags and insignia displayed on parade, the military music, the marching formations and drill instructors' cadenced calls—of the idealized organization, the "brotherhood" to which they will be admitted as full members if they submit and conform. Nowhere in the armed forces are the military courtesies so elaborately observed, the staffs' uniforms so immaculate (some DIs change several times a day), and the ritual aspects of military life so highly visible as on a basic training establishment.

Even the seeming inanity of close-order drill has a practical role in the conversion process. It has been over a century since mass formations of men were of any use on the battlefield, but every army in the world still drills its troops, especially during basic training, because marching in formation, with every man moving his body in the same way at the same moment, is a direct physical way of learning two things a soldier must believe: that orders have to be obeyed automatically and instantly, and that you are no longer an individual, but part of a group.

The recruits' total identification with the other members of their unit is the most important lesson of all, and everything possible is done to foster it. They spend almost every waking moment together—a recruit alone is an anomaly to be looked into at once—and during most of that time they are enduring shared hardships. They also undergo collective punishments, often for the misdeed or omission of a single individual (talking in the ranks, a bed not swept under during barracks inspection), which is a highly effective way of suppressing any tendencies toward individualism. And, of course, the DIs place relentless emphasis on competition with other "serials" in training: There may be something infinitely pathetic to outsiders about a marching group of anonymous recruits chanting, "Lift your heads and hold them high, 3313 is a-passin' by," but it doesn't seem like that to the men in the ranks.

Nothing is quite so effective in building up a group's morale and solidarity, though, as a steady diet of small triumphs. Quite early in basic training, the recruits begin to do things that seem, at first sight, quite dangerous: descend by ropes from 50-foot towers, cross yawning gaps hand-over-hand on high wires (known as the Slide for Life, of course), and the like. The common denominator is that these activities are daunting but not really dangerous: The ropes will prevent anyone from falling to his death off the rappelling tower, and there is a pond of just the right depth—deep enough to cushion a falling man, but not deep enough that he is likely to drown—under the Slide for Life. The goal is not to kill recruits, but to build up their confidence as individuals and as a group by allowing them to overcome apparently frightening obstacles.

You have an enemy here at Parris Island. The enemy that you're going to have at Parris Island is in every one of us. It's in the form of cowardice. The most rewarding experience you're going to have in recruit training is standing on line every evening, and you'll be able to look into each other's eyes, and you'll be able to say to each other with your eyes: "By God, we've made it one more day! We've defeated the coward."

—Captain Pingree, USMC

Number on deck, sir, 45 . . . highly motivated, truly dedicated, rompin', stompin', bloodthirsty, kill-crazy United States Marine Corps recruits, SIR!

—Marine chant, Parris Island, 1982

If somebody does fail a particular test, he tends to be alone, for the hurdles are deliberately set low enough that most recruits can clear them if they try. In any large group of people there is usually a goat: someone whose intelligence or manner or lack of physical stamina marks him for failure and contempt. The competent drill instructor, without deliberately setting up this unfortunate individual for disgrace, will use his failure to strengthen the solidarity and confidence of the rest. When one hapless young man fell off the Slide for Life into the pond, for example, his drill instructor shouted the usual invective—"Well, get out of the water. Don't contaminate it all day"— and then delivered the payoff line: "Go back and change your clothes. You're useless to your unit now."

"Useless to your unit" is the key phrase, and all the recruits know that what it means is "useless *in battle*." The Marine drill instructors at Parris Island know exactly what they are doing to the recruits, and why. They are not rear-echelon people filling comfortable jobs, but the most dedicated and intelligent NCOs the Marine Corps can find; even now, many of them have combat experience. The Corps has a clear-eyed understanding of precisely what it is training its recruits for—combat—and it ensures that those who do the training keep that objective constantly in sight.

The DIs "stress" the recruits, feed them their daily ration of synthetic triumphs over apparent obstacles, and bear in mind all the time that the goal is to instill the foundations for the instinctive, selfless reactions and the fierce group loyalty that is what the recruits will need if they ever see combat. They are arch-manipulators, fully conscious of it, and utterly unashamed. These kids have signed up as Marines, and they could well see combat; this is the way they have to think if they want to live.

I've seen guys come to Vietnam from all over. They were all sorts of people that had been scared—some of them had been scared all their life and still scared. Some of them had been a country boy, city boys—you know, all different kinds of people—but when they got in combat they all reacted the same—99 percent of them reacted the same. . . . A lot of it is training here at Parris Island, but the other part of it is survival. They know if they don't conform—conform I call it, but if they don't react in the same way other people are reacting, they won't survive. That's just it. You know, if you don't react together, then nobody survives.

—USMC drill instructor, Parris Island, 1982

When I went to boot camp and did individual combat training they said if you walk into an ambush what you want to do is just do a right face—you just turn right or left, whichever way the fire is coming from, and assault. I said, "Man, that's crazy. I'd never do anything like that. It's stupid."

. . .

The first time we came under fire, on Hill 1044 in Operation Beauty Canyon in Laos, we did it automatically. Just like you look at your watch to see what time it is. We done a right face, assaulted the hill—a fortified position with concrete bunkers emplaced, machine guns, automatic weapons—and we took it. And we killed—I'd estimate probably 35 North Vietnamese soldiers in the assault, and we only lost three killed. I think it was about two or three, and about eight or ten wounded.

. . .

But you know, what they teach you, it doesn't faze you until it comes down to the time to use it, but it's in the back of your head, like, What do you do when you come to a stop sign? It's in the back of your head, and you react automatically.

—USMC sergeant, 1982

Combat is the ultimate reality that Marines—or any other soldiers, under any flag—have to deal with. Physical fitness, weapons training, battle drills, are all indispensable elements of basic training, and it is absolutely essential that the recruits learn the attitudes of group loyalty and interdependency which will be their sole hope of survival and success in combat. The training inculcates or fosters all of those things, and even by the halfway point in the 11-week course, the recruits are generally responding with enthusiasm to their tasks.

. . .

In basic training establishments, . . . the malleability is all one way: in the direction of submission to military authority and the internalization of military values. What a place like Parris Island produces when it is successful, as it usually is, is a soldier who will kill because that is his job.

NOTES

1. Leonard Cottrell, *The Warrior Pharaohs* (London: Evans Brothers, 1968).
2. Samuel Rolbart, *The Israeli Soldier* (New York: A. S. Barnes, 1970), p. 206.

PART IV

Groups and Social Structure

15

ROLE MAKING AND DECISION MAKING WITHIN THE WORKING CLASS

NORMA WILLIAMS

The following four selections explore groups and social structure. The basic components of social structure are the roles and social statuses of individuals. Over the course of a lifetime, people occupy numerous statuses and roles. A *status* is a social position an individual holds within a group or a social system. A *role* is a set of expectations about the behavior assigned to a particular social status. Each role helps to define the nature of interaction with others and contributes to social organization by creating patterns of interpersonal and group relationships. Because we modify social roles more than we do our social statuses, roles are the dynamic aspect of social status. In this reading, Norma Williams investigates the mutability of roles in her study of Mexican American families.

T wo contradictory conclusions regarding decision making between husbands and wives are expressed in the social science literature. One is the importance of "machismo" as an all-encompassing form of male domination. The other is the egalitarian nature of the relationship between husbands and wives.

. . .

I am intent upon casting the issue of conjugal power relationships into a social context broader in scope than that of other research. There is now a vast body of literature that seeks to assess the power relations that exist between husbands and wives with respect to decision making on specific issues, for example, the purchase of a car, or the disciplining of children. Even so, McDonald (1980), among others, has observed that our understanding of conjugal power relationships leaves much to be desired, and he suggests that alternative approaches need to be explored. Most of the research has been carried out from the perspective of some version of exchange theory. But this orientation has definite limitations for understanding how husbands and wives arrive at decisions. The processual nature of decision making (including the give-and-take of negotiation) is typically overlooked. In part this is because most of the research on decision making has employed closed-ended questions, and it is almost impossible to track social processes over time with this methodological tool. Of even greater theoretical import, apparently no student of the family has examined the decision-making process within the context of role making. We know that husbands and wives in the broader society have for some decades been remaking their roles, and in the process they have been redefining each other's influence and power (Hertz 1986; Gerson 1985). In a more general sense, no one seems to have placed specific decision-making patterns within a broader interactional context and, in line with this, interpreted the nature of the power relationships between husbands and wives.

. . .

Role Making by Husbands and Wives: A Clarification of Issues

We are now at the point where we can uncover the nature of role making by husbands and wives as well as the resistance to this process. But the succeeding analysis requires that we have a clear understanding of the concept of "role making." This in turn leads us to elaborate on some rather fundamental sociological issues.

Ralph Turner (1962) introduced the concept of role making into sociological literature over a quarter of a century ago. Although his essay has been widely cited, the idea of role making has been utilized explicitly by only a few researchers in the course of analyzing empirical data. Turner has done so to some extent (e.g., Turner and Shosid 1976),[1] and so has Zurcher (1983). To be sure, many social scientists who have examined the changing roles of men and women in the past two decades have implicitly employed some form of the role-making framework (e.g., Gerson 1985) but they have yet to grasp the theoretical orientation that underlies the analysis of their data.

The basic premise of role making is that human agents take an active part in restructuring, or attempting to restructure, their own roles. Role making is different from role taking. Role taking, which calls for adopting the expectations of others in the course of one's actions, emphasizes social stability. In taking the role of others, human beings tend to act according to how they believe others expect them to act. In role making, however, human beings are not just being reactive; they are also proactive in that they are striving to create new roles for themselves. Role making involves role taking, but role taking does not necessarily involve role making.[2] This distinction is essential to an understanding of how Mexican Americans, especially women, are redefining their place in the social order.

When we consider the role-making process, we are led to give special attention to the "social mind." Most symbolic interactionists have emphasized the idea of the self. Certainly the concept of the self, which is always social in nature, is a crucial one and is part and parcel of my analysis. However, it is because of the social mind, not the social self, that persons are able to engage in social calculations and reflective thought and empathize with others and thus respond to new and complex situations in a variety of ways and create new roles for themselves. The social mind emerges only in the context of interaction with others; one's mind is not a fixed biological entity. How we learn to think arises within the concept of interaction with other persons.

Because of the social mind, persons come to have a social or collective memory. They store past experiences (albeit selectively) and use this memory as they respond to changing social circumstances. Thus, Mexican American husbands and wives have a memory of the traditional role expectations. My stress on the social mind is in keeping with the efforts of certain social scientists to give it greater prominence in the understanding of social interaction (Collins 1989; Smith 1982; Vaughan and Sjoberg 1984).[3]

To interpret the data regarding the actions of Mexican American wives and husbands, we must elaborate on, as well as modify, Turner's formulation regarding role making. Turner stressed that role making takes place in situations that are vague and ambiguous. But we must also realize that human agents create new roles by remaking traditional role expectations. It is this latter situation that receives major attention in the succeeding analysis. Then, too, resistance to role making occurs—a pattern that Turner did not examine. Thus, empirically, we come to grasp role making by recognizing the resistance to it. Such resistance to role making by wives, for example, is found not only within the familial context but also within the community and organizational setting (McCall and Simmons 1982). My fieldwork experience leads me to conclude that we cannot comprehend the issues regarding role making unless we consider negative reactions to the remaking of traditional expectations concerning how wives (and husbands) should act in everyday life. Again, recognizing the dialectical process between role making and the resistance to it enables us to discern the emergence of new kinds of conjugal relationships among Mexican Americans.

Specific Role-Making Patterns

But just what kinds of role making are occurring among working-class husbands and wives? Social scientists argue that women, especially women in the Anglo middle class, are taking the lead in reshaping their roles (cf. Stryker and Statham 1985). No research reports have delineated this process for Mexican American working-class women. Husbands and wives were very aware that fundamental changes in their relationship with each other had occurred over time. This was particularly true for those who had been married for a number of years. A number of women took the view that the men were not as dominant today as in the early years of marriage. This pattern is high-lighted in the comments of one wife who, in discussing her changing rela-tionship with her husband, indicated:

> *Whatever he said went like that. I'm not so timid now. I have some say. If I don't like what he does, I'll tell him so. Before we did not communicate with each other. He was a very dominating person, and even my friends noticed this pattern.*

The men replayed the themes of the wives. In the early years of mar-riage, "I said something and that was it." Today, the husbands stress that there is more discussion with their wives.

While changes in the roles of husbands and wives were apparent to the participants, the couples were unable to define just what was going on. Only after a rather extended period in the field did I sort out the fundamental role-making pattern that is taking place among working-class women. Essentially the women are striving to attain a new personal, as well as social, identity for themselves. One's personal identity can be quite private (or personal), whereas one's social identity is public (Weigert 1983). The issue is not equal-ity but the search for a separate identity on the part of the wives.

The wives' newfound personal and social identity sets them apart from traditional Mexican American women. Strikingly, none of the working-class women in Austin and Corpus Christi (and Kingsville as well) expected to fol-low the traditional mourning patterns if they became widowed. That women no longer sustain a symbolic social identity with their husbands after the lat-ter's death certainly reflects a major change from the past. Moreover, the hus-bands did not expect them to follow this traditional pattern.

A somewhat separate identity is essential today if a woman is to carry out certain activities within the public sphere after her husband's death. In view of the fragmentation of the traditional extended family, a widow can no longer rely on relatives to shop for groceries or carry out basic tasks for her-self and her family. Also, the demands of the workplace do not permit these women to engage in extended mourning rites. Thus they have had to do more than take the roles of others; they have had to reshape, often in a reflec-tive manner, their own roles in the light of the major structural changes that have been occurring in modern urban communities.

But greater specificity is required in detailing this search for a separate identity. For the working-class women, three types of role-making patterns can be delineated. Most of the working-class women reflect Type II, discussed below.

Type I: A Personal (but Limited Social) Identity

A very few of the women have achieved a personal identity apart from that of their husbands, but they have been unable to translate this into a meaning-ful social (i.e., public) identity. In their own private way they view themselves as separate from their husbands. But the lack of a broader social network of family, friends, or fellow workers has made it impossible for them to establish the kind of social identity they long for, one that would provide public support for their personal identity.

The experiences of one Mexican American woman serve to illustrate this pattern. During the interviews, she complained that she did not have an ID card issued by the Department of Public Safety. She had heard that she could obtain one, but her husband was unwilling to assist her in this endeavor, and she lacked a network of friends or a kinship system that could help her. She needed transportation as well as assistance in filling out the proper papers. Her lack of social identity had been embarrassing; for instance, she had at times mistakenly been identified as a Mexican national, although she was born in the United States and is a Mexican American.

After a couple of interviews, she asked me to help her secure an ID, and I agreed to assist her. Her husband did not object, in part because I was an "outsider" and in part because of my educational status. After she obtained her ID, she was able, for example, to cash checks, and she was therefore elated with her newfound social identity. The ID dramatizes the need for a separate identity if one is to carry out even minimal activities, such as cashing checks, within the impersonal, public sphere of a contemporary urban setting. College-educated women take these matters for granted.

Type II: An Emerging Personal and Social Identity

Most of the working-class married women I interviewed or encountered in my fieldwork were in the process of attaining a degree of personal and social identity (i.e., autonomy) apart from that of their husbands. This identity has come to be achieved, and is expressed, in a variety of ways. It typically involves support by relatives, friends, or persons in the workplace. Moreover, it may involve personal achievements outside the home that reinforce the fact that the woman in question does indeed command special skills and knowledge that make her different from her husband. Also, it involves the learning of social skills, including negotiation and image management, that make it possible for a wife to cope more effectively with her husband's resistance to her emerging identity.

First, as to the support system, one of the most crucial kinds consists of older children, especially daughters. In several instances, daughters attending a university in another community encouraged their mothers to visit them. In one case, the husband reluctantly permitted his wife to travel without him, and the wife commented as follows:

> *I used to drive all that way to see my daughter. My husband could not go, so I drove it. I was not familiar with the roads, but I did it.*

These concrete actions signified the wife's independence from her husband and served as a significant step in creating a sense of her social identity or autonomy.

Thus, daughters who become better educated than their mothers play a role in socializing the latter into creating a new identity, and at times they are able to intervene with their fathers and persuade them to become less rigid in their expectations.

Second, the development of a personal and social identity depends not only on a support system but also on the attainment of new social skills and knowledge.

The newfound identity of these working-class women is given credibility by their special knowledge or achievements in the public sphere. One woman had taken the lead in helping some of her fellow workers obtain their general equivalency diploma (GED). She proved to herself that she could act independently of her husband, and that she could do so in an effective manner. In addition, a number of women took pride in their ability to budget effectively and shop for bargains. This practical knowledge provided their families, especially the children, with opportunities they might otherwise lack. As a result of this situation, many respondents were reflectively aware of having created a personal and social identity that differed greatly from that of their mothers and grandmothers. This permitted them to cope with a variety of demands associated with everyday urban life.

Third, new social skills are important in helping women build a personal and social identity apart from that of their husbands. Working-class women must learn how to negotiate with their spouses, and they may also learn how to use impression management (Goffman 1959). They are reflectively aware of the fact that they may have to act differently at work than at home in order to cope with the tensions that develop between their husbands' more traditional expectations and the new expectations that arise at work. Therefore, some women conceal certain information about their activities in the workplace from their husbands. For example, one working-class woman had baked a cake for a party on the job, but her husband ate part of it. She had not told him what the cake was for because he would have disapproved of her "partying" at work, and she feared that he would have insisted that she quit her job.

Another pattern that emerged was that these women learned to modify their husbands' positions through effecting incremental, rather than drastic, changes. One woman indicated that she purposely makes small changes in the way she does things. Her husband "yells about it," but then he gets used to it, and then she makes other little changes. He tends to forget some of what occurred, and though he resists each change, after a time he comes to accept the reality that new expectations have arisen.

Many of these wives are aware of the need for "strategies" that will permit them to attain a greater degree of personal and social identity. They know they have not achieved the identity they aspire to, but they also realize that they have made strides in modifying their husband's actions. And most of the husbands are cognizant of the new social relationship that is emerging and begrudgingly accept many of the changes.

Type III: A Personal and Social Identity (with Reservations)

As with the Type I working-class married woman, the Type III woman, based on my interviews and fieldwork, is rare. I encountered only a few such women in my research in Austin, Corpus Christi, and Kingsville. One married woman, who was over 40, indicated that she was ready to do something different with her life. She conceded that it would be easier for her than for other women her age to make a change because she had greater financial security than other women she knew. And there were few constraints on her. She was not working and had time to think about what to do with her life.

Yet another woman in this category speaks for herself:

I have the financial security now and I am braver. I still have more to do. I am 44, I've got money, a good car and my kids are behind me. Now, if I am not home in time to make dinner, he can make a sandwich. We've been together a long time and he knows how to make a sandwich. I have had to stand my ground. Two years ago I wanted to go to school to study for a radiologist. He didn't let me. He said I didn't have to. I got my GED. Recently . . . I made a stand that I'm going out and I do. I go out during the day with friends to go out to eat. Not at night. I guess I was scared to go out. I always felt the obligation that I had to come home to cook.

These women stand apart from the typical working-class women I encountered. Because of their relative financial security, and convinced that they have played a major role in helping their husbands to achieve success, these women have developed a personal and social identity that brings them somewhat closer to the identity that college-educated women . . . take for granted.

Resistance to Role Making

Throughout the preceding discussion, I have alluded to the husbands' resistance to the emerging social and personal identity of their wives. Working-class women recognize that their spouses often object to the fact that they are breaking away from traditional expectations. This resistance results in part from the fact that husbands do not wish to give up their traditional power and privilege (Goode 1983). But it also reflects the fact that their social power is anchored in a cultural tradition that the husbands remember and deem important. Without a social memory of their past, the husbands would be less rigid.

Still, the roadblocks to change that men construct can be exaggerated, for they are at the same time revising some of their expectations regarding their wives' actions. As the wives have been in the process of attaining a separate personal and social identity, they have been able to negotiate a new role for themselves. In Austin I discovered a small group of men who were self-critical about their roles. These men, who were members of a church group, pointed out to one another, for instance, that they should not be so overbearing with their wives, or so "macho."

The general resistance by husbands to role making is only one aspect of the problem faced by working-class Mexican American women. There is also resistance to role making by these women from the organizational structure of the community as a whole. This is a complex process, for Mexican American women are "twice a minority" (cf. Melville 1980). Although the majority sector often assumes that it treats minorities fairly, in fact it negates them within a variety of contexts. Mexican American women are negated because of both their gender and their ethnicity. In comparison to the professional group, working-class women seem to experience greater discrimination outside the home in terms of ethnicity than in terms of gender. Although both forms of negation exist, that relating to ethnicity seems more immediate in their interaction in the larger community setting. With regard to the work world, a number of women expressed the view that Anglos "can do anything to you."

This negation—first on the basis of ethnicity and second on the basis of gender—in the public sphere makes these women highly tentative about participating in a variety of activities that are of special interest to them. For example, a number of working-class women asked me for information and assistance in dealing with the school system. They wanted to help their children, but they felt rather powerless in coping with the schools. One reason for this is a lack of confidence in their personal and social identity. In turn, this insecurity is reinforced by their fear of discrimination because of their ethnicity and gender. Their problems are compounded by their lack of knowledge about the school system and their lack of skills in serving as brokers between their children and school officials. Specifically, they lack knowledge of how to cope effectively with the forms they are expected to sign, some of which are intended more to protect the school system than to assist the children.

The resistance to role making by Mexican American women within the community seems to compel them to greater reliance on their husbands and families. This situation generates difficulties because their husbands' resistance to the creation of new roles (noted above) limits their ability to deal more effectively with community structures. Generally speaking, the patterns of discrimination within the community place constraints on role making by Mexican American working-class women in significant ways.

The activities of working-class women as twice a minority also bring other issues to light. Just how do these women cope with the contradictory role expectations regarding ethnicity and gender in the public sphere, as well as the tensions that result from their husbands' resistance to change in the familial sphere? These women cannot simply rely on the patterns of managing role tensions or conflicts outlined by Goode (1973). He speaks, for example, of the use of compartmentalization in managing role conflicts. The women use this technique to some extent; however, reality calls for them to live with what Zurcher (1986) aptly terms a "cognitive dialectic." They must deal with contradictory role expectations—some of which are humiliating and socially painful. Many symbolic interactionists (as well as other social psychologists) downplay the contradictions that persons face in their daily lives. Yet, a number of decades ago Komarovsky (1946) analyzed the contradictory sex-role expectations for women in the privileged majority sector of U.S. society. The contradictions for minority women such as Mexican Americans are greater and have a more profound impact on the actions of these women.

NOTES

1. It is significant that Turner did not employ the concept of role making in his major work *Family Interaction* (1970), even though he was the person who formulated the concept of role making some years earlier.

2. For more detailed information on some of the theoretical issues involved in role making, see Turner (1985). In this chapter, Turner places his own formulation within the context of modern social-psychological theory, and he discusses problems that he did not delineate in his first essay on this subject. For a theoretical and methodological evaluation of the concept of role making, see Williams (1989).

   Much work needs to be done in clarifying various theoretical and empirical issues with respect to role making. One of the areas demanding special attention is the relationship between role taking and role making. Few sociologists have grasped the significance of the basic differences between these concepts. The problems are compounded by the complex conceptual issues involved in the concept of role (Biddle 1986).

3. Most symbolic interactionists, and sociologists in general, have overlooked the fact that Mead's most influential book was *Mind, Self and Society* (1934). In fact, until recently the issue of the mind was generally ignored by sociologists.

   The concept of the "social mind" is being rehabilitated in sociological theory. Randall Collins' (1989) article in *Symbolic Interaction*, and responses to it by various sociologists, will likely stimulate renewed interest in this orientation.

   A number of issues regarding the social mind cannot be addressed in this article. Although I emphasize the cognitive aspects of the social mind, I realize that the social mind also encompasses emotions such as empathy that are an integral aspect of human interaction.

REFERENCES

Biddle, B. J. 1986. "Recent Developments in Role Theory." *Annual Review of Sociology* 12:67–92.

Collins, R. 1989. "Toward a Neo-Meadian Sociology of Mind." *Symbolic Interaction* 12:1–32.

Gerson, K. 1985. *Hard Choices: How Women Decide about Work, Career, and Motherhood.* Berkeley: University of California Press.

Goffman, E. 1959. *The Presentation of Self in Everyday Life.* Garden City, NY: Doubleday/Anchor.

Goode, W. J. 1973. *Explorations in Social Theory.* New York: Oxford University Press.

———. 1983. "Why Men Resist." Pp. 201–18 in *Family in Transition,* edited by A. Skolnick and J. Skolnick. 4th ed. Boston: Little, Brown.

Hertz, R. 1986. *More Equal than Others: Women and Men in Dual-Career Marriages.* Berkeley: University of California Press.

Komarovsky, M. 1946. "Cultural Contradictions and Sex Roles." *American Journal of Sociology* 52:184–89.

McCall, G. & J. L. Simmons. 1982. *Social Psychology: A Sociological Approach*. New York: Free Press.

McDonald, G. W. 1980. "Family Power: The Assessment of a Decade of Theory and Research, 1970–1979." *Journal of Marriage and the Family* 42:841–54.

Mead, G. H. 1934. *Mind, Self and Society*. Chicago: University of Chicago Press.

Melville, M., ed. 1980. *Twice a Minority: Mexican American Women*. St. Louis: C. V. Mosby.

Smith, C. W. 1982. "On the Sociology of Mind." Pp. 221–28 in *Explaining Human Behavior*, edited by P. Secord. Beverly Hills: Sage.

Stryker, S. and A. Statham. 1985. "Symbolic Interaction and Role Theory." Pp. 311–78 in *The Handbook of Social Psychology*, Vol 1., edited by G. Lindzey and E. Aronson. New York: Random House.

Turner, R. 1962. "Role Taking: Process Versus Conformity." Pp. 20–39 in *Human Behavior and Social Processes*, edited by A. Rose. London: Routledge and Kegan Paul.

———. 1970. *Family Interaction*. New York: Wiley.

——— and N. Shosid. 1976. "Ambiguity and Interchangeability in Role Attribution: The Effect of Alter's Response." *American Sociological Review* 41:993–1006.

———. 1985. "Unanswered Questions in the Convergence Between Structuralist and Interactionist Role Theories." Pp. 22–36 in *Micro-Sociological Theory Perspectives on Sociological Theory*, Vol. 2, edited by H. J. Helle and S. N. Eisenstadt. Beverly Hills: Sage.

Vaughan, T. R. and G. Sjoberg. 1984. "The Individual and Bureaucracy: An Alternative Meadian Interpretation." *Journal of Applied Behavioral Science* 20:57–69.

Weigert, A. J. 1983. "Identity: Its Emergence within Sociological Psychology." *Symbolic Interaction* 6:183–206.

Williams, N. 1989. "Theoretical and Methodological Issues in the Study of Role-making." In *Studies in Symbolic Interaction: A Research Annual*, Vol. 10, edited by N. Denzin. Greenwich: JAI Press.

Zurcher, L. A. 1983. *Social Roles: Conformity, Conflict and Creativity*. Beverly Hills: Sage.

———. 1986. "The Bureaucratizing of Impulse: Self-Conception in the 1980's." *Symbolic Interaction* 9:169–78.

16

SLIM'S TABLE

MITCHELL DUNEIER

This selection by Mitchell Duneier is a study of a *primary group* that exists in a Chicago-area cafeteria. Every day, a group of men come together at Slim's Table to discuss local events. As the reading by Duneier shows, Slim's Table is similar to other primary groups in that it is small, intimate, and informal. Examples of other primary groups are families, friendship cliques, sororities and fraternities, gangs, neighborhood coffee klatches, and small work groups. Thus, primary groups emerge when people live or work closely together.

They both came of age at the height of segregation. Sixty-five, a lifelong Chicagoan, Slim is a black mechanic in a back-alley garage in the ghetto. Bart, white, and 10 years older, is a retired file clerk who grew up in the rural South. Both are regular patrons of the Valois "See Your Food" cafeteria.

I first met Bart during my early days as a university student, long before I ever set foot inside Valois. Like many older residents of the Hyde Park neighborhood, he ate regularly in the cafeteria of International House, or I-House, as it was called, a dormitory for graduate students close to the University of Chicago campus.

Tall and skeletal in his mid-70s, Bart dressed in fine suits and sported a Dobbs hat. Sometimes when he'd be sitting alone at one of the cafeteria's long wooden tables, I'd join him and ask about his past. He did not have any strong family ties. His only brother lived in Colorado, and he hadn't seen him in about five years. They spoke on the telephone no more than once a year. He had retired from a long career as a clerk at Swift's, one of the major meat-packing companies, during the era when Chicago was still "hog butcher for the world." Then he took a job as a file clerk at one of Chicago's largest law firms.

Bart moved to Hyde Park in 1928 to attend the University of Chicago as a premedical student and supported himself for a time by working at the Streets of Paris section of the 1933 Century of Progress Exposition. He had little to say about that experience. He had been a ticket collector at the entrance to the shows but had never gone inside to look.

Bart was a very incurious person, one of many odd human beings who become attached to a university community as students and continue the association for decades. His explanation for not marrying was that "some people just never find a person to jive with." His biggest dream had been to become a physician like his father, but the hardships of the Depression made it impossible for him to continue his studies.

He wasn't bitter about his life. They only resentment he ever displayed was toward blacks in the local community. With the southern drawl of the Kentucky town in which he had been raised, he often complained that Hyde Park had long ago turned into a "high-class slum."

Because I thought about Bart only when I saw him sitting in "his" chair after dinner at I-House, many weeks may have gone by before I realized that the old man had been absent for some time. I wondered if he had taken ill. Months passed with no sign of him. I asked the front desk clerk and other residents if they had seen Bart. No one had, and I finally decided that he might have died.

Two years later, when I entered Valois Cafeteria for the first time, I was startled to see Bart sitting by himself eating a bowl of radishes, amidst black men sipping coffee at the surrounding tables. On a chair next to him was the same Dobbs hat I had seen him wearing before he abandoned I-House. He asked me how I had been and inquired about some of the people he remembered from the dormitory cafeteria. He told me that although he had liked being around the students, prices there were high and the quality of food very poor. He had been eating at Valois for a year. I asked what he could tell me about the restaurant, which is known locally by its motto "See Your Food."

"I don't know anything about the place."

"But you eat here every day?"

"Yes, but I don't pay any attention to the place. I just eat my meal and go home."

As our conversation came to a close, he informed me that I might direct my questions about Valois to the owner.

Over the weeks and months that followed, I would see Bart constantly. Despite his claims, he seemed to be well aware of the other habitual patrons of the restaurant, including the group of black regulars that congregated at Slim's table.

I came to learn that Slim's table has, for over a decade, been the meeting place of a group of black men who regularly patronize this cafeteria on the margin of the ghetto. Slim, who comes to the restaurant every day is usually joined by Harold, a self-employed exterminator; Cornelius, a retired meter inspector; Ted, a film developer for *Playboy Magazine* who received an honorable discharge from the army after 20 years of service; and Earl, an administrator at the Chicago Board of Education. These and others constitute a core group that frequents the restaurant daily. Besides them, hundreds of other black men frequent Valois less often, some only on weekends. Ties binding members of the larger collectivity have developed over decades, and it is not uncommon for someone entering the restaurant to be playfully scolded by Slim or his buddies: "Now, don't you go hiding from us again" or "Come by and see us more often," if he has been absent for any significant amount of time.

The spectrum of social classes among the black men is very broad. At one end of the spectrum are a few men like Earl from the Board of Education, middle class and college educated. In the middle, most of the men are solidly working class. At the other end of the spectrum are a significant number who have been downwardly mobile in their later years and have incomes which would place them among the working poor. These are individuals whose wages would place them at or below the poverty line.[1] But even this description is tidier than the reality because most of the men have social characteristics which would place them in various classes at the same time.[2] Most of the men live in small apartments in Hyde Park or local ghettos, but some like Slim own small homes. By the standards of mainstream American society, none of these men are members of the "underclass" or "undeserving poor," though they are sometimes treated as such by whites from the nearby university.

These black men were very much aware of Bart. Sometimes they would refer to him as "the gentleman" because he wore a Dobbs hat and a suit and tie. And then, after another year had passed and they had come to regard his eccentricities with affection, as Bartie. Although Bart seemed to want to remain detached from the blacks around him, he had a neighborly, jocular relationship with them. He found himself inextricably drawn into the social life at Valois as the men began to greet him cordially.

. . .

For the black regulars, passing time at Valois consists of participating in the same rhythm of various routinized episodes that yield both companionship and solitude. These repetitive sequences are significant because they guarantee the recurrent presence of close acquaintances while establishing them as people who have "things to do." The routines of most of the men therefore demonstrate full awareness of the times when they might be in the way at the cafeteria. Rather than put themselves in the position of spending too much time in one place, they make a point of developing routines that show a certain independence of the establishment. No matter how gratifying collective life can be, excessive time spent in one place can demean a man. This is why routines also function to guard the individual against a likely challenge to his pride. Self-respecting people cannot help experiencing a certain amount of embarrassment when they appear to others to have nothing to do and no place to go. As Luther, a newsstand attendant, says: "A man without things to do is not a man."

Clearly defined personal activities and repetitive processes are constituents of both individual autonomy and collective solidarity. Collective life among the black regulars is therefore characterized by intermittence and recurrence. The same people are usually present at similar times each day or week. But gatherings do not necessarily occur among them with that same regularity. Collective life does not consist of a continuous flow of interaction among all the members. It is, rather, a now-and-then phenomenon that occurs with some unpredictability, in varying arrangements, from day to day. A few habitués routinely sit alone at separate tables and only join members of the larger collectivity on rare occasions; many choose to sit by themselves at least sometimes. Most participate in a variety of subgroups drawn from the wider collectivity of black men. It is not uncommon for individuals to begin by sitting with a small group, later to change partners or move to another table by themselves. Often men who gather at one table will engage in constant conversation; at other times those same men will sit quietly with one another or simply make occasional comments while reading their newspapers in each other's presence. The average length of these gatherings is about 45 minutes but it is not unusual for men to sit together for twice that length of time.

Some of the black cafeteria regulars are retired, others still work. Hanging out, not unlike traditional forms of work,[3] is organized around specific bundles of tasks that need to be accomplished if only to satisfy obligations to oneself. The example of Drake is illustrative. He is a retired butcher who brings lottery tickets to the Greek owners every night in exchange for reimbursement and a cup of tea with lemon. He sometimes works as a substitute at the newsstand on the same block as the restaurant. Seven days a week he travels on the bus from his nursing home, eight blocks away in the ghetto, to Fifty-third Street. Men like Drake create satisfactions for themselves by establishing, in their times of leisure, conditions not unlike those of their former jobs.

Drake's day is organized into tasks. At 10:30 A.M., when he goes to Wendy's to have a cup of coffee and read his morning paper, he is engaging in the first important event of the day. After sitting for three-quarters of an hour, he stretches, glances at the clock, looks around the restaurant, and then goes back to his newspaper. At 11:30 he gets up and goes next door to Valois. What is the significance of Drake's moving from one restaurant to another at the same time every day? The answer might be found in a particular aspect of the world of work which molded him. Most regularly employed people discover that within a job boredom can be minimized by changing the form of activity from time to time.[4] Drake's routine consists of different activities that make the day more interesting than it would be if he were to spend all of his time in one place.

Once he is inside the cafeteria, Drake sits down to talk with his buddies for a few minutes. He comments on the news of the day and makes predictions about future baseball or football games. He says hello and shakes hands with the men he regularly sees. Having checked in, Drake walks up to the front counter where he joshes with the Greeks and orders his usual. When he sits down, he always goes alone to the same table. He sits with his newspaper for at least 45 minutes. At Wendy's he reads the sports section; at Valois he reads the business section. He reads the paper in the same order every day. After he finishes reading, he looks at the clock and shows signs of restlessness, stretching and turning his head. Soon he rises, orders a refill of tea, and joins friends at another table. He is likely to stay with these same people until he leaves the cafeteria at 1:00 P.M.

What is the significance of the various activities this man has built into the time he spends at any one place? It would be simpler merely to observe that Drake goes to Wendy's at a certain time and moves along to the cafeteria. But as just one part of his day illustrates, each event consists of a variety of separate activities. The man who spends his life on a regular job learns to conceive of work as a series of self-contained tasks. This is not the same, of course, as changing the form of activity when Drake moves from Wendy's to Valois. Conceiving of the period spent in one place as a series of self-contained activities keeps a long stretch of time in the same place from seeming interminable.

Hanging out consists of discovering types of activity that result in predictable and desired amounts of companionship, conviviality, and solitude, and the ability to bring about new experiences by changing the conditions within each type of activity. Contrasts and choices among the alternatives are made manifest after men have been inside the cafeteria for an extended period of time. It is common for them to alter the conditions of passing time by joining new people at other tables or even by moving away from a group to sit alone for a period of time. The social world is large enough—especially when the cafeteria is crowded—to ensure that each man can sit with many others without ever getting tired of their company. It is through such processes that men with time on their hands avoid boredom.

There are middle-class people in the Hyde Park neighborhood who view the black men at Valois as bums and loafers. But the men involved—like Drake—experience their days as productive. They have been molded by the ideals and necessities of the conditions of their work. The black regulars seem to be temperamentally suited to establishing routines that provide maximum satisfaction[5] from simply keeping busy, engaging in a range of repetitious activities from day to day. This enables them to preserve their self-esteem and to feel they are taking part in chosen activities, rather than residual ones, and this in turn helps them to feel that their own lives are meaningful.

Although the men often congregate at the same table, it is not unusual for them to settle in separately, without even acknowledging the presence of those with whom they sat only a day or a meal earlier. Normally they mingle with the same general group of sitting buddies, but not always. Sometimes the same men might sit together no more than once every few weeks. But regardless of the extent to which collective life is intermittent, individuals do tend to be present on the same schedules each day. There is always a balance between co-presence and intermittence.

Few of these men are disposed to elicit constant affirmation from their friends and acquaintances. Often, many weeks can pass between the interactions of two people who have warm feelings for one another. In such a context, the "insult" plays an important role in communication. A harmonious relationship is often acknowledged and affirmed through the use of rough words. Here Johnson walked into the restaurant and noticed Claude, whom he had not seen for a while.

"Hey you little fat-faced fucker, where have you been?"

Happy to see his friend, Claude replied joyously, "Dirty bum! You senile old man! When the hell are you going to retire?"

Playful insults of this kind have a role in the now-and-then structure of interaction at Valois.[6] They enable regulars who have not seen one another for a period of time to reaffirm the warmth that existed the last time they were together. Boldness and effrontery serve to remind men that although time has passed, each still has a place in the others' hearts. These ritual indications are symbolic of the stability of relationships, assuring men even as autonomous as these that their importance to others inside the cafeteria is by no means precarious from encounter to encounter.

Regardless of the extent to which collective life takes on a now-and-then character, such rhythmic sequences bring about the recurrent presence of the same group of others in a man's life. Although interaction is frequently interrupted, the routines of those involved are nevertheless important to the group. They are the vehicle by which the black men can depend upon the recurrent presence of specific others in their lives.

If a man is asked why he hangs out with the same people at the same times throughout the year, he may say, as one man did to me, that it is just happenstance or he may deny the existence of repetitive sequences altogether, so as not to imply that he is a creature of habit. But if some do not recognize or admit to their own routines, they are the exception rather than the rule. In fact, the very significance of routines to collective life is sometimes a topic of discussion among the men themselves. Most of them are capable of describing in general terms the sequences they see from day to day. They also show specific awareness of the time patterns of each of their companions. The image of collective life in the minds of group members is partly a function of each man's awareness of the routines of his associates. The sense that one is a member of a collective life is served by knowledge that he participates in a common repetitive process.

A man places a value on his own recurrent patterns and on those of his friends as well. This is the case not only for those with whom he sits frequently but also for persons he encounters at more unpredictable intervals. Comments and questions like "You're late tonight" or "Why have you been late the last few nights?" or "Where have you been? We were worried about you!" are heard over and over again. Whether explicitly stated or not, one reason many men come to the cafeteria at particular times is that they are expected—and they expect others to be there as well. As Leroy says, "Sometimes when I'm tired I know I should come down to Valois because everybody else be coming. People expect to see you. It's part of the day." Particular routines are a vehicle by which both self-respect and companionship with the same people are maintained. The expectation of regular participation in collective life is one of the greatest single sources of support a man can find—short of a wife and children.

Although they are occasionally intolerant of middle-class blacks or university students, the black regulars usually grant unconditional acceptance to other members of their own group, treating one another with respect and socializing with discretion. These poor and solidly working-class black men are notably different from the prevailing stereotypes about them. Despite the contradictory ways in which they are treated by their society, they are consistently directed by standards within themselves.

Though the black regulars sometimes use humor to embarrass their associates in a good-natured way, they do not usually attempt to humiliate them or put them in their place. For them, the disposition to be frank about their own personal weaknesses rather than to create fictions which might serve to increase others' sense of their worth is proper behavior. These remarks about Slim, intended to explain why he is popular, emphasize the significance of sincerity to group members. Harold says: "As far as Slim goes, I like his honesty. Slim sits up there and tells me about people, about what is happening to him. And he is honest about it. He won't cover up what's happened to him. Slim will come around and tell it like it is. He'll say, 'Look, I don't mind giving her all the money, but she shouldn't mistreat me.' That's the way it is. It's Slim's honesty that I like."

. . .

The disposition to be honest rather than to create fictions that might serve to prop up others' sense of one's own value is the true achievement of worth in the eyes of their associates. These are not men who find it necessary to show others what "kinda studs"[7] they are. By living in accordance with principles such as pride, civility, sincerity, and discretion, these men confirm for themselves—rather than proving to others—that they possess some of the most important human virtues. Thus they make evident the extraordinary strength of their sense of self and their ease with their own selves. In each of these qualities one recognizes a different aspect of the fixed conception of self-worth that inheres in these men. Quiet satisfaction, pride, inner strength, and a genuine expressiveness without effusiveness here coalesce in a type of masculinity that is certainly more widespread in reality than in current accounts of the black male in the mass media and in sociology. Slim and his sitting buddies have created a caring community that crosses boundaries of race. The men transcend the usual limits of the male role. They are vulnerable and expressive while living with resolve and remaining directed by standards within themselves.

NOTES

1. For an excellent article, see Mary Jo Bane and David Ellwood, "Is American Business Working for the Poor?" *Harvard Business Review* (September–October, 1991), pp. 58–66. See also Ellwood, *Poor Support: Poverty and the American Family* (New York: Basic Books, 1988).
2. In this book, I adopt the assumptions about social class enunciated by Christopher Jencks, who writes,

    We use terms such as "middle class" and "underclass" because we know that occupation, income, educational credentials, cognitive skills, a criminal record, out-of-wedlock childbearing, and other personal characteristics are somewhat correlated with one another. Class labels provide a shorthand device for describing people who differ along many of these dimensions simultaneously. The term "middle class," for example, evokes someone who has attended college, holds a steady job, earns an adequate income, got married before having children, and has never murdered, raped, robbed, or assaulted anyone. The term "underclass," in contrast, conjures up a chronically jobless high school dropout who has had two or three children out of wedlock, has very little money to support them, and probably has either a criminal record or a history of welfare dependence.

Relatively few people fit either of these stereotypes perfectly. Many people are "middle class" in some respects, "working class" in others, and "underclass" in still others. Those who use class labels always assume, however, that everyone is a member of some class or another. In order to assign everyone to a class, they allow their classes to be internally heterogeneous. If they assign people to classes on the basis of how they make their living, for example, they allow the members of these classes to differ with regard to income, educational credentials, cognitive skills, family structure, and arrest record. Everyone who stops to think recognizes that the world is untidy in this sense. We use class labels precisely because we want to make the world seem tidier than it is. The purpose of these labels is to draw attention to the differences between classes. But by emphasizing differences between classes, such labels inevitably encourage us to forget about the much larger differences that exist *within* classes.

See Christopher Jencks, *Rethinking Social Policy* (Cambridge, MA: Harvard University Press, 1992).

Thus a man like Ted, who works for *Playboy* magazine in the photographic lab and retired from a long career in the army, might be considered a member of the working class by virtue of the jobs he has held. His use of large words might demonstrate a verbal ability associated with a middle-class education. His many trips abroad might also show a middle-class orientation, and his views may fluctuate between a working-class orientation most of the time and a middle-class orientation on occasions.

A man like Jackson, a crane operator and longshoreman, who saw much of the world during the Korean war, will engage in a conversation about Paris that might normally be expected from a middle-class person. He reads newspapers and a high school history book and has a working knowledge of Western history. But he lives in a small one-bedroom apartment, has no telephone, and writes all of his checks at the currency exchange. His wages put him below the poverty line. He has a small wardrobe and very few possessions and can only afford to eat one meal a day.

Because of the difficulties involved in any system of classification, I am wary of making claims regarding what these men typify within the class structure of the black community. Though most of their occupations, lifestyles, and values place them in the working and lower-working class, I leave it to readers to draw their own conclusions for individual members of the group. With regard to the composition of the black class structure, William Julius Wilson writes, "To be somewhat schematic, of the 29 million American blacks, about 20 percent are in the professional middle class, with another 15 percent in noncredentialed white-collar positions. About 33 percent are working class, with half of them vulnerable to job loss, and 33 percent poor. I'd say about half of that poor population is truly disadvantaged, a sort of destitute population." "The Poor Image of Black Men," *New Perspectives Quarterly* 8, no. 3 (summer 1991): 26.

Readers can draw their own conclusions from the table (cited in Martin Kilson and Clement Cottingham, "Thinking about Race Relations," *Dissent* [Fall 1991], p. 521), which summarizes some relevant statistics.

3. Everett Hughes, *The Sociological Eye* (New Brunswick, NJ: Transaction Books, 1984), p. 311.

4. See S. Wyatt and J. A. Fraser, *The Effects of Monotony in Work* (London: His Majesty's Stationery Office, 1929); Elton Mayo, *The Human Problems of an Industrial Civilization* (New York: Macmillan, 1933).

5. These personality characteristics are similar to those described in Wyatt and Fraser, *The Effects of Monotony.*

6. Many accounts of African American language patterns take note of insults which tend to be ritualized. The insults at Valois do not take the form of rhymes or other stereotyped language. For comparisons with ritual insults, see William Labov, "Rules for Ritual Insults," in *Studies in Social Interaction,* ed. David Sudnow (New York: Free Press, 1978); see also Gerald D. Suttles, "Friendship as a Social Institution," in *Social Relationships,* George J. McCall et al. (Chicago: Aldine, 1970), pp. 95–135. For a comparison, see Elijah Anderson, *A Place on the Corner* (Chicago: University of Chicago Press, 1978).

7. This was the phrase used by Elijah Anderson to describe the behavioral tendencies of lower- and working-class men on the street corner. See Anderson, *A Place on the Corner,* p. 51.

17

WOMEN OF THE KLAN

KATHLEEN M. BLEE

This reading by Kathleen Blee is an example of sociological research done with a secondary group. *Secondary groups* tend to be larger, less intimate, and more formal than primary groups. Moreover, most secondary groups are utilitarian in that they serve some function. Blee looks at the history of the Women's Ku Klux Klan (WKKK) and the group characteristics that distinguish this organization from the all-male KKK. Blee finds that the WKKK had a particular social structure that enabled it to obtain a large membership in a short period of time.

Judge R. M. Mann of the second division circuit court in Little Rock, Arkansas, officially chartered the Women of the Ku Klux Klan on June 10, 1923. Its national headquarters were set up in a three-room office in the Ancient Order of United Workmen hall in Little Rock, Arkansas, at some distance from the male Klan's Atlanta headquarters to symbolize the purported independence of the new women's order from its male counterpart.[1]

Membership in the WKKK was open to white Gentile female native-born citizens over 18 years of age who owed no allegiance to any foreign government or sect, that is, who were not Catholic, Socialist, Communist, or so forth. Applicants were required to have been resident in a Klan jurisdiction for at least six months and to be endorsed by at least two Klanswomen or a WKKK kleagle or Imperial Commander. Klanswomen swore to investigate "carefully and personally" the qualifications and background of every candidate they proposed for office. Dues of $10 included one robe and helmet but did not apply to wives of men who were members of the original Klan or a similar organization during Reconstruction. The national offices of the WKKK were supported (in lavish style) by a portion of all dues; an Imperial Tax (a per capita assessment); profits from the sale of regalia, uniforms, stationery, jewelry, and costumes; and by interest and profits from investments.[2]

... The WKKK declared itself an organization "by women, for women, and of women [that] no man is exploiting for his individual gain." The structure of the new women's Klan, worked out in a meeting of WKKK leaders in Asheville, North Carolina, would focus on specific functions and each would have a corresponding task department. The major areas of work for the WKKK's initial efforts were Americanism, education, public amusements, legislation, child welfare and delinquency, citizenship, civics, law enforcement, disarmament, peace, and politics.[3]

. . .

The charter membership of the new WKKK numbered 125,000 women. Most lived in the Midwest, Northwest, and Ozarks region, strongholds of the KKK. Not satisfied with a membership drawn from among the wives, sisters, sweethearts, and mothers of Klansmen, [WKKK leaders] immediately embarked on a recruiting trip throughout the West and Northwest, increasing the WKKK's overall membership and giving the new organization visibility in other regions. [Leaders] also hired female field agents and kleagles who worked with KKK kleagles to bring the message of the women's Klan to all areas of the country. WKKK kleagles, initially often the wives and sisters of KKK officers, worked on a commission basis, retaining a percentage of the initiation dues collected from each new Klanswoman. Organizers used techniques proven effective in the men's Klan: they recruited through personal, family, and work contacts and held highly publicized open meetings to reach politically inactive women and women not from Klan families. In addition, WKKK kleagles worked to recruit women through existing organizations. Female nativist and patriotic societies, in particular, were courted by WKKK organizers who sought to persuade them to merge into the new national women's Klan organization.[4]

Organizers for the women's Klan were effective. Within four months, the WKKK claimed that its membership had doubled to 250,000. By November 1923, 36 states had chapters of the Women of the Ku Klux Klan. Throughout 1924 the WKKK continued to grow, accepting girls over 16 years old and chartering 50 locals a week in 1924. The following year an influential anti-Klan commentator declared that at least three million women had been initiated into the women's Klan. His estimate was no doubt inflated, perhaps by projecting from the recruitment successes of the strong Ohio and Indiana WKKK realms; indeed, modern scholars judge the entire 1920s Klan to have enrolled no more than three to five million members. It is clear, however, that the WKKK attracted a great many women within a short time.[5]

It is impossible to determine the exact number or location of WKKK chapters across the country in the absence of organizational records, but we can estimate the expansion of the women's Klan by examining the pages of Klan periodicals. During the mid-1920s the *Fellowship Forum* published news about WKKK chapters, women's rights organizations, and women's clubs—mingled with recipes and fashion tips. The September 1925 issue carried news from local WKKK chapters in 11 states: New York, Connecticut, Pennsylvania, Michigan, Ohio, Virginia, West Virginia, Kansas, Oklahoma, Texas, and Colorado. Most chapters were located in small towns; the exceptions were those of Oklahoma City and Norfolk. The following September, in 1926, the *Fellowship Forum* included news from WKKK chapters in 16 states: New York, Pennsylvania, Maryland, Virginia, Georgia, Florida, Illinois, Indiana, Ohio, Iowa, Minnesota, Wisconsin, Michigan, Nebraska, California, Washington, and in the District of Columbia as well. Again, most chapters were located outside major metropolitan areas although most members of the WKKK, as of the male Ku Klux Klan, probably resided in large or middle-sized cities. Other issues of the *Fellowship Forum* show a similar geographical dispersion of the women's Klan. Many chapters clustered in Pennsylvania, Ohio, Indiana, Michigan, and New York—states where the KKK was also strong—but chapters existed in the West, on the Atlantic Coast, and along the North-South border.[6]

. . .

In chartering its new women's organization, the Klan emphasized the role of women as helpmates to Klansmen. Women's cooperation and assistance were needed, Klansmen insisted, to ensure that the political agenda of the men's Klan could be implemented. The KKK press talked often of the WKKK as its "women's auxiliary" and argued that the men's Klan had created the WKKK with the same ideals and principles as its father organization.[7]

Klansmen were unsure, however, about what Klan membership would mean for women. Women might be convenient symbols for mobilizing men into the Klan, but women's actual political participation was another matter. An early advertisement written by the KKK to solicit members for an organization of Klanswomen illustrates the men's ambivalence. Although it was a recruitment pitch for the WKKK, the advertisement also pointed to a fearful potential in political involvement to masculinize women. Many worry, the ad suggested, that "giving [women] the ballot would foster masculine boldness and restless independence, which might detract from the modesty and virtue of womanhood." To this dilemma, the KKK posed as a solution the creation of a separate organization for Klanswomen. The WKKK would allow women to be politically active without "sacrifice of that womanly dignity and modesty we all admire." The key to the delicate balancing act between a "masculine" and a "feminine" political involvement, according to the KKK, was acquiescence of Klanswomen in the political agenda of Klansmen. By adopting as a whole the Klan's agenda of support for white Protestantism, the English language, public schools, the Bible, and immigration restrictions, women could exercise their newly granted enfranchisement without relying on "masculine" traits of political judgment and strategizing.[8]

A related tactic of recruitment for the women's organization stressed women's political *potential*. Although ostensibly supporting women's involvement in politics, this approach emphasized women's ignorance and limited abilities in the political arena. Excluded from the world of political debate, white Protestant women had developed only a "moral influence" in politics. Their special roles in the family and home gave women good political instincts, the Klan argued, but not mature political judgment. Women now needed to be taught (by men) those principles and attitudes that the world of politics required: clear thinking, intelligence, and collective and individual responsibility for maintaining the principles of Anglo-Saxon Protestantism. Women might have gained the ballot by law, but the ability to use it intelligently required further education—an education the Klan was prepared to provide through its women's organization.

. . .

The WKKK advertised its ability to champion the goals of white womanhood as a standard recruiting tool for new members. Its Washington chapter, for example, argued that white Protestant native-born women had common political interests and would be more effective in pursuing those interests if they were politically organized. Their recruitment advertisement posed a number of questions for women to consider:

> *Are you interested in the welfare of our Nation?*
> *As an enfranchised woman are you interested in Better Government?*
> *Do you not wish for the protection of Pure Womanhood?*
> *Shall we uphold the sanctity of the American Home?*
> *Should we not interest ourselves in Better Education for our children?*
> *Do we not want American teachers in our American schools?*

"Patriotic women," those who answered these questions in the affirmative, were needed in the women's Klan. Protestant white women, the WKKK insisted, shared a concern for their children's education and the welfare of the country. It is the "duty of the American Mother" to stamp out vice and immorality in the nation. Joining the Klan was an effective avenue for the political work that white Protestant women needed to do.[9]

The Women's Klan

To understand the nature of the new women's Klan, we need to examine the beliefs, organizations, rituals, and activities of the WKKK in comparison with those of the men's order. But we must use caution in our comparison.

When Klanswomen swore to uphold the "sanctity of the home and chastity of womanhood" they echoed the words, but not necessarily the sentiments, of their male Klan counterparts. Although a simple listing of WKKK and KKK principles and rituals would suggest that there was little difference between the two organizations, we must understand how these were interpreted and justified by each organization.

Beliefs

On one level, many principles of the new women's Klan appear identical to the racist and xenophobic politics of the first and second men's Klans. The WKKK supported militant patriotism, national quotas for immigration, racial segregation, and antimiscegenation laws. Klanswomen cited the need to safeguard the "eternal supremacy" of the white race against a "rising tide of color" and decried Catholic and Jewish influence in politics, the schools, the media, and the business world. [Lulu] Markwell [of Arkansas, the first Imperial Commander of the WKKK,] . . . saw the mission of the women's Klan as "fighting for the same principles as the Knights of the Ku Klux Klan," although she reserved for the WKKK a special interest in "work peculiar to women's organization, such as social welfare work [and] the prevention of juvenile delinquency." [10]

Like the men's Klan, the WKKK often used politically palatable symbols to present its agenda of nativism and racial hatred to the public. It called for separation of church from state when crusading against Roman Catholic political influence, for free public schools when seeking to destroy parochial schools, and for the purity of race when seeking racial segregation and restricted immigration. In private, the racial bigotry of the WKKK was fully as vicious as that of the KKK, as in Klanswomen's condemnation of "mulatto leaders forced to remain members of the negro group [who] aspire to white association because of their white blood [thus] boldly preaching racial equality." [11]

But if many of the WKKK's basic principles followed existing doctrines of the men's Klan, women and men did not always have a common perception of the problems that required Klan action. Klansmen of the 1920s denounced interracial marriage for its destructive genetic outcomes; their Klan forefathers fought interracial sexuality to maintain white men's sexual access to white and black women. Klanswomen, however, saw a different danger in miscegenation: the destruction of white marriages by untrustworthy white men who "betray their own kind."

In many cases, women and men in the Klan took different messages from common symbols. Klansmen praised womanhood to underscore the correctness of male supremacy; Klanswomen used the symbol to point out the inequities that women faced in society and politics. Klansmen sought political inspiration in the "great achievements" of white American Protestantism, but

Klanswomen read history differently. Rather than mimicking the men's empty gestures of praise for "true American women" in the past, the WKKK complained that women had been excluded from public politics throughout most of this glorious history, even though "our mothers have ever been Klanswomen at heart, sharing with our fathers the progress and development of our country." Klanswomen embraced the KKK's racist, anti-Catholic, and anti-Semitic agenda and symbols of American womanhood but they used these to argue as well for equality for white Protestant women.[12]

Organization

For the most part the WKKK adopted the militaristic hierarchical style of the KKK. An Excellent Commander served as president, with a four-year term of office and responsibility for issuing, suspending, and revoking the charters of locals and realms (state organizations). Next in the chain of command was the klaliff (vice-president), who acted as presiding officer of the Imperial Klonvokation; the klokard (lecturer), responsible for disseminating Klankraft; and the kludd (chaplain), who presided over Klan ritual. Other major officers included the kligrapp (secretary), bonded for $25,000 to handle minor Klan funds; the Klabee (treasurer), bonded for $50,000 to handle major Klan funds; and the officers of Klan ritual and ceremony, including the kladd (conductor), klagoro (inner guard), klexter (outer guard), night hawk (in charge of candidates), klokan (investigator and auditor), and kourier (messenger).

Each realm or group of realms of the WKKK was organized by a Major Kleagle with subjurisdictions organized by minor kleagles and supervised by a series of Realm Commanders and Imperial Commanders. Upon retirement from office, Excellent Commanders became Klan Regents, Realm Commanders became Grand Regents, and Imperial Commanders became Imperial Regents. In keeping with the military arrangement of the WKKK, nearly all offices were subdivided into further levels of authority. The rank of kourier, for example, was subdivided into that of kourier private, corporal, sergeant, lieutenant, captain, major, and colonel. Ranks carried more than symbolic authority, as failure to obey the command of an officer was defined as insubordination and could bring harsh punishment.[13]

The similarity between the organization of the male and female Klans is significant. Consistently, WKKK denied that it was like the auxiliary of a fraternal association, "merely a social order for social purposes." Instead, Klanswomen embraced the mixture of individualism and deference to authority that characterized the male Klan. Like Klansmen, Klanswomen had at least ostensible opportunities to rise within the organization through individual effort and talent; both organizations used a strict command hierarchy. In this, the WKKK claimed to stand apart from the outside world that discouraged women from individual efforts and achievements. By valuing both obedience and individual effort, the WKKK would "inculcate patriotism, upbuild character, and develop true clannishness among women."[14]

Other features of the WKKK show the contrasting aspects of obedience and commonality that characterized the KKK. Like their male counterparts, Klanswomen typically wore white robes with masks and helmets, although some chapters used red robes. Masks were clearly intended to disguise the identity of Klanswomen in public, but the WKKK insisted that masks had only a symbolic purpose. Through masking Klanswomen hid their individuality as well as identity, exemplifying the Klan motto "not for self, but for others." Similar claims were made about Klan robes. Although in fact officers' robes had more colors and accoutrements, Klanswomen asserted that their robes symbolized the equality of all women within Klankraft. Robes set Klanswomen apart from the invidious world of social class distinctions in fashion, leveling the divisions of wealth so pervasive in alien society. "As we look upon a body of women robed in white we realize that we are on a common level of sisterhood and fraternal union." [15]

The detailed laws and regulations of the WKKK ensured obedience to authority. Women, no less than men, were expected to conduct themselves according to klannish principles. The WKKK treated as major offenses those of treason to the Klan, violating the oath of allegiance, disrespect of virtuous womanhood, violation of the U.S. Constitution, the "pollution" of Caucasian blood through miscegenation, and other acts unworthy of a Klanswoman. Minor offenses included profane language or vulgarity during a klonklave, acts against the best interest of the Klan or a Klanswoman, and refusal or failure to obey the Excellent Commander. The Excellent Commander assessed penalties for minor offenses; a tribunal handled major offenses. Violators faced reprimand, suspension, banishment forever, or complete ostracism.

Ritual

At least as central as laws and hierarchy to both women's and men's Klans was an elaborate and intricate web of ceremonials, rites, and protocols designed to increase members' commitment to the order and to sharpen the distinctions between insiders and outsiders ("aliens"). Like the men's Klan, the WKKK used threatening, frightening, and challenging rituals to ensure loyalty and instill fear in its members. Both the WKKK and the KKK referred to themselves as "invisible empires," conveying the Klan's aspirations to universal jurisdiction. Secret klannish words gave members an immediate way to recognize sister and brother Klan members. In Klan ceremonies, days of the week were not Sunday, Monday, and so forth as in the alien world but were desperate, dreadful, desolate, doleful, dismal, deadly, and dark. Weeks of the month became weird, wonderful, wailing, weeping, and woeful. January through December were labeled appalling, frightful, sorrowful, mournful, horrible, terrible, alarming, furious, fearful, hideous, gloomy, and bloody.

The Klan changed historical time as well, setting it to the ascendancy of white Gentile Americans. The reign of Incarnation included all time up to the American Revolution. A first reign of Reincarnation lasted from the beginning of the revolutionary war until the organization of the first Ku Klux Klan in 1866. A second reign of Reincarnation extended from 1866 to 1872, the collapse of the first KKK. The third reign of Reincarnation began in 1915, the reorganization of the KKK, and extended from the present into the future.[16]

The naturalization klonklave was typical of women's Klan rituals. An altar was placed in the center of a room or in an open-air gathering place surrounded by stations with water, a Bible, a flag, and a sword. WKKK officers entered the klonklave, kissed the flag, proceeded to the altar, and saluted the Excellent Commander or other presiding officer, raising their masks to reveal their identities to this official. When all officers were assembled, the kladd certified that everyone present was a valid member of the WKKK. The entrance to the building or park was secured by the klexter and klagoro and then all masks were removed.

Once assembled, officers were questioned about the seven sacred symbols of Klankraft in a ritualized catechism oddly patterned after the catechism ritual of the Roman Catholic church. Each officer repeated a litany of symbols: the Bible (God), fiery cross (sacrifice and service), flag (U.S. Constitution), sword (law enforcement and national defense), water (purity of life and unity of purpose), mask (secrecy, unselfishness, and banishment of individuality), and robe (purity and equality). Between each restatement of Klan doctrine, the audience and officers sang a Christian hymn.

During the naturalization ceremony, a klokard led the class of candidates through the oath of admission. Candidates swore that they were serious, qualified for admission, believers in klannishness, and willing to practice klannishness toward other Klanswomen and work for the eternal maintenance of white supremacy. Candidates then were greeted by officers and members and congratulated for their "womanly decision to forsake the world of selfishness and fraternal alienation and emigrate to the delectable bounds of the Invisible Empire and become its loyal citizens." At this point, the Excellent Commander conferred the obligation and oath of admission on the assembled candidates and baptized the new members by pouring water and saying:

> *With this transparent, life-giving, powerful God-given fluid, more precious and far more significant than all the sacred oils of the ancients, I set you apart from the women of your daily association to the great and honorable task you have voluntarily allotted yourselves as citizens of the Invisible Empire, Women of the Ku Klux Klan. As Klanswomen, may your character be as transparent, your life purpose as powerful, your motive in all things as magnanimous and as pure, and your Klannishness as real and as faithful as the manifold drops herein.*

As a quartet of Klanswomen sang and the assembly prayed, the klannish initiates responded with their own ritual. They dipped fingers in water and touched their shoulders, saying "In body," and their foreheads, saying "In mind," then waved their hands in the air, saying "In spirit," and made a circle above their heads saying "In life." The klokard then imparted the secret signs and words of the Klan. The ceremony closed with an opportunity to raise issues from the floor (probably an infrequent occurrence), followed by a restatement of the need for secrecy in the presence of aliens. The night hawk extinguished the fiery cross, the kludd performed a benediction, and the klonklave was declared closed.[17]

Ceremonies for higher levels in the WKKK followed a similar pattern, although more was required of the candidates. Acceptance into the second-degree obligation, the highest rank below officer level, required candidates to make pledges against slandering other Klanswomen or Klansmen, against materialism, and against selfishness and similar temptations. Candidates for advanced degrees also made greater pledges of duty, swearing that "when pleasure interferes with my duty as Klanswoman . . . I will set aside pleasure"; they affirmed their loyalty, vowing not to recommend "faithless, contemptuous, careless, or indifferent" women for advancement in the order.[18]

Activities

It is difficult to compare the political practices of the women's and men's Klans, as both varied considerably across the nation and over time but the national agendas of each organization give some indication of the differences. The political agenda of the men's Klan ranged from infiltration into legislative and judicial politics on the state, municipal, and county level to acts of violence and terroristic intimidation against Jews, Catholics, and blacks. Many Klansmen, though, used the KKK as primarily a male fraternity, a social club of like-minded white Protestants.[19]

The women's Klan similarly showed a range of activities and purposes. On a national level, the women's Klan worked to legitimate the violence and terrorism of the men's order. It published and distributed a detailed guide to the proper display of the American flag and a pocket-sized version of the U.S. Constitution and circulated a card reminding Protestants to attend church faithfully; each item prominently displayed the WKKK logo. The WKKK involved itself in national legislative politics, although without much success. It actively supported the creation of a federal Department of Education to bolster public schools and undermine parochial education and opposed U.S. membership in the World Court. Although it claimed to be interested in safeguarding white Protestant children and the home, the WKKK opposed a 1924 bill outlawing child labor on the grounds that it was "a Communistic, Bolshevistic scheme." That same year Klanswomen were active in blocking an attempt by anti-Klan forces to introduce a plank in the national Democratic party platform condemning the Ku Klux Klan.[20]

At times the women's Klan sought to portray itself as an organization of social work and social welfare. One national WKKK speaker announced that she left social work for the "broader field of Klankraft" because of the Klan's effectiveness in promoting morality and public welfare. Many chapters claimed to collect food and money for the needy, although these donations typically went to Klan families, often to families of Klan members arrested for rioting and vigilante activities. A powerful Florida WKKK chapter operated a free day nursery, charging that Catholic teachers had ruined the local public schools.[21]

Some WKKK chapters ran homes for wayward girls. These homes served two purposes: to protect the virtue of Protestant women who were tempted by a life of vice and to underscore the danger faced by delinquent girls placed in Catholic-controlled reform schools. The Shreveport, Louisiana, WKKK chapter, for example, based its fund-raising for a Protestant girls' home on the story of a woman whose unhappy fate it was to be sent to a Catholic reform home after being convicted of selling whiskey and prostituting her teenaged daughters.[22]

Another activity of many WKKK locals was the crusade against liquor and vice. WKKK chapters worked to "clean up" a motion picture industry in which they claimed Jewish owners spewed a steady diet of immoral sex onto the screen. Other chapters fought against liquor, as evidenced by the case of Myrtle Cook, a Klanswoman and president of the Vinton, Iowa, WCTU, who was assassinated for documenting the names of suspected bootleggers. In death, Cook was eulogized by Klanswomen and WCTU members alike; all business in Vinton was suspended for the two hours of the funeral.[23]

WKKK chapters in many states were active also in campaigns to prohibit prenuptial religious agreements about future children, bar interracial marriage, outlaw the Knights of Columbus (a Catholic fraternal society), remove Catholic encyclopedias from public schools, bar the use of Catholic contractors by public agencies, and exclude urban (i.e., Jewish and Catholic) vacationers in majority-Protestant suburban resorts.[24]

Some WKKK locals, though, functioned largely for the personal and financial success of their members. F. C. Dunn of Lansing, Michigan, made a fortune after introducing her invention, a new antiseptic powder, at a local WKKK meeting.[25]

Klanswomen tended not to be involved in physical violence and rioting, but there were exceptions. In the aftermath of a 1924 Klan riot in Wilkinsburg, Pennsylvania, Mamie H. Bittner, a 39-year-old mother of three children and member of the Homestead, Pennsylvania, WKKK testified that she, along with thousands of other Klanswomen paraded through town, carrying heavy maple riot clubs. Moreover, Bittner claimed that the WKKK was teaching its members to murder and kill in the interest of the Klan.[26]

The activities of the women's Klan were shaped largely by the existing political agenda of the men's Klan. It is not accurate, however, to portray the WKKK as a dependent auxiliary of the men's order. Klanswomen created a distinctive ideology and political agenda that infused the Klan's racist and nativist goals with ideas of equality between white Protestant women and men. The ideology and politics of Klanswomen and Klansmen were not identical, though at many points they were compatible. But women and men of the Klan movement sometimes found themselves in contention as women changed from symbols to actors in the Klan.

The difference between the women's and men's Klan grew from an underlying message in the symbol of white womanhood. By using gender and female sexual virtue as prime political symbols, the Klan shaped its identity through intensely masculinist themes, as an organization of real men. Clearly, this was an effective recruitment strategy for the first Klan. But in the 1920s, as both financial and political expediency and significant changes in women's political roles prompted the Klan to accept female members, an identity based on symbols of masculine exclusivity and supremacy became problematic. In addition, if Klansmen understood that defending white womanhood meant safeguarding white Protestant supremacy and male supremacy, many women heard the message differently. The WKKK embraced ideas of racial and religious privilege but rejected the messages of white female vulnerability. In its place Klanswomen substituted support for women's rights and a challenge to white men's political and economic domination.

NOTES

1. *Arkansas Gazette,* June 10, 1923, 1.
2. WKKK, *Constitution and Laws* (WKKK, 1927).
3. *Fellowship Forum,* Feb. 23, 1924, p. 6; Nov. 17, 1923, p. 6; *Imperial Night-Hawk,* Oct. 31, 1923, p. 1; Aug. 1, 1923, p. 8.
4. *The Truth;* also, *Fiery Cross,* July 13, 1923, p. 1; Sue Wilson Abbey ("The Ku Klux Klan in Arizona, 1921–25," *Journal of Arizona History* 14 [Spring 1973]: 10–30) discusses how Tom Akers was sent to organize the Phoenix, Arizona, chapter of the WKKK in 1923; Loucks, *The Ku Klux Klan in Pennsylvania,* pp. 150–56; *Arkansas Gazette,* June 10, 1925, p. 1.
5. *Arkansas Gazette,* Oct. 7, 1923, p. 12; see also *Imperial Night-Hawk,* Oct. 31, 1923, p. 1; *New York Times,* Nov. 7, 1923, p. 15; Kenneth Jackson, *The Ku Klux Klan;* William M. Likins, *The Ku Klux Klan, Its Rise and Fall; Patriotism Capitalized or Religion Turned into Gold* (privately published, 1925).
6. See Kenneth Jackson, *The Ku Klux Klan; Fellowship Forum,* 1924–1928.
7. *Imperial Night-Hawk,* June 13, 1923, p. 5; Aug. 8, 1923, p. 6.
8. *Fiery Cross,* Mar. 2, 1923, p. 4; *Fellowship Forum,* June 2, 1923, p. 8.
9. *Watcher on the Tower,* Sept. 15, 1923, p. 12.
10. *Imperial Night-Hawk,* June 20, 1923, p. 8.
11. WKKK, *Ideals of the Women of the Ku Klux Klan* (WKKK, 1923), pp. 2–3, 4–5; WKKK *Women of America!,* pp. 6–7, 9–10, 13–14 (WKKK, ca. 1923); WKKK, *Kreed* (WKKK, ca. 1924).
12. WKKK, *Women of America!;* WKKK, *Constitution and Laws,* pp. 6–7; WKKK, *Kreed;* WKKK, *Ideals,* pp. 2–3, 4–5; *Imperial Night-Hawk,* June 20, 1923, p. 8; May 14, 1924, p. 7; advertisement in *Dawn,* Aug. 11, 1923, p. 2.
13. WKKK, *Constitution and Laws.* From statement by Victoria Rogers, Major Kleagle for the Realm of Illinois, in *Dawn,* Feb. 2, 1924, p. 12.
14. WKKK, *Women of America!*
15. WKKK, *Catalogue of Official Robes and Banners* (WKKK, ca. 1923); WKKK, *Kloran or Ritual of the WKKK* (WKKK, 1923).
16. WKKK, *Constitution and Laws.*
17. WKKK, *Kloran or Ritual of the WKKK.* The *New York Times* (Aug. 19, 1923, p. 2) has

detailed coverage of a naturalization ceremony involving 700 members of the women's Klan in Allenwood, New Jersey.

18. WKKK, *Second Degree Obligation of the Women of the Ku Klux Klan* (WKKK, n.d.); see also WKKK, *Installation Ceremonies of the Women of the Ku Klux Klan* (WKKK, n.d.).

19. Hiram Evans, *The Menace* and *The Attitude of the Knights of the Ku Klux Klan toward the Roman Catholic Hierarchy* (KKK, ca. 1923).

20. WKKK, *Flag Book* (WKKK, 1923); Ku Klux Klan record collection (hereafter cited as KKK), Indiana State Library; WKKK, *U.S. Constitution* (WKKK, n.d.); *Fiery Cross*, Oct. 10, 1924, p. 5; *Fellowship Forum*, July 5, 1924, pp. 6–7.

21. *Fellowship Forum*, Sept. 19, 1925, p. 6; July 5, 1924; Mar. 3, 1926, p. 6. The anonymous speaker is identified only as a "Klan female speaker." January 1925 issues of the *Fellowship Forum* have other examples of such self-promotion, as does that of May 1, 1926, p. 7; see also Chalmers, *Hooded Americanism*.

22. *Imperial Night-Hawk*, May 9, 1923, p. 2; see also *New York Times*, July 11, 1926, p. 7.

23. *Arkansas Gazette,* Sept. 8, 1925, p. 1; *Fiery Cross*, Mar. 30, 1923, p. 5; *Fellowship Forum,* Jan. 24, 1925, p. 6; *New York Times*, Sept. 9, 1925, p. 1; Sept. 19, 1925, p. 20; Sept. 11, 1925, p. 5.

24. *New York Times*, June 3, 1923, sect.1, pt. 2, p. 8; *Fellowship Forum*, Jan. 24, 1925, p. 6; *New York Times*, Mar. 21, 1922, p. 6; Dec. 8, 1922, p. 9; *Imperial Night-Hawk*, May 9, 1923, p. 3; *Fiery Cross*, Oct. 10, 1924, p. 5; *Fellowship Forum*, Jan. 17, 1925, p. 6; July 5, 1924, p. 6. For a detailed analysis of the conflict over the Klan during the 1924 election, especially during the Democratic party convention, see Lee Allen, "The McAdoo Campaign for the Presidential Nomination of 1924," *Journal of Southern History* 29 (1963): 211–18; "The Klan and the Democrats," *Literary Digest*, June 14, 1924, pp. 12–13; Rice, *Ku Klux Klan*; Chalmers, *Hooded Americanism*, pp. 282–90.

25. *Fiery Cross*, July 18, 1924, p. 6. In an odd twist—"because of their affiliation with the KKK"—two women were excluded from the will of a third woman with whom they had lived for 16 years (will of Alice Reid, filed in surrogate's court in Brooklyn in 1928 and reported in the *New York Times*, Oct. 10, 1928, p. 16).

26. Testimony of Mamie H. Bittner in U.S. District Court for the Western District of Pennsylvania, *Knights of the Ku Klux Klan, Plaintiff, v. Rev. John F. Strayer et al., Defendants*, 1928 (Equity 1897 in National Archives–Philadelphia Branch; William M. Likins, *The Trail of the Serpent* (n.p., 1928), pp. 64–67.

18

THE VIEW FROM EAST SWALLOW

KAI ERIKSON

Communities are another type of social structure often studied by sociologists. This selection by Kai Erikson investigates what happens to a community after the discovery of an environmentally toxic condition. Erikson argues that disasters change the relationships between individuals and between individuals and social structures. As the gas spill in this middle-class neighborhood in Fort Collins, Colorado, illustrates, the community itself is forever altered as the disaster takes center stage in the individuals' lives.

In the summer of 1985 the operators of a Royal Petroleum service station on the corner of South College Avenue and East Swallow Road in Fort Collins, Colorado, discovered that they had been experiencing significant inventory shortages over a period of several years. They solved the leakage problem by replacing three "incontinent" underground tanks.

Later that year David and Patricia Losser, who lived in the first house down East Swallow Road, were alarmed by a sharp smell that seemed to fill their home. It turned out not to be natural gas, as they at first supposed, but vapors drifting to the surface from underground pools of petroleum. By year's end the Lossers had been forced to evacuate, and in the months that followed, waves of concern began to radiate in slow-motion ripples down East Swallow Road as people came to understand that a plume of petroleum was moving eastward with the sureness of a glacier. Before long, 16 families living within the affected area (together with a handful of others who owned property in the neighborhood) brought suit against Royal Petroleum and another oil company.

East Swallow Road is a pleasant residential street with neatly spaced ranch-style houses and comfortable backyards. To a stranger visiting in 1989, the only evidences of turmoil on that block-long stretch of homes were a fierce and incongruous chain link fence around what had been the Losser home marked by a sign warning of "danger" and an occasional monitoring well protruding from a private lawn or a public street.

The residents of East Swallow lived for the most part on modest incomes. Roughly half of them (averaging 71 years old) were retired, and the other half (averaging a shade under 50) were well into what most of them would call their middle years. So it was an older group, as such neighborhoods go. Only two of the 16 households contained younger children, and the parents in both cases were in their 40s.

The East Swallow neighborhood belonged at the very center of the American social landscape occupationally: a machinist, a bookkeeper, a construction foreman, a teacher; a handful of people in sales, government service, and clerical work of one kind or another; another handful trying to make a go of home businesses.

And it belonged at the center of the American social landscape geographically. Most of the retired residents came from small towns in the Middle West (South Dakota, Iowa, Nebraska, Missouri), and while the younger residents often came from farther afield, most of them had spent their adult lives in that part of the country and expected to continue to do so. Even though the neighborhood itself was relatively new, many of the residents were living in the first homes they had ever owned, and most were living in the last homes they expected to own.

So it was an altogether familiar grouping of Americans, acquainted with hard work, tuned to small-town values, entitled to the feeling that they had earned whatever comforts and securities had come their way.

. . .

The residents of East Swallow, seen as a group, have been damaged appreciably by the gasoline spill [resulting from the service station's leaking tanks] and the events that followed. The apprehension and stress reported by virtually everyone in the neighborhood are a product not only of inner psychological struggles but of the fact that a good part of the immediate social world on which people depend for security and coherence—home, neighborhood, wider community—has been harmed in decisive ways.

The degree of dread and anxiety expressed by the plaintiff group [in the suit they filed against Royal Petroleum] is so sharp and so widely shared that it becomes a sociological finding as well as a clinical one, if only in the sense that it can be said to form the prevailing social temper—the culture, even—of the whole community.

It can take the form of a tension so profound that it results in something approaching real physical distress:

> *That bothers me more than anything. And I just tie up in a knot. My muscles are tight and tense and I am nervous. I can't relax, I can't enjoy myself. . . . I just tie up in such a knot that my muscles hurt. It's my muscles and my legs and my thighs and my back and my neck and shoulders. It's such a tension and I can't let go. . . . It hurts. It just plain—you can't see stress—it just hurts.*

> *Physically ill? Sleepless nights, if that's physically ill—yes, I have had them. Being nervous, upset, sometimes sullen, snappy—if those are physical symptoms, then I'll clarify it: Yes, I have had them. But I haven't had a big lump grow on the end of my nose. No parts have fallen off.*

It can take the form of an apprehension so deep that it almost dominates one's spirit.

> *I don't know if I have come across with this yet or not, but I have a lot of fear, a lot of fear. I have fear for my family, I have fear for myself. I have a lot of anger. . . . I went from a human being that I felt I was an average, good, human being—caring, loving. I'm full of anger. I'm full of frustration. I'm full of fear. I have a lot of emotions. I feel that my life has gone from a normal to a real hellish, hellish situation.*

> *I fear for myself having been exposed to it, for my parents who are still exposed to it. Everyone in the neighborhood. I fear an explosion. That something may set off a spark and blow the entire thing up. I fear for my parents' health, my future health, what effects this may have on me.*

It can take the form of a sense of helplessness and a feeling of upset so overwhelming that it makes strong, resolute, and remarkably capable men cry (this is from the deposition of a burly man of 50 used to controlling the spaces he occupies):

No, we never wanted to sell that house. We wanted to stay. But—you got to excuse me. Shit. Excuse me. You know, hell, I can't explain this. I am like a bawling baby anymore. It is just something that happens, and I can't control it. I'm sorry. . . . But this has been pure hell. I've never experienced anything like this in my life. I never dreamed it would happen to me, but, goddamn, it did. I want to tear things up. I want to argue with people. I want to fight. And that's not me.

And it affects the youngest members of the community every bit as much as their elders. The comments below were both made by mothers, the first speaking of a 14-year-old son, and the second of a six-year-old son.

Well, he asked me the other day, "How are we in danger? We're just fine here." I said to him that we are breathing fumes and they are not good for your health and we could come up with a disease of some kind or cancer or something and he had a funny look on his face. Maybe it finally hit him. He's old enough, and you're hearing this and it's sinking in.

I have told him that there is a gasoline spill, and we will move out to my sister's house upon indication. And they want to know why. We told them because we believe that the house is unsafe to live in. That it makes us sick and we want to stay where it is healthier. . . . [W]hen they were at my sister's house and we were going to town for the day, he would say, "I don't want to go to the gas house." That's his words.

The intensity and persistence of such feelings will be no source of surprise to social and behavioral scientists familiar with accidents involving toxic poisons. . . . The evidence from communities that have been affected by toxic contamination together with other findings that have recently emerged from the new field of risk assessment is now quite compelling: People in general find accidents involving toxins a good deal more threatening than both natural hazards of even the most dangerous kind and mechanical mishaps of considerable destructive power. Toxic poisons clearly unnerve human beings in new and special ways.

For one thing, it is by now a familiar finding that toxic emergencies are often harder to deal with than natural ones because they are not framed by distinct beginnings or ends. The danger one is exposed to has no duration, no natural term; and as a result one remains in a permanent state of alarm and anxiety.

. . .

For all practical purposes, then, the accident is still in progress, and it involves agents that are all the more dreaded because they cannot be detected by the usual human senses. People worry that the accident still in progress may yet result in explosions:

When I think I want to do something within the house or out in the yard I hesi-
tate. What if I should drill holes to put in a post? What if I ignite something? I
stop and hesitate. I'm very careful about that—about any trash around, any
matches around, or anything like that. I don't want to start an explosion on my
property.

Scared. Scared. And especially when I found out later on that the fumes were on
this side of the street. It's the fumes that can blow you up. The gasoline won't ex-
plode, but fumes will. . . . And you just sit here, like on a time bomb, waiting for
whatever, I guess.

And people worry that the accident still in progress may have done—and
may yet do—lasting harm to themselves or their loved ones. The point is not
that most plaintiffs have reason to suppose that dreadful things have already
happened to them, although the great majority of them express real concerns
about what the future has in store for them medically and some are convinced that the health of those who live in their households has already been
affected. The problem is that they can never know what is happening to
them or has already happened to them, and so they remain—despite themselves, as often as not—on constant alert:

I know when they tested in the soil there was hydrocarbons next door in the
ground, so I know it's there. I know it's locked in the soil. And the thing that
bothers me here . . . is that every time something happens, especially to the chil-
dren healthwise, you wonder if it isn't because of this or if it isn't aggravated by
this. . . . A cold isn't just a cold. It becomes "Is this gasoline-related?" And then
you get on this guilt trip wondering if it's on account of that.

I mean no tests have been done on my property. I don't know whether it's con-
taminated or not. . . . I have a regular physical every year. No big deal. I'm al-
ways overweight but healthy, you know—that kind of stuff. But the last time
I went in I had a raised liver count on one enzyme. No big deal. Just one thing.
Just barely. But then you think "Oh shit, could it be from the—" I mean I'm not
supposed to be exposed to it, but maybe I am.

All of these feelings together form a community climate that is the context of the other points I plan to make here.

Members of the plaintiff group report a very strong sense of being out of
control, of being caught up in forces that capture them and take them over.
They feel helpless, pushed around, worked over, pummeled.

These feelings of helplessness and vulnerability are so common in moments of crisis, as we noted earlier, that they are one of the identifying psychological symptoms of "trauma" and a prominent feature of what is now
widely called "the disaster syndrome." But they have a special urgency in
places like East Swallow—first because toxic poisons are still absorbed into
the very tissue of the neighborhood, leaving the persons who live there vulnerable, and second because the slowness of all efforts to find redress leaves

them more or less frozen in place, unable to take charge of their own destinies or even to cope effectively. Plaintiffs speak of being "hostages" or "prisoners," of being "besieged" and "trapped":

> *A disaster. I'd say it's a neighborhood of pretty unhappy, hurting people, stuck in a situation that they can't get out of. . . . We feel helpless. We feel trapped. We feel—you have no control, no control.*

It is hard to think of a more basic tenet of the American way—and maybe even especially for those who come from small towns and farms, as the majority of these plaintiffs do—than that individuals should be independent and self-reliant, free to chart their own lives, to take care of their own families, and to command the spaces they earn title to.

. . .

The residents of East Swallow who were exposed to the effects of the gasoline spill complain—with considerable justice, one has to assume—that the value of their homes has declined precipitously as a result of recent events. In one sense, of course, that is a financial matter and outside the scope of this report: Plaintiffs have invested large amounts of capital into the dwellings they occupy, and they are understandably concerned about the safety of those investments. For many, maybe most of them, it is not just a matter of losing a valuable possession; it is a matter of placing a life's savings at risk.

> *Well, it doesn't make me feel sick or it doesn't make me feel nervous to the extent that my hands shake, but when we think about the loss of our property, the value of our property, it concerns us very much. Most of our estate is in that home. . . . [I]f we would lose our property, if it would be condemned and we move out, it's possible that we would lose everything we own.*

> *Well, we feel that the value of our property has taken a nose dive. It is our only security. We don't feel that it's stable. If we can't sell it, we can't relocate, we can't move, we can't expand or change. We feel that we're sort of stuck.*

But it is also clear that the people of East Swallow have invested a great deal more than money in their homes. They have invested great quantities of time, energy, skill, devotion, pride. They have invested a part of themselves, in short, and when something happens to that property, the part of the self that was thus invested is at risk. People experience damage done to the homes they cherish as damage to themselves.

It is well understood by social and behavioral scientists who are familiar with accidents of this kind that the loss of a home can be profoundly traumatic. I wrote in my report on the Buffalo Creek flood of 1972, for example, that a home in which a person has made a real personal investment "is not simply an expression of one's taste; it is the outer edge of one's personality, a part of the self itself. And the loss of that part of the self . . . is akin to the loss of flesh." Other researchers have come to the same general conclusion. A well-known study of a tornado in Texas, for instance, reported that people who had lost their homes felt as though "they had lost part of themselves." And an equally well-known study of an urban relocation project in the East End of Boston was entitled, simply, "Grieving for a Lost Home."[1]

The East Swallow plaintiffs have not—yet—lost their homes, and I do not mean to suggest that they have suffered in the same way as the people of Buffalo Creek. But the feelings they experience are of the same kind. Those who assume that they will need to move elsewhere to resume a normal and healthy life are grieving for lost homes even while they remain resident in them. And those who expect to remain are acutely aware that damage may have been done to their homes and has certainly been done to the land on which they stand. In either event, the damage is experienced as an insult to and an assault on the persons who live in it. To a sociologist, then, the complaints expressed by the residents of East Swallow speak of injuries to their sense of personal security and pride as well as injuries to their purses. And such injuries are felt all the more sharply in places like East Swallow because so many of the residents expected to live out their lives in the shelter of those homes.

The woman who said in an interview, "I have sadness thinking that we might have to leave; we've put a lot of work into this house and I really don't want, really, anyone else to live here," is very clearly speaking of something far more than a possession. The home she thinks she will have to leave is a part of her, an extension of her person. The two persons quoted below, a wife and a husband in early middle age, share that feeling deeply:

Our home has always been our castle. We feel very good about it, and it houses everything we have. Our whole lives are right here. We've always felt good about it. And now to feel that it isn't good—that's hard to deal with. . . . And I have this feeling that if I move away then somebody else is going to come in and they're going to benefit from everything I put in it. And it's mine! *I don't want to give it to you!*

It's become—it's a dwelling, it's not what it was. It was kind of—I don't know—it was sort of an integral part of our life, it was almost like a friend. It's just a house now. When everyone else was, you know, building up a little equity and then moving onto the next new trendy neighborhood, we just kind of stayed where we were and shaped it to ourselves.

To many plaintiffs, it is almost as if the home, once having been a living thing, is now dead or dying. There is no point in breathing any kind of personality or distinctive character into it, of continuing the process of shaping it to one's needs and preferences, because no one knows how much it has been depreciated in any of the several senses of that term. In this respect, too, life is on hold:

[Y]ou hate to put all the work into it and not know what's going to come out. I mean there's things I'd like to do. I mean I'd like to paint the house. I'd like to

dig up a couple of trees and plant some others. But by the same token, I don't know what's going to happen. I'd hate to put in all that work and then the place blow up or something.

Just lethargic. We used to always do things in the house. Obviously we don't want to do it anymore because of the situation. At Christmas time we went out and bought a limited edition print. We can't do anything permanent in the house, so we'll get a nice picture. We had it framed, we got it back, it was finally done on about our anniversary. It's sitting in the bedroom on the floor. Haven't put it up. Just haven't felt like doing it. . . . Why bother, you know.

The long and anxious wait for some kind of resolution, moreover, is made all the more difficult by the fact that, to begin with, people are afraid of their homes and see them as places of danger, and yet, paradoxically, are afraid to leave them for anything more than a few short stretches of time. It can be a painful dilemma. On the one hand, the home may be so perilous that it is unfair to expose other people—children particularly—to it:

I don't want [my children] to be in here at all, really, any more. I feel that they're better off if I visit them. It's a fear that is intangible.

I used to do a lot of baby-sitting for friends. Younger people that would like to go out, I would baby sit their kids and they could bring them to my house. Then I thought if there are fumes around here that I am not detecting, could they possibly be harmful to somebody's child? . . . So I don't keep these children any more.

I would like to use my yard for parties and things [but] I just don't feel like—you always kind of have to think: "Should I expose other people to possible contamination by having them over?"

On the other hand, people are afraid to leave the house exactly because they appreciate how many things could go wrong in their absence. The speaker above who described her reluctance to invite her children to the house also said:

I've gotten to be more or less of a recluse. I'm frightened to leave for fear something might happen. . . . Like I was almost a prisoner. Almost a hostage, more or less. Keeping me here because I'm frightened to go away. . . . I'm scared to death to leave this property.

That is a familiar feeling in the neighborhood. "You cannot go out of town and really be at peace of mind about whether your property is going to be there or something else is going to happen until you get back," said one man at his deposition. "What are you worried is going to happen?" he was asked. "Fire, explosion, whatever," was the answer. Another neighbor said:

And it's an awful feeling to leave your house and in your mind wonder: "Is the house going to be here when we come back?" We don't dare take a vacation, we just don't dare.

So people find themselves trapped in homes they no longer value or even trust. What ought to be a hearth, a safe haven, a source of pride, a place of comfort, now becomes something spoiled, dangerous, and even hateful—a process Michael Edelstein calls "the inversion of home":[2]

> *Well, yeah, [my feelings] have gone 180 degrees in that we just don't enjoy the home any more. It's not a thing of pleasure. It's just a big albatross to us. . . . There just isn't any enjoyment there. Well, it's just turned into a complete nightmare. I don't think any of the neighbors enjoy their homes any more. And we're all just looking forward to the day that we can turn the key and walk away.*

> *The house doesn't have the love and the care and everything that goes into making a home anymore. The yard doesn't. Our whole lifestyle has changed from tender loving care to being with something you're fearful of, something you resent, something you lose interest in.*

One resident of East Swallow—speaking, without having that in mind, for all her neighbors—summed the matter up perfectly:

> *One of the major ways is by not feeling that we could live there safely. . . . Also the fear of the vapors, the fear of the gasoline odors—never knowing how strong they may be, never knowing when they may appear, . . . never knowing if they become explosive. You don't have friends over, you don't have your children have their friends over, you don't want to encourage others to expose themselves to harm. You don't enjoy or even have any desire to maintain your property and increase its value because you feel that it has no value because of the gasoline spill and the contamination underneath it. Why make it more refined? Why upgrade it? It would be money wasted.*

Sociologists and other social and behavioral scientists have known for a long time that a secure sense of community is important to the well-being of people in general. Individuals may vary in the strength of their need for communal structures, but the longing for and dependence on some form of communality can be said to be natural for humankind. It is a fair rule of thumb, moreover, that people who come from rural and small-town backgrounds, as most of the East Swallow plaintiffs do, feel a greater need to gather together into continuing communities than is the case for people of a more urban background.

The East Swallow neighborhood is not a long-standing, traditional community as is the case for New England villages, Appalachian hollows, or even the midwestern farm communities from which so many of the plaintiffs have come. Most of the residents seem to favor neighborhoods in which a fair degree of social distance is observed and a sense of individual privacy respected, but, at the same time, in which one can count on a caring and warm human surrounding. "We did not socialize . . . a whole lot," said one woman, "and yet if somebody went someplace and needed to have a paper picked up or mail picked up, any of us would have been willing to do it." And another woman, expressing views common to the majority of her neighbors, said:

I don't have what you call a back-door policy of neighboring, you know—run in and out, chummy all the time. No, I can't say that. We are all friendly and speak to one another and usually at the mailbox or something like that. No, we're not chummy neighbors.

Still, it is clear that most of them are what the mountain folk of Appalachia often call "neighbor people." That is, they seek communal settings in which persons can be counted on to look after one another, to share a feeling of neighborliness, and together to form a buffer zone behind which they can feel safe and comfortable. It is an old dream for many, and especially those who move to new neighborhoods with the expectation of spending their final years there. So the story of East Swallow is not that of a place with a long past, now disrupted; it is the story of a place with an emerging future, now threatened. The loss is of a different kind, but it is a sharp and painful one all the same.

A sense of community depends upon a sense of place. A community is grounded. It has location. It belongs to, is a part of, a given territory. Nothing could be clearer from the available evidence, however, that the residents of East Swallow see the space in which their community is located as soiled and contaminated in some profoundly disturbing way, and such a perception can hardly help but disrupt the feelings of communality that are so crucial a part of neighborly living. It is "a disaster area," "a misery," "a dump." Not every resident of East Swallow would agree with the young woman who called it "the most horrible place in the world," but all would acknowledge that they are now part of what seems to be a blighted, half-ruined landscape.

Something foul has worked its way into the very atmosphere of the community. Everything seems dirtied, contaminated, polluted:

The neighborhood, I mean it's really deceptive. It's like looking at someone who has cancer and you think they look healthy on the outside but you know they are not. That is the way this neighborhood is. I like the house, I like the location, but I don't like the fact that it's on contaminated ground.

Everyone in the community assumes that substantial quantities of gasoline are still to be found in the land under their feet, gathering in dangerous pockets underground, continuing to migrate, and ready to do further harm. The place is not only contaminated, then, but dangerous, requiring people to live with thoughts like these:

At one time my sprinkler system became disengaged . . . so consequently, the west section of my lawn started to dry out. And then I really investigated and found out and had it repaired. But in the interim I was scared to death someone would throw a cigarette on my lawn . . . and cause the neighborhood to go up. Really, I was frantic.

The uncertainty, I think. . . . For instance, they are doing work over on the Foothills Fashion Mall, which is south of our home, and they have an enormous trench dug over there—I would guess six feet or so deep. I saw a man standing in it. . . . He was working down inside this trench and he was smoking a cigarette. . . . And, frankly, I was terrified to be walking by while he was smoking. . . . I mean it was very scary not knowing whether I was going to explode walking by.

It is easy to appreciate that when one lives with such preoccupations as those, uncertainty and fear become the prevailing moods of the community— a constant, nagging, persistent worrying about what has happened in the past and what might yet happen in the future. "We're living over a time bomb," people say; "we're sitting on a stick of dynamite," we're "standing in quicksand."

On the one hand, the residents of the neighborhood have forged a new closeness in the process of facing such adversity together. The event "has certainly brought us closer together as a neighborhood," said one resident, "it's been, really, a positive thing in that sense." But that blessing, on the other hand—if indeed one can even call it that—has a bitter edge. For one thing, it increases the size of the circle of those whose troubles one must share and take into account:

And since the gas spill, we have been forced to become more intimate. And, in a way, that's actually going to make it worse, because now when I worry, I don't just have [my family] to worry about, I have the Owens and the Browns and the Overtons and . . . If you don't have a neighborhood that is homogeneous and engages in coffee klatch type activities, then you wouldn't know all those things about other people. And you wouldn't know how badly their lives have been affected by the same thing that's been destroying my life.

And, maybe more to the point, neighborhood gatherings are so focused on the spill and the miseries it later caused that the normal affairs of everyday life— the kinds of things neighbors usually discuss over the back fence—scarcely ever enter the conversation. The accident has moved into the center of the community's sense of itself.

I think as far as the neighbors are concerned, it's brought us closer to them than probably we would have. That's kind of a mixed blessing, you know. I mean it's been nice to get to know all the other people here, but the circumstances for it are not always pleasant, so a lot of times when we do get together it's—instead of fun or chit-chat, it's commiserating a little bit about our problems and that sort of thing.

In part, then, the neighborhood came together and became stronger in the course of what most of its members consider a real struggle, and the irony of the situation is that the success of that community may very well mean its dispersal.

People in society are insulated emotionally, so to speak, by layers of human warmth that surround them like concentric circles. The first of those circles, obviously, is the one occupied by the family niche. And the second, just as obviously, is occupied by the immediate neighborhood. Both of these inner layers of comfort and support have been greatly damaged in East Swallow by the spill and the events surrounding it. The home no longer has the feel of a family hearth and the neighborhood is now held together in the most fragile of ways—not by the bonds of communality but by the urgency of a disaster.

NOTES

1. Kai Erikson, *Everything in Its Path* (New York: Simon & Schuster, 1976); Harry Estill Moore, *Tornadoes over Texas* (Austin: University of Texas Press, 1958); and Marc Fried, "Grieving for a Lost Home," in *The Urban Condition*, ed. Leonard J. Duhl (New York: Basic Books, 1963).
2. Michael Edelstein, *Contaminated Communities: The Social and Psychological Impacts of Residential Toxic Exposure* (Boulder, CO: Westview Press, 1988).

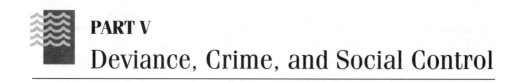

PART V
Deviance, Crime, and Social Control

19

ON BEING SANE IN INSANE PLACES

DAVID L. ROSENHAN

Sociologists have a long-standing interest in the study of social deviance, which is explored in the next four readings. *Deviance* is the recognized violation of social norms. As norms cover a wide range of human behavior, deviant acts are plentiful in any given society. Moreover, whether a person is labeled deviant depends on how others perceive, define, and respond to that person's behavior. In this selection, David L. Rosenhan explores the social deviance of mental illness and the consequences of labeling people "sane" or "insane."

If sanity and insanity exist . . . how shall we know them? The question is neither capricious nor itself insane. However much we may be personally convinced that we can tell the normal from the abnormal, the evidence is simply not compelling. It is commonplace, for example, to read about murder trials wherein eminent psychiatrists for the defense are contradicted by equally eminent psychiatrists for the prosecution on the matter of the defendant's sanity. More generally, there is a great deal of conflicting data on the reliability, utility, and meaning of such terms as *sanity, insanity, mental illness,* and *schizophrenia.*[1] Finally, as early as 1934, Benedict suggested that normality and abnormality are not universal.[2] What is viewed as normal in one culture may be seen as quite aberrant in another. Thus, notions of normality and abnormality may not be quite as accurate as people believe they are.

To raise questions regarding normality and abnormality is in no way to question the fact that some behaviors are deviant or odd. Murder is deviant. So, too, are hallucinations. Nor does raising such questions deny the existence of the personal anguish that is often associated with "mental illness." Anxiety and depression exist. Psychological suffering exists. But normality and abnormality, sanity and insanity, and the diagnoses that flow from them may be less substantive than many believe them to be.

At its heart, the question of whether the sane can be distinguished from the insane (and whether degrees of insanity can be distinguished from each other) is a simple matter: Do the salient characteristics that lead to diagnoses reside in the patients themselves or in the environments and contexts in which observers find them? From Bleuler, through Kretchmer, through the formulations of the recently revised *Diagnostic and Statistical Manual* of the American Psychiatric Association, the belief has been strong that patients present symptoms, that those symptoms can be categorized, and, implicitly, that the sane are distinguishable from the insane. More recently, however, this belief has been questioned. Based in part on theoretical and anthropological considerations, but also on philosophical, legal, and therapeutic ones, the view has grown that psychological categorization of mental illness is useless at best and downright harmful, misleading, and pejorative at worst. Psychiatric diagnoses, in this view, are in the minds of the observers and are not valid summaries of characteristics displayed by the observed.[3, 4, 5]

Gains can be made in deciding which of these is more nearly accurate by getting normal people (that is, people who do not have, and have never suffered, symptoms of serious psychiatric disorders) admitted to psychiatric hospitals and then determining whether they were discovered to be sane and, if so, how. If the sanity of such pseudopatients were always detected, there would be *prima facie* evidence that a sane individual can be distinguished from the insane context in which he is found. Normality (and presumably abnormality) is distinct enough that it can be recognized wherever it occurs, for it is carried within the person. If, on the other hand, the sanity of the pseudopatients were never discovered, serious difficulties would arise for those who support traditional modes of psychiatric diagnosis. Given that the hospital staff was not incompetent, that the pseudopatient had been behaving as sanely as he had been outside of the hospital, and that it had never been previously suggested that he belonged in a psychiatric hospital, such an unlikely outcome would support the view that psychiatric diagnosis betrays little about the patient but much about the environment in which an observer finds him.

This article describes such an experiment. Eight sane people gained secret admission to twelve different hospitals.[6] Their diagnostic experiences constitute the data of the first part of this article; the remainder is devoted to a description of their experiences in psychiatric institutions. Too few psychiatrists and psychologists, even those who have worked in such hospitals, know what the experience is like. They rarely talk about it with former patients, perhaps because they distrust information coming from the previously insane. Those who have worked in psychiatric hospitals are likely to have adapted so thoroughly to the settings that they are insensitive to the impact of that experience. And while there have been occasional reports of researchers who submitted themselves to psychiatric hospitalization,[7] these researchers have commonly remained in the hospitals for short periods of time, often with the knowledge of the hospital staff. It is difficult to know the extent to which they were treated like patients or like research colleagues. Nevertheless, their reports about the inside of the psychiatric hospital have been valuable. This article extends those efforts.

Pseudopatients and Their Settings

The eight pseudopatients were a varied group. One was a psychology graduate student in his 20s. The remaining seven were older and "established." Among them were three psychologists, a pediatrician, a psychiatrist, a painter, and a housewife. Three pseudopatients were women, five were men. All of them employed pseudonyms, lest their alleged diagnoses embarrass them later. Those who were in mental health professions alleged another occupation in order to avoid the special attentions that might be accorded by staff, as a matter of courtesy or caution, to ailing colleagues.[8] With the exception of myself (I was the first pseudopatient and my presence was known to the hospital administrator and chief psychologist and, so far as I can tell, to them alone), the presence of pseudopatients and the nature of the research program were not known to the hospital staffs.[9]

The settings were similarly varied. In order to generalize the findings, admission into a variety of hospitals was sought. The 12 hospitals in the sample were located in five different states on the East and West coasts. Some were old and shabby, some were quite new. Some were research-oriented, others not. Some had good staff-patient ratios, others were quite understaffed. Only one was a strictly private hospital. All of the others were supported by state or federal funds, or in one instance, by university funds.

After calling the hospital for an appointment, the pseudopatient arrived at the admissions office complaining that he had been hearing voices. Asked what the voices said, he replied that they were often unclear, but as far as he could tell they said "empty," "hollow," and "thud." The voices were unfamiliar and were of the same sex as the pseudopatient. The choice of these symptoms was occasioned by their apparent similarity to existential symptoms. Such symptoms are alleged to arise from painful concerns about the perceived meaninglessness of one's life. It is as if the hallucinating person were saying, "My life is empty and hollow." The choice of these symptoms was also determined by the *absence* of a single report of existential psychoses in the literature.

Beyond alleging the symptoms and falsifying name, vocation, and employment, no further alterations of person, history, or circumstances were made. The significant events of the pseudopatient's life history were presented as they had actually occurred. Relationships with parents and siblings, with spouse and children, with people at work and in school, consistent with the aforementioned exceptions, were described as they were or had been. Frustrations and upsets were described along with joys and satisfactions. These facts are important to remember. If anything, they strongly biased the subsequent results in favor of detecting sanity, since none of their histories or current behaviors were seriously pathological in any way.

Immediately upon admission to the psychiatric ward, the pseudopatient ceased simulating *any* symptoms of abnormality. In some cases, there was a brief period of mild nervousness and anxiety, since none of the pseudopatients really believed that they would be admitted so easily. Indeed, their shared fear was that they would be immediately exposed as frauds and greatly embarrassed. Moreover, many of them had never visited a psychiatric ward; even those who had, nevertheless had some genuine fears about what might happen to them. Their nervousness, then, was quite appropriate to the novelty of the hospital setting, and it abated rapidly.

Apart from that short-lived nervousness, the pseudopatient behaved on the ward as he "normally" behaved. The pseudopatient spoke to patients and staff as he might ordinarily. Because there is uncommonly little to do on a psychiatric ward, he attempted to engage others in conversation. When asked by the staff how he was feeling, he indicated that he was fine, that he no longer experienced symptoms. He responded to instructions from attendants, to calls for medication (which was not swallowed), and to dining-hall instructions. Beyond such activities as were available to him on the admissions ward, he spent his time writing down his observations about the ward, its patients, and the staff. Initially these notes were written "secretly," but as it soon became clear that no one much cared, they were subsequently written on standard tablets of paper in such public places as the dayroom. No secret was made of these activities.

The pseudopatient, very much as a true psychiatric patient, entered a hospital with no foreknowledge of when he would be discharged. Each was told that he would have to get out by his own devices, essentially by convincing the staff that he was sane. The psychological stresses associated with hospitalization were considerable, and all but one of the pseudopatients desired to be discharged almost immediately after being admitted. They were, therefore, motivated not only to behave sanely, but to be paragons of cooperation. That their behavior was in no way disruptive is confirmed by nursing reports, which have been obtained on most of the patients. These reports uniformly indicate that the patients were "friendly," "cooperative," and "exhibited no abnormal indications."

The Normal Are Not Detectably Sane

Despite their public "show" of sanity, the pseudopatients were never detected. Admitted, except in one case, with a diagnosis of schizophrenia,[10] each was discharged with a diagnosis of schizophrenia "in remission." The label "in remission" should in no way be dismissed as a formality, for at no time during any hospitalization had any question been raised about any pseudopatient's simulation. Nor are there any indications in the hospital records that the pseudopatient's status was suspect. Rather, the evidence is strong that, once labeled schizophrenic, the pseudopatient was stuck with that label. If the pseudopatient was to be discharged, he must naturally be "in remission"; but he was not sane, nor, in the institution's view, had he ever been sane.

The uniform failure to recognize sanity cannot be attributed to the quality of the hospitals, for, although there were considerable variations among them, several are considered excellent. Nor can it be alleged that there was simply not enough time to observe the pseudopatients. Length of hospitalization ranged from seven to 52 days, with an average of 19 days. The pseudopatients were not, in fact, carefully observed, but this failure clearly speaks more to the traditions within psychiatric hospitals than to lack of opportunity.

Finally, it cannot be said that the failure to recognize the pseudopatients' sanity was due to the fact that they were not behaving sanely. While there was clearly some tension present in all of them, their daily visitors could detect no serious behavioral consequences—nor, indeed, could other patients. It was quite common for the patients to "detect" the pseudopatients' sanity. During the first three hospitalizations, when accurate counts were kept, 35 of a total of 118 patients on the admissions ward voiced their suspicions, some vigorously. "You're not crazy. You're a journalist, or a professor [referring to the continual note-taking]. You're checking up on the hospital." While most of the patients were reassured by the pseudopatient's insistence that he had been sick before he came in but was fine now, some continued to believe that the pseudopatient was sane throughout his hospitalization.[11] The fact that the patients often recognized normality when staff did not raises important questions.

Failure to detect sanity during the course of hospitalization may be due to the fact that physicians operate with a strong bias toward what statisticians call the type 2 error.[12] This is to say that physicians are more inclined to call a healthy person sick (a false positive, type 2) than a sick person healthy (a false negative, type 1). The reasons for this are not hard to find: It is clearly more dangerous to misdiagnose illness than health. Better to err on the side of caution, to suspect illness even among the healthy.

But what holds for medicine does not hold equally well for psychiatry. Medical illnesses, while unfortunate, are not commonly pejorative. Psychiatric diagnoses, on the contrary, carry with them personal, legal, and social stigmas.[13] It was therefore important to see whether the tendency toward diagnosing the sane insane could be reversed. The following experiment was arranged at a research and teaching hospital whose staff had heard these findings but doubted that such an error could occur in their hospital. The staff was informed that at some time during the following three months, one or more pseudopatients would attempt to be admitted into the psychiatric hospital. Each staff member was asked to rate each patient who presented himself at admissions or on the ward according to the likelihood that the patient was a pseudopatient. A 10-point scale was used, with a 1 and 2 reflecting high confidence that the patient was a pseudopatient.

Judgments were obtained on 193 patients who were admitted for psychiatric treatment. All staff who had had sustained contact with or primary responsibility for the patient—attendants, nurses, psychiatrists, physicians, and psychologists—were asked to make judgments. Forty-one patients were alleged, with high confidence, to be pseudopatients by at least one member of the staff. Twenty-three were considered suspect by at least one psychiatrist. Nineteen were suspected by one psychiatrist and one other staff member. Actually, no genuine pseudopatient (at least from my group) presented himself during this period.

The experiment is instructive. It indicates that the tendency to designate sane people as insane can be reversed when the stakes (in this case, prestige and diagnostic acumen) are high. But what can be said of the 19 people who were suspected of being "sane" by one psychiatrist and another staff member? Were these people truly "sane," or was it rather the case that in the course of avoiding the type 2 error the staff tended to make more errors of the first sort—calling the crazy "sane"? There is no way of knowing. But one thing is certain: Any diagnostic process that lends itself so readily to massive errors of this sort cannot be a very reliable one.

The Stickiness of Psychodiagnostic Labels

Beyond the tendency to call the healthy sick—a tendency that accounts better for diagnostic behavior on admission than it does for such behavior after a lengthy period of exposure—the data speak to the massive role of labeling in psychiatric assessment. Having once been labeled schizophrenic, there is nothing the pseudopatient can do to overcome the tag. The tag profoundly colors others' perceptions of him and his behavior.

From one viewpoint, these data are hardly surprising, for it has long been known that elements are given meaning by the context in which they occur. Gestalt psychology made this point vigorously, and Asch[14] demonstrated that there are "central" personality traits (such as "warm" versus "cold") which are so powerful that they markedly color the meaning of other information in forming an impression of a given personality.[15] "Insane," "schizophrenic," "manic-depressive," and "crazy" are probably among the most powerful of such central traits. Once a person is designated abnormal, all of his other behaviors and characteristics are colored by that label. Indeed, that label is so powerful that many of the pseudopatients' normal behaviors were overlooked entirely or profoundly misinterpreted. Some examples may clarify this issue.

Earlier I indicated that there were no changes in the pseudopatient's personal history and current status beyond those of name, employment, and, where necessary, vocation. Otherwise, a veridical description of personal history and circumstances was offered. Those circumstances were not psychotic. How were they made consonant with the diagnosis of psychosis? Or were those diagnoses modified in such a way as to bring them into accord with the circumstances of the pseudopatient's life, as described by him?

As far as I can determine, diagnoses were in no way affected by the relative health of the circumstances of a pseudopatient's life. Rather, the reverse occurred: The perception of his circumstances was shaped entirely by the diagnosis. A clear example of such translation is found in the case of a pseudopatient who had had a close relationship with his mother but was rather remote from his father during his early childhood. During adolescence and beyond, however, his father became a close friend, while his relationship with his mother cooled. His present relationship with his wife was characteristically close and warm. Apart from occasional angry exchanges, friction was minimal. The children had rarely been spanked. Surely there is nothing especially pathological about such a history. Indeed, many readers may see a similar pattern in their own experiences, with no markedly deleterious consequences. Observe, however, how such a history was translated in the psychopathological context, this from the case summary prepared after the patient was discharged.

> This white 39-year-old male . . . manifests a long history of considerable ambivalence in close relationships, which begins in early childhood. A warm relationship with his mother cools during adolescence. A distant relationship to his father is described as becoming very intense. Affective stability is absent. His attempts to control emotionality with his wife and children are punctuated by angry outbursts and, in the case of the children, spankings. And while he says that he has several good friends, one senses considerable ambivalence embedded in those relationships also.

The facts of the case were unintentionally distorted by the staff to achieve consistency with a popular theory of the dynamics of schizophrenic reaction.[16] Nothing of an ambivalent nature had been described in relations with parents, spouse, or friends. To the extent that ambivalence could be inferred, it was probably not greater than is found in all human relationships. It is true the pseudopatient's relationships with his parents changed over time, but in the ordinary context that would hardly be remarkable—indeed, it might very well be expected. Clearly, the meaning ascribed to his verbalizations (that is, ambivalence, affective instability) was determined by the diagnosis: schizophrenia. An entirely different meaning would have been ascribed if it were known that the man was "normal."

All pseudopatients took extensive notes publicly. Under ordinary circumstances, such behavior would have raised questions in the minds of observers, as, in fact, it did among patients. Indeed, it seemed so certain that the notes would elicit suspicion that elaborate precautions were taken to remove them from the ward each day. But the precautions proved needless. The closest any staff member came to questioning these notes occurred when one pseudopatient asked his physician what kind of medication he was receiving and began to write down the response. "You needn't write it," he was told gently. "If you have trouble remembering, just ask me again."

If no questions were asked of the pseudopatients, how was their writing interpreted? Nursing records for three patients indicate that the writing was seen as an aspect of their pathological behavior. "Patient engages in writing behavior" was the daily nursing comment on one of the pseudopatients who was never questioned about his writing. Given that the patient is in the hospital, he must be psychologically disturbed. And given that he is disturbed, continuous writing must be a behavioral manifestation of that disturbance, perhaps a subset of the compulsive behaviors that are sometimes correlated with schizophrenia.

One tacit characteristic of psychiatric diagnosis is that it locates the sources of aberration within the individual and only rarely within the complex of stimuli that surrounds him. Consequently, behaviors that are stimulated by the environment are commonly misattributed to the patient's disorder. For example, one kindly nurse found a pseudopatient pacing the long hospital corridors. "Nervous, Mr. X?" she asked. "No, bored," he said.

The notes kept by pseudopatients are full of patient behaviors that were misinterpreted by well-intentioned staff. Often enough, a patient would go "berserk" because he had, wittingly or unwittingly, been mistreated by, say, an attendant. A nurse coming upon the scene would rarely inquire even cursorily into the environmental stimuli of the patient's behavior. Rather, she assumed that his upset derived from his pathology, not from his present interactions with other staff members. Occasionally, the staff might assume that the patient's family (especially when they had recently visited) or other patients had stimulated the outburst. But never were the staff found to assume that one of themselves or the structure of the hospital had anything to do with a patient's behavior. One psychiatrist pointed to a group of patients who were sitting outside the cafeteria entrance half an hour before lunchtime. To a group of young residents he indicated that such behavior was characteristic of the oral-acquisitive nature of the syndrome. It seemed not to occur to him that there were very few things to anticipate in the psychiatric hospital besides eating.

A psychiatric label has a life and an influence of its own. Once the impression has been formed that the patient is schizophrenic, the expectation is that he will continue to be schizophrenic. When a sufficient amount of time has passed, during which the patient has done nothing bizarre, he is considered to be in remission and available for discharge. But the label endures beyond discharge, with the unconfirmed expectation that he will behave as a schizophrenic again. Such labels, conferred by mental health professionals, are as influential on the patient as they are on his relatives and friends, and it should not surprise anyone that the diagnosis acts on all of them as a self-fulfilling prophecy. Eventually, the patient himself accepts the diagnosis, with all of its surplus meanings and expectations, and behaves accordingly.[17]

The inferences to be made from these matters are quite simple. Much as Zigler and Phillips have demonstrated that there is enormous overlap in the symptoms presented by patients who have been variously diagnosed,[18] so there is enormous overlap in the behaviors of the sane and the insane. The sane are not "sane" all of the time. We lose our tempers "for no good reason." We are occasionally depressed or anxious, again for no good reason. And we may find it difficult to get along with one or another person—again for no reason that we can specify. Similarly, the insane are not always insane. Indeed, it was the impression of the pseudopatients while living with them that they were sane for long periods of time—that the bizarre behaviors upon which their diagnoses were allegedly predicated constituted only a small fraction of their total behavior. If it makes no sense to label ourselves permanently depressed on the basis of an occasional depression, then it takes evidence that is presently available to label all patients insane or schizophrenic on the basis of bizarre behaviors or cognitions. It seems more useful, as Mischel[19] has pointed out, to limit our discussions to *behaviors*, the stimuli that provoke them, and their correlates.

It is not known why powerful impressions of personality traits, such as "crazy" or "insane," arise. Conceivably, when the origins of and stimuli that give rise to a behavior are remote or unknown, or when the behavior strikes us as immutable, trait labels regarding the *behavior* arise. When, on the other hand, the origins and stimuli are known and available, discourse is limited to the behavior itself. Thus, I may hallucinate because I am sleeping, or I may hallucinate because I have ingested a peculiar drug. These are termed sleep-induced hallucinations, or dreams, and drug-induced hallucinations, respectively. But when the stimuli to my hallucinations are unknown, that is called craziness, or schizophrenia—as if that inference were somehow as illuminating as the others.

The Consequences of Labeling and Depersonalization

Whenever the ratio of what is known to what needs to be known approaches zero, we tend to invent "knowledge" and assume that we understand more than we actually do. We seem unable to acknowledge that we simply don't know. The needs for diagnosis and remediation of behavioral and emotional problems are enormous. But rather than acknowledge that we are just embarking on understanding, we continue to label patients "schizophrenic," "manic-depressive," and "insane," as if in those words we had captured the essence of understanding. The facts of the matter are that we have known for a long time that diagnoses are often not useful or reliable, but we have nevertheless continued to use them. We now know that we cannot distinguish insanity from sanity. It is depressing to consider how that information will be used.

Not merely depressing, but frightening. How many people, one wonders, are sane but not recognized as such in our psychiatric institutions? How many have been needlessly stripped of their privileges of citizenship, from the right to vote and drive to that of handling their own accounts? How many have feigned insanity in order to avoid the criminal consequences of their behavior, and conversely, how many would rather stand trial than live interminably in a psychiatric hospital—but are wrongly thought to be mentally ill? How many have been stigmatized by well-intentioned, but nevertheless erroneous, diagnoses? On the last point, recall again that a "type 2 error" in psychiatric diagnosis does not have the same consequences it does in medical diagnosis. A diagnosis of cancer that has been found to be in error is cause for celebration. But psychiatric diagnoses are rarely found to be in error. The label sticks, a mark of inadequacy forever.

NOTES

1. P. Ash, *Journal of Abnormal and Social Psychology* 44 (1949): 272; A. T. Beck, *American Journal of Psychiatry* 119 (1962): 210; A. T. Boisen, *Psychiatry* 2 (1938): 233; J. Kreitman, *Journal of Mental Science* 107 (1961): 876; N. Kreitman, P. Sainsbury, J. Morrisey, J. Towers, and J. Scrivener, *Journal of Mental Science* 107 (1961): 887; H. O. Schmitt, and C. P. Fonda, *Journal of Abnormal Social Psychology* 52 (1956): 262; W. Seeman, *Journal of Nervous Mental Disorders* 118 (1953):541. For analysis of these artifacts and summaries of the disputes, see J. Zubin, *Annual Review of Psychology* 18 (1967): 373; L. Phillips and J. G. Draguns, *Annual Review of Psychology* 22 (1971): 447.

2. R. Benedict, *Journal of General Psychology* 10 (1934): 59.

3. See in this regard Howard Becker, *Outsiders: Studies in the Sociology of Deviance* (New York: Free Press, 1963); B. M. Braginsky, D. D. Braginsky, and K. Ring, *Methods of Madness: The Mental Hospital as a Last Resort* (New York: Holt, Rinehart and Winston, 1969); G. M. Crocetti and P. V. Lemkau, *American Sociological Review* 30 (1965): 577; Erving Goffman, *Behavior in Public Places* (New York: Free Press, 1964); R. D. Laing, *The Divided Self: A Study of Sanity and Madness* (Chicago: Quadrangle, 1960); D. L. Phillips, *American Sociological Review* 28 (1963): 963; T. R. Sarbin, *Psychology Today* 6 (1972): 18; E. Schur, *American Journal of Sociology* 75 (1969): 309; Thomas Szasz, *The Myth of Mental Illness: Foundations of a Theory of Mental Illness* (New York: Hoeber Harper, 1963). For a critique of some of these views, see W. R. Gave, *American Sociological Review* 35 (1970): 873.

4. Erving Goffman, *Asylums* (Garden City, NY: Doubleday, 1961).

5. T. J. Scheff, *Being Mentally Ill: A Sociological Theory* (Chicago: Aldine, 1966).

6. Data from a ninth pseudopatient are not incorporated in this report because, although his sanity went undetected, he falsified aspects of his personal history, including his marital status and parental relationships. His experimental behaviors therefore were not identical to those of the other pseudopatients.

7. A. Barry, *Bellevue Is a State of Mind* (New York: Harcourt Brace Jovanovich, 1971); I. Belknap, *Human Problems of a State Mental Hospital* (New York: McGraw-Hill, 1956); W. Caudill, F. C. Redlich, H. R. Gilmore, and E. B. Brody, *American Journal of Orthopsychiatry* 22 (1952): 314; A. R. Goldman, R. H. Bohr, and T. A. Steinberg, *Professional Psychology* 1 (1970): 427; *Roche Report* 1, no. 13 (1971): 8.

8. Beyond the personal difficulties that the pseudopatient is likely to experience in the hospital, there are legal and social ones that, combined, require considerable attention before entry. For example, once admitted to a psychiatric institution, it is difficult, if not impossible, to be discharged on short notice, state law to the contrary notwithstanding. I was not sensitive to these difficulties at the outset of the project, nor to the personal and situational emergencies that can arise, but later a writ of habeas corpus was prepared for each of the entering pseudopatients and an attorney was kept "on call" during every hospitalization. I am grateful to John Kaplan and Robert Bartels for legal advice and assistance in these matters.

9. However distasteful such concealment is, it was a necessary first step to examining these questions. Without concealment, there would have been no way to know how valid these experiences were; nor was there any way of knowing whether whatever detections occurred were a tribute to the diagnostic acumen of the staff or to the hospital's rumor network. Obviously, since my concerns are general ones that cut across individual hospitals and staffs, I have respected their anonymity and have eliminated clues that might lead to their identification.

10. Interestingly, of the 12 admissions, 11 were diagnosed as schizophrenic and one, with the identical symptomatology, as manic-depressive psychosis. This diagnosis has a more favorable prognosis, and it was given by the only private hospital in our sample. On the relations between social class and psychiatric diagnosis, see A. B. Hollinghead and F. C. Redlich, *Social Class and Mental Illness: A Community Study* (New York: Wiley, 1958).

11. It is possible, of course, that patients have quite broad latitudes in diagnosis and therefore are inclined to call many people sane, even those whose behavior is patently aberrant. However, although we have no hard data on this matter, it was our distinct impression that this was not the case. In many instances, patients not only singled us out for attention, but came to imitate our behaviors and styles.

12. Scheff, *Being Mentally Ill.*

13. J. Cumming and E. Cumming, *Community Mental Health* 1 (1965): 135; A. Farina and K. Ring, *Journal of Abnormal Psychology* 40 (1965): 47; H. E. Freeman and O. G. Simmons, *The Mental Patient Comes Home* (New York: Wiley, 1963); W. J. Johannsen, *Mental Hygiene* 53 (1969): 218; A. S. Linsky, *Social Psychology* 5 (1970): 166.

14. S. E. Asch, *Abnormal Social Psychology* 41 (1946): 258; S. E. Asch, *Social Psychology* (New York: Prentice-Hall, 1952).

15. See also I. N. Mensch and J. Wishner, *Journal of Personality* 16 (1947): 188; J. Wishner, *Psychological Review* 67 (1960): 96; J. S. Bruner and K. R. Tagiuri in *Handbook of Social Psychology*, vol. 2, ed. G. Lindzey (Cambridge, MA: Addison-Wesley, 1954), pp. 634–54; J. S. Bruner, D. Shapiro, and R. Tagiuri in *Person Perception and Interpersonal Behavior*, ed. R. Tagiuri and L. Petrullo (Stanford, CA: Stanford University Press, 1958), pp. 277–88.

16. For an example of a similar self-fulfilling prophecy, in this instance dealing with the "central" trait of intelligence, see R. Rosenthal and L. Jacobson, *Pygmalion in the Classroom* (New York: Holt, Rinehart and Winston, 1968).

17. Scheff, *Being Mentally Ill.*

18. E. Zigler and L. Phillips, *Journal of Abnormal and Social Psychology* 63 (1961): 69. See also R. K. Freudenberg and J. P. Robertson, *A.M.A. Archives of Neurological Psychiatry* 76 (1956): 14.

19. W. Mischel, *Personality and Assessment* (New York: Wiley, 1968).

20

ANOREXIA NERVOSA AND BULIMIA
The Development of Deviant Identities

PENELOPE A. McLORG • DIANE E. TAUB

Symbolic interactionists claim that deviance is relative depending on the situation and who is perceiving the act of deviance. Thus, according to *labeling theory*, people label certain acts as deviant and others as normal. This reading by Penelope A. McLorg and Diane E. Taub further illustrates this subjective process of deviance identification. McLorg and Taub employ labeling theory to explain how eating disorders have become defined as deviant behaviors and how some young women acquire deviant identities by modifying their self-concepts to conform to the societal labels of a person with an eating disorder.

Introduction

Current appearance norms stipulate thinness for women and muscularity for men; these expectations, like any norms, entail rewards for compliance and negative sanctions for violations. Fear of being overweight—of being visually deviant—has led to a striving for thinness, especially among women. In the extreme, this avoidance of overweight engenders eating disorders, which themselves constitute deviance. Anorexia nervosa, or purposeful starvation, embodies visual as well as behavioral deviation; bulimia, binge-eating followed by vomiting and/or laxative abuse, is primarily behaviorally deviant.

Besides a fear of fatness, anorexics and bulimics exhibit distorted body images. In anorexia nervosa, a 20–25 percent loss of initial body weight occurs, resulting from self-starvation alone or in combination with excessive exercising, occasional binge-eating, vomiting and/or laxative abuse. Bulimia denotes cyclical (daily, weekly, for example) binge-eating followed by vomiting or laxative abuse; weight is normal or close to normal (Humphries et al. 1982). Common physical manifestations of these eating disorders include menstrual cessation or irregularities and electrolyte imbalances; among behavioral traits are depression, obsessions/compulsions, and anxiety (Russell 1979; Thompson and Schwartz 1982).

Increasingly prevalent in the past two decades, anorexia nervosa and bulimia have emerged as major health and social problems. Termed an epidemic on college campuses (Brody, as quoted in Schur 1984, p. 76), bulimia affects 13 percent of college students (Halmi et al. 1981). Less prevalent, anorexia nervosa was diagnosed in 0.6 percent of students utilizing a university health center (Stangler and Printz 1980). However, the overall mortality rate of anorexia nervosa is 6 percent (Schwartz and Thompson 1981) to 20 percent (Humphries et al. 1982); bulimia appears to be less life-threatening (Russell 1979).

Particularly affecting certain demographic groups, eating disorders are most prevalent among young, white, affluent (upper-middle to upper class) women in modern, industrialized countries (Crisp 1977; Willi and Grossman 1983). Combining all of these risk factors (female sex, youth, high socioeconomic status, and residence in an industrialized country), prevalence of anorexia nervosa in upper class English girls' schools is reported at 1 in 100 (Crisp et al. 1976). The age of onset for anorexia nervosa is bimodal at 14.5 and 18 years (Humphries et al. 1982); the most frequent age of onset for bulimia is 18 (Russell 1979).

Eating disorders have primarily been studied from psychological and medical perspectives.[1] Theories of etiology have generally fallen into three categories: the ego psychological (involving an impaired child-maternal environment); the family systems (implicating enmeshed, rigid families); and the endocrinological (involving a precipitating hormonal defect). Although relatively ignored in previous studies, the sociocultural components of anorexia nervosa and bulimia (the slimness norm and its agents of reinforcement, such as role models) have been postulated as accounting for the recent, dramatic increases in these disorders (Boskind-White 1985; Schwartz et al. 1982).[2]

Medical and psychological approaches to anorexia nervosa and bulimia obscure the social facets of the disorders and neglect the individuals' own definitions of their situations. Among the social processes involved in the development of an eating disorder is the sequence of conforming behavior, primary deviance, and secondary deviance. Societal reaction is the critical mediator affecting the movement through the deviant career (Becker 1973). Within a framework of labeling theory, this study focuses on the emergence of anorexic and bulimic identities, as well as on the consequences of being career deviants.

Methodology

Sampling and Procedures

Most research on eating disorders has utilized clinical subjects or nonclinical respondents completing questionnaires. Such studies can be criticized for simply counting and describing behaviors and/or neglecting the social construction of the disorders. Moreover, the work of clinicians is often limited by therapeutic orientation. Previous research may also have included individuals who were not in therapy on their own volition and who resisted admitting that they had an eating disorder.

Past studies thus disregard the intersubjective meanings respondents attach to their behavior and emphasize researchers' criteria for definition as anorexic or bulimic. In order to supplement these sampling and procedural designs, the present study utilizes participant observation of a group of self-defined anorexics and bulimics.[3] As the individuals had acknowledged their eating disorders, frank discussion and disclosure were facilitated.

Data are derived from a self-help group, BANISH, Bulimics/Anorexics in Self-Help, which met at a university in an urban center of the mid-South. Founded by one of the researchers (D.E.T.), BANISH was advertised in local newspapers as offering a group experience for individuals who were anorexic or bulimic. Despite the local advertisements, the campus location of the meeting may have selectively encouraged university students to attend. Nonetheless, in view of the modal age of onset and socioeconomic status of individuals with eating disorders, college students have been considered target populations (Crisp et al. 1976; Halmi et al. 1981).

The group's weekly two-hour meetings were observed for two years. During the course of this study, 30 individuals attended at least one of the meetings. Attendance at meetings was varied: Ten individuals came nearly every Sunday; five attended approximately twice a month; and the remaining 15 participated once a month or less frequently, often when their eating problems were "more severe" or "bizarre." The modal number of members at meetings was 12. The diversity in attendance was to be expected in self-help groups of anorexics and bulimics

> Most people's involvement will not be forever or even a long time. Most people get the support they need and drop out. Some take the time to help others after they themselves have been helped but even they may withdraw after a time. It is a natural and in many cases *necessary* process (emphasis in original). (American Anorexia/Bulimia Association, 1983)

Modeled after Alcoholics Anonymous, BANISH allowed participants to discuss their backgrounds and experiences with others who empathized. For many members, the group constituted their only source of help; these respondents were reluctant to contact health professionals because of shame, embarrassment, or financial difficulties.

In addition to field notes from group meetings, records of other encounters with all members were maintained. Participants visited the office of one of the researchers (D.E.T.), called both researchers by phone, and invited them to their homes or out for a cup of coffee. Such interaction facilitated genuine communication and mutual trust. Even among the 15 individuals who did not attend the meetings regularly, contact was maintained with 10 members on a monthly basis.

Supplementing field notes were informal interviews with 15 group members, lasting from two to four hours. Because they appeared to represent more extensive experience with eating disorders, these interviewees were chosen to amplify their comments about the labeling process, made during group meetings. Conducted near the end of the two-year observation period, the interviews focused on what the respondents thought antedated and maintained their eating disorders. In addition, participants described others' reactions to their behaviors as well as their own interpretations of these reactions. To protect the confidentiality of individuals quoted in the study, pseudonyms are employed.

Description of Members

The demographic composite of the sample typifies what has been found in other studies (Crisp 1977; Fox and James 1976; Herzog 1982; Schlesier-Stropp 1984). Group members' ages ranged from 19 to 36, with the modal age being 21. The respondents were white, and all but one were female. The sole male and three of the females were anorexic; the remaining females were bulimic.[4]

Primarily composed of college students, the group included four nonstudents, three of whom had college degrees. Nearly all members derived from upper-middle or lower-upper-class households. Eighteen students and two nonstudents were never married and uninvolved in serious relationships; two nonstudents were married (one with two children); two students were divorced (one with two children); and six students were involved in serious relationships. The duration of eating disorders ranged from three to 15 years.

Conforming Behavior

In the backgrounds of most anorexics and bulimics, dieting figures prominently, beginning in the teen years (Crisp 1977; Johnson et al. 1982; Lacey et al. 1986). As dieters, these individuals are conformist in their adherence to the cultural norms emphasizing thinness (Garner et al. 1980; Schwartz et al. 1982). In our society, slim bodies are regarded as the most worthy and attractive; overweight is viewed as physically and morally unhealthy—"obscene," "lazy," "slothful," and "gluttonous" (DeJong 1980; Ritenbaugh 1982; Schwartz et al. 1982).

Among the agents of socialization promoting the slimness norm is advertising. Female models in newspaper, magazine, and television advertisements are uniformly slender. In addition, product names and slogans exploit the thin orientation; examples include "Ultra Slim Lipstick," "Miller Lite," and "Virginia Slims." While retaining pressures toward thinness, an Ayds commercial attempts a compromise for those wanting to savor food: "Ayds . . . so you can taste, chew, and enjoy, while you lose weight." Appealing particularly to women, a nationwide fast-food restaurant chain offers low-calorie selections, so individuals can have a "license to eat." In the latter two examples, the notion of enjoying food is combined with the message to be slim. Food and restaurant advertisements overall convey the pleasures of eating, whereas advertisements for other products, such as fashions and diet aids, reinforce the idea that fatness is undesirable.

Emphasis on being slim affects everyone in our culture, but it influences women especially because of society's traditional emphasis on women's appearance. The slimness norm and its concomitant narrow beauty standards exacerbate the objectification of women (Schur 1984). Women view themselves as visual entities and recognize that conforming to appearance expectations and "becoming attractive object[s] [are] role obligation[s]" (Laws, as quoted in Schur 1984:66). Demonstrating the beauty motivation behind dieting, a recent Nielson survey indicated that of the 56 percent of all women aged 24 to 54 who dieted during the previous year, 76 percent did so for cosmetic, rather than health, reasons (Schwartz et al. 1982). For most female group members, dieting was viewed as a means of gaining attractiveness and appeal to the opposite sex. The male respondent, as well, indicated that "when I was fat, girls didn't look at me, but when I got thinner, I was suddenly popular."

In addition to responding to the specter of obesity, individuals who develop anorexia nervosa and bulimia are conformist in their strong commitment to other conventional norms and goals. They consistently excel at school and work (Bruch 1981; Humphries et al. 1982; Russell 1979), maintaining high aspirations in both areas (Lacey et al. 1986; Theander 1970). Group members generally completed college-preparatory courses in high school, aware from an early age that they would strive for a college degree. Also, in college as well as high school, respondents joined honor societies and academic clubs.

Moreover, pre-anorexics and -bulimics display notable conventionality as "model children" (Humphries et al. 1982, p. 199), "the pride and joy" of their parents (Bruch 1981, p. 215), accommodating themselves to the wishes of others. Parents of these individuals emphasize conformity and value achievement (Bruch 1981). Respondents felt that perfect or near-perfect grades were expected of them; however, good grades were not rewarded by parents, because "A's" were common for these children. In addition, their parents suppressed conflicts, to preserve the image of the "all-American family" (Humphries et al. 1982). Group members reported that they seldom, if ever, heard their parents argue or raise their voices.

Also conformist in their affective ties, individuals who develop anorexia nervosa and bulimia are strongly, even excessively, attached to their parents. Respondents' families appeared close-knit, demonstrating palpable emotional ties. Several group members, for example, reported habitually calling home at prescribed times, whether or not they had any news. Such families have been termed "enmeshed" and "overprotective," displaying intense interaction and concern for members' welfare (Minuchin et al. 1978; Selvini-Palazzoli 1978). These qualities could be viewed as marked conformity to the norm of familial closeness.[5]

Another element of notable conformity in the family milieu of pre-anorexics and -bulimics concerns eating, body weight/shape, and exercising (Humphries et al. 1982; Kalucy et al. 1977). Respondents reported their fathers' preoccupation with exercising and their mothers' engrossment in food preparation. When group members dieted and lost weight, they received an extraordinary amount of approval. Among the family, body size became a matter of "friendly rivalry." One bulimic informant recalled that she, her mother, and her coed sister all strived to wear a size 5, regardless of their heights and body frames. Subsequent to this study, the researchers learned that both the mother and sister had become bulimic.

As pre-anorexics and -bulimics, group members thus exhibited marked conformity to cultural norms of thinness, achievement, compliance, and parental attachment. Their families reinforced their conformity by adherence to norms of family closeness and weight/body shape consciousness.

Primary Deviance

Even with familial encouragement, respondents, like nearly all dieters (Chernin 1981), failed to maintain their lowered weights. Many cited their lack of willpower to eat only restricted foods. For the emerging anorexics and bulimics, extremes such as purposeful starvation or binging accompanied by vomiting and/or laxative abuse appeared as "obvious solutions" to the problem of retaining weight loss. Associated with these behaviors was a regained feeling of control in lives that had been disrupted by a major crisis. Group members' extreme weight-loss efforts operated as coping mechanisms for entering college, leaving home, or feeling rejected by the opposite sex.

The primary inducement for both eating adaptations was the drive for slimness: With slimness came more self-respect and a feeling of superiority over "unsuccessful dieters." Brian, for example, experienced a "power trip" upon consistent weight loss through starvation. Binges allowed the purging respondents to cope with stress through eating while maintaining a slim appearance. As former strict dieters, Teresa and Jennifer used binging/purging as an alternative to the constant self-denial of starvation. Acknowledging their parents' desires for them to be slim, most respondents still felt it was a conscious choice on their part to continue extreme weight-loss efforts. Being thin became the "most important thing" in their lives—their "greatest ambition."

In explaining the development of an anorexic or bulimic identity, Lemert's (1951, 1967) concept of primary deviance is salient. Primary deviance refers to a transitory period of norm violations which do not affect an individual's self-concept or performance of social roles. Although respondents were exhibiting anorexic or bulimic behavior, they did not consider themselves to be anorexic or bulimic.

At first, anorexics' significant others complimented their weight loss, expounding on their new "sleekness" and "good looks." Branch and Eurman (1980, p. 631) also found anorexics' families and friends describing them as "well groomed," "neat," "fashionable," and "victorious." Not until the respondents approached emaciation did some parents or friends become concerned and withdraw their praise. Significant others also became increasingly aware of the anorexics' compulsive exercising, preoccupation with food preparation (but not consumption), and ritualistic eating patterns (such as cutting food into minute pieces and eating only certain foods at prescribed times).

For bulimics, friends or family members began to question how the respondents could eat such large amounts of food (often in excess of 10,000 calories a day) and stay slim. Significant others also noticed calluses across the bulimics' hands, which were caused by repeated inducement of vomiting. Several bulimics were "caught in the act," bent over commodes. Generally, friends and family required substantial evidence before believing that the respondents' binging or purging was no longer sporadic.

Secondary Deviance

Heightened awareness of group members' eating behavior ultimately led others to label the respondents "anorexic" or "bulimic." Respondents differed in their histories of being labeled and accepting the labels. Generally first termed anorexic by friends, family, or medical personnel, the anorexics initially vigorously denied the label. They felt they were not "anorexic enough," not skinny enough; Robin did not regard herself as having the "skeletal" appearance she associated with anorexia nervosa. These group members found it difficult to differentiate between socially approved modes of weight loss—eating less and exercising more—and the extremes of those behaviors. In fact, many of their activities—cheerleading, modeling, gymnastics, aerobics—reinforced their pursuit of thinness. Like other anorexics, Chris felt she was being "ultra-healthy," with "total control" over her body.

For several respondents, admitting they were anorexic followed the realization that their lives were disrupted by their eating disorder. Anorexics' inflexible eating patterns unsettled family meals and holiday gatherings. Their regimented lifestyle of compulsively scheduled activities—exercising, school, and meals—precluded any spontaneous social interactions. Realization of their adverse behaviors preceded the anorexics' acknowledgment of their subnormal body weight and size.

Contrasting with anorexics, the binge/purgers, when confronted, more readily admitted that they were bulimic and that their means of weight loss was "abnormal." Teresa, for example, knew "very well" that her bulimic behavior was "wrong and unhealthy," although "worth the physical risks." While the bulimics initially maintained that their purging was only a temporary weight-loss method, they eventually realized that their disorder represented a "loss of control." Although these respondents regretted the self-indulgence, "shame," and "wasted time," they acknowledged their growing dependence on binging/purging for weight management and stress regulation.

The application of anorexic or bulimic labels precipitated secondary deviance, wherein group members internalized these identities. Secondary deviance refers to norm violations which are a response to society's labeling: "secondary deviation . . . becomes a means of social defense, attack or adaptation to the overt and covert problems created by the societal reaction to primary deviance" (Lemert 1967, p. 17). In contrast to primary deviance, secondary deviance is generally prolonged, alters the individual's self-concept, and affects the performance of his/her social roles.

As secondary deviants, respondents felt that their disorders "gave a purpose" to their lives. Nicole resisted attaining a normal weight because it was not "her"—she accepted her anorexic weight as her "true" weight. For Teresa, bulimia became a "companion"; and Julie felt "every aspect of her life," including time management and social activities, was affected by her bulimia. Group members' eating disorders became the salient element of their self-concepts, so that they related to familiar people and new acquaintances as anorexics or bulimics. For example, respondents regularly compared their body shapes and sizes with those of others. They also became sensitized to comments about their appearance, whether or not the remarks were made by someone aware of their eating disorder.

With their behavior increasingly attuned to their eating disorders, group members exhibited role engulfment (Schur 1971). Through accepting anorexic or bulimic identities, individuals centered activities around their deviant role, downgrading other social roles. Their obligations as students, family members, and friends became subordinate to their eating and exercising rituals. Socializing, for example, was gradually curtailed because it interfered with compulsive exercising, binging, or purging.

Labeled anorexic or bulimic, respondents were ascribed a new status with a different set of role expectations. Regardless of other positions the individuals occupied, their deviant status, or master status (Becker 1973; Hughes 1958), was identified before all others. Among group members, Nicole, who was known as the "school's brain," became known as the "school's anorexic." No longer viewed as conforming model individuals, some respondents were termed "starving waifs" or "pigs."   .

Because of their identities as deviants, anorexics' and bulimics' interactions with others were altered. Group members' eating habits were scrutinized by friends and family and used as a "catch-all" for everything negative that happened to them. Respondents felt self-conscious around individuals who knew of their disorders; for example, Robin imagined people "watching and whispering" behind her. In addition, group members believed others expected them to "act" anorexic or bulimic. Friends of some anorexic group members never offered them food or drink, assuming continued disinterest on the respondents' part. While being hospitalized, Denise felt she had to prove to others she was not still vomiting, by keeping her bathroom door open. Other bulimics, who lived in dormitories, were hesitant to use the restroom for normal purposes lest several friends be huddling at the door, listening for vomiting. In general, individuals interacted with the respondents largely on the basis of their eating disorder; in doing so, they reinforced anorexic and bulimic behaviors.

Bulimic respondents, whose weight-loss behavior was not generally detectable from their appearance, tried earnestly to hide their bulimia by binging and purging in secret. Their main purpose in concealment was to avoid the negative consequences of being known as a bulimic. For these individuals, bulimia connoted a "cop-out": Like "weak anorexics," bulimics pursued thinness but yielded to urges to eat. Respondents felt other people regarded bulimia as "gross" and had little sympathy for the sufferer. To avoid these stigmas or "spoiled identities," the bulimics shrouded their behaviors.

Distinguishing types of stigma, Goffman (1963) describes discredited (visible) stigmas and discreditable (invisible) stigmas. Bulimics, whose weight was approximately normal or even slightly elevated, harbored discreditable stigmas. Anorexics, on the other hand, suffered both discreditable and discredited stigmas—the latter due to their emaciated appearance. Certain anorexics were more reconciled than the bulimics to their stigmas: For Brian, the "stigma of anorexia was better than being fat." Common to the stigmatized individuals was an inability to interact spontaneously with others. Respondents were constantly on guard against topics of eating and body size.

Both anorexics and bulimics were held responsible by others for their behavior and presumed able to "get out of it if they tried." Many anorexics reported being told to "just eat more," while bulimics were enjoined to simply "stop eating so much." Such appeals were made without regard for the complexities of the problem. Ostracized by certain friends and family members, anorexics and bulimics felt increasingly isolated. For respondents, the self-help group presented a nonthreatening forum for discussing their disorders. Here, they found mutual understanding, empathy, and support. Many participants viewed BANISH as a haven from stigmatization by "others."

Group members, as secondary deviants, thus endured negative consequences, such as stigmatization, from being labeled. As they internalized the labels anorexic or bulimic, individuals' self-concepts were significantly influenced. When others interacted with the respondents on the basis of their eating disorders, anorexic or bulimic identities were encouraged. Moreover, group members' efforts to counteract the deviant labels were thwarted by their master status.

Discussion

Previous research on eating disorders has dwelt almost exclusively on medical and psychological facets. Although necessary for a comprehensive understanding of anorexia nervosa and bulimia, these approaches neglect the social processes involved. The phenomena of eating disorders transcend concrete disease entities and clinical diagnoses. Multifaceted and complex, anorexia nervosa and bulimia require a holistic research design, in which sociological insights must be included.

A limitation of medical/psychiatric studies, in particular, is researchers' use of a priori criteria in establishing salient variables. Rather than utilizing predetermined standards of inclusion, the present study allows respondents to construct their own reality. Concomitant to this innovative approach to eating disorders is the selection of a sample of self-admitted anorexics and bulimics. Individuals' perceptions of what it means to become anorexic or bulimic are explored. Although based on a small sample, findings can be used to guide researchers in other settings.

With only 5 to 10 percent of reported cases appearing in males (Crisp 1977; Stangler and Printz 1980), eating disorders are primarily a women's aberrance. The deviance of anorexia nervosa and bulimia is rooted in the visual objectification of women and attendant slimness norm. Indeed, purposeful starvation and binging/purging reinforce the notion that "a society gets the deviance it deserves" (Schur 1979, p. 71). As recently noted (Schur 1984), the sociology of deviance has generally bypassed systematic studies of women's norm violations. Like male deviants, females endure label applications, internalizations, and fulfillments.

The social processes involved in developing anorexic or bulimic identities comprise the sequence of conforming behavior, primary deviance, and secondary deviance. With a background of exceptional adherence to conventional norms, especially the striving for thinness, respondents subsequently exhibit the primary deviance of starving or binging/purging. Societal reaction to these behaviors leads to secondary deviance, wherein respondents' self-concepts and master statuses become anorexic or bulimic. Within this framework of labeling theory, the persistence of eating disorders, as well as the effects of stigmatization, are elucidated.

Although during the course of this research some respondents alleviated their symptoms through psychiatric help or hospital treatment programs, no one was labeled "cured." An anorexic is considered recovered when weight is normal for two years; a bulimic is termed recovered after being symptom-free for one and one-half years (American Anorexia/Bulimia Association Newsletter 1985). Thus deviance disavowal (Schur 1971), or efforts after normalization to counteract deviant labels, remains a topic for future exploration.

NOTES

1. Although instructive, an integration of the medical, psychological, and socio-cultural perspectives on eating disorders is beyond the scope of this paper.
2. Exceptions to the neglect of sociocultural factors are discussions of sex-role socialization in the development of eating disorders. Anorexics' girlish appearance has been interpreted as a rejection of femininity and womanhood (Bruch 1981; Orbach 1979, 1985). In contrast, bulimics have been characterized as over-conforming to traditional female sex roles (Boskind-Lodahl 1976).
3. Although a group experience for self-defined bulimics has been reported (Boskind-Lodahl 1976), the researcher, from the outset, focused on Gestalt and behaviorist techniques within a feminist orientation.
4. One explanation for fewer anorexics than bulimics in the sample is that, in the general population, anorexics are outnumbered by bulimics at 8 or 10 to 1 (Lawson, as reprinted in American Anorexia/Bulimia Association Newsletter 1985, p. 1). The proportion of bulimics to anorexics in the sample is 6.5 to 1. In addition, compared to bulimics, anorexics may be less likely to attend a self-help group as they have a greater tendency to deny the existence of an eating problem (Humphries et al. 1982). However, the four anorexics in the present study were among the members who attended the meetings most often.
5. Interactions in the families of anorexics and bulimics might seem deviant in being inordinately close. However, in the larger societal context, the family members epitomize the norms of family cohesiveness. Perhaps unusual in their occurrence, these families are still within the realm of conformity. Humphries and colleagues (1982, p. 202) refer to the "highly enmeshed and protective" family as part of the "idealized family myth."

REFERENCES

American Anorexia/Bulimia Association. 1983, April. Correspondence.
American Anorexia/Bulimia Association Newsletter. 1985. 8(3).
Becker, Howard S. 1973. *Outsiders.* New York: Free Press.
Boskind-Lodahl, Marlene. 1976. "Cinderella's Stepsisters: A Feminist Perspective on Anorexia Nervosa and Bulimia." *Signs, Journal of Women in Culture and Society* 2:342–56.

Boskind-White, Marlene. 1985. "Bulimarexia: A Sociocultural Perspective." Pp. 113–26 in *Theory and Treatment of Anorexia Nervosa and Bulimia: Biomedical, Sociocultural and Psychological Perspectives*, edited by S. W. Emmett. New York: Brunner/Mazel.

Branch, C. H. Hardin and Linda J. Eurman. 1980. "Social Attitudes toward Patients with Anorexia Nervosa." *American Journal of Psychiatry* 137:631–32.

Bruch, Hilda. 1981. "Developmental Considerations of Anorexia Nervosa and Obesity." *Canadian Journal of Psychiatry* 26:212–16.

Chernin, Kim. 1981. *The Obsession: Reflections on the Tyranny of Slenderness*. New York: Harper & Row.

Crisp, A. H. 1977. "The Prevalence of Anorexia Nervosa and Some of Its Associations in the General Population." *Advances in Psychosomatic Medicine* 9:38–47.

Crisp, A. H., R. L. Palmer, and R. S. Kalucy. 1976. "How Common Is Anorexia Nervosa? A Prevalence Study." *British Journal of Psychiatry* 128:549–54.

DeJong, William. 1980. "The Stigma of Obesity: The Consequences of Naive Assumptions Concerning the Causes of Physical Deviance." *Journal of Health and Social Behavior* 21:75–87.

Fox, K. C. and N. McI. James. 1976. "Anorexia Nervosa: A Study of 44 Strictly Defined Cases." *New Zealand Medical Journal* 84:309–12.

Garner, David M., Paul E. Garfinkel, Donald Schwartz, and Michael Thompson. 1980. "Cultural Expectations of Thinness in Women." *Psychological Reports* 47:483–91.

Goffman, Erving. 1963. *Stigma*. Englewood Cliffs, NJ: Prentice-Hall.

Halmi, Katherine A., James R. Falk, and Estelle Schwartz. 1981. "Binge-Eating and Vomiting: A Survey of a College Population." *Psychological Medicine* 11:697–706.

Herzog, David B. 1982. "Bulimia: The Secretive Syndrome." *Psychosomatics* 23:481–83.

Hughes, Everett C. 1958. *Men and Their Work*. New York: Free Press.

Humphries, Laurie L., Sylvia Wrobel, and H. Thomas Wiegert. 1982. "Anorexia Nervosa." *American Family Physician* 26:199–204.

Johnson, Craig L., Marilyn K. Stuckey, Linda D. Lewis, and Donald M. Schwartz. 1982. "Bulimia: A Descriptive Survey of 316 Cases." *International Journal of Eating Disorders* 2(1):3–16.

Kalucy, R. S., A. H. Crisp, and Britta Harding. 1977. "A Study of 56 Families with Anorexia Nervosa." *British Journal of Medical Psychology* 50:381–95.

Lacey, Hubert J., Sian Coker, and S. A. Birtchnell. 1986. "Bulimia: Factors Associated with Its Etiology and Maintenance." *International Journal of Eating Disorders* 5:475–87.

Lemert, Edwin M. 1951. *Social Pathology*. New York: McGraw-Hill.

———. 1967. *Human Deviance, Social Problems and Social Control*. Englewood Cliffs, NJ: Prentice-Hall.

Minuchin, Salvador, Bernice L. Rosman, and Lester Baker. 1978. *Psychosomatic Families: Anorexia Nervosa in Context*. Cambridge, MA: Harvard University Press.

Orbach, Susie. 1979. *Fat Is a Feminist Issue*. New York: Berkeley.

———. 1985. "Visibility/Invisibility: Social Considerations in Anorexia Nervosa—A Feminist Perspective." Pp. 127–38 in *Theory and Treatment of Anorexia Nervosa and Bulimia: Biomedical, Sociocultural and Psychological Perspectives*, edited by S. W. Emmett. New York: Brunner/Mazel.

Ritenbaugh, Cheryl, 1982. "Obesity as a Culture-Bound Syndrome." *Culture, Medicine and Psychiatry* 6:347–61.

Russell, Gerald. 1979. "Bulimia Nervosa: An Ominous Variant of Anorexia Nervosa." *Psychological Medicine* 9:429–48.

Schlesier-Stropp, Barbara. 1984. "Bulimia: A Review of the Literature." *Psychological Bulletin* 95:247–57.

Schur, Edwin M. 1971. *Labeling Deviant Behavior*. New York: Harper & Row.

———. 1979. *Interpreting Deviance: A Sociological Introduction*. New York: Harper & Row.

————. 1984. *Labeling Women Deviant: Gender, Stigma, and Social Control.* New York: Random House.

Schwartz, Donald M. and Michael G. Thompson. 1981. "Do Anorectics Get Well? Current Research and Future Needs." *American Journal of Psychiatry* 138:319–23.

Schwartz, Donald M., Michael G. Thompson, and Craig L. Johnson. 1982. "Anorexia Nervosa and Bulimia: The Socio-cultural Context." *International Journal of Eating Disorders* 1(3):20–36.

Selvini-Palazzoli, Mara. 1978. *Self-Starvation: From Individual to Family Therapy in the Treatment of Anorexia Nervosa.* New York: Jason Aronson.

Stangler, Ronnie S. and Adolph M. Printz. 1980. "DSM-III: Psychiatric Diagnosis in a University Population." *American Journal of Psychiatry* 137:937–40.

Theander, Sten. 1970. "Anorexia Nervosa." *Acta Psychiatrica Scandinavica Supplement* 214:24–31.

Thompson, Michael G. and Donald M. Schwartz. 1982. "Life Adjustment of Women with Anorexia Nervosa and Anorexic-like Behavior." *International Journal of Eating Disorders* 1(2):47–60.

Willi, Jurg and Samuel Grossman. 1983. "Epidemiology of Anorexia Nervosa in a Defined Region of Switzerland." *American Journal of Psychiatry* 140:564–67.

21

DISCLOSING ILLNESS

KATHY CHARMAZ

We often stigmatize people whom we consider to be deviant, such as the mentally ill and women who have eating disorders. Other deviant groups in the United States, such as gangs, the homeless, and persons with HIV/AIDS, also are heavily stigmatized. In this reading, Kathy Charmaz illustrates how another stigmatized group in our society, people who are chronically ill, struggle with negative labels and stigmas associated with their illnesses.

I think that emotionally I would feel like if I got sick again that the same stuff would happen again in terms of that I would be real alone, and that I would have to deal with everything alone, that I couldn't tell anyone that I was sick and that I wouldn't be able to take care of myself, but that I wouldn't be able to ask for help. And to be in that is a real double bind, you know?

Sara Shaw became ill 16 years ago. After several years of having her symptoms discounted, she received a diagnosis of lupus erythematosus, which was changed to mixed collagen disease five years ago. She made the above statement nine years ago. Two years after that interview, she said, "If I were to start going with somebody pretty heavily, how would I tell them about having been sick, the possibility that I could be sick again—that scares me to death." I asked, "So it's not something that comes up in your friendships?" She said:

> *Yeah, actually everyone that I've talked to or been real close to that I'm friends with, I've told that I was sick. I don't tend to say that I'm sick now. I don't tend to say it in terms of the present tense, or in terms of an ongoing, a chronic illness. . . . But I also wonder if anyone would understand if I were to get involved with somebody to the point of marriage, the point of sharing lives. I have very little balance on that question.*

Three years later, Sara disclosed, "I don't think I do trust anybody in terms of letting them know about having been sick, even though I'm not sick now. That's something like that is kind of secret." Subsequently, two years later, seven years after her first statement above, she remarked:

> *It's [her illness and near-death experience] like a prestige thing now, I mean that I've gone through a near-death experience at ALU [the university where she worked] is like, I mean I'm one level higher, you know, for that. . . . That comes out quickly, you know, in whatever way it comes out. That started [for her] with FPI [a psychological institute specializing in intensive workshops using simulated families to work on family-of-origin issues]. . . . I was able to bring that out and say I had a lot of fears . . . around having—being intimate and letting people know, you know, that I had had, that I get sick sometimes and because I talked to them about everything, the people that I'm close to in that family. . . . I never thought I could say stuff like that because then I thought that they would need, they would feel that they would need to change me, or heal me, or fix me. And we don't have to do that to each other, we're just sharing our lives, that's it, you know. So that's real new. Yeah, but I do that now. I'm not seeing anybody romantically, so I haven't had to deal with that. Uhm, but I think I would tell because what's happened is I'm not willing enough to abandon myself to where I wouldn't bring that up. I would want someone to know now.*

To tell or not to tell? How much to tell? Risk disclosure but face rejection? Sara Shaw pondered over these questions for years. When she first became ill, the young man with whom she lived left three days before her exploratory surgery. Later, when her doctor told her that she would need care, she found that she had no one on whom she could rely. Not surprisingly, she grew secretive about her past illness and any present symptoms. Disclosing illness meant heavy risks.

For Sara Shaw, like others, disclosing illness meant revealing her feelings and vulnerabilities. Disclosing is a form of telling in which someone reveals self. When one discloses illness, facts and feelings about it touch one's self-concept and self-esteem (Jourard 1971; Zerubavel 1982). Still, an individual's stance toward disclosure may change with time, as Sara's did, as experiences change and as new perspectives are gained.

How do chronically ill people handle telling others about their illnesses? What does disclosure and avoiding disclosure mean to them?[1] When do they disclose? How do they manage their emotions about disclosing? What concerns do ill people have about others' responses to their disclosures?

Dilemmas of Disclosing Illness

Chronically ill people wonder what they *should* tell and what they *need* to tell others about their illnesses. Kathleen Lewis, who has lupus erythematosus, begins her book, "'How are you?' can perhaps become the most difficult question a chronically ill person needs to learn to answer" (1985, p. 3). Telling anything about illness can mean revealing potentially discrediting information about self (Schneider and Conrad 1980, 1983). Telling often means exposing hidden feelings. Telling sometimes means straining relationships. Telling can also mean risking loss of control and autonomy (Cozby 1973). Hence, some men and women will not tell family, friends, and associates that they have a chronic illness, and many others avoid updating people about their conditions. Other ill people take the risk or feel compelled to apprise select individuals about their situations.

Telling does not end. Physicians can impart bad news and depart (Clark and La Beff 1982; Glaser 1966; Glaser and Strauss 1965; Sudnow 1967; Taylor 1988). Unlike physicians, chronically ill people must tell and retell their news to many people and frequently do so at each step along the path that their illness takes. Moreover, they must live with the telling.

Perhaps most fundamentally, young and middle-aged adults risk losing acceptance by telling; older adults risk losing autonomy. Young and middle-aged adults can find themselves ignored, rejected, and stigmatized when they disclose their illnesses (Goffman 1963; Hopper 1981; Schneider and Conrad 1983). Not only must they handle their feelings about telling, but also they must handle their feelings about another's response to being told. Lovers, spouses, friends, and jobs may vanish from their lives. Of course, older adults experience these responses, too, but many older adults, particularly single elderly women, already have only a frail hold on their autonomy. Adult children or service providers, concerned about the safety of these elderly people or the quality of their housekeeping, may see their illness as a reason to grasp more control over them. For these older adults, telling means losing control over their homes, their mobility, their money, their decisions—in short, their lives. Meanwhile, they also must handle losing their health.

Thus the dilemmas of disclosing turn on control—control of identity, control over information, control over emotional response, and control over one's life. Hence, avoiding disclosure entirely, maintaining distance, metering disclosures, censoring information, and pacing disclosures all become ways of preserving control.

Avoiding Disclosure

Given the potential costs, avoiding disclosure can be a natural response to illness. Avoiding disclosure takes a different twist than concealing illness. When people avoid disclosure, they try to circumvent or minimize others' attending to their health status. Concealing illness often takes an enormous amount of commitment, planning, and work. When people conceal illness, they shroud it in secrecy. Avoiding disclosure can be easier and may reflect a spontaneous decision during the course of a conversation. By avoiding disclosure, people try to keep their illness understated in a relationship, or in their lives, more generally. Certainly an underlying reason for either concealing illness or for avoiding disclosure turns on whether someone grants illness any reality at all, and, if so, what kind of reality.

Both concealing illness and avoiding disclosure distance illness from self and avoid stigma. Yet a serious exacerbation can puncture a long-maintained secrecy. As her disability progressed, Tina Reidel tried to hide it in public and, thus, attempted to avoid stigma. During a recent interview, she described the embarrassment she had felt that morning when she could hardly walk through a department store:

> When I got up, after having my makeup done, I felt like I could hardly walk and I kept thinking, "I hope nobody notices, you know, that I'm really this way, that I can hardly walk." . . . It's like I think that other people could perceive the way I perceive myself, but they can't. So it's like I try to keep it hidden. . . . I think it's real embarrassing. You know, like say if someone can see that I can hardly walk or something, I'm all stooped over or you know, I catch a glimpse of myself in ah, like a window, it's very shocking sometimes what I see.

I asked, "In which way?" She said,

> Well, I can see that, other people can see is that, you know, my leg, I can hardly walk on it. And I feel like somehow I'm not a whole person and . . . people can look at it and feel sympathetic, but they can look at you and see you as being less than whole, you know. . . . And ah, it's frightening, I guess. . . . This idea of getting foot surgery and it's really scary because I don't think I'd be able to walk for about three months; I'd have to wear those bunny boots [removable casts]. And just the idea of like trying to go out in the world and it being like more apparent, that's the scariest part. It's not so much the pain I'd go through or anything, it's just that they'd know. It's like I'd be—you know, people could see.

A visible disability does not permit choice about whom to tell, when to tell, or how to tell. Under these conditions, information about self once held private becomes public knowledge and floods *self* as well as potentially flooding interaction. At that point, ill people often feel forced to face their feelings and values about disability.

Until disability becomes a visible and continuing fact, someone who avoids disclosure can more readily treat illness as a temporary interruption, rather than as a chronic condition. The possibility of effective medical procedures in the future can further this stance. For example, a kidney dialysis patient looked well, functioned quite well at work, and believed that he was in much better shape than other patients on the dialysis unit. Since he did not want to be identified as ill or disabled, he told no one beyond his family about his illness. He said, "I'm not really ill at all from this thing. And I'm perfectly able to keep working. It takes a little time to be on the machine, but I just schedule around it. It's really a very minor part of my life. And who knows? A transplant might become available and then this [dialysis] will be over."

Further, avoiding disclosure limits the reality of illness to self and for others. Lara Corbert recalled her first episode: "I remember not talking a lot about it, not telling a lot of people. Talking about it would make it real and I didn't want to think of it as permanent." Thus, avoiding disclosure allows claiming other identities than illness. To the extent that concealing illness and avoiding disclosure work, these strategies limit stigma and support preferred self-images.

Perhaps more commonly, ill people refuse to grant illness legitimacy to shape their lives and self-concepts. They do not wish to exploit their illness to their advantage. Bonnie Presley toyed with telling her accounting teacher that her illness had prevented her from completing an assignment. She said, "It's almost like you'd be using it, do you know what I mean? It sort of feels like that. You know about—with teachers—you hear about all these teachers and they say this guy said this and this girl said this and 'I have so many people lose their grandmothers,' and, you know, all these excuses for not doing their work. But everybody else has reasons too why they can't get it done, so I'm no different."

People with invisible illnesses often refused to grant legitimacy to the special needs that their illnesses engendered, and therefore, they chose not to disclose. Occasionally, they deferred to someone else's physical needs. For example, when the elevator stopped running just before my seminar, a student who used a wheelchair phoned to request that the class meet on the lawn. The class members agreed but several weeks later, a student who had multiple sclerosis told me, "I should have never gone out with the class; it was just too hot for me that day and I can't take the heat, but at the time, I thought Connie's needs were greater than mine. So I didn't say anything."

Potential Losses and Risks

In addition to the ultimate risks of losing acceptance and autonomy, ill people face immediate interactional risks: (1) being rejected and stigmatized for disclosing and for having an illness (cf. Ponse 1976), (2) being unable to handle others' responses, and (3) losing control over their emotions.

When people believe that they risk losing—or assuredly will lose—

status or self-esteem, they avoid disclosing illness. Lin Bell would not tell her co-workers when she had angina attacks. Instead, she tried to hide when she took her nitroglycerine so that her temporary distress would remain unnoticed. However, her tactics did not always work. She said:

Somebody saw me and you know how word gets around. I was hiding behind a cage, kind of bent over, taking [the pill]—well she went running to the supervisor and he sent someone else over to see how I was doing—I was just having an angina attack. No worse than what I had before the heart attack. Now they're scared to death that I'm going to have one there. And I don't want them to think that I can't keep up, 'cause they don't have to give me a light duty assignment. There's a lot of pressures in this world.

The people who'll support me are fine—it's—it's the ones who think they're being my friend by running and saying, you know, "Watch Lin, she'll go lay down or something." If I do—if they do that too often, the . . . [management] is going to say, "Hey, let's get her out of here. Why pay $13.00 an hour to somebody who can't keep up?"

Most men and women want to be known for attributes other than illness. Therefore, they will conceal illness or avoid disclosures when they see that illness could cloud other people's images and judgments of them. They will not take the risk. Because photojournalist Roger Ressmeyer would not allow his diabetes to flood his identity, he decided not to disclose it at work. During one incident, he risked possible residual brain damage or even death from insulin shock rather than request minimal help—and thereby disclose his illness. He writes:

I had forgotten to bring some food along. I napped intermittently, vaguely aware that the insulin injection I had taken earlier that morning was reaching its peak and my need for food was becoming critical. But I was too tired and embarrassed to mention my rapidly worsening condition to the well-known news photographer next to me, or to the driver or to anyone who might have had the apple or candy that would have saved me.

When I awoke, as from a dream, I was horrified to discover that I was standing on the street in front of a deli in Cocoa Beach with a half-empty bottle of orange juice in my hand. My head was throbbing and my body was shuddering. Hours had obviously passed, since the printed image of the shuttle launch stared at me from a newspaper rack. I had no recall of walking to the deli, or the missing hours. Many diabetics have accidents under exactly the same conditions but some angel must have been watching me. (1983, p. 8)

Knotty problems, shaky relationships, and harsh judgments make disclosing a dilemma. Subsequently, people avoid disclosing for months, or even years. To an older woman, her husband's alcoholism and consequent chronic illnesses seemed much more pressing than her own illness and growing disability. Though she had known for five years that she had lupus erythe-matosus, she had not told her husband about it. Tenuous or hostile relations can also increase an individual's proclivity not to tell. For example, a middle-aged man with cancer faced an uncertain future. Three years earlier, he had divorced his wife after a hostile separation and a nasty legal battle. Although he had severed contact with her and their daughter, he continued to feel unrelenting rage toward his ex-wife whom, he believed, had poisoned their daughter against him. He vowed that the first news either of them would have about his illness would be in his obituary.

Fear of being thought of as a complainer or whiner dissuades people from discussing their illnesses. Christine Danforth said:

> *If you have lupus, I mean one day it's my liver; one day it's my joints; one day it's my head, and it's like people really think you're a hypochondriac if you keep complaining about different ailments. . . . It's like you don't want to say any-thing because people are going to start thinking, you know, "God, don't go near her, all she is—is complaining about this." And I think that's why I never say anything because I feel like everything I have is related one way or another to the lupus but most of the people don't know I have lupus, and even those that do are not going to believe that 10 different ailments are the same thing. And I don't want anybody saying, you know, [that] they don't want to come around me be-cause I complain.*

A tendency to avoid disclosure intensifies when ill people had not talked about previous illnesses or feelings. Christine Danforth's father had died a painful death from cancer, but no one in the family had ever discussed his pain and suffering. Similar patterns repeat themselves. Christine believed that her mother knew her diagnosis but not what it meant. Not only did Christine resist revealing her discomfort, but also, when she did disclose, others did not believe her. She said, "My friends would call and say 'Let's go here or let's go there,' and I'd say, 'I can't; I just can't walk,' and they'd say, 'Pulling another Elise [her sister who as a child used her back injury as an ex-cuse to get out of chores], huh?' So I never, ever would say that I hurt when they called. Ever."

Once ill people have proof that others will use their disclosures against them, they guard against disclosing. Even people who had earlier revealed their feelings, as well as their conditions, become circumspect and guarded after discovering that someone used their disclosures against them. Patricia Kennedy recalled that for a lengthy period, "I became very, very careful." Like many other ill people, she learned to answer questions about how she was feeling by saying, "I'm fine."

Having a condition that everyone "knows" about raises special risks of disclosing. These conditions elicit probing questions about health habits and regimen, which, in turn, can escalate into continuing criticism. Though irri-tating enough to have one's private behavior relegated to public discourse and evaluation, the criticism can sting already open wounds. And when this happens, the judgments stick. Such criticism reflects an objectified version of similar silent inner dialogues ill people have long had in which they berate themselves about their difficulties or failures in following their regimens. Lin Bell remarked:

> *I think the not telling is that I smoke. . . . I am so guilty for that. And yet I'm not willing to quit. And when you tell somebody you smoke and you have heart disease, a little computer in their head goes, "Hey, this person is self-destructive," and I'm tired of hearing that, 'cause I'm not. I know that I'm smoking, Kathy; I know that it doesn't help me. But I am not self-destructive. I don't have a death wish at all.*

Risking disclosure extends into whether to claim having special needs, or to acknowledge hardships, long after everyone knows the diagnosis. Maureen Murphy's employers had forced her to take a disability leave for a year because of her diagnosis of multiple sclerosis. When she returned to work, they switched her to a less physically demanding job in another department with much less pay. After not working for a year, she felt grateful to have a job at all and therefore concealed any indication that the work was too strenuous for her. She recalled, "When I first started [working] there, I was doing filing and that got me tired, but I remember, you know, 'cause they didn't know what—where I would fit in, and so they decided to let me file for a little. And I didn't dare say a thing about being tired because I thought, 'Oh, God, they'll bounce me out of here,' you know. And, oh, that first day I was ready to drop."

Similar issues arise in relationships. For example, his respiratory therapist observed that keeping pace with his much healthier wife wore out a 68-year-old man with emphysema and heart disease. But he wouldn't tell his wife that he needed to slow down because he felt so guilty about draining their finances for his care. He wanted, at least, to help her with daily chores. He risked more rapid deterioration to gain a more favorable image in her eyes. For single ill people, the mere thought of repeatedly explaining their inability to maintain a new friend's pace can stifle romantic involvement.

Conceptions of illness as private lead to avoiding disclosure. For many people, facts and feelings about illness rank with sex and finances for deserving privacy. Maintaining this privacy becomes part of a creditable self. Bonnie Presley remarked, "I'd like to feel better before I have a relationship. I guess maybe I'm not willing to share it." I asked, "Share it?" She said:

> *Share when I don't feel good—share things like that. I'm not willing—I mean I don't tell my daughter very often—I don't tell her. . . . I know people who call and tell me real personal things and I just think, "God, this person doesn't even know me and you're telling me that?" I can't do that.*
>
> *It's [feeling ill]; it's private; it's mine. In a relationship, you'd have to share. If somebody doesn't feel good and they don't want to talk about it, then living alone seems like the answer. You don't have to explain.*

Should family, friends, and acquaintances think that the person's illness, treatments, or symptoms are stigmatizing, they may demand that he or she keep quiet about them. Thus, avoiding disclosure naturally follows. Ill people, like this woman who had a bowel dysfunction, find "that I can talk about this disease but I can't find anyone to listen." Although she spoke freely about her pain and sudden diarrhea to immediate co-workers, they cut her off. She needed support and care from her lover, but he could not tolerate the dirt and disorder her condition caused and therefore he either ignored or castigated her. As Mitteness (1987) points out, bodily control is a prerequisite to competent adult status. Thus, the lack of such control goes beyond forcing disclosure; it threatens to elicit judgments of inadequacy and incompetence. To the extent that others impose their judgments and that ill people share them, they will avoid both disclosures and situations in which their symptoms might become apparent (Conrad 1987; Mitteness 1987; Reif 1975).

Even without having symptoms that undermine bodily functions, ill people often fear negative responses, revealed through direct statements, gestures, and tone. Usually after their first serious episode, ill people will tell everyone all the details about their illness, hospitalization, and doctor's advice. Although initially interested, other people soon weary of these conversations and begin to treat the ill person as diminished, a malingerer, or an object of fleeting pity. Occasionally, ill people's friends and acquaintances told them that they looked "better" but their tone and expression belied their statements. Not surprisingly then, ill people prop themselves up for social occasions with the help of their closest intimates. They try to present a public face preserved from the past, only to collapse when they return home (Bury 1982). While still convalescing, an older man with heart disease attended the office Christmas party. He attempted to look as vigorous as possible. He rested for long hours before, dressed nattily, rehearsed a ready repertoire of jokes and quips, and minimized any overexertion in getting there. Afterwards, he spent three days recovering from the event. By preserving a public face, these people avoid or minimize others' negative judgments that link their state of health with their being. Preserving an earlier public face also protects a current self-conception. To the extent that ill people preserve that public face, they can more easily maintain the same feelings about self.

By modifying certain disclosures, metering some disclosures, and censoring still others, an individual can provide continuity with a past self or protect a now fragile or vulnerable self. After a turbulent first marriage that ended with her husband's death, a young widow looked forward to a happy second marriage. She asked her fiancé if he could be happy with someone who could not play tennis with him. She had a minor, but visible, disability and high fatigue. Though her doctor had diagnosed her as having multiple sclerosis, she vacillated between not accepting the diagnosis and doubting it. To her, doubting the accuracy of the diagnosis justified not telling her fiancé about it. She said, "'Cause I do wonder about this [having MS], you know. I think the hardest thing is for me not knowing really whether I have it or not, so I can't see whether I should, you know, make things—jeopardize things by saying that." By avoiding this disclosure, she maintained continuity with a preferred self but risked later recriminations and feeling guilty about deception.

Interaction with others may lead an ill person to censor disclosure. For example, after a woman had snubbed Tina Reidel, she then censored her disclosures. She recalled, "When she next asked how my arthritis was, I said really quickly, '*Don't ask.*'" She reflected:

> *Some people I feel I can bring in. Other people I have to keep out. . . . When they see me, it's as if they are thinking all these other thoughts—like, "Should I go up to her?" or "What's she thinking?" They're thinking about me—I can pick it up. But they're not spontaneous. They don't just go, "Oh, hi, Tina," or "Good to see you." Like that girl who knew me; I thought it was very awkward for her to stand in front of me and talk to the other person and not acknowledge me. So what it equates in my mind is: Why should I bare my vulnerability to this person? They don't even care.*

NOTE

1. Throughout the article, I focus on disclosing, although I note where disclosing fits with other forms of telling and how it compares with them.

REFERENCES

Bury, Michael. 1982. "Chronic Illness as Disruption." *Sociology of Health and Illness* 4:167–82.

Clark, Robert E. and Emily E. Le Beff. 1982. "Death Telling: Managing the Delivery of Bad News." *Journal of Health and Social Behavior* 23:366–80.

Conrad, Peter. 1987. "The Experience of Illness: Recent and New Directions." Pp. 1–32 in *Research in the Sociology of Health Care: The Experience and Management of Chronic Illness*, Volume 6, edited by Julius A. Roth and Peter Conrad. Greenwich, CT: JAI Press.

Cozby, Paul C. 1973. "Self-Disclosure: A Literature Review." *Psychological Bulletin* 79:73–91.

Glaser, Barney G. 1966. "Disclosure of Terminal Illness." *Journal of Health and Human Behavior* 7:83–91.

Glaser, Barney G. and Anselm L. Strauss. 1965. *Awareness of Dying*. Chicago: Aldine.

Goffman, Erving. 1963. *Stigma*. Englewood Cliffs, NJ: Prentice-Hall.

Hopper, Susan. 1981. "Diabetes as a Stigmatized Condition." *Social Science and Medicine* 15B:11–19.

Jourard, Sidney. 1971. *The Transparent Self*. New York: Van Nostrand.

Lewis, Kathleen. 1985. *Successful Living with Chronic Illness*. Wayne, NJ: Avery.

Mitteness, Linda S. 1987. "So What Do You Expect When You're 85?: Urinary Incontinence in Late Life." Pp. 177–220 in *Research in the Sociology of Health Care: The Experience and Management of Chronic Illness*, edited by Julius A. Roth and Peter Conrad. Greenwich, CT: JAI Press.

Ponse, Barbara. 1976. "Secrecy in the Lesbian World." *Urban Life* 5:313–38.

Reif, Laura. 1975. "Ulcerative Colitis: Strategies for Managing Life." Pp. 81–88 in *Chronic Illness and the Quality of Life*, edited by Anselm L. Strauss and Barney G. Glaser. St. Louis: Mosby.

Ressmeyer, Roger. July 10, 1983. "A Day to Day Struggle." Pp. 1–8 in *California Living, San Francisco Chronicle & Examiner.*

Schneider, Joseph W. and Peter Conrad. 1980. "In the Closet with Illness: Epilepsy, Stigma Potential, and Information Control." *Social Problems* 28:32–44.

Schneider, Joseph W. and Peter Conrad. 1983. *Having Epilepsy.* Philadelphia: Temple University Press.

Sudnow, David. 1967. *Passing On: The Social Organization of Dying.* Englewood Cliffs, NJ: Prentice-Hall.

Taylor, Kathryn M. 1988. "Telling Bad News: Physicians and the Disclosure of Undesirable Information." *Sociology of Health & Illness* 10:109–32.

Zerubavel, Eviatar. 1982. "Personal Information and Social Life." *Symbolic Interaction* 5:97–109.

22

FRATERNITIES AND RAPE ON CAMPUS

PATRICIA YANCEY MARTIN • ROBERT A. HUMMER

Conflict theory suggests that, in our society, whom and what the label "deviant" is place on is based primarily on relative power. Those who have more authority and control define what is "normal" and what is deviant. Moreover, conflict theorists argue that social norms, including laws, generally reflect the interests of the rich and powerful. Thus, historically, we have property laws to protect against the theft of property of the land-owning classes and domestic laws that protect the status of men, as patriarchs, within the family. The reading by Patricia Yancey Martin and Robert A. Hummer exemplifies this process, in which the privileged attempt to socially construct deviance and crime to their advantage. In particular, Martin and Hummer analyze the social norms and rituals of male fraternities that contribute to the high incidence of violence against women on many college campuses.

Rapes are perpetrated on dates, at parties, in chance encounters, and in specially planned circumstances. That group structure and processes, rather than individual values or characteristics, are the impetus for many rape episodes was documented by Blanchard (1959) 30 years ago (also see Geis 1971), yet sociologists have failed to pursue this theme (for an exception, see Chancer 1987). A recent review of research (Muehlenhard and Linton 1987) on sexual violence, or rape, devotes only a few pages to the situational contexts of rape events, and these are conceptualized as potential risk factors for individuals rather than qualities of rape-prone social contexts.

Many rapes, far more than come to the public's attention, occur in fraternity houses on college and university campuses, yet little research has analyzed fraternities at American colleges and universities as rape-prone contexts (cf. Ehrhart and Sandler 1985). Most of the research on fraternities reports on samples of individual fraternity men. One group of studies compares the values, attitudes, perceptions, family socioeconomic status, psychological traits (aggressiveness, dependence), and so on, of fraternity and nonfraternity men (Bohrnstedt 1969; Fox, Hodge, and Ward 1987; Kanin 1967; Lemire 1979; Miller 1973). A second group attempts to identify the effects of fraternity memberships over time on the values, attitudes, beliefs, or moral precepts of members (Hughes and Winston 1987; Marlowe and Auvenshine 1982; Miller 1973; Wilder, Hoyt, Doren, Hauck, and Zettle 1978; Wilder, Hoyt, Surbeck, Wilder, and Carney 1986). With minor exceptions, little research addresses the group and organizational context of fraternities or the social construction of fraternity life (for exceptions, see Letchworth 1969; Longino and Kart 1973; Smith 1964).

Gary Tash, writing as an alumnus and trial attorney in his fraternity's magazine, claims that over 90 percent of all gang rapes on college campuses involve fraternity men (1988, p. 2). Tash provides no evidence to substantiate this claim, but students of violence against women have been concerned with fraternity men's frequently reported involvement in rape episodes (Adams and Abarbanel 1988). Ehrhart and Sandler (1985) identify over 50 cases of gang rape on campus perpetrated by fraternity men, and their analysis points to many of the conditions that we discuss here. Their analysis is unique in focusing on conditions in fraternities that make gang rapes of women by fraternity men both feasible and probable. They identify excessive alcohol use, isolation from external monitoring, treatment of women as prey, use of pornography, approval of violence, and excessive concern with competition as precipitating conditions to gang rape (also see Merton 1985; Roark 1987).

The study reported here confirmed and complemented these findings by focusing on both conditions and processes. We examined dynamics associated with the social construction of fraternity life, with a focus on processes that foster the use of coercion, including rape, in fraternity men's relations with women. Our examination of men's social fraternities on college and university campuses as groups and organizations led us to conclude that fraternities are a physical and sociocultural context that encourages the sexual coercion of women. We make no claim that all fraternities are "bad" or that all fraternity men are rapists. Our observations indicated, however, that rape is especially probable in fraternities because of the kinds of organizations they are, the kinds of members they have, the practices their members engage in, and a virtual absence of university or community oversight. Analyses that lay blame for rapes by fraternity men on "peer pressure" are, we feel, overly simplistic (cf. Burkhart 1989; Walsh 1989). We suggest, rather, that fraternities create a sociocultural context in which the use of coercion in sexual relations with women is normative and in which the mechanisms to keep this pattern of behavior in check are minimal at best and absent at worst. We conclude that unless fraternities change in fundamental ways, little improvement can be expected.

Methodology

Our goal was to analyze the group and organizational practices and conditions that create in fraternities an abusive social context for women. We developed a conceptual framework from an initial case study of an alleged gang rape at Florida State University that involved four fraternity men and an 18-year-old coed. The group rape took place on the third floor of a fraternity house and ended with the "dumping" of the woman in the hallway of a neighboring fraternity house. According to newspaper accounts, the victim's blood-alcohol concentration, when she was discovered, was .349 percent, more than three times the legal limit for automobile driving and an almost lethal amount. One law enforcement officer reported that sexual intercourse occurred during the time the victim was unconscious: "She was in a life-threatening situation" (*Tallahassee Democrat* 1988b). When the victim was found, she was comatose and had suffered multiple scratches and abrasions. Crude words and a fraternity symbol had been written on her thighs (*Tampa Tribune* 1988). When law enforcement officials tried to investigate the case, fraternity members refused to cooperate. This led, eventually, to a five-year ban of the fraternity from campus by the university and by the fraternity's national organization.

In trying to understand how such an event could have occurred, and how a group of over 150 members (exact figures are unknown because the fraternity refused to provide a membership roster) could hold rank, deny knowledge of the event, and allegedly lie to a grand jury, we analyzed newspaper articles about the case and conducted open-ended interviews with a variety of respondents about the case and about fraternities, rapes, alcohol use, gender relations, and sexual activities on campus. Our data included over 100 newspaper articles on the initial gang rape case; open-ended interviews with Greek (social fraternity and sorority) and non-Greek (independent) students (N = 20); university administrators (N = 8, five men, three women); and alumni advisers to Greek organizations (N = 6). Open-ended interviews were held also with judges, public and private defense attorneys, victim advocates, and state prosecutors regarding the processing of sexual assault cases. Data were analyzed using the grounded theory method (Glaser 1978; Martin and Turner 1986). In the following analysis, concepts generated from the data analysis are integrated with the literature on men's social fraternities, sexual coercion, and related issues.

Fraternities and the Social Construction of Men and Masculinity

Our research indicated that fraternities are vitally concerned—more than with anything else—with masculinity (cf. Kanin 1967). They work hard to create a macho image and context and try to avoid any suggestion of "wimpishness," effeminacy, and homosexuality. Valued members display, or are willing to go along with, a narrow conception of masculinity that stresses competition, athleticism, dominance, winning, conflict, wealth, material possessions, willingness to drink alcohol, and sexual prowess vis-à-vis women.

Valued Qualities of Members

When fraternity members talked about the kind of pledges they prefer, a litany of stereotypical and narrowly masculine attributes and behaviors was recited and feminine or women-associated qualities and behaviors expressly denounced (cf. Merton 1985). Fraternities seek men who are "athletic," "big guys," good in intramural competition, "who can talk college sports." Males "who are willing to drink alcohol," "who drink socially," or "who can hold their liquor" are sought. Alcohol and activities associated with the recreational use of alcohol are cornerstones of fraternity social life. Nondrinkers are viewed with skepticism and rarely selected for membership.[1]

Fraternities try to avoid "geeks," nerds, and men said to give the fraternity a "wimpy" or "gay" reputation. Art, music, and humanities majors, majors in traditional women's fields (nursing, home economics, social work, education), men with long hair, and those whose appearance or dress violate current norms are rejected. Clean-cut, handsome men who dress well (are clean, neat, conforming, fashionable) are preferred. One sorority woman commented that "the top ranking fraternities have the best-looking guys."

One fraternity man, a senior, said his fraternity recruited "some big guys, very athletic" over a two-year period to help overcome its image of wimpiness. His fraternity had won the interfraternity competition for highest grade-point average several years running but was looked down on as "wimpy, dancy, even gay." With their bigger, more athletic recruits, "our reputation improved; we're a much more recognized fraternity now." Thus a fraternity's reputation and status depends on members' possession of stereotypically masculine qualities. Good grades, campus leadership, and community service are "nice" but masculinity dominance—for example, in athletic events, physical size of members, athleticism of members—counts most.

Certain social skills are valued. Men are sought who "have good personalities," are friendly, and "have the ability to relate to girls" (cf. Longino and Kart 1973). One fraternity man, a junior, said: "We watch a guy [a potential pledge] talk to women . . . we want guys who can relate to girls." Assessing a pledge's ability to talk to women is, in part, a preoccupation with homosexuality and a conscious avoidance of men who seem to have effeminate manners or qualities. If a member is suspected of being gay, he is ostracized and informally drummed out of the fraternity. A fraternity with a reputation as wimpy or tolerant of gays is ridiculed and shunned by other fraternities. Militant heterosexuality is frequently used by men as a strategy to keep each other in line (Kimmel 1987).

Financial affluence or wealth, a male-associated value in American culture, is highly valued by fraternities. In accounting for why the fraternity involved in the gang rape that precipitated our research project had been recognized recently as "the best fraternity chapter in the United States," a university official said: "They were good-looking, a big fraternity, had lots of BMWs [expensive, German-made automobiles]." After the rape, newspaper stories described the fraternity members' affluence, noting the high number of members who owned expensive cars (*St. Petersburg Times* 1988).

The Status and Norms of Pledgeship

A pledge (sometimes called an associate member) is a new recruit who occupies a trial membership status for a specific period of time. The pledge period (typically ranging from 10 to 15 weeks) gives fraternity brothers an opportunity to assess and socialize new recruits. Pledges evaluate the fraternity also and decide if they want to become brothers. The socialization experience is structured partly through assignment of a Big Brother to each pledge. Big Brothers are expected to teach pledges how to become a brother and to support them as they progress through the trial membership period. Some pledges are repelled by the pledging experience, which can entail physical abuse; harsh discipline; and demands to be subordinate, follow orders, and engage in demeaning routines and activities, similar to those used by the military to "make men out of boys" during boot camp.

Characteristics of the pledge experience are rationalized by fraternity members as necessary to help pledges unite into a group, rely on each other, and join together against outsiders. The process is highly masculinist in execution as well as conception. A willingness to submit to authority, follow orders, and do as one is told is viewed as a sign of loyalty, togetherness, and unity. Fraternity pledges who find the pledge process offensive often drop out. Some do this by openly quitting, which can subject them to ridicule by brothers and other pledges, or they may deliberately fail to make the grades necessary for initiation or transfer schools and decline to reaffiliate with the fraternity on the new campus. One fraternity pledge who quit the fraternity he had pledged described the experience during pledgeship as follows:

> *This one guy was always picking on me. No matter what I did, I was wrong. One night after dinner, he and two other guys called me and two other pledges into the chapter room. He said, "Here X, hold this 25 pound bag of ice at arms' length 'til I tell you to stop." I did it even though my arms and hands were*

killing me. When I asked if I could stop, he grabbed me around the throat and lifted me off the floor. I thought he would choke me to death. He cussed me and called me all kinds of names. He took one of my fingers and twisted it until it nearly broke. . . . I stayed in the fraternity for a few more days, but then I decided to quit. I hated it. Those guys are sick. They like seeing you suffer.

Fraternities' emphasis on toughness, withstanding pain and humiliation, obedience to superiors, and using physical force to obtain compliance contributes to an interpersonal style that deemphasizes caring and sensitivity but fosters intragroup trust and loyalty. If the least macho or most critical pledges drop out, those who remain may be more receptive to, and influenced by, masculinist values and practices that encourage the use of force in sexual relations with women and the covering up of such behavior (cf. Kanin 1967).

Norms and Dynamics of Brotherhood

Brother is the status occupied by fraternity men to indicate their relations to each other and their membership in a particular fraternity organization or group. Brother is a male-specific status; only males can become brothers, although women can become "Little Sisters," a form of pseudomembership. "Becoming a brother" is a rite of passage that follows the consistent and often lengthy display by pledges of appropriately masculine qualities and behaviors. Brothers have a quasi-familial relationship with each other, are normatively said to share bonds of closeness and support, and are sharply set off from nonmembers. Brotherhood is a loosely defined term used to represent the bonds that develop among fraternity members and the obligations and expectations incumbent upon them (cf. Marlowe and Auvenshine [1982] on fraternities' failure to encourage "moral development" in freshman pledges).

Some of our respondents talked about brotherhood in almost reverential terms, viewing it as the most valuable benefit of fraternity membership. One senior, a business-school major who had been affiliated with a fairly high-status fraternity throughout four years on campus, said:

Brotherhood spurs friendship for life, which I consider its best aspect, although I didn't see it that way when I joined. Brotherhood bonds and unites. It instills values of caring about one another, caring about community, caring about ourselves. The values and bonds [of brotherhood] continually develop over the four years [in college] while normal friendships come and go.

Despite this idealization, most aspects of fraternity practice and conception are more mundane. Brotherhood often plays itself out as an overriding concern with masculinity and, by extension, femininity. As a consequence, fraternities comprise collectivities of highly masculinized men with attitudinal qualities and behavior norms that predispose them to sexual coercion of women (cf. Kanin 1967; Merton 1985; Rapaport and Burkhart 1984). The norms of masculinity are complemented by conceptions of women and femininity that are equally distorted and stereotyped and that may enhance the probability of women's exploitation (cf. Ehrhart and Sandler 1985; Sanday 1981, 1986).

Practices of Brotherhood

Practices associated with fraternity brotherhood that contribute to the sexual coercion of women include a preoccupation with loyalty, group protection and secrecy, use of alcohol as a weapon, involvement in violence and physical force, and an emphasis on competition and superiority.

Loyalty, Group Protection, and Secrecy   Loyalty is a fraternity preoccupation. Members are reminded constantly to be loyal to the fraternity and to their brothers. Among other ways, loyalty is played out in practices of group protection and secrecy. The fraternity must be shielded from criticism. Members are admonished to avoid getting the fraternity into trouble and to bring all problems "to the chapter" (local branch of a national social fraternity) rather than to outsiders. Fraternities try to protect themselves from close scrutiny and criticism by the Interfraternity Council (a quasi-governing body composed of representatives from all social fraternities on campus), their fraternity's national office, university officials, law enforcement, the media, and the public. Protection of the fraternity often takes precedence over what is procedurally, ethically, or legally correct. Numerous examples were related to us of fraternity brothers' lying to outsiders to "protect the fraternity."

Group protection was observed in the alleged gang rape with which we began our study. Except for one brother, a rapist who turned state's evidence, the entire remaining fraternity membership was accused by university and criminal justice officials of lying to protect the fraternity. Members consistently failed to cooperate even though the alleged crimes were felonies, involved only four men (two of whom were not even members of the local chapter), and the victim of the crime nearly died. According to a grand jury's findings, fraternity officers repeatedly broke appointments with law enforcement officials, refused to provide police with a list of members, and refused to cooperate with police and prosecutors investigating the case (*Florida Flambeau* 1988).

Secrecy is a priority value and practice in fraternities, partly because full-fledged membership is premised on it (for confirmation, see Ehrhart and Sandler 1985; Longino and Kart 1973; Roark 1987). Secrecy is also a boundary-maintaining mechanism, demarcating in-group from out-group, us from them. Secret rituals, handshakes, and mottoes are revealed to pledge brothers as they are initiated into full brotherhood. Since only brothers are supposed to know a fraternity's secrets, such knowledge affirms membership in the fraternity and separates a brother from others. Extending secrecy tactics from protection of private knowledge to protection of the fraternity from criticism is a predictable development. Our interviews indicated that individual members knew the difference between right and wrong, but fraternity norms that emphasize loyalty, group protection, and secrecy often overrode standards of ethical correctness.

Alcohol as Weapon   Alcohol use by fraternity men is normative. They use it on weekdays to relax after class and on weekends to "get drunk," "get crazy," and "get laid." The use of alcohol to obtain sex from women is pervasive—in other words, it is used as a weapon against sexual reluctance. According to several fraternity men whom we interviewed, alcohol is the major tool used to gain sexual mastery over women (cf. Adams and Abarbanel 1988; Ehrhart and Sandler 1985). One fraternity man, a 21-year-old senior, described alcohol to gain sex as follows: "There are girls that you know will fuck, then some you have to put some effort into it. . . . You have to buy them drinks or find out if she's drunk enough."

A similar strategy is used collectively. A fraternity man said that at parties with Little Sisters: "We provide them with 'hunch punch' and things get wild. We get them drunk and most of the guys end up with one." "'Hunch punch,'" he said, "is a girls' drink made up of overproof alcohol and powdered Kool-Aid, no water or anything, just ice. It's very strong. Two cups will do a number on a female." He had plans in the next academic term to surreptitiously give hunch punch to women in a "prim and proper" sorority because "having sex with prim and proper sorority girls is definitely a goal." These women are a challenge because they "won't openly consume alcohol and won't get openly drunk as hell." Their sororities have "standards committees" that forbid heavy drinking and easy sex.

In the gang rape case, our sources said that many fraternity men on campus believed the victim had a drinking problem and was thus an "easy make." According to newspaper accounts, she had been drinking alcohol on the evening she was raped; the lead assailant is alleged to have given her a bottle of wine after she arrived at his fraternity house. Portions of the rape occurred in a shower, and the victim was reportedly so drunk that her assailants had difficulty holding her in a standing position (*Tallahassee Democrat* 1988a). While raping her, her assailants repeatedly told her they were members of another fraternity under the apparent belief that she was too drunk to know the difference. Of course, if she was too drunk to know who they were, she was too drunk to consent to sex (cf. Allgeier 1986; Tash 1988).

One respondent told us that gang rapes were wrong and can get one expelled, but he seemed to see nothing wrong in sexual coercion one-on-one. He seemed unaware that the use of alcohol to obtain sex from a woman is grounds for a claim that a rape occurred (cf. Tash 1988). Few women on campus (who also may not know these grounds) report date rapes, however; so the odds of detection and punishment are slim for fraternity men who use alcohol for "seduction" purposes (cf. Byington and Keeter 1988; Merton 1985).

Violence and Physical Force   Fraternity men have a history of violence (Ehrhart and Sandler 1985; Roark 1987). Their record of hazing, fighting, property destruction, and rape has caused them problems with insurance companies

(Bradford 1986; Pressley 1987). Two university officials told us that fraternities "are the third riskiest property to insure behind toxic waste dumps and
amusement parks." Fraternities are increasingly defendants in legal actions
brought by pledges subjected to hazing (Meyer 1986; Pressley 1987) and by
women who were raped by one or more members. In a recent alleged gang
rape incident at another Florida university, prosecutors failed to file charges
but the victim filed a civil suit against the fraternity nevertheless (*Tallahassee
Democrat* 1989).

Competition and Superiority   Interfraternity rivalry fosters in-group identification and out-group hostility. Fraternities stress pride of membership and
superiority over other fraternities as major goals. Interfraternity rivalries
take many forms, including competition for desirable pledges, size of pledge
class, size of membership, size and appearance of fraternity house, superiority in intramural sports, highest grade-point averages, giving the best parties,
gaining the best or most campus leadership roles, and, of great importance,
attracting and displaying "good looking women." Rivalry is particularly intense over members, intramural sports, and women (cf. Messner 1989).

Fraternities' Commodification of Women

In claiming that women are treated by fraternities as commodities, we mean
that fraternities knowingly, and intentionally, *use* women for their benefit.
Fraternities use women as bait for new members, as servers of brothers'
needs, and as sexual prey.

Women as Bait   Fashionable attractive women help a fraternity attract new
members. As one fraternity man, a junior, said, "They are good bait." Beautiful, sociable women are believed to impress the right kind of pledges and give
the impression that the fraternity can deliver this type of woman to its members. Photographs of shapely, attractive coeds are printed in fraternity bro-
chures and videotapes that are distributed and shown to potential pledges.
The women pictured are often dressed in bikinis, at the beach, and are pictured hugging the brothers of the fraternity. One university official says such
recruitment materials give the message: "Hey, they're here for you, you can
have whatever you want," and "We have the best-looking women. Join us
and you can have them too." Another commented: "Something's wrong when
males join an all-male organization as the best place to meet women. It's so
illogical."

Fraternities compete in promising access to beautiful women. One fraternity man, a senior, commented that "the attraction of girls [i.e., a fraternity's success in attracting women] is a big status symbol for fraternities."
One university official commented that the use of women as a recruiting tool
is so well entrenched that fraternities that might be willing to forgo it say
they cannot afford to unless other fraternities do so as well. One fraternity
man said, "Look, if we don't have Little Sisters, the fraternities that do will
get all the good pledges." Another said, "We won't have as good a rush [the

period during which new members are assessed and selected] if we don't have these women around."

In displaying good-looking, attractive, skimpily dressed, nubile women to potential members, fraternities implicitly, and sometimes explicitly, promise sexual access to women. One fraternity man commented that "part of what being in a fraternity is all about is the sex" and explained how his fraternity uses Little Sisters to recruit new members:

> We'll tell the sweetheart [the fraternity's term for Little Sister], "You're gorgeous; you can get him." We'll tell her to fake a scam and she'll hang all over him during a rush party, kiss him, and he thinks he's done wonderful and wants to join. The girls think it's great too. It's flattering for them.

Women as Servers   The use of women as servers is exemplified in the Little Sister program. Little Sisters are undergraduate women who are rushed and selected in a manner parallel to the recruitment of fraternity men. They are affiliated with the fraternity in a formal but unofficial way and are able, indeed required, to wear the fraternity's Greek letters. Little Sisters are not full-fledged fraternity members, however; and fraternity national offices and most universities do not register or regulate them. Each fraternity has an officer called Little Sister Chairman who oversees their organizations and activities. The Little Sisters elect officers among themselves, pay monthly dues to the fraternity, and have well-defined roles. Their dues are used to pay for the fraternity's social events, and Little Sisters are expected to attend and hostess fraternity parties and hang around the house to make it a "nice place to be." One fraternity man, a senior, described Little Sisters this way: "They are very social girls, willing to join in, be affiliated with the group, devoted to the fraternity." Another member, a sophomore, said: "Their sole purpose is social—attend parties, attract new members, and 'take care' of the guys."

Our observations and interviews suggested that women selected by fraternities as Little Sisters are physically attractive, possess good social skills, and are willing to devote time and energy to the fraternity and its members. One undergraduate woman gave the following job description for Little Sisters to a campus newspaper:

> It's not just making appearances at all the parties but entails many more responsibilities. You're going to be expected to go to all the intramural games to cheer the brothers on, support and encourage the pledges, and just be around to bring some extra life to the house. [As a Little Sister] you have to agree to take on a new responsibility other than studying to maintain your grades and managing to keep your checkbook from bouncing. You have to make time to be a part of the fraternity and support the brothers in all they do. (*The Tomahawk* 1988)

The title of Little Sister reflects women's subordinate status; fraternity men in a parallel role are called Big Brothers. Big Brothers assist a sorority primarily with the physical work of sorority rushes, which, compared to fraternity rushes, are more formal, structured, and intensive. Sorority rushes take place in the daytime and fraternity rushes at night so fraternity men are free to help. According to one fraternity member, Little Sister status is a benefit to women because it gives them a social outlet and "the protection of the brothers." The gender-stereotypic conceptions and obligations of these Little Sister and Big Brother statuses indicate that fraternities and sororities promote a gender hierarchy on campus that fosters subordination and dependence in women, thus encouraging sexual exploitation and the belief that it is acceptable.

Women as Sexual Prey   Little Sisters are a sexual utility. Many Little Sisters do not belong to sororities and lack peer support for refraining from unwanted sexual relations. One fraternity man (whose fraternity has 65 members and 85 Little Sisters) told us they had recruited "wholesale" in the prior year to "gets lots of new women." The structural access to women that the Little Sister program provides and the absence of normative supports for refusing fraternity members' sexual advances may make women in this program particularly susceptible to coerced sexual encounters with fraternity men.

Access to women for sexual gratification is a presumed benefit of fraternity membership, promised in recruitment materials and strategies and through brothers' conversations with new recruits. One fraternity man said: "We always tell the guys you get sex all the time, there's always new girls. . . . After I became a Greek, I found out I could be with females at will." A university official told us that, based on his observations, "no one [i.e., fraternity men] on this campus wants to have 'relationships.' They just want to have fun [i.e., sex]." Fraternity men plan and execute strategies aimed at obtaining sexual gratification, and this occurs at both individual and collective levels.

Individual strategies include getting a woman drunk and spending a great deal of money on her. As for collective strategies, most of our undergraduate interviewees agreed that fraternity parties often culminate in sex and that this outcome is planned. One fraternity man said fraternity parties often involve sex and nudity and can "turn into orgies." Orgies may be planned in advance, such as the Bowery Ball party held by one fraternity. A former fraternity member said of this party:

> The entire idea behind this is sex. Both men and women come to the party wearing little or nothing. There are pornographic pinups on the walls and usually porno movies playing on the TV. The music carries sexual overtones. . . . They just get schnockered [drunk] and, in most cases, they also get laid.

When asked about the women who come to such a party, he said: "Some Little Sisters just won't go. . . . The girls who do are looking for a good time, girls who don't know what it is, things like that."

Other respondents denied that fraternity parties are orgies but said that sex is always talked about among the brothers and they all know "who each other is doing it with." One member said that most of the time, guys have sex with their girlfriends "but with socials, girlfriends aren't allowed to come and it's their [members'] big chance [to have sex with other women]." The use of alcohol to help get women into bed is a routine strategy at fraternity parties.

Conclusions

In general, our research indicated that the organization and membership of fraternities contribute heavily to coercive and often violent sex. Fraternity houses are occupied by same-sex (all men) and same-age (late teens, early 20s) peers whose maturity and judgment is often less than ideal. Yet fraternity houses are private dwellings that are mostly off-limits to, and away from scrutiny of, university and community representatives, with the result that fraternity house events seldom come to the attention of outsiders. Practices associated with the social construction of fraternity brotherhood emphasize a macho conception of men and masculinity, a narrow, stereotyped conception of women and femininity, and the treatment of women as commodities. Other practices contributing to coercive sexual relations and the cover-up of rapes include excessive alcohol use, competitiveness, and normative support for deviance and secrecy (cf. Bogal-Allbritten and Allbritten 1985; Kanin 1967).

Some fraternity practices exacerbate others. Brotherhood norms require "sticking together" regardless of right or wrong; thus rape episodes are unlikely to be stopped or reported to outsiders, even when witnesses disapprove. The ability to use alcohol without scrutiny by authorities and alcohol's frequent association with violence, including sexual coercion, facilitates rape in fraternity houses. Fraternity norms that emphasize the value of maleness and masculinity over femaleness and femininity and that elevate the status of men and lower the status of women in members' eyes undermine perceptions and treatment of women as persons who deserve consideration and care (cf. Ehrhart and Sandler 1985; Merton 1985).

Androgynous men and men with a broad range of interests and attributes are lost to fraternities through their recruitment practices. Masculinity of a narrow and stereotypical type helps create attitudes, norms, and practices that predispose fraternity men to coerce women sexually, both individually and collectively (Allgeier 1986; Hood 1989; Sanday 1981, 1986). Male athletes on campus may be similarly disposed for the same reasons (Kirshenbaum 1989; Telander and Sullivan 1989).

Research into the social contexts in which rape crimes occur and the social constructions associated with these contexts illumine rape dynamics on campus. Blanchard (1959) found that group rapes almost always have a leader who pushes others into the crime. He also found that the leader's latent homosexuality, desire to show off to his peers, or fear of failing to prove himself a man are frequently an impetus. Fraternity norms and practices contribute to the approval and use of sexual coercion as an accepted tactic in relations with women. Alcohol-induced compliance is normative, whereas, presumably, use of a knife, gun, or threat of bodily harm would not be because the woman who "drinks too much" is viewed as "causing her own rape" (cf. Ehrhart and Sandler 1985).

Our research led us to conclude that fraternity norms and practices influence members to view the sexual coercion of women, which is a felony crime, as sport, a contest, or a game (cf. Sato 1988). This sport is played not between men and women but between men and men. Women are the pawns or prey in the interfraternity rivalry game; they prove that a fraternity is successful or prestigious. The use of women in this way encourages fraternity men to see women as objects and sexual coercion as sport. Today's societal norms support young women's right to engage in sex at their discretion, and coercion is unnecessary in a mutually desired encounter. However, nubile young women say they prefer to be "in a relationship" to have sex while young men say they prefer to "get laid" without a commitment (Muehlenhard and Linton 1987). These differences may reflect, in part, American puritanism and men's fears of sexual intimacy or perhaps intimacy of any kind. In a fraternity context, getting sex without giving emotionally demonstrates "cool" masculinity. More important, it poses no threat to the bonding and loyalty of the fraternity brotherhood (cf. Farr 1988). Drinking large quantities of alcohol before having sex suggests that "scoring" rather than intrinsic sexual pleasure is a primary concern of fraternity men.

Unless fraternities' compositions, goals, structures, and practices change in fundamental ways, women on campus will continue to be sexual prey for fraternity men. As all-male enclaves dedicated to opposing faculty and administration and to cementing in-group ties, fraternity members eschew any hint of homosexuality. Their version of masculinity transforms women, and men with womanly characteristics, into the out-group. "Womanly men" are ostracized; feminine women are used to demonstrate members' masculinity. Encouraging renewed emphasis on their founding values (Longino and Kart 1973), service orientation and activities (Lemire 1979), or members' moral development (Marlowe and Auvenshine 1982) will have little effect on fraternities' treatment of women. A case for or against fraternities cannot be made by studying individual members. The fraternity qua group and organization is at issue. Located on campus along with many vulnerable women, embedded in a sexist society, and caught up in masculinist goals, practices, and values, fraternities' violation of women—including forcible rape—should come as no surprise.

NOTE

1. Recent bans by some universities on open-keg parties at fraternity houses have resulted in heavy drinking before coming to a party and an increase in drunkenness among those who attend. This may aggravate, rather than improve, the treatment of women by fraternity men at parties.

REFERENCES

Adams, Aileen and Gail Abarbanel. 1988. *Sexual Assault on Campus: What Colleges Can Do.* Santa Monica, CA: Rape Treatment Center.

Allgeier, Elizabeth. 1986. "Coercive versus Consensual Sexual Interactions." G. Stanley Hall Lecture to American Psychological Association Annual Meeting, Washington, DC, August.

Blanchard, W. H. 1959. "The Group Process in Gang Rape." *Journal of Social Psychology* 49:259–66.

Bogal-Allbritten, Rosemarie B., and William L. Allbritten. 1985. "The Hidden Victims: Courtship Violence among College Students." *Journal of College Student Personnel* 43:201–4.

Bohrnstedt, George W. 1969. "Conservatism, Authoritarianism and Religiosity of Fraternity Pledges." *Journal of College Student Personnel* 27:36–43.

Bradford, Michael. 1986. "Tight Market Dries Up Nightlife at University." *Business Insurance* (March 2):2, 6.

Burkhart, Barry. 1989. Comments in Seminar on Acquaintance/Date Rape Prevention: A National Video Teleconference, February 2.

Burkhart, Barry R. and Annette L. Stanton. 1985. "Sexual Aggression in Acquaintance Relationships." Pp. 43–65 in *Violence in Intimate Relationships*, edited by G. Russell. Englewood Cliffs, NJ: Spectrum.

Byington, Diane B., and Karen W. Keeter. 1988. "Assessing Needs of Sexual Assault Victims on a University Campus." Pp. 23–31 in *Student Services: Responding to Issues and Challenges.* Chapel Hill: University of North Carolina Press.

Chancer, Lynn S. 1987. "New Bedford, Massachusetts, March 6, 1983–March 22, 1984: The 'Before and After' of a Group Rape." *Gender & Society* 1:239–60.

Ehrhart, Julie K. and Bernice R. Sandler. 1985. *Campus Gang Rape: Party Games?* Washington, DC: Association of American Colleges.

Farr, K. A. 1988. "Dominance Bonding through the Good Old Boys Sociability Network." *Sex Roles* 18:259–77.

Florida Flambeau. "Pike Members Indicted in Rape." (May 19):1, 5.

Fox, Elaine, Charles Hodge, and Walter Ward. 1987. "A Comparison of Attitudes Held by Black and White Fraternity Members." *Journal of Negro Education* 56:521–34.

Geis, Gilbert. 1971. "Group Sexual Assaults." *Medical Aspects of Human Sexuality* 5:101–13.

Glaser, Barney G. 1978. *Theoretical Sensitivity: Advances in the Methodology of Grounded Theory.* Mill Valley, CA: Sociology Press.

Hood, Jane. 1989. "Why Our Society is Rape-Prone." *New York Times,* May 16.

Hughes, Michael J. and Roger B. Winston, Jr. 1987. "Effects of Fraternity Membership on Interpersonal Values." *Journal of College Student Personnel* 45:405–11.

Kanin, Eugene J. 1967. "Reference Groups and Sex Conduct Norm Violations." *The Sociological Quarterly* 8:495–504.

Kimmel, Michael, ed. 1987. *Changing Men: New Directions in Research on Men and Masculinity.* Newbury Park, CA: Sage.

Kirshenbaum, Jerry. 1989. "Special Report, an American Disgrace: A Violent and Unprecedented Lawlessness Has Arisen among College Athletes in All Parts of the Country." *Sports Illustrated* (February 27):16–19.

Lemire, David. 1979. "One Investigation of the Stereotypes Associated with Fraternities and Sororities." *Journal of College Student Personnel* 37:54–57.

Letchworth, G. E. 1969. "Fraternities Now and in the Future." *Journal of College Student Personnel* 10:118–22.

Longino, Charles F., Jr. and Cary S. Kart. 1973. "The College Fraternity: An Assessment of Theory and Research." *Journal of College Student Personnel* 31:118–25.

Marlowe, Anne F. and Dwight C. Auvenshine. 1982. "Greek Membership: Its Impact on the Moral Development of College Freshmen." *Journal of College Student Personnel* 40:53–57.

Martin, Patricia Yancey and Barry A. Turner. 1986. "Grounded Theory and Organizational Research." *Journal of Applied Behavioral Science* 22:141–57.

Merton, Andrew. 1985. "On Competition and Class: Return to Brotherhood." *Ms.* (September):60–65, 121–22.

Messner, Michael. 1989. "Masculinities and Athletic Careers." *Gender & Society* 3:71–88.

Meyer, T. J. 1986. "Fight against Hazing Rituals Rages on Campuses." *Chronicle of Higher Education* (March 12):34–36.

Miller, Leonard D. 1973. "Distinctive Characteristics of Fraternity Members." *Journal of College Student Personnel* 31:126–28.

Muehlenhard, Charlene L. and Melaney A. Linton. 1987. "Date Rape and Sexual Aggression in Dating Situations: Incidence and Risk Factors." *Journal of Counseling Psychology* 34:186–96.

Pressley, Sue Anne. 1987. "Fraternity Hell Night Still Endures." *Washington Post* (August 11): B1.

Rapaport, Karen, and Barry R. Burkhart. 1983. "Personality and Attitudinal Characteristics of Sexually Coercive College Males." *Journal of Abnormal Psychology* 93:216–21.

Roark, Mary L. 1987. "Preventing Violence on College Campuses." *Journal of Counseling and Development* 65:367–70.

St. Petersburg Times. 1988. "A Greek Tragedy." (May 29):1F, 6F.

Sanday, Peggy Reeves. 1981. "The Socio-Cultural Context of Rape: A Cross-Cultural Study." *Journal of Social Issues* 37:5–27.

———. 1986. "Rape and the Silencing of the Feminine." Pp. 84–101 in *Rape*, edited by S. Tomaselli and R. Porter. Oxford: Basil Blackwell.

Sato, Ikuya. 1988. "Play Theory of Delinquency: Toward a General Theory of 'Action.'" *Symbolic Interaction* 11:191–212.

Smith, T. 1964. "Emergence and Maintenance of Fraternal Solidarity." *Pacific Sociological Review* 7:29–37.

Tallahassee Democrat. 1988a. "FSU Fraternity Brothers Charged" (April 27):1A, 12A.

———. 1988b. "FSU Interviewing Students about Alleged Rape" (April 24):1D.

———. 1989. "Woman Sues Stetson in Alleged Rape" (March 19):3B.

Tampa Tribune. 1988. "Fraternity Brothers Charged in Sexual Assault of FSU Coed." (April 27):6B.

Tash, Gary B. 1988. "Date Rape." *The Emerald of Sigma Pi Fraternity* 75(4):1–2.

Telander, Rick and Robert Sullivan. 1989. "Special Report, You Reap What You Sow." *Sports Illustrated* (February 27):20–34.

The Tomahawk. 1988. "A Look Back at Rush, A Mixture of Hard Work and Fun" (April/May):3D.

Walsh, Claire. 1989. Comments in Seminar on Acquaintance/Date Rape Prevention: A National Video Teleconference, February 2.

Wilder, David H., Arlyne E. Hoyt, Dennis M. Doren, William E. Hauck, and Robert D. Zettle. 1978. "The Impact of Fraternity and Sorority Membership on Values and Attitudes." *Journal of College Student Personnel* 36:445–49.

Wilder, David H., Arlyne E. Hoyt, Beth Shuster Shurbeck, Janet C. Wilder, and Patricia Imperatrice Carney. 1986. "Greek Affiliation and Attitude Change in College Students." *Journal of College Student Personnel* 44:510–19.

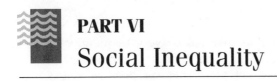

PART VI
Social Inequality

23

CLASS, STATUS, PARTY

MAX WEBER

In the following four selections, we investigate social inequality that results from social class membership. *Social class* refers to categories of people who share common economic interests in a stratification system. Sociologists utilize various indicators to measure social class. For example, *socioeconomic status* (SES) is calculated using income, educational attainment, and occupational status. Sociologists also employ subjective indicators of social class, such as attitudes and values, class identification, and consumption patterns. Using both subjective and objective indicators, Max Weber defines social class as a group of persons who share a "class situation" of similar life chances and economic interests. The following reading is an excerpt from Weber's classic essay on social stratification, which illustrates his concern with the distribution of power and honor among different social status groups.

Economically Determined Power and the Social Order

Law exists when there is a probability that an order will be upheld by a specific staff of men who will use physical or psychical compulsion with the intention of obtaining conformity with the order, or of inflicting sanctions for infringement of it.[1] The structure of every legal order directly influences the distribution of power, economic or otherwise, within its respective community. This is true of all legal orders and not only that of the state. In general, we understand by "power" the chance of a man or of a number of men to realize their own will in a communal action even against the resistance of others who are participating in the action.

"Economically conditioned" power is not, of course, identical with "power" as such. On the contrary, the emergence of economic power may be the consequence of power existing on other grounds. Man does not strive for power only in order to enrich himself economically. Power, including economic power, may be valued "for its own sake." Very frequently the striving for power is also conditioned by the social "honor" it entails. Not all power, however, entails social honor: The typical American Boss, as well as the typical big speculator, deliberately relinquishes social honor. Quite generally, "mere economic" power, and especially "naked" money power, is by no means a recognized basis of social honor. Nor is power the only basis of social honor. Indeed, social honor, or prestige, may even be the basis of political or economic power, and very frequently has been. Power, as well as honor, may be guaranteed by the legal order, but, at least normally, it is not their primary source. The legal order is rather an additional factor that enhances the chance to hold power or honor; but it cannot always secure them.

The way in which social honor is distributed in a community between typical groups participating in this distribution we may call the "social order." The social order and the economic order are, of course, similarly related to the "legal order." However, the social and the economic order are not identical. The economic order is for us merely the way in which economic goods and services are distributed and used. The social order is of course conditioned by the economic order to a high degree, and in its turn reacts upon it.

Now: "classes," "status groups," and "parties" are phenomena of the distribution of power within a community.

Determination of Class-Situation by Market-Situation

In our terminology, "classes" are not communities; they merely represent possible, and frequent, bases for communal action. We may speak of a "class" when (1) a number of people have in common a specific causal component of their life chances, insofar as (2) this component is represented exclusively by economic interests in the possession of goods and opportunities for income, and (3) is represented under the conditions of the commodity or labor markets. [These points refer to "class situation," which we may express more briefly as the typical chance for a supply of goods, external living conditions, and personal life experiences, insofar as this chance is determined by the amount and kind of power, or lack of such, to dispose of goods or skills for the sake of income in a given economic order. The term "class" refers to any group of people that is found in the same class situation.]

It is the most elemental economic fact that the way in which the disposition over material property is distributed among a plurality of people, meeting competitively in the market for the purpose of exchange, in itself creates specific life chances. According to the law of marginal utility this mode of distribution excludes the non-owners from competing for highly valued goods; it favors the owners and, in fact, gives to them a monopoly to acquire such goods. Other things being equal, this mode of distribution monopolizes the opportunities for profitable deals for all those who, provided with goods, do not necessarily have to exchange them. It increases, at least generally, their power in price wars with those who, being propertyless, have nothing to offer but their services in native form or goods in a form constituted through their own labor, and who above all are compelled to get rid of these products in order barely to subsist. This mode of distribution gives to the propertied a monopoly on the possibility of transferring property from the sphere of use as a "fortune," to the sphere of "capital goods"; that is, it gives them the entrepreneurial function and all chances to share directly or indirectly in returns on capital. All this holds true within the area in which pure market conditions prevail. "Property" and "lack of property" are, therefore, the basic categories of all class situations. It does not matter whether these two categories become effective in price wars or in competitive struggles.

Within these categories, however, class situations are further differentiated: on the one hand, according to the kind of property that is usable for returns; and, on the other hand, according to the kind of services that can be offered in the market. Ownership of domestic buildings; productive establishments; warehouses; stores, agriculturally usable land, large and small holdings—quantitative differences with possibly qualitative consequences; ownership of mines; cattle; men (slaves); disposition over mobile instruments of production, or capital goods of all sorts, especially money or objects that can be exchanged for money easily and at any time; disposition over products of one's own labor or of others' labor differing according to their various distances from consumability; disposition over transferable monopolies of any kind—all these distinctions differentiate the class situations of the propertied just as does the "meaning" which they can and do give to the utilization of property, especially to property which has money equivalence. Accordingly, the propertied, for instance, may belong to the class of rentiers or to the class of entrepreneurs.

Those who have no property but who offer services are differentiated just as much according to their kinds of services as according to the way in which they make use of these services, in a continuous or discontinuous relation to a recipient. But always this is the generic connotation of the concept of class: that the kind of chance in the *market* is the decisive moment which presents a common condition for the individual's fate. "Class situation" is, in this sense, ultimately "market situation." The effect of naked possession *per se*, which among cattle breeders gives the non-owning slave or serf into the power of the cattle owner, is only a forerunner of real "class" formation. However, in the cattle loan and in the naked severity of the law of debts in such communities, for the first time mere "possession" as such emerges as decisive for the fate of the individual. This is very much in contrast to the agricultural communities based on labor. The creditor-debtor relation becomes the basis of "class situations" only in those cities where a "credit market," however primitive, with rates of interest increasing according to the extent of dearth and a factual monopolization of credits, is developed by a plutocracy. Therewith "class struggles" begin.

Those men whose fate is not determined by the chance of using goods or services for themselves on the market, e.g., slaves, are not, however, a "class" in the technical sense of the term. They are, rather, a "status group."

Communal Action Flowing from Class Interest

According to our terminology, the factor that creates "class" is unambiguously economic interest, and indeed, only those interests involved in the existence of the "market." Nevertheless, the concept of "class-interest" is an ambiguous one: Even as an empirical concept it is ambiguous as soon as one understands by it something other than the factual direction of interests following with a certain probability from the class situation for a certain "average" of those people subjected to the class situation. The class situation and other circumstances remaining the same, the direction in which the individual worker, for instance, is likely to pursue his interests may vary widely, according to whether he is constitutionally qualified for the task at hand to a high, to an average, or to a low degree. In the same way, the direction of interests may vary according to whether or not a *communal* action of a larger or smaller portion of those commonly affected by the "class situation," or even an association among them, e.g., a "trade union," has grown out of the class situation from which the individual may or may not expect promising results. [Communal action refers to that action which is oriented to the feeling of the actors that they belong together. Societal action, on the other hand, is oriented to a rationally motivated adjustment of interests.] The rise of societal or even of communal action from a common class situation is by no means a universal phenomenon.

The class situation may be restricted in its effects to the generation of essentially *similar* reactions, that is to say, within our terminology, of "mass actions." However, it may not have even this result. Furthermore, often merely an amorphous communal action emerges. For example, the "murmuring" of the workers known in ancient oriental ethics: the moral disapproval of the work-master's conduct, which in its practical significance was probably equivalent to an increasingly typical phenomenon of precisely the latest industrial development, namely, the "slowdown" (the deliberate limiting of work effort) of laborers by virtue of tacit agreement. The degree in which "communal action" and possibly "societal action," emerges from the "mass actions" of the members of a class is linked to general cultural conditions, especially to those of an intellectual sort. It is also linked to the extent of the contrasts that have already evolved, and is especially linked to the *transparency* of the connections between the causes and the consequences of the "class situation." For however different life chances may be, this fact in itself, according to all experience, by no means gives birth to "class action" (communal action by the members of a class). The fact of being conditioned and the results of the class situation must be distinctly recognizable. For only then the contrast of life chances can be felt not as an absolutely given fact to be accepted, but as a resultant from either (1) the given distribution of property, or (2) the structure of the concrete economic order. It is only then that people may react against the class structure not only through acts of an intermittent and irrational protest, but in the form of rational association. There have been "class situations" of the first category (1), of a specifically naked and transparent sort, in the urban centers of antiquity and during the Middle Ages; especially then, when great fortunes were accumulated by factually monopolized trading in industrial products of these localities or in foodstuffs. Furthermore, under certain circumstances, in the rural economy of the most diverse periods, when agriculture was increasingly exploited in a profit-making manner. The most important historical example of the second category (2) is the class situation of the modern "proletariat."

Types of "Class Struggle"

Thus every class may be the carrier of any one of the possibly innumerable forms of "class action," but this is not necessarily so: In any case, a class does not in itself constitute a community. To treat "class" conceptually as having the same value as "community" leads to distortion. That men in the same class situation regularly react in mass actions to such tangible situations as economic ones in the direction of those interests that are most adequate to their average number is an important and after all simple fact for the understanding of historical events. Above all, this fact must not lead to that kind of pseudo-scientific operation with the concepts of "class" and "class interests" so frequently found these days, and which has found its most classic expression in the statement of a talented author, that the individual may be in error concerning his interests but that the "class" is "infallible" about its interests. Yet, if classes as such are not communities, nevertheless class situations emerge only on the basis of communalization. The communal action that brings forth class situations, however, is not basically action between members of the identical class; it is an action between members of different classes. Communal actions that directly determine the class situation of the worker and the entrepreneur are the labor market, the commodities market, and the capitalistic enterprise. But, in its turn, the existence of a capitalistic enterprise presupposes that a very specific communal action exists and that it is specifically structured to protect the possession of goods *per se*, and especially the power of individuals to dispose, in principal freely, over the means of production. The existence of a capitalistic enterprise is preconditioned by a specific kind of "legal order." Each kind of class situation, and above all when it rests upon the power of property *per se*, will become most clearly efficacious when all other determinants of reciprocal relations are, as far as possible, eliminated in their significance. It is in this way that the utilization of the power of property in the market obtains its most sovereign importance.

Now "status groups" hinder the strict carrying through of the sheer market principle. In the present context they are of interest to us only from this one point of view. Before we briefly consider them, note that not much of a general nature can be said about the more specific kinds of antagonism between "classes" (in our meaning of the term). The great shift, which has been going on continuously in the past, and up to our times, may be summarized, although at the cost of some precision: The struggle in which class situations are effective has progressively shifted from consumption credit toward, first, competitive struggles in the commodity market and, then, toward price wars on the labor market. The "class struggles" of antiquity—to the extent that they were genuine class struggles and not struggles between status groups— were initially carried on by indebted peasants, and perhaps also by artisans threatened by debt bondage and struggling against urban creditors. For debt bondage is the normal result of the differentiation of wealth in commercial cities, especially in seaport cities. A similar situation has existed among cattle breeders. Debt relationships as such produced class action up to the time of Cataline. Along with this, and with an increase in provision of grain for the city by transporting it from the outside, the struggle over the means of sustenance emerged. It centered in the first place around the provision of bread and the determination of the price of bread. It lasted throughout antiquity and the entire Middle Ages. The propertyless as such flocked together against those who actually and supposedly were interested in the dearth of bread. This fight spread until it involved all those commodities essential to the way of life and to handicraft production. There were only incipient discussions of wage disputes in antiquity and in the Middle Ages. But they have been slowly increasing up into modern times. In the earlier periods they were completely secondary to slave rebellions as well as to fights in the commodity market.

The propertyless of antiquity and of the Middle Ages protested against monopolies, preemption, forestalling, and the withholding of goods from the market in order to raise prices. Today the central issue is the determination of the price of labor.

This transition is represented by the fight for access to the market and for the determination of the price of products. Such fights went on between merchants and workers in the putting-out system of domestic handicraft during the transition to modern times. Since it is quite a general phenomenon we must mention here that the class antagonisms that are conditioned through the market situation are usually most bitter between those who actually and directly participate as opponents in price wars. It is not the rentier, the shareholder, and the banker who suffer the ill will of the worker, but almost exclusively the manufacturer and the business executives who are the direct opponents of workers in price wars. This is so in spite of the fact that it is precisely the cash boxes of the rentier, the share-holder, and the banker into which the more or less "unearned" gains flow, rather than into the pockets of the manufacturers or of the business executives. This simple state of affairs has very frequently been decisive for the role the class situation has played in the formation of political parties. For example, it has made possible the varieties of patriarchal socialism and the frequent attempts—formerly, at least—of threatened status groups to form alliances with the proletariat against the "bourgeoisie."

Status Honor

In contrast to classes, *status groups* are normally communities. They are, however, often of an amorphous kind. In contrast to the purely economically determined "class situation" we wish to designate as "status situation" every typical component of the life fate of men that is determined by a specific, positive or negative, social estimation of *honor.* This honor may be connected with any quality shared by a plurality, and, of course, it can be knit to a class situation: Class distinctions are linked in the most varied ways with status distinctions. Property as such is not always recognized as a status qualification, but in the long run it is, and with extraordinary regularity. In the subsistence economy of the organized neighborhood, very often the richest man is simply the chieftain. However, this often means only an honorific preference. For example, in the so-called pure modern "democracy," that is, one devoid of any expressly ordered status privileges for individuals, it may be that only the families coming under approximately the same tax class dance with one another. This example is reported of certain smaller Swiss cities. But status honor need not necessarily be linked with a "class situation." On the contrary, it normally stands in sharp opposition to the pretensions of sheer property.

Both propertied and propertyless people can belong to the same status group, and frequently they do with very tangible consequences. This "equality" of social esteem may, however, in the long run become quite precarious. The "equality" of status among the American "gentlemen," for instance, is expressed by the fact that outside the subordination determined by the different functions of "business," it would be considered strictly repugnant— wherever the old tradition still prevails—if even the richest "chief," while playing billiards or cards in his club in the evening, would not treat his "clerk" as in every sense fully his equal in birthright. It would be repugnant if the American "chief" would bestow upon his "clerk" the condescending "benevolence" marking a distinction of "position," which the German chief can never dissever from his attitude. This is one of the most important reasons why in America the German "clubby-ness" has never been able to attain the attraction that the American clubs have.

Guarantees of Status Stratification

In content, status honor is normally expressed by the fact that above all else a specific *style of life* can be expected from all those who wish to belong to the circle. Linked with this expectation are restrictions on "social" intercourse (that is, intercourse which is not subservient to economic or any other of business's "functional" purposes). These restrictions may confine normal marriages to within the status circle and may lead to complete endogamous closure. As soon as there is not a mere individual and socially irrelevant imitation of another style of life, but an agreed-upon communal action of this closing character, the "status" development is under way.

In its characteristic form, stratification by "status groups" on the basis of conventional styles of life evolves at the present time in the United States out of the traditional democracy. For example, only the resident of a certain street ("the street") is considered as belonging to "society," is qualified for social intercourse, and is visited and invited. Above all, this differentiation evolves in such a way as to make for strict submission to the fashion that is dominant at a given time in society. This submission to fashion also exists among men in America to a degree unknown in Germany. Such submission is considered to be an indication of the fact that a given man *pretends* to qualify as a gentleman. This submission decides, at least *prima facie*, that he will be treated as such. And this recognition becomes just as important for his employment chances in "swank" establishments, and above all, for social intercourse and marriage with "esteemed" families, as the qualification for dueling among Germans in the Kaiser's day. As for the rest: certain families resident for a long time, and, of course, correspondingly wealthy, e.g., "F.F.V., i.e. First Families of Virginia," or the actual or alleged descendants of the "Indian Princess" Pocahontas, of the Pilgrim fathers, or of the Knickerbockers, the members of almost inaccessible sects and all sorts of circles setting themselves apart by means of any other characteristics and badges—all these elements usurp "status" honor. The development of status is essentially a question of stratification resting upon usurpation. Such usurpation is the normal origin of almost all status honor. But the road from this purely conventional situation to legal privilege, positive or negative, is easily traveled as soon as a certain stratification of the social order has in fact been "lived in" and has achieved stability by virtue of a stable distribution of economic power.

· · ·

Status Privileges

For all practical purposes, stratification by status goes hand in hand with a monopolization of ideal and material goods or opportunities, in a manner we have come to know as typical. Besides the specific status honor, which always rests upon distance and exclusiveness, we find all sorts of material monopolies. Such honorific preferences may consist of the privilege of wearing special costumes, of eating special dishes taboo to others, of carrying arms—which is most obvious in its consequences—the right to pursue certain non-professional dilettante artistic practices, e.g., to play certain musical instruments. Of course, material monopolies provide the most effective motives for the exclusiveness of a status group; although, in themselves, they are rarely sufficient, almost always they come into play to some extent. Within a status circle there is the question of intermarriage: The interest of the families in the monopolization of potential bridegrooms is at least of equal importance and is parallel to the interest in the monopolization of daughters. The daughters of the circle must be provided for. With an increased inclosure of the status group, the conventional preferential opportunities for special employment grow into a legal monopoly of special offices for the members. Certain goods become objects for monopolization by status groups. In the typical fashion these include "entailed estates" and frequently also the possessions of serfs or bondsmen and, finally, special trades. This monopolization occurs positively when the status group is exclusively entitled to own and to manage them; and negatively when, in order to maintain its specific way of life, the status group must *not* own and manage them.

The decisive role of a "style of life" in status "honor" means that status groups are the specific bearers of all "conventions." In whatever way it may be manifest, all "stylization" of life either originates in status groups or is at least conserved by them. Even if the principles of status conventions differ greatly, they reveal certain typical traits, especially among those strata which are most privileged. Quite generally, among privileged status groups there is a status disqualification that operates against the performance of common physical labor. This disqualification is now "setting in" in America against the old tradition of esteem for labor. Very frequently every rational economic pursuit, and especially "entrepreneurial activity," is looked upon as a disqualification of status. Artistic and literary activity is also considered as degrading work as soon as it is exploited for income, or at least when it is connected with hard physical exertion. An example is the sculptor working like a mason in his dusty smock as over against the painter in his salon-like "studio" and those forms of musical practice that are acceptable to the status group.

NOTE

1. *Wirtschaft und Gesellschaft,* part III, chap. 4, pp. 631–40. The first sentence in paragraph one and the several definitions in this chapter which are in brackets do not appear in the original text. They have been taken from other contexts of *Wirtschaft und Gesellschaft.*

24

THE AMERICAN UPPER CLASS

G. WILLIAM DOMHOFF

This selection is taken from G. William Domhoff's book, *Who Rules America Now?* Using both subjective and objective indicators of social class status, Domhoff finds that in addition to wealth, the upper class shares a distinctive lifestyle through participation in various social institutions. Domhoff argues that not only is there a cohesive upper class in the United States, but also that the upper class has a disproportionate share of power through their control over economic and political decision making in this country.

Introduction

If there is an American upper class, it must exist not merely as a collection of families who feel comfortable with each other and tend to exclude outsiders from their social activities. It must exist as a set of interrelated social institutions. That is, there must be patterned ways of organizing the lives of its members from infancy to old age, and there must be mechanisms for socializing both the younger generation and new adult members who have risen from lower social levels. If the class is a reality, the names and faces may change somewhat over the years, but the social institutions that underlie the upper class must persist with remarkably little change over several generations. . . .

Training the Young

From infancy through young adulthood, members of the upper class receive a distinctive education. This education begins early in life in preschools that frequently are attached to a neighborhood church of high social status. Schooling continues during the elementary years at a local private school called a day school. The adolescent years may see the student remain at day school, but there is a strong chance that at least one or two years will be spent away from home at a boarding school in a quiet rural setting. Higher education will be obtained at one of a small number of heavily endowed private universities. Harvard, Yale, Princeton, and Stanford head the list, followed by smaller Ivy League schools in the East and a handful of other small private schools in other parts of the country. Although some upper-class children may attend public high school if they live in a secluded suburban setting, or go to a state university if there is one of great esteem and tradition in their home state, the system of formal schooling is so insulated that many upper-class students never see the inside of a public school in all their years of education.

This separate educational system is important evidence for the distinctiveness of the mentality and lifestyle that exists within the upper class, for schools play a large role in transmitting the class structure to their students. Surveying and summarizing a great many studies on schools in general, sociologist Randall Collins concludes: "Schools primarily teach vocabulary and inflection, styles of dress, aesthetic tastes, values and manners."[1]

The training of upper-class children is not restricted to the formal school setting, however. Special classes and even tutors are a regular part of their extracurricular education. This informal education usually begins with dancing classes in the elementary years, which are seen as more important for learning proper manners and the social graces than for learning to dance. Tutoring in a foreign language may begin in the elementary years, and there are often lessons in horseback riding and music as well. The teen years find the children of the upper class in summer camps or on special travel tours, broadening their perspectives and polishing their social skills.

The linchpins in the upper-class educational system are the dozens of boarding schools that were developed in the last half of the nineteenth and the early part of the twentieth centuries, with the rise of a nationwide upper class whose members desired to insulate themselves from an inner city that was becoming populated by lower-class immigrants. Baltzell concludes that these schools became "surrogate families" that played a major role "in creating an upper-class subculture on almost a national scale in America."[2] The role of boarding schools in providing connections to other upper-class social institutions is also important. As one informant explained to Ostrander in her interview study of upper-class women: "Where I went to boarding school, there were girls from all over the country, so I know people from all over. It's helpful when you move to a new city and want to get invited into the local social clubs."[3]

Consciously molded after their older and more austere British counterparts, it is within these several hundred schools that a unique style of life is inculcated through such traditions as the initiatory hazing of beginning students, the wearing of school blazers or ties, compulsory attendance at chapel services, and participation in esoteric sports such as lacrosse, squash, and crew. Even a different language is adopted to distinguish these schools from public schools. The principal is a headmaster or rector, the teachers are sometimes called masters, and the students are in forms, not grades. Great emphasis is placed upon the building of "character." The role of the school in preparing the future leaders of America is emphasized through the speeches of the headmaster and the frequent mention of successful alumni.*. . .

Whatever university upper-class students attend, they tend to socialize together as members of a small number of fraternities, sororities, eating clubs, and secret societies, perpetuating to some extent the separate existence of a day or boarding school. As sociologist C. Wright Mills explained, it is not merely a matter of going to a Harvard or a Yale but to the right Harvard or Yale.

> That is why in the upper social classes, it does not by itself mean much merely to have a degree from an Ivy League college. That is assumed: the point is not Harvard, but which Harvard? By Harvard, one means Porcellian, Fly, or A.D.: by Yale, one means Zeta Psi or Fence or Delta Kappa Epsilon: by Princeton, Cottage, Tifer, Cap and Gown or Ivy.[4]

From kindergarten through college, then, schooling is very different for members of the upper class from what it is for most Americans, and it teaches them to be distinctive in many ways. In a country where education is highly valued and the overwhelming majority attend public schools, less than one student in a hundred is part of this private system that primarily benefits members of the upper class and provides one of the foundations for the old-boy and old-girl networks that will be with them throughout their lives.

Social Clubs

Just as private schools are a pervasive feature in the lives of upper-class children, so, too, are private social clubs a major point of orientation in the lives of upper-class adults. These clubs also play a role in differentiating members of the upper class from other members of society. According to Baltzell, "the club serves to place the adult members of society and their families within the social hierarchy." He quotes with approval the suggestion by historian Crane Brinton that the club "may perhaps be regarded as taking the place of those extensions of the family, such as the clan and the brotherhood, which have disappeared from advanced societies."[5] Conclusions similar to Baltzell's resulted from an interview study in Kansas City: "Ultimately, say upper-class Kansas Citians, social standing in their world reduces to one issue: Where does an individual or family rank on the scale of private club memberships and informal cliques."[6]

---

*The Episcopal priest who served as headmaster at Choate from 1908 to 1947 often exhorted his students: "Ask not what your school can do for you, but what you can do for your school." This line was adapted slightly by one of his students, John F. Kennedy, who in 1961 as president of the United States asked his fellow citizens in a stirring patriotic speech: "Ask not what your country can do for you, but what you can do for your country."

The clubs of the upper class are many and varied, ranging from family-oriented country clubs and downtown men's and women's clubs to highly specialized clubs for yachtsmen, sportsmen, gardening enthusiasts, and fox hunters. Many families have memberships in several different types of clubs, but the days when most of the men by themselves were in a half dozen or more clubs faded before World War II. Downtown men's clubs originally were places for having lunch and dinner, and occasionally for attending an evening performance or a weekend party. But as upper-class families deserted the city for large suburban estates, a new kind of club, the country club, gradually took over some of these functions. The downtown club became almost entirely a luncheon club, a site to hold meetings, or a place to relax on a free afternoon. The country club, by contrast, became a haven for all members of the family. It offered social and sporting activities ranging from dances, parties, and banquets to golf, swimming, and tennis. Special group dinners were often arranged for all members on Thursday night, the traditional maid's night off across the United States. . . .

Initiation fees, annual dues, and expenses vary from a few thousand dollars in downtown clubs to tens of thousands of dollars in some country clubs, but money is not the primary barrier in gaining membership to a club. Each club has a very rigorous screening process before accepting new members. Most require nomination by one or more active members, letters of recommendation from three to six members, and interviews with at least some members of the membership committee. Names of prospective members are sometimes posted in the clubhouse, so all members have an opportunity to make their feelings known to the membership committee. Negative votes by two or three members of what is typically a 10-to-20 person committee often are enough to deny admission to the candidate.

The carefulness with which new members are selected extends to a guarding of club membership lists, which are usually available only to club members. Older membership lists are sometimes given to libraries by members or their surviving spouses, and some members will give lists to individual researchers, but for most clubs there are no membership lists in the public domain. Our request to 15 clubs in 1981 for membership lists for research purposes was refused by 12 of the clubs and left unanswered by the other three.

Not every club member is an enthusiastic participant in the life of the club. Some belong out of tradition or a feeling of social necessity. One woman told Ostrander the following about her country club: "We don't feel we should withdraw our support even though we don't go much." Others mentioned a feeling of social pressure: "I've only been to [the club] once this year. I'm really a loner, but I feel I have to go and be pleasant even though I don't want to." Another volunteered: "I think half the members go because they like it and half because they think it's a social necessity."[7]

People of the upper class often belong to clubs in several cities, creating a nationwide pattern of overlapping memberships. These overlaps provide further evidence for the social cohesion within the upper class. An indication of the nature and extent of this overlapping is revealed by our study of membership lists for 20 clubs in several major cities across the country, including the Links in New York, the Century Association in New York, the Duquesne in Pittsburgh, the Chicago in Chicago, the Pacific Union in San Francisco, and the California in Los Angeles. Using a clustering technique based on Boolean algebra, the study revealed there was sufficient overlap among 18 of the 20 clubs to form three regional groupings and a fourth group that provided a bridge between the two largest regional groups. The several dozen men who were in three or more of the clubs were especially important in creating the overall pattern. At the same time, the fact that these clubs often have from 1,000 to 2,000 members makes the percentage of overlap within this small number of clubs relatively small, ranging from a high of 20 to 30 percent between clubs in the same city to as low as 1 or 2 percent in clubs at opposite ends of the country.[8]

One of the most central clubs in this network, the Bohemian Club of San Francisco, is also the most unusual and widely known club of the upper class. Its annual two-week encampment in its 2,700-acre Bohemian Grove 75 miles north of San Francisco brings together the social elite, celebrities, and government officials for relaxation and entertainment. A description of this gathering provides the best possible insight into the role of clubs in uniting the upper class.[9]

The huge forest retreat called the Bohemian Grove was purchased by the club in the 1890s. Bohemians and their guests number anywhere from 1,500 to 2,000 for the three weekends in the encampment, which is always held during the last two weeks in July, when it almost never rains in northern California. However, there may be as few as 400 men in residence in the middle of the week, for most return to their homes and jobs after the weekends. During their stay the campers are treated to plays, symphonies, concerts, lectures, and political commentaries by entertainers, musicians, scholars, and government officials. They also trapshoot, canoe, swim, drop by the Grove art gallery, and take guided tours into the outer fringe of the mountain forest. But a stay at the Bohemian Grove is mostly a time for relaxation and drinking in the modest lodges, bunkhouses, and even teepees that fit unobtrusively into the landscape along the two or three macadam roads that join the few "developed" acres within the Grove. It is like a summer camp for the power elite and their entertainers.

The men gather in little camps of about 10 to 30 members during their stay. Each of the approximately 120 camps has its own pet name, such as Sons of Toil, Cave Man, Mandalay, Toyland, Owl's Nest, Hill Billies, and Parsonage. A group of men from Los Angeles named their camp Lost Angels, and the men in the Bohemian chorus call their camp Aviary. Some camps are noted for special drinks, brunches, or luncheons, to which they invite members from other camps. The camps are a fraternity system within the larger fraternity.

There are many traditional events during the encampment, including plays called the High Jinx and the Low Jinx. But the most memorable event, celebrated every consecutive year since 1880, is the opening ceremony, called the Cremation of Care. This ceremony takes place at the base of a 40-foot Owl Shrine constructed out of poured concrete and made even more resplendent by the mottled forest mosses that cover much of it. The Owl Shrine is only one of many owl symbols and insignias to be found in the Grove and the downtown clubhouse, for the owl was adopted early in the club's history as its mascot or totem animal.

The opening ceremony is called the Cremation of Care because it involves the burning of an effigy named Dull Care, who symbolizes the burdens and responsibilities that these busy Bohemians now wish to shed temporarily. More than 60 Bohemians take part in the ceremony as priests, acolytes, torch bearers, brazier bearers, boatmen, and woodland voices. After many flowery speeches and a long conversation with Dull Care, the high priest lights the fire with the flame from the Lamp of Fellowship, located on the "Altar of Bohemia" at the base of the shrine. The ceremony, which has the same initiatory functions as those of any fraternal or tribal group, ends with fireworks, shooting, and the playing of "There'll Be a Hot Time in the Old Town Tonight." The attempt to create a sense of cohesion and solidarity among the assembled is complete.

As the case of the Bohemian Grove and its symbolic ceremonies rather dramatically illustrate, there seems to be a great deal of truth to the earlier-cited suggestion by Crane Brinton that clubs may have the function within the upper class that the clan or brotherhood has in tribal societies. With their restrictive membership policies, initiatory rituals, private ceremonials, and great emphasis on tradition, clubs carry on the heritage of primitive secret societies. They create within their members an attitude of prideful exclusiveness that contributes greatly to an in-group feeling and a sense of fraternity within the upper class. . . .

Marriage and Family Continuity

The institution of marriage is as important in the upper class as it is in any level of American society, and it does not differ greatly from other levels in its patterns and rituals. Only the exclusive site of the occasion and the lavishness of the reception distinguish upper-class marriages.

The prevailing wisdom within the upper class is that children marry someone of their own social class. The women interviewed by Ostrander, for example, felt that marriage was difficult enough without differences in "interests" and "background," which seemed to be the code words for class in discussions of marriage. Marriages outside the class were seen as likely to end in divorce.[10]. . .

The general picture for social class and marriage in the United States is suggested in a statistical study of neighborhoods and marriage patterns in the San Francisco area. Its results are very similar to the Philadelphia study using the *Social Register.* Of 80 grooms randomly selected from the highest-level neighborhoods, court records showed that 51 percent married brides of a comparable level. The rest married women from middle-level neighborhoods; only one or two married women from lower-level residential areas. Conversely, 63 percent of 81 grooms from the lowest-level neighborhoods married women from comparable areas, with under 3 percent having brides from even the lower end of the group of top neighborhoods. Completing the picture, most of the 82 men from middle-level areas married women from the same types of neighborhoods, but about 10 percent married into higher-level neighborhoods. Patterns of intermarriage, then, suggest both stability and some upward mobility through marriage into the upper class.[11]. . .

It seems likely, then, that the American upper class is a mixture of old and new members. There is both continuity and social mobility, with the newer members being assimilated into the lifestyle of the class through participation in the schools, clubs, and other social institutions described in this chapter. There may be some tensions between those newly arrived and those of established status, as novelists and journalists love to point out, but what they have in common soon outweighs their differences. This point is well demonstrated in the social affiliations and attitudes of highly successful Jewish businessmen, who become part of the upper class as they rise in the corporate community.[12]

The Preoccupations of the Upper Class

Members of the upper class do not spend all their time in social activities. Contrary to stereotypes, most members of the upper class are and have been hardworking people, even at the richest levels. In a study of the 90 richest men for 1950, for example, Mills found that only 26 percent were men of leisure.[13]

By far the most frequent preoccupation of men of the upper class is business and finance. This point is most clearly demonstrated through studying the occupations of boarding school alumni. A classification of the occupations of a sample of the graduates of four private schools—Saint Mark's, Groton, Hotchkiss, and Andover—for the years 1906 and 1926 showed that the most frequent occupation for all but the Andover graduates was some facet of finance and banking. Others became presidents of medium-size businesses or practiced corporation law with a large firm. Only a small handful went to work as executives for major national corporations. Andover, with a more open curriculum and a far greater number of scholarship students at the time, produced many more people who ended up in middle management, particularly in 1926, when 44 percent of the graduates were in such positions. The second area of concentration for the Andover alumni was as owners or presidents of medium-size businesses. Only 8 percent went into banking and finance, and only 4 percent into law.[14]. . .

Although finance, business, and law are the most typical occupations of upper-class males, there is no absence of physicians, architects, museum officials, and other professional occupations. This fact was demonstrated most systematically in Baltzell's study of the Philadelphians listed in *Who's Who in America* for 1940; 39 percent of the Philadelphian architects and physicians listed in *Who's Who* for that year were also listed in the *Social Register,* as were 35 percent of the museum officials. These figures are close to the 51 percent for lawyers and the 42 percent for businessmen, although they are far below the 75 percent for bankers, clearly the most elite profession in Philadelphia at that time.[15]

Less systematic studies also suggest this wide range of professional occupations. Our classification of the occupations listed by Saint Paul's alumni in the spring 1965 issue of the alumni journal found 7 physicians, 7 academic scholars, and 4 authors in addition to the 20 financiers and 16 businessmen, which were once again the most frequent occupations. The remainder of the sample was divided among small numbers of ministers (5), government officials (4), private school teachers (4), military officers (2), architects (2), playwrights (1), and lawyers (1). Although this study can be considered no more than a set of examples, it is consistent with the findings of Baltzell on Philadelphia 25 years earlier.

The feminine half of the upper class has different preoccupations than those of men. Our study of a large sample of the upper-class women included in *Who's Who in American Women* for 1965 showed the most frequent activity of upper-class women to be that of civic worker or volunteer, which includes a wide range of welfare, cultural, and civic activities. Second on the list was author or artist followed by a career in journalism, where upper-class women are involved in both the management and writing of newspapers and magazines. Finally, women of the upper class were found in academic positions as teachers, administrators, and trustees at leading boarding schools and colleges for women.[16]

The most informative and intimate look at the preoccupations of the feminine half of the upper class is provided in Ostrander's interview study. It revealed the women to be people of both power and subservience, playing decision-making roles in numerous cultural and civic organizations, but also accepting traditional roles at home vis-à-vis their husbands and children. By asking the women to describe a typical day and to explain which activities were most important to them, Ostrander found that the role of community volunteer is a central preoccupation of upper-class women, having significance as a family tradition and as an opportunity to fulfill an obligation to the community. One elderly woman involved for several decades in both the arts and human services explained: "If you're privileged, you have a certain responsibility. This was part of my upbringing; it's a tradition, a pattern of life that my brothers and sisters do too."[17]. . .

Despite this emphasis on volunteer work, the women placed high value on family life. They arranged their schedules to be home when children came home from school (30 of the 38 had three or more children), and they emphasized that their primary concern was to provide a good home for their husbands. Several of them wanted to have greater decision-making power over their inherited wealth, but almost all of them wanted to be in the traditional roles of wife and mother, at least until their children were grown. . . .

Numerous anecdotal examples also show that some members of the upper class even lead lives of failure, despite all the opportunities available to them. Although members of the upper class are trained for leadership and given every opportunity to develop feelings of self-confidence, there are some who fail in school, become involved with drugs and alcohol, or become mentally disturbed. Once again, however, this cannot be seen as evidence for a lack of cohesion in the upper class, for there are bound to be individual failures of this nature in any group.

Deviants and failures do exist within the upper class, then, but it seems likely that a majority of its male members are at work in business, finance, and corporate law, and that most of the female members are equally busy as civic volunteers and homemakers. Members of both sexes have plenty of time for clubs, vacations, and party going, but their major preoccupations are in the world of work. . . .

Conclusion

The evidence [here] suggests that there is an interacting and intermarrying upper social stratum or social elite in America that is distinctive enough in its institutions, source and amount of income, and lifestyle to be called an "upper class." This upper class makes up about 0.5 percent of the population, a rough estimate that is based upon the number of students attending independent private schools, the number of listings in past *Social Registers* for several cities, and detailed interview studies in Kansas City and Boston.[18]

Not everyone in this nationwide upper class knows everyone else, but everybody knows somebody who knows someone in other areas of the country thanks to a common school experience, a summer at the same resort, or membership in the same social club. With the social institutions described in this [article] as the undergirding, the upper class at any given historical moment consists of a complex network of overlapping social circles that are knit together by the members they have in common and by the numerous signs of equal social status that emerge from a similar lifestyle. Viewed from the standpoint of social psychology, the upper class is made up of innumerable face-to-face small groups that are constantly changing in their composition as people move from one social setting to another.

Research work in both sociology and social psychology demonstrates that constant interaction in small-group settings leads to the social cohesion that is considered to be an important dimension of a social class.[19] This social cohesion does not in and of itself demonstrate that members of the upper class are able to agree among themselves on general issues of economic and governmental policy. But it is important to stress that social cohesion is one of the factors that makes it possible for policy coordination to develop. Indeed, research in social psychology demonstrates that members of socially cohesive groups are eager to reach agreement on issues of common concern to them. They are more receptive to what other members are saying, more likely to trust each other, and more willing to compromise, which are no small matters in any collection of human beings trying to get something accomplished.[20]

The more extravagant social activities of the upper class—the debutante balls, the expensive parties, the jet-setting to spas and vacation spots all over the world, the involvement with exotic entertainers—are often viewed by pluralists and Marxists alike as superfluous trivialities best left to society page writers. However, there is reason to believe that these activities play a role both in solidifying the upper class and in maintaining the class structure. Within the class, these occasions provide an opportunity for members to show each other that they are similar to each other and superior to the average citizen. As political scientist Gabriel Almond suggested in his 1941 study of the New York upper class and its involvement in city politics: "The elaborate private life of the plutocracy serves in considerable measure to separate them out in their own consciousness as a superior, more refined element."[21] Then, too, the values upon which the class system is based are conveyed to the rest of the population in this conspicuous consumption. Such activities make clear that there is a gulf between members of the upper class and ordinary citizens, reminding everyone of the hierarchical nature of the society. Social extravaganzas bring home to everyone that there are great rewards for success, helping to stir up the personal envy that can be a goad to competitive striving.

In sociological terms, the upper class comes to serve as a "reference group." Sociologist Harold Hodges, in a discussion of his findings concerning social classes in the suburban areas south of San Francisco, expresses the power of the upper class as a reference group in the following way: "Numerically insignificant—less than one in every 500 Peninsula families is listed in the pages of the *Social Register*—the upper class is nonetheless highly influential as a 'reference group': a membership to which many aspire and which infinitely more consciously or unconsciously imitate."[22]

Exhibiting high social status, in other words, is a way of exercising power. It is a form of power rooted in fascination and enchantment. It operates by creating respect, envy, and deference in others. Considered less important than force or economic power by social scientists who regard themselves as tough-minded and realistic, its role as a method of control in modern society goes relatively unnoticed despite the fact that power was originally in the domain of the sacred and the magical.[23]

Whatever the importance that is attached to prestige and social status as mechanisms of power, this [reading] has demonstrated the power of the upper class through the disproportionate amount of wealth and income that its members possess. As [has been] argued [elsewhere] . . . such disparities are evidence for class power if it is assumed that wealth and income are highly valued in American society. However, the case for the hypothesis that the American upper class is a ruling class will not rest solely on reference group power and inequalities in the wealth and income distributions.

NOTES

1. Randall Collins, "Functional and Conflict Theories of Educational Stratification," *American Sociological Review* 36 (1971): 1010.
2. E. Digby Baltzell, *Philadelphia Gentlemen: The Making of a National Upper Class* (Glencoe, IL: Free Press, 1958), p. 160.
3. Susan Ostrander, "A Study of Upper Class Women" (book manuscript to be published by Temple University Press, 1984), p. 174; Steven B. Levine, "The Rise of the American Boarding Schools" (senior honors thesis, Harvard University, 1978), pp. 5–6; "Boys' Schools," *Fortune*, January 1936; Erving Goffman, *Asylums* (Chicago: Aldine, 1961); Michael Gordon, "Changing Patterns of Prep School Placements," *Pacific Sociological Review*, Spring 1969; Jack Trumpbour, "Private Schools" (research memo, 1980); Peter J. Nelligan, "The Cate School and the Upper Class" (term paper, University of California at Santa Barbara, 1971); G. William Domhoff, "The Women's Page as a Window on the Ruling Class," in *Hearth and Home: Images of Women in the Mass Media,* ed. Gaye Tuchman, Arlene K. Daniels, and James Benet (New York: Oxford University Press, 1978).
4. C. Wright Mills, *The Power Elite* (New York: Oxford University Press, 1956), p. 67.
5. Baltzell, *Philadelphia Gentlemen*, p. 373.
6. Richard P. Coleman and Lee Rainwater, *Social Standing in America* (New York: Basic Books, 1978), p. 144; Sophy Burnham, *The Landed Gentry* (New York: G. P. Putnam's Sons, 1978).
7. Ostrander, "A Study of Upper Class Women," p. 204.
8. Philip Bonacich and G. William Domhoff, "Latent Classes and Group Membership," *Social Networks* 3 (1981). . . . For an earlier analysis of this matrix using a technique developed by Bonacich that is based on matrix algebra, see G. William Domhoff, "Social Clubs, Political Groups, and Corporations: A Network Study of Ruling-Class Cohesiveness," *The Insurgent Sociologist,* Spring 1975.
9. G. William Domhoff, *The Bohemian Grove and Other Retreats* (New York: Harper & Row, 1974); G. William Domhoff, "Politics among the Redwoods," *The Progressive*, January 1981.
10. Ostrander, "A Study of Upper Class Women," p. 169.
11. Robert C. Tryon, "Identification of Social Areas by Cluster Analysis: A General Method with an Application to the San Francisco Bay Area," *University of California Publications in Psychology* 8 (1955); Robert C. Tryon, "Predicting Group Differences in Cluster Analysis: The Social Areas Problem," *Multivariate Behavioral Research* 2 (1967).
12. Richard L. Zweigenhaft and G. William Domhoff, *Jews in the Protestant Establishment* (New York: Praeger, 1982).
13. Mills, *Power Elite*, p. 108.

14. Levine, "Rise of the American Boarding Schools," pp. 128–30.

15. Baltzell, *Philadelphia Gentlemen*, pp. 51–65.

16. G. William Domhoff, *The Higher Circles* (New York: Random House, 1970), pp. 41–43.

17. Ostrander, "A Study of Upper Class Women," p. *xx*.

18. G. William Domhoff, *Who Rules America?* (Englewood Cliffs, NJ: Prentice-Hall, 1967), pp. 7n–8n; "Private Schools Search for a New Social Role," *National Observer*, August 26, 1968, p. 5; Coleman and Rainwater, *Social Standing in America*, p. 148. For a summary of many studies that concludes that "Capital S Society" in the United States includes "probably no more than four-tenths of one percent in large cities, and even a smaller proportion in smaller communities," see Richard P. Coleman and Bernice L. Neugarten, *Social Status in the City* (San Francisco: Jossey-Bass, 1971), p. 270.

19. Domhoff, *Bohemian Grove*, pp. 89–90, for a summary of this research.

20. Dorwin Cartwright and Alvin Zander, *Group Dynamics* (New York: Harper & Row, 1960), p. 89; Albert J. Lott and Bernice E. Lott, "Group Cohesiveness as Interpersonal Attraction," *Psychological Bulletin* 64 (1965): 291–96; Michael Argyle, *Social Interaction* (Chicago: Aldine, 1969), pp. 220–23.

21. Gabriel Almond, "Plutocracy and Politics in New York City" (Ph.D. dissertation, University of Chicago, 1941), p. 108.

22. Harold M. Hodges, Jr., "Peninsula People: Social Stratification in a Metropolitan Complex," in *Education and Society*, ed. Warren Kallenbach and Harold M. Hodges, Jr. (Columbus, OH: Merrill, 1963), p. 414.

23. See Norman O. Brown, *Life against Death* (London: Routledge & Kegan Paul, 1959), pp. 242, 249–52, for a breathtaking argument on the roots of power in the sacred and the psychological. For one attempt to apply the argument to the class structure, see G. William Domhoff, "Historical Materialism, Cultural Determinism, and the Origin of the Ruling Classes," *Psychoanalytical Review*, no. 2 (1969). For a discussion that rightly announces itself as "the first extensive treatise on prestige as a social control system," see William J. Goode, *The Celebration of Heroes: Prestige as a Social Control System* (Berkeley, CA: University of California Press, 1978).

25

DECLINING FORTUNES
The Withering of the American Dream

KATHERINE S. NEWMAN

A fascinating aspect of social stratification research is the documentation of *social reproduction*, the process through which a social class reproduces and maintains itself. For example, the upper class preserves its higher position in society through social rituals, social networks, and influence in the major social institutions. Unfortunately, social reproduction has not been as easy for the U.S. middle class. In this reading, Katherine Newman reports on the falling standard of living among the middle class. The postwar middle-class advantages of home ownership, college educations, and secure jobs are harder to obtain now. In short, many middle-class Americans are discovering that no matter how hard they work, the American Dream of economic prosperity is no longer within their reach.

Lauren Caulder was born in the halcyon days of the 1950s, when prosperity was a given and the formula for achieving it was clear. You drove yourself in school, got into a respectable college, picked a practical career, and pushed ahead with your nose to the grindstone. At the end of this long march lay the accoutrements of the good life: homeownership, family, and the security of a middle-class standard of living. Even as the currents of the American cultural revolution of the late 1960s swirled around her, Lauren doggedly followed the prescription for entry into the middle class and landed the kind of job that should have made it all possible, as a mid-level administrator of a federal lending program.

Something went awry in Lauren's life in the 1980s. Just when the fruits of her labor should have begun to pay off, the carrot at the end of the stick began to shrivel. Homeownership, that essential piece of the American dream, became an impossibility. Prices escalated to ridiculous levels and closed Lauren out. Unable to afford her own home, Lauren thought she could at least enjoy the benefits of her hard work through an occasional shopping spree or a winter holiday on a sunny island. Instead she discovered that even without the burden of a mortgage, she was still boxed in by a budget that never seemed to stretch far enough for the odd, spontaneous purchase. These days, every dime in her bankbook is committed: She is reasonably solvent, but there is no room for indulgence. This would not be such a problem if Lauren were just starting out; she could afford to wait her turn. But she is nearly 40 years old now. All that lies ahead is endless penny-pinching, without much equity to show for it:

> Every time I think I've made a financial breakthrough, something comes along that knocks me right out of the water. You think, okay, finally everything is paid off. Great, now we can start saving for such and such. Car breaks down. No use fixing it anymore. You've got to buy a new one or worse yet pay for a $750 transmission job. There you go. Now you're back in the hole, charged up on your credit card. . . . Something always comes along to wipe out everything that you might think is a winning achievement. You never seem to get over the hump and put it behind you.

Why has Lauren's standard of living fallen so far short of what she thought it would be? Her father, a quiet man of working-class origins and modest means, worked all his life in the advertising industry as a copywriter. Together with his wife, who stayed home to raise the Caulder clan, he was able to buy into a comfortable suburban community and give Lauren and her siblings a solid high school education at the local public school, swimming lessons at "the club," a chance to learn a musical instrument, and occasional travel to interesting vacation spots. Mr. Caulder's life is testimony to the great American dream: His hard work paid off in a better life for himself and his kids. His upward mobility ensured that serious want never intruded into Lauren's childhood.

The Caulder children were raised to respect traditional virtues of family and frugality, but they were also provided the emblems of affluence that were, after all, part of the reason their parents labored so hard. What was an achievement to be proud of for Mr. Caulder's generation became an expectation, a norm, an entitlement in his daughter's generation. If you became a certain kind of person—educated, cultivated, serious, motivated, hardworking—you were entitled to expect the same benefits in your life. Remaining a card-carrying member of the middle class was the most natural state of existence imaginable for baby boomers like Lauren who were raised amid its splendors.

But as Lauren left the 1980s behind—the decade dubbed by the media, the president, and a passel of economists as the longest period of expansion in the economy's postwar history—all she could see was the lifestyle she had taken for granted receding farther and farther from her grasp. She is better educated than her father; her job pays more than his ever did; she has a professional identity that her mother never even dreamed of—she should be sitting on top of the world. At the very least, Lauren tells herself, she and her husband are entitled to do as well as her parents did on one modest salary. Yet the gap between what should be and what is feels as large as the Grand Canyon:

> I'll never have what my parents had. I can't even dream of that. I'm living a lifestyle that's way lower than it was when I was growing up and it's depressing. You know it's a rude awakening when you're out in the world on your own. . . . I took what was given to me and tried to use it the best way I could. Even if you are a hard worker and you never skipped a beat, you followed all the rules, did everything they told you you were supposed to do, it's still horrendous. *They lied to me.* You don't get where you were supposed to wind up. At the end of the road it isn't there. I worked all those years and then I didn't get to candy land. The prize wasn't there, damn it.

Lauren is a member of the first generation since the Great Depression that can expect to have a *lower* standard of living than its parents. Children of the post–World War II economic boom, they entered adulthood in an era of economic uncertainty, where news of shuttered factories, bankruptcies, junk-bond nightmares, and white-collar unemployment is the stuff of daily headlines. Gone is the notion that each generation improves on the lot of its parents. In its stead comes the dread Lauren feels: She is on a treadmill that will never support a lifestyle even remotely like the one she knew as a child. Where Lauren's parents could expect to live in a nice house at low cost, have a family when they felt like it, and support their expenses on a single income, Lauren knows that she cannot afford a house, that she and her husband both have to work, and that children are a luxury that will be hard to afford.

Lauren's father, Andrew, a widower for some eight years now, recently sold the house he had owned for 30 years. This lovely New England-style home—too big for a man alone, with its four bedrooms and a large yard—had cost him $15,000 in the late 1950s, nearly twice his yearly income. While that was no small amount of money for Andrew, the 4 percent veteran's mortgage he received as thanks for his military service brought the cost within reach. The Caulder homestead fetched an astounding $400,000 in 1990, a sum so vast it makes Lauren laugh and weep at the same time. There is simply no way she can imagine ever earning enough money to buy her natal home now, or anything even remotely similar.

If Lauren could scale back her expectations, change her ambitions with every fluctuation of the consumer price index, she would have lower blood pressure. Instead, she boils over at being so tightly constrained, so unable to see past this month's paycheck:

> I'm not able to go anywhere. The lack of upward mobility and foreseeing no way out of my current situation is very frustrating. I couldn't take a more expensive apartment, couldn't buy a new car, can't take a vacation I want to take. It's just being frustrated everywhere I turn. Not being able to do the things you want to do with the money you are earning to enjoy your life. Being constantly browbeaten by the economy.

Most perplexing of all from Lauren's perspective is the fact that she always resisted the temptation to deviate and instead stuck to the straight and narrow path that was supposed to ensure that this would not happen. She followed the rules: She didn't party too much or get involved in drugs. She finished a respectable college degree, and she has steadily worked her way up the public-sector hierarchy to a responsible, even important, job. In her youth, the rewards for this good behavior were forthcoming, and she was lulled into the expectation that goodies come to those who work and wait. It seems a cruel hoax:

> I've always killed myself for a reason. I killed myself in school to get the good grades, and that was the reward, thank you very much. I got my A's. All the way along, I was rewarded in just the way I was supposed to be. . . . That was what the book said. And then you get out here to the real world and suddenly the last chapter is a sad joke. You're told you work hard for a living and you can buy a house in [your hometown], or the next town down the line that's a little cheaper. But its not true and it's really very perturbing.

Lauren sees the real world as a rude awakening from a perfect childhood. Her upbringing made her naive and gullible. Unseen forces have taken advantage of her faith in the work ethic, leaving her feeling duped.

Americans are an optimistic lot. It is part of our cultural heritage, if not our daily experience, to assume that even when times are tough, the situation is bound to improve. Even in the depths of the Great Depression, the government tried to capitalize on the average Joe's belief that prosperity was just around the corner. Unfortunately, the members of Lauren's generation do not see the economy in this light. They are beginning to believe that the slump they have experienced is permanent, something they will have to get used to, even though they find this "fact" difficult to accept. Although they have lost their optimism, they have yet to come to terms with the new reality of downward mobility.

Baby boomers find it hard to accept their lot because more than their own lot is at stake. The fall they have experienced relative to their parents may well have serious consequences for their own children. Wendy Norman, a high school classmate of Lauren's, spends a lot of time thinking about the advantages her parents conferred upon her: comfort and enrichment without extravagance—ballet lessons, the occasional theater trip, and lazy summer days down at the pool. While Wendy was lucky to have all these things, her parents were fortunate too. The economic history of the 1950s made it possible for them to do far more for Wendy than their own parents had been able to do for them in the dreary days of the Great Depression. The Normans took pride and pleasure in being able to provide Wendy with so many advantages. Wendy is fairly certain, however, that she will *not* experience the satisfaction that comes from knowing that she has "done right" by her own kids:

> I guess our grandparents and our parents, what kept them moving and motivated was that they were trying to do for their children. Improve their children's lot. I think they achieved that and for the most part were probably happy in it. That gave them the happiness, the self-fulfillment. I don't think we have that in our generation.

Wendy and her baby-boom counterparts across the nation are worried that those critical advantages, those aspects of personal biography social scientists call "cultural capital," may be lost to their own children in the 1980s and 1990s. Their kids may have to settle for less: for mediocre schools, libraries that are closing down due to lack of revenue, and residence in less affluent communities with fewer amenities.

Today's middle-class parents are only too aware of how disastrous such a scenario could be. Children who do not go to good high schools have a hard time finding their way into competitive colleges. They are disadvantaged in their efforts to get into professional schools or to land high-paying jobs. In short, the connection between cultural advantage and social prestige has never been more definitive, particularly in the eyes of those baby-boom parents who were themselves the beneficiaries of middle-class advantage. Wendy knows all too well that she would be doing even *worse* in the 1990s were it not for the educational credentials her parents bestowed upon her. She is bombarded daily with headlines that proclaim education the key to the nation's prosperity, along with daily public hand-wringing over the quality of America's schools. The message is abundantly clear: Her child's future depends upon the resources she provides. If these are less than what it takes, Wendy's kids will pay the price.

If the baby-boom generation is bewildered and disturbed by this turn of events, their parents—the generation that entered adulthood in the affluent years following World War II—are even more confused. They see themselves as living proof of the vitality of the American dream. Children of the Great Depression who were raised in cramped working-class enclaves of the nation's cities, they came of age in a time of war and emerged into peacetime to the benefits of the GI Bill, the VA mortgage, cheap land, a booming housing market, and a seemingly endless expansion in every conceivable industry.[1] Young men whose fathers crossed the Atlantic in steerage (and were satisfied to land a steady job in a sweatshop), ended up in America's finest universities and fueled an unprecedented expansion of the country's middle class. They became engineers, doctors, lawyers, businessmen—the first professionals in their family lines. Opportunity seemed limitless. As these postwar parents tell the story, those who were willing to work hard could literally make their dreams come true.

John Reinhardt certainly saw the world in these terms. John married Helen, his high school sweetheart, just before shipping out to serve in the European theater in 1945. After John was released from the army four years later, the Reinhardts moved in with his parents to save enough money to find a place of their own. Apartments were scarce in the immediate postwar years, but ironically houses were getting cheaper and more accessible than they had ever been before. The Reinhardts moved to suburban New Jersey and laid down some roots:

> We lived in a small house with two bedrooms and a big yard. It was a corner plot; it was like a quarter of an acre and it was one of those houses that were designed for GIs, right after the war. You could buy it for $11,990—can you imagine that? Ten percent down—all you needed was $1,100! Which I had to borrow from my father!

The Reinhardts had two children in that home. When the third was imminent, they traded up to a four-bedroom colonial in a more affluent community. Moving up was virtually effortless, for it was financed out of the steady accumulation of equity that came to suburban homeowners during the 1950s. By the time Gerry, the Reinhardts' fourth child, came along in 1952, the family was settled, secure, and able to enjoy the spacious country atmosphere of their home. John had always assumed that little Gerry would repeat his own performance and set up a family of his own nearby, but as he sees it now, the mountains Gerry has to climb are far too steep:

> Everything he does now is so much more expensive than what we did at a comparable age. He has to keep up with the times and it isn't easy. . . . We were always raised that your rent shouldn't exceed one week's pay. That's a good rule of thumb. Today the young people can't do that. Today they're spending two weeks' pay to keep an apartment! I feel sorry for them. And the young married people today can't go out and buy a house for $11,990 like I did. They have to pay $100,000. Where do they get it from? I'm not talking about people who inherit money or their parents give them money, I'm talking about hard-working kids that have to save. . . . Today a car costs more than what I paid for my house!

John and Gerry, father and son, see themselves as part of a single family unit with a common history. Yet in the space of one generation, so much has changed in the landscape of the U.S. economy that fathers and sons have come to inhabit different Americas. John finds this truth deeply troubling; his effort to understand why his son cannot lay hold to his rightful station as a local homeowner remains unsatisfied. John is not ready to accept the notion that Gerry's life will never equal his own from a material point of view. He wants to know to whom he can assign the blame for this most un-American reversal of fortune.

Both generations—those who rode the wave of postwar affluence and those who have fallen into the trough of postindustrial decline—pose this question now, largely in the privacy of their homes and in conversation with friends. The declining fortunes of the baby-boom cohort, while the subject of an occasional magazine piece or newspaper article, have yet to become the platform for a social movement or the rallying cry of a new-age politician. Indeed, for many Americans the personal strain of coping with disappointed expectations and dashed ambitions is so great that little energy is left for analyzing their own experience as symptomatic of far-reaching, structural disorders in the U.S. economy.

. . .

What Happened to the American Dream?

From the perspective of the boomers and their parents, a series of intertwined forces derailed the "normal" trajectory that is supposed to make it possible for children to surpass their parents. Although Pleasanton residents are not economists and do not lay claim to professional expertise in these matters, they have a fairly good grasp of the immediate culprits that have complicated their lives. Four related phenomena typically crop up when they explain the erosion of their slice of the American dream: escalating housing prices, occupational insecurity, blocked mobility on the job, and the cost-of-living squeeze that has penalized the boomer generation, even when they have more education and better jobs than their parents.

The extraordinary inflation of housing prices comes as no news to postwar parents. By sitting tight and doing almost nothing, they have seen the value of their most important asset rise to levels that are, by their own standards, stratospheric. In the course of the 1980s real estate became a language and a way of life. Dinner-party gossip revolved around how much houses on the block were going for and who was making a killing on what piece of property. It seemed, and still seems to many in Pleasanton, as though there was nothing else to talk about, nothing as captivating as money being made in the form of four-bedroom colonials. The Renfrew family can provide instant quotations on the cost of the homes that run in their comparatively well-heeled family. When asked to describe the lifestyle of their now-grown children, Mr. Renfrew responded with what has become a well-understood shorthand:

> Let's put it this way, our son lives in a million-dollar house, our daughter in Boston an $800,000 house. [Our house] is about a $400,000 house and our daughter [who lives nearby] has about a $500,000 house. So that puts it in perspective.

In public, people like the Renfrews would shake their heads in amazement over these numbers. In private they became almost giddy over the sudden wealth acquired by simply staying put.

The odd thing about this sudden wealth was that it made the process of accumulating capital effortless, almost magical. Compared to working for a living, real estate profits were incredibly easy to pile up. Dumb luck—being in the right place at the right time—and some modest resources were all that was needed to get into the game.

. . .

Of course, the escalating cost of housing is not the only divide separating the postwar parents from their baby-boom children. Jobs are harder to find and far more insecure in all respects. Pleasanton's progeny were well-educated by any standard, and they parlayed that advantage into job qualifications that often exceeded anything their parents had had to offer employers in years gone by. The sons of skilled blue-collar workers earned college degrees and became accountants. The daughters of nonworking, high school-educated mothers nearly all went on to higher education, often finding jobs as teachers or managers. Yet even with these credentials, success did not come easily to the boomers. Where their parents found an expanding job market with an inexhaustible thirst for their talents, they have found a crowded, competitive market that often deems them expendable.

Security is not easy to come by these days; it is a concern that looms very large in the lives of those who were raised in the prosperous, stable 1950s and the roaring, expansive 1960s. Contractions, leveraged buyouts, bankrupt-cies, layoffs, and general despair over the state of American competitive-ness—these are the headlines in today's business pages. Nothing in the boomers' upbringing, schooling, or early experience in the labor market pre-pared them for what we must all confront now: The U.S. economy cannot provide the kind of job opportunities or personal security that the country took for granted only a generation ago.

. . .

In the 1980s a new habit began to spread through corporate America, a tradition of declining loyalty of firm to worker and a consequent wariness among younger employees of depending upon any job for permanent secu-rity.[2] We are used to the fact that our manufacturing industries are on the skids and few of Pleasanton's progeny were headed in that direction. They were, and are now, white-collar material. But this has hardly protected them, their parents, or their friends from the shakeouts and shutdowns that have plagued the service industries. New York City, where many Pleasanton boomers work, has lost over one hundred thousand jobs since 1987, many of them white-collar positions.[3] Martin O'Rourke watched an older, longtime employee get the ax, and it scared him enough to abandon the corporate world altogether. His fear was well justified, since few age groups have been spared the pressure of mounting layoffs and white-collar dislocation. Many a 30- and 40-year-old has been handed a pink slip in the long aftermath of the 1987 stock market crash.[4]

Among those who *have* managed to escape the abyss of unemployment in the 1980s and the early 1990s, other problems have contributed to an inter-generational decline. Upward mobility within the ranks of American firms is leveling out at an earlier age for baby boomers than was true for their fathers in the expansive postwar period. When business was booming in the United States, management pyramids just kept on growing. Newly minted B.A.'s (courtesy of the G.I. Bill) flooded into the marketplace and advanced quickly up the ranks. Business growth remained strong as they reached their 40s, and this was reflected in continuous career growth. For these postwar men, careers tended to level off in their 50s and to begin the slow descent to retire-ment as they entered their 60s. While some were caught and crushed by the years of high unemployment in the early 1980s, most managed to escape the crunch of the Reagan recession and are still coasting on reasonable pensions and high home equity.

Sons and daughters who began their careers in the 1970s and 1980s have encountered both tremendous competition for the "good jobs" and flatter job pyramids, which level off at distressingly early ages. . . .

. . .

Under the best of circumstances only a few of the millions of baby boomers will see advancement into executive ranks. Many will see the zenith of their careers arrive in their 40s, leaving 20 or 30 more years of their work lives with unchanged horizons (if they are lucky enough to escape the pressures of downsizing or business collapse). Beyond the boredom that leveling off entails lie important financial consequences: Boomers will not see the continued salary increases that might eventually put them on a par with their parents. Leveling off, coupled with increasingly frequent recessions or inflationary pressures, will translate into a long-term erosion of their standard of living, a standard that already falls short of their initial expectations.

The combination of high housing costs, occupational insecurity, and slowing potential for advancement in the workplace has subjected the baby-boom generation to an intense squeeze.[5] Yet the demands upon their resources, far from slowing, have only accelerated. Now in the midst of their childbearing years, they face mounting costs for everything from clothing to child care, from education to transportation. The proportion of their income that must go toward these essentials seems, from their parents' perspective, far more than was required in "the good old days." As one 1950s mother put it, her children are working hard not to get ahead of her but in order to keep from slipping even farther backward:

> Our income was so low when we first got married, but we got a brand-new auto for $1,800. Our son David earns $20,000 teaching kids. For him a new car costs $16,000. It's just the proportion! When I went to Radcliffe, it cost $3,200 a year. Maybe my father was only earning $9,000. But for David, Harvard would cost $20,000 a year and that's a lot more than one-third of his father's income. . . . Usually there's an improvement in each generation and what they're able to get. But I think with our kids they're going backwards. They have a much more austere kind of lifestyle.

Disparities between generations along these basic economic lines inevitably leads to strain and a background jealousy. Boomers do not wish their parents ill or feel that their good fortune was undeserved. They just want to know why the run of luck did not hold long enough to include them, why they have to put up with the penny-pinching that Lauren Caulder complains of so bitterly:

> You just sit there and look, and watch how everything that seemed reasonable to wish for has somehow flown—I really think in the last two or three years. Partly because there's so many of us pushing prices up. . . . It's not as if it's a mystery why this should be happening. It's just a shame that you have to wake up and smell the coffee like that.

Lauren believes that an arbitrary force intervened to ruin things for her. She has to pay the penalty for living in an era of economic disarray, for being part of a generation so huge it has overwhelmed every market it touches—from the schools, to the professions, and no doubt some day to the retirement homes. But it is often hard for her to hold on to this structural explanation, this macropicture of demography and economics, interest rates, and international competition. What she *can* see is the discordant biography that puts her own childhood experience of normal middle-class existence out of reach now that she has reached middle age.

Many boomers have had the good fortune to exceed their parents in education and in occupational prestige. Unfortunately, superior credentials no longer seem to "buy" a superior, or even equal, lifestyle. Mary Flory's experience is a case in point. Her parents are working-class people who were able to settle in Pleasanton when that was still possible for families of modest means. Mary and her husband have moved up in the world; he, in particular, is an educated white-collar man. Nonetheless, they have fallen way behind Mary's parents in terms of the lifestyle they can afford:

> My father was an elevator operator all his life. My husband is a teacher. I would have thought right away of course we could afford to live in Pleasanton. We have better jobs. But we couldn't. There is no way we could live there. I really couldn't believe that I couldn't live in the town that I grew up in. I don't know what it says.

American culture is based in large part on an underlying social Darwinism that sees justice in the rule of survival of the fittest. We believe that those who are well equipped to compete will reap material rewards and that, conversely, those who cannot "cut the mustard" will (and should) suffer deprivation. For the past 50 years or more the dominance of white-collar work in the U.S. prestige hierarchy has meant that we define the "fittest" as those who are educated and who can lay claim to a professional identity.[6] According to this view of the natural order, blue-collar employment should not be rewarded nearly as well as "mental" work. Jobs that require a strong back are honorable enough, but they do not deserve the kind of payoff that "thought" jobs do.

In Mary Flory's case, the reverse rule seems to apply. Her respectable but unskilled father could afford to buy into Pleasanton, but her educated, professional husband is locked out. The upside-down quality of this arrangement is entirely illegitimate from Mary's point of view, and there is considerable cultural support for her way of thinking. There is no justice in the notion that Mr. Flory was in the right place at the right time, whereas Mary and her husband had the bad taste to be born at the wrong historical moment. It is an arbitrary feature of postwar history. Yet arbitrariness barely begins to capture Mary's response. She is angry, frustrated, and above all bewildered by this reversal of what "ought to be."

. . .

For most of Pleasanton's boomers, the cost-of-living squeeze is here to stay. They do not see any way out of this mess, and this conclusion in and of itself is a source of depression. Weathering hard times is one thing; accepting that the intergenerational slide is a permanent fact of life is quite another. Nevertheless, as Cathy Larson sees it, there is no reason for the realistic person to see the situation in a rosier light:

> This has gone on for so long, I don't know why it should be any different tomorrow. You know, you tell yourself constantly that you can get over the hump. But it's just an ongoing thing. It's a life of credit cards. It's a life of bills. It's a life of living beyond your means.

In Cathy's life, financial limitations create what she calls a "low burning thing," a subtext of constraint, a feeling that she is not free. This, above all, is the meaning of the intergenerational slide: The freedom to consume is cut short, the ability to plan for the long run is limited, and the bitter sense of rules turned inside out makes people feel, to use Cathy's words, like "it was all a big lie."

NOTES

1. Glen Elder discusses the fate of this generation in his important book *Children of the Great Depression: Social Change in Life Experience* (Chicago: University of Chicago Press, 1974).
2. For an ethnographic study of workers' views of American industry, see Katherine S. Newman, *Falling from Grace: The Experience of Downward Mobility in the American Middle Class* (New York: Free Press, 1988), chap. 6; and Katherine S. Newman, "Turning Your Back on Tradition: Symbolic Analysis and Moral Critique in a Plant Shutdown," *Urban Anthropology* 14, no. 1–3 (1985): 109–50.
3. "Workers Must Choose as Jobs Move," *New York Times*, April 11, 1991, p. B1.
4. Parents of the boomer generation find these trends equally frightening. The unpredictable swings in the local economy are all too reminiscent of earlier economic disasters they lived through as children in the Depression. As Simon Rittenberg sees it, things are just going from bad to worse:

   > I think there are going to be a lot of psychological breakdowns because of this economic uncertainty. I really do. I hope to hell it doesn't happen and I don't think it will be as severe as what my parents went through [in the 30s], but I see it happening. You pick up the *New York Times* this morning, Wang Corporation is laying off two thousand people. Oh boy, that's a lot of people. Mobil Oil, Esso, they're all laying off people. The economics of these takeovers that are taking place and then selling these companies in parts only means one thing: The people lose jobs, the companies do not exist after they get through cutting them up.

5. After 1973 growth of real wages and thus growth of family income stagnated. As a result, individuals who came of age during this period face what Frank Levy calls an "inequality of prospects" relative to the generation that came before them. Levy, *Dollars and Dreams: The Changing American Income Distribution* (New York: Norton, 1987); and Frank S. Levy and Richard C. Michael, *The Economic Future of American Families: Income and Wealth Trends* (Washington, DC: Urban Institute, 1991).
6. See Kathryn Dudley, *End of the Line* (Chicago: University of Chicago Press, 1993). Dudley offers an interesting discussion of this Darwinist ideology in practice in Kenosha, Wisconsin, where auto workers are being told they deserve to lose their jobs and standard of living to the white-collar elites since they had never really deserved these benefits in the first place.

26

THE USES OF POVERTY
The Poor Pay All

HERBERT J. GANS

If the American Dream is becoming unobtainable for the middle class, it was never a reality for the poor. Instead, the indigent struggle to meet the economic requirements of everyday survival. This reading by Herbert J. Gans provides a functional analysis of poverty. Contrary to the conflict theory views of Weber and Domhoff, where power is the central characteristic of class relations, the functionalist view of social class is concerned with how stratification may benefit society. Utilizing this perspective, Gans outlines the benefits or functions that the poor serve in our society.

Some years ago Robert K. Merton applied the notion of functional analysis to explain the continuing though maligned existence of the urban political machine: If it continued to exist, perhaps it fulfilled latent—unintended or unrecognized—positive functions. Clearly it did. Merton pointed out how the political machine provided central authority to get things done when a decentralized local government could not act, humanized the services of the impersonal bureaucracy for fearful citizens, offered concrete help (rather than abstract law or justice) to the poor, and otherwise performed services needed or demanded by many people but considered unconventional or even illegal by formal public agencies.

Today, poverty is more maligned than the political machine ever was; yet it, too, is a persistent social phenomenon. Consequently, there may be some merit in applying functional analysis to poverty, in asking whether it also has positive functions that explain its persistence.

Merton defined functions as "those observed consequences [of a phenomenon] which make for the adaptation of adjustment of a given [social] system." I shall use a slightly different definition; instead of identifying functions for an entire social system, I shall identify them for the interest groups, socioeconomic classes, and other population aggregates with shared values that "inhabit" a social system. I suspect that in a modern heterogeneous society, few phenomena are functional or dysfunctional for the society as a whole, and that most result in benefits to some groups and costs to others. Nor are any phenomena indispensable; in most instances, one can suggest what Merton calls "functional alternatives" or equivalents for them, i.e., other social patterns or policies that achieve the same positive functions but avoid the dysfunction. [In the following discussion, positive functions will be abbreviated as functions and negative functions as dysfunctions. Functions and dysfunctions, in the planner's terminology, will be described as benefits and costs.]

Associating poverty with positive functions seems at first glance to be unimaginable. Of course, the slumlord and the loan shark are commonly known to profit from the existence of poverty, but they are viewed as evil men, so their activities are classified among the dysfunctions of poverty. However, what is less often recognized, at least by the conventional wisdom, is that poverty also makes possible the existence or expansion of respectable professions and occupations, for example, penology, criminology, social work, and public health. More recently, the poor have provided jobs for professional and paraprofessional "poverty warriors," and for journalists and social scientists, this author included, who have supplied the information demanded by the revival of public interest in poverty.

Clearly, then, poverty and the poor may well satisfy a number of positive functions for many nonpoor groups in American society. I shall describe 13 such functions—economic, social, and political—that seem to me most significant.

The Functions of Poverty

First, the existence of poverty ensures that society's "dirty work" will be done. Every society has such work: physically dirty or dangerous, temporary, dead-end and underpaid, undignified, and menial jobs. Society can fill these jobs by paying higher wages than for "clean" work, or it can force people who have no other choice to do the dirty work—and at low wages. In America, poverty functions to provide a low-wage labor pool that is willing—or, rather, unable to be *un*willing—to perform dirty work at low cost. Indeed, this function of the poor is so important that in some Southern states, welfare payments have been cut off during the summer months when the poor are needed to work in the fields. Moreover, much of the debate about the Negative Income Tax and the Family Assistance Plan has concerned their impact on the work incentive, by which is actually meant the incentive of the poor to do the needed dirty work if the wages therefrom are no larger than the income grant. Many economic activities that involve dirty work depend on the poor for their existence: restaurants, hospitals, parts of the garment industry, and "truck farming," among others, could not persist in their present form without the poor.

Second, because the poor are required to work at low wages, they subsidize a variety of economic activities that benefit the affluent. For example, domestics subsidize the upper-middle and upper classes, making life easier for their employers and freeing affluent women for a variety of professional, cultural, civic, and partying activities. Similarly, because the poor pay a higher proportion of their income in property and sales taxes, among others, they subsidize many state and local governmental services that benefit more affluent groups. In addition, the poor support innovation in medical practice as patients in teaching and research hospitals and as guinea pigs in medical experiments.

Third, poverty creates jobs for a number of occupations and professions that serve or "service" the poor, or protect the rest of society from them. As already noted, penology would be minuscule without the poor, as would the police. Other activities and groups that flourish because of the existence of poverty are the numbers game, the sale of heroin and cheap wines and liquors, pentecostal ministers, faith healers, prostitutes, pawn shops, and the peacetime army, which recruits its enlisted men mainly from among the poor.

Fourth, the poor buy goods others do not want and thus prolong the economic usefulness of such goods—day-old bread, fruit and vegetables that would otherwise have to be thrown out, secondhand clothes, and deteriorating automobiles and buildings. They also provide incomes for doctors, lawyers, teachers, and others who are too old, poorly trained, or incompetent to attract more affluent clients.

In addition to economic functions, the poor perform a number of social functions.

Fifth, the poor can be identified and punished as alleged or real deviants in order to uphold the legitimacy of conventional norms. To justify the desirability of hard work, thrift, honesty, and monogamy, for example, the defenders of these norms must be able to find people who can be accused of being lazy, spendthrift, dishonest, and promiscuous. Although there is some evidence that the poor are about as moral and law abiding as anyone else, they are more likely than middle-class transgressors to be caught and punished when they participate in deviant acts. Moreover, they lack the political and cultural power to correct the stereotypes that other people hold of them and thus continue to be thought of as lazy, spendthrift, etc., by those who need living proof that moral deviance does not pay.

Sixth, and conversely, the poor offer vicarious participation to the rest of the population in the uninhibited sexual, alcoholic, and narcotic behavior in which they are alleged to participate and which, being freed from the constraints of affluence, they are often thought to enjoy more than the middle classes. Thus many people, some social scientists included, believe that the poor not only are more given to uninhibited behavior (which may be true, although it is often motivated by despair more than by lack of inhibition) but derive more pleasure from it than affluent people (which research by Lee Rainwater, Walter Miller, and others shows to be patently untrue). However, whether the poor actually have more sex and enjoy it more is irrelevant; so long as middle-class people believe this to be true, they can participate in it vicariously when instances are reported in factual or fictional form.

Seventh, the poor also serve a direct cultural function when culture created by or for them is adopted by the more affluent. The rich often collect artifacts from extinct folk cultures of poor people; and almost all Americans listen to the blues, Negro spirituals, and country music, which originated among the Southern poor. Recently they have enjoyed the rock styles that were born, like the Beatles, in the slums; and in the last year, poetry written by ghetto children has become popular in literary circles. The poor also serve as culture heroes, particularly, of course, to the left; but the hobo, the cowboy, the hipster, and the mythical prostitute with a heart of gold have performed this function for a variety of groups.

Eighth, poverty helps to guarantee the status of those who are not poor. In every hierarchial society someone has to be at the bottom; but in American society, in which social mobility is an important goal for many and people need to know where they stand, the poor function as a reliable and relatively permanent measuring rod for status comparisons. This is particularly true for the working class, whose politics is influenced by the need to maintain status distinctions between themselves and the poor, much as the aristocracy must find ways of distinguishing itself from the *nouveaux riches.*

Ninth, the poor also aid the upward mobility of groups just above them in the class hierarchy. Thus a goodly number of Americans have entered the middle class through the profits earned from the provision of goods and services in the slums, including illegal or nonrespectable ones that upper-class and upper-middle-class businessmen shun because of their low prestige. As a result, members of almost every immigrant group have financed their upward mobility by providing slum housing, entertainment, gambling, narcotics, etc., to later arrivals—most recently to blacks and Puerto Ricans.

Tenth, the poor help to keep the aristocracy busy, thus justifying its continued existence. "Society" uses the poor as clients of settlement houses and beneficiaries of charity affairs; indeed, the aristocracy must have the poor to demonstrate its superiority over other elites who devote themselves to earning money.

Eleventh, the poor, being powerless, can be made to absorb the costs of change and growth in American society. During the nineteenth century, they did the backbreaking work that built the cities; today, they are pushed out of their neighborhoods to make room for "progress." Urban renewal projects to hold middle-class taxpayers in the city and expressways to enable suburbanites to commute downtown have typically been located in poor neighborhoods, since no other group will allow itself to be displaced. For the same reason, universities, hospitals, and civic centers also expand into land occupied by the poor. The major costs of the industrialization of agriculture have been borne by the poor, who are pushed off the land without recompense; and they have paid a large share of the human cost of the growth of American power overseas, for they have provided many of the foot soldiers for Vietnam and other wars.

Twelfth, the poor facilitate and stabilize the American political process. Because they vote and participate in politics less than other groups, the political system is often free to ignore them. Moreover, since they can rarely support Republicans, they often provide the Democrats with a captive constituency that has no other place to go. As a result, the Democrats can count on their votes, and be more responsive to voters—for example, the white working class—who might otherwise switch to the Republicans.

Thirteenth, the role of the poor in upholding conventional norms (see the *fifth* point, above) also has a significant political function. An economy based on the ideology of laissez-faire requires a deprived population that is allegedly unwilling to work or that can be considered inferior because it must accept charity or welfare in order to survive. Not only does the alleged moral deviancy of the poor reduce the moral pressure on the present political economy to eliminate poverty, but socialist alternatives can be made to look quite unattractive if those who will benefit most from them can be described as lazy, spendthrift, dishonest, and promiscuous.

The Alternatives

I have described 13 of the more important functions poverty and the poor satisfy in American society, enough to support the functionalist thesis that poverty, like any other social phenomenon, survives in part because it is useful to society or some of its parts. This analysis is not intended to suggest that because it is often functional, poverty *should* exist, or that it *must* exist. For one thing, poverty has many more dysfunctions than functions; for another, it is possible to suggest functional alternatives.

For example, society's dirty work could be done without poverty, either by automation or by paying "dirty workers" decent wages. Nor is it necessary for the poor to subsidize the many activities they support through their low-wage jobs. This would, however, drive up the costs of these activities, which would result in higher prices to their customers and clients. Similarly, many of the professionals who flourish because of the poor could be given other roles. Social workers could provide counseling to the affluent, as they prefer to do anyway; and the police could devote themselves to traffic and organized crime. Other roles would have to be found for badly trained or incompetent professionals now relegated to serving the poor, and someone else would have to pay their salaries. Fewer penologists would be employable, however. And pentecostal religion could probably not survive without the poor—nor would parts of the second- and third-hand-goods market. And in many cities, "used" housing that no one else wants would then have to be torn down at public expense.

Alternatives for the cultural functions of the poor could be found more easily and cheaply. Indeed, entertainers, hippies, and adolescents are already serving as the deviants needed to uphold traditional morality and as devotees of orgies to "staff" the fantasies of vicarious participation.

The status functions of the poor are another matter. In a hierarchial society, some people must be defined as inferior to everyone else with respect to a variety of attributes, but they need not be poor in the absolute sense. One could conceive of a society in which the "lower class," though last in the pecking order, received 75 percent of the median income, rather than 15–40 percent, as is now the case. Needless to say, this would require considerable income redistribution.

The contribution the poor make to the upward mobility of the groups that provide them with goods and services could also be maintained without the poor's having such low incomes. However, it is true that if the poor were more affluent, they would have access to enough capital to take over the provider role, thus competing with, and perhaps rejecting, the "outsiders." (Indeed, owing in part to antipoverty programs, this is already happening in a number of ghettos, where white storeowners are being replaced by blacks.) Similarly, if the poor were more affluent, they would make less willing clients for upper-class philanthropy, although some would still use settlement houses to achieve upward mobility, as they do now. Thus "Society" could continue to run its philanthropic activities.

The political functions of the poor would be more difficult to replace. With increased affluence the poor would probably obtain more political power and be more active politically. With higher incomes and more political power, the poor would be likely to resist paying the costs of growth and change. Of course, it is possible to imagine urban renewal and highway projects that properly reimbursed the displaced people, but such projects would then become considerably more expensive, and many might never be built. This, in turn, would reduce the comfort and convenience of those who now benefit from urban renewal and expressways. Finally, hippies could serve also as more deviants to justify the existing political economy—as they already do. Presumably, however, if poverty were eliminated, there would be fewer attacks on that economy.

In sum, then, many of the functions served by the poor could be replaced if poverty were eliminated, but almost always at higher costs to others, particularly more affluent others. Consequently, a functional analysis must conclude that poverty persists not only because it fulfills a number of positive functions but also because many of the functional alternatives to poverty would be quite dysfunctional for the affluent members of society. A functional analysis thus ultimately arrives at much the same conclusion as radical sociology, except that radical thinkers treat as manifest what I describe as latent: that social phenomena that are functional for affluent or powerful groups and dysfunctional for poor or powerless ones persist; that when the elimination of such phenomena through functional alternatives would generate dysfunctions for the affluent or powerful, they will continue to persist; and that phenomena like poverty can be eliminated only when they become dysfunctional for the affluent or powerful, or when the powerless can obtain enough power to change society.

GENDER

27

THE BURDEN OF WOMANHOOD

JOHN WARD ANDERSON • MOLLY MOORE

Gender stratification, examined in the next four selections, refers to those social systems in which socioeconomic resources and political power are distributed on the basis of one's sex and gender. In any social system, we can
measure the gendered distribution of resources and rewards to see whether
men or women have a higher social status. Objective indices of gender inequality include income, educational attainment, wealth, occupational status, mortality rates, and access to social institutions. The following reading
by John Ward Anderson and Molly Moore examines the social status of
women in several countries, including India, Pakistan, and Kenya. Anderson and Moore illuminate the cultural, religious, and legal practices that
define women's status as inferior to that of men and often deprive women of
basic human rights.

GANDHI NAGAR, India

When Rani returned home from the hospital cradling her newborn
daughter, the men in the family slipped out of her mud hut while
she and her mother-in-law mashed poisonous oleander seeds into
a dollop of oil and forced it down the infant's throat. As soon as darkness fell,
Rani crept into a nearby field and buried her baby girl in a shallow, un-
marked grave next to a small stream.

"I never felt any sorrow," Rani, a farm laborer with a weather-beaten
face, said through an interpreter. "There was a lot of bitterness in my heart
toward the baby because the gods should have given me a son."

Each year hundreds and perhaps thousands of newborn girls in India
are murdered by their mothers simply because they are female. Some women
believe that sacrificing a daughter guarantees a son in the next pregnancy. In
other cases, the family cannot afford the dowry that would eventually be demanded for a girl's marriage.

And for many mothers, sentencing a daughter to death is better than
condemning her to life as a woman in the Third World, with cradle-to-grave
discrimination, poverty, sickness and drudgery.

"In a culture that idolizes sons and dreads the birth of a daughter, to
be born female comes perilously close to being born less than human," the

Indian government conceded in a recent report by its Department of Women and Child Development.

While women in the United States and Europe—after decades of struggling for equal rights—often measure sex discrimination by pay scales and seats in corporate board rooms, women in the Third World gauge discrimination by mortality rates and poverty levels.

"Women are the most exploited among the oppressed," says Karuna Chanana Ahmed, a New Delhi anthropologist who has studied the role of women in developing countries. "I don't think it's even possible to eradicate discrimination, it's so deeply ingrained."

. . . From South America to South Asia, women are often subjected to a lifetime of discrimination with little or no hope of relief.

As children, they are fed less, denied education, and refused hospitalization. As teenagers, many are forced into marriage, sometimes bought and sold like animals for prostitution and slave labor. As wives and mothers, they are often treated little better than farmhands and baby machines. Should they outlive their husbands, they frequently are denied inheritance, banished from their homes and forced to live as beggars on the streets.

The scores of women interviewed [for the series from which this selection was taken]—from destitute villages in Brazil and Bangladesh, to young professionals in Cairo, to factory workers in China—blamed centuries-old cultural and religious traditions for institutionalizing and giving legitimacy to gender discrimination.

Although the forms of discrimination vary tremendously among regions, ethnic groups, and age levels in the developing world, Shahla Zia, an attorney and women's activist in Islamabad, Pakistan, says there is a theme: "Overall, there is a social and cultural attitude where women are inferior—and discrimination tends to start at birth."

In many countries, a woman's greatest challenge is an elemental one: simply surviving through a normal life cycle. In South Asia and China, the perils begin at birth, with the threat of infanticide.

Like many rural Indian women, Rani, now 31, believed that killing her daughter $3\frac{1}{2}$ years ago would guarantee that her next baby would be a boy. Instead, she had another daughter.

"I wanted to kill this child also," she says, brushing strands of hair from the face of the two-year-old girl she named Asha, or Hope. But her husband got scared because all these social workers came and said, 'Give us the child.'" Ultimately, Rani was allowed to keep her. She pauses. "Now I have killed, and I still haven't had any sons."

Amravati, who lives in a village near Rani in the Indian state of Tamil Nadu, says she killed two of her own day-old daughters by pouring scalding chicken soup down their throats, one of the most widely practiced methods of infanticide in southern India. She showed where she buried their bodies— under piles of cow dung in the tiny courtyard of her home.

"My mother-in-law and father-in-law are bedridden," says Amravati, who has two living daughters. "I have no land and no salary, and my husband met with an accident and can't work. Of course it was the right decision. I need a boy. Even though I have to buy clothes and food for a son, he will grow on his own and take care of himself. I don't have to buy him jewelry or give him a 10,000-rupee [$350] dowry."

Sociologists and government officials began documenting sporadic examples of female infanticide in India about 10 years ago. The practice of killing newborn girls is largely a rural phenomenon in India; although its extent has not been documented, one indication came in a recent survey by the Community Services Guild of Madras, a city in Tamil Nadu. Of the 1,250 women questioned, the survey concluded that more than half had killed baby daughters.

In urban areas, easier access to modern medical technology enables women to act before birth. Through amniocentesis, women can learn the sex of a fetus and undergo sex-selective abortions. At one clinic in Bombay, of 8,000 abortions performed after amniocentesis, 7,999 were of female fetuses, according to a recent report by the Indian government. To be sure, female infanticide and sex-selective abortion are not unique to India. Social workers in other South Asian states believe that some communities also condone the practice. In China, one province has had so many cases of female infanticide that a half-million bachelors cannot find wives because they outnumber women their age by 10 to 1, according to the official New China News Agency.

The root problems, according to village women, sociologists, and other experts, are cultural and economic. In India, a young woman is regarded as a temporary member of her natural family and a drain on its wealth. Her parents are considered caretakers whose main responsibility is to deliver a chaste daughter, along with a sizable dowry, to her husband's family.

"They say bringing up a girl is like watering a neighbor's plant," says R. Venkatachalam, director of the Community Services Guild of Madras. "From birth to death, the expenditure is there." The dowry, he says, often wipes out a family's life savings but is necessary to arrange a proper marriage and maintain the honor of the bride's family.

After giving birth to a daughter, village women "immediately start thinking, 'Do we have the money to support her through life?' and if they don't, they kill her," according to Vasanthai, 20, the mother of an 18-month-old girl and a resident of the village where Rani lives. "You definitely do it after two or three daughters. Why would you want more?"

Few activists or government officials in India see female infanticide as a law-and-order issue, viewing it instead as a social problem that should be eradicated through better education, family planning, and job programs. Police officials say few cases are reported and witnesses seldom cooperate.

"There are more pressing issues," says a top police official in Madras. "Very few cases come to our attention. Very few people care."

———

Surviving childbirth is itself an achievement in South Asia for both mother and baby. One of every 18 women dies of a pregnancy-related cause, and more than one of every 10 babies dies during delivery.

For female children, the survival odds are even worse. Almost one in every five girls born in Nepal and Bangladesh dies before age 5. In India, about one-fourth of the 12 million girls born each year die by age 15.

The high death rates are not coincidental. Across the developing world, female children are fed less, pulled out of school earlier, forced into hard labor sooner and given less medical care than boys. According to numerous studies, girls are handicapped not only by the perception that they are temporary members of a family, but also by the belief that males are the chief breadwinners and therefore more deserving of scarce resources.

Boys are generally breast-fed longer. In many cultures, women and girls eat leftovers after the men and boys have finished their meals. According to a joint report by the United Nations Children's Fund and the government of Pakistan, some tribal groups do not feed high-protein foods such as eggs and meat to girls because of the fear it will lead to early puberty.

Women are often hospitalized only when they have reached a critical stage of illness, which is one reason so many mothers die in childbirth. Female children, on the other hand, often are not hospitalized at all. A 1990 study of patient records at Islamabad Children's Hospital in Pakistan found that 71 percent of the babies admitted under age 2 were boys. For all age groups, twice as many boys as girls were admitted to the hospital's surgery, pediatric intensive care and diarrhea units.

Mary Okumu, an official with the African Medical and Research Foundation in Nairobi, says that when a worker in drought-ravaged northern Kenya asked why only boys were lined up at a clinic, the worker was told that in times of drought, many families let their daughters die.

"Nobody will even take them to a clinic," Okumu says. "They prefer the boy to survive."

For most girls, however, the biggest barrier—and the one that locks generations of women into a cycle of discrimination—is lack of education.

Across the developing world, girls are withdrawn from school years before boys so they can remain at home and lug water, work the fields, raise younger siblings, and help with other domestic chores. By the time girls are 10 or 12 years old, they may put in as much as an eight-hour work day, studies show. One survey found that a young girl in rural India spends 30 percent of her waking hours doing household work, 29 percent gathering fuel and 20 percent fetching water.

Statistics from Pakistan demonstrate the low priority given to female education: Only one-third of the country's schools—which are sexually segregated—are for women, and one-third of those have no building. Almost 90 percent of the women over age 25 are illiterate. In the predominantly rural state of Baluchistan, less than 2 percent of women can read and write.

In Islamic countries such as Pakistan and Bangladesh, religious concern about interaction with males adds further restrictions to females' mobility. Frequently, girls are taken out of school when they reach puberty to limit their contact with males—though there exists a strong impetus for early marriages. In Bangladesh, according to the United Nations, 73 percent of girls are married by age 15, and 21 percent have had at least one child.

———

Across South Asia, arranged marriages are the norm and can sometimes be the most demeaning rite of passage a woman endures. Two types are common—bride wealth, in which the bride's family essentially gives her to the highest bidder, and dowry, in which the bride's family pays exorbitant amounts to the husband's family.

In India, many men resort to killing their wives—often by setting them afire—if they are unhappy with the dowry. According to the country's Ministry of Human Resource Development, there were 5,157 dowry murders in 1991—one every hour and 42 minutes.

After being bartered off to a new family, with little education, limited access to health care, and no knowledge of birth control, young brides soon become young mothers. A woman's adulthood is often spent in a near constant state of pregnancy, hoping for sons.

According to a 1988 report by India's Department of Women and Child Development: "The Indian woman on an average has eight to nine pregnancies, resulting in a little over six live births, of which four or five survive. She is estimated to spend 80 percent of her reproductive years in pregnancy and lactation." Because of poor nutrition and a hard workload, she puts on about nine pounds during pregnancy, compared with 22 pounds for a typical pregnant woman in a developed country.

A recent study of the small Himalayan village of Bemru by the New Delhi-based Center for Science and the Environment found that "birth in most cases takes place in the cattle shed," where villagers believe that holy cows protect the mother and newborn from evil spirits. Childbirth is considered unclean, and the mother and her newborn are treated as "untouchables" for about two weeks after delivery.

"It does not matter if the woman is young, old or pregnant, she has no rest, Sunday or otherwise," the study said, noting that women in the village did 59 percent of the work, often laboring 14 hours a day and lugging loads $1\frac{1}{2}$ times their body weight. "After two or three . . . pregnancies, their stamina gives up, they get weaker, and by the late 30s are spent out, old and tired, and soon die."

Studies show that in developing countries, women in remote areas can spend more than two hours a day carrying water for cooking, drinking, cleaning and bathing, and in some rural areas they spend the equivalent of more than 200 days a year gathering firewood. That presents an additional hazard: The International Labor Organization found that women using wood fuels in India inhaled carcinogenic pollutants that are the equivalent of smoking 20 packs of cigarettes a day.

Because of laws relegating them to a secondary status, women have few outlets for relaxation or recreation. In many Islamic countries, they are not allowed to drive cars, and their appearance in public is so restricted that they are banned from such recreational and athletic activities as swimming and gymnastics.

In Kenya and Tanzania, laws prohibit women from owning houses. In Pakistan, a daughter legally is entitled to half the inheritance a son gets when their parents die. In some criminal cases, testimony by women is legally given half the weight of a man's testimony, and compensation for the wrongful death of a woman is half that for the wrongful death of a man.

———

After a lifetime of brutal physical labor, multiple births, discrimination, and sheer tedium, what should be a woman's golden years often hold the worst indignities. In India, a woman's identity is so intertwined and subservient to her husband's that if she outlives him, her years as a widow are spent as a virtual nonentity. In previous generations, many women were tied to their husband's funeral pyres and burned to death, a practice called *suttee* that now rarely occurs.

Today some widows voluntarily shave their heads and withdraw from society, but more often a spartan lifestyle is forced upon them by families and a society that place no value on old, single women. Widowhood carries such a stigma that remarriage is extremely rare, even for women who are widowed as teenagers.

In some areas of the country, women are forced to marry their dead husband's brother to ensure that any property remains in the family. Often they cannot wear jewelry or a *bindi*—the beauty spot women put on their foreheads—or they must shave their heads and wear a white sari. Frequently, they cannot eat fish or meat, garlic or onions.

"The life of a widow is miserable," says Aparna Basu, general secretary of the All India Women's Conference, citing a recent study showing that more than half the women in India age 60 and older are widows, and their mortality rate is three times higher than that of married women of the same age.

In South Asia, women have few property or inheritance rights, and a husband's belongings usually go to sons and occasionally daughters. A widow must rely on the largess of her children, who often cast their mothers on the streets.

Thousands of destitute Indian widows make the pilgrimage to Vrindaban, a town on the outskirts of Agra where they hope to achieve salvation by praying to the god Krishna. About 1,500 widows show up each day at the Shri Bhagwan prayer house, where in exchange for singing "Hare Rama, Hare Krishna" for eight hours, they are given a handful of rice and beans and 1.5 rupees, or about 5 cents.

Some widows claim that when they stop singing, they are poked with sticks by monitors, and social workers allege that younger widows have been sexually assaulted by temple custodians and priests.

On a street there, an elderly woman with a *tilak* on her forehead—white chalk lines signifying that she is a devout Hindu widow—waves a begging cup at passing strangers.

"I have nobody," says Paddo Chowdhury, 65, who became a widow at 18 and has been in Vrindaban for 30 years. "I sit here, shed my tears and get enough food one way or another."

28

NO MAN'S LAND
Men's Changing Commitments to Family and Work

KATHLEEN GERSON

In recent years, we have experienced radical transformations in the social norms governing the lives of women and men. Of particular interest is the impact increasing numbers of employed women have on families and on individual lives. Most U.S. women work outside the home. For some women, this provides a second income to help meet the expenses of child care and other family costs; for others, employment is their only source of income and financial support. These changes in women's lives also signify great modifications in the lives of men. In the following reading, Kathleen Gerson explores how men's lives and gender roles within the family have altered in recent years.

Received models of fatherhood are not writ in the stars or in our genes. Our ancestors knew a very different pattern than our own, and our descendants may have another that is no less different. Fatherhood, history reminds us, is a cultural invention.

—JOHN DEMOS, "THE CHANGING FACES OF FATHERHOOD"

To make sense of men's lives, we first need to lay some myths to rest. Consider the belief that breadwinning is a traditional or natural pattern with a long legacy. In fact, men's behavior and our wider cultural ideals about manhood have not consistently conformed to this model throughout American history.[1] To the contrary, the idea that men should provide sole or primary economic support for their households in lieu of participating in domestic work did not develop until the emergence of industrial capitalism and only gradually came to describe the behavior of most men. However much some may mourn its decline, the good-provider ethic has not been a continuous historical pattern. It was the product of social forces

that converged in one fleeting era, and its reign as a predominant form of behavior and a prevailing cultural ethic has been relatively short-lived.

. . .

Contemporary American men have inherited an ambiguous legacy. The
"lone man against the world" image extolled in popular myth has its roots in
the early period of preindustrial expansion, when men could, and often did,
leave home and family to seek their fortunes alone. Yet the preindustrial period also offers a vision of men and women jointly shouldering the risks and
responsibilities of work and family. Both visions have persisted in American
mythology, but each lost a large share of real-life adherents as industrial capitalism developed throughout the nineteenth and twentieth centuries.[2] The
rise of the wage-earning worker produced a new definition of manhood and,
indeed, a new kind of man.

. . .

The rise of the primary-breadwinning husband, based on the ideal of a
family wage and the "protection" of women and children, provided some
obvious benefits. It afforded middle-class women and children relief from
the sometimes dangerous and often squalid conditions of early industrial
workplaces. It freed children from the burdens of wage earning, allowing
them an extended childhood devoted to learning and play under the watch-
ful eyes of mothers, teachers, and other female caretakers. As the sociologist
Viviana Zelizer points out, children became economically "useless," but socially "priceless."[3]

Despite these real benefits, the barring of women from highly paid, secure
jobs reinforced and exaggerated inequality between men and women and between adults and children. The "modern family" became synonymous with
a sharp differentiation between the sexes, a glorification of the mother-child
bond, and an expectation that men should provide economically for their
wives and children.

The consolidation of the modern family, with its reliance on a male family wage, transformed the justification for male control over women and
children. Patriarchal dominance could no longer be easily asserted as a male
birthright; men now had to earn it through economic success in the marketplace. Male power and privilege became tied to good jobs that paid enough
to support the family in a certain degree of comfort. In exchange for assuming economic responsibilities, men "earned" the right—and gained the economic power—to head the household and to control the family purse strings.

. . .

In this early period, the growth of the female labor force did not appear
to threaten the preeminence of the male breadwinner. After all, the vast ma-

jority of women workers were young, single, childless, and only temporarily employed. Marriage and pregnancy sent most employed women home to care for newly acquired husbands and children. The economic prosperity that followed the Great Depression and World War II, coupled with veterans' benefits and preferential treatment for male workers, gave male breadwinning a new boost and temporarily suppressed the long-term erosion of the good-provider pattern. However insignificant the emergence of large numbers of employed women may have appeared at the outset, it was a portent of more widespread changes to come.

When changes did become apparent, they made a revolutionary transformation in women's lives.[4] Streaming into the labor force in ever-increasing numbers, women have developed a commitment to the workplace that has come to resemble the career pattern once reserved for men. A burgeoning proportion has also postponed or rejected marriage, reduced their reproductive rates to an unprecedented low, and fashioned a variety of alternatives to full-time mothering. By the mid-1970s, over half of all American women of working age were in the labor force, and the birthrate had dropped below the replacement rate of 2.2 children per woman for the first time in American history.

Since then, women's movement into the work force has continued unabated, topping 58 percent for all working-age women in 1990 and accounting for two out of every three mothers with preschool children. Since the precipitous rise in women's employment rate is fueled by the entry of younger rather than older cohorts of women, the percentage of mothers with young children who are employed has risen faster than the percentage of all women who are employed. . . .

Men have also undergone a revolution in family and work commitments, albeit a quieter one. Since 1970, men's earnings have stagnated, eroding their ability to earn a "family wage." From 1979 to 1988, the median hourly wage for men fell 5 percent, and the bottom 75 percent of the male work force experienced wage reductions.[5] For white men serving as a family's only breadwinner, median inflation-adjusted income fell 22 percent between 1976 and 1984.[6] Families have been able to maintain a comparable standard of living only because women have joined the work force and experienced slightly rising wages.[7] Men's relative economic contributions to family survival have thus declined over the last several decades, while pressure for them to share in the work of the home has mounted.

Although the economic prospects of most men have contracted, their options about whether to share their earnings with women and children have expanded. The rise in divorce, nonmarital sexual partnerships, and out-of-wedlock childbearing has given men an escape hatch from the demands of primary breadwinning.[8] Many men may now find it difficult to support a family alone, but they have a choice about what to do instead; they can rely on an employed partner to share the pressures of economic survival, or they can simply remain single and thereby keep their earnings to themselves.

. . .

Now, as in an earlier era, "good providers" vie with "autonomous men" and "involved husbands and fathers" for ideological and social support. But no clear successor has taken the place of the once-ascendant but now embattled ethos of male breadwinning. Contemporary men—whether primary breadwinners, husbands and fathers in dual-earner marriages, or confirmed bachelors—face new choices and circumstances. Models from the past, however unambiguous or attractive, provide little help in navigating these uncertain waters.

Alternative Paths in Men's Development

Just as it is incorrect to assume that men's breadwinning is a pattern that has prevailed throughout American history, it is also erroneous to assume that contemporary men are a homogeneous group. Despite the common belief that a shared set of experiences binds all or most men together, modern men inherit an ambiguous cultural legacy and face a variety of social circumstances. Pushed and pulled in diverse ways, they are moving in different directions. Some continue to choose breadwinning, but others are forging alternative paths. To make sense of this diversity, we need to distill the complexity of men's lives into some general patterns. In particular, men differ in two important ways: whether or not they developed a breadwinning outlook in childhood, and whether or not they have sustained or changed their outlooks over time.

Among men who expected to become breadwinners, some have maintained this outlook into and throughout adulthood, following a stable path toward good providing. But others experienced unexpected change, either moving away from family commitments or moving toward parental caretaking.

Men who did not develop a breadwinning outlook in childhood have followed a similar range of paths. Some of these men have sustained an autonomous outlook. Others have undergone some kind of change, either becoming breadwinners despite an earlier reluctance or unexpectedly turning toward involvement in child rearing.

These six paths do not exhaust all of the complicated patterns emerging among contemporary men, but they illustrate some of the most important contours of change. Taking a close look at how individuals are traversing these alternative routes provides a way to decipher how and why men are changing. Consider, then, the paths taken by the following middle-class and working-class men.

Jim and Brian come from very different economic backgrounds, but they share a life trajectory toward breadwinning:

Jim grew up in a comfortable home located in a well-to-do suburb outside a major Eastern city. His parents moved there shortly after his birth, attracted by the spacious lawns and high-quality public schools that seemed ideal for their children. Each day, his father commuted to work in the city, leaving Jim and his sisters in the care of their mother.

His parents stressed education, and his father's income as an advertising executive ensured Jim's access to a good college. From his earliest memories, Jim aimed for and expected to achieve professional status. In his eyes, a professional job would provide the income to support a wife and children in the same degree of comfort he enjoyed as a child. It would also bestow him with the mark of success.

In college, Jim partied more than he studied, and his grades suffered accordingly. Though a pre-med student, he had little chance of being accepted into an accredited U.S. medical school. But being a doctor seemed the most appealing way to achieve the material and social rewards he desired, so Jim gained entry to a less selective medical school abroad. Four years later, he returned to the United States with a medical degree and an appointment as an intern at a small suburban hospital.

In his late 20s, with the demanding—and impoverished—years of medical training behind him, Jim met and married Theresa, a nurse five years his junior. She shared his vision of creating a home and family in which he earned the bread and she baked it. Jim was finally able to cash in on his "investment" in a lucrative, if demanding, private practice, and he and his wife are expecting their first child. She has quit her nursing job to devote all her time to child rearing, and he puts in long hours as a doctor to support his growing family in style.

Although less privileged and further along in his work and family "careers," Brian has followed a path parallel to Jim's:

Brian grew up in a modest attached house in a crowded Irish neighborhood on the outskirts of a large city. His father was a plumber who loyally stayed with the same company, despite low pay and poor working conditions. His mother, a devout Catholic, never held a paid job or, to his recollection, expressed any desire to do so. She seemed content to look after her six children.

Brian spent his boyhood playing in the crowded streets of his neighborhood. He never enjoyed school and, like his father, preferred to work with his hands rather than his head. When his father was able to get him a plumbing apprenticeship, he jumped at the opportunity to quit school at 17 and learn a "useful trade." His parents, who stressed hard work and making a good living, were happy with this decision.

After completing his training, Brian went to work as a plumber for his father's boss. He also married his neighborhood girlfriend, Donna, shortly after they discovered she was pregnant. He can't say he "really loved" her, but it was the "right thing to do." Besides, she shared his background and outlook on life, and the timing seemed right. Shunning birth control, they had two daughters within the first three years of marriage and planned for an even larger family.

As his family grew, Brian chafed under the insecure working conditions of private contracting. When the opportunity arose, he took the appropriate civil service exams and moved to a more secure job with the city. He has been there ever since. Now that he has four children to feed, he cannot afford to leave. The security, pension benefits, and other protections of a civil service job offset his irritation with tedious working conditions and bureaucratic procedures.

Today, Brian, Donna, and their four children share a small but comfortable house in a working-class suburb. Donna "rules the roost" and complains that he is never home. He rejoins that he has to work overtime and take extra jobs "off the books" to meet the heavy expenses of a large family. He also admits he prefers hanging out with the guys to "taking orders" from Donna at home. She has no desire to work, and in any case he would not "allow" it until the youngest child begins school. They both agree that "a mother belongs at home."

Jim and Brian found the social and economic support to maintain their early outlooks on work, family, and breadwinning. Indeed, both attributed their later success to following the model their parents had set for them. And why not? They had little reason to question the logic and value of their upbringing, since the promises of their childhood were relatively easy to fulfill. Through hard work, they reason, they have been able to obtain the rewards of being a man: supportive wives to care for their homes, healthy children to carry on their names, sufficient income to meet their material aspirations, and the respect of family and friends for having accomplished so much at home and at work.

Other men, however, have not found the process of becoming a breadwinner as straightforward or attractive as they had anticipated. Beginning with similar backgrounds and aspirations, Walter, Alan, Robert, and Larry moved away from primary breadwinning over time, although not in the same direction:

Walter's background, like Jim's, was solidly middle class. His father was a modestly successful accountant, who supported his family and was "moderately" involved in raising his young son and daughter. His mother was home daily, never feeling the need or desire to work outside the home. Walter "always assumed" he would marry and have children some day. He knew he would be a professional, too.

He was good in math and science and attracted to the financial rewards promised by a medical career. But he was not attracted to the pressures and long training doctors must endure. He thus chose dentistry, a well-paying but less demanding medical occupation.

In college, Walter had his first serious relationship with a woman and married her three years later. His wife worked as a film editor but quit when their son was born. By then, Walter was making ample money in his private practice, and she had hit a dead end in her career. They moved to the suburbs, and he commuted to work in the city each day.

But Walter gradually tired of his life at work and at home. His private practice was lucrative but uninspiring and excruciatingly predictable. He longed for more time to himself, but the financial demands of a nonemployed wife and child made that impossible.

Walter also became estranged from his family. Commuting kept him away from home much of the time, and his resentment of their dependence on him made tensions high when he was there. These tensions created a subtle but palpable barrier between him and his young son.

By the time it came, Walter's divorce merely ratified his emotional distance from his family. It also allowed him to move to the city, where the emotional distance took physical form. He now lives close to his office, but has cut back on his working hours to enjoy the leisure activities that city living affords. He pays only modest alimony, since his ex-wife now works, and his child-support payments are less than the expenses he bore when married. He tries to see his son every weekend, but his new girlfriend is taking an increasing amount of his time. Mostly, he says, he likes being alone.

Alan also avoided parental commitments even though he initially held a breadwinning orientation:

Alan was raised by his grandparents. His parents were divorced before he was five, and his memories of his father are dim. He lived with his mother and maternal grandparents, who were like parents to him. His grandfather took his father's place as family breadwinner and patriarch. His grandmother "spoiled" him, and he remembers her as "terrific."

Alan's expectations for the future were vague, but he was confident he could "take care of whatever came up." He always "figured" he'd get married and get a job. He gravitated toward retail sales, where his relaxed, unaffected charm made finding jobs easy.

Alan went to work right after high school selling hard goods in a department store. He was an effective salesman and able to make "good money" on commission. With money in his pockets, he married young, had a child, and became a breadwinning father when he was barely into his 20s.

After a few years, an economic recession hit, sales fell drastically, and Alan found himself out of work. He was not especially concerned; he knew he could find another job and was happy to enjoy his leisure until the unemployment checks ran out. His wife, however, was horrified at Alan's sudden change of fortune. When she asked for a divorce, Alan learned that she was involved with another man.

Within weeks of his wife's revelation, divorce proceedings were under way. In court, she asked for and gained full custody of their daughter, citing Alan's poor work record and lack of involvement with their child. She also claimed Alan assaulted her, although Alan denies this vehemently.

When the divorce was final, Alan's wife moved across the country with her new boyfriend, taking his young daughter far away. Alan considered contesting his ex-wife's move, but he believed the judge would not support him and would have little power to enforce compliance even if he did. After several attempts to contact his daughter, all of which his ex-wife opposed, Alan ceased trying to be a father. He has not seen or heard from his daughter for over a decade.

Since his divorce, Alan has held a variety of jobs and remarried twice. He rarely stays at one job for long, choosing instead to alternate between periods of work and periods of play. He has no desire to have any more children. He prefers the freedom of childlessness to the risk of loss that fatherhood would entail.

Walter and Alan turned away from an initial adherence to the good-provider ethic toward an ethic that stresses personal freedom and autonomy.

Like them, Robert and Larry expected to become primary breadwinners but ultimately rejected this pattern. Instead of distancing themselves from domestic life, however, these two men embraced parental involvement, developing ties to their children that extend far beyond providing for economic needs alone:

Robert grew up in the privileged surroundings of an affluent suburb. His father, a doctor, provided a stern, imposing, and demanding figure for his two sons. His mother also had a strong personality, but fewer outlets for its expression. She worked part-time, but poured most of her considerable energy into her family. Both parents stressed discipline and achievement. Robert was not close to his father, but he did respect his father's accomplishments. Like his father, he expected to become a successful doctor and good provider for his own wife and children.

In college, Robert realized that science was not his strength and that becoming a doctor was not his, but his father's, aspiration. He switched to a humanities major over both parents' objections and went on to graduate school in art education. He liked working with people, especially children, and eventually became a high school teacher.

In his early 20s, he married a fellow teacher. They had two children, a boy and a girl. Since he and his wife earned limited incomes but enjoyed flexible schedules as teachers, they both continued to work and shared fairly equally in the child-care duties not absorbed by day-care centers and baby-sitters. Robert found himself to be a devoted and nurturing father, far different than his own father had been. Indeed, he took to parenthood with greater enthusiasm than did his wife.

Shortly after the birth of their second child, the marriage began to deteriorate. Robert's wife became dissatisfied with teaching and began to feel "confined" by marriage and motherhood. As she struck out on a new career in advertising, they "grew apart." Divorce seemed a welcome relief to both, but Robert was determined not to lose his children. They agreed on a joint custody arrangement, in which the children split their time equally between the two parents. This arrangement gave her the freedom she desired and him the parental involvement he needed. The divorce reinforced rather than undermined the shared caretaking that had already developed between them.

Robert now lives with his new wife, Rhonda, an editor with a publishing company, in an apartment a few blocks away from his former wife. His children, now nearing their teens, have rooms in each dwelling and move back and forth easily between their two homes. They spend every other week with Robert, who proudly displays their art on the apartment's walls. He has remained a devoted teacher and has recently begun to write innovative educational texts. He is eager to have another child with Rhonda.

Larry's economic origins were more modest, but he held equally traditional expectations:

Larry's father was a boat captain, and from his earliest memory that is what Larry wanted to become. As the oldest son, he was often looked to as the man around the house during his father's frequent absences at sea. Larry's mother, a strong woman who stressed the values of hard work and honesty, doted on him. His father died when Larry was in his teens, but his father's pension kept the family out of poverty.

Larry joined the seafarers' apprentice program shortly after high school graduation. It takes years to become a licensed captain and many are never accepted into the ranks of this elite group, but Larry was confident that his father's connections, combined with his own skills, would secure a place for him among the captains' ranks.

For seven years he worked as a crew member on tugboats that pulled barges out to sea. The work was tedious, but he was learning to be a captain and never doubted that his promotion would come at the end of the probationary period. During this period, he married and had two children. His wife, Rita, continued to work as a flight attendant. In addition to recognizing the need for two incomes, she was committed to working and aimed, as she still does, for a promotion to management. They have been able to coordinate two erratic work schedules so that one parent has always been home to care for their toddlers or get them to the baby-sitter.

Several years ago, Larry's lifelong dream was shattered. The board refused to promote him to captain's rank. If he remains at sea, he will have to do so as a member of the crew. Rita, he says, has kept him "afloat" economically and spiritually during this rough time. As he has struggled to adjust to his thwarted ambitions and to search for new, if less stimulating, work in the everyday world of the "land-locked," his family, and especially his children, has become the emotional center of his world.

Unlike their own distant fathers, Robert and Larry actively participate in rearing and providing emotional sustenance to their young children. Although unexpected, parenting has become one of their most fulfilling life experiences. They not only share but *enjoy* sharing the economic and nurturing responsibilities of parenthood. It is difficult to distinguish their contributions to the family from those of their wives. The trajectories of these involved fathers provide a sharp contrast to those of Jim and Brian, who remained stable breadwinners, and of Walter and Alan, who avoided parental involvement, even though all three groups grew up with similar aspirations.

Those early aspirations are quite different than those of the following six men, who grew up hoping to find freedom and to avoid the demands of becoming a good provider. Gus and Tony never veered from the path they initially hoped to pursue:

Gus grew up in a small Southern town. His mother was a full-time homemaker, and his father a lawyer who worked out of a small office attached to their home. Unlike most fathers of his era, Gus's father was close at hand and even joined the family for lunch whenever the children were home. Both parents were well educated and stressed professional careers and marriage for their three children. Gus, however, was a gifted artist and wanted to find an occupation that drew on his artistic skills. He also felt bored and confined by small-town family life, attracted instead to the glamour and excitement that a big city promised.

Despite his parents' wishes, Gus moved to New York City after high school graduation to pursue his interest in art and design. In place of the comfort and security of small-town life, New York offered insecurity and economic hardship, but also the freedom from "middle-class" values and the opportunity to explore alternative lifestyles. He enrolled in a design school, subsisted on part-time jobs, and moved in with a woman he met at school.

After finishing the design program with honors, he took a job as designer-planner for a social service agency. Living with a woman, however, confirmed Gus's aversion to family life. He found sharing an apartment, much less his life, too confining. As her demands for commitment escalated, he concluded that he preferred living alone, where he could be free to devote his time to work.

As middle age approaches, Gus has few regrets. He has become increasingly self-confident in his work and has grown restive with the limits of working in a bureaucracy. He plans to start his own business soon. Although a risky move, Gus can afford to take it, for he has avoided the economic and social entanglements of marriage and fatherhood. Children appeal to him in the abstract, but the concrete circumstances necessary to become a father do not. His own material needs are few, and time rather than money is his most valued resource. He breathes a sigh of relief that he has managed to avoid the "trap" of family life and is grateful to his sister for giving his parents the grandchild they so desired. He feels little nostalgia for the small-town world he long ago left behind.

Like Gus, Tony never wished to become a father or a breadwinner, and his aspirations did not undergo significant change:

> Tony was not completely averse to having a child of his own; it just never seemed like a realistic goal. Orphaned as a young boy, he was sent to live with his older sisters, dividing his time between the two so that he would be less of a burden to each. As soon as he was old enough to earn money, he worked at any odd job he could find. The lack of financial resources made college out of the question. He did not like school anyway. When his uncle offered him the chance to be a mechanic in his gas station, he quit school in the tenth grade and began to support himself.
>
> Within a few years his uncle hit hard times and let Tony go. Tony was good with his hands and always able to find work, but no job lasted more than a year, and none seemed to provide much promise for the future. He moved aimlessly from one job to another until he finally joined the army. His army stint was short and comparatively painless, since he was sent to Europe instead of Southeast Asia. Once discharged, he returned to his sister's home and the modest but bearable life he had left behind.
>
> Not long after his return, Tony met Vickie, a teenager who lived down the street. Over her father's strong objections, they began to date steadily and were soon making plans to marry. She seemed to

have the self-confidence and ambition that Tony lacked. She began working and saving money for the house they would buy someday. Tony went along, handing over most of his pay to her. She stayed in school, graduated, and trained to become a nurse. She also pushed Tony to apply for a job with the city, where he was hired as a provisional worker.

As soon as Vickie reached the age of consent, they married and settled into a bungalow financed primarily by her savings. Since that time, they have discussed having children, but she states flatly that she is too ambitious to take the time out to raise a child and that, with high blood pressure, a pregnancy would threaten her health. As a provisional worker, Tony does not earn enough money to support a family alone in the style his wife wishes. He hopes to find job security someday, but holds little hope that the work will pay well. He nevertheless has no desire to be a househusband. He hates housework and leaves most of it to Vickie, who demands a high standard of cleanliness. His marriage gives him more of a family than he ever expected, and he feels no need to press for a child over his wife's objections. Her judgment has proved correct so far, and he is willing, indeed happy, to abide by her preferences.

Despite the cultural and social injunctions that encourage men to trade personal freedom for family responsibilities, specific social circumstances converged to reinforce Gus's and Tony's early aversion to the breadwinning ethic. They differ from Paul and Steve, who both moved from an early rejection of breadwinning toward conformity to the good-provider pattern:

> Paul was a child of the 60s. Raised in a solidly middle-class family, he concluded in adolescence that he wanted no part of the establishment to which his parents belonged. At the height of the youth rebellion, he moved to Vermont with Nancy, his college girlfriend, where they opened a store together. They were happy as equal partners in their food store, and although some extramarital affairs brought strains to the marriage, their commitment to each other survived. Following one especially rough period, when his wife got seriously involved with another lover, they decided to forgo all extramarital liaisons and cement their bond to each other by having a child. They shared in the care of their young daughter, just as they shared in the running of the store.
>
> Paul was very happy living the life of a country hippie, but "making ends meet" got difficult. Expecting a second child and facing the economic burdens that parenthood brings, he and Nancy decided to move back to "civilization" in search of jobs with steady paychecks.
>
> With the proceeds from selling their country store as a down payment, they bought a house in the suburbs and went looking for jobs in the "real world." Hindered by her lack of work experience, Nancy was disappointed to find nothing better than a low-paying

job as a clerk-typist. Paul was more fortunate, landing a job on the bottom rung of a social service agency. His managerial skills, concern for the needy, and sheer energy were appreciated and rewarded. Paul found himself moving up the ladder of success despite himself. He missed the time work took away from being with his family, and especially his two young children, but the rewards of success were seductive.

Within a few years, Paul was making enough money to enable Nancy to quit her job. She had never planned to become a house-wife, but her job was leading her nowhere. Paul urged her to stay home, for he was working 60 hours a week and felt someone needed to be with the kids.

Now an agency director, Paul feels remorse when Nancy and the kids complain of his long days and nights at work. He admits he has discovered work ambitions he once scorned, but he loves his job and the lifestyle it affords him. Much to his own surprise, he has become a breadwinner and a member of the establishment.

Steve also became a breadwinner without ever intending to do so:

From as far back as he can remember, Steve recalls that he was wild. His parents tried to keep him off the streets, but as soon as he was big enough to stand up to his father, he was out of the house and hanging out with the guys. He sought in his friends the warmth and camaraderie he never had from his unaffectionate father, a military man with a cold, stern demeanor. His friends offered more than sup-port, however. By the time he graduated from high school, he was well schooled in sex and drugs. He made no plans for the future.

Following a brief period of immersion in the hippie countercul-ture, he was drafted and sent to Vietnam. There he acquired several tattoos and a serious heroin addiction. By the time he returned home, his life had less direction than ever. He drifted from job to job; what-ever income he could muster was quickly depleted to support his drug habit, and he sought work that enabled him to stay high as of-ten as possible. His strongest memory of that period is being fired from a mail-carrier job for driving a truck while stoned.

Eventually he moved in with Elaine, who seemed to care about him in ways he had never known before. With a steady job of her own, she urged him to break his drug habit and aim for something better in life. He joined a methadone program and gave up the "hard stuff." When Elaine got pregnant, they married.

Faced with the new and overwhelming responsibilities of father-hood, Steve panicked and reverted to drugs as the most convenient escape. Elaine supported him and their child singlehandedly. He found that arrangement even harder to take and moved out of the house they had purchased with the help of his in-laws.

On his own for the first time in years, Steve realized how accustomed he had become to domesticity and how little pleasure he now derived from his freedom. On the advice of a friend, he applied for a job working with computers. He tested well, for he had always had an aptitude for math. In his new job as a computer programmer, he discovered talents he never thought he had and a love of work he had never known. Recognizing his talent, his boss offered him a promotion.

Elaine agreed to let him move back in with her and their young daughter if he would stay straight. She had tired of the double burden of full-time work and sole responsibility for child rearing. Steve was now earning enough to support the whole family, and she was ready to have another child.

Off drugs for two years, Steve is now a full-time breadwinner. Elaine works part-time to provide some extra income, but she spends most of her time caring for their two young children. Steve gets up every morning looking forward to a job he enjoys. He expects to be promoted to management soon and ultimately plans to run the whole department. In his view, the support of his boss and his wife saved his life.

Paul's and Steve's stories show how strong the social pull toward breadwinning can remain for some. In contrast, the life histories of Frank and Todd demonstrate how the pull toward the good-provider model is waning for others:

Frank grew up in a Midwestern household, where a stress on education and achievement groomed him for the fast track of occupational accomplishment. Although his parents also stressed "family values," Frank sensed that making money and climbing the corporate ladder were more important ingredients of success than marriage and family. From as early as he can remember, Frank recalls that work ambitions crowded out any strong desire to have children.

Proving himself to be an able student and a dedicated worker, Frank launched a promising career as a corporate economist after completing graduate school. He fell easily into the habit of working 80-hour weeks, usually arriving home only to eat a quick meal and fall into bed. His hard work and quick intelligence were rewarded with frequent promotions and hefty raises. In the early years, amid work demands and rewards, he hardly noticed that a personal life was missing.

By his late 20s, however, Frank had begun to sense an emptiness in the skewed balance of his life. He was growing weary of long days at the office and short nights alone. He started to drop in bars after work and even gambled on a few blind dates. Within a few years, Frank met Sharon, a woman he could envision sharing his life with. She, too, was a busy professional who shared his enthusiasm for hard work. She moved in with him. They settled into the busy life of two childless professionals and married after a few years.

Several years into the marriage, Sharon began to raise the subject of children. Her pleas to start a family increased in frequency, but Frank hardly noticed. He was too pressured at work and did not need another responsibility. He had never taken her suggestions seriously, for he knew she was as committed to working as he.

One morning, Sharon announced she was leaving. She explained that he was too distant, inaccessible, and tied to his work; she wanted a more balanced life, with a child and with more sharing and intimacy. Frank had heard these complaints before and so was skeptical of her sincerity, but when he arrived home that night she was gone. He was devastated. The prospect of losing Sharon made him realize how much he needed and loved her, how important their life together had become to him.

After a few days of disorientation and despair, Frank came to a fateful conclusion: for the first time since adolescence, he realized some things mattered more to him than money, success, and power. He resigned from his high-pressured job and set about to find less demanding employment. His occupational future looked less promising, but he looked forward to having more time to pursue other pleasures.

It took months to convince Sharon that she meant more to Frank than his job did, but after six months of separation she agreed to reunite. They bought a home in a nearby suburb.

Frank and Sharon now have a four-year-old daughter. As an assistant vice president in a major corporation, Frank is an achiever by most people's standards. He nevertheless feels downwardly mobile compared to the goals he once set for himself and the path he once traveled. He will never be president of any corporation; nor does he wish to be. Instead, he leaves the office by 5:30 each day so that he can relieve the baby-sitter. As he awaits Sharon's return from work, he bathes his daughter and prepares her for bed. He marvels at how much joy he has found as a father and how little regret he feels for choosing a slower track.

Like Frank, Todd moved from avoiding family life to becoming closely involved in rearing his young daughter and deeply committed to supporting his wife's professional career:

Todd's memories of his mother are vague, for she died of leukemia before he started school. His father was a hard-working insurance salesman who could barely support his two young sons, even working nights to bring in extra cash. He had neither the time nor the desire to be their mother as well as their father, and soon married his deceased wife's sister to provide a mother for his boys. Not without bitterness, Todd remembers his father as an emotionally remote man in a marriage devoid of passion, tied to a secure but ultimately unfulfilling job. His father stressed these conservative values to his sons, warning them that if they did not work hard at school and go to college, they would end up as ditchdiggers or on the breadline.

Todd viewed his father's life as sadly truncated and did not wish to pursue the same safe but constrained existence. Instead, he wanted to be a singer or an actor. Freedom, excitement, and self-fulfillment, not security, were his life goals. After a few frustrating semesters at a local community college, Todd left home with a small suitcase and a guitar. He moved to Florida to eke out a living singing in coffeehouses while he developed his musical and acting skills.

But freedom proved an elusive goal for Todd. The Vietnam War was growing abroad, and the draft board was breathing down his neck. With no student or health deferments to shield him, Todd decided to enlist before he was drafted. Like countless other working-class boys of his generation, he decided that defending his country was the right thing to do.

Todd came back from the war irrevocably changed. The experience had been painful enough, but the discrimination he encountered on his return added insult to injury. He could not land a decent job as, time after time, the image of the unstable Vietnam vet foreclosed employment possibilities. He moved from one temporary job to another, pursuing his dream of a music and acting career in his spare time. He also married, but divorced within several years as financial and other difficulties took their toll on the relationship. When he did, he left a son in his ex-wife's care.

One night, Todd met and was immediately attracted to a self-confident, assertive, and graceful woman named Sally. As a professional dancer, she knew what she wanted and where she was going. They moved in together, and he found a satisfaction that he had never known when he was "free."

Then Todd had another good experience. Through a special program for displaced Vietnam veterans, he was offered, and accepted, a job as a water and sewer repairer—work he would have rejected a decade earlier as boring and restrictive, beneath his abilities. Much to his surprise, he enjoyed the physical work and the split-shift hours. For the first time in his adult life, he had a steady income and a secure job. With Sally's career as a professional dancer and teacher blossoming, they felt ready to get married and have a child.

Todd is now delighted to take care of his infant daughter during the day while Sally takes and teaches her dance classes. In the evenings, he digs ditches and repairs pipes, chuckling to himself that he has ended up just as his father warned he would. But he has never been so happy and already looks forward to having another

child. He still dreams of an acting career, but his priorities have
changed: A strong, supportive relationship with his wife and close
involvement in raising his daughter now come before all else. He
feels a deep sadness that his own distant (and now deceased) father
missed the joy he is now experiencing taking care of his child. He
also regrets that he could not care for the child of his first marriage
as he now does for his daughter.

These life histories suggest some of the most prevalent patterns of commitment that have emerged as men's choices have diversified over the last
several decades. They show not only that men can develop a variety of expectations and desires in childhood but also that these outlooks may be sustained or changed as men encounter unexpected circumstances later in life.

Regardless of class background, young boys confront a contradictory
and ambiguous array of definitions about what it means to be a man. They
may accept the good-provider ethic, or they may develop a more skeptical
view of breadwinning. For those who aspire to breadwinning, marriage, fatherhood, and a good job offer the promise of domestic power and public
prestige. For those who do not, breadwinning commitments are more likely
to appear risky and dangerous. On the one hand, failure to become a "good
enough" provider or a "successful enough" worker means failing more fundamentally as a man. On the other, successful breadwinning can trap one in
boring work or stifling domestic obligations. From this perspective, the
search for personal autonomy offers a more promising route to manhood
than does lifelong commitment to marriage, parenthood, and work success.

Both of these outlooks are deeply rooted in the American cultural tradition to which children are exposed.[9] Yet adopting either as a child is no guarantee of achieving it as an adult. Rather, men may sustain, modify, or reject
their early outlooks as they grow up and face the unexpected contingencies
of adult life. As men have encountered new options and constraints, they
have built their lives in a variety of ways. Many have developed outlooks
that bear little resemblance either to earlier cultural definitions of manhood
or to the aspirations they held as children.[10]

Either by sustaining or unexpectedly developing a breadwinning outlook, some men have reaffirmed the good-provider ethic. Either by maintaining an early outlook or by moving away from parenthood in adulthood,
other men have stressed a more autonomous vision of manhood. Still others
who expected to become breadwinners or to remain autonomous have become caretakers and nurturers instead. Each of these patterns contains much
diversity, and the variations among men can be as much a matter of degree
as a matter of fundamental difference. Yet comparisons between those who
underwent significant change from their early outlooks and those who did
not make all paths instructive.

These paths provide a framework for moving beyond a uniform vision
of men to examine a range of choices and outlooks. By identifying the crucial

events and experiences that propelled men down these different paths, we can uncover the causes, shape, and consequences of change in men's lives.

NOTES

1. For discussions of the history of fatherhood and masculinity, see Jessie Bernard, "The Good Provider Role: Its Rise and Fall," *American Psychologist* 36 (1981): 1–12; J. Bloom-Feshbach, "Historical Perspectives on the Father's Role," in *The Role of the Father in Child Development,* ed. Michael E. Lamb (New York: Wiley, 1981); and John Demos, "The Changing Faces of Fatherhood," in *Past, Present, and Personal: The Family and the Life Course in American History,* ed. John Demos (New York: Oxford University Press, 1986), pp. 41–66.

   For overviews of historical changes in American family patterns, see Sara M. Evans, *Born for Liberty: A History of Women in America* (New York: Free Press, 1989); Steven Mintz and Susan Kellogg, *Domestic Revolutions: A Social History of American Family Life* (New York: Free Press, 1988), and Arlene Skolnick, *Embattled Paradise: The American Family in an Age of Uncertainty* (New York: Basic Books, 1991).

2. R. W. Connell, "The Big Picture: Masculinities in Recent World History," unpublished manuscript, 1992.

3. Viviana A. Zelizer, *Pricing the Priceless Child* (New York: Basic Books, 1985).

4. Ralph E. Smith, *The Subtle Revolution: Women at Work* (Washington, DC: Urban Institute, 1979).

5. Lawrence Mishel and David M. Frankel, *The State of Working America* (Armonk, NY: M. E. Sharpe, 1991), pp. 78–81.

6. Kevin Phillips, *The Politics of Rich and Poor: Wealth and the American Electorate in the Reagan Aftermath* (New York: HarperCollins, 1990).

7. Mishel and Frankel, *The State of Working America,* p. 81.

8. U.S. Bureau of the Census, *Population Profile of the United States, 1991,* Current Population Reports, Special Studies, Ser. P-23, no. 173 (Washington, DC: U.S. Government and Printing Office, 1991).

9. Ann Swidler, "Love and Adulthood in American Culture," in *Themes of Work and Love in Adulthood,* ed. Neil J. Smelser and Erik H. Erikson (Cambridge, MA: Harvard University Press, 1980), pp. 120–47.

10. Robert S. Weiss, *Staying the Course: The Emotional and Social Lives of Men Who Do Well at Work* (New York: Free Press, 1990).

29

THE GLASS ESCALATOR
Hidden Advantages for Men
in the "Female" Professions

CHRISTINE L. WILLIAMS

Sociologists argue that individuals learn gender roles and gender stereotyping through socialization. Moreover, gender roles often are assigned dichotomously to each sex with men and women expected to fulfill different family and occupational roles. Thus, women traditionally have been assigned the roles of homemaker, nurse, teacher, and secretary. This reading by Christine L. Williams is an analysis of what happens when men enter traditionally defined "female" occupations. Williams' in-depth interviews reveal the advantages and disadvantages experienced by male nurses, teachers, librarians, and social workers.

T he sex segregation of the U.S. labor force is one of the most perplexing and tenacious problems in our society. Even though the proportion of men and women in the labor force is approaching parity (particularly for younger cohorts of workers) (U.S. Department of Labor 1991, p. 18), men and women are still generally confined to predominantly single-sex occupations. Forty percent of men or women would have to change major occupational categories to achieve equal representation of men and women in all jobs (Reskin and Roos 1990, p. 6), but even this figure underestimates the true degree of sex segregation. It is extremely rare to find specific jobs where equal numbers of men and women are engaged in the same activities in the same industries (Bielby and Baron 1984).

Most studies of sex segregation in the workforce have focused on women's experiences in male-dominated occupations. Both researchers and advocates for social change have focused on the barriers faced by women who try to integrate predominantly male fields. Few have looked at the "flipside" of occupational sex segregation: the exclusion of men from predominantly female occupations (exceptions include Schreiber 1979; Williams 1989; Zimmer 1988). But the fact is that men are less likely to enter female sex-typed occupations than women are to enter male-dominated jobs (Jacobs 1989). Reskin and Roos, for example, were able to identify 33 occupations in which female representation increased by more than nine percentage points between 1970 and 1980, but only three occupations in which the proportion of men increased as radically (1990:20–21).

In this paper, I examine men's underrepresentation in four predominantly female occupations—nursing, librarianship, elementary school teaching, and social work. Throughout the twentieth century, these occupations have been identified with "women's work"—even though prior to the Civil War, men were more likely to be employed in these areas. These four occupations, often called the female "semi-professions" (Hodson and Sullivan 1990), today range from 5.5 percent male (in nursing) to 32 percent male (in social work). These percentages have not changed substantially in decades. In fact, two of these professions—librarianship and social work—have experienced declines in the proportions of men since 1975. Nursing is the only one of the four experiencing noticeable changes in sex composition, with the proportion of men increasing 80 percent between 1975 and 1990. Even so, men continue to be a tiny minority of all nurses.

. . .

Methods

I conducted in-depth interviews with 76 men and 23 women in four occupations from 1985 to 1991. Interviews were conducted in four metropolitan areas: San Francisco/Oakland, California; Austin, Texas; Boston, Massachusetts; and Phoenix, Arizona. These four areas were selected because they show considerable variation in the proportions of men in the four professions. For example, Austin has one of the highest percentages of men in nursing (7.7 percent), whereas Phoenix's percentage is one of the lowest (2.7 percent) (U.S. Bureau of the Census 1980). The sample was generated using "snowballing" techniques. Women were included in the sample to gauge their feelings and responses to men who enter "their" professions.

. . .

Discrimination in Hiring

Contrary to the experience of many women in the male-dominated professions, many of the men and women I spoke to indicated that there is a *preference* for hiring men in these four occupations. A Texas librarian at a junior high school said that his school district "would hire a male over a female."

I: Why do you think that is?

R: Because there are so few, and the . . . ones that they do have, the library directors seem to really . . . think they're doing great jobs. I don't know, maybe they just feel they're being progressive or something, [but] I have had a real sense that they really appreciate having a male, particularly at the junior high. . . . As I said, when seven of us lost our jobs from the high schools and were redistributed, there were only four positions at junior high, and I got one of them. Three of the librarians, some who had been here longer than I had with the school district, were put down in elementary school as librarians. And I definitely think that being male made a difference in my being moved to the junior high rather than an elementary school.

Many of the men perceived their token status as males in predominantly female occupations as an *advantage* in hiring and promotions. I asked an Arizona teacher whether his specialty (elementary special education) was an unusual area for men compared to other areas within education. He said,

> Much more so. I am extremely marketable in special education. That's not why I got into the field. But I am extremely marketable because I am a man.

In several cases, the more female-dominated the specialty, the greater the apparent preference for men. For example, when asked if he encountered any problem getting a job in pediatrics, a Massachusetts nurse said,

> No, no, none. . . . I've heard this from managers and supervisory-type people with men in pediatrics: "It's nice to have a man because it's such a female-dominated profession."

However, there were some exceptions to this preference for men in the most female-dominated specialties. In some cases, formal policies actually barred men from certain jobs. This was the case in some rural Texas school districts, which refused to hire men in the youngest grades (K–3). Some nurses also reported being excluded from positions in obstetrics and gynecology wards, a policy encountered more frequently in private Catholic hospitals.

But often the pressures keeping men out of certain specialties were more subtle than this. Some men described being "tracked" into practice areas within their professions which were considered more legitimate for men. For example, one Texas man described how he was pushed into administration and planning in social work, even though "I'm not interested in writing policy; I'm much more interested in research and clinical stuff." A nurse who is interested in pursuing graduate study in family and child health in Boston said he was dissuaded from entering the program specialty in favor of a concentration in "adult nursing." A kindergarten teacher described the difficulty of finding a job in his specialty after graduation: "I was recruited immediately to start getting into a track to become an administrator. And it was men who recruited me. It was men that ran the system at that time, especially in Los Angeles."

This tracking may bar men from the most female-identified specialties within these professions. But men are effectively being "kicked upstairs" in the process. Those specialties considered more legitimate practice areas for men also tend to be the most prestigious, better paying ones. A distinguished kindergarten teacher, who had been voted citywide "Teacher of the Year," told me that even though people were pleased to see him in the classroom, "there's been some encouragement to think about administration, and there's been some encouragement to think about teaching at the university level or something like that, or supervisory-type position." That is, despite his aptitude and interest in staying in the classroom, he felt pushed in the direction of administration.

The effect of this "tracking" is the opposite of that experienced by women in male-dominated occupations. Researchers have reported that many women encounter a "glass ceiling" in their efforts to scale organizational and professional hierarchies. That is, they are constrained by invisible barriers to promotion in their careers, caused mainly by sexist attitudes of men in the highest positions (Freeman 1990). In contrast to the "glass ceiling," many of the men I interviewed seem to encounter a "glass escalator."

Often, despite their intentions, they face invisible pressures to move up in their professions. As if on a moving escalator, they must work to stay in place.

A public librarian specializing in children's collections (a heavily female-dominated concentration) described an encounter with this "escalator" in his very first job out of library school. In his first six-months' evaluation, his supervisors commended him for his good work in storytelling and related activities, but they criticized him for "not shooting high enough."

> Seriously. That's literally what they were telling me. They assumed that because I was a male—and they told me this—and that I was being hired right out of graduate school, that somehow I wasn't doing the kind of management-oriented work that they thought I should be doing. And as a result, really they had a lot of bad marks, as it were, against me on my evaluation. And I said I couldn't believe this!

Throughout his 10-year career, he has had to struggle to remain in children's collections.

The glass escalator does not operate at all levels. In particular, men in academia reported some gender-based discrimination in the highest positions due to their universities' commitment to affirmative action. Two nursing professors reported that they felt their own chances of promotion to deanships were nil because their universities viewed the position of nursing dean as a guaranteed female appointment in an otherwise heavily male-dominated administration. One California social work professor reported his university canceled its search for a dean because no minority male or female candidates had been placed on their short list. It was rumored that other schools on campus were permitted to go forward with their searches—even though they also failed to put forward names of minority candidates—because the higher administration perceived it to be "easier" to fulfill affirmative action goals in the social work school. The interviews provide greater evidence of the "glass escalator" at work in the lower levels of these professions.

Of course, men's motivations also play a role in their advancement to higher professional positions. I do not mean to suggest that the men I talked to all resented the informal tracking they experienced. For many men, leaving the most female-identified areas of their professions helped them resolve internal conflicts involving their masculinity. One man left his job as a school social worker to work in a methadone drug treatment program not because he was encouraged to leave by his colleagues, but because "I think there was some macho shit there, to tell you the truth, because I remember feeling a little uncomfortable there . . . ; it didn't feel right to me." Another social worker, employed in the mental health services department of a large urban area in California, reflected on his move into administration:

> The more I think about it, through our discussion, I'm sure that's a large part of why I wound up in administration. It's okay for a man to do the administration. In fact, I don't know if I fully answered a question that you asked a little while ago about how did being male contribute to my

advancing in the field. I was saying it wasn't because I got any special favoritism as a man, but . . . I think . . . because I'm a man, I felt a need to get into this kind of position. I may have worked harder toward it, may have competed harder for it, than most women would do, even women who think about doing administrative work.

Elsewhere I have speculated on the origins of men's tendency to define masculinity through single-sex work environments (Williams 1989). Clearly, personal ambition does play a role in accounting for men's movement into more "male-defined" arenas within these professions. But these occupations also structure opportunities for males independent of their individual desires or motives.

The interviews suggest that men's underrepresentation in these professions cannot be attributed to discrimination in hiring or promotions. Many of the men indicated that they received preferential treatment because they were men. Although men mentioned gender discrimination in the hiring process, for the most part they were channeled into the more "masculine" specialties within these professions, which ironically meant being "tracked" into better-paying and more prestigious specialties.

Supervisors and Colleagues: The Working Environment

Researchers claim that subtle forms of workplace discrimination push women out of male-dominated occupations (Jacobs 1989; Reskin and Hartmann 1986). In particular, women report feeling excluded from informal leadership and decision-making networks, and they sense hostility from their male co-workers, which makes them feel uncomfortable and unwanted (Carothers and Crull 1984). Respondents in this study were asked about their relationships with supervisors and female colleagues to ascertain whether men also experienced "poisoned" work environments when entering gender atypical occupations.

A major difference in the experience of men and women in nontraditional occupations is that men in these situations are far more likely to be supervised by a member of their own sex. In each of the four professions I studied, men are overrepresented in administrative and managerial capacities, or, as is the case of nursing, their positions in the organizational hierarchy are governed by men (Grimm and Stern 1974; Phenix 1987; Schmuck 1987; Williams 1989; York, Henley and Gamble 1987). Thus, unlike women who enter "male fields," the men in these professions often work under the direct supervision of other men.

Many of the men interviewed reported that they had good rapport with their male supervisors. Even in professional school, some men reported extremely close relationships with their male professors. For example, a Texas librarian described an unusually intimate association with two male professors in graduate school:

> I can remember a lot of times in the classroom there would be discussions about a particular topic or issue, and the conversation would spill over into their office hours, after the class was over. And even though there were . . . a couple of the other women that had been in on the discussion, they weren't there. And I don't know if that was preferential or not . . . it certainly carried over into personal life as well. Not just at the school and that sort of thing. I mean, we would get together for dinner . . .

. . .

Other men reported similar closeness with their professors. A Texas psychotherapist recalled his relationships with his male professors in social work school:

> I made it a point to make a golfing buddy with one of the guys that was in administration. He and I played golf a lot. He was the guy who kind of ran the research training, the research part of the master's program. Then there was a sociologist who ran the other part of the research program. He and I developed a good friendship.

This close mentoring by male professors contrasts with the reported experience of women in nontraditional occupations. Others have noted a lack of solidarity among women in nontraditional occupations. Writing about military academies, for example, Yoder describes the failure of token women to mentor succeeding generations of female cadets. She argues that women attempt to play down their gender difference from men because it is the source of scorn and derision.

> Because women felt unaccepted by their male colleagues, one of the last things they wanted to do was to emphasize their gender. Some women thought that, if they kept company with other women, this would highlight their gender and would further isolate them from male cadets. These women desperately wanted to be accepted as cadets, not as *women* cadets. Therefore, they did everything from not wearing skirts as an option with their uniforms to avoiding being a part of a group of women. (Yoder 1989:532)

Men in nontraditional occupations face a different scenario—their gender is construed as a *positive* difference. Therefore, they have an incentive to bond together and emphasize their distinctiveness from the female majority.

. . .

Openly gay men may encounter less favorable treatment at the hands of their supervisors. For example, a nurse in Texas stated that one of the physicians he worked with preferred to staff the operating room with male nurses exclusively—as long as they weren't gay. Stigma associated with homo-sexuality leads some men to enhance, or even exaggerate their "masculine" qualities, and may be another factor pushing men into more "acceptable" specialties for men.

Not all men who work in these occupations are supervised by men. Many of the men interviewed who had female bosses also reported high lev-els of acceptance—although levels of intimacy with women seemed lower than with other men. In some cases, however, men reported feeling shut out from decision making when the higher administration was constituted en-tirely by women. I asked an Arizona librarian whether men in the library profession were discriminated against in hiring because of their sex:

> Professionally speaking, people go to considerable lengths to keep that kind of thing out of their [hiring] deliberations. Personally, is another matter. It's pretty common around here to talk about the "old girl network." This is one of the few libraries that I've had any intimate knowledge of which is actually controlled by women. . . . Most of the de-partment heads and upper-level administrators are women. And there's an "old girl network" that works just like the "old boy network," except that the important conferences take place in the women's room rather than on the golf course. But the political mechanism is the same, the ex-clusion of the other sex from decision making is the same. The reasons are the same. It's somewhat discouraging . . .

Although I did not interview many supervisors, I did include 23 women in my sample to ascertain their perspectives about the presence of men in their professions. All of the women I interviewed claimed to be supportive of their male colleagues, but some conveyed ambivalence. For example, a so-cial work professor said she would like to see more men enter the social work profession, particularly in the clinical specialty (where they are under-represented). Indeed, she favored affirmative action hiring guidelines for men in the profession. Yet, she resented the fact that her department hired "another white male" during a recent search.

. . .

Even outside work, most of the men interviewed said they felt fully ac-cepted by their female colleagues. They were usually included in informal socializing occasions with the women—even though this frequently meant attending baby showers or Tupperware parties. Many said that they de-clined offers to attend these events because they were not interested in "women's things," although several others claimed to attend everything: The minority men I interviewed seemed to feel the least comfortable in these informal contexts. One social worker in Arizona was asked about socializing with his female colleagues:

> I: So in general, for example, if all the employees were going to get together to have a party, or celebrate a bridal shower or whatever, would you be invited along with the rest of the group?
>
> R: They would invite me, I would say, somewhat reluctantly. Being a black male, working with all white females, it did cause some outside problems. So I didn't go to a lot of functions with them . . .
>
> I: You felt that there was some tension there on the level of your acceptance . . . ?
>
> R: Yeah. It was OK working, but on the outside, personally, there was some tension there. It never came out, that they said, "Because of who you are we can't invite you" (laughs), and I wouldn't have done anything anyway. I would have probably respected them more for saying what was on their minds. But I never felt completely in with the group.

Some single men also said they felt uncomfortable socializing with married female colleagues because it gave the "wrong impression." But in general, the men said that they felt very comfortable around their colleagues and described their work places as very congenial for men. It appears unlikely, therefore, that men's underrepresentation in these professions is due to hostility toward men on the part of supervisors or women workers.

Discrimination from "Outsiders"

The most compelling evidence of discrimination against men in these professions is related to their dealings with the public. Men often encounter negative stereotypes when they come into contact with clients or "outsiders"—people they meet outside of work. For instance, it is popularly assumed that male nurses are gay. Librarians encounter images of themselves as "wimpy" and asexual. Male social workers describe being typecast as "feminine" and "passive." Elementary school teachers are often confronted by suspicions that they are pedophiles. One kindergarten teacher described an experience that occurred early in his career, which was related to him years afterward by his principal:

> He indicated to me that parents had come to him and indicated to him that they had a problem with the fact that I was a male. . . . I recall almost exactly what he said. There were three specific concerns that the parents had: One parent said, "How can he love my child; he's a man." The second thing that I recall, he said the parent said, "He has a beard." And the third thing was, "Aren't you concerned about homosexuality?"

Such suspicions often cause men in all four professions to alter their work behavior to guard against sexual abuse charges, particularly in those specialties requiring intimate contact with women and children.

Men are very distressed by these negative stereotypes, which tend to undermine their self-esteem and to cause them to second-guess their motivations for entering these fields. A California teacher said,

> If I tell men that I don't know, that I'm meeting for the first time, that that's what I do, . . . sometimes there's a look on their faces that, you know, "Oh, couldn't get a real job?"

When asked if his wife, who is also an elementary school teacher, encounters the same kind of prejudice, he said,

> No, it's accepted because she's a woman. . . . I think people would see that as a . . . step up, you know. "Oh, you're not a housewife, you've got a career. That's great . . . that you're out there working. And you have a daughter, but you're still out there working. You decided not to stay home, and you went out there and got a job." Whereas for me, it's more like I'm supposed to be out working anyway, even though I'd rather be home with [my daughter].

Unlike women who enter traditionally male professions, men's movement into these jobs is perceived by the "outside world" as a step down in status. This particular form of discrimination may be most significant in explaining why men are underrepresented in these professions. Men who otherwise might show interest in and aptitudes for such careers are probably discouraged from pursuing them because of the negative popular stereotypes associated with the men who work in them. This is a crucial difference from the experience of women in nontraditional professions: "My daughter, the physician," resonates far more favorably in most people's ears than "my son, the nurse."

Many of the men in my sample identified the stigma of working in a female-identified occupation as the major barrier to more men entering their professions. However, for the most part, they claimed that these negative stereotypes were not a factor in their own decisions to join these occupations. Most respondents didn't consider entering these fields until well into adulthood, after working in some related occupation. Several social workers and librarians even claimed they were not aware that men were a minority in their chosen professions. Either they had no well-defined image or stereotype, or their contacts and mentors were predominantly men. For example, prior to entering library school, many librarians held part-time jobs in university libraries, where there are proportionally more men than in the profession generally. Nurses and elementary school teachers were more aware that mostly women worked in these jobs, and this was often a matter of some concern to them. However, their choices were ultimately legitimized by mentors, or by encouraging friends or family members who implicitly reassured them that entering these occupations would not typecast them as feminine. In some cases, men were told by recruiters there were special advancement opportunities for men in these fields, and they entered them expecting rapid promotion to administrative positions.

> I: Did it ever concern you when you were making the decision to enter nursing school, the fact that it is a female-dominated profession?
>
> R: Not really. I never saw myself working on the floor. I saw myself pretty much going into administration, just getting the background and then getting a job someplace as a supervisor and then working, getting up into administration.

Because of the unique circumstances of their recruitment, many of the respondents did not view their occupational choices as inconsistent with a male gender role, and they generally avoided the negative stereotypes directed against men in these fields.

Indeed, many of the men I interviewed claimed that they did not encounter negative professional stereotypes until they had worked in these fields for several years. Popular prejudices can be damaging to self-esteem and probably push some men out of these professionals altogether. Yet, ironically, they sometimes contribute to the "glass escalator" effect I have been describing. Men seem to encounter the most vituperative criticism from the public when they are in the most female-identified specialties. Public concerns sometimes result in their being shunted into more "legitimate" positions for men. A librarian formerly in charge of a branch library's children's collection, who now works in the reference department of the city's main library, describes his experience:

> R: Some of the people [who frequented the branch library] complained that they didn't want to have a man doing the storytelling scenario. And I got transferred here to the central library in an equivalent job . . . I thought that I did a good job. And I had been told by my supervisor that I was doing a good job.
>
> I: Have you ever considered filing some sort of lawsuit to get that other job back?
>
> R: Well, actually, the job I've gotten now . . . well, it's a reference librarian; it's what I wanted in the first place. I've got a whole lot more authority here. I'm also in charge of the circulation desk. And I've recently been promoted because of my new stature, so . . . no, I'm not considering trying to get that other job back.

The negative stereotypes about men who do "women's work" can push men out of specific jobs. However, to the extent that they channel men into more "legitimate" practice areas, their effects can actually be positive. Instead of being a source of discrimination, these prejudices can add to the "glass escalator effect" by pressuring men to move *out* of the most female-identified areas, and *up* to those regarded more legitimate and prestigious for men.

Author's Note: This research was funded in part by a faculty grant from the University of Texas at Austin. I also acknowledge the support of the sociology departments of the University of California, Berkeley; Harvard University; and Arizona State University. I would like to thank Judy Auerbach, Martin Button, Robert Nye, Teresa Sullivan, Debra Umberson, Mary Waters, and the reviewers at *Social Problems* for their comments on earlier versions of this paper. © 1992 by the Society for the Study of Social Problems. Reprinted from *Social Problems*, Vol. 39, No. 3, August 1992, pp. 253–67 by permission.

REFERENCES

Bielby, William T. and James N. Baron. 1984. "A Woman's Place Is with Other Women: Sex Segregation within Organizations." Pp. 27–55 in *Sex Segregation in the Workplace: Trends, Explanations, Remedies*, edited by Barbara Reskin. Washington, DC: National Academy Press.

Carothers, Suzanne C. and Peggy Crull. 1984. "Contrasting Sexual Harassment in Female-Dominated and Male-Dominated Occupations." Pp. 220–27 in *My Troubles Are Going to Have Trouble with Me: Everyday Trials and Triumphs of Women Workers*, edited by Karen B. Sacks and Dorothy Remy. New Brunswick, NJ: Rutgers University Press.

Freeman, Sue J. M. 1990. *Managing Lives: Corporate Women and Social Change*. Amherst, MA: University of Massachusetts Press.

Grimm, James W. and Robert N. Stern. 1974. "Sex Roles and Internal Labor Market Structures: The Female Semi-Professions." *Social Problems* 21:690–705.

Hodson, Randy and Teresa Sullivan. 1990. *The Social Organization of Work*. Belmont, CA: Wadsworth Publishing Co.

Jacobs, Jerry. 1989. *Revolving Doors: Sex Segregation and Women's Careers*. Stanford, CA: Stanford University Press.

Phenix, Katherine. 1987. "The Status of Women Librarians." *Frontiers* 9:36–40.

Reskin, Barbara and Heidi Hartmann. 1986. *Women's Work, Men's Work: Sex Segregation on the Job*. Washington, DC: National Academy Press.

Reskin, Barbara and Patricia Roos. 1990. *Job Queues, Gender Queues: Explaining Women's Inroads into Male Occupations*. Philadelphia: Temple University Press.

Schmuck, Patricia A. 1987. "Women School Employees in the United States." Pp. 75–97 in *Women Educators: Employees of Schools in Western Counties*, edited by Patricia A. Schmuck. Albany: State University of New York Press.

Schreiber, Carol. 1979. *Men and Women in Transitional Occupations*. Cambridge, MA: MIT Press.

U.S. Bureau of the Census. 1980. *Detailed Population Characteristics*, vol. 1, Ch. D. Washington, DC: Government Printing Office.

U.S. Department of Labor. Bureau of Labor Statistics. 1991. *Employment and Earnings*. Washington, DC: Government Printing Office.

Williams, Christine L. 1989. *Gender Differences at Work: Women and Men in Nontraditional Occupations*. Berkeley: University of California Press.

Yoder, Janice D. 1989. "Women at West Point: Lessons for Token Women in Male-Dominated Occupations." Pp. 523–37 in *Women: A Feminist Perspective*, edited by Jo Freeman. Mountain View, CA: Mayfield Publishing Company.

York, Reginald O., H. Carl Henley, and Dorothy N. Gamble. 1987. "Sexual Discrimination in Social Work: Is It Salary or Advancement?" *Social Work* 32:336–40.

Zimmer, Lynn. 1988. "Tokenism and Women in the Workplace." *Social Problems* 35:64–77.

30

TREATING HEALTH
Women and Medicine

BARBARA KATZ ROTHMAN • MARY BETH CASCHETTA

Gender inequality has enormous consequences for women, men, and society. Gender inequality reinforces and perpetuates *sexism,* which is prejudice and discrimination against a person on the basis of his or her sex. The costs and consequences of sexism are extensive and include the wage gap, the feminization of poverty, high rates of female victimization as a result of male violence, and psychological and physical health problems in both women and men. This selection by Barbara Katz Rothman and Mary Beth Caschetta reveals the rampant sexism within the institution of medicine, both historically and currently. Specifically, the authors examine how the institution of medicine has defined and treated women and their illnesses differently from those of men.

Women are not only people: *Woman* is a subject one can specialize in within medicine. However, except for sex organs and reproduction, women have not been studied or treated adequately by the medical establishment. At the moment, when a woman enters the health delivery system, her body is essentially divided among specialists. Obstetricians and gynecologists, for example, are medicine's, and perhaps society's, generally recognized "experts" on the subject of women, though technically they provide care for only reproduction and the functioning of sex organs.[1] *Obstetrics* is the branch of medicine limited to the care of women during pregnancy, labor, and the time surrounding childbirth,[2] a practice that tried to supplant midwifery. *Gynecology* is the "science of the diseases of women, especially those affecting the sex organs."[3] Diseases that frequently affect women and do not involve the sex organs, such as thyroid disease, rheumatoid arthritis, adult-type diabetes, osteoporosis, and depression, have not been studied in women.[4] Conditions occurring more frequently in women of color, for example, hypertension, alcoholism, and cardiovascular diseases, have, until very recently, received no attention at all.

At its simplest, a medical specialty can be seen as arising out of preexisting needs. People have heart attacks: The medical specialty of cardiology develops. Or the amount of knowledge generated in a field grows so enormously that no one person can hope to master it all. Physicians then "carve out" their own areas of specialization. Increasing knowledge about cancer thus led to the specialty of, and the subspecialties within, oncology. By looking at the history of emerging specialties, their successes and failures, we can tell a lot about medical needs and knowledge. For instance, an attempt by urologists in 1891 to develop an "andrology" specialty for men came to nothing.[5] Technically, there is no "science" of the study of men, comparable to the specialties devoted to women and their reproductive functions. This may be because most of generalized medicine is already geared toward men and the male body, and women are treated as special cases in that they are different from men.

But the development of a medical specialty is not necessarily the creation of a key for an already existing lock. Medical needs do not necessarily predate the specialty, even though the specialty is presumably organized to meet those needs. This has been made quite clear in the work of Thomas Szasz on the expansion of medicine into such "social problem" areas as alcoholism, gambling, and suicide.[6] Medicine does not have "cures" for these problems, but by defining them in medical terms, as a sickness, the physician gains political control over the societal response: Punishment becomes "treatment," desired or not, successful or not. Similarly, medicine can be viewed as a tool in the political control over women's sexuality, childbirth, lactation, menopause, and general health and well-being. Such medical control has rarely been based on superior ability to deal with these concerns.

Exclusion of Women from Research

In 1985, the United States Public Health Service reported a general lack of research data on women and a limited understanding of women's general health needs.[7] Because menstrual cycles are said to constitute a separate variable affecting test results,[8] researchers have used menses as an excuse to exclude women from research. A woman's period "muddies" the research data, so to speak. Additionally, medical experts have been, and continue to be, reluctant to perform studies on women of childbearing age, because experimental treatments or procedures may affect their reproductive capabilities and/or a potential fetus.[9]

The exclusion of females from medical research is so institutionalized that even female rats are commonly excluded from early basic research, on which most medical decisions rest. The result of female exclusion from human research is that most medical recommendations made to the general population are extrapolated from the Caucasian male body.[10] Therefore, the original research on the ability of aspirin to prevent coronary artery disease was done exclusively on men,[11] although it had been known for some time that heart disease is a leading killer of women. The original testing of antidepressant drugs on men[12] did not anticipate the fact that the constant doses appropriate for men may in women sometimes be too high or too low, due to the natural hormonal changes during the menstrual cycle.[13]

As expected, this astounding lack of research concerning women's biology has enormous impact on the individual experiences of women seeking care and results in inadequate health care. For instance, more women than men die from heart disease each year, yet women with heart trouble are less likely to receive treatment, even when symptoms clearly indicate severe heart trouble exists.[14] And while lung cancer is the number-one cancer killer of women, they are twice as likely as men *not* to be tested for lung cancer.[15] Additionally, while AIDS is a leading killer of women in many urban areas, the official definition of AIDS—which is actually a series of infections and cancers that occur when the immune system is weakened by the human immunodeficiency virus (HIV)—did not originally include many of the HIV-related conditions in women because what is known about HIV disease is derived principally from research on men.[16] Therefore, significant numbers of women who die of HIV-related complications do so without an actual diagnosis of AIDS.[17]

The medical specialists clash over women and AIDS: Infectious disease experts claim not to know about the gynecological infections and cancers of HIV, and gynecologists claim not to understand the general manifestations of HIV. Internists generally do not look for HIV infection in women. Therefore undercounting of women in the epidemic is enormous: Women are denied disability entitlements to which they are entitled; their illness goes misdiagnosed and untreated; and research efforts are skewed, distorting general knowledge of the scope of the AIDS epidemic.

Problems with "Women" as a Medical Category

It is important to understand that the medical term *women* almost always assumes white, middle-class females. The significance of this short-sighted view of a diverse population is wide-reaching. For instance, biological racial differences and socioeconomic impacts on illness are only now coming to light, although they have long been suspected. Studies show that compared to whites, Asians may achieve significantly higher blood serum levels when given certain drugs; osteoporosis is more prevalent in white women; and black women have a significantly higher rate of low birth weights, a fact often blamed on inner-city socioeconomic status, yet Latina women in similar inner-city situations birth far fewer low-weight babies.[18] Nonetheless, until recently, medicine has ignored differences among real people, including gender and race.

Doctors, Midwives, and Other Struggles for Power

. . .

In the nineteenth and early twentieth centuries midwives and physicians were in direct competition for patients, and not only for their fees. Newer, more clinically oriented medical training demanded "teaching material," so that even immigrant and poor women were desired as patients.[19] The displacement of the midwife by the male obstetrician can be better understood in terms of this competition than as an ideological struggle or as "scientific advancement." Physicians, unlike the unorganized, disenfranchised midwives, had access to the power of the state through their professional associations. They were thus able to control licensing legislation, restricting the midwife's sphere of activity and imposing legal sanctions against her in state after state.[20]

The legislative changes were backed up by the medical establishment's attempt to win public disapproval for midwifery and support for obstetrics. Physicians accused midwives of ignorance and incompetence and attacked midwifery practices as "meddlesome." Rather than upgrading the practice of midwifery by teaching the skills physicians thought necessary, the profession of medicine refused to train women either as midwives or as physicians.[21] Physicians argued repeatedly that medicine was the appropriate profession to handle birth because "normal pregnancy and parturition are exceptions and to consider them to be normal physiologic conditions was a fallacy."[22] Childbirth was redefined as a medical rather than a social event, and the roles and care surrounding it were reorganized to suit medical needs.[23]

Once professional dominance was established in the area of childbirth, obstetrics rapidly expanded into the relatively more sophisticated area of gynecology. The great obstetricians of the nineteenth century were invariably gynecologists (and of course were all men).[24] Among other effects, this linking of obstetrics and gynecology further reinforced the obstetrical orientation toward pathology.

Medical Control and Women

One of the earliest uses of the developing field of gynecology was the overt social control of women through surgical removal of various sexual organs. Surgical removal of the clitoris (clitoridectomy) or, less dramatically, its foreskin (circumcision) and removal of the ovaries (oopherectomy or castration) were used to check women's "mental disorders." The first gynecologist to do a clitoridectomy was an Englishman, in 1858.[25] In England, the procedure was harshly criticized and was not repeated by others after the death of the originator in 1860. In America, however, clitoridectomies were done regularly from the late 1860s until at least 1904,[26] and then sporadically until as recently as the late 1940s.[27] The procedure was used to terminate sexual desire or sexual behavior, something deemed pathological in women. Circumcisions were done on women of all ages to stop masturbation up until at least 1937.[28]

More widespread than clitoridectomies or circumcisions were oopherectomies for psychological "disorders." Interestingly, the female gonads were

removed not when women were "too female"—i.e., too passive or dependent—but when women were too masculine—assertive, aggressive, "un-
ruly." Oopherectomies for "psychiatric" reasons were done in America
between 1872 and 1946.[29] (By the 1940s, prefrontal lobotomies were gaining
acceptance as psychosurgery.)

The developing medical control of women was not limited to extreme
cures for psychiatric problems. The physical health and stability of even the
most socially acceptable women were questioned. Simply by virtue of gender, women were (and are) subject to *illness labeling.*

One explanation for women's vulnerability to illness labeling lies in the
functionalist approach to the sociology of health. Talcott Parsons has pointed
out that it is a functional requirement of any social system that there be a basic level of health of its members.[30] Any definition of illness that is too lenient
would disqualify too many people from fulfilling their functions and would
impose severe strains on the social system. System changes, such as war, can
make changes in standards of health and illness generally set for members.
This works on an individual level as well, standards of health and illness being related to social demands: A mild headache will excuse a student from
attending class but not from taking final exams. A logical extension of this is
that the less valued a person's or group's contribution to society, the more
easily are such people labeled ill.

Women are not always seen as functional members of society, as people
doing important things. This has historically and cross-culturally been especially true of the women of the upper classes in patriarchal societies, where it
is a mark of status for a man to be able to afford to keep a wife who is not
performing any useful function. A clear, if horrifying, example of this is the
traditional Chinese practice of foot-binding. By crippling girls, men were
able to show that they could afford to have wives and daughters who did
nothing. It is a particularly disturbing example of conspicuous consumption.
In their historical analysis of the woman patient, *Complaints and Disorders,*
Barbara Ehrenreich and Deirdre English speak of the European-American
"lady of leisure" of the late nineteenth and early twentieth centuries. "She
was the social ornament that proved a man's success; her idleness, her deli-
cacy, her child-like ignorance of 'reality' gave a man the 'class' that money
alone could not provide." [31]

Menstruation and the Body as Machine

The practice of creating physical deformity in women can be seen in our history as well. A woman researcher who studied menstrual problems among
college women, between 1890 and 1920 found that women in the earlier period probably were somewhat incapacitated by menstruation, just as the
gynecologists of the day were claiming. However, the researcher did not attribute the menstrual problems to women's "inherent disabilities" or "over-

growth of the intellect" as did the male physicians; she related it to dress styles. Women in the 1890s carried some 15 pounds of skirts and petticoats, hanging from a tightly corseted waist. As skirts got lighter and waists were allowed to be larger, menstruation ceased to be the problem it had been.[32] In the interest of science, women might try the experiment of buckling themselves into a painfully small belt and hanging a 15-pound weight from it. One might expect weakness, fatigue, shortness of breath, even fainting: all the physical symptoms of women's "inherent" disability. And consider further the effects of bleeding as a treatment for the problem.

It follows from Parsons' analysis that, in addition to suffering by created physical disabilities (the bound feet of the Chinese, the deforming corsetry of our own history), women were more easily *defined* as sick when they were not seen as functional social members. At the same time in our history that the upper-class women were "delicate," "sickly," and "frail," the working-class women were well enough to perform the physical labor of housework, both their own and that of the upper classes, as well as to work in the factories and fields. "However sick or tired working class women might have been, they certainly did not have the time or money to support a cult of invalidism. Employers gave no time off for pregnancy or recovery from childbirth, much less for menstrual periods, though the wives of these same employers often retired to bed on all these occasions."[33] The working-class women were seen as strong and healthy; for them, pregnancy, menstruation, and menopause were not allowed to be incapacitating.

These two factors—the treatment of the body as a machine and the lesser functional importance assigned to women—still account for much of the medical treatment of women. Contemporary physicians do not usually speak of the normal female reproductive functions as diseases. The exception, to be discussed below, is menopause. The other specifically female reproductive functions—menstruation, pregnancy, childbirth, and lactation—are regularly asserted in medical texts to be normal and healthy phenomena. However, these statements are made within the context of teaching the medical "management," "care," "supervision," and "treatment" of each of these "conditions."

Understood in limited mechanical terms, each of these normal female conditions or happenings is a complication or stress on an otherwise normal system. Medicine has fared no better than has any other discipline in developing a working model of women that does not take men as the comparative norm. For example, while menstruation is no longer viewed as a disease, it is seen as a complication in the female system, contrasted to the reputed biological stability of the supposedly noncycling male.[34] As recently as 1961, the *American Journal of Obstetrics and Gynecology* was still referring to women's "inherent disabilities" in explanations of menstruation:

> Women are known to suffer at least some inconvenience during certain phases of the reproductive cycle, and often with considerable mental

and physical distress. Woman's awareness of her inherent disabilities is thought to create added mental and in turn physical changes in the total body response, and there result problems that concern the physician who must deal with them.[35]

Premenstrual syndrome (PMS) is probably the most recent and most stunning example of the construction of women's normal functions as disease. According to the medical model, PMS manifests as emotional, physical, and behavioral conditions, characterized by more than 150 "symptoms," any number of which a woman might "suffer" during a specific phase of her menstrual cycle. Symptoms are always negative and include the following, to name a few: tension, irritability, forgetfulness, depression, mood swings, anger, muscle pains, cramps, craving for sweets or alcohol, headaches, crying jags, panic attacks, suicidal depressions, and bouts of violent or abusive behavior.[36]

The cause of PMS is thought to be a physiologic abnormality or an abnormal response to normal hormonal changes during the seventh to tenth day before the menstrual period starts. However, the most current research shows that no such abnormalities could be consistently identified and linked to women who are diagnosed as having PMS.[37] Nonetheless, an abundance of hypotheses link PMS to medical causes. For instance, the syndrome has been attributed to an overproduction of estrogen, under- and overproduction of progesterone, a disturbance in the estrogen/progesterone balance, water retention, salt retention, an insulin imbalance, a liver malfunction, stress, and inadequate nutrition.[38] To accommodate "treatment" for the new medical condition, PMS clinics have sprung up across the United States, offering "diagnoses" of the syndrome by pelvic exam and blood tests that cost anywhere from $200 to $500.[39]

There is much debate about whether PMS is a true medical entity or a social phenomenon that medicalizes the menstrual cycle in order to enforce social control over women. Emily Martin explores current conceptions of women's role in society and women's bodies by examining accounts of the language used to describe PMS and its foremost "symptom," anger.[40] Martin writes:

> The problems of men in these accounts are caused by outside circumstances and other people (women). The problems of women are caused by their own internal failure, seen as a biological malfunction. What is missing is any consideration of why, in Western societies, women might feel extreme rage at a time when their usual emotional controls are reduced.[41]

Pregnancy and the Mother-Host

Research on contraception displays mechanistic biases. The claim has been made that contraceptive research has concentrated on the female rather than the male because of the sheer number of potentially vulnerable links in the female chain of reproductive events.[42] Reproduction is clearly a more complicated process for the female than the male. While we might claim that it is safer to interfere in a simpler process, medicine has tended to view the number of points in the female reproductive process as distant entities. Reproduction is dealt with not as a complicated organic process but as a series of discrete points, like stations on an assembly line, with more for female than for male.

The alternative to taking the female system as a complication of the "basic" or "simpler" male system is of course to take female as the working norm. In this approach, a pregnant woman is compared only to pregnant women, a lactating breast compared only to other lactating breasts. Pregnancy and lactation are accepted not only as nominally healthy variations but as truly normal states. To take the example of pregnancy, women *are* pregnant; pregnancy is not something they "have" or "catch" or even "contain." It involves physical changes; these are not, as medical texts frequently call them, "symptoms" of pregnancy. Pregnancy is not a disease, and its changes are no more symptoms than the growth spurt and development of pubic hair are symptomatic of puberty. There may be diseases or complications of pregnancy, but the pregnancy itself is neither disease nor complication.

In contrast, medicine's working model of pregnancy is a woman with an insulated parasitic capsule growing inside. The pregnancy, while physically located within the woman, is still seen as external to her, not a part of her. The capsule within has been seen as virtually omniscient and omnipotent, reaching out and taking what it needs from the mother-host, at her expense if necessary, while protected from all that is bad or harmful.

The pregnancy, in this medical model, is almost entirely a mechanical event in the mother. She differs from the nonpregnant woman only in the presence of this thing growing inside her. Differences other than the mechanical are accordingly seen as symptoms to be treated, so that the woman can be kept as "normal" as possible through the "stress" of the pregnancy. Pregnancy in this model is not seen necessarily as inherently unhealthy, but it is frequently associated with changes other than the growth of the uterus and its contents, and these changes are seen as unhealthy. For example, hemoglobin (iron) is lower in pregnant women than nonpregnant, making pregnant women appear (by nonpregnant standards) anemic. They are then treated for this anemia with iron supplements. Water retention, or edema, is greater in pregnant women than nonpregnant ones, so pregnant women are treated with limits placed on their salt intake and with diuretics. Pregnant women tend to gain weight over that accounted for by the fetus, placenta, and amniotic fluid. They are treated for this weight gain with strict diets, sometimes even with "diet pills." And knowing that these changes are likely to occur in pregnant women, American doctors generally have tried to treat all pregnant women with iron supplements, with limits on salt and calorie intake, and sometimes with diuretics. This attempt to cure the symptoms has brought up not only strict diets to prevent normal weight gain and diuretics to prevent normal fluid retention but also the dangerous drugs, from tha-

lidomide to Bendectin, to prevent nausea. Each of these "cures" has had devastating effects: fetal malformation, maternal and fetal illness, even death.

What is particularly important to note is that these "treatments" of entirely normal phenomena are frequently not perceived by the medical profession as interventions or disruptions. Rather, the physician sees himself
as assisting nature, restoring the woman to normality. Janet Bogdan, in her
study of the development of obstetrics, reports that in the 1800s, a noninter-
ventionist physician, as opposed to a "regular" physician, would give a laboring woman some castor oil or milk of magnesia, catheterize her, bleed her
a pint or so, administer ergot, and use poultices to blister her. "Any of these
therapies would be administered in the interests of setting the parturient up
for an easier, less painful labor and delivery, while still holding to the belief
that the physician was letting nature take its course." [43] Dorothy Wertz says
that medicine currently has redefined "natural childbirth," in response to
consumer demand for it, to include any of the following techniques: spinal
or epidural anesthesia, inhalation anesthesia in the second stage of labor, for-
ceps, episiotomy, induced labor.[44] Each of these techniques increases the
risks of childbirth for mothers and babies.[45] Under the title "Normal Delivery," an obstetric teaching film shows "the use of various drugs and procedures used to facilitate normal delivery." Another "Normal Delivery" film is
"a demonstration of a normal, spontaneous delivery, including a paracervi-
cal block, episiotomy."

As the technologies of both "curing" and "diagnosis" grow more powerful, the danger increases. The extraordinary rise in cesarean sections starting
in the 1970s in the United States provides a striking example of this. Refine-
ments in anesthesiology, and to a lesser extent in surgery itself, have made
the cesarean section a much safer procedure in recent years. While it is not,
and cannot be, as safe as an unmedicated vaginal birth—a section is major
abdominal surgery, and all anesthesia entails risk—it is unquestionably safer
today than it was 20 or 40 years ago. Thus, the "cure" is more readily used.
But what is the disease? The disease is labor, of course. While medicine now
claims that pregnancy and labor are not diseases per se, they are always considered in terms of "riskiness": labor is at best "low risk" and is increasingly
often defined as "high risk." At first only labors defined as high risk, but
now even low-risk labors, are routinely being monitored electronically. The
electronic fetal monitor has a belt that wraps around the pregnant belly, thus
preventing normal walking and movement, and an electrode that goes into
the vagina and literally screws into the top of the baby's head. Contractions,
fetal heartbeat, and fetal scalp blood are all continuously monitored. With all
of this diagnostic sophistication, "fetal distress" can be detected—and presumably cured, by cesarean section. The National Center for Health Services
Research announced as far back as 1978 that electronic fetal monitoring may
do more harm than good, citing among other things the dangers of the rapidly
increasing cesarean section rate, but monitoring is still receiving widespread
medical acceptance.[46]

Menopause and the End of the Femininity Index

The use of estrogens provides an even better example of how medicine views the body as a machine that can be "run" or managed without being changed. Estrogens are female hormones; in medicine they are seen as femininity in a jar. In the widely selling *Feminine Forever*, Dr. Robert A. Wilson, pushing "estrogen-replacement therapy" for all menopausal women, calls estrogen levels, as detected by examination of cells from the vagina, a woman's "femininity index."[47] As estrogen levels naturally drop off after menopause a woman, according to Wilson, is losing her femininity. Interestingly, estrogen levels are also quite low while a woman is breastfeeding, something not usually socially linked to a "loss of feminity."

Menopause remains the one normal female process that is still overtly referred to as a disease in the medical literature. To some physicians, menopause is a "deficiency disease," and the use of estrogens is restoring the woman to her "normal" condition. Here we must reconsider the question of women's functional importance in the social system. Middle-aged housewives have been called the last of the "ladies of leisure," having outlived their social usefulness as wife-mothers and having been allowed no alternatives. While oopherectomies and clitoridectomies are no longer being done on upper-class women as they were a hundred years ago, to cure all kinds of dubious ills, older women are having hysterectomies (surgical removal of the uterus) at alarming rates.[48] Much more typical of modern medicine, however, is the use of chemical rather than surgical "therapy." Because the social changes and demands for readjustment of middle age roughly coincide with the time of menopause, menopause becomes the "illness" for which women can be treated.

Estrogens have been used in virtually every stage of the female reproductive cycle, usually with the argument that they return the woman to normal or are a "natural" treatment. Estrogens are used to keep adolescent girls from getting "unnaturally" tall; to treat painful menstruation; as contraception, supposedly mimicking pregnancy; as a chemical abortion in the "morning after" pill; to replace supposedly missing hormones and thus to prevent miscarriages; to dry up milk and return women to the "normal" nonlactating state; and to return menopausal women to the "normal" cycling state. For all the claims of normality and natural treatment, at this writing approximately half of these uses of estrogens have been shown to cause cancer. The use of estrogens in pregnancy was the first to be proved carcinogenic: Daughters of women who had taken estrogens (notably DES, a synthetic estrogen) are at risk for the development of a rare cancer of the vagina.[49] The sequential birth-control pill was taken off the market as the danger of endometrial cancer (cancer of the lining of the uterus) became known,[50] and, similarly, estrogens taken in menopause have been shown to increase the risk of endometrial cancer by as much as 14 times after seven years of use.[51]

The model of the body as a machine that can be regulated, controlled, and managed by medical treatments is not working. "Femininity" or physical "femaleness" is not something that comes in a jar and can be manipulated. Nor are women accepting the relegation to secondary functional importance, as wives and mothers of men. In rejecting the viewpoint that women bear men's children for them, women are reclaiming their bodies. When pregnancy is seen not as the presence of a (man's) fetus in a woman but as a condition of the woman herself, attitudes toward contraception, infertility, abortion, and childbirth all change. When pregnancy is perceived as a condition of the woman, then abortion, for example, is primarily a response to that condition.

Changing Feminist Perspectives

In the 1970s, the reemergence of the feminist movement brought about a new focus on women and health that called attention to medicine's treatment of female patients. Women's health advocates rejected not only the "specialty treatment" offered women by the medical establishment but in fact the whole medical system. These women opted for methods of care outside of the system altogether and urged the mobilization of self-help groups, self-examinations, and women's clinics. Self-help and lay midwifery groups have worked, and continue to work, outside of the medical system, redefining women's health. They taught, and continue to teach, women how to examine their own bodies, not in the never-ending search for pathology in which physicians are trained, but to learn more about health.

Contemporary women's health advocates also reject the specialty care approach, but do so by emphasizing women's inclusion into the system. These new feminists, operating at a time separated from their foremothers by a decade of conservative politics and an ailing, underfunded health care system, demand access to primary medical attention for women of all classes, colors, and cultures. Additionally, they emphasize a need for women's general health care that is based on a sound scientific understanding of female biology. These health advocates are geared toward consumerism within medicine, seeking better medical care and access for a wider range of services and a more inclusive population of women. Better trained, more knowledgeable, and more humane health care workers are a high priority, as is care that is based on the realities of women's lives.

Demanding better access, however, may not address the problem that medical care in the United States consists of an overmedicalization of the female body, a primary treatment focus on women's reproduction, and a general lack of information about female biology. And do we want physicians to be "treating" our health? Do we agree with what physicians consider to be illness in women? Do we want to urge comprehensive care that overmedicalizes the female body? It is entirely possible for a woman to fit herself for a diaphragm, do a pap smear and a breast examination (all with help and instruction if she needs it), and never adopt the patient role. It is also possible for a woman to go through a pregnancy and birth her baby with good, knowledgeable, caring help without becoming a patient under the supervision of a physician.

Women have been imbued with the medical model of women's bodies and health. And it is essential, whether working within or outside of the system, to redefine women in women's terms and to redefine physical normality within the context of the female body. This is not a problem unique to health. It is an essential feminist issue.

NOTES

1. Diana Scully and Pauline Bart, "A Funny Thing Happened on the Way to the Orifice: Women and Gynecology Textbooks," *American Journal of Sociology* 78 (1971): 1045–50.
2. *Gould Medical Dictionary*, 3rd ed. (New York: McGraw-Hill, 1972): 1056.
3. *Gould Medical Dictionary*, p. 658.
4. Karen Johnson and Charlea Massion, "Why a Women's Medical Specialty?" *Ms.* 11, no. 3 (1991): 68–69.
5. G. J. Barker-Benfield, *The Horrors of the Half-Known Life* (New York: Harper & Row, 1976).
6. Thomas Szasz, *The Theology of Medicine* (New York: Harper Colophon, 1977).
7. U.S. Public Health Service, "Women's Health: Report of the Public Health Service Task Force on Women's Health Issues," Washington, DC: U.S. Department of Health and Human Services, 1985.
8. A. Hamilton and C. Perry, "Sex Related Differences in Clinical Drug Response: Implications for Women's Health," *Medical Women's Association* 38 (1983): 126–37.
9. Council on Ethical and Judicial Affairs of the American Medical Association, "Gender Disparities in Clinical Decision Making," *Journal of the American Medical Association* 266 (1991): 559–62.
10. Paul Cotton, "Is There Still Too Much Extrapolation from Data on Middle-Aged White Men?" *Journal of the American Medical Association* 263 (1990): 1049–50.
11. Joann E. Manson et al., "A Prospective Study of Aspirin Use and Primary Prevention of Cardiovascular Disease in Women," *Journal of the American Medical Association* 266 (1991): 521–27.
12. A. Raskin, "Age-Sex Differences in Response to Antidepressant Drugs," *Journal of Nervous Mental Disease* 159 (1974): 120–30.
13. Paul Cotton, "Examples Abound of Gaps in Medical Knowledge Because of Groups Excluded from Scientific Study," *Journal of the American Medical Association* 263 (1990): 1051–52.
14. N. K. Wenger, "Gender, Coronary Artery Disease, and Coronary Bypass Surgery," *Annals of Internal Medicine* 112 (1985): 557–58.
15. Council on Ethical and Judicial Affairs of the American Medical Association, "Gender Disparities in Clinical Decision Making," *Journal of the American Medical Association* 266 (1991): 559–62.
16. Howard Minkoff and Jack DeHovitz, "Care of Women Infected with the Human Immunodeficiency Virus," *Journal of the American Medical Association* 266 (1991): 2253–58.
17. Susan Chu et al., "Impact of the Human Immunodeficiency Virus Epidemic on

Mortality in Women of Reproductive Age, United States," *Journal of the American Medical Association* 264 (1990): 225–29.

18. Cotton, "Examples Abound," pp. 1051–52.

19. Barbara Ehrenreich and Deirdre English, *Witches, Midwives and Nurses* (Old Westbury, NY: Feminist Press, 1973), p. 33.

20. Datha Clapper Brack, "The Displacement of the Midwife: Male Domination in a Formerly Female Occupation" (unpublished, 1976).

21. Janet Carlisle Bogdan, "Nineteenth Century Childbirth: Its Context and Meaning" (paper presented at the third Berkshire Conference on the History of Women, June 9–11, 1976), p. 8.

22. Frances E. Kobrin, "The American Midwife Controversy: A Crisis in Professionalization," *Bulletin of the History of Medicine* (1966): 353.

23. Brack, "Displacement of the Midwife," p. 1.

24. Barker-Benfield, *The Horrors of the Half-Known Life*, p. 83.

25. Ibid., p. 120.

26. Ibid.

27. Barbara Ehrenreich and Deirdre English, *Complaints and Disorders* (Old Westbury, NY: Feminist Press, 1973).

28. Barker-Benfield, *The Horrors of the Half-Known Life*, p. 120.

29. Ibid., p. 121.

30. Talcott Parsons, "Definitions of Health and Illness in Light of American Value Systems," in *Patients, Physicians and Illnesses*, ed. E. Gartly Jaco (New York: Free Press, 1958).

31. Ehrenreich and English, *Complaints and Disorders*, p. 16.

32. Vern Bullough and Martha Voght, "Women, Menstruation and Nineteenth-Century Medicine" (paper presented at the 45th annual meeting of the American Association for the History of Medicine, 1972).

33. Ehrenreich and English, *Complaints and Disorders*, p. 47.

34. Estelle Ramey, "Men's Cycles (They Have Them Too, You Know)," *Ms.* (1972): 8–14.

35. Milton Abramson and John R. Torghele, *American Journal of Obstetrics and Gynecology* (1961): 223.

36. Lynda Madaras and Jane Paterson, M.D., *Womancare: A Gynecological Guide to Your Body* (New York: Avon Books, 1984), p. 601.

37. Peter J. Schmidt, M.D., Lynnette K. Nieman, et al., "Lack of Effect of Induced Menses on Symptoms in Women with Premenstrual Syndrome," *The Journal of the American Medical Association* 324, no. 17 (1991): 1174–79.

38. Madaras and Paterson, p. 604.

39. Ellen Switzer, "PMS, the Return of Raging Hormones," *Working Woman*, Oct. 1983, pp. 123–27.

40. Emily Martin, "Premenstrual Syndrome: Discipline, Work, Anger in Late Industrial Societies," in *Blood Magic: The Anthology of Menstruation*, ed. Thomas Buckley and Alma Gottlieb (Berkeley: University of California Press, 1988), pp. 161–81.

41. Ibid., 174.

42. Sheldon Segal, "Contraceptive Research: A Male Chauvinist Plot?" *Family Planning Perspectives* (July 1972): 21–25.

43. Janet Carlisle Bogdan, "Nineteenth Century Childbirth: The Politics of Reality" (paper presented at the 71st annual meeting of the American Sociological Association, 1976), p. 11.

44. Dorothy C. Wertz, "Childbirth as a Controlled Workspace: From Midwifery to

Obstetrics" (paper presented at the 71st annual meeting of the American Socio-logical Association, 1976), p. 15.

45. Doris Haire, *The Cultural Warping of Childbirth* (Hillside, NJ: International Child-birth Education Association, 1972).

46. See Barbara Katz Rothman, *In Labor: Women and Power in the Birthplace* (New York: Norton, 1982), for a fuller discussion of the medicalization of the maternity cycle and developing alternatives.

47. Robert A. Wilson, *Feminine Forever* (New York: Pocket Books, 1968).

48. John Bunker, "Surgical Manpower," *New England Journal of Medicine* 282 (1970): 135–44.

49. Arthur Herbst, J. Ulfelder, and D. C. Poskanzer, "Adenocarcinoma of the Vagina," *New England Journal of Medicine* 284 (1971): 871–81.

50. Barbara Seaman and Gideon Seaman, *Women and the Crisis in Sex Hormones* (New York: Rawson Associates, 1977), p. 78.

51. Harry Ziel and William Finkle, "Estrogen Replacement Therapy," *New England Journal of Medicine* 293 (1975): 1167–70.

RACE AND ETHNICITY

31

THE PROBLEM OF THE TWENTIETH CENTURY IS THE PROBLEM OF THE COLOR LINE

W.E.B. DU BOIS

Race and ethnicity are the topics explored in the next four selections. This reading by W.E.B. Du Bois, "The Problem of the Twentieth Century Is the Problem of the Color Line," describes the U.S. system of racial apartheid. Du Bois, a well-known sociologist, wrote the first essay based on that title in 1901. In this selection, written in 1950, Du Bois analyzes the changing patterns of racial relations since the turn of the century. Even though some progress had been made in 50 years, Du Bois concludes that the color line is still visible in everyday life in America.

We are just finishing the first half of the twentieth century. I remember its birth in 1901. There was the usual discussion as to whether the century began in 1900 or 1901; but, of course, 1901 was correct. We expected great things . . . peace; the season of war among nations had passed; progress was the order . . . everything going forward to bigger and better things. And then, not so openly expressed, but even more firmly believed, the rule of white Europe and America over black, brown, and yellow peoples.

I was 32 years of age in 1901, married, and a father, and teaching at Atlanta University with a program covering a hundred years of study and investigation into the condition of American Negroes. Our subject of study at that time was education: the college-bred Negro in 1900, the Negro common school in 1901. My own attitude toward the twentieth century was expressed in an article which I wrote in the *Atlantic Monthly* in 1901. It said:

> The problem of the Twentieth Century is the problem of the color-line . . . I have seen a land right merry with the sun, where children sing, and rolling hills lie like passioned women wanton with harvest. And there in the King's Highway sat, and sits, a figure veiled and bowed, by which the Traveler's footsteps hasten as they go. On the tainted air broods fair. Three centuries' thought have been the raising and unveiling of that bowed human soul; and now behold, my fellows, a century now for the duty and the deed! The problem of the Twentieth Century is the problem of the color-line.

This is what we hoped, to this we Negroes looked forward; peace, progress and the breaking of the color line. What has been the result? We know it all too well . . . war, hate, the revolt of the colored peoples and the fear of more war.

In the meantime, where are we; those 15,000,000 citizens of the United States who are descended from the slaves, brought here between 1600 and 1900? We formed in 1901, a separate group because of legal enslavement and emancipation into caste conditions, with the attendant poverty, ignorance, disease, and crime. We were an inner group and not an integral part of the American nation; but we were exerting ourselves to fight for integration.

The burden of our fight was in seven different lines. We wanted education; we wanted particularly the right to vote and civil rights; we wanted work with adequate wage; housing, without segregation or slums; a free press to fight our battles, and (although in those days we dare not say it) social equality.

In 1901 our education was in perilous condition, despite what we and our white friends had done for 30 years. The Atlanta University Conference said in its resolutions of 1901:

> We call the attention of the nation to the fact that less than one million of the three million Negro children of school age are at present regularly attending school, and these attend a session which lasts only a few months. We are today deliberately rearing millions of our citizens in ignorance and at the same time limiting the rights of citizenship by educational qualifications. This is unjust.

More particularly in civil rights, we were oppressed. We not only did not get justice in the courts, but we were subject to peculiar and galling sorts of injustice in daily life. In the latter half of the nineteenth century, where we first get something like statistics, no less than 3,000 Negroes were lynched without trial. And in addition to that we were subject continuously to mob violence and judicial lynching.

In political life we had, for 25 years, been disfranchised by violence, law, and public opinion. The 14th and 15th amendments were deliberately violated and the literature of the day in book, pamphlet, and daily press, was widely of opinion that the Negro was not ready for the ballot, could not use it intelligently, and that no action was called for to stop his political power from being exercised by Southern whites like Tillman and Vardaman.

We did not have the right or opportunity to work at an income which would sustain a decent and modern standard of life. Because of a past of chattel slavery, we were for the most part common laborers and servants, and a very considerable proportion were still unable to leave the plantations where they worked all their lives for next to nothing.

There were a few who were educated for the professions and we had many good artisans; that number was not increasing as it should have been, nor were new artisans being adequately trained. Industrial training was popular, but funds to implement it were too limited, and we were excluded from unions and the new mass industry.

We were housed in slums and segregated districts where crime and disease multiplied, and when we tried to move to better and healthier quarters we were met by segregation ordinance if not by mobs. We not only had no social equality, but we did not openly ask for it. It seemed a shameful thing to beg people to receive us as equals and as human beings; that was something we argued "that came and could not be fetched." And that meant not simply that we could not marry white women or legitimize mulatto bastards, but we could not stop in a decent hotel, nor eat in a public restaurant nor attend the theater, nor accept an invitation to a private white home, nor travel in a decent railway coach. When the "public" was invited, this did not include us and admission to colleges often involved special consideration if not blunt refusal.

Finally we had poor press . . . a few struggling papers with little news and inadequately expressed opinion, with small circulation or influence and almost no advertising.

This was our plight in 1901. It was discouraging, but not hopeless. There is no question but that we had made progress, and there also was no doubt but what that progress was not enough to satisfy us or to settle our problems.

We could look back on a quarter century of struggle which had its results. We had schools; we had teachers; a few had forced themselves into the leading colleges and were tolerated if not welcomed. We voted in Northern cities, owned many decent homes and were fighting for further progress. Leaders like Booker Washington had perceived wide popular approval and a Negro literature had begun to appear.

But what we needed was organized effort along the whole front, based on broad lines of complete emancipation. This came with the Niagara Movement in 1906 and the NAACP in 1909. In 1910 came the Crisis magazine and the real battle was on.

What have we gained and accomplished? The advance has not been equal on all fronts, nor complete on any. We have not progressed with closed ranks like a trained army, but rather with serried and broken ranks, with wide gaps and even temporary retreats. But we have advanced. Of that there can be no atom of doubt.

First of all in education; most Negro children today are in school and most adults can read and write. Unfortunately this literacy is not as great as the census says. The draft showed that at least a third of our youth are illiterate. But education is steadily rising. Six thousand bachelor degrees are awarded to Negroes each year and doctorates in philosophy and medicine are not uncommon. Nevertheless as a group, American Negroes are still in the lower ranks of learning and adaptability to modern conditions. They do not read widely, their travel is limited and their experience through contact with the modern world is curtailed by law and custom.

Secondly, in civil rights, the Negro has perhaps made his greatest advance. Mob violence and lynching have markedly decreased. Three thousand Negroes were lynched in the last half of the nineteenth century and five hundred in the first half of the twentieth. Today lynching is comparatively rare. Mob violence also has decreased, but is still in evidence, and summary and unjust court proceedings have taken the place of open and illegal acts. But the Negro has established, in the courts, his legal citizenship and his right to be included in the Bill of Rights. The question still remains of "equal but separate" public accommodations, and that is being attacked. Even the institution of "jim-crow" in travel is tottering. The infraction of the marriage situation by law and custom is yet to be brought before the courts and public opinion in a forcible way.

Third, the right to vote on the part of the Negro is being gradually established under the 14th and 15th amendments. It was not really until 1915 that the Supreme Court upheld this right of Negro citizens and even today the penalties of the 14th amendment have never been enforced. There are 7,000,000 possible voters among American Negroes and of these it is a question if more than 2,000,000 actually cast their votes. This is partly from the national inertia, which keeps half of all American voters away from the polls; but even more from the question as to what practical ends the Negro shall cast his vote.

He is thinking usually in terms of what he can do by voting to better his condition and he seldom gets a chance to vote on this matter. On the wider implications of political democracy he has not yet entered; particularly he does not see the economic foundations of present civilization and the necessity of his attacking the rule of corporate wealth in order to free the labor group to which he belongs.

Fourth, there is the question of occupation. There are our submerged classes of farm labor and tenants: our city laborers, washerwomen and scrub-women and the mass of lower-paid servants. These classes still form a majority of American Negroes and they are on the edge of poverty, with the ignorance, disease, and crime that always accompany such poverty.

If we measure the median income of Americans, it is $3,000 for whites and $2,000 for Negroes. In Southern cities, seven percent of the white families and 30 percent of the colored families receive less than $1,000 a year. On the other hand, the class differentiation by income among Negroes is notable: the number of semiskilled and skilled artisans has increased or will as membership in labor unions. Professional men have increased, especially teachers and less notably, physicians, dentists, and lawyers.

The number of Negroes in business has increased; mostly in small retail businesses, but to a considerable extent in enterprises like insurance, real estate and small banking, where the color line gives Negroes certain advantages and where, too, there is a certain element of gambling. Also beyond the line of gambling, numbers of Negroes have made small fortunes in antisocial enterprises. All this means that there has arisen in the Negro group a distinct stratification from poor to rich. Recently I polled 450 Negro families belonging to a select organization 45 years old. Of these families, 127 received over $10,000 a year and a score of these over $25,000; 200 families received from $5,000 to $10,000 a year and 86 less than $5,000.

This is the start of a tendency which will grow; we are beginning to follow the American pattern of accumulating individual wealth and of considering that this will eventually settle the race problem. On the other hand, the whole trend of the thought of our age is toward social welfare; the prevention of poverty by more equitable distribution of wealth, and business for general welfare rather than private profit. There are few signs that these ideals are guiding Negro development today. We seem to be adopting increasingly the ideal of American culture.

Housing has, of course, been a point of bitter pressure among Negroes, because the attempt to segregate the race in its living conditions has not only kept the more fortunate ones from progress, but it has confined vast numbers of Negro people to the very parts of cities and country districts where they have fewest opportunities and least social contacts. They must live largely in slums, in contact with criminals and with fewest of the social advantages of government and human contact. The fight against segregation has been carried on in the courts and shows much progress against city ordinances, against covenants which make segregation hereditary.

Literature and art have made progress among Negroes, but with curious handicaps. An art expression is normally evoked by the conscious and unconscious demand of people for portrayal of their own emotion and experience. But in the case of the American Negroes, the audience, which embodies the demand and which pays sometimes enormous price for satisfaction, is not the Negro group, but the white group. And the pattern of what the white group wants does not necessarily agree with the natural desire of Negroes.

The whole of Negro literature is therefore curiously divided. We have writers who have written, not really about Negroes, but about the things which white people, and not the highest class of whites, like to hear about Negroes. And those who have expressed what the Negro himself thinks and feels, are those whose books sell to few, even of their own people; and whom most folk do not know. This has not made for the authentic literature which the early part of this century seemed to promise. To be sure, it can be said that American literature today has a considerable amount of Negro expression and influence, although not as much as once we hoped.

Despite all this we have an increasing number of excellent Negro writers who make the promise for the future great by their real accomplishment. We have done something in sculpture and painting, but in drama and music we have markedly advanced. All the world listens to our singers, sings our music, and dances to our rhythms.

In science, our handicaps are still great. Turner, a great entomologist, was worked to death for lack of laboratory, just never had the recognition he richly deserved; and Carver was prisoner of his inferiority complex. Notwithstanding this, our real accomplishment in biology and medicine; in history and law; and in the social sciences has been notable and widely acclaimed. To this in no little degree is due our physical survival, our falling death rate, and our increased confidence in our selves and in our destiny.

The expression of Negro wish and desire through a free press has greatly improved as compared with 1900. We have a half dozen large weekly papers with circulations of a hundred thousand or more. Their news coverage is immense, even if not discriminating. But here again, the influence of the American press on us has been devastating. The predominance of advertising over opinion, the desire for income rather than literary excellence and the use of deliberate propaganda, has made our press less of a power than it could be, and leaves wide chance for improvement in the future.

In comparison with other institutions, the Negro church during the twentieth century has lost ground. It is no longer the dominating influence that it used to be, the center of social activity and of economic experiment. Nevertheless, it is still a powerful institution in the lives of a numerical majority of American Negroes if not upon the dominant intellectual classes. There has been a considerable increase in organized work for social progress through the church, but there has also been a large increase of expenditure for buildings, furnishings, and salaries; and it is not easy to find any increase in moral stamina or conscientious discrimination within church circles.

The scandal of deliberate bribery in election of bishops and in the holding of positions in the churches without a hierarchy has been widespread. It is a critical problem now as to just what part in the future the church among Negroes is going to hold.

Finally there comes the question of social equality, which, despite efforts on the part of thinkers, white and black, is after all the main and fundamental problem of race in the United States. Unless a human being is going to have all human rights, including not only work, but friendship, and if mutually desired, marriage and children, unless these avenues are open and free, there can be no real equality and no cultural integration.

It has hitherto seemed utterly impossible that any such solution of the Negro problem in America could take place. The situation was quite similar to the problem of the lower classes of laborers, serfs and servants in European nations during the sixteenth, seventeenth, and eighteenth centuries. All nations had to consist of two separate parts and the only relations between them was employment and philanthropy.

That problem has been partly solved by modern democracy, but modern democracy cannot succeed unless the peoples of different races and religions are also integrated into the democratic whole. Against this, large numbers of Americans have always fought and are still fighting, but the progress despite this has been notable. There are places in the United States, especially in large cities like New York and Chicago, where the social differences between the races has, to a large extent, been nullified and there is a meeting on terms of equality which would have been thought impossible a half century ago.

On the other hand, in the South, despite religion, education, and reason, the color line, although perhaps shaken, still stands, stark and unbending, and to the minds of most good people, eternal. Here lies the area of the last battle for the complete rights of American Negroes.

Within the race itself today there are disquieting signs. The effort of Negroes to become Americans of equal status with other Americans is leading them to a state of mind by which they not only accept what is good in America, but what is bad and threatening so long as the Negro can share equally. This is peculiarly dangerous at this epoch in the development of world culture.

After two world wars of unprecedented loss of life, cruelty, and destruction, we are faced by the fact that the industrial organization of our present civilization has in it something fundamentally wrong. It went to pieces in the first world war because of the determination of certain great powers excluded from world rule to share in that rule, by acquisition of the labor and materials of colonial peoples. The attempt to recover from the cataclysm resulted in the collapse of our industrial system, and a second world war.

In spite of the propaganda which has gone on, which represents America as the leading democratic state, we Negroes know perfectly well, and ought to know even better than most, that America is not a successful democracy and that until it is, it is going to drag down the world. This nation is ruled by corporate wealth to a degree which is frightening. One thousand persons own the United States and their power outweighs the voice of the mass of American citizens. This must be cured, not by revolution, not by war and violence, but by reason and knowledge.

Most of the world is today turning toward the welfare state; turning against the idea of production for individual profit toward the idea of production for use and for the welfare of the mass of citizens. No matter how difficult such a course is, it is the only course that is going to save the world and this we American Negroes have got to realize.

We may find it easy now to get publicity, reward, and attention by going along with the reactionary propaganda and war hysteria which is convulsing this nation, but in the long run America will not thank its black children if they help it go the wrong way, or retard its progress.

32

"IS THIS A WHITE COUNTRY, OR WHAT?"

LILLIAN B. RUBIN

In this reading, Lillian Rubin presents her findings of racial hostility among working-class white ethnics. Rubin finds that the "color line" has been redefined to include immigrants and all people of color. Using interviews and document analysis, Rubin compares the anti-immigrant, racist beliefs of her respondents with actual demographic data on immigration and social opportunities in the United States.

"They're letting all these coloreds come in and soon there won't be any place left for white people," broods Tim Walsh, a 33-year-old white construction worker. "It makes you wonder: Is this a white country, or what?"

It's a question that nags at white America, one perhaps that's articulated most often and most clearly by the men and women of the working class. For it's they who feel most vulnerable, who have suffered the economic contractions of recent decades most keenly, who see the new immigrants most clearly as direct competitors for their jobs.

It's not whites alone who stew about immigrants. Native-born blacks, too, fear the newcomers nearly as much as whites—and for the same economic reasons. But for whites the issue is compounded by race, by the fact that the newcomers are primarily people of color. For them, therefore, their economic anxieties have combined with the changing face of America to create a profound uneasiness about immigration—a theme that was sounded by nearly 90 percent of the whites I met, even by those who are themselves first-generation, albeit well-assimilated, immigrants.

Sometimes they spoke about this in response to my questions; equally often the subject of immigration arose spontaneously as people gave voice to their concerns. But because the new immigrants are predominantly people of color, the discourse was almost always cast in terms of race as well as immigration, with the talk slipping from immigration to race and back again as if these are not two separate phenomena. "If we keep letting all them foreigners in, pretty soon there'll be more of them than us and then what will this country be like?" Tim's wife, Mary Anne, frets. "I mean, this is *our* country, but the way things are going, white people will be the minority in our own country. Now does that make any sense?"

Such fears are not new. Americans have always worried about the strangers who came to our shores, fearing that they would corrupt our society, dilute our culture, debase our values. So I remind Mary Anne, "When your ancestors came here, people also thought we were allowing too many foreigners into the country. Yet those earlier immigrants were successfully integrated into the American society. What's different now?"

"Oh, it's different, all right," she replies without hesitation. "When my people came, the immigrants were all white. That makes a big difference."

"Why do you think that's so?"

"I don't know; it just is, that's all. Look at the black people; they've been here a long time, and they still don't live like us—stealing and drugs and having all those babies."

"But you were talking about immigrants. Now you're talking about blacks, and they're not immigrants."

"Yeah, I know," she replies with a shrug. "But they're different, and there's enough problems with them, so we don't need any more. With all these other people coming here now, we just have more trouble. They don't talk English; and they think different from us, things like that."

Listening to Mary Anne's words I was reminded again how little we Americans look to history for its lessons, how impoverished is our historical memory. For, in fact, being white didn't make "a big difference" for many of those earlier immigrants. The dark-skinned Italians and the eastern European Jews who came in the late nineteenth and early twentieth centuries didn't look very white to the fair-skinned Americans who were here then. Indeed, the same people we now call white—Italians, Jews, Irish—were seen as another race at that time. Not black or Asian, it's true, but an alien other, a race apart, although one that didn't have a clearly defined name. Moreover, the racist fears and fantasies of native-born Americans were far less contained then than they are now, largely because there were few social constraints on their expression.

When, during the nineteenth century, for example, some Italians were taken for blacks and lynched in the South, the incidents passed virtually unnoticed. And if Mary Anne and Tim Walsh, both of Irish ancestry, had come to this country during the great Irish immigration of that period, they would have found themselves defined as an inferior race and described with the same language that was used to characterize blacks: "low-browed and savage, grovelling and bestial, lazy and wild, simian and sensual."[1] Not only during that period but for a long time afterward as well, the U.S. Census Bureau counted the Irish as a distinct and separate group, much as it does today with the category it labels "Hispanic."

But there are two important differences between then and now, differences that can be summed up in a few words: the economy and race. Then, a growing industrial economy meant that there were plenty of jobs for both immigrant and native workers, something that can't be said for the contracting economy in which we live today. True, the arrival of the immigrants, who were more readily exploitable than native workers, put Americans at a disadvantage and created discord between the two groups. Nevertheless, work was available for both.

Then, too, the immigrants—no matter how they were labeled, no matter how reviled they may have been—were ultimately assimilable, if for no other reason than that they were white. As they began to lose their alien ways, it became possible for native Americans to see in the white ethnics of yesteryear a reflection of themselves. Once this shift in perception occurred, it was possible for the nation to incorporate them, to take them in, chew them up, digest them, and spit them out as Americans—with subcultural variations not always to the liking of those who hoped to control the manners and mores of the day, to be sure, but still recognizably white Americans.

Today's immigrants, however, are the racial other in a deep and profound way. It's true that race is not a fixed category, that it's no less an *idea* today than it was yesterday. And it's also possible, as I have already suggested, that we may be witness to social transformation from race to ethnicity among some of the most assimilated—read: middle-class—Asians and Latinos. But even if so, there's a long way to go before that metamorphosis is realized. Meanwhile, the immigrants of this era not only bring their own language and culture, they are also people of color—men, women, and children whose skin tones are different and whose characteristic features set them apart and justify the racial categories we lock them into.[2] And integrating masses of people of color into a society where race consciousness lies at the very heart of our central nervous system raises a whole new set of anxieties and tensions.

It's not surprising, therefore, that racial dissension has increased so sharply in recent years. What is surprising, however, is the passion for ethnicity and the preoccupation with ethnic identification among whites that seems suddenly to have burst upon the public scene. . . .

. . .

What does being German, Irish, French, Russian, Polish mean to someone who is an American? It's undoubtedly different for recent immigrants than for those who have been here for generations. But even for a relative newcomer, the inexorable process of becoming an American changes the meaning of ethnic identification and its hold on the internal life of the individual. Nowhere have I seen this shift more eloquently described than in a recent op-ed piece published in the *New York Times.* The author, a Vietnamese refugee writing on the day when Vietnamese either celebrate or mourn the fall of Saigon, depending on which side of the conflict they were on, writes:

> Although I sometimes mourn the loss of home and land, it's the American landscape and what it offers that solidify my hyphenated identity.
> . . . Assimilation, education, the English language, the American 'I'—these have carried me and many others further from that beloved tropical country than the C-130 ever could. . . . When did this happen? Who knows? One night, America quietly seeps in and takes hold of one's mind and body, and the Vietnamese soul of sorrows slowly fades away. In the morning, the Vietnamese American speaks a new language of materialism: his vocabulary includes terms like career choices, down payment, escrow, overtime.[3]

A new language emerges, but it lives, at least for another generation, alongside the old one; Vietnamese, yes, but also American, with a newly developed sense of self and possibility—an identity that continues to grow stronger with each succeeding generation. It's a process we have seen repeated throughout the history of American immigration. The American world reaches into the immigrant communities and shapes and changes the people who live in them.[4] By the second generation, ethnic identity already is attenuated; by the third, it usually has receded as a deeply meaningful part of life.

Residential segregation, occupational concentration, and a common language and culture—these historically have been the basis for ethnic solidarity and identification. As strangers in a new land, immigrants banded together, bound by their native tongue and shared culture. The sense of affinity they felt in these urban communities was natural; they were a touch of home, of the old country, of ways they understood. Once within their boundaries, they could feel whole again, sheltered from the ridicule and revulsion with which they were greeted by those who came before them. For whatever the myth about America's welcoming arms, nativist sentiment has nearly always been high and the anti-immigrant segment of the population large and noisy.

Ethnic solidarity and identity in America, then, was the consequence of the shared history each group brought with it, combined with the social and psychological experience of establishing themselves in the new land. But powerful as these were, the connections among the members of the group were heightened and sustained by the occupational concentration that followed—the Irish in the police departments of cities like Boston and San Francisco, for example, the Jews in New York City's garment industry, the east central Europeans in the mills and mines of western Pennsylvania.[5]

As each ethnic group moved into the labor force, its members often became concentrated in a particular occupation, largely because they were helped to find jobs there by those who went before them. For employers, this ethnic homogeneity made sense. They didn't have to cope with a babel of different languages, and they could count on the older workers to train the newcomers and keep them in line. For workers, there were advantages as well. It meant that they not only had compatible workmates, but that they weren't alone as they faced the jeers and contempt of their American-born counterparts. And perhaps most important, as more and more ethnic peers filled the available jobs, they began to develop some small measure of control in the workplace.

The same pattern of occupational concentration that was characteristic of yesterday's immigrant groups exists among the new immigrants today, and for the same reasons. The Cubans in Florida and the Dominicans in New York,[6] the various Asian groups in San Francisco, the Koreans in Los Angeles and New York—all continue to live in ethnic neighborhoods; all use the networks established there to find their way into the American labor force.[7]

For the white working-class ethnics whose immigrant past is little more than part of family lore, the occupational, residential, and linguistic chain has been broken. This is not to say that white ethnicity has ceased to be an observable phenomenon in American life. Cities like New York, Chicago, and San Francisco still have white ethnic districts that influence their culture, especially around food preferences and eating habits. But as in San Francisco's North Beach or New York's Little Italy, the people who once created vibrant neighborhoods, where a distinct subculture and language remained vividly alive, long ago moved out and left behind only the remnants of the commercial life of the old community. As such transformations took place, ethnicity became largely a private matter, a distant part of the family heritage that had little to do with the ongoing life of the family or community.

What, then, are we to make of the claims to ethnic identity that have become so prominent in recent years? Herbert Gans has called this identification "symbolic ethnicity"—that is, ethnicity that's invoked or not as the individual chooses.[8] Symbolic ethnicity, according to Gans, has little impact on a person's daily life and, because it is not connected to ethnic structures or activities—except for something like the wearing of the green on St. Patrick's Day—it makes no real contribution to ethnic solidarity or community.

The description is accurate. But it's a mistake to dismiss ethnic identification, even if only symbolic, as relatively meaningless. Symbols, after all, become symbolic precisely because they have meaning. In this case, the symbol has meaning at two levels: One is the personal and psychological, the other is the social and political.

At the personal level, in a nation as large and diverse as ours—a nation that defines itself by its immigrant past, where the metaphor for our national identity has been the melting pot—defining oneself in the context of an ethnic group is comforting. It provides a sense of belonging to some recognizable and manageable collectivity—an affiliation that has meaning because it's connected to the family where, when we were small children, we first learned about our relationship to the group. As Vilma Janowski, a 24-year-old first-generation Polish-American who came here as a child put it: "Knowing there's other people like you is really nice. It's like having a big family, even if you don't ever really see them. It's just nice to know they're there. Besides, if I said I was American, what would it mean? Nobody's just American."

Which is true. Being an American is different from being French or Dutch or any number of other nationalities because, except for Native Americans, there's no such thing as an American without a hyphen somewhere in the past. To identify with the front end of that hyphen is to maintain a connection—however tenuous, illusory, or sentimentalized—with our roots. It sets us apart from others, allows us the fantasy of uniqueness—a quest given particular urgency by a psychological culture that increasingly emphasizes the development of the self and personal history. Paradoxically, however, it also gives us a sense of belonging—of being one with others like ourselves—that helps to overcome some of the isolation of modern life.

But these psychological meanings have developed renewed force in recent years because of two significant sociopolitical events. The first was the civil rights movement with its call for racial equality. The second was the change in the immigration laws, which, for the first time in nearly half a century, allowed masses of immigrants to enter the country.

It was easy for northern whites to support the early demands of the civil rights movement when blacks were asking for the desegregation of buses and drinking fountains in the South. But supporting the black drive to end discrimination in jobs, housing, and education in the urban North was quite another matter—especially among those white ethnics whose hold on the ladder of mobility was tenuous at best and with whom blacks would be most likely to compete, whether in the job market, the neighborhood, or the classroom. As the courts and legislatures around the country began to honor some black claims for redress of past injustices, white hackles began to rise.

It wasn't black demands alone that fed the apprehensions of whites, however. In the background of the black civil rights drive, there stood a growing chorus of voices, as other racial groups—Asian Americans, Latinos, and Native Americans—joined the public fray to seek remedy for their own grievances. At the same time that these home-grown groups were making their voices heard and, not incidentally, affirming their distinctive cultural heritages and calling for public acknowledgment of them, the second great wave of immigration in this century washed across our shores.

After having closed the gates to mass immigration with the National Origins Act of 1924, Congress opened them again when it passed the Immigration Act of 1965.[9] This act, which was a series of amendments to the McCarran-Walter Act of 1952, essentially jettisoned the national origins provisions of earlier law and substituted overall hemisphere caps. The bill, according to immigration historian Roger Daniels, "changed the whole course of American immigration history" and left the door open for a vast increase in the numbers of immigrants.[10]

More striking than the increase in numbers has been the character of the new immigrants. Instead of the large numbers of western Europeans whom the sponsors had expected to take advantage of the new policy, it has been the people of Asia, Latin America, and the Caribbean who rushed to the boats. "It is doubtful if any drafter or supporter of the 1965 act envisaged this result," writes Daniels.[11] In fact, when members of Lyndon Johnson's administration, under whose tenure the bill became law, testified before Congress, they assured the legislators and the nation that few Asians would come in under the new law.[12]

This is a fascinating example of the unintended consequences of a political act. The change in the law was sponsored by northern Democrats who sought to appeal to their white ethnic constituencies by opening the gates to their countrymen once again—that is, to the people of eastern and southern Europe whom the 1924 law had kept out for nearly half a century. But those same white ethnics punished the Democratic Party by defecting to the Republicans during the Reagan-Bush years, a defection that was at least partly related to their anger about the new immigrants and the changing racial balance of urban America.

During the decade of the 1980s, 2.5 million immigrants from Asian countries were admitted to the United States, an increase of more than 450 percent over the years between 1961 and 1970, when the number was slightly less than half a million. In 1990 alone, nearly as many Asian immigrants—one-third of a million—entered the country as came during the entire decade of the 1960s. Other groups show similarly noteworthy increases. Close to three-quarters of a million documented Mexicans crossed the border in the single year of 1990, compared to less than half a million during all of the 1960s. Central American immigration, too, climbed from just under one hundred thousand between 1961 and 1970 to more than triple that number during the 1980s. And immigrants from the Caribbean, who numbered a little more than half a million during the 1960s, increased to over three-quarters of a million in the years between 1981 and 1989.[13]

Despite these large increases and the perception that we are awash with new immigrants, it's worth noting that they are a much smaller proportion of the total population today, 6.2 percent, than they were in 1920, when they were a hefty 13.2 percent of all U.S. residents.[14] But the fact that most immigrants today are people of color gives them greater visibility than ever before.

Suddenly, the nation's urban landscape has been colored in ways unknown before. In 1970, the California cities that were the site of the original research for *Worlds of Pain* were almost exclusively white. Twenty years later, the 1990 census reports that their minority populations range from 54 to 69 percent. In the nation at large, the same census shows nearly one in four

Americans with African, Asian, Latino, or Native American ancestry, up from one in five in 1980.[15] So dramatic is this shift that whites of European descent now make up just over two-thirds of the population in New York State, while in California they number only 57 percent. In cities like New York, San Francisco, and Los Angeles whites are a minority—accounting for 38, 47, and 37 percent of residents, respectively. Twenty years ago the white population in all these cities was over 75 percent.[16]

The increased visibility of other racial groups has focused whites more self-consciously than ever on their own racial identification. Until the new immigration shifted the complexion of the land so perceptibly, whites didn't think of themselves as white in the same way that Chinese know they're Chinese and African Americans know they're black. Being white was simply a fact of life, one that didn't require any public statement, since it was the definitive social value against which all others were measured. "It's like everything's changed and I don't know what happened," complains Marianne Bardolino. "All of a sudden you have to be thinking all the time about these race things. I don't remember growing up thinking about being white like I think about it now. I'm not saying I didn't know there was coloreds and whites; it's just that I didn't go along thinking, *Gee, I'm a white person.* I never thought about it at all. But now with all the different colored people around, you have to think about it because they're thinking about it all the time."

"You say you feel pushed now to think about being white, but I'm not sure I understand why. What's changed?" I ask.

"I told you," she replies quickly, a small smile covering her impatience with my question. "It's because they think about what they are, and they want things their way, so now I have to think about what I am and what's good for me and my kids." She pauses briefly to let her thoughts catch up with her tongue, then continues. "I mean, if somebody's always yelling at you about being black or Asian or something, then it makes you think about being white. Like, they want the kids in school to learn about their culture, so then I think about being white and being Italian and say: What about my culture? If they're going to teach about theirs, what about mine?"

To which America's racial minorities respond with bewilderment. "I don't understand what white people want," says Gwen Tomalson. "They say if black kids are going to learn about black culture in school, then white people want their kids to learn about white culture. I don't get it. What do they think kids have been learning about all these years? It's all about white people and how they live and what they accomplished. When I was in school you wouldn't have thought black people existed for all our books ever said about us."

As for the charge that they're "thinking about race all the time," as Marianne Bardolino complains, people of color insist that they're forced into it by a white world that never lets them forget. "If you're Chinese, you can't forget it, even if you want to, because there's always something that reminds you," Carol Kwan's husband, Andrew, remarks tartly. "I mean, if Chinese kids get good grades and get into the university, everybody's worried and you read about it in the papers."

While there's little doubt that racial anxieties are at the center of white concerns, our historic nativism also plays a part in escalating white alarm. The new immigrants bring with them a language and an ethnic culture that's vividly expressed wherever they congregate. And it's this also, the constant reminder of an alien presence from which whites are excluded, that's so troublesome to them.

The nativist impulse isn't, of course, given to the white working class alone. But for those in the upper reaches of the class and status hierarchy—those whose children go to private schools, whose closest contact with public transportation is the taxicab—the immigrant population supplies a source of cheap labor, whether as nannies for their children, maids in their households, or workers in their businesses. They may grouse and complain that "nobody speaks English anymore," just as working-class people do. But for the people who use immigrant labor, legal or illegal, there's a payoff for the inconvenience—a payoff that doesn't exist for the families in this study but that sometimes costs them dearly.[17] For while it may be true that American workers aren't eager for many of the jobs immigrants are willing to take, it's also true that the presence of a large immigrant population—especially those who come from developing countries where living standards are far below our own—helps to make these jobs undesirable by keeping wages depressed well below what most American workers are willing to accept.[18]

Indeed, the economic basis of our immigration policies too often gets lost in the lore that we are a land that says to the world, "Give me your tired, your poor, your huddled masses, yearning to breathe free."[19] I don't mean to suggest that our humane impulses are a fiction, only that the reality is far more complex than Emma Lazarus' poem suggests. The massive immigration of the nineteenth and early twentieth centuries didn't just happen spontaneously. America may have been known as the land of opportunity to the Europeans who dreamed of coming here—a country where, as my parents once believed, the streets were lined with gold. But they believed these things because that's how America was sold by the agents who spread out across the face of Europe to recruit workers—men and women who were needed to keep the machines of our developing industrial society running and who, at the same time, gave the new industries a steady supply of hungry workers willing to work for wages well below those of native-born Americans.

The enormous number of immigrants who arrived during that period accomplished both those ends. In doing so, they set the stage for a long history of antipathy to foreign workers. For today, also, one function of the new immigrants is to keep our industries competitive in a global economy. Which simply is another way of saying that they serve to depress the wages of native American workers.

It's not surprising, therefore, that working-class women and men speak so angrily about the recent influx of immigrants. They not only see their jobs and their way of life threatened, they feel bruised and assaulted by an environment that seems suddenly to have turned color and in which they feel like strangers in their own land. So they chafe and complain: "They come here to take advantage of us, but they don't really want to learn our ways," Beverly Sowell, a 33-year-old white electronics assembler, grumbles irritably. "They live different than us; it's like another world how they live. And they're so clannish. They keep to themselves, and they don't even *try* to learn English. You go on the bus these days and you might as well be in a foreign country; everybody's talking some other language, you know, Chinese or Spanish or something. Lots of them have been here a long time, too, but they don't care; they just want to take what they can get."

But their complaints reveal an interesting paradox, an illuminating glimpse into the contradictions that beset native-born Americans in their relations with those who seek refuge here. On the one hand, they scorn the immigrants; on the other, they protest because they "keep to themselves." It's the same contradiction that dominates black–white relations. Whites refuse to integrate blacks but are outraged when they stop knocking at the door, when they move to sustain the separation on their own terms—in black theme houses on campuses, for example, or in the newly developing black middle-class suburbs.

I wondered, as I listened to Beverly Sowell and others like her, why the same people who find the lifeways and languages of our foreign-born population offensive also care whether they "keep to themselves."

"Because like I said, they just shouldn't, that's all," Beverly says stubbornly. "If they're going to come here, they should be willing to learn our ways—you know what I mean, be real Americans. That's what my grandparents did, and that's what they should do."

"But your grandparents probably lived in an immigrant neighborhood when they first came here, too," I remind her.

"It was different," she insists. "I don't know why; it was. They wanted to be Americans; these here people now, I don't think they do. They just want to take advantage of this country."

She stops, thinks for a moment, then continues, "Right now it's awful in this country. Their kids come into the schools, and it's a big mess. There's not enough money for our kids to get a decent education, and we have to spend money to teach their kids English. It makes me mad. I went to public school, but I have to send my kids to Catholic school because now on top of the black kids, there's all these foreign kids who don't speak English. What kind of an education can kids get in a school like that? Something's wrong when plain old American kids can't go to their own schools.

"Everything's changed, and it doesn't make sense. Maybe you get it, but I don't. We can't take care of our own people and we keep bringing more and more foreigners in. Look at all the homeless. Why do we need more people here when our own people haven't got a place to sleep?"

"Why do we need more people here?"—a question Americans have asked for two centuries now. Historically, efforts to curb immigration have come during economic downturns, which suggests that when times are good, when American workers feel confident about their future, they're likely to be more generous in sharing their good fortune with foreigners. But when the economy falters, as it did in the 1990s, and workers worry about having to compete for jobs with people whose standard of living is well below their own, resistance to immigration rises. "Don't get me wrong; I've got nothing against these people," Tim Walsh demurs. "But they don't talk English, and they're used to a lot less, so they can work for less money than guys like me can. I see it all the time; they get hired and some white guy gets left out."

It's this confluence of forces—the racial and cultural diversity of our new immigrant population; the claims on the resources of the nation now being made by those minorities who, for generations, have called America their home; the failure of some of our basic institutions to serve the needs of our people; the contracting economy, which threatens the mobility aspirations of working-class families—all these have come together to leave white workers feeling as if everyone else is getting a piece of the action while they get nothing. "I feel like white people are left out in the cold," protests Diane Johnson, a 28-year-old white single mother who believes she lost a job as a bus driver to a black woman. "First it's the blacks; now it's all those other colored people, and it's like everything always goes their way. It seems like a white person doesn't have a chance anymore. It's like the squeaky wheel gets the grease, and they've been squeaking and we haven't," she concludes angrily.

Until recently, whites didn't need to think about having to "squeak"—at least not specifically as whites. They have, of course, organized and squeaked at various times in the past—sometimes as ethnic groups, sometimes as workers. But not as whites. As whites they have been the dominant group, the favored ones, the ones who could count on getting the job when people of color could not. Now suddenly there are others—not just individual others but identifiable groups, people who share a history, a language, a culture, even a color—who lay claim to some of the rights and privileges that formerly had been labeled "for whites only." And whites react as if they've been betrayed, as if a sacred promise has been broken. They're white, aren't they? They're *real* Americans, aren't they? This is their country, isn't it?

NOTES

1. David R. Roediger, *The Wages of Whiteness* (New York: Verso, 1991), p. 133.
2. I'm aware that many Americans who have none of the characteristic features associated with their African heritage are still defined as black. This is one reason why I characterize race as an idea, not a fact. Nevertheless, the main point I am making here still holds—that is, the visible racial character of a people makes a difference in whether white Americans see them as assimilable or not.
3. *New York Times*, April 30, 1993.
4. For an excellent historical portrayal of the formation of ethnic communities among the east central European immigrants in Pennsylvania, the development

of ethnic identity, and the process of Americanization, see Ewa Morawska, *For Bread with Butter* (New York: Cambridge University Press, 1985).

5. Ibid.

6. Alejandro Portes and Ruben G. Rumbaut, *Immigrant America* (Berkeley: University of California Press, 1990).

7. One need only walk the streets of New York to see the concentration of Koreans in the corner markets and the nail care salons that dot the city's landscape.

   In San Francisco the Cambodians now own most of the donut shops in the city. It all started when, after working in such a shop, an enterprising young Cambodian combined the family resources and opened his own store and bakery. He now has 20 shops and has been instrumental in helping his countrymen open more, all of them buying their donuts from his bakery.

8. Herbert Gans, "Symbolic Ethnicity: The Future of Ethnic Groups and Cultures in America," *Ethnic and Racial Studies* 2 (1979): 1–18.

9. Despite nativist protests, immigration had proceeded unchecked by government regulation until the end of the nineteenth century. The first serious attempt to restrict immigration came in 1882 when, responding to the clamor about the growing immigration of Chinese laborers to California and other western states, Congress passed the Chinese Exclusion Act. But European immigration remained unimpeded. In the years between 1880 and 1924, twenty-four million newcomers arrived on these shores, most of them eastern and southern Europeans, all bringing their own language and culture, and all the target of pervasive bigotry and exploitation by native-born Americans. By the early part of the twentieth century, anti-immigration sentiments grew strong enough to gain congressional attention once again. The result was the National Origins Act of 1924, which established the quota system that sharply limited immigration, especially from the countries of southern and eastern Europe.

10. Roger Daniels, *Coming to America: A History of Immigration and Ethnicity in American Life* (New York: HarperCollins, 1990), pp. 338–44.

11. Daniels, *Coming to America*, p. 341, writes further, "In his Liberty Island speech Lyndon Johnson stressed the fact that he was redressing the wrong done [by the McCarran-Walter Act] to those 'from southern or eastern Europe,' and although he did mention 'developing continents,' there was no other reference to Asian or Third World immigration."

12. For a further review of the Immigration Act of 1965, see chapter 13 (pp. 328–49) of *Coming to America*.

13. *Statistical Abstract*, U.S. Bureau of the Census (1992), Table 8, p. 11.

14. *Statistical Abstract*, U.S. Bureau of the Census (1992), Table 45, p. 42.

15. *Statistical Abstract*, U.S. Bureau of the Census (1992), Table 18, p. 18, and Table 26, p. 24.

16. U.S. Bureau of the Census, *Population Reports*, 1970 and 1990. Cited in Mike Davis, "The Body Count," *Crossroads* (June 1993). The difference in the racial composition of New York and San Francisco explains, at least in part, why black–white tensions are so much higher in New York City than they are in San Francisco. In New York, 38 percent of the population is now white, 30 percent black, 25 percent Hispanic, and 7 percent Asian. In San Francisco, whites make up 47 percent of the residents, blacks 11 percent, Hispanics 14 percent, and Asians 29 percent. Thus, blacks in New York reflect the kind of critical mass that generally sparks racial prejudices, fears, and conflicts. True, San Francisco's Asian population—three in ten of the city's residents—also form that kind of critical and noticeable mass. But whatever the American prejudice against Asians, and however much it has been

acted out in the past, Asians do not stir the same kind of fear and hatred in white hearts as do blacks.

17. Zoë Baird, the first woman ever to be nominated to be attorney general of the United States, was forced to withdraw when it became known that she and her husband had hired an illegal immigrant as a nanny for their three-year-old child. The public indignation that followed the revelation came largely from people who were furious that, in a time of high unemployment, American workers were bypassed in favor of cheaper foreign labor.

18. This is now beginning to happen in more skilled jobs as well. In California's Silicon Valley, for example, software programmers and others are being displaced by Indian workers, people who are trained in India and recruited to work here because they are willing to do so for lower wages than similarly skilled Americans (*San Francisco Examiner*, February 14, 1993).

19. From Emma Lazarus' "The New Colossus," inscribed at the base of the Statue of Liberty in New York's harbor, the gateway through which most of the immigrants from Europe passed as they came in search of a new life.

33

LA GÜERA

CHERRÍE MORAGA

Race is a creation of culture that reflects social distinctions and power. To say that race is a social construction, however, does not mean that race is not real. Many people believe in the existence of discrete biological racial categories. Sociologists are concerned not only with how race and ethnicity are defined but also with the consequences of those distinctions. The following reading by Cherríe Moraga highlights the individual consequences resulting from the social construction of race. In this narrative, Moraga articulates her personal experience with the ambiguities and resulting inequalities of racial identity. What is particularly insightful in Moraga's discussion is her explicit linkage between racial inequality and other systems of oppression, such as those created by the stratification of social class, gender, and sexual orientation. Thus, racism is interconnected with sexism, classism, and homophobia.

It requires something more than personal experience to gain a philosophy or point of view from any specific event. It is the quality of our response to the event and our capacity to enter into the lives of others that help us to make their lives and experiences our own.

—EMMA GOLDMAN[1]

I am the very well-educated daughter of a woman who, by the standards in this country, would be considered largely illiterate. My mother was born in Santa Paula, Southern California, at a time when much of the central valley there was still farmland. Nearly 35 years later, in 1948, she was the only daughter of six to marry an Anglo, my father.

I remember all of my mother's stories, probably much better than she realizes. She is a fine storyteller, recalling every event of her life with the vividness of the present, noting each detail right down to the cut and color of her dress. I remember stories of her being pulled out of school at the ages of five, seven, nine, and eleven to work in the fields, along with her brothers and sisters; stories of her father drinking away whatever small profit she was able to make for the family; of her going the long way home to avoid meeting him on the street, staggering toward the same destination. I remember stories of my mother lying about her age in order to get a job as a hat-check girl at Agua Caliente Racetrack in Tijuana. At 14, she was the main support of the family. I can still see her walking home alone at 3 A.M., only to turn all of her salary and tips over to her mother, who was pregnant again.

The stories continue through the war years and on: walnut-cracking factories, the Voit Rubber factory, and then the computer boom. I remember my mother doing piecework for the electronics plant in our neighborhood. In the late evening, she would sit in front of the T.V. set, wrapping copper wires into the backs of circuit boards, talking about "keeping up with the younger girls." By that time, she was already in her mid-50s.

Meanwhile, I was college-prep in school. After classes, I would go with my mother to fill out job applications for her, or write checks for her at the supermarket. We would have the scenario all worked out ahead of time. My mother would sign the check before we'd get to the store. Then, as we'd approach the checkstand, she would say—within earshot of the cashier—"oh honey, you go 'head and make out the check," as if she couldn't be bothered with such an insignificant detail. No one asked any questions.

I was educated, and wore it with a keen sense of pride and satisfaction, my head propped up with the knowledge, from my mother, that my life would be easier than hers. I was educated; but more than this, I was "la güera": fair-skinned. Born with the features of my Chicana mother, but the skin of my Anglo father, I had it made.

No one ever quite told me this (that light was right), but I knew that being light was something valued in my family (who were all Chicano, with the exception of my father). In fact, everything about my upbringing (at least what occurred on a conscious level) attempted to bleach me of what color I did have. Although my mother was fluent in it, I was never taught much Spanish at home. I picked up what I did learn from school and from overheard snatches of conversation among my relatives and mother. She often called other lower-income Mexicans "braceros," or "wet-backs," referring to herself and her family as "a different class of people." And yet, the real story was that my family, too, had been poor (some still are) and farmworkers. My mother can remember this in her blood as if it were yesterday. But this is something she would like to forget (and rightfully), for to her, on a basic economic level, being Chicana meant being "less." It was through my mother's desire to protect her children from poverty and illiteracy that we became "anglocized"; the more effectively we could pass in the white world, the better guaranteed our future.

From all of this, I experience, daily, a huge disparity between what I was born into and what I was to grow up to become. Because (as Goldman suggests) these stories my mother told me crept under my "güera" skin. I had no choice but to enter into the life of my mother. *I had no choice.* I took her life into my heart, but managed to keep a lid on it as long as I feigned being the happy, upwardly mobile heterosexual.

When I finally lifted the lid to my lesbianism, a profound connection with my mother reawakened in me. It wasn't until I acknowledged and confronted my own lesbianism in the flesh, that my heartfelt identification with and empathy for my mother's oppression—due to being poor, uneducated, and Chicana—was realized. My lesbianism is the avenue through which I have learned the most about silence and oppression, and it continues to be the most tactile reminder to me that we are not free human beings.

You see, one follows the other. I had known for years that I was a lesbian, had felt it in my bones, had ached with the knowledge, gone crazed with the knowledge, wallowed in the silence of it. Silence *is* like starvation. Don't be fooled. It's nothing short of that, and felt most sharply when one has had a full belly most of her life. When we are not physically starving, we have the luxury to realize psychic and emotional starvation. It is from this starvation that other starvations can be recognized—if one is willing to take the risk of making the connection—if one is willing to be responsible to the result of the connection. For me, the connection is an inevitable one.

What I am saying is that the joys of looking like a white girl ain't so great since I realized I could be beaten on the street for being a dyke. If my sister's being beaten because she's black, it's pretty much the same principle. We're both getting beaten any way you look at it. The connection is blatant; and in the case of my own family, the difference in the privileges attached to looking white instead of brown are merely a generation apart.

In this country, lesbianism is a poverty—as is being brown, as is being a woman, as is being just plain poor. The danger lies in ranking the oppressions. *The danger lies in failing to acknowledge the specificity of the oppression.* The danger lies in attempting to deal with oppression purely from a theoretical base. Without an emotional, heartfelt grappling with the source of our own oppression, without naming the enemy within ourselves and outside of us, no authentic, nonhierarchical connection among oppressed groups can take place.

When the going gets rough, will we abandon our so-called comrades in a flurry of racist/heterosexist/what-have-you panic? To whose camp, then, should the lesbian of color retreat? Her very presence violates the ranking and abstraction of oppression. Do we merely live hand to mouth? Do we merely struggle with the "ism" that's sitting on top of our own heads?

The answer is yes, I think first we do; and we must do so thoroughly and deeply. But to fail to move out from there will only isolate us in our own oppression—will only insulate, rather than radicalize us.

To illustrate: a gay male friend of mine once confided to me that he continued to feel that, on some level, I didn't trust him because he was male; that he felt, really, if it ever came down to a "battle of the sexes," I might kill him. I admitted that I might very well. He wanted to understand the source of my distrust. I responded, "You're not a woman. Be a woman for a day. Imagine being a woman." He confessed that the thought terrified him because, to him, being a woman meant being raped by men. He *had* felt raped by men; he wanted to forget what that meant. What grew from that discussion was the realization that in order for him to create an authentic alliance with me, he must deal with the primary source of his own sense of oppression. He must, first, emotionally come to terms with what it feels like to be a victim. If he—or anyone—were to truly do this, it would be impossible to discount the oppression of others, except by again forgetting how we have been hurt.

And yet, oppressed groups are forgetting all the time. There are instances of this in the rising black middle class, and certainly an obvious trend of such "unconsciousness" among white gay men. Because to remember may mean giving up whatever privileges we have managed to squeeze out of this society by virtue of our gender, race, class, or sexuality.

Within the women's movement, the connections among women of different backgrounds and sexual orientations have been fragile, at best. I think this phenomenon is indicative of our failure to seriously address ourselves to some very frightening questions: How have I internalized my own oppression? How have I oppressed? Instead, we have let rhetoric do the job of poetry. Even the word *oppression* has lost its power. We need a new language, better words that can more closely describe women's fear of and resistance to one another; words that will not always come out sounding like dogma.

What prompted me in the first place to work on an anthology by radical women of color was a deep sense that I had a valuable insight to contribute, by virtue of my birthright and background. And yet, I don't really understand firsthand what it feels like being shitted on for being brown. I understand much more about the joys of it—being Chicana and having family are synonymous for me. What I know about loving, singing, crying, telling stories, speaking with my heart and hands, even having a sense of my own soul comes from the love of my mother, aunts, cousins . . .

But at the age of 27, it is frightening to acknowledge that I have internalized a racism and classism, where the object of oppression is not only someone outside of my skin, but the someone inside my skin. In fact, to a large degree, the real battle with such oppression, for all of us, begins under the skin. I have had to confront the fact that much of what I value about being Chicana, about my family, has been subverted by anglo culture and my own cooperation with it. This realization did not occur to me overnight. For example, it wasn't until long after my graduation from the private college I'd attended in Los Angeles, that I realized the major reason for my total alienation from and fear of my classmates was rooted in class and culture. CLICK.

Three years after graduation, in an apple orchard in Sonoma, a friend of mine (who comes from an Italian Irish working-class family) says to me, "Cherríe, no wonder you felt like such a nut in school. Most of the people there were white and rich." It was true. All along I had felt the difference, but not until I had put the words "class" and "color" to the experience, did my feelings make any sense. For years, I had berated myself for not being as "free" as my classmates. I completely bought that they simply had more guts than I did—to rebel against their parents and run around the country hitchhiking, reading books, and studying "art." They had enough privilege to be atheists, for chrissake. There was no one around filling in the disparity for me between their parents, who were Hollywood filmmakers, and my parents, who wouldn't know the name of a filmmaker if their lives depended on it (and precisely because their lives didn't depend on it, they couldn't be bothered). But I knew nothing about "privilege" then. White was right. Period. I could pass. If I got educated enough, there would never be any telling.

Three years after that, another CLICK. In a letter to Barbara Smith, I wrote:

> I went to a concert where Ntosake Shange was reading. There, everything exploded for me. She was speaking a language that I knew—in the deepest parts of me—existed, and that I had ignored in my own feminist studies and even in my own writing. What Ntosake caught in me is the realization that in my development as a poet, I have, in many ways, denied the voice of my brown mother—the brown in me. I have acclimated to the sound of a white language, which, as my father represents it, does not speak to the emotions in my poems—emotions which stem from the love of my mother.
>
> The reading was agitating. Made me uncomfortable. Threw me into a week-long terror of how deeply I was affected. I felt that I had to start all over again. That I turned only to the perceptions of white middle-class women to speak for me and all women. I am shocked by my own ignorance.

Sitting in that auditorium chair was the first time I had realized to the core of me that for years I had disowned the language I knew best—ignored the words and rhythms that were the closest to me. The sounds of my mother and aunts gossiping—half in English, half in Spanish—while drinking cerveza in the kitchen. And the hands—I had cut off the hands in my poems. But not in conversation; still the hands could not be kept down. Still they insisted on moving.

The reading had forced me to remember that I knew things from my roots. But to remember puts me up against what I don't know. Shange's reading agitated me because she spoke with power about a world that is both alien and common to me: "the capacity to enter into the lives of others." But you can't just take the goods and run. I knew that then, sitting in the Oakland auditorium (as I know in my poetry), that the only thing worth writing about is what seems to be unknown and, therefore, fearful.

The "unknown" is often depicted in racist literature as the "darkness" within a person. Similarly, sexist writers will refer to fear in the form of the vagina, calling it "the orifice of death." In contrast, it is a pleasure to read works such as Maxine Hong Kingston's *Woman Warrior,* where fear and alienation are described as "the white ghosts." And yet, the bulk of literature in this country reinforces the myth that what is dark and female is evil. Consequently, each of us—whether dark, female, or both—has in some way *internalized* this oppressive imagery. What the oppressor often succeeds in doing is simply *externalizing* his fears, projecting them into the bodies of women, Asians, gays, disabled folks, whoever seems most "other."

> call me
> roach and presumptuous
> nightmare on your white pillow
> your itch to destroy
> the indestructible
> part of yourself
>
> —AUDRE LORDE[2]

But it is not really difference the oppressor fears so much as similarity. He fears he will discover in himself the same aches, the same longings as those of the people he has shitted on. He fears the immobilization threatened by his own incipient guilt. He fears he will have to change his life once he has seen himself in the bodies of the people he has called different. He fears the hatred, anger, and vengeance of those he has hurt.

This is the oppressor's nightmare, but it is not exclusive to him. We women have a similar nightmare, for each of us in some way has been both oppressed and the oppressor. We are afraid to look at how we have failed each other. We are afraid to see how we have taken the values of our oppressor into our hearts and turned them against ourselves and one another. We are afraid to admit how deeply "the man's" words have been ingrained in us.

To assess the damage is a dangerous act. I think of how, even as a feminist lesbian, I have so wanted to ignore my own homophobia, my own hatred of myself for being queer. I have not wanted to admit that my deepest personal sense of myself has not quite "caught up" with my "woman-identified" politics. I have been afraid to criticize lesbian writers who choose to "skip over" these issues in the name of feminism. In 1979, we talk of "old gay" and "butch and femme" roles as if they were ancient history. We toss them aside as merely patriarchal notions. And yet, the truth of the matter is that I have sometimes taken society's fear and hatred of lesbians to bed with me. I have sometimes hated my lover for loving me. I have sometimes felt "not woman enough" for her. I have sometimes felt "not man enough." For a lesbian trying to survive in a heterosexist society, there is no easy way around these emotions. Similarly, in a white-dominated world, there is little getting around racism and our own internalization of it. It's always there, embodied in someone we least expect to rub up against.

When we do rub up against this person, *there* then is the challenge. *There* then is the opportunity to look at the nightmare within us. But we usually shrink from such a challenge.

Time and time again, I have observed that the usual response among white women's groups when the "racism issue" comes up is to deny the difference. I have heard comments like, "Well, we're open to *all* women; why don't they (women of color) come? You can only do so much . . ." But there is seldom any analysis of how the very nature and structure of the group itself may be founded on racist or classist assumptions. More importantly, so often the women seem to feel no loss, no lack, no absence when women of color are not involved; therefore, there is little desire to change the situation. This has hurt me deeply. I have come to believe that the only reason women of a privileged class will dare to look at *how* it is that *they* oppress, is when they've come to know the meaning of their own oppression. And understand that the oppression of others hurts them personally.

The other side of the story is that women of color and working-class women often shrink from challenging white middle-class women. It is much easier to rank oppressions and set up a hierarchy, rather than take responsibility for changing our own lives. We have failed to demand that white women, particularly those who claim to be speaking for all women, be accountable for their racism.

The dialogue has simply not gone deep enough.

I have many times questioned my right to even work on an anthology which is to be written "exclusively by Third World women." I have had to look critically at my claim to color, at a time when, among white feminist ranks, it is a "politically correct" (and sometimes peripherally advantageous) assertion to make. I must acknowledge the fact that, physically, I have had a *choice* about making that claim, in contrast to women who have not had such a choice, and have been abused for their color. I must reckon with the fact that for most of my life, by virtue of the very fact that I am white-looking, I identified with and aspired toward white values, and that I rode the wave of that Southern California privilege as far as conscience would let me.

Well, now I feel both bleached and beached. I feel angry about this—the years when I refused to recognize privilege, both when it worked against me, and when I worked it, ignorantly, at the expense of others. These are not settled issues. That is why this work feels so risky to me. It continues to be discovery. It has brought me into contact with women who invariably know a hell of a lot more than I do about racism, as experienced in the flesh, as revealed in the flesh of their writing.

I think: What is my responsibility to my roots—both white and brown, Spanish-speaking and English? I am a woman with a foot in both worlds; and I refuse the split. I feel the necessity for dialogue. Sometimes I feel it urgently.

But one voice is not enough, nor two, although this is where dialogue begins. It is essential that radical feminists confront their fear of and resistance to each other, because without this, there *will* be no bread on the table. Simply, we will not survive. If we could make this connection in our heart of hearts, that if we are serious about a revolution—better—if we seriously believe there should be joy in our lives (real joy, not just "good times"), then we need one another. We women need each other. Because my / your solitary, self-asserting "go-for-the-throat-of-fear" power is not enough. The real power, as you and I well know, is collective. I can't afford to be afraid of you, nor you of me. If it takes head-on collisions, let's do it: This polite timidity is killing us.

As Lorde suggests in the passage I cited earlier, it is in looking to the nightmare that the dream is found. There, the survivor emerges to insist on a future, a vision, yes, born out of what is dark and female. The feminist movement must be a movement of such survivors, a movement with a future.

NOTES

1. Alix Kates Shulman, "Was My Life Worth Living?" *Red Emma Speaks* (New York: Random House, 1972), p. 388.
2. From "The Brown Menace or Poem to the Survival of Roaches," *The New York Head Shop and Museum* (Detroit: Broadside, 1974), p. 48.

34

NAVIGATING PUBLIC PLACES

JOE R. FEAGIN • MELVIN P. SIKES

Racism is any prejudice or discrimination against an individual or a group based on their race, ethnicity, or some other perceived difference. The following reading by Joe R. Feagin and Melvin P. Sikes documents the common and everyday discrimination experienced by middle-class African Americans. Utilizing research based on over 200 interviews, Feagin and Sikes find that their respondents encounter a disturbing and extensive amount of both individual and institutional discrimination. Moreover, Feagin and Sikes report that since discrimination often involves racial stereotyping, verbal harassment, and even the threat or occurrence of violence, the consequences of discrimination on the individual are enormous.

T ITLE II of the most important civil rights act of this century, the 1964 Civil Rights Act, stipulates that "all persons shall be entitled to the full and equal enjoyment of the goods, services, facilities, privileges, advantages, and accommodations of any place of public accommodation . . . without discrimination or segregation on the ground of race, color, religion, or national origin." Yet, as we approach the twenty-first century, this promise of full and equal enjoyment of the public places and accommodations of the United States is far from reality for African Americans.

Not long ago Debbie Allen, a movie star and television producer, recounted a painful experience with discrimination at a Beverly Hills jewelry store. A white clerk, possibly stereotyping Allen as poor or criminal, refused to show her some jewelry. Allen was so incensed that she used the incident as the basis for an episode on a television show. Across the country in Tamarac, Florida, a 20-year-old black man, wearing a Syracuse University cap and hoping to invest his savings, visited a branch of Great Western Bank seeking information. After stopping at other banks, he returned to Great Western, got more information, and then went to his car to review the materials. There he was surrounded by sheriff's deputies with guns drawn, handcuffed, and read his rights. The deputies questioned him for some time before dismissing the report of white bank employees that the black man looked like a bank robber.[1]

Discrimination in Public Accommodations

In this chapter the middle-class respondents challenge us to reflect on their experiences with discrimination as they move into traditionally white public accommodations, such as upscale restaurants and department stores, and through public streets once the territory only of whites. They frequently report that their middle-class resources and status provide little protection against overt discrimination. Although there are, at least in principle, some social restraints on hostile white behavior in public accommodations, African Americans often experience hostility and mistreatment when they venture into spaces where many whites question the presence of a black person.

In the authors' experience many middle-class African Americans can relate several recent stories of being treated poorly by whites in public accommodations officially made hospitable by decades of civil rights laws. In our respondents' accounts restaurants are one site of hostile treatment, as are stores, hotels, and places of amusement. A black minister in a predominantly white denomination described his experience at a restaurant near a southern religious camp:

> We were refused service, because they said they didn't serve black folk. It was suggested that if we stayed there any longer, that there was a possibility that our tires would be slashed. We finally stayed long enough for them to say, "Well, I'll tell you what. We will serve

you something to go, but you cannot come inside. We refuse that."
And it was a situation that—I was not prepared for that. I was angry.
I was humiliated, and I wanted to do something. I wanted to kick
some ass.[2]

Given the threat of violence, he did not respond aggressively to this exclusion, but internalized his anger. Such encounters are not isolated events for many middle-class black Americans. The minister described yet another incident in a southern metropolis:

I was at this place called Joe's restaurant. I had to go into Joe's because I came up in that community. Joe's is a barbecue place that is right by the auto plant, so all of the executives from the plant would come there for lunch. I went there with a guy who was successful. [I] thought I was a decent black person, came in wearing a suit and tie, sat down, and I noticed that, you know, these white boys kept coming in, and the waitress kept on looking over me. And I eventually said to her, "Ma'am, I'd like to order." She said, "Well, you're going to have to wait." And I complained to the owner and he proceeded to cuss me out. Told me that I didn't have "no goddamn business" in that restaurant telling them who they ought to serve and when they ought to serve them. Told me that. I came up in the neighborhood, been eating there for years, and it suddenly dawned on me that white folk will take your money, but to them in their minds you're still a nigger. They're able to separate economics from dealing with relationships between them and black folk. He challenged me to a fight, and this was another source of humiliation. I said to myself, "If I fought this man in his restaurant with there being a hundred white boys that'll substantiate whatever story he told, they could lynch me and say that I hung myself, you know." I left. I've never gone back to that place. But I've always thought about burning it down.

In spite of the 1964 Civil Rights Act black customers today encounter poor service or are refused service. Even with the growth of black economic resources, there seems to be some conflict within many white business owners between taking the dollars blacks can spend and recoiling from dealing with blacks.

In such events the person being rudely treated or ignored is usually quite conscious of the historical context of the interaction, as can be seen in the minister's allusion to lynching. In another account, a black news director at a television station described an incident in which she and her boyfriend responded very differently to an act of discrimination and the anger it provoked in them:

He was waiting to be seated. . . . He said, "You go to the bathroom and I'll get the table. . . ." He was standing there when I came back; he continued to stand there. The restaurant was almost empty. There were waiters, waitresses, and no one seated. And when I got back to him, he was ready to leave, and said, "Let's go." I said, "What happened to our table?" He wasn't seated. So I said, "No, we're not leaving, please." And he said, "No, I'm leaving." So we went outside, and we talked about it. And what I said to him was, you have to be aware of the possibilities that this is not the first time that this has happened at this restaurant or at other restaurants, but this is the first time it has happened to a black news director here or someone who could make an issue of it, or someone who is prepared to make an issue of it.

So we went back inside after I talked him into it and, to make a long story short, I had the manager come. I made most of the people who were there (while conducting myself professionally the whole time) aware that I was incensed at being treated this way. . . . I said, "Why do you think we weren't seated?" And the manager said, "Well, I don't really know." And I said, "Guess." He said, "Well, I don't know, because you're black?" I said, "Bingo. Now isn't it funny that you didn't guess that I didn't have any money (and I opened up my purse and I said, because I certainly have money). And isn't it odd that you didn't guess that it's because I couldn't pay for it because I've got two American Express cards and a Master Card right here. I think it's just funny that you would have assumed that it's because I'm black." . . . And then I took out my [business] card and gave it to him and said, "If this happens again, or if I hear of this happening again, I will bring the full wrath of an entire news department down on this restaurant." And he just kind of looked at me. "Not [just] because I am personally offended. I am. But because you have no right to do what you did, and as a people we have lived a long time with having our rights abridged."

There were probably three or four sets of diners in the restaurant and maybe five waiters/waitresses. They watched him [her boyfriend] standing there waiting to be seated. His reaction to it was that he wanted to leave. I understood why he would have reacted that way, because he felt that he was in no condition to be civil. He was ready to take the place apart and . . . sometimes it's appropriate to behave that way. We hadn't gone the first step before going on to the next step. He didn't feel that he could comfortably and calmly take the first step, and I did. So I just asked him to please get back in the restaurant with me, and then you don't have to say a word, and let me handle it from there. It took some convincing, but I had to appeal to his sense of, this is not just you, this is not just for you. We are finally in a position as black people where there are some of us who can genuinely get their attention. And if they don't want to do this because it's right for them to do it, then they'd better do it because they're afraid to do otherwise. If it's fear, then fine, instill the fear.

Discrimination here was not the "No Negroes" exclusion of the recent past, but rejection in the form of poor service. Again a black person's skin color took precedence over money. The black response has changed too, since the 1950s and 1960s, from deference to indignant, vigorous confrontation. Here the assertive black response and the white backtracking are typical of "negotiation" that can occur in racial confrontations today.

In recounting this incident this black professional mentions black "rights" several times. Clearly imbedded in her response is a theory of rights that she, like many African Americans, holds as a part of her worldview. Her response signals the impact of the tradition of civil rights struggle, and civil rights laws, on the life perspective of African Americans. Also of interest here is her mention of her credit cards and other middle-class resources. A quick reading of her statement, and that of other black middle-class people who mention similar trappings of success, might lead to the conclusion that middle-class blacks expect to be treated better than poorer blacks because they have worked hard and have money. But this does not seem to be the meaning of such references. Instead, this woman is outraged that the obvious evidence of hard work and achievements does not protect her from racial discrimination. She has achieved certain elements of the American dream, but they are not sufficient.

A close look at the experience of middle-class African Americans is important to understand the racial backwardness of contemporary U.S. society, for it confirms that no amount of hard work, money, and success can protect a black person from the destructive impact of racial stereotyping and discrimination. In this [article] we show that middle-class black Americans, just like other black Americans, have terrible experiences with everyday racism. But we show much more than that. We also demonstrate that racial stereotyping and discrimination operate independently of the real identities and achievements of specifically targeted black individuals.

The ability of middle-class African Americans to act forcefully against discrimination by whites marks a change from a few decades ago when very few had the resources to fight back successfully. Black Americans have always fought against discrimination, but in earlier decades such fights were usually doomed to failure if not injury. In this account, the woman's ability as a professional to bring a television news team to the restaurant enabled her to take assertive action. This example also underscores the complexity of the interaction in some situations of discrimination, for not only is there a confrontation with a white manager over mistreatment but also a negotiation between the black individuals over how to respond.

It is an effective antidiscrimination strategy on the part of black Americans to make the confrontations public. An executive at a financial institution in an East Coast city recounted his experience with a pattern of poor service in a restaurant, explaining his decision to confront the discriminators:

> I took the staff here to a restaurant that had recently opened in the prestigious section of the city, and we waited while other people got waited on, and decided that after about a half hour that these people don't want to wait on us. I happened to have been in the same

restaurant a couple of evenings earlier, and it took them about 45 minutes before they came to wait on me and my guest. So, on the second incident, I said, this is not an isolated incident, this is a pattern, because I had spoken with some other people who had not been warmly received in the restaurant. So, I wrote a letter to the owners . . . and sent copies to the city papers. That's my way of expressing myself and letting the world know. You have to let people, other than you and the owner know. You have to let others know you're expressing your dismay at the discrimination or the barrier that's presented to you. I met with the owners. Of course, they wanted to meet with their attorneys with me, because they wanted to sue me. I told them they're welcome to do so. I don't have a thing, but fine they can do it. It just happens that I knew their white attorney. And he more or less vouched that if I had some concern that it must have been legitimate in some form. When the principals came in, one of the people who didn't wait on me was one of the owners who happened to be waiting on everybody else. We resolved the issue by them inviting me to come again, and if I was fairly treated, or if I would come on several occasions and if I was fairly treated I would write a statement of retraction. I told them I would not write a retraction, I would write a statement with regard to how I was treated. Which I ultimately did. And I still go there today, and they speak to me, and I think the pattern is changed to a great degree.

The time- and energy-consuming aspects of publicly confronting discrimination are apparent in this account. The respondent invested much of himself in a considered response to a recurring problem. Forcing whites to renegotiate, especially by using negative publicity, can bring about changes. The arrival on the restaurant scene of middle-class black Americans with substantial resources has at least created situations that force whites into explicit negotiating.

Whites often enter into this "bargaining" situation with tacit assumptions and cultural expectations about black powerlessness. In the two previous examples we see the black professionals establishing "power credibility," as the whites decide that they are not bluffing. It is important to note that the whites here are not just the blue-collar whites often said to be the primary source of whatever bigotry remains in the United States. Those doing the discrimination include middle-class whites, a fact that signals the importance of race over class in much racial interaction.

That discrimination against black customers and employees in white-owned restaurants is widespread has become evident in several court suits filed since 1990 against national chains, including Denny's, Shoney's, and the International House of Pancakes (IHOP). In December 1991, for example, several groups of black college students were reportedly turned away from a Milwaukee IHOP restaurant and told that it was closed, while white customers were allowed in. In 1993 a federal judge ordered the restaurant to pay a settlement for the discrimination. Also in 1993, the Denny's chain, found to have a pattern of discrimination by the U.S. Justice Department, reached an agreement with the Department in which executives promised to train employees in nondiscriminatory behavior and to include more minorities in its advertising. This settlement did not affect a class-action discrimination suit by 32 black customers who reportedly had suffered discrimination in several Denny's restaurants in California. Moreover, in mid-1993 six black secret service agents also sued the chain, alleging discrimination at a Denny's in Annapolis, Maryland. The black agents reported that while they waited for service for nearly an hour, white agents and other white patrons were promptly served.[3] After much bad publicity, Denny's joined in an important agreement with the NAACP to work to end discrimination in its restaurants.[4]

As revealed in the court cases, restaurant discrimination has recently included long waits while whites are served, special cover fees applied only to blacks, and prepayment requirements only for black customers.[5] In the Shoney's case, the chain was sued over discrimination against black employees. According to the *St. Petersburg Times,* top officers in the white-run firm were well known for their antiblack views, and local managers were discouraged from hiring black employees. In a 1992 landmark agreement the company agreed to pay $115 million, the most ever, to employees who could prove racial discrimination.[6]

Restaurants are only one site of discrimination. Daily life inevitably involves contact with clerks and managers in various retail and grocery stores. A utility company executive in an eastern city described how her family was treated in a small store:

> I can remember one time my husband had picked up our son . . .
> from camp; and he'd stopped at a little store in the neighborhood
> near the camp. It was hot, and he was going to buy him a snowball.
> . . . This was a very old, white neighborhood, and it was just a little
> sundry store. But the proprietor had a little window where people
> could come up and order things. Well, my husband and son had
> gone into the store. And he told them, "Well, I can't give it to you
> here, but if you go outside to the window, I'll give it to you." And
> there were other people in the store who'd been served [inside]. So,
> they just left and didn't buy anything.

The old white neighborhood in which this episode occurred exemplifies the racial-territorial character of many cities even today. The poor service here seems a throwback to the South of the 1950s, where deferential blacks were served only at the back of a store. This man chose not to confront the white person nor to acquiesce abjectly but rather to leave. Here the effect on the white man was probably inconsequential because there was no confrontation and interracial negotiation. The long-run importance of a service site may well affect a black person's choice of how to respond to such discrimination. The store in this example was not important to the black family just passing through the area. The possibility of returning might have generated a more confrontational response.

Another problem that black shoppers face, especially in department and grocery stores, is the common white assumption that they are likely shoplifters. This is true in spite of the fact that national crime statistics show that most shoplifters are white. For several months in late 1991 a news team at KSTP-TV in Minneapolis conducted a field study of discrimination against black shoppers in several local department stores. Members of the team took jobs as security personnel in the stores, and black and white shoppers were sent into the stores in order to observe the reactions of white security personnel. The ensuing television report, "Who's Minding the Store?" showed how many black customers became the targets of intensive surveillance from white security guards, who neglected white shoppers when black shoppers were in the stores. As a result of the documentary, local black leaders called for a boycott of one of the store chains. Soon a number of the local stores changed their surveillance and security procedures.[7] Excessive surveillance of black customers in department and other stores was reported by some we interviewed. A black professional in the North commented on how she deals with whites who harass her with excessive surveillance and other acts of rejection:

> [I have faced] harassment in stores, being followed around, being questioned about what are you going to purchase here. . . . I was in an elite department store just this past Saturday and felt that I was being observed while I was window shopping. I in fact actually ended up purchasing something, but felt the entire time I was there—I was in blue jeans and sneakers, that's how I dress on a Saturday—I felt that I was being watched in the store as I was walking through the store—what business did I have there, what was I going to purchase, that kind of thing. . . . There are a few of those white people that won't put change in your hand, touch your skin. That doesn't need to go on. [Do you tell them that?] Oh, I do, I do. That is just so obvious. I usually [speak to them] if they're rude in the manner in which they deal with people. [What do they say about that?] Oh, stuff like, "Oh, excuse me," and some who are really unconscious about it, say "Excuse me," and put the change in your hand. That's happened. But I've watched other people be rude, and I've been told to mind my own business. [But you still do it?] Oh, sure, because for the most part I think that people do have to learn to think for themselves, and demand respect for themselves. . . . I find my best weapon of defense is to educate them, whether it's in the store, in a line, at the bank, any situation, I teach them. And you take them

by surprise because you tell them and show them what they should be doing, and what they should be saying, and how they should be thinking. And they look at you because they don't know how to process you. They can't process it because you've just shown them how they should be living, and the fact that they are cheating themselves, really, because the racism is from fear. The racism is from lack of education.

A number of racial stereotypes are evident in this account. Whites with images of black criminality engage in excessive surveillance, and whites with images of black dirtiness will not touch black hands or skin. Black shoppers at all income levels report being ignored when in need of service and the unwillingness of some whites even to touch their hands. Why such a reaction to black bodies? In a speculative Freudian analysis of white racism, Joel Kovel has argued that for centuries whites have irrationally connected blackness, and black bodies, with fecal matter and dirt. In his view, whites are somehow projecting onto the darkness of the black outgroup personal inclinations, desires, and fears that cannot be openly and honestly acknowledged.[8]

A common black response to contemporary discrimination is evident here. Rather than withdrawing when facing such discrimination, this professional sometimes protracts the interaction with verbal confrontation. She notes the surprise effect of calling whites on the carpet for discrimination, which she sees as grounded in fear and ignorance. Interrupting the normal flow of an interaction to change a one-way experience into a two-way experience forces whites into unaccustomed situations in which they are unsure how to respond.

Middle-class African Americans enter many settings where few blacks have been before. A news anchorperson for an East Coast television station reported on an incident at a luxury automobile dealer:

I knew I wanted to buy a Porsche, but I didn't know which model. So, on my day off, I went into a Porsche dealership in the city I used to work in. . . . And I was dressed like I normally do when I'm off. I'm into working out a lot, so I'm in sweatsuits, baseball caps, sunglasses quite a bit. So I dashed into this place dressed like that, and I must have walked around the show room floor for 20 minutes. No salesperson ever walked up to me and asked me, "Can I help you? Can I give you some information?" Nothing. I got the impression, the opinion, that they generally thought that this person, being black, being dressed in a sweatsuit, cannot hardly afford to be in here buying a Porsche. He's wasting my time, so I'm not even going to bother. And I knew that. So I specifically, the next day on my lunch hour, dressed in my work clothes, having just come off the air, I walked into that showroom. And I said, "Can I see the general manager?" And they got the general manager for me. And I said to the general

manager, "I was in here yesterday." Well, I said, "First of all, I want
to buy that Porsche there, the most expensive one on the floor." And
I also told him, "Just yesterday I was in here, I was looking in, and I
was hoping I could get some information, and oddly none of your
sales people ever asked me if they could help me." . . . And there is
prejudice, discrimination and racism, and things like that go on.
Once they found out who I was, they bent over backward [to wait
on me].

White salespeople apparently took the cue from this man's color and clothing and stereotyped him as moneyless, an assumption that the victim challenged the next day when he engaged in an unexpected confrontation. This
chronic mistreatment by white salespeople, while white shoppers are generally treated with greater respect, is infuriating for black customers. It is clear
from our interviews that African Americans must prepare themselves for
this sort of encounter, for they never know when they will be shown normal
respect and courtesy as customers or when they must "front" (dress in a certain way, talk in a certain way) in order to receive the treatment accorded a
comparable white customer.

Among several respondents who discussed discrimination at retail
stores, the manager of a career development organization, who found that
discrimination by clerks is common, had a repertoire of responses for dealing with it:

If you're in a store—and let's say the person behind the counter is
white—and you walk up to the counter, and a white person walks
up to the counter, and you know you were there before the white
customer, the person behind the counter knows you were there first,
and it never fails, they always go, "Who's next." Ok. And what I've
done, if they go ahead and serve the white person first, then I will
immediately say, "Excuse me, I was here first, and we both know I
was here first." . . . If they get away with it once, they're going to get
away with it more than once, and then it's going to become something else. And you want to make sure that folks know that you're
not being naive, that you really see through what's happening. Or if
it's a job opportunity or something like that, too, same thing. You
first try to get a clear assessment of what's really going on and sift
through that information, and then . . . go from there.

In discussions with middle-class black Americans across the nation, both our
respondents and a variety of informants and journalists, we heard many
similar accounts of white clerks "looking through" black customers and only
"seeing" whites farther back in line. Such incidents suggest that much of the
hostility manifest in white actions is based on a deep-lying, perhaps even
subconscious or half-conscious, aversion to black color and persona. This executive also spoke of her coping process, one that begins with sifting infor-

mation before deciding on action. Frequently choosing immediate action, she forces whites to face the reality of their behavior.

The dean of a black college who travels in various parts of the United States described the often complex process of evaluating and responding to the mistreatment that has plagued him in public accommodations:

> When you're in a restaurant and . . . you notice that blacks get seated near the kitchen. You notice that if it's a hotel, your room is near the elevator, or your room is always way down in a corner somewhere. You find that you are getting the undesirable rooms. And you come there early in the day and you don't see very many cars on the lot and they'll tell you that this is all we've got. Or you get the room that's got a bad television set. You know that you're being discriminated against. And of course you have to act accordingly. You have to tell them, "Okay, the room is fine, [but] this television set has got to go. Bring me another television set." So in my personal experience, I simply cannot sit and let them get away with it and not let them know that I know that that's what they are doing. . . .
>
> When I face discrimination, first I take a long look at myself and try to determine whether or not I am seeing what I think I'm seeing in 1989, and if it's something that I have an option [about]. In other words, if I'm at a store making a purchase, I'll simply walk away from it. If it's at a restaurant where I'm not getting good service, I first of all let the people know that I'm not getting good service, then I [may] walk away from it. But the thing that I have to do is to let people know that I know that I'm being singled out for separate treatment. And then I might react in any number of ways—depending on where I am and how badly I want whatever it is that I'm there for.

These recurring incidents in public accommodations illustrate the cumulative nature of discrimination. The dean first takes care to assess the incident and avoid jumping to conclusions. One must be constantly prepared on everyday excursions to assess accurately what is happening and then to decide on an appropriate response. What is less obvious here is the degree of pain and emotional drain that such a constant defensive stance involves.

NOTES

1. Lena Williams, "When Blacks Shop, Bias often Accompanies a Sale," *New York Times,* April 30, 1991, pp. A1, A9.
2. Names and places in interview quotes have been disguised or eliminated to protect anonymity. Some quotes have been lightly edited for grammar and to delete excessive pause phrases like "you know" and "uh."
3. National Public Radio, "Weekend Edition," May 29, 1993.
4. Associated Press, "Denny's to Monitor Treatment of Blacks," *Gainesville Sun,* May 30, 1993, p. 7A.

5. Judy Pasternak, "Service Still Skin Deep for Blacks," *Los Angeles Times*, April 1, 1993, p. A1.
6. Martin Dyckman, "Lawyers Can Be Heroes Too," *St. Petersburg Times*, April 11, 1993, p. 3D.
7. Bill McAuliffe, "Black Leaders Call for Boycott of Local Carsons Stores," *Star Tribune*, December 10, 1991, p. 1B.
8. Joel Kovel, *White Racism*, rev. ed. (New York: Columbia University Press, 1984).

PART VII
Social Institutions

35

THE POWER ELITE

C. WRIGHT MILLS

Who really governs in the United States? In this selection, C. Wright Mills argues that the most important decisions in this country are made by a cohesive "power elite." This power elite consists of the top leaders in three areas: The corporate elite is made up of the executives from large companies; the military elite is the senior officers; and the small political elite includes the president and top officials in the executive and legislative branches. According to Mills' argument, this group of elite officials all know each other and act in unison when critical decisions must be made. This selection is the first of four addressing power and politics.

The powers of ordinary men are circumscribed by the everyday worlds in which they live, yet even in these rounds of job, family, and neighborhood they often seem driven by forces they can neither understand nor govern. "Great changes" are beyond their control, but affect their conduct and outlook nonetheless. The very framework of modern society confines them to projects not their own, but from every side, such changes now press upon the men and women of the mass society, who accordingly feel that they are without purpose in an epoch in which they are without power.

But not all men are in this sense ordinary. As the means of information and of power are centralized, some men come to occupy positions in American society from which they can look down upon, so to speak, and by their decisions mightily affect, the everyday worlds of ordinary men and women. They are not made by their jobs; they set up and break down jobs for thousands of others; they are not confined by simple family responsibilities; they can escape. They may live in many hotels and houses, but they are bound by no one community. They need not merely "meet the demands of the day and hour"; in some part, they create these demands, and cause others to meet them. Whether or not they profess their power, their technical and political experience of it far transcends that of the underlying population. What Jacob

357

Burckhardt said of "great men," most Americans might well say of their elite: "They are all that we are not."

The power elite is composed of men whose positions enable them to transcend the ordinary environments of ordinary men and women; they are in positions to make decisions having major consequences. Whether they do or do not make such decisions is less important than the fact that they do occupy such pivotal positions: Their failure to act, their failure to make decisions, is itself an act that is often of greater consequence than the decisions they do make. For they are in command of the major hierarchies and organizations of modern society. They rule the big corporations. They run the machinery of the state and claim its prerogatives. They direct the military establishment. They occupy the strategic command posts of the social structure, in which are now centered the effective means of the power and the wealth and the celebrity which they enjoy.

The power elite are not solitary rulers. Advisers and consultants, spokesmen and opinion makers are often the captains of their higher thought and decision. Immediately below the elite are the professional politicians of the middle levels of power, in the Congress and in the pressure groups, as well as among the new and old upper classes of town and city and region. Mingling with them, in curious ways which we shall explore, are those professional celebrities who live by being continually displayed but are never, so long as they remain celebrities, displayed enough. If such celebrities are not at the head of any dominating hierarchy, they do often have the power to distract the attention of the public or afford sensations to the masses, or, more directly, to gain the ear of those who do occupy positions of direct power. More or less unattached, as critics of morality and technicians of power, as spokesmen of God and creators of mass sensibility, such celebrities and consultants are part of the immediate scene in which the drama of the elite is enacted. But that drama itself is centered in the command posts of the major institutional hierarchies.

The truth about the nature and the power of the elite is not some secret which men of affairs know but will not tell. Such men hold quite various theories about their own roles in the sequence of event and decision. Often they are uncertain about their roles, and even more often they allow their fears and their hopes to affect their assessment of their own power. No matter how great their actual power, they tend to be less acutely aware of it than of the resistances of others to its use. Moreover, most American men of affairs have learned well the rhetoric of public relations, in some cases even to the point of using it when they are alone, and thus coming to believe it. The personal awareness of the actors is only one of the several sources one must examine in order to understand the higher circles. Yet many who believe that there is no elite, or at any rate none of any consequence, rest their argument upon what men of affairs believe about themselves, or at least assert in public.

There is, however, another view: Those who feel, even if vaguely, that a compact and powerful elite of great importance does now prevail in America often base that feeling upon the historical trend of our time. They have felt, for example, the domination of the military event, and from this they infer that generals and admirals, as well as other men of decision influenced by them, must be enormously powerful. They hear that the Congress has again abdicated to a handful of men decisions clearly related to the issue of war or peace. They know that the bomb was dropped over Japan in the name of the United States of America, although they were at no time consulted about the matter. They feel that they live in a time of big decisions; they know that they are not making any. Accordingly, as they consider the present as history, they infer that at its center, making decisions or failing to make them, there must be an elite of power.

On the one hand, those who share this feeling about big historical events assume that there is an elite and that its power is great. On the other hand, those who listen carefully to the reports of men apparently involved in the great decisions often do not believe that there is an elite whose powers are of decisive consequence.

Both views must be taken into account, but neither is adequate. The way to understand the power of the American elite lies neither solely in recognizing the historic scale of events nor in accepting the personal awareness reported by men of apparent decision. Behind such men and behind the events of history, linking the two, are the major institutions of modern society. These hierarchies of state and corporation and army constitute the means of power; as such they are now of a consequence not before equaled in human history—and at their summits, there are now those command posts of modern society which offer us the sociological key to an understanding of the role of the higher circles in America.

Within American society, major national power now resides in the economic, the political, and the military domains. Other institutions seem off to the side of modern history, and, on occasion, duly subordinated to these. No family is as directly powerful in national affairs as any major corporation; no church is as directly powerful in the external biographies of young men in America today as the military establishment; no college is as powerful in the shaping of momentous events as the National Security Council. Religious, educational, and family institutions are not autonomous centers of national power; on the contrary, these decentralized areas are increasingly shaped by the big three, in which developments of decisive and immediate consequence now occur.

Families and churches and schools adapt to modern life; governments and armies and corporations shape it; and, as they do so, they turn these lesser institutions into means for their ends. Religious institutions provide chaplains to the armed forces where they are used as a means of increasing the effectiveness of its morale to kill. Schools select and train men for their jobs in corporations and their specialized tasks in the armed forces. The extended family has, of course, long been broken up by the industrial revolution, and now the son and the father are removed from the family, by compulsion if need be, whenever the army of the state sends out the call. And the symbols of all these lesser institutions are used to legitimate the power and the decisions of the big three.

The life-fate of the modern individual depends not only upon the family into which he was born or which he enters by marriage, but increasingly upon the corporation in which he spends the most alert hours of his best years; not only upon the school where he is educated as a child and adolescent, but also upon the state which touches him throughout his life; not only upon the church in which on occasion he hears the word of God, but also upon the army in which he is disciplined.

If the centralized state could not rely upon the inculcation of nationalist loyalties in public and private schools, its leaders would promptly seek to modify the decentralized educational system. If the bankruptcy rate among the top 500 corporations were as high as the general divorce rate among the 37 million married couples, there would be economic catastrophe on an international scale. If members of armies gave to them no more of their lives than do believers to the churches to which they belong, there would be a military crisis.

Within each of the big three, the typical institutional unit has become enlarged, has become administrative, and, in the power of its decisions, has become centralized. Behind these developments there is a fabulous technology, for as institutions, they have incorporated this technology and guide it, even as it shapes and paces their developments.

The economy—once a great scatter of small productive units in autonomous balance—has become dominated by two or three hundred giant corporations, administratively and politically interrelated, which together hold the keys to economic decisions.

The political order, once a decentralized set of several dozen states with a weak spinal cord, has become a centralized, executive establishment which has taken up into itself many powers previously scattered, and now enters into each and every cranny of the social structure.

The military order, once a slim establishment in a context of distrust fed by state militia, has become the largest and most expensive feature of government, and, although well-versed in smiling public relations, now has all the grim and clumsy efficiency of a sprawling bureaucratic domain.

In each of these institutional areas, the means of power at the disposal of decision makers have increased enormously; their central executive powers have been enhanced; within each of them modern administrative routines have been elaborated and tightened up.

As each of these domains becomes enlarged and centralized, the consequences of its activities become greater, and its traffic with the others increases. The decisions of a handful of corporations bear upon military and political as well as upon economic developments around the world. The decisions of the military establishment rest upon and grievously affect political life as well as the very level of economic activity. The decisions made within the political domain determine economic activities and military programs. There is no longer, on the one hand, an economy, and, on the other hand, a political order containing a military establishment unimportant to politics and to money making. There is a political economy linked, in a thousand ways, with military institutions and decisions. On each side of the world-split running through central Europe and around the Asiatic rimlands, there is an ever-increasing interlocking of economic, military, and political structures. If there is government intervention in the corporate economy, so is there corporate intervention in the governmental process. In the structural sense, this triangle of power is the source of the interlocking directorate that is most important for the historical structure of the present.

The fact of the interlocking is clearly revealed at each of the points of crisis of modern capitalist society—slump, war, and boom. In each, men of decision are led to an awareness of the interdependence of the major institutional orders. In the nineteenth century, when the scale of all institutions was smaller, their liberal integration was achieved in the automatic economy, by an autonomous play of market forces, and in the automatic political domain, by the bargain and the vote. It was then assumed that out of the imbalance and friction that followed the limited decisions then possible a new equilibrium would in due course emerge. That can no longer be assumed, and it is not assumed by the men at the top of each of the three dominant hierarchies.

For given the scope of their consequences, decisions—and indecisions—in any one of these ramify into the others, and hence top decisions tend either to become coordinated or to lead to a commanding indecision. It has not always been like this. When numerous small entrepreneurs made up the economy, for example, many of them could fail and the consequences still remain local; political and military authorities did not intervene. But now, given political expectations and military commitments, can they afford to allow key units of the private corporate economy to break down in slump? Increasingly, they do intervene in economic affairs, and as they do so, the controlling decisions in each order are inspected by agents of the other two, and economic, military, and political structures are interlocked.

At the pinnacle of each of the three enlarged and centralized domains, there have arisen those higher circles which make up the economic, the political, and the military elites. At the top of the economy, among the corporate rich, there are the chief executives; at the top of the political order, the members of the political directorate; at the top of the military establishment, the elite of soldier-statesmen clustered in and around the Joint Chiefs of Staff and the upper echelon. As each of these domains has coincided with the others, as decisions tend to become total in their consequence, the leading men in each of the three domains of power—the warlords, the corporation chieftains, the political directorate—tend to come together, to form the power elite of America.

The higher circles in and around these command posts are often thought of in terms of what their members possess: They have a greater share than other people of the things and experiences that are most highly valued. From this point of view, the elite are simply those who have the most of what there is to have, which is generally held to include money, power, and prestige—as well as all the ways of life to which these lead. But the elite are not simply those who have the most, for they could not "have the most" were it not for their positions in the great institutions. For such institutions are the necessary bases of power, of wealth, and of prestige, and at the same time, the chief means of exercising power, of acquiring and retaining wealth, and of cashing in the higher claims for prestige.

By the powerful we mean, of course, those who are able to realize their will, even if others resist it. No one, accordingly, can be truly powerful unless he has access to the command of major institutions, for it is over these institutional means of power that the truly powerful are, in the first instance, powerful. Higher politicians and key officials of government command such institutional power; so do admirals and generals, and so do the major owners and executives of the larger corporations. Not all power, it is true, is anchored in and exercised by means of such institutions, but only within and through them can power be more or less continuous and important.

Wealth also is acquired and held in and through institutions. The pyramid of wealth cannot be understood merely in terms of the very rich; for the great inheriting families, as we shall see, are now supplemented by the corporate institutions of modern society: Every one of the very rich families has been and is closely connected—always legally and frequently managerially as well—with one of the multimillion-dollar corporations.

The modern corporation is the prime source of wealth, but, in latter-day capitalism, the political apparatus also opens and closes many avenues to wealth. The amount as well as the source of income, the power over consumer's goods as well as over productive capital, are determined by position within the political economy. If our interest in the very rich goes beyond their lavish or their miserly consumption, we must examine their relations to modern forms of corporate property as well as to the state; for such relations now determine the chances of men to secure big property and to receive high income.

Great prestige increasingly follows the major institutional units of the social structure. It is obvious that prestige depends, often quite decisively, upon access to the publicity machines that are now a central and normal feature of all the big institutions of modern America. Moreover, one feature of these hierarchies of corporation, state, and military establishment is that their top positions are increasingly interchangeable. One result of this is the accumulative nature of prestige. Claims for prestige, for example, may be initially based on military roles, then expressed in and augmented by an educational institution run by corporate executives, and cashed in, finally, in the political order, where, for General Eisenhower and those he represents, power and prestige finally meet at the very peak. Like wealth and power, prestige tends to be cumulative: The more of it you have, the more you can get. These values also tend to be translatable into one another: The wealthy find it easier than the poor to gain power; those with status find it easier than those without it to control opportunities for wealth.

If we took the one hundred most powerful men in America, the one hundred wealthiest, and the one hundred most celebrated away from the institutional positions they now occupy, away from their resources of men and women and money, away from the media of mass communication that are now focused upon them—then they would be powerless and poor and uncelebrated. For power is not of a man. Wealth does not center in the person of the wealthy. Celebrity is not inherent in any personality. To be celebrated, to be wealthy, to have power requires access to major institutions, for the institutional positions men occupy determine in large part their chances to have and to hold these valued experiences.

The people of the higher circles may also be conceived as members of a top social stratum, as a set of groups whose members know one another, see one another socially and at business, and so, in making decisions, take one another into account. The elite, according to this conception, feel themselves to be, and are felt by others to be, the inner circle of "the upper social classes." They form a more or less compact social and psychological entity; they have become self-conscious members of a social class. People are either accepted into this class or they are not, and there is a qualitative split, rather than merely a numerical scale, separating them from those who are not elite. They are more or less aware of themselves as a social class and they behave toward one another differently from the way they do toward members of other classes. They accept one another, understand one another, marry one another, tend to work and to think if not together at least alike.

Now, we do not want by our definition to prejudge whether the elite of the command posts are conscious members of such a socially recognized class, or whether considerable proportions of the elite derive from such a clear and distinct class. These are matters to be investigated. Yet in order to be able to recognize what we intend to investigate, we must note something that all biographies and memoirs of the wealthy and the powerful and the eminent make clear: No matter what else they may be, the people of these higher circles are involved in a set of overlapping "crowds" and intricately connected "cliques." There is a kind of mutual attraction among those who "sit on the same terrace"—although this often becomes clear to them, as well as to others, only at the point at which they feel the need to draw the line; only when, in their common defense, they come to understand what they have in common, and so close their ranks against outsiders.

The idea of such ruling stratum implies that most of its members have similar social origins, that throughout their lives they maintain a network of informal connections, and that to some degree there is an interchangeability of position between the various hierarchies of money and power and celebrity. We must, of course, note at once that if such an elite stratum does exist, its social visibility and its form, for very solid historical reasons, are quite different from those of the noble cousinhoods that once ruled various European nations.

That American society has never passed through a feudal epoch is of decisive importance to the nature of the American elite, as well as to American society as a historic whole. For it means that no nobility or aristocracy, established before the capitalist era, has stood in tense opposition to the higher bourgeoisie. It means that this bourgeoisie has monopolized not only wealth but prestige and power as well. It means that no set of noble families has commanded the top positions and monopolized the values that are generally held in high esteem; and certainly that no set has done so explicitly by inherited right. It means that no high church dignitaries or court nobilities, no entrenched landlords with honorific accouterments, no monopolists of high army posts have opposed the enriched bourgeoisie and in the name of birth and prerogative successfully resisted its self-making.

But this does *not* mean that there are no upper strata in the United States. That they emerged from a "middle class" that had no recognized aristocratic superiors does not mean they remained middle class when enormous increases in wealth made their own superiority possible. Their origins and their newness may have made the upper strata less visible in America than elsewhere. But in America today there are in fact tiers and ranges of wealth and power of which people in the middle and lower ranks know very little and may not even dream. There are families who, in their well-being, are quite insulated from the economic jolts and lurches felt by the merely prosperous and those farther down the scale. There are also men of power who in quite small groups make decisions of enormous consequence for the underlying population.

36

MONEY TALKS
Corporate PACs and Political Influence

DAN CLAWSON • ALAN NEUSTADTL • DENISE SCOTT

Sociological research supports the thesis that a power elite exists in this country. A point of debate is the degree of interconnection among the three groups—the corporate, military, and political elites. Nonetheless, current social research still indicates that power is concentrated among a few social groups and institutions, as shown in a recent study discussed in this selection by Dan Clawson, Alan Neustadtl, and Denise Scott. After investigating 309 corporate political action committees (PACs), the authors conclude that PACs, which represent corporate interests, ensure that the concerns of Big Business are heard on Capitol Hill.

Ⅰn the past 20 years, political action committees, or PACs, have transformed campaign finance. The chair of the PAC at one of the 25 largest manufacturing companies in the United States explained to us why his corporation has a PAC:

> The PAC gives you access. It makes you a player. These congressmen, in particular, are constantly fundraising. Their elections are very expensive and getting increasingly expensive each year. So they have an on-going need for funds.
>
> It profits us in a sense to be able to provide some funds because in the provision of it you get to know people, you help them out. There's no real quid pro quo. There is nobody whose vote you can count on, not with the kind of money we are talking about here. But the PAC gives you access, puts you in the game.
>
> You know, some congressman has got X number of ergs of energy, and here's a person or a company who wants to come see him and give him a thousand dollars, and here's another one who wants to just stop by and say hello. And he only has time to see one. Which one? So the PAC's an attention getter.

Most analyses of campaign finance focus on the candidates who receive the money, not on the people and political action committees that give it. PACs are entities that collect money from many contributors, pool it, and then make donations to candidates. Donors may give to a PAC because they are in basic agreement with its aims, but once they have donated they lose direct control over their money, trusting the PAC to decide which candidates should receive contributions.

Corporate PACs have unusual power that has been largely unexamined. In this [reading] we begin the process of giving corporate PACs, and business–government relations in general, the scrutiny they deserve. By far the most important source for our analysis is a set of in-depth interviews we conducted with corporate executives who direct and control their corporations' political activity. The insight these interviews provide into the way corporate executives think, the goals they pursue, and the methods they use to achieve those goals is far more revealing than most analyses made by outside critics. We think most readers will be troubled, as we are, by the worldview and activities of corporate PAC directors. . . .

Why Does the Air Stink?

Everybody wants clean air. Who could oppose it? "I spent seven years of my life trying to stop the Clean Air Act," explained the PAC director for a major corporation that is a heavy-duty polluter. Nonetheless, he was perfectly willing to use his corporation's PAC to contribute to members of Congress who voted for the act:

> How a person votes on the final piece of legislation often is not representative of what they have done. Somebody will do a lot of things during the process. How many guys voted against the Clean Air Act? But during the process some of them were very sympathetic to some of our concerns.

In the world of Congress and political action committees things are not always what they seem. Members of Congress want to vote for clean air, but they also want to receive campaign contributions from corporate PACs and pass a law that business accepts as "reasonable." The compromise solution to this dilemma is to gut the bill by crafting dozens of loopholes inserted in private meetings or in subcommittee hearings that don't receive much (if any) attention in the press. Then the public vote on the final bill can be nearly unanimous: Members of Congress can assure their constituents that they voted for the final bill and their corporate PAC contributors that they helped weaken the bill in private. We can use the Clean Air Act of 1990 to introduce and explain this process.

The public strongly supports clean air and is unimpressed when corporate officials and apologists trot out their normal arguments: "Corporations are already doing all they reasonably can to improve environmental quality"; "we need to balance the costs against the benefits"; "people will lose their jobs if we make controls any stricter." The original Clean Air Act was passed in 1970, revised in 1977, and not revised again until 1990. Although the initial goal of its supporters was to have us breathing clean air by 1975, the deadline for compliance has been repeatedly extended—and the 1990 legislation provides a new set of deadlines to be reached sometime far in the future.

Because corporations control the production process unless the government specifically intervenes, any delay in government action leaves corporations free to do as they choose. Not only have laws been slow to come, but corporations have fought to delay or subvert implementation. The 1970 law ordered the Environmental Protection Agency (EPA) to regulate the hundreds of poisonous chemicals that are emitted by corporations, but as William Greider notes, "In 20 years of stalling, dodging, and fighting off court orders, the EPA has managed to issue regulatory standards for a total of seven toxics."[1]

Corporations have done exceptionally well politically, given the problem they face: The interests of business often are diametrically opposed to those of the public. Clean air laws and amendments have been few and far between, enforcement is ineffective, and the penalties for infractions are minimal. On the one hand, corporations have had to pay billions; on the other hand, the costs to date are a small fraction of what would be needed to clean up the environment.

This corporate struggle for the right to pollute takes place on many fronts. One front is public relations: The Chemical Manufacturers Association took out a two-page Earth Day ad in the *Washington Post* to demonstrate its concern for the environment; coincidentally many of the corporate signers are also on the EPA's list of high-risk producers.[2] Another front is research: Expert studies delay action while more information is gathered. The federally funded National Acid Precipitation Assessment Program (NAPAP) took 10 years and $600 million to figure out whether acid rain was a problem. Both business and the Reagan administration argued that no action should be taken until the study was completed.[3] The study was discredited when its summary of findings minimized the impact of acid rain—even though this did not accurately represent the expert research in the report. But the key site of struggle has been Congress, where for years corporations have succeeded in defeating environmental legislation. In 1987, utility companies were offered a compromise bill on acid rain, but they "were very adamant that they had beat the thing since 1981 and they could always beat it," according to Representative Edward Madigan (R–Ill.).[4] Throughout the 1980s the utilities defeated all efforts at change, but their intransigence probably hurt them when revisions finally were made.

The stage was set for a revision of the Clean Air Act when George Bush was elected as "the environmental president" and George Mitchell, a strong supporter of environmentalism, became the Senate majority leader. But what sort of clean air bill would it be? "What we wanted," said Richard Ayres, head of the environmentalists' Clean Air Coalition, "is a health-based standard— one-in-1-million cancer risk." Such a standard would require corporations to clean up their plants until the cancer risk from their operations was reduced to one in a million. "The Senate bill still has the requirement," Ayres said, "but there are 40 pages of extensions and exceptions and qualifications and loopholes that largely render the health standard a nullity."[5] Greider reports, for example, that "according to the EPA, there are now 26 coke ovens that pose a cancer risk greater than 1 in 1,000 and six where the risk is greater than 1 in 100. Yet the new clean-air bill will give the steel industry another 30 years to deal with the problem."[6]

This change from what the bill was supposed to do to what it did do came about through what corporate executives like to call the "access" process. The main aim of most corporate political action committee contributions is to help corporate executives attain "access" to key members of Congress and their staffs. Corporate executives (and corporate PAC money) work to persuade the member of Congress to accept a carefully predesigned loophole that sounds innocent but effectively undercuts the stated intention of the bill. Representative Dingell (D–Mich.), chair of the House Committee on Energy and Commerce, is a strong industry supporter; one of the people we interviewed called him "the point man for the Business Roundtable on clean air." Representative Waxman (D–Calif.), chair of the Subcommittee on Health and the Environment, is an environmentalist. Observers of the Clean Air Act legislative process expected a confrontation and contested votes on the floor of the Congress.

The problem for corporations was that, as one Republican staff aide said, "If any bill has the blessing of Waxman and the environmental groups, unless it is totally in outer space, who's going to vote against it?"[7] But corporations successfully minimized public votes. Somehow Waxman was persuaded to make behind-the-scenes compromises with Dingell so members didn't have to publicly side with business against the environment during an election year.[8] Often the access process leads to loopholes that protect a single corporation; but for "clean" air, most special deals targeted entire industries, not specific companies. The initial bill, for example, required cars to be able to use strictly specified cleaner fuels. But the auto industry wanted the rules loosened, and Congress eventually modified the bill by incorporating a variant of a formula suggested by the head of General Motors' fuels and lubricants department.

Nor did corporations stop fighting after they gutted the bill through amendments. Business pressed the EPA for favorable regulations to implement the law: "The cost of this legislation could vary dramatically, depending on how EPA interprets it," said William D. Fay, vice president of the National Coal Association, who headed the hilariously misnamed Clean Air Working Group, an industry coalition that fought to weaken the legislation.[9] An EPA aide working on acid rain regulations reported, "We're having a hard time getting our work done because of the number of phone calls we're getting" from corporations and their lawyers.

Corporations trying to convince federal regulators to adopt the "right" regulations don't rely exclusively on the cogency of their arguments. They often exert pressure on a member of Congress to intervene for them at the EPA or other agency. Senators and representatives regularly intervene on behalf of constituents and contributors by doing everything from straightening out a Social Security problem to asking a regulatory agency to explain why it is pressuring a company. This process—like campaign finance—usually follows accepted etiquette. In addressing a regulatory agency the senator does not say, "Lay off my campaign contributors, or I'll cut your budget." One standard phrasing for letters asks regulators to resolve the problem "as quickly as possible within applicable rules and regulations."[10] No matter how mild and careful the inquiry, the agency receiving the request is certain to give it extra attention; only after careful consideration will they refuse to make any accommodation.

The power disparity between business and environmentalists is enormous during the legislative process but even larger thereafter. When the Clean Air Act passed, corporations and industry groups offered positions, typically with large pay increases, to congressional staff members who wrote the law. The former congressional staff members who work for corporations know how to evade the law and can persuasively claim to EPA that they know what Congress intended. Environmental organizations pay substantially less than Congress and can't afford large staffs. They are rarely able to become involved in the details of the administrative process or influence implementation and enforcement.[11]

Having pushed Congress for a law, and the Environmental Protection Agency for regulations, allowing as much pollution as possible, business then went to the Quayle Council for rules allowing even more pollution. Vice President J. Danforth Quayle's Council, technically the Council on Competitiveness, was created by President Bush specifically to help reduce regulations on business. Quayle told the *Boston Globe* "that this council has an 'open door' to business groups and that he has a bias against regulations."[12] The Council reviews, and can override, all federal regulations, including those by the EPA setting the limits at which a chemical is subject to regulation. The council also recommended that corporations be allowed to increase their polluting emissions if a state did not object within seven days of the proposed increase. Corporations thus have multiple opportunities to win. If they lose in Congress, they can win at the regulatory agency; if they lose there, they can try again at the Quayle Council. If they lose there, they can try to reduce the money available to enforce regulations, tie up the issue in the courts, or accept a minimal fine.

The operation of the Quayle Council probably would have received little publicity, but reporters discovered that the executive director of the Council, Allan Hubbard, had a clear conflict of interest. Hubbard chaired the biweekly White House meetings on the Clean Air Act. He owns half of World Wide Chemical, received an average of more than a million dollars a year in profits from it while directing the Council, and continues to attend quarterly stockholder meetings. According to the *Boston Globe*, "Records on file with the Indianapolis Air Pollution Control Board show that World Wide Chemical emitted 17,000 to 19,000 pounds of chemicals into the air last year."[13] The company "does not have the permit required to release the emissions," "is putting out nearly four times the allowable emissions without a permit, and could be subject to a $2,500-a-day penalty," according to David Jordan, director of the Indianapolis Air Pollution Board.[14]

In business-government relations attention focuses on scandal. It is outrageous that Hubbard will personally benefit by eliminating regulations that his own company is violating, but the key issue here is not this obvious conflict of interest. The real issue is the *system* of business-government relations, and especially of campaign finance, that offers business so many opportunities to craft loopholes, undermine regulations, and subvert enforcement. Still worse, many of these actions take place outside of public scrutiny. If the Quayle Council were headed by a Boy Scout we'd still object to giving business yet another way to use backroom deals to increase our risk of getting cancer. In *Money Talks* we try to analyze not just the exceptional cases, but the day-to-day reality of corporate-government relations. . . .

Myth One: Key Votes Are the Issue

Many critics of PACs and campaign finance seem to feel that a corporate PAC officer walks into a member's office and says, "Senator, I want you to vote against the Clean Air Act. Here's $5,000 to do so." This view, in this crude form, is simply wrong. The (liberal) critics who hold this view seem to reason as follows: (1) we know that PAC money gives corporations power in relation to Congress; (2) power is the ability to make someone do something against their will; (3) therefore campaign money must force members to switch their votes on key issues. We come to the same conclusion about the outcome—corporate power in relation to Congress—but differ from conventional critics on both the understanding of power and the nature of the process through which campaign money exercises its influence.

The debate over campaign finance is frequently posed as, "Did special interests buy the member's vote on a key issue?" Media accounts as well as most academic analyses in practice adopt this approach.[15] With the question framed in this way, we have to agree with the corporate political action committee directors we interviewed, who answered, "No, they didn't." But they believed it followed that they have no power and maybe not even any influence, and we certainly don't agree with that. If power means the ability to force a member of Congress to vote a certain way on a major bill, corporate PACs rarely have power. However, corporations and their PACs have a great deal of power if power means the ability to exercise a field of influence that shapes the behavior of other social actors. In fact, corporations have effective hegemony: Some alternatives are never seriously considered, and others seem natural and inevitable; some alternatives generate enormous controversy and costs, and others are minor and involve noncontroversial favors. Members of Congress meet regularly with some people, share trust, discuss the issues honestly off the record, and become friends, while other people have a hard time getting in the door much less getting any help. Members don't have to be forced; most of them are eager to do favors for corporations and do so without the public's knowledge. If citizens did understand what was happening their outrage might put an end to the behavior, but even if the favors are brought to light the media will probably present them as at least arguably good public policy.

High-Visibility Issues

Corporate PAC officers could stress two key facts: First, on important highly visible issues they cannot determine the way a member of Congress votes; second, even for low-visibility issues the entire process is loose and uncertain. The more visible an issue, the less likely that a member's vote will be determined by campaign contributions. If the whole world is watching, a member from an environmentally conscious district can't vote against the Clean Air Act because it is simply too popular. An April 1990 poll by Louis Harris and Associates reported that when asked, "Should Congress make the 1970 Clean Air Act stricter than it is now, keep it about the same, or make it less strict?" 73 percent of respondents answered, "Make it stricter"; 23 percent, "Keep it about the same"; and only 2 percent, "Make it less strict" (with 2 percent not sure).[16] Few members could risk openly voting against such sentiments. To oppose the bill they'd have to have a very good reason—perhaps that it would cost their district several hundred jobs, perhaps that the bill was fatally flawed, but never, never, never that they had been promised $5,000, $10,000, or $50,000 for doing so.

The PAC officers we interviewed understood this point, although they weren't always careful to distinguish between high- and low-visibility issues. (As we discuss below, we believe low-visibility issues are an entirely different story.) Virtually all access-oriented PACs went out of their way at some point in the interview to make it clear that they do not and could not buy a member's vote on any significant issue. No corporate official felt otherwise; moreover, these opinions seemed genuine and not merely for public consumption. They pointed out that the maximum legal donation by a PAC is $5,000 per candidate per election. Given that in 1988 the cost of an average winning House campaign was $388,000 and for the Senate $3,745,000,[17] no individual company can provide the financial margin of victory in any but the closest of races. A member of Congress would be a fool to trade 5 percent of the district's votes for the maximum donation an individual PAC can make ($5,000) or even for 10 times that amount. Most PACs therefore feel they have little influence. Even the one person who conceded possible influence in some rare circumstances considered it unlikely:

> You certainly aren't going to be able to buy anybody for $500 or $1,000 or $10,000. It's a joke. Occasionally something will happen where everybody in one industry will be for one specific solution to a problem, and they may then also pour money to one guy. And he suddenly looks out and says, "I haven't got $7,000 coming in from this group, I've got $70,000." That might get his attention: "I've got to support what they want." But that's a rarity, and it doesn't happen too often. Most likely, after the election he's going to rationalize that it wasn't that important and they would have supported him anyway. I just don't think that PACs are that important.

This statement by a senior vice president at a large *Fortune* 500 company probably reflects one part of the reality: Most of the time members' votes can't be bought; occasionally a group of corporations support the same position and combine resources to influence a member's vote even on a major contested issue. Even if that happens, the member's behavior is far from certain.

Low-Visibility Issues and Nonissues

This is true only if we limit our attention to highly visible, publicly contested issues. Most corporate PACs, and most government relations units, focus only a small fraction of their time, money, and energy on the final votes on such issues. So-called access-oriented PACs have a different purpose and style. Their aim is not to influence the member's public vote on the final piece of legislation, but rather to be sure that the bill's wording exempts their company from the bill's most costly or damaging provisions. If tax law is going to be changed, the aim of the company's government relations unit, and its associated PAC, is to be sure that the law has built-in loopholes that protect the company. The law may say that corporate tax rates are increased, and that's what the media and the public think, but section 739, subsection J, paragraph iii, contains a hard-to-decipher phrase. No ordinary mortal can figure out what it means or to whom it applies, but the consequence is that the company doesn't pay the taxes you'd think it would. For example, the 1986 Tax "Reform" Act contained a provision limited to a single company, identified as a "corporation incorporated on June 13, 1917, which has its principal place of business in Bartlesville, Oklahoma."[18] With that provision in the bill, Philips Petroleum didn't mind at all if Congress wanted to "reform" the tax laws.

Two characteristics of such provisions structure the way they are produced. First, by their very nature such provisions, targeted at one (or at most a few) corporations or industries, are unlikely to mobilize widespread business support. Other businesses may not want to oppose these provisions, but neither are they likely to make them a priority, though the broader the scope the broader the support. Business as a whole is somewhat uneasy about very narrow provisions, although most corporations and industry trade associations feel they must fight for their own. Peak business associations such as the Business Roundtable generally prefer a "clean" bill with clear provisions favoring business in general rather than a "Christmas tree" with thousands of special-interest provisions. Most corporations play the game, however, and part of playing the game is not to object to or publicize what other corporations are doing. But they don't feel good about what they do, and if general-interest business associations took a stand they would probably speak against, rather than in favor of, these provisions.

Second, however, these are low-visibility issues; in fact, most of them are not "issues" at all in that they are never examined or contested. The corporation's field of power both makes the member willing to cooperate and gets the media and public to in practice accept these loopholes as noncontroversial. Members don't usually have to take a stand on these matters or be willing to face public scrutiny. If the proposal does become contested, the member probably can back off and drop the issue with few consequences, and the corporation probably can go down the hall and try again with another member. . . .

What Is Power?

Our analysis is based on an understanding of power that differs from that usually articulated by both business and politicians. The corporate PAC directors we interviewed insisted that they have no power:

> If you were to ask me what kind of access and influence do we have, being roughly the 150th largest PAC, I would have to tell you that on the basis of our money we have zero. . . . If you look at the level of our contributions, we know we're not going to buy anybody's vote, we're not going to rent anybody, or whatever the cliches have been over the years. We know that.

The executives who expressed these views[19] used the word *power* in roughly the same sense that it is usually used within political science, which is also the way the term was defined by Max Weber, the classical sociological theorist. Power, according to this common conception, is the ability to make someone do something against his or her will. If that is what power means, then corporations rarely have power in relation to members of Congress. . . . In this regard we agree with the corporate officials we interviewed: A PAC is not in a position to say to a member of Congress, "Either you vote for this bill, or we will defeat your bid for reelection." Rarely do they even say, "Vote for this bill, or you won't get any money from us." Therefore, if power is the ability to make someone do something against his or her will, then PAC donations rarely give corporations power over members of Congress.

This definition of power as the ability to make someone do something against his or her will is what Steven Lukes[20] calls a *one-dimensional view of power*. A *two-dimensional view* recognizes the existence of nondecisions: A potential issue never gets articulated or, if articulated by someone somewhere, never receives serious consideration. In 1989 and 1990 one of the major political battles, and a focus of great effort by corporate PACs, was the Clean Air Act. Yet 20 or 30 years earlier, before the rise of the environmental movement, pollution was a nonissue: It simply didn't get considered, although its effects were, in retrospect, of great importance. In one Sherlock Holmes story the key clue is that the dog didn't bark.[21] A two-dimensional view of power makes the same point: In some situations no one notices power is being exercised—because there is no overt conflict.

Even this model of power is too restrictive, however, because it still focuses on discrete decisions and nondecisions. Tom Wartenberg . . . argues instead for a *field theory of power* that analyzes social power as similar to a magnetic field. A magnetic field alters the motion of objects susceptible to magnetism. Similarly, the mere presence of a powerful social agent alters social space for others and causes them to orient to the powerful agent.[22] One of the executives we interviewed took it for granted that "if we go see the congressman who represents [a city where the company has a major plant], where 10,000 of our employees are also his constituents, we don't need a

PAC to go see him." The corporation is so important in that area that the member has to orient himself or herself in relation to the corporation and its concerns. In a different sense, the mere act of accepting a campaign contribution changes the way a member relates to a PAC, creating a sense of obligation and need to reciprocate. The PAC contribution has altered the member's social space, his or her awareness of the company and wish to help it, even if no explicit commitments have been made.

Business Is Different

Power therefore is not just the ability to force people to do something against their will; it is most effective (and least recognized) when it shapes the field of action. Moreover, business's vast resources, influence on the economy, and general legitimacy place it on a different footing from other so-called special interests. Business donors are often treated differently from other campaign contributors. When a member of Congress accepts a $1,000 donation from a corporate PAC, goes to a committee hearing, and proposes "minor" changes in a bill's wording, those changes are often accepted without discussion or examination. The changes "clarify" the language of the bill, perhaps legalizing higher levels of pollution for a specific pollutant or exempting the company from some tax. The media do not report on this change, and no one speaks against it. . . .

Even groups with great social legitimacy encounter more opposition and controversy than business faces for proposals that are virtually without public support. Contrast the largely unopposed commitment of more than $500 billion for the bailout of savings and loan associations with the sharp debate, close votes, and defeats for the rights of men and women to take *unpaid* parental leaves. Although the classic phrase for something noncontroversial that everyone must support is to call it a "motherhood" issue, and it would cost little to guarantee every woman the right to an unpaid parental leave, nonetheless this measure generated intense scrutiny and controversy, ultimately going down to defeat. Few people are prepared to publicly defend pollution or tax evasion, but business is routinely able to win pollution exemptions and tax loopholes. Although cumulatively these provisions may trouble people, individually most are allowed to pass without scrutiny. *No analysis of corporate political activity makes sense unless it begins with a recognition that the PAC is a vital element of corporate power, but it does not operate by itself. The PAC donation is always backed by the wider range of business power and influence.*

Corporations are different from other special-interest groups not only because business has far more resources, but also because of this acceptance and legitimacy. When people feel that "the system" is screwing them, they tend to blame politicians, the government, the media—but rarely business. Although much of the public is outraged at the way money influences elections and public policy, the issue is almost always posed in terms of what politicians do or don't do. This pervasive double standard largely exempts business from criticism. We, on the other hand, believe it is vital to scrutinize business as well. . . .

The Limits to Business Power

We have argued that power is more than winning an open conflict, and business is different from other groups because of its pervasive influence on our society—the way it shapes the social space for all other actors. These two arguments, however, are joined with a third: a recognition of, in fact an insistence on, the limits to business power. We stress the power of business, but business does not feel powerful. As one executive said to us,

> I really wish that our PAC in particular, and our lobbyists, had the influence that is generally perceived by the general population. If you see it written in the press, and you talk to people, they tell you about all that influence that you've got, and frankly I think that's far overplayed, as far as the influence goes. Certainly you can get access to a candidate, and certainly you can get your position known; but as far as influencing that decision, the only way you influence it is by the providing of information.

Executives believe that corporations are constantly under attack, primarily because government simply doesn't understand that business is crucial to everything society does but can easily be crippled by well-intentioned but unrealistic government policies. A widespread view among the people we interviewed is that "far and away the vast majority of things that we do are literally to protect ourselves from public policy that is poorly crafted and nonresponsive to the needs and realities and circumstances of our company." These misguided policies, they feel, can come from many sources—labor unions, environmentalists, the pressure of unrealistic public-interest groups, the government's constant need for money, or the weight of its oppressive bureaucracy. Simply maintaining equilibrium requires a pervasive effort: If attention slips for even a minute, an onerous regulation will be imposed or a precious resource taken away. To some extent such a view is an obvious consequence of the position of the people we interviewed: If business could be sure of always winning, the government relations unit (and thus their jobs) would be unnecessary; if it is easy to win, they deserve little credit for their victories and much blame for defeats. But evidently the corporation agrees with them, since it devotes significant resources to political action of many kinds, including the awareness and involvement of top officials. Chief executive officers and members of the board of directors repeatedly express similar views. . . .

Like the rest of us, business executives can usually think of other things they'd like to have but know they can't get at this time or that they could win but wouldn't consider worth the price that would have to be paid. More important, the odds may be very much in their favor, their opponents may be hobbled with one hand tied behind their back, but it is still a contest requiring pervasive effort. Perhaps once upon a time business could simply make its wishes known and receive what it wanted; today corporations must form PACs, lobby actively, make their case to the public, run advocacy ads, and engage in a multitude of behaviors that they wish were unnecessary. From the outside we are impressed with the high success rates over a wide range of issues and with the lack of a credible challenge to the general authority of business. From the inside they are impressed with the serious consequences of occasional losses and with the continuing effort needed to maintain their privileged position.

NOTES

1. William Greider, "Whitewash: Is Congress Conning Us on Clean Air?" *Rolling Stone*, June 14, 1990, pp. 37–39, 146.
2. Ibid.
3. Margaret E. Kriz, "Dunning the Midwest," *National Journal* (April 14, 1990), pp. 893–97.
4. Ibid., p. 41.
5. Quoted in Greider, "Whitewash," p. 40.
6. Ibid.
7. Margaret E. Kriz, "Politics at the Pump," *National Journal* (June 2, 1990), p. 1328.
8. Information in this paragraph is from Kriz, "Politics at the Pump," pp. 1328–29.
9. Why can't industry just come out and name its groups "Polluters for Profit" or the "Coalition for Acid Rain Preservation" (CARP)? All quotes in this paragraph are from Carol Matlack, "It's Round Two in Clean Air Fight," *National Journal* (January 26, 1991), p. 226.
10. Charles R. Babcock and Helen Dewar, "Keating Fallout: Senators Draw Own Lines on When to Intervene," *Washington Post*, January 16, 1991, p. A17.
11. Matlack, "It's Round Two in Clean Air Fight," p. 227.
12. Michael Kranish, "House Panel to Probe Waiver for Quayle Aide," *Boston Globe*, November 21, 1991, p. 17.
13. Ibid.
14. Michael Kranish, "Quayle Aide's Firm Is Linked to Pollution: Official Works on Emission Rules," *Boston Globe*, November 20, 1991, p. 4.
15. Janet M. Grenzke, "PACs and the Congressional Supermarket: The Currency Is Complex," *American Journal of Political Science* 33 (1989): 1–24; James B. Kau and Paul H. Rubin, *Congressmen, Constituents, and Contributors* (Boston: Maratinus Nijhof, 1982); Alan Neustadtl, "Interest-Group PACsmanship: An Analysis of Campaign Contributions, Issue Visibility, and Legislative Impact," *Social Forces* 69 (1991): 549–64.
16. "Opinion Outlook: Views on the American Scene," *National Journal* 22 (April 28, 1990): 1052.
17. David B. Magleby and Candice J. Nelson, *The Money Chase: Congressional Campaign Finance Reform* (Washington, DC: Brookings Institution, 1990), p. 36.
18. Gary Klott, "Senators Won Many Exceptions in Bill to Aid Specific Taxpayers," *New York Times*, June 6, 1986, pp. D1–D2.
19. Their views on this, as on other issues, are sometimes complicated and contradic-

tory, and at other points in the same interview the person might take a different position.

20. Steven Lukes, *Power: A Radical View* (New York: Macmillan, 1974).

21. Theodore J. Eismeier and Philip H. Pollock III, "The Retreat from Partisanship: Why the Dog Didn't Bark in the 1984 Election," *Business Strategy and Public Policy*, edited by Alfred A. Marcus, Allen M. Kaufman, and David R. Beam (Westport, CT: Quorum Books, 1987), pp. 137–47.

22. Thomas Wartenberg, *The Forms of Power: From Domination to Transformation* (Philadelphia: Temple University Press, 1990), pp. 66–67, 74.

37

THE MASS MEDIA AS A POWER INSTITUTION

MARTIN N. MARGER

This selection by Martin N. Marger also exemplifies C. Wright Mills' notion of the power elite. As Marger argues, even though Mills recognized 40 years ago that the mass media could be an effective tool of manipulation, Mills could not have imagined how powerful the institution of the mass media would become. In fact, Marger situates the media alongside the government and the economy as one of the most dominant institutions in society. Marger explains the magnitude of the mass media's authority by analyzing the ownership and control of media industries, the content of media information, and the effects the media have on public opinion and political awareness.

In contemporary societies, the two major institutions of power—government and economy—must be joined by a third—the mass media—to complete any scheme of societal power. Although not formally a part of either government or the economy, the mass media are integrally tied to both, and both rely on the mass media to function as they do. Moreover, the mass media have substantial independent resources that make them a formidable institution of power in their own right.

The Societal Role of the Mass Media

The mass media are of two types: print and electronic. Print media are books, magazines, and newspapers; electronic media are television, radio, and films. To refer to them as *mass* media implies that their communicative realm is extremely broad, often encompassing the entire society. In modern societies, the mass media serve several vital functions. They are agents of socialization, instructing people in the norms and values of their society and generally transmitting the society's culture. They are sources of information, supplying citizens with knowledge about their society and especially about the political economy. They function as propaganda mechanisms through which powerful units of the government and economy seek to persuade the public either to support their policies (government) or to buy their consumer products (corporations). Finally, they serve as agents of legitimacy, generating mass belief in (and acceptance of) dominant political and economic institutions.

Given these vital functions, three queries are of fundamental importance in examining the mass media's power in modern societies. The first concerns their control and accessibility: Who owns or controls the mass media, and how much access to them is afforded individuals and groups in the society? The second question pertains to their content: What do the media present to the public, and who makes decisions regarding that content? The third question concerns the effects of mass media on public opinion and political awareness: To what extent do the mass media shape people's views of events and personalities in their society and the world, and how do the media transmit ideology?

Most media research during the past several decades has focused on the United States. The following discussion, therefore, pertains to the power of the mass media primarily in American society. Most of the patterns and tendencies apparent in the United States, however, are increasingly characteristic of the mass media in other industrial societies.

Media Control and Accessibility

Control and accessibility of the mass media in the United States and increasingly in other industrial societies are determined primarily by the economic context within which the media function and by their place in the political economy.

In the United States, the mass media operate almost entirely as privately owned enterprises. In most other industrial societies, newspapers are privately owned but television and radio are at least partially public corporations that compete within a mixed public-private system. Television and radio in Canada, for example, are dominated by the state-run Canadian Broadcasting Corporation (CBC), although there are also several privately owned television and radio networks. A similar system exists in Britain, where the electronic media are a mixture of public and commercial corporations. Only in autocratic societies like China are the media fully state controlled; in these societies, the media are organized and operated to implement the government's social and political policies (Wright, 1986). In recent years, there has been a movement in most societies toward the dominance of privately owned and operated electronic media, although the United States remains unique in the extent of private ownership and control. Moreover, although the electronic media are nominally regulated by government, they operate with far fewer restrictions in the United States than in other societies. Meanwhile, a global trend toward convergence of national networks and companies into transnational units is increasingly evident (Schiller, 1989).

The mass media are huge corporations (or parts of corporate conglomerates) whose primary objective, like all enterprises in a capitalist economy, is to maximize their profits. Like most industries in the American political economy, the mass media are concentrated in a few giant corporate units and thus constitute an oligopoly. Vast multifaceted companies composed of newspaper chains, radio and television stations, and recording, motion-picture, and publishing units dominate the media industry. Among the 1,600 United States daily newspapers, about a dozen corporations control more than half the circulation. The Knight-Ridder chain, for example, owns newspapers throughout the United States with three million in daily circulation, including the *Detroit Free Press*, the *Miami Herald*, the *Philadelphia Inquirer*, and numerous smaller dailies. Gannett owns *USA Today* as well as 88 other dailies with six million in circulation. Although 11,000 individual magazine titles are published in the United States, a handful of corporations derive most of the magazine revenue (Time-Warner alone controls more than 40 percent of magazine business), and among more than 2,500 book publishing companies, a half-dozen corporations sell most books. Three major studios control most of the movie business, and three corporations draw most of the audience and revenue of the television industry (Bagdikian 1989). Edward Herman and Noam Chomsky have identified 24 media giants that basically control the industry. Twenty-three of these companies had assets in excess of $1 billion in 1986 and three-quarters of them earned after-tax profits of over $100 million (Herman and Chomsky 1988).

One must also consider the scope and diversity of these companies' media holdings and activities. Time-Warner, for example, is made up of Warner Brothers Pictures (movies), dozens of popular mass circulation magazines (including *Time* and *Life*), cable television companies, and book companies. NBC is part of the RCA Corporation, which, in turn, is part of General Electric. CBS and Capital Cities/ABC are massive media conglomerates that own numerous television and radio stations, cable television networks, and magazine, recording, book publishing, and motion picture companies.

Topping off this narrow media concentration are the wire service companies, which accumulate news stories. A large proportion of the items appearing in every mass circulation newspaper in the United States comes from the wires of the Associated Press (AP) or United Press International (UPI). Newspapers subscribe to these services, which become the major source of stories. A few of the larger newspaper companies operate their own wire services and also supply other smaller papers. Thus, in the coverage of national or international news, the difference from one newspaper to another is ordinarily slight. Radio and television news, to a lesser degree, also rely on these wire services.

It is apparent, then, that in the United States, as in most industrial societies, ownership and control of the mass media are extremely concentrated. This concentration parallels the tendency of all political and economic institutions in modern societies to converge into fewer and more powerful units. All other aspects of media power, including their content and effects, are colored by this fact.

In modern societies, to publicly communicate views or ideas requires use of the media. A critical concern, therefore, is not only who owns or controls the media but also who has access to them. In modern societies, only government and big business have the resources—money, authority, and influence—to employ the media regularly and effectively.

As privately owned enterprises, the major goal of the various media is to generate revenue. This objective requires that the media cater primarily to those who can pay to put their views on the air or into print: the major corporations, which use the media primarily to create demand for their products and services through advertising. Consider that a 30-second television commercial on Super Bowl Sunday in 1992 cost $850,000; or that Procter and Gamble spends almost $1.5 billion each year on media advertising. Advertising not only serves to create demand but also provides corporations with a means of creating a positive public image. General Electric, for example, tells the public that "we bring good things to life." Most corporations convey similar messages in which they are portrayed not as profit-seeking enterprises but as compassionate, publicly responsible citizens.

Government access to the media is founded not on financial power but on the fact that the media are closely interwoven with government, particularly at the national level. Put simply, the relationship between government and media is symbiotic; neither can function effectively without the other. As a regulated industry in the United States, the media must take into account the interests of government elites. More importantly, however, the media are heavily dependent on government elites as their major source of political information, which is the core of news. In fact, it is the actions of government elites that dominate news as presented by both print and electronic media. Moreover, much of the news transmitted by the mass media is prepared by government agencies. Studies have indicated that not only are government officials the source of most news but most news stories are drawn from situations over which newsmakers "have either complete or substantial control" (Sigal 1973).

Power elites, particularly those in the realm of government, can easily gain access to the mass media simply because they possess credibility among the public as well as among the media elite. Their accounts of events and policies are more likely to be accepted and thus become part of the news format than accounts and interpretations provided by other sources (Gans 1979). Moreover, in gathering information, the mass media ordinarily follow the path of least resistance; this means relying on official sources for information. As Herman and Chomsky (1988, p. 19) have noted, "Taking information from sources that may be presumed credible reduces investigative expense, whereas material from sources that are not prima facie credible, or that will elicit criticism and threats, requires careful checking and costly research."

Government elites, however, are equally dependent on the mass media. This dependency stems from their need to employ the media to convey their messages to the public and thus shape and influence public opinion. Political leaders today rarely engage in face-to-face communication with the masses. Instead, they speak primarily through the electronic media in soundbites and project their images through photo opportunities. Political dialogue, particularly at the national level, is increasingly reduced to creating impressions (Postman 1985). This process reaches a high point in the orchestration of pseudo-events, that is, carefully scripted and staged events that are designed to create favorable public images but that have little basis in reality (Boorstin 1961).

Mass Media Content

The mass media exercise considerable power independently of both government and business. This power is particularly significant in their role as gatekeepers of political, economic, and social information—what is ordinarily termed "news." As information gatekeepers, it is the media who define what news is or what is socially significant. As suppliers of vital information, the mass media in modern societies are unequaled. They have become our window on the world, and it is through them that we learn about key events, personalities, and other so-called news. The media, in other words, have become a source of reality itself. As Ben Bagdikian (1971, pp. xii–xiii) has put it: "For most of the people of the world, for most of the events of the world, what the news systems do not transmit did not happen. To that extent, the world and its inhabitants are what the news media say they are."

Given the media's strong influence on the molding of political, economic, and social reality, a key power issue concerns the decision-making process of news selection and presentation. Like critical decisions of government and the economy, this process is essentially an elite function. Events become newsworthy, and thus of importance to the society, only after they have been selected by the communications elite—editors, journalists, and media executives (Cohen and Young 1973; Epstein 1974; Gans 1979; Tuchman 1978). It is the media elite, therefore, who are largely responsible for molding the public's conception of political, economic, and social events and conditions. The media elite must therefore be added to corporate and governmental elites as top decision makers in the United States and other modern societies.

What are the consequences of this concentration of control over the shaping of sociopolitical reality? Here we must consider the political-economic context of the mass media in the United States and most other modern societies. First, because the major media operate as business enterprises, the media elite, when making content decisions, must take into account the interests of the dominant economic groups—the large corporations—that supply them with revenue. Second, given their symbiotic relationship with government, these decisions must be weighed against the interests of political elites. The result is that ideas or movements outside the political and economic mainstream receive little attention. In U.S. elections, for example, minor parties and candidates are generally treated by the mass media as curiosities, not as legitimate contenders. Hence, political debate is narrowly limited to the two major parties in the mainstream political arena, parties that rarely differ fundamentally on policy or philosophical issues. In short, ruling business and political elites are best situated to exercise influence over the content of the mass media.

With maximum access to the mass media as well as the ability to shape news, elites of the political economy are able not only to place their issues on the political agenda but also to define them in ways "likely to influence their resolution" (Bennett 1988, p. 96). Parties, organizations, and individuals who advocate serious economic or political change but lack financial and political resources have a very difficult time communicating their messages through the mass media. It is true that challenges to established authority are often given attention by newspaper and, particularly, television journalism. But this is due primarily to the fact that "the logic of audience maintenance favors conflict between easily recognizable groups" (Epstein 1974, p. 269). Coverage is not provided in acknowledgment of the legitimacy of challenging groups or to present the substance of their protest (Gitlin 1980).

The emphasis on official perspectives results in limited public understanding of the nature of political, economic, and social problems and how they might be resolved. Rarely do the mass media subject the dominant political economy to serious scrutiny and criticism. "The political world," Lance Bennett (1988, p. 96) has explained, "becomes a caricature drawn out of unrealistic stereotypes, predictable political postures, and superficial images." Moreover, even when attention is drawn to societal shortcomings by public affairs or news programs or investigative journalists, it is done in the spirit of the dominant ideology. That is, problems are presented as the products of deviant individuals or groups within the context of an otherwise healthy social system. The *systemic* origins of chronic problems are rarely explained or even acknowledged. As David Paletz and Robert Entman (1981, p. 167) have observed, "The mass media have never given powerless Americans the necessary information to link the ubiquitous rotten apples to the structure of the barrel." Questioning the structure and functioning of dominant political and economic institutions is clearly beyond the capabilities of the mass media (Gans 1979; Gitlin 1980; Parenti 1986).

The bias of mass media content toward the dominant system should not be seen, however, as the result of government and economic elites conspiring with media editors, journalists, and executives. The media elite express dominant values largely unconsciously: They see themselves as objective news commentators, not bearers of opinion. As Herbert Gans (1979, pp. 39–40) has noted, "The values in the news are rarely explicit and must be found between the lines—in what actors and activities are reported or ignored, and in how they are described." Political objectivity, therefore, is not political neutrality. Critical information presented by the media, in the form of news and public affairs, is framed by dominant values and shaped by power elites, no matter how seemingly objective the presentation may be (Iyengar and Kinder 1987). Moreover, the very notion of objectivity among the media is illusory. As Paletz and Entman (1981, p. 22) have explained, "to edit is to interpret, to speak is to define, to communicate is to structure reality." Hence, the media, by their very nature, cannot be objective.

The inability of the mass media to present issues to the public in a thorough and critical manner is largely a result of their commercial imperatives. News, like other aspects of mass media, must be sold as a consumer product. This requires that it be presented in an entertainment format, and, as Bennett (1988) has explained, be personalized, dramatized, fragmented, and normalized. It is personalized in the sense that it "gives preference to the individual actors and human-interest angles in events while downplaying institutional and political considerations that establish the social contexts for those events" (p. 26). Similarly, the media seek out dramatic events and personalities to which viewers and readers can relate, rather than events and personalities that may be more politically significant though less glamorous and fascinating. The entertainment format of news forces it to be presented in unrelated bits and pieces rather than as a meaningful whole. As a result, news becomes a series of what Neil Postman (1985) has called "decontextualized facts," comparable to background music. Finally, information presented as news is filtered through traditional themes and images of the society, thereby assuring the viewer or reader of the merit of dominant institutions and discrediting challenges to them.

In short, although they may engage in social criticism, the mass media frame their presentations in a way that legitimizes the prevailing political economy. Although there is no blatant censorship of media content in the United States as there is in a totalitarian society, an implicit understanding exists on the part of the media elite regarding their role in upholding the status quo. Self-censorship by the media is reinforced when they anticipate the reactions of political and economic elites and alter their presentations in advance. At times, of course, more blatant attempts at censorship may arise, as when corporate advertisers exert direct pressure to influence the content of the media or when government elites pressure the media to "toe the line" (Gans 1979). Although the media elite may resist these pressures, more often their ideological perspectives are fully compatible with those of political and economic elites, and they may therefore have little inclination to follow a path not basically in line with those views. Moreover, although the media commonly present opposing sides of social and political issues, the two perspectives are only narrowly divergent and the issues are presented in ideologically safe stereotypes. The irony of modern communications systems is that despite the profusion of messages with which the citizenry is bombarded daily, the absence of a thorough exploration of issues by the mass media results in an increasingly uninformed public.

It is also important to consider the essentially passive role of the citizenry in the communications system of most modern societies. In essence, political communication flows only in one direction. The media are virtually unchallenged by consumers. There is little effective feedback from those who read newspapers and especially from those who watch television. Thus, as Mills explained almost four decades ago, there is a growing tendency for mass media to be tools of manipulation rather than channels for the interchange of opinion: "In the primary public the competition of opinions goes on between people holding views in the service of their interests and their reasoning. But in the mass society of media markets, competition, if any, goes on between the manipulators with their mass media on the one hand, and the people receiving their propaganda on the other" (1956, p. 305).

Although viewers and readers, as consumers, can choose not to buy a newspaper or watch a television program, the mass media operate in an oligopolistic market domestically and, increasingly, in an integrated international market. Hence, consumer choices are limited and, in the end, it is the producers—in this case the newspapers and television networks—who make critical decisions about the product and who exercise control over its supply and demand.

Media Effects

Concentrated media power, in the form of constricted ownership and control of content, does not necessarily guarantee to the users of the media—primarily government and big business—that the effects they desire, that is, public acceptance and internalization of their messages, will be produced. To what extent are the media effective in molding public opinion and shaping people's versions of political and social reality?

Although sociologists and communications experts are not certain about the precise effects of the mass media on socialization or how the media modify the influences of other socializers like the family and the school (Comstock 1980; Gerbner 1967), it appears that the media are becoming the chief means through which people construct their versions of social reality. Well before the advent of television, Walter Lippmann (1922) explained how the mass media, by selectively reporting and interpreting events and personalities, determine the pictures in our heads (stereotypes, as he referred to them) that shape our social worlds. With the predominance of television, this "reality-shaping" function of the mass media has become much more complete. Television serves increasingly in this capacity because few can escape its influence. Only sleep and work occupy more of Americans' time than television viewing. Most important, the mass media serve as the primary organs of political communication, setting the framework of public discourse, solidifying the legitimacy of powerful institutions and elites, and transmitting the society's dominant ideology.

The mediated version of social reality presented by television, newspapers, and other media is most evident in the communication of news. "News," as has been suggested, is hardly a complete or precise picture of societal or world events. Rather, it is a picture constructed by the media elite who select and interpret events, processes, and personalities. From an almost infinite number of happenings that occur each day, only a few are chosen for transmission as news. Beyond the realm of our personal lives, the issues that concern us are therefore the issues defined for us by the media elite as important and worthy of our attention.

In the early years of research on the effects of mass media on public attitudes and beliefs, the prevalent view was that media had a direct and significant influence. Starting in the 1940s, research seemed to reverse this view, concluding instead that the power of the mass media had been exaggerated. The new perspective held that viewers and readers were not to be seen as a "mass," but rather as individual consumers whose interpretations of media presentations were modified by social class, ethnicity, religion, and other social variables (Lazarsfeld et al. 1948). People exposed themselves to the media selectively, it was suggested, so that media messages generally had the effect of simply reaffirming people's prior beliefs and views. V. O. Key (1964, p. 357) warned against overestimating the effectiveness of the mass media in conveying the same messages to all people: "The flow of the messages of the mass media," he wrote, "is rather like dropping a handful of confetti from the rim of the Grand Canyon with the object of striking a man astride a burro on the canyon floor. In some measure chance determines which messages reach what targets." This "minimal-effects" view remains today among some media observers. Albert Gollin (1988, p. 43), for example, has written that "People bring to their encounters with the mass media a formidable array of established habits, motives, social values and perceptual defenses that screen out, derail the intent or limit the force of media messages. The media certainly do affect people in obvious and subtle ways. But no simple 1:1 relationship exists between content or intent and effects."

More recently, researchers have pointed out that the minimal-effects view was based on perceived changes, brought about by the media, in attitudes about political issues. What was overlooked, however, was the impact of mass media on creating a public *awareness* of issues. This has become known as the "agenda-setting function" of the mass media (McCombs and Shaw 1972). Communications researchers have explained that although television and other mass media may not be overly effective in telling us *what* to think, they are extremely effective in telling us what and whom to think *about* (Shaw and McCombs 1977; Iyengar and Kinder 1987). Issues emphasized by the media become the issues regarded by viewers and readers as significant. As the media shift their emphasis to new issues, public perceptions change correspondingly. Moreover, Iyengar and Kinder (1987) have suggested a kind of media power that goes one step beyond agenda setting, which they call "priming." Priming refers to changes in the standards that people use in making political choices and judgments. As news, especially television news, shifts its attention from one issue to another, governments and political leaders are judged on their performance regarding those issues. Thus, by drawing attention to some aspects of political life at the expense of others, television helps bring to mind certain bits of political memory while others are ignored.

The mass media not only transmit descriptions of events and personalities but, more importantly, they convey the society's dominant ideology. It is in this sense that the media are agents of social control, used by power elites not only to communicate and legitimize their policies and actions but to stabilize the political and economic systems by generating allegiance among the public. As Todd Gitlin has explained:

> The media bring a manufactured public world into private space. From within their private crevices, people find themselves relying on the media for concepts, for images of their heroes, for guiding information, for emotional charges, for a recognition of public values, for symbols in general, even for language. Of all the institutions of daily life, the media specialize in orchestrating everyday consciousness—by virtue of their pervasiveness, their accessibility, their centralized symbolic capacity. They name the world's parts, they certify reality *as* reality—and when their certifications are doubted and opposed, as they surely are, it is those same certifications that limit the terms of effective opposition. To put it simply: the mass media have become core systems for the distribution of ideology. (1980, pp. 1–2)

We should not assume that the presentation of news is the mass media's only way of creating support for the society's dominant ideology and institutions. In modern societies, news and public affairs represent only a small portion of all media fare, particularly of television. The remaining entertainment, and especially the advertising that constantly accompanies it, is no less reflective and supportive of the society's prevailing value system (Bagdikian 1983; Goldsen 1977; Parenti 1986).

In recognizing the enormous power of mass media in modern societies to portray a particular version of reality, it should be understood that this is not consummate power. The ability of the media to propagate dominant values and shape political reality is by no means absolute. More specialized media (i.e., non–mass media), especially books and magazines, regularly present alternative and dissenting views. Moreover, dissident views are given coverage by the mass media once those views have gained at least some credibility. Nor can the media create problems that are nonexistent or conceal those that do exist (Iyengar and Kinder 1987).

Acknowledging the less-than-total power of mass media to influence people's social and political worlds, however, should not lead to an underestimation of the power of this institution. In all modern societies, control of information is critical: Whoever controls the means of communication has great power. Marx posited that those who control the society's means of material production are the most powerful. It might be claimed that in modern societies, great power hinges on control of the means of information—the media. This is the reason that political and economic elites make great efforts to dominate the media and to control the flow of information. Those who exert significant control over the media or who can freely gain access to them are able to exercise great influence in determining the views, images, and ideas that will become part of the public consciousness.

REFERENCES

Bagdikian, Ben. 1971. *The Information Machines*. New York: Harper & Row.
——. 1983. *The Media Monopoly*. Boston: Beacon.
——. 1989. "Missing from the News," *The Progressive* 53 (August): 32–34.
Bennett, W. Lance. 1988. *News: The Politics of Illusion*. 2nd ed. New York: Longman.
Boorstin, Daniel J. 1961. *The Image: A Guide to Pseudo-Events in America*. New York: Harper & Row.
Cohen, Stanley and Jock Young, eds. 1973. *The Manufacture of News*. London: Constable.
Comstock, George. 1980. "The Impact of Television on American Institutions." Pp. 28–44 in *Readings in Mass Communication: Concepts and Issues in the Mass Media*, edited by Michael Emery and Ted Curtis Smythe. 4th ed. Dubuque, IA: Wm. C. Brown.
Epstein, Edwin Jay. 1974. *News from Nowhere*. New York: Vintage.
Gans, Herbert J. 1979. *Deciding What's News*. New York: Pantheon.
Gerbner, G. 1967. "An Institutional Approach to Mass Communications Research." Pp. 429–51 in *Communication: Theory and Research*, edited by L. Thayer. Springfield, IL: Charles C. Thomas.
Gitlin, Todd. 1980. *The Whole World Is Watching*. Berkeley: University of California Press.
Goldsen, Rose K. 1977. *The Show and Tell Machine: How Television Works and Works You Over*. New York: Dell.
Gollin, Albert E. 1988. "Media Power: On Closer Inspection, It's Not That Threatening." Pp. 41–44 in *Impacts of Mass Media*, edited by Ray Eldon Hiebert and Carol Reuss. 2nd ed. New York: Longman.
Herman, Edward S. and Noam Chomsky. 1988. *Manufacturing Consent: The Political Economy of the Mass Media*. New York: Pantheon.
Iyengar, Shanto and Donald R. Kinder. 1987. *News That Matters: Television and American Opinion*. Chicago: University of Chicago Press.
Key, V. O., Jr. 1964. *Public Opinion and American Democracy*. New York: Knopf.
Lazarsfeld, Paul, Bernard Berelson, and H. Gaudet. 1948. *The People's Choice*. New York: Columbia University Press.
Lippmann, Walter. 1922. *Public Opinion*. New York: Macmillan.
McCombs, Maxwell and Donald Shaw. 1972. "The Agenda-Setting Function of Mass Media," *Public Opinion Quarterly* 36:176–87.

Mills, C. Wright. 1956. *The Power Elite.* New York: Oxford University Press.

Paletz, David L. and Robert M. Entman. 1981. *Media Power Politics.* New York: Free Press.

Parenti, Michael. 1986. *Inventing Reality: The Politics of the Mass Media.* New York: St. Martin's.

Postman, Neil. 1985. *Amusing Ourselves to Death: Public Discourse in the Age of Show Business.* New York: Penguin.

Schiller, Herbert I. 1989. *Culture, Inc.: The Corporate Takeover of Public Expression.* New York: Oxford University Press.

Shaw, Donald L. and Maxwell E. McCombs. 1977. *The Emergence of American Political Issues: The Agenda-Setting Function of the Press.* St. Paul: West Publishers.

Sigal, Leon V. 1973. *Reporters and Officials: The Organization and Politics of News Reporting.* Lexington, MA: Heath.

Tuchman, Gaye. 1978. *Making News.* New York: Free Press.

Wright, Charles R. 1986. *Mass Communication: A Sociological Perspective.* 3rd ed. New York: Random House.

38

THE AGE OF GLOBALIZATION

RICHARD J. BARNET • JOHN CAVANAGH

This reading by Richard J. Barnet and John Cavanagh is an excerpt from their recent book, *Global Dreams: Imperial Corporations and the New World Order.* Barnet and Cavanagh explore how the global economy is reshaping the international division of labor and affecting millions of individual lives. The rise of multinational corporations and the inability of nation states to regulate them has numerous consequences for capitalists and workers. Barnet and Cavanagh discuss several implications of increasing globalization on both developed and developing countries.

I

A quarter century ago, pictures taken from space of a fragile blue ball swathed in a thin membrane of life-sustaining vapors altered forever the way we envision our planet. Spaceship Earth offered a unifying metaphor to awaken planetary consciousness. Today more and more human beings are in touch with one another than ever before. Billions more, without even knowing it, are becoming entangled across great distances in global webs that are transforming their lives.

The world is getting smaller, as people like to say, but it is not coming together. Indeed, as economies are drawn closer, nations, cities, and neighborhoods are being pulled apart. The processes of global economic integration are stimulating political and social disintegration. Family ties are severed, established authority is undermined, and the bonds of local community are strained. Like cells, nations are multiplying by dividing.

We are all participants in one way or another in an unprecedented political and economic happening, but we cannot make sense of it. We know that we are supposed to think globally, but it is hard to wrap the mind even around a city block, much less a planet. No wonder we are at the mercy of buzzwords and sound bites. "Globalization" is the most fashionable word of the 1990s, so portentous and wonderfully patient as to puzzle Alice in Wonderland and thrill the Red Queen because it means precisely whatever the user says it means. Just as poets and songwriters celebrated the rise of modern nationalism, so in our day corporate managers, environmental prophets, business philosophers, rock stars, and writers of advertising copy offer themselves as poet laureates of the global village. But much breathless talk about globalization we hear all around us is what the late Clare Boothe Luce used to call globaloney.

The emerging global order is spearheaded by a few hundred corporate giants, many of them bigger than most sovereign nations. Ford's economy is larger than Saudi Arabia's and Norway's. Philip Morris's annual sales exceed New Zealand's gross domestic product. The multinational corporation of 20 years ago carried on separate operations in many different countries and tailored its operations to local conditions. In the 1990s large business enterprises, even some smaller ones, have the technological means and strategic vision to burst old limits—of time, space, national boundaries, language, custom, and ideology. By acquiring earth-spanning technologies, by developing products that can be produced anywhere and sold everywhere, by spreading credit around the world, and by connecting global channels of communication that can penetrate any village or neighborhood, these institutions we normally think of as economic rather than political, private rather than public, are becoming the world empires of the twenty-first century. The architects and managers of these space-age business enterprises understand that the balance of power in world politics has shifted in recent years from territorially bound governments to companies that can roam the world. As the hopes and pretensions of government shrink almost everywhere, these imperial corporations are occupying public space and exerting a more profound influence over the lives of ever larger numbers of people.

II

. . . While hundreds of millions of people in the world are playing their part in creating the ties that bind across great distances, a few hundred business enterprises control the human energy, capital, and technology that are making it happen. They are the midwives of the new world economy.

Global corporations are the first secular institutions run by men (and a handful of women) who think and plan on a global scale. Things that managers of multinational companies dreamed of 20 years ago are becoming reality—Coca-Cola's ads that reach billions in the same instant, Citibank's credit cards for Asian yuppies, Nike's network for producing millions of sports shoes in factories others paid for. A relatively few companies with worldwide connections dominate the four intersecting webs of global commercial activity on which the new world economy largely rests: the Global Cultural Bazaar; the Global Shopping Mall; the Global Workplace; and the Global Financial Network.

These worldwide webs of economic activity have already achieved a degree of global integration never before achieved by any world empire or nation-state. The driving force behind each of them can be traced in large measure to the same few hundred corporate giants with headquarters in the United States, Japan, Germany, France, Switzerland, the Netherlands, and the United Kingdom. The combined assets of the top 300 firms now make up roughly a quarter of the productive assets in the world.[1]

The Global Cultural Bazaar is the newest of the global webs, and the most nearly universal in its reach. Films, television, radio, music, magazines, T-shirts, games, toys, and theme parks are the media for disseminating global images and spreading global dreams. Rock stars and Hollywood blockbusters are truly global products. All across the planet people are using the same electronic devices to watch or listen to the same commercially produced songs and stories. Thanks to satellite, cable, and tape recorders, even autocratic governments are losing the tight control they once had over the flow of information and their hold on the fantasy lives of their subjects.

Even in culturally conservative societies in what we still call the Third World the dinner hour is falling victim to television. In bars, teahouses, and cafés and in living quarters around the world the same absence of conversation and human interaction is noticeable as family members, singly or together, sit riveted in front of a cathode tube. As in the United States, Europe, and Japan, centuries-old ways of life are disappearing under the spell of advanced communication technologies. The cultural products most widely distributed around the world bear the stamp "Made in the U.S.A.," and almost any Hollywood film or video is bound to offend traditional values somewhere. Scenes depicting independent women, amorous couples, and kids talking back to parents upset all sorts of people across the globe as assaults on family, religion, and order. Because the steady streams of global commercial products in many places, including parts of the United States, are feared as barbarian intrusions, they are provoking local and nationalist backlashes, often carried out in the name of God.

. . .

The Global Shopping Mall is a planetary supermarket with a dazzling spread of things to eat, drink, wear, and enjoy. We will explore the rise of global advertising, distribution, and marketing and examine their impacts. Dreams of affluent living are communicated to the farthest reaches of the globe, but only a minority of the people in the world can afford to shop at the Mall. Of the 5.4 billion people on earth, almost 3.6 billion have neither cash nor credit to buy much of anything. A majority of people on the planet are at most windowshoppers.

. . .

The Global Workplace is a network of factories, workshops, law offices, hospitals, restaurants, and all sorts of other places where goods are produced, information is processed, and services of every description are rendered. Everything from cigarettes to cars contains materials from dozens of countries pieced together in a global integrated assembly line driven by the logic of the bottom line. Data processors, law offices, advertising agencies, and insurance companies have become global assembly lines of a different sort. A worldwide labor market for creative merchandising ideas, computer knowledge, patient fingers, managerial know-how, and every other marketable skill coexists with a global labor pool in which more and more of us, from the chief executive officer to the wastebasket emptier, are swimming. Hundreds of millions more of the world's uprooted and dispossessed are desperate to jump in.

The Ford Motor Company played a historic role in the development of mass production, and in many ways it is the American-based automaker that has most successfully adapted to the post–mass production era, the most avid in trying to develop a car that can be sold anywhere in the world, and the most resourceful in making transnational alliances with its Japanese competitors. The pressures on Ford and its competitors to cut labor costs have had a profound effect on the world labor market. A look at a range of other industries, too, including clothing, information processing, and electronics, brings the true dimensions of the global job crisis into sharper focus. . . . There is much data that point to a stark reality: A huge and increasing proportion of human beings are not needed and will never be needed to make goods or to provide services because too many people in the world are too poor to buy them.

The Global Financial Network is a constantly changing maze of currency transactions, global securities, MasterCards, euroyen, swaps, ruffs, and an ever more innovative array of speculative devices for repackaging and reselling money. This network is much closer to a chain of gambling casinos than to the dull gray banks of yesteryear. Twenty-four hours a day, trillions of dollars flow through the world's major foreign-exchange markets as bits of data traveling at split-second speed.[2] No more than 10 percent of this staggering sum has anything to do with trade in goods and services.[3] International traffic in money has become an end in itself, a highly profitable game. John Maynard Keynes, who had intimations of how technology might one day be harnessed in the service of nonrecreational gambling, predicted the rise of this "casino economy," as he called it. Yet as banking activities have become more global and more speculative, the credit needs of billions of people and millions of small businesses are not met.

. . .

Viewed together, these four webs offer a picture very different from that of a global village. The Global Cultural Bazaar is reaching the majority of households with its global dreams. Much smaller numbers are playing any role at all in the three networks that produce, market, and finance the world's goods and services. In the new world economy, there is a huge gulf between the beneficiaries and the excluded and, as world population grows, it is widening.

III

. . .

The most disturbing aspect of this [global] system is that the formidable power and mobility of global corporations are undermining the effectiveness of national governments to carry out essential policies on behalf of their people. Leaders of nation-states are losing much of the control over their own territory they once had. More and more, they must conform to the demands of the outside world because the outsiders are already inside the gates. Business enterprises that routinely operate across borders are linking far-flung pieces of territory into a new world economy that bypasses all sorts of established political arrangements and conventions. Tax laws intended for another age, traditional ways to control capital flows and interest rates, full-employment policies, and old approaches to resource development and environmental protection are becoming obsolete, unenforceable, or irrelevant.

National leaders no longer have the ability to comprehend, much less control, these giants because they are mobile, and like the mythic Greek figure Proteus they are constantly changing appearances to suit different circumstances. The shifting relationships between the managers of global corporations and political authorities are creating a new political reality almost everywhere.

An extraordinary global machine has been developed to make, sell, and service commodities and to render all manner of services, but no political ideology or economic theory has yet evolved to take account of the tectonic shift that has occurred. The modern nation-state, that extraordinary legacy of Madison, Napoleon, Bolívar, Lincoln, Bismarck, Wilson, Roosevelt, Stalin, Mao, Nehru, Kenyatta, and the millions all over the world who have sacrificed and died for it, looks more and more like an institution of a bygone age. In much of Asia, Africa, and Latin America, the state is collapsing under the weight of debt, bloated bureaucracy, and corruption. Local peoples' movements and surprisingly sophisticated informal economic arrangements, many of them off the books and beyond the reach of government, are growing up to fill the vacuum. The United States, although still the largest national economy and by far the world's greatest military power, is increasingly subject to the vicissitudes of a world economy no nation can dominate. Foreign trade and investment have become much more important to the U.S. economy. A generation ago the sum of all U.S. exports and imports amounted to around 10 percent of the gross national product. Today it is more than 25 percent.[4] In the process, the economic health of the United States has become increasingly at the mercy of decisions of foreign corporations, banks, governments, and investors.

However, the nation-state is far from disappearing. On the contrary, the Cold War victory has unleashed a revival of nationalism, a bloody nightmare in the Balkans that is a prototype of the national security crises of the 1990s. Every ethnic group and religious faction, it seems, wants its own national banner. National governments everywhere are getting bigger, but are neither more effective nor popular. In Ronald Reagan's America and Margaret Thatcher's Britain, the size and budget of the state expanded even as these leaders denounced government and preached "privatization." It is altogether obvious that what governments do or fail to do is still important. Politicians and generals determine when and where the dogs of war are unleashed, not corporate chairmen or commodity traders. National governments, acting either unilaterally or in concert, still set the rules under which the world economy functions, and national policies for economic development continue to exert a profound influence on the competitive positions of particular corporations. But the nation-state everywhere faces a crisis of redefinition without a practical ideology that confronts the realities of the emerging global order.

As the twentieth century draws to a close, much of the official truth that sustained and guided governments for 50 years or more has collapsed and new political visions are in short supply. The repudiation of socialism is of course the most spectacular ideological turnabout of the 1990s, but the inexorable intrusions of a world economy over which national governments exercise diminishing control have drained other established political orthodoxies of meaning and power. Like Leninism, Keynesianism was premised on the idea that national economies were real. Within the borders of a nation-state, at least within militarily powerful, advanced industrial nations, government could provide economic stability, development, and social progress. The Leninists believed they could accomplish these worthy objectives through state planning and a command economy. The Keynesians thought it could all be done more humanely by more modest government intervention in the marketplace, essentially by adjusting interest and tax rates and by well-targeted government spending.

What it takes to manage a successful national economy in the new global environment to achieve stability and growth without destroying people, crushing their spirit, or wrecking the environment is as yet unknown. Political programs can stimulate short-term booms, but all across the political spectrum long-term economic management has become a mystery since nothing quite works as theory predicts. Juggling interest rates and exchange rates, raising and lowering taxes, all produce unwelcome surprises. As politicians across the political spectrum are learning, staking one's reputation on promises of prosperity is not the best way to get your name emblazoned on a bridge. The same global economic changes that hastened the breakdown of the Cold War order are still straining nations everywhere.

The ideas for navigating the transition to the postnational order that beckons as the only apparent alternative to anarchic disorder and the breakup of nations are not likely to originate in corporate boardrooms. The interests and self-defined responsibilities of corporate leaders are global but parochial; their eyes are on the global market, but most of the world's people remain invisible. Hundreds of millions are now residents in the global village being created by the great corporations, but billions more are not and have no such prospects. "Going global" is a strategy for picking and choosing from a global menu. Vast areas of the world and the people who live there are written off. Contrast corporate globalism with past notions of world civilization. Even when they espoused a universal spirit, aspiring world cultures were rooted in particular places. Athens. Rome. Constantinople. But the ideology of the age of globalization celebrates the liberation from passionate attachments to any specific piece of territory. This is quite different from the universal consciousness of which poets, philosophers, and prophets have dreamed through the ages.

IV

As the processes of globalization accelerate, the more conscious we become of the pull of localism in all its forms. For most people across the world, place and rootedness are as important as ever. Their very identity is tied to a place, and they cannot conceive of living anywhere else, for they are dependent on a piece of ground for their livelihood and on a particular culture and language for their sense of well-being. For them the forces of globalization are a threat. Hundreds of millions of people over the last generation have been uprooted from the land because of the spread of export agriculture or industrial development, or they have been drawn to the city by the pull of urban life. But unlike peripatetic lawyers, executives, rock stars, and other jet-age nomads who see the world as a giant menu of personal and professional choices, most of these people have no better prospects than marginal employment in the capital city or a life of insecurity in a faraway land. As people migrate to the great cities of the world, largely in response to global economic and cultural integration in its various forms, old ways of life, family traditions, child-rearing practices, and local authority structures are swept away. All this is creating a crisis not just of politics but of culture.

Global integration has many positive aspects . . . but in the late twentieth century there is strong evidence that, as national economies become increasingly intertwined, nations are breaking up in many different ways, and no alternative community is yet on the horizon. For some regions and city blocks all around the world, globalization brings unparalleled prosperity. For others on another continent or just across town the consequence may be crushing poverty. The inhabitants of a penthouse apartment on the Upper East Side of Manhattan are drawn by taste, style, habit, and outlook into a closer relationship with similarly situated citizens of Brussels, Rio, or Tokyo and further and further away from poorer, less mobile residents who may live a block or two away.

As traditional communities disappear and ancient cultures are overwhelmed, billions of human beings are losing the sense of place and sense of self that give life meaning. The fundamental political conflict in the opening decades of the new century, we believe, will not be between nations or even between trading blocs but between the forces of globalization and the territorially based forces of local survival seeking to preserve and to redefine community.

NOTES

1. "A Survey of Multinationals," *Economist,* March 27, 1993, pp. 5–6.
2. James Robinson, CEO, American Express, to Executives Club, Chicago, September 1989.
3. *Wall Street Journal,* September 18, 1992.
4. In 1965, the figure was 10.8 percent; in 1990 it was 25.9 percent. Calculated from Council of Economic Advisers, *Economic Report of the President* (Washington, DC: U.S. Government Printing Office, 1991).

THE ECONOMY AND WORK

39

MANIFESTO OF THE COMMUNIST PARTY

KARL MARX • FRIEDRICH ENGELS

The economy and work are the focus of the next four readings. The first selection in this group is an excerpt from the classic "Manifesto of the Communist Party," written by Karl Marx and Friedrich Engels in 1848. Students often are surprised to discover the currency of many of the topics discussed by Marx and Engels. Specifically, Marx and Engels foresaw the rise of global capitalism. They also accurately described exploitive industrial conditions and the oppositional interests of workers and capitalists. Even though Marx and Engels are criticized for not foreseeing the rise of other social agents (such as the middle class, the government, and unions) in mediating the conflict between capitalists and workers, their theory of class struggle and revolution is still provocative and a source for worldwide social change.

The history of all hitherto existing society is the history of class struggles.

Freeman and slave, patrician and plebeian, lord and serf, guild-master and journeyman, in a word, oppressor and oppressed, stood in constant opposition to one another, carried on an uninterrupted, now hidden, now open fight, a fight that each time ended, either in a revolutionary reconstitution of society at large, or in the common ruin of the contending classes.

In the earlier epochs of history, we find almost everywhere a complicated arrangement of society into various orders, a manifold gradation of social rank. In ancient Rome we have patricians, knights, plebeians, slaves; in the Middle Ages, feudal lords, vassals, guild-masters, journeymen, apprentices, serfs; in almost all of these classes, again, subordinate gradations.

The modern bourgeois society that has sprouted from the ruins of feudal society has not done away with class antagonisms. It has but established new classes, new conditions of oppression, new forms of struggle in place of the old ones.

Our epoch, the epoch of the bourgeoisie, possesses, however, this distinctive feature: It has simplified the class antagonisms. Society as a whole is more and more splitting up into two great hostile camps, into two great classes directly facing each other: Bourgeoisie and Proletariat.

From the serfs of the Middle Ages sprang the chartered burghers of the earliest towns. From these burgesses the first elements of the bourgeoisie were developed.

The discovery of America, the rounding of the Cape, opened up fresh ground for the rising bourgeoisie. The East-Indian and Chinese markets, the colonization of America, trade with the colonies, the increase in the means of exchange and in commodities generally, gave to commerce, to navigation, to industry, an impulse never before known, and thereby, to the revolutionary element in the tottering feudal society, a rapid development.

The feudal system of industry, under which industrial production was monopolized by closed guilds, now no longer sufficed for the growing wants of the new markets. The manufacturing system took its place. The guild-masters were pushed on one side by the manufacturing middle class; division of labour between the different corporate guilds vanished in the face of division of labour in each single workshop.

Meantime the markets kept ever growing, the demand ever rising. Even manufacture no longer sufficed. Thereupon, steam and machinery revolutionized industrial production. The place of manufacture was taken by the giant, Modern Industry, the place of the industrial middle class, by industrial millionaires, the leaders of whole industrial armies, the modern bourgeois.

Modern industry has established the world-market, for which the discovery of America paved the way. This market has given an immense development to commerce, to navigation, to communication by land. This development has, in its turn, reacted on the extension of industry; and in proportion as industry, commerce, navigation, railways extended, in the same proportion the bourgeoisie developed, increased its capital, and pushed into the background every class handed down from the Middle Ages.

We see, therefore, how the modern bourgeoisie is itself the product of a long course of development, of a series of revolutions in the modes of production and of exchange.

Each step in the development of the bourgeoisie was accompanied by a corresponding political advance of that class. An oppressed class under the sway of the feudal nobility, an armed and self-governing association in the mediaeval commune; here independent urban republic (as in Italy and Germany), there taxable "third estate" of the monarchy (as in France), afterwards, in the period of manufacture proper, serving either the semi-feudal or the absolute monarchy as a counterpoise against the nobility, and, in fact, corner-stone of the great monarchies in general, the bourgeoisie has at last, since the establishment of Modern Industry and of the world-market, conquered for itself, in the modern representative State, exclusive political sway. The execution of the modern State is but a committee for managing the common affairs of the whole bourgeoisie.

The bourgeoisie, historically, has played a most revolutionary part.

The bourgeoisie, wherever it has got the upper hand, has put an end to all feudal, patriarchal, idyllic relations. It has pitilessly torn asunder the motley feudal ties that bound man to his "natural superiors," and has left remaining no other nexus between man and man than naked self-interest, than callous "cash payment." It has drowned the most heavenly ecstasies of religious fervor, of chivalrous enthusiasm, of philistine sentimentalism, in the icy water of egotistical calculation. It has resolved personal worth into exchange value, and in place of the numberless indefeasible chartered freedoms, has set up that single, unconscionable freedom—Free Trade. In one word, for exploitation, veiled by religious and political illusions, it has substituted naked, shameless, direct, brutal exploitation.

The bourgeoisie has stripped of its halo every occupation hitherto honored and looked up to with reverent awe. It has converted the physician, the lawyer, the priest, the poet, the man of science, into its paid wage-labourers.

The bourgeoisie has torn away from the family its sentimental veil, and has reduced the family relation to a mere money relation.

The bourgeoisie has disclosed how it came to pass that the brutal display of vigor in the Middle Ages, which Reactionists so much admire, found its fitting complement in the most slothful indolence. It has been the first to show what man's activity can bring about. It has accomplished wonders far surpassing Egyptian pyramids, Roman aqueducts, and Gothic cathedrals; it has conducted expeditions that put in the shade all former Exoduses of nations and crusades.

The bourgeoisie cannot exist without constantly revolutionizing the instruments of production, and thereby the relations of production, and with them the whole relations of society. Conservation of the old modes of production in unaltered form, was, on the contrary, the first condition of existence for all earlier industrial classes. Constant revolutionizing of production, uninterrupted disturbance of all social conditions, everlasting uncertainty and agitation distinguish the bourgeois epoch from all earlier ones. All fixed, fast-frozen relations, with their train of ancient and venerable prejudices and opinions, are swept away, all new-formed ones become antiquated before they can ossify. All that is solid melts into air, all that is holy is profaned, and man is at last compelled to face with sober senses, his real conditions of life, and his relations with his kind.

The need of a constantly expanding market for its products chases the bourgeoisie over the whole surface of the globe. It must nestle everywhere, settle everywhere, establish connexions everywhere.

The bourgeoisie has through its exploitation of the world-market given a cosmopolitan character to production and consumption in every country. To the great chagrin of Reactionists, it has drawn from under the feet of industry the national ground on which it stood. All old-established national industries have been destroyed or are daily being destroyed. They are dislodged by new industries, whose introduction becomes a life and death question for all civilized nations, by industries that no longer work up indigenous raw material, but raw material drawn from the remotest zones; industries whose products are consumed, not only at home, but in every quarter of the globe. In place of the old wants, satisfied by the productions of the country, we find new wants, requiring for their satisfaction the products of distant lands and climes. In place of the old local and national seclusion and self-sufficiency, we have intercourse in every direction, universal inter-dependence of nations. And as in material, so also in intellectual production. The intellectual creations of individual nations become common property. National one-sidedness and narrow-mindedness become more and more impossible, and from the numerous national and local literatures, there arises a world literature.

The bourgeoisie, by the rapid improvement of all instruments of production, by the immensely facilitated means of communication, draws all, even the most barbarian, nations into civilization. The cheap prices of its commodities are the heavy artillery with which it batters down all Chinese walls, with which it forces the barbarians' intensely obstinate hatred of foreigners to capitulate. It compels all nations, on pain of extinction, to adopt the bourgeois mode of production; it compels them to introduce what it calls civilization into their midst, *i.e.,* to become bourgeois themselves. In one word, it creates a world after its own image.

The bourgeoisie has subjected the country to the rule of the towns. It has created enormous cities, has greatly increased the urban population as compared with the rural, and has thus rescued a considerable part of the population from the idiocy of rural life. Just as it has made the country dependent on the towns, so it has made barbarian and semi-barbarian countries dependent on the civilized ones, nations of peasants on nations of bourgeois, the East on the West.

The bourgeoisie keeps more and more doing away with the scattered state of the population, of the means of production, and of property. It has agglomerated population, centralized means of production, and has concentrated property in a few hands. The necessary consequence of this was political centralization. Independent, or but loosely connected provinces, with separate interests, laws, governments and systems of taxation, became lumped together into one nation, with one government, one code of laws, one national class-interest, one frontier and one customs-tariff.

The bourgeoisie, during its rule of scarce one hundred years, has created more massive and more colossal productive forces than have all preceding generations together. Subjection of Nature's forces to man, machinery, application of chemistry to industry and agriculture, steam-navigation, railways, electric telegraphs, clearing of whole continents for cultivation, canalization of rivers, whole populations conjured out of the ground—what earlier century had even a presentiment that such productive forces slumbered in the lap of social labour?

We see then: the means of production and of exchange, on whose foundation the bourgeoisie built itself up, were generated in feudal society. At a certain stage in the development of these means of production and of exchange, the conditions under which feudal society produced and exchanged, the feudal organization of agriculture and manufacturing industry, in one word, the feudal relations of property became no longer compatible with the already developed productive forces; they became so many fetters. They had to be burst asunder; they were burst asunder.

Into their place stepped free competition, accompanied by a social and political constitution adapted to it, and by the economical and political sway of the bourgeois class.

A similar movement is going on before our own eyes. Modern bourgeois society with its relations of production, of exchange and of property, a society that has conjured up such gigantic means of production and of exchange, is like the sorcerer, who is no longer able to control the powers of the nether world whom he has called up by his spells. For many a decade past the history of industry and commerce is but the history of the revolt of modern productive forces against modern conditions of production, against the property relations that are the conditions for the existence of the bourgeoisie and of its rule. It is enough to mention the commercial crises that by their periodical return put on its trial, each time more threateningly, the existence of the entire bourgeois society. In these crises a great part not only of the existing products, but also of the previously created productive forces, are periodically destroyed. In these crises there breaks out an epidemic that, in all earlier epochs, would have seemed an absurdity—the epidemic of over-production. Society suddenly finds itself put back into a state of momentary barbarism; it appears as if a famine, a universal war of devastation had cut off the supply of every means of subsistence; industry and commerce seem to be destroyed; and why? Because there is too much civilization, too much means of subsistence, too much industry, too much commerce. The productive forces at the disposal of society no longer tend to further the development of the conditions of bourgeois property; on the contrary, they have become too powerful for these conditions, by which they are fettered, and so soon as they overcome these fetters, they bring disorder into the whole of bourgeois society, endanger the existence of bourgeois property. The conditions of bourgeois society are too narrow to comprise the wealth created by them. And how does the bourgeoisie get over these crises? On the one hand by enforced destruction of a mass of productive forces; on the other, by the conquest of new markets, and by the more thorough exploitation of the old ones. That is to say, by paving the way for more extensive and more destructive crises, and by diminishing the means whereby crises are prevented.

The weapons with which the bourgeoisie felled feudalism to the ground are now turned against the bourgeoisie itself.

But not only has the bourgeoisie forged the weapons that bring death to itself; it has also called into existence the men who are to wield those weapons—the modern working class—the proletarians.

In proportion as the bourgeoisie, *i.e.,* capital, is developed, in the same proportion is the proletariat, the modern working class, developed—a class of labourers, who live only so long as they find work, and who find work only so long as their labour increases capital. These labourers, who must sell themselves piece-meal, are a commodity, like every other article of commerce, and are consequently exposed to all the vicissitudes of competition, to all the fluctuations of the market.

Owing to the extensive use of machinery and to division of labour, the work of the proletarians has lost all individual character, and consequently, all charm for the workman. He becomes an appendage of the machine, and it is only the most simple, most monotonous, and most easily acquired knack, that is required of him. Hence, the cost of production of a workman is restricted, almost entirely, to the means of subsistence that he requires for his maintenance, and for the propagation of his race. But the price of a commodity, and therefore also of labour, is equal to its cost of production. In proportion, therefore, as the repulsiveness of the work increases, the wage decreases. Nay more, in proportion as the use of machinery and division of labour increases, in the same proportion the burden of toil also increases, whether by prolongation of the working hours, by increase of the work exacted in a given time or by increased speed of the machinery, etc.

Modern industry has converted the little workshop of the patriarchal master into the great factory of the industrial capitalist. Masses of labourers, crowded into the factory, are organised like soldiers. As privates of the industrial army they are placed under the command of a perfect hierarchy of officers and sergeants. Not only are they slaves of the bourgeois class, and of the bourgeois State; they are daily and hourly enslaved by the machine, by the over-looker, and, above all, by the individual bourgeois manufacturer himself. The more openly this despotism proclaims gain to be its end and aim, the more petty, the more hateful and the more embittering it is.

The less the skill and exertion of strength implied in manual labour, in other words, the more modern industry becomes developed, the more is the labour of men superseded by that of women. Differences of age and sex have no longer any distinctive social validity for the working class. All are instruments of labour, more or less expensive to use, according to their age and sex.

No sooner is the exploitation of the labourer by the manufacturer, so far, at an end, that he receives his wages in cash, than he is set upon by the other portions of the bourgeoisie, the landlord, the shopkeeper, the pawnbroker, etc.

40

DOLLARS AND DIPLOMAS

KATHRYN MARIE DUDLEY

This reading is an excerpt from Kathryn Marie Dudley's book, *The End of the Line: Lost Jobs, New Lives in Postindustrial America.* Dudley spent two years researching the impact of an automotive plant closure in Kenosha, Wisconsin, on individuals and on the community. In this selection, Dudley describes how deindustrialization has affected three different workers and their families. Dudley is especially concerned with educational attainment and how it affects the employment opportunities of laid-off workers.

At 38 years old, Steve Miller had 18 years' seniority at the auto plant. In another 12 years he would have been eligible for early retirement. Without this goal to work toward, Steve feels confused and disoriented.

It's really hard to describe the feeling that you have when all of a sudden you don't have a job anymore—especially after all them years. You're under pressure every day, and you just don't know how you can relieve that pressure. You're kinda in limbo. You're kinda hung out at the end of the pole to dry. It's a tough situation. You don't know where you're gonna go, or what you're gonna do for a living. I worry about the kids, how I'm gonna get them through college. It's rough . . . it's pretty bad.

For industrial workers at the peak of their working lives, job loss instantly nullifies the principle of seniority around which so much of their life has been structured. It used to be that seniority protected you from the waves of layoffs so frequent in the volatile auto industry. And every year worked at the plant built up "equity" in the substantial retirement package you could plan on receiving at the end of 30 years. But a plant closing forecloses this sense of working toward a secure future. In the Kenosha shutdown, many workers were under 40 and thus too young to qualify for the special retirement benefits Chrysler agreed to give older workers dislocated by the plant closing.[1] Two years shy of 40, Steve feels his 18 years of seniority are now almost worthless:

> I'll get partial pension when I'm 60 and no insurance. But if I was 40 years old, I could get my partial pension when I'm 55 *and* insurance. If they wouldn't have closed down, in two more years, then at least after 55, I'd have my insurance. But they cut it off at 40 years of age, and anybody that was under 40 [gets] nothing.

Workers know that a partial pension is better than no pension at all, but they share an overriding feeling that they are the victims of a cruel hoax. After all, they weren't banking on a partial pension. Many pushed themselves to continue working at the auto plant year after year because the promise of retirement benefits made it seem worthwhile. Most had every intention of staying until they reached that goal. It is as if they have charted the course of their lives with a compass fixed steadily on the north pole and have come halfway around the world only to discover someone has moved the goal.[2]

Connie Miller shares her husband's feeling of constant pressure since the closing was announced. She worries whether Steve will find a decent job, one that can support a family of four on a single income and allow them to maintain their present lifestyle:

> I could think about finding a job too, you know, but we really feel strongly about the mom being home with the kids. [Our daughter] is a year and a half. We don't want anyone else raising her. That was one of the nice things about Steve working at the plant—and probably for other people, too—that it enabled me to stay home with the kids and only work very part-time. Instead of like having to go and work some dumb job, and ship them off to a day care and let someone else raise them. We just don't believe in that.

Women like Connie belong to a generation for which the nature of family roles is far more open to individual choice than ever in our nation's history. Connie herself worked in the auto plant for several years before her son was born and has always planned to return to work when her daughter starts school. But as a mother, she feels strongly that her proper social role, if not moral obligation, is to stay home while the children are young.

Actions that may seem economically counterproductive—such as turning down a promising job offer, staying at home with young children, and holding out for largely nonexistent factory work—make sense when understood as a last line of defense against the psychological trauma inflicted by involuntary job loss.[3] Next to the family, employment is the dominant social institution in working people's lives. The workplace is more than just a place where we earn money. Through its organization and rules, it structures our daily lives by providing certain unavoidable categories of experience. In this sense work meets enduring human needs for time structure, activity, social contacts, participation in a collective purpose, and knowledge of one's place in society.[4] Steve and Connie Miller are struggling to maintain their customary lifestyle and honor the commitments to family that this entails, but the foundations of their blue-collar world have collapsed.

Where Have All the Good Jobs Gone?

For American workers in Steve Miller's position—relatively young men with high-school educations who lose jobs in manufacturing—finding a comparable replacement is virtually impossible. Getting another job is no longer just a matter of putting in applications at other factories down the street. High-paying industrial jobs have been drying up all over the region for years. Even if Steve is lucky enough to hire in at another local factory, wage rates there will be in the range of five to seven dollars an hour—half what he was earning at the auto plant. If his experience is like that of most dislocated workers in the United States today, he can expect to suffer a 37 percent cut in pay during his first year of unemployment.[5]

For this reason the search for new work often feels like a no-win proposition. The competition seems too fierce, and the pie too small, to generate much hope of success. Steve admits that a lack of optimism makes it difficult for him to pursue all the job leads he knows he should. "I think there's just too many people out there looking for a good job that pays decent wages," he says with a sigh. "We're just afraid there aren't enough good jobs to go around," Connie adds anxiously. "There weren't before [the auto plant] shut down, and now there's even less."

By a "good" job, the Millers mean one that pays a middle-income wage to a person with a high-school education who is willing to work full time at a job in heavy industrial production. Connie's fear that there are fewer and fewer jobs of this type is well justified. Jobs in the middle range of the wage distribution *are* harder to find. As economists Bennett Harrison and Barry Bluestone report in their book *The Great U-Turn*, there has been a dramatic

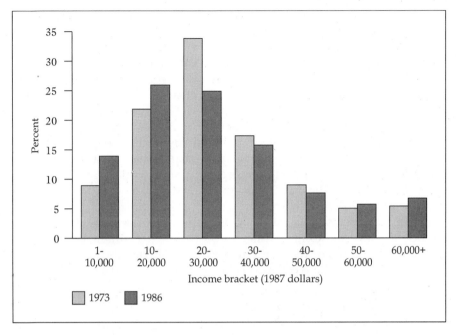

FIGURE 40.1   Earnings distribution of prime-age men (men aged 25 to 55 who worked at least one hour a year) 1973 and 1986.

Data from Frank Levy, "Incomes, Families, and Living Standards," in *American Living Standards,* ed. Robert E. Litan, Robert Z. Lawrence, and Charles L. Schultze (Washington, DC: Brookings Institution, 1988), p. 122, Figure 4–3. Calculations based on CPS microdata files.

decline in the creation of good-paying jobs since the early 1970s. From 1963 to 1973 almost nine out of every ten new jobs created paid middle-income wages. From 1979 to 1986 that figure shrank to only one in two.[6] The impact of this "job shortage" can be seen in the earnings distribution of men who are 25 to 55 years old (see Figure 40.1).

The largest drop has been in the percentage of men earning $20,000 to $50,000 a year. This is precisely the income category that Steve and Connie Miller consider "middle class," and indeed, by this reckoning Kenosha's autoworkers were all squarely in the middle class. As they look for work in today's labor market, they are increasingly faced with a choice between high-paying jobs that require a college education or technical degree and "bad" jobs that pay less than they are accustomed to. The economic profile is not simply a picture of the "disappearing" middle class; it also reveals a steady trend toward a *polarization of incomes.* The proportion of workers earning less than $20,000 grew substantially in the 1980s, and the proportion earning over $50,000 also increased in size. Only the group in the middle has shrunk.

There is a marked regional dimension to the current pattern of income polarization. The Midwest, hardest hit by the decline of manufacturing employment, has witnessed the obliteration of virtually all new job creation in the middle-wage category.[7] As good-paying industrial jobs vanish, new employment in the rust belt has been almost entirely in the low-wage service sector of the economy (see Table 40.1). Even for those who remain in the middle class, it has become harder and harder to support a family on one paycheck. In contrast to the rising incomes of the postwar years, most of today's workers have seen their earnings fall over the past 25 years. For the 80 percent of the United States population classified as "production and non-supervisory" workers—for example, factory workers, construction workers, restaurant and clerical workers, nurses, and teachers—average adjusted weekly earnings dropped from $375.73 in 1973 to $335.20 in 1989 (see Figure 40.2).

In an economy where incomes are not growing, the only way workers can improve their standard of living is by moving into higher-paying jobs. They can no longer stay in the same job and expect to see the real value of

TABLE 40.1   Percentage of Net Job Growth by Region, 1963–1986

	1963–1973	1973–1979	1979–1986
Northeast			
Low stratum[a]	(29.6)[d]	38.5	24.7
Middle stratum[b]	88.4	69.9	51.3
High stratum[c]	41.2	(8.4)	23.9
Midwest			
Low stratum	(5.2)	16.5	96.0
Middle stratum	81.4	80.8	(4.8)
High stratum	23.8	2.7	8.8
South			
Low stratum	(13.2)	16.2	33.7
Middle stratum	98.0	76.3	52.8
High stratum	15.2	7.5	13.5
West			
Low stratum	5.1	16.4	29.8
Middle stratum	75.7	71.4	60.1
High stratum	19.2	12.2	10.1
New England			
Low stratum	(70.7)	29.6	16.6
Middle stratum	117.9	66.7	61.8
High stratum	52.8	3.8	21.6

[a]Low stratum = earnings of less than $11,104 a year (in 1985 dollars).
[b]Middle stratum = earnings of $11,105 to $44,412 a year.
[c]High stratum = earnings of $44,413 a year or more.
[d]Negative numbers are given in parentheses.

Source: Bennett Harrison and Barry Bluestone, *The Great U-Turn: Corporate Restructuring and the Polarizing of America* (New York: Basic Books, 1988).

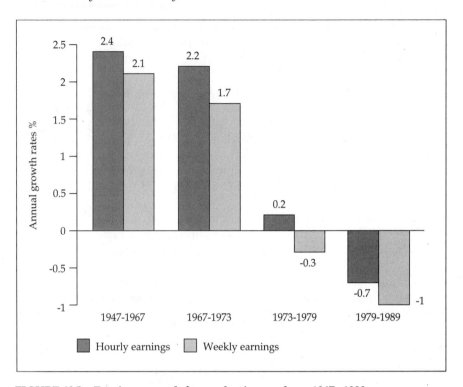

FIGURE 40.2   Earnings growth for production workers, 1947–1989.

Data from Lawrence Mishel and David M. Frankel, *The State of Working America, 1990–91 Edition*. Economic Policy Institute (Armonk, NY: M. E. Sharpe, 1991), p. 74, Figure 3B.

their earnings rise over time as they could during the postwar years. For workers dislocated from good manufacturing jobs, this makes prospects in the service sector twice as grim. Not only will their initial wages be lower, but they cannot hope to see their earnings improve over time. The standard of living they lost with a high-paying industrial job will in all likelihood never be recovered.

Harsh realities like these demand an explanation. Why are millions of industrial workers losing their jobs and falling out of the middle class? Because our work is invested with moral meaning, we are not comfortable with the idea that misfortune of this magnitude can befall anyone at any time. We have a pressing need to determine whether this suffering was caused by something people did or is due to forces beyond their control. Are dislocated workers victims in need of emergency aid, or do they in some sense deserve this particular fate? How we interpret this situation will guide our behavior in the marketplace and, even more important, determine how we judge the behavior of others. Social scientists, policy makers, and the residents of factory towns all across the United States are forced to make this moral judgment every time new employment data are released, every time a new bill on industrial policy crosses lawmakers' desks, every time a plant closes.

Deindustrialization

When the Millers reflect on what has happened to them, they blame the United States government for allowing American corporations to move good jobs out of the country. Connie speaks for many Kenoshans caught in the plant closing:

> What galls me the most about the whole affair was that [Chrysler] shipped that one auto line to Mexico to build them there and put our people *here* out of work. I just don't think that's right. And [American businesses] do that with so many things! In the future, I see you're gonna have a rich class and a poor class and that's gonna be it. And I don't think that's right!

The "export" of manufacturing jobs is certainly an important dimension of the problem American workers face. Over the past 25 years, United States companies have built more than 1,800 manufacturing plants in Mexico.[8] These *maquiladora* factories employ more than 500,000 nonunion laborers under a program sponsored by the Mexican government, which guarantees American businesses a low tariff on the goods they ship back into the United States.

Capital flight—the diversion of corporate funds from investment in domestic plants and equipment into speculation, foreign ventures, mergers, and acquisitions—is the primary culprit that economists Barry Bluestone and Bennett Harrison point to in their definitive account of what is happening to the United States economy, *The Deindustrialization of America. Deindustrialization,* as they define it, is more than a descriptive term applied to the closing of industrial plants: It is the "widespread, systematic disinvestment in the nation's basic productive capacity."[9] During the 1980s, Bluestone and Harrison argue, the overseas investments strategies of United States corporations changed dramatically. Instead of investing in domestic production for foreign markets, major industrial firms began producing goods abroad for import back into the United States market.[10] During the late 1970s and 1980s, disinvestment in domestic operations showed up on corporate balance sheets as "excess production capacity," and thousands of idled factories were closed.[11]

Economists disagree on the exact causes and nature of this trend, but few dispute that manufacturing employment in the industrial Midwest has been in free fall for the past two decades.[12] At no other time since the Great Depression has employment in manufacturing plunged so far so fast. From the 1950s through the end of the 1970s, at least 1.5 million manufacturing jobs were *added* to the economy every decade (see Figure 40.3). This pattern abruptly reversed itself in the 1980s. Between 1978 and 1982, one out of every four

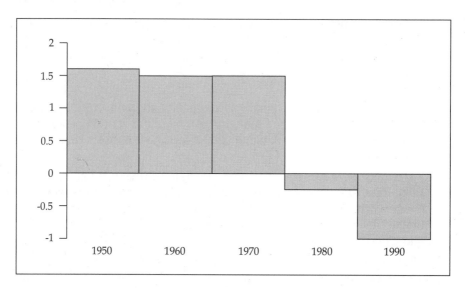

FIGURE 40.3   Creation and destruction of manufacturing jobs (in millions).
(Projection for the 1990s is based on current trends.)
Data from Donald L. Barlett and James B. Steele, *America: What Went Wrong?* (Kansas City, MO: Andrews and McMeel, 1992), p. 18.

industrial jobs was eliminated in the nation's largest manufacturing companies.[13] As domestic firms continued to slash payrolls and close aging factories at an unprecedented rate during the 1980s, the number of manufacturing jobs lost soared past 850,000 in 1988.[14] If the 1980s rate of plant closures, layoffs, and forced retirements continues unabated, more than one million industrial jobs will be eliminated by the end of the century.[15] During the 1950s and 1960s, one-third of all working Americans had jobs in manufacturing. That figure fell to 20 percent in the 1970s, and by the end of the 1980s, only 17 percent of the workforce remained employed in manufacturing.[16] Today fewer people than ever before can earn a living making things with their hands.

What Difference Does Education Make?

Donna Clausen is the wife of a tavern owner and the mother of four. She was among the thousands of autoworkers laid off in 1984. Just before her unemployment compensation ran out, Donna took a job at a local factory that was paying $3.75 an hour—a drastic cut from the $14 an hour she had been earning at American Motors. For much of the next year Donna and her family struggled to make ends meet. To their immense relief, Chrysler stepped in and called Donna back to work during the summer of 1986. It took the Clausens several months to get out from under the pile of bills that had accumulated during this 19-month layoff. "Even when the [1988] announcement of the closing came, that was the first week my check was clear, except for groceries," Donna recalls. "I was so happy—until I heard about the closing . . . that didn't make me too happy."

Like so many other Kenosha autoworkers, Donna learned about the plant closing while sitting at the kitchen table with her family, eating supper and listening to the evening news on television:

> It hit me like a rock. It was *terrible.* I waited until my kids were in the front room, and I said something to my husband. Because of going through what I did in '85, and you know, starting with the $3.75, I told him now maybe I can understand these families where the spouse is killing his children and his spouse and committing suicide. I said I can understand that now. He just looked at me really scared and told me I'd never said something so scary before. It's just . . . like my *heart* was ripped out. It's that I had to start all over again.

In the Clausen household, Donna's job at the Motors had enabled her husband, Teddy, to take the risk of buying a tavern and going into business for himself. Even when forced to work for lower wages during her layoff, Donna's steady paycheck saw the family through many bumpy months at the tavern, where cash flow is typically erratic and unreliable. Teddy's Bar and Grill is several blocks from the main plant. Weary autoworkers relaxing after each shift were the mainstay of his business. The Clausens know they cannot rely on tavern receipts alone to get them through this critical time in their lives. With the plant gone, what will become of the bar and Teddy's first stab at entrepreneurial independence? Donna's deepest fear is that she will see everything they have worked for evaporate before their eyes:

> I would rather [kill myself] than have to put [my kids] through not having enough food or a good place to live. I'm not talking no hundred thousand dollar home. I'm just talking about a *nice* home. I don't want my kids to have to play out in the street because I can't afford to keep them out of the street. There's just too many kids that live that way now. Too many kids I see at the school that come half-dressed. And I just couldn't. . . . I would rather not be here than have to put my kids through that.

For a growing number of families, the difference between a precarious place just above the nation's poverty line and middle-class status is the contribution a working wife makes to the household income. This is especially true when women take on the challenge of industrial work, which is still dominated by men. Many women find the challenge more than worth the effort. Their income in durable goods industries is generally three to four times the earnings of "pink-collar" workers in the service sector.[17] Donna and her female co-workers often earn as much as the men they marry, or more; and many are divorced or widowed, struggling to support children on their own.

For families in which both parents are high school graduates, the second income provided by a working woman is often the only way to maintain a middle-class standard of living. Over the past two decades, the wages of high school–educated men have fallen significantly (see Figure 40.4); much of the "vanishing middle class" can be attributed to their reduced earnings.[18] Americans without college degrees constitute about 75 percent of the population, and their average incomes are now about 16 percent lower than they were in 1970.[19]

The earnings of men and women with college educations have not increased since 1971. From 1971 to 1986, however, the wage gap between college- and high school–educated men doubled to 49 percent, with male college graduates earning, on average, almost twice as much as less highly educated counterparts.[20] The only group to see little or no change in average earnings has been female high school graduates. Although stagnant wages are clearly preferable to falling wages, if these women are married to men who are also high school graduates, they must deal with the pressure of a declining family income.

Losing a steady income, insurance, and the perquisites of seniority is not all Donna has in mind when she experiences the terror of having to start over. Like many other autoworkers in Kenosha, her life has been shaped from her earliest years by cultural and emotional ties to the world of work in

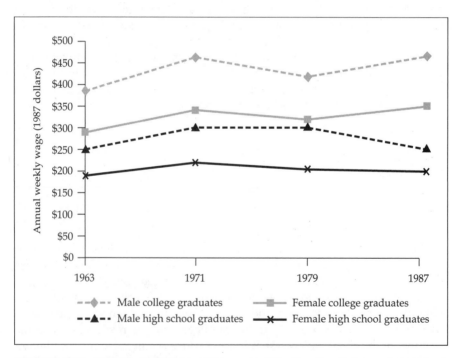

FIGURE 40.4 Wages of workers with one to five years' experience, by sex and education, 1963–1987.

Data from Lawrence Mishel and David M. Frankel, *The State of Working America, 1990–91 Edition,* Economic Policy Institute (Armonk, NY: M. E. Sharpe, 1991), p. 98, Table 3.21.

the auto factory. Both of her parents worked at American Motors, bringing home enough on payday to raise six children out in rural Kenosha County. They were by no means rich, but there was always food on the table and a roof over their heads. Donna has special memories of riding into town with her grandparents to pick up her parents at the factory gates. Uncles and cousins who had jobs in the plant would be getting off work too, and it was like an informal family reunion almost every day.

After high school, Donna enrolled in a secretarial course at the community college, but two semesters left her thoroughly discouraged with the tedium of office work and the prospect of low wages. When she got her job in the plant at age 20, two sisters were already working there, and the fourth joined them a year later. For Donna, as for many others of her generation, automaking was "in the blood," and the plant itself was at the heart of an intricate web of family and community ties.

Changing Demand for Labor

Autoworkers like Steve Miller and Donna Clausen are caught in the crosscurrents of economic and industrial change. On one hand, they are victims of the overall economic slowdown that is affecting every sector of the labor market. College education or not, United States workers in all but the highest income brackets have had difficulty getting ahead or simply trying to make ends meet. On the other hand, Steve and Donna are being edged out of the shrinking manufacturing sector, and this has enormous consequences for their ability to find new jobs at comparable pay. Taken together, these two trends create an uncertain, if not bleak, employment picture for workers of their age, educational background, and region of the country.

In the early 1970s almost 50 percent of the workforce employed in goods-producing industries—manufacturing, mining, and construction—had no more than four years' high school education. These production workers typically earned 10 percent to 14 percent more per year than similarly educated workers in the service sector.[21] As seniority-based layoffs ravaged the ranks of industrial labor during the 1970s and 1980s, young workers were the hardest hit. Not only were they the first to be laid off, but by the late 1970s jobs had become so scarce they couldn't get hired at most factories in the first place. The age distribution in the Kenosha plant clearly reflected this demographic squeeze. Like a top-heavy tower of blocks, the older workforce teetered over a small number of people in the 18- to 29-year-old range.

The changing demand for labor in manufacturing and services industries has dramatically altered the kinds of job opportunities open to young workers. The proportion of young, high school–educated men who work in goods-producing industries fell sharply from about 50 percent in 1973 to 42 percent in 1986 (see Figure 40.5). Women with high school diplomas were also less likely to work in goods-producing jobs than in 1973. Industry shifts

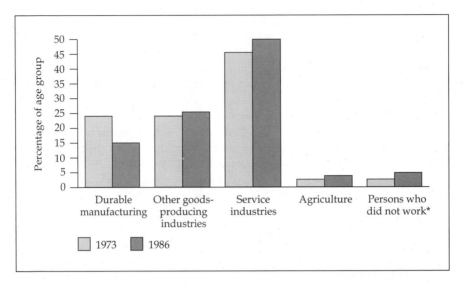

FIGURE 40.5   Distribution of men aged 25 to 34 with four years of high school across industrial sectors, 1973 and 1986.

(*Refers to persons who did not work at all during the year, including the unemployed, the disabled, and those who were out of the labor force voluntarily.)

Data from Frank Levy, "Incomes, Families, and Living Standards," in *American Living Standards,* ed. Robert E. Litan, Robert Z. Lawrence, and Charles L. Schultze (Washington, DC: Brookings Institution, 1988), p. 152, from Table 4.12.

do not appear to be affecting young men with college educations, however. Although the earnings of these men stagnated during the 1980s, service-sector employment alone cannot account for this slowdown. Indeed, rather than losing ground in manufacturing, college-educated workers were slightly more likely to be employed in goods production at the end of the decade (Figure 40.6).

These contrasting employment pictures tell us that the experience of industrial decline differs profoundly for people with different educational credentials. College-educated workers have been stung by economic contraction, but the transition to a postindustrial society has had minimal impact, if any, on their employment opportunities. A starkly different situation confronts those with high school educations. Not only have they seen their real earning power decline, but their chances of employment in high-paying manufacturing industries have decreased substantially. The way workers interpret this situation is rarely as pragmatic or instrumental as economists and labor market analysts would lead us to believe. More education is not always the best choice.

Luis Ramirez is the 34-year-old son of a Mexican American sharecropper. He and his wife came to Kenosha in the early 1970s when her family, working as migrant laborers, came north to pick crops. Luis' first job at AMC

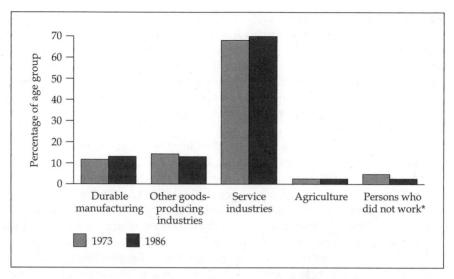

FIGURE 40.6 **Distribution of men aged 25 to 34 with four years of college across industrial sectors, 1973 and 1986.**

(*Refers to persons who did not work at all during the year, including the unemployed, the disabled, and those who were out of the labor force voluntarily.)

Data from Frank Levy, "Incomes, Families, and Living Standards," in *American Living Standards*, ed. Robert E. Litan, Robert Z. Lawrence, and Charles L. Schultze (Washington, DC: Brookings Institution, 1988), p. 152, from Table 4.12.

was spot welding car bodies—one of the most strenuous and unpleasant jobs in the plant. Despite his strength and his capacity for hard physical labor, Luis admits ruefully, there were many times when he thought about quitting and going back down south. But eventually he was able to move out of welding and onto that part of the line called the trim department, where most interior and exterior parts—from seat belts to taillights—are installed. He has been in trim ever since, for a total of 15 years at the plant.

Luis heard about the plant closing on the car radio as he was driving to work. His first thought was that he shouldn't have bought the car he was driving, purchased secondhand a month earlier. Then he began to wonder if the news could be believed:

> Can't be. I wasn't officially notified! They've made mistakes before. But that's the only thing on your mind from then on. You want to get the newspaper outa the way. You want to get to a more reliable source, if there can be a reliable source. You want to hear it from someone directly, someone you trust. Who that is, I don't know.

In truth, there is no reliable source where blue-collar workers—or most other workers, for that matter—can get the information they need to anticipate industrial trends and workforce reductions. The management of

American corporations is virtually a "black box" to the general public, academic institutions, and the United States government. Data about the linkages between industry, employment, and community upheaval are generally limited to what the industry itself decides to report.[22] Workers faced with a plant closing have little choice but to accept the word of industry spokesmen and assume that the company has good reasons for what it is doing. But as Luis says, representatives of the company are the last people autoworkers are inclined to trust.

Within the next week Luis must decide whether to accept a transfer to Chrysler's transmission plant in Kokomo, Indiana, or to begin a 16-week course on air-conditioning and refrigeration at a local technical college, where Chrysler will pick up the tab for tuition. Luis has three more months of unemployment benefits, so at least he can count on that income while he is going to school—but afterward, will there be a job waiting for him in this new field? "I've got two paths before me," Luis says, "and they both are . . . they both look promising. Which is good, I mean, for me. Some people, I guess, don't have that clear of a choice. Some are a lot worse [off] than I am in that sense. But it's just the anxiety—the tension—of having to deal with it, I mean, that's all part of life, true, but . . . I don't know, maybe it didn't have to happen in the first place."

Being forced to make a decision about a career change is quite different from choosing to make a career change. Not only must you deal with anxiety of the unknown, which is "all part of life," you must also come to terms with what you have lost—again, not what you have voluntarily given up, but what has been taken from you. If Luis chooses to go to school—not, I should point out, in a field of his own choosing, but simply in a class where there happened to be an opening during this summer session—he will give up 18 years' seniority with Chrysler and all the retirement benefits he might accrue with continued employment. "And I hate to throw that away," he says. But deciding to go to Kokomo isn't without drawbacks either. "If I go to Indiana, I don't know if it will be permanent."

Luis runs an anxious hand through his thick black hair and looks at me as if I might provide the answer he is seeking. I encourage him to talk about his concerns in Indiana. "Well," he continues, "will I be laid off again, as this roller coaster thing has been going? Or do I keep chasing Chrysler around? Or do I just drop them and pursue a different career, where hopefully it will be a lot more steady?"

As we talk, I learn that Luis has been through a retraining program before. When he was laid off two years ago from AMC, he took a course in electronic servicing, for which he got a "vocational diploma." He had been told that it would be a course on TV/VCR repair, which looked interesting to him, given the four other courses he had to choose from. Once in the class, however, it became apparent that he was being trained to do electronic servicing for large factory machinery, not the smaller repairs he had envisioned. Luis stuck with the course even so, hoping that at the very least it would help him find a steady job. But once he graduated he quickly discovered that this training was of very little practical use in the labor market. To enter a career in this field, he would have to go to school part-time for another three years to get an associate degree; and beyond that, most employees require four years of on-the-job experience. Getting through the whole program seemed like a very slow process. When Luis was called back to the plant in 1987, he had no difficulty deciding what to do.

I ask him why he went back to the plant. As he reflects on this a moment, he smiles with pleasure at the memory:

> I was *happy* to go. You got that work family, I was telling you about. You've spent years in that plant. That's part of your life. All your buddies are there. The familiar surroundings are there. Your routine is there. The paycheck is there every week. I mean, the money is good. It's something that's sort of like a habit—a habit that's your *life*. Whereas, you're entering a new area, an unknown area, if you stick with school in another field. And it's . . . well, a different area, a whole new start. You don't know what to expect. You don't know how much you're going to be earning. You can't plan anything because you're wondering, Well, what if I make so much and I can do this or that? And there [at the plant], you know what you can do. You know how much you can limit yourself or how far you can step out.

When Luis talks of auto work as "a habit that's my life," he is talking about something much more important than a comfortable routine. Our sense of self—our subjectively experienced identity and feeling of self-worth—is intimately bound up with the kind of work we do. An occupational identity doesn't come from flipping through a college catalog and fantasizing about the person we might become if we take certain courses; it doesn't even come from taking the courses and receiving certificates and diplomas. It comes, Luis explains, from performing the jobs we know how to do and feeling that our actions are valued by others in the marketplace:

> Your identity doesn't depend on the actual [company or person] you're working for. I think it's mostly what you're doing. For 15 years I've been in the automaking industry. I think there's a pride in being an autoworker. Yeah, you can identify with that field. You can be a carpenter, you can be a plumber, you can be a what-have-you. But I chose that. There's a lot of people involved. I think maybe I'm a people person. I like people, friends. That's got a lot to do, in my life, [with what] satisfies me.

So much for the image of autoworkers as depersonalized automatons. Work has meaning because it is truly one of the few ways in American society that people can demonstrate their moral worth. Every occupation provides a stage on which our moral character can be displayed, and an attentive audience from whom we seek validation and applause. But unlike middle-class professionals, who can transport their educational credentials and job history from place to place, industrial workers demonstrate their ability on the shopfloor and compile a track record that is inseparable from their place of employment. Linking place, culture, and identity, Luis describes how auto work has shaped his life:

> Kenosha has a history of [automaking], and it's the pride of being part of it. You know, it started way before my time, and just belonging to that group—there's a sense of *pride* in it. Like I say, being a part of the autoworker family. I think that's where it's at. You can . . . like I'm going to school and probably'll get into another field maybe, if I choose that. And I don't know, maybe years from now I'll be proud of being in that refrigerator/air-conditioning family. But this will always, I think, be Number One Son. The other will be probably a stepchild. [Auto work] brought me up, from being a kid, let's say, to being an adult. It's been with me all my life . . . you know, a *friend*. It's brought me a lot of good friends, a lot of material things. And I've expanded with it, grown with it.

Luis pauses, and then adds simply, *"It's been me."*

What does the future hold for workers like Luis? For families like the Clausens and the Millers? Much will depend on the choices they make. Much will depend on the state of the economy. And the two, of course, are intertwined. Individual choices and economic trends are linked by cultural systems of meaning that guide people's behavior in the marketplace and invest that behavior with moral significance. Whether or not these autoworkers go back to school or find another factory job, their lives, their sense of self, and their understanding of American society have been irrevocably changed. The American dream has failed them, and they feel betrayed. Hard work— the sweat in your eyes, backbreaking labor of the assembly line—has not brought them the success and economic advancement bestowed upon their parents' generation. . . .

Much has changed since Eli Chinoy first posed a question like this to industrial laborers. The autoworkers he spoke with in the early 1950s found meaning in a distinctive version of the success ethic that fit in well with an era of economic expansion and Cold War truths. Today Kenosha's autoworkers face an uncertain world and an uncharted future. For them, on one level, the American dream is dead. The optimistic spin of the wheel of fortune has turned treacherous and foreboding. On another level, however, the dream lives. It lives in autoworkers' feisty hope of redemption and interpersonal understanding. . . . Economic change affects far more than our workaday lives. It subtly alters the ways we evaluate hard work and success, and it challenges our sense of community at the deepest level.

NOTES

1. Two retirement programs were available to Kenosha autoworkers. The first, called "30 and out," allowed workers who had 30 years' seniority to retire with a guaranteed income, which worked out to be about $15,050 a year, plus a total insurance program. About 1,800 Chrysler workers were eligible for benefits under this pro-

gram. Under a second plan, called "special early," workers who were over 40 years old and had over 10 years' seniority at the time of the shutdown could "grow into" their retirement plan. At age 55, full insurance coverage would be reinstated, and these workers could then begin to draw monthly retirement benefits at a rate calculated by multiplying their total years of service by $26. Since this type of retirement program would cover about half the workers in the plant, it was understandably high on the union's list of contract priorities during negotiations with Chrysler.

2. Dislocated or "displaced" workers are defined as those who had stable employment in jobs with satisfactory pay and every reason to expect continued employment up to retirement, have been laid off with little chance of recall, and are unlikely to find new employment at or near their customary rates of pay using their familiar skills. Under this definition, operatives (production workers) in basic manufacturing account for about half of all displaced workers since 1980. Gary B. Hansen, "Layoffs, Plant-Closings, and Worker Displacement in America: Serious Problems That Need a National Solution," *Journal of Social Issues* 44, no. 4 (1988): 153–71.

3. Dislocated workers frequently appear to act irresponsibly during the early phases of the job hunt. Employment opportunities are commonly declined in preference for a more desirable, appropriate job, regardless of the low likelihood of finding one. Job counselors often consider this behavior self-defeating and unrealistic. As Ramsay and Joan Liem have suggested, however, this "strategy" can also be seen as a form of resistance to the "job skidding" that has affected many underemployed workers during the 1980s. The jobs resistant workers refuse to take pay significantly less than their previous employment, confer much lower status, and demand a significant accommodation in lifestyle—not only of workers but of their families as well. The Liems argue that the strategies of holding out, turning to part-time work, and exploiting the underground economy are short-term responses to unemployment that reflect survivors' resourcefulness and unwillingness to compromise their integrity. The Liems see in this behavior evidence that the unemployed retain their own priorities and actively dispute the external redefinition of their social status. Ramsay Liem and Joan Liem, "Psychological Effects of Unemployment on Workers and Their Families," *Journal of Social Issues,* 44, no. 4 (1988): 87–105.

4. From a psychological perspective, exclusion from employment is a threat to mental health because it frustrates needs that can be met only in the organized, purposeful company of others. Thus psychological studies of unemployment usually focus on the fit (or lack of fit) between job loss and human needs. The mental state of the unemployed is most often explained by reference to two basic factors: the sudden drop and steady decline in the standard of living, and the loss of the habitual way of life that having a job entails. How people cope (or fail to cope) with this frustration is the key research problem in most psychological studies of unemployment. Frank Furstenberg, "Work Experience and Family Life," in *Work and the Quality of Life,* ed. J. O'Toole (Cambridge: MIT Press, 1974), pp. 341–60; S. Kasl and S. Cobb, "Some Mental Health Consequences of Plant Closings," in *Mental Health and the Economy,* ed. L. Ferman and J. Gordus (Kalamazoo, MI: Upjohn Institute, 1979), pp. 255–300; Marie Jahoda, "Economic Recessions and Mental Health: Some Conceptual Issues," *Journal of Social Issues* 44, no. 4 (1988): 13–23; Patricia Voydanoff and Brenda W. Donnelly, "Economic Distress, Family Coping, and Quality of Family Life," in *Families and Economic Distress: Coping Strategies and Social Policy,* ed. P. Voydanoff and L. Majka (Beverly Hills, CA: Sage, 1988), pp. 97–115.

5. This figure is based on data from the government's Displaced Worker Survey for 1979–1983. The earnings loss drops to 20 percent in the next year and remains more or less at that level through the fifth year. Michael Podgursky and Paul Swaim, "Dislocated Workers and Earnings Loss: Estimates from the Dislocated Worker

Survey," Department of Economics, University of Massachusetts-Amherst, March 1985.

6. Bennett Harrison and Barry Bluestone, *The Great U-Turn: Corporate Restructuring and the Polarizing of America* (New York: Basic Books, 1993), pp. 121–23.

7. While production jobs in the nation declined 29.7 percent from 1979 to 1984, the decline in Great Lakes rust belt cities was 45.3 percent. Richard Child Hill and Cynthia Negrey, "Deindustrialization in the Great Lakes," *Urban Affairs Quarterly* 22, no. 4 (June 1987): 580–97.

8. Donald L. Barlett and James B. Steele, *America: What Went Wrong?* (Kansas City, MO: Andrews and McMeel, 1992), p. 35.

9. Barry Bluestone and Bennett Harrison, *The Deindustrialization of America: Plant Closings, Community Abandonment, and the Dismantling of Basic Industry* (New York: Basic Books, 1982).

10. Overseas investment did not have an adverse impact on domestic employment early in the postwar period. Workers actually benefited from the export of capital, insofar as it kept corporate profits high and gave the unions considerable bargaining flexibility. Only when United States jobs began to be exported along with United States capital did unions start to suffer from the problems of international production and economic integration. For an excellent analysis, see Kim Moody, *An Injury to All: The Decline of American Unionism* (London: Verso Press, 1988).

11. The impact of deindustrialization on communities, workers, and their families is measured by how long it takes for workers dislocated by a mass layoff or plant shutdown to find new employment at comparable pay. Some have argued that deindustrialization is simply a myth. This argument rests on the observation that total manufacturing employment in 1980 remained almost identical to its 1973 level. If there has been no decrease in the total number of industrial workers, so this line of reasoning goes, how can it be said that the country is deindustrializing? As Barry Bluestone has pointed out, however, it is wrong to assume that aggregate employment patterns reflect a situation in which there is perfect interindustry and interregional worker mobility. In other words, workers who lose highly paid union jobs in a particular part of the country still suffer the effects of deindustrialization even if new manufacturing jobs are created in other geographic regions (often at lower nonunion wages). Aggregate, macrolevel data cannot be used as a measure of the social costs incurred by capital flight. Bluestone, "Is Deindustrialization a Myth? Capital Mobility versus Absorptive Capacity in the US Economy," *Annals of the American Academy of Political and Social Science* 475 (September 1984): 39–51.

12. Economists who attribute the loss of good-paying jobs to industrial shifts point to the lower and inherently unequal incomes earned in the service sector. See Robert Kuttner, "The Declining Middle," *Atlantic Monthly* 252 (July 1983): 60–72; Lester C. Thurow, "The Disappearance of the Middle Class," *New York Times*, February 5, 1984; and Barry Bluestone and Bennett Harrison, "The Great American Job Machine: The Proliferation of Low-Wage Employment in the US Economy," a study prepared for the Joint Economic Committee of the U.S. Congress, Washington, DC, December 1986. Other economists argue that the newly created jobs are high-status, white-collar jobs that more often than not support a middle-class standard of living. See, for example, *Economic Report of the President*, February 1988, pp. 60–61; Marvin H. Kosters and Murray N. Ross, "A Shrinking Middle Class?" *Public Interest*, no. 90 (Winter 1988): 3–27; and Robert J. Samuelson, "The American Job Machine," *Newsweek*, February 23, 1987.

13. Candee Harris, "The Magnitude of Job Loss from Plant Closings and the Generation of Replacement Jobs: Some Recent Evidence," *Annals of the American Academy of Political and Social Science* 475 (September 1984): 15–27.

14. D. S. Hamermesh, "What Do We Know about Worker Displacement in the US?" *Industrial Relations* 28 (1989): 51–60.

15. Barlett and Steele, *America*, p. 18.

16. Ibid.

17. Mary Lindenstein Walshok, *Blue-Collar Women: Pioneers on the Male Frontier* (New York: Anchor Books, 1981), and Ellen Israel Rosen, *Bitter Choices: Blue-Collar Women in and out of Work* (Chicago: University of Chicago Press, 1987).

18. Women's earnings are systematically below those of men, but as Frank Levy points out, the proportion of women earning more than $20,000 a year rose from 16 percent in 1973 to 27 percent in 1986. This increase in working women's incomes is masked by the substantial decline in the earnings of working men. Frank Levy, *Dollars and Dreams: The Changing American Income Distribution* (New York: W. W. Norton, 1987).

19. Lawrence Mischel and David M. Frankel, *The State of Working America, 1990–91 Edition* (Armonk, NY: Economic Policy Institute, 1991), pp. 93–95.

20. Levy, *Dollars and Dreams*, p. 127.

21. Ibid., pp. 127–128, Table 4–4.

22. As anthropologist Carol MacLennan points out, knowledge about the auto industry can be gleaned only from a few broad measures of production and employment compiled by the United States Census and the Bureau of Labor Statistics. Some information about the industry is available through trade publications, but the reporting in these publications is not always consistent, and sources are often unknown. This "black box" is a result of the cultural assumption that, in the right economic environment, business will behave in ways that are beneficial to society as a whole. Given this bias, policy efforts to address industrial problems tend to focus not on matters internal to industry, but on correcting imbalances in society and the economy. As a result, knowledge about the industrial factors that do affect social life is generally lacking. Carol A. MacLennan, "Political Response to Economic Loss: The Automotive Crisis of 1979–1982," *Urban Anthropology* 14, nos. 1–3 (1985): 21–57.

41

OVER THE COUNTER
McDonald's

ROBIN LEIDNER

Robin Leidner's case study, "Over the Counter: McDonald's," takes us inside one employment organization and reveals what it is like to work there. Leidner shows how McDonald's employees are intensively socialized. She also illustrates how the work is reduced to simple steps, and therefore, routinized, so that managers and owners can maintain the most control over their product and over their employees. This process of increased routinization in the work place has a long history in industrialization, especially within factory work. Many social analysts, including Karl Marx (1818–1883), have argued that the routinization of work leads to workers' feeling alienated from their products and from their sense of selves.

O rganizations have many ways of obtaining the cooperation of participants, ranging from persuasion and enticement to force and curtailment of options. All organizations "hope to make people want to do what the organization needs done" (Biggart 1989, p. 128), but when they cannot count on success in manipulating people's desires they can do their best to compel people to act in the organization's interests.

Organizations choose strategies that rely on socialization and social control in varying mixtures that are determined by the aims of the organization, the constraints set by the organizational environment and the nature of the work, and the interests and resources of the parties involved. In service-providing organizations, upper-level management must concern itself with the wishes and behavior of service recipients and various groups of workers.[1] For each group, service organizations try to find the most effective and least costly ways to get people to act in the organizations' interests, proffering various carrots and sticks, making efforts to win hearts and minds, closing off choices.

Organizations that routinize work exert control primarily by closing off choices. There is much room for variation, however, in what aspects of the work organizations will choose to routinize, how they go about it, and how much freedom of decision making remains. Moreover, even when routines radically constrain choice, organizations still must socialize participants and set up systems of incentives and disincentives to ensure the compliance of workers and customers.

. . . McDonald's . . . take[s] routinization to extremes . . . includ[ing] predetermination of action and transformation of character . . . McDonald's stresses minute specification of procedures, eliminating most decision making for most workers, although it does make some efforts to standardize operations by transforming the characters of its store-level managers. . . .

This . . . [selection] show[s] how the compan[y's] approaches to routinizing the work of those who interact with customers depend largely on the predictability of service recipients' behavior, which in turn depends on the kinds of resources the organizations have available to channel consumer behavior. . . . At McDonald's . . . the routines sharply limit the workers' autonomy without giving them much leverage over customers.

McDonald's

No one ever walks into a McDonald's and asks, "So, what's good today?" except satirically. The heart of McDonald's success is its uniformity and predictability. Not only is the food supposed to taste the same every day everywhere in the world, but McDonald's promises that every meal will be served quickly, courteously, and with a smile. Delivering on that promise over 20 million times a day in 54 countries is the company's colossal challenge (*McDonald's Annual Report* for 1990, p. 2). Its strategy for meeting that challenge draws on scientific management's most basic tenets: Find the One Best Way to do every task and see that the work is conducted accordingly.[2]

To ensure that all McDonald's restaurants serve products of uniform quality, the company uses centralized planning, centrally designed training programs, centrally approved and supervised suppliers, automated machinery and other specially designed equipment, meticulous specifications, and systematic inspections. To provide its customers with a uniformly pleasant "McDonald's experience," the company also tries to mass produce friendliness, deference, diligence, and good cheer through a variety of socialization and social control techniques. Despite sneers from those who equate uniformity with mediocrity, the success of McDonald's has been spectacular.

McFacts

By far the world's largest fast-food company, McDonald's has over 11,800 stores worldwide (*McDonald's Annual Report* for 1990, p. 1), and its 1990 international sales surpassed those of its three largest competitors combined (Berg 1991 sec. 3, p. 6).[3] In the United States, consumer familiarity with Mc-Donald's is virtually universal: The company estimates that 95 percent of U.S. consumers eat at a McDonald's at least once a year (Koepp 1987, p. 58). McDonald's 1990 profits were $802.3 million, the third highest profits of any retailing company in the world (*Fortune* 1991, p. 179). At a time when the ability of many U.S. businesses to compete on the world market is in question, McDonald's continues to expand around the globe—most recently to Morocco—everywhere remaking consumer demand in its own image.

As politicians, union leaders, and others concerned with the effects of the shift to a service economy are quick to point out, McDonald's is a major employer. McDonald's restaurants in the United States employ about half a million people (Bertagnoli 1989, p. 33), including one out of 15 first-time job seekers (Wildavsky 1989, p. 30). The company claims that 7 percent of all current U.S. workers have worked for McDonald's at some time (Koepp 1987, p. 59). Not only has McDonald's directly influenced the lives of millions of workers, but its impact has also been extended by the efforts of many kinds of organizations, especially in the service sector, to imitate the organizational features they see as central to McDonald's success.

. . .

The relentless standardization and infinite replication that inspire both horror and admiration are the legacy of Ray Kroc, a salesman who got into the hamburger business in 1954, when he was 52 years old, and created a worldwide phenomenon.[4] His inspiration was a phenomenally successful hamburger stand owned by the McDonald brothers of San Bernardino, California. He believed that their success could be reproduced consistently through carefully controlled franchises, and his hamburger business succeeded on an unprecedented scale. The basic idea was to serve a very few items of strictly uniform quality at low prices. Over the years, the menu has expanded somewhat and prices have risen, but the emphasis on strict, detailed standardization has never varied.

. . .

Enforcement of McDonald's standards has been made easier over the years by the introduction of highly specialized equipment. Every company-owned store in the United States now has an "in-store processor," a computer system that calculates yields and food costs, keeps track of inventory and cash, schedules labor, and breaks down sales by time of day, product, and worker (*McDonald's Annual Report* for 1989, p. 29). In today's McDonald's, lights and buzzers tell workers exactly when to turn burgers or take fries out of the fat, and technologically advanced cash registers, linked to the computer system, do much of the thinking for window workers. Specially designed ketchup dispensers squirt exactly the right amount of ketchup on each burger in the approved flower pattern. The french-fry scoops let workers fill a bag and set it down in one continuous motion and help them gauge the proper serving size.

The extreme standardization of McDonald's products, and its workers, is closely tied to its marketing. The company advertises on a massive scale—in 1989, McDonald's spent $1.1 billion systemwide on advertising and promotions (*McDonald's Annual Report* for 1989, p. 32). In fact, McDonald's is the single most advertised brand in the world (*Advertising Age* 1990, p. 6).[5] The national advertising assures the public that it will find high standards of quality, service, and cleanliness at every McDonald's store. The intent of the strict quality-control standards applied to every aspect of running a McDonald's outlet, from proper cleaning of the bathrooms to making sure the hamburgers are served hot, is to help franchise owners keep the promises made in the company's advertising.[6]

The image of McDonald's outlets promoted in the company's advertising is one of fun, wholesomeness, and family orientation. Kroc was particularly concerned that his stores not become teenage hangouts, since that would discourage families' patronage. To minimize their attractiveness to teenage loiterers, McDonald's stores do not have jukeboxes, video games, or even telephones. Kroc initially decided not to hire young women to work behind McDonald's counters for the same reason: "They attracted the wrong kind of boys" (Boas and Chain 1976, p. 19).

You Deserve a Break Today: Conditions of Employment

Although McDonald's does not want teenagers to hang out on its premises, it certainly does want them to work in the stores. Almost half of its U.S. employees are under 20 years old (Wildavsky 1989, p. 30). In recent years, as the McDonald's chain has grown faster than the supply of teenagers, the company has also tried to attract senior citizens and housewives as workers. What people in these groups have in common is a preference or need for part-time work, and therefore a dearth of alternative employment options. Because of this lack of good alternatives, and because they may have other means of support for themselves and their dependents, many people in these groups are willing to accept jobs that provide less than subsistence wages.

Traditionally, McDonald's has paid most of its employees the minimum wage, although labor shortages have now forced wages up in some parts of the country, raising the average hourly pay of crew people to $4.60 by 1989 (Gibson and Johnson 1989, p. B1). Benefits such as health insurance and sick days are entirely lacking for crew people at most franchises. In fact, when the topic of employee benefits was introduced in a class lecture at McDonald's management training center, it turned out to refer to crew meetings, individual work-evaluation sessions, and similar programs to make McDonald's management seem accessible and fair.

The lack of more tangible benefits is linked to the organization of employment at McDonald's as part-time work. According to the manager of the franchise I studied, all McDonald's hourly employees are officially part-time workers, in that no one is guaranteed a full work week. The company's labor practices are designed to make workers bear the costs of uncertainty based on fluctuation in demand. McDonald's places great emphasis on having no more crew people at work at any time than are required by customer flow at that period, as measured in half-hour increments. Most workers therefore have fluctuating schedules, and they are expected to be flexible about working late or leaving early depending on the volume of business.

Not surprisingly, McDonald's employee-turnover rates are extremely high. Turnover averaged 153 percent in 1984, and 205 percent in 1985 (training center lecture). These high rates are partly attributable to the large percentage of teenage workers, many of whom took the job with the intention of working for only a short time. However, the limited job rewards, both financial and personal, of working at McDonald's are certainly crucial contributing factors.

Some argue that the conditions of employment at McDonald's are unproblematic to the workers who take them. If we assume that most McDonald's workers are teenagers who are in school and are not responsible for supporting themselves or others, then many of the features of McDonald's work do not seem so bad. Fringe benefits and employment security are relatively unimportant to them, and the limited and irregular hours of work may actually be attractive (see Greenberger and Steinberg 1986). These arguments are less persuasive when applied to other McDonald's employees, such as mothers of young children, and retirees, although those workers might similarly appreciate the part-time hours, and access to other forms of income and benefits could make McDonald's employment conditions acceptable, if not desirable. Employment security would not be important to the many people who choose to work at McDonald's as a stopgap or for a limited period.[7] Many of the workers at the franchise I studied had taken their jobs with the intention of holding them only temporarily, and many were being supported by their parents. However, other workers there were trying to support themselves and their dependents on earnings from McDonald's, sometimes in combination with other low-paying jobs.

. . .

McDonald's wants both managers and workers to dedicate themselves to the values summed up in its three-letter corporate credo, "QSC." Quality, service, and cleanliness are the ends that the company's thousands of rules and specifications are intended to achieve. Kroc promised his customers QSC,[8] and he believed firmly that if, at every level of the organization, McDonald's workers were committed to providing higher-quality food, speedier service, and cleaner surroundings than the competition, the success of the enterprise was assured. McDonald's extraordinarily elaborate training programs are designed both to teach McDonald's procedures and standards and to instill and enforce corporate values.

Kroc approached his business with a zeal and dedication that even he regarded as religious: "I've often said that *I believe in God, family, and McDonald's—and in the office that order is reversed*" (Kroc with Anderson 1977, p. 124 [emphasis in the original]). Throughout the organization, Kroc is still frequently quoted and held up as a model, and nowhere is his ongoing influence more apparent than at Hamburger University.

Taking Hamburgers Seriously: Training Managers

McDonald's main management training facility is located on 80 beautifully landscaped acres in Oak Brook, Illinois, a suburb of Chicago. Its name, Hamburger University, captures the thoroughness and intensity with which McDonald's approaches management training, and it also suggests the comic possibilities of immersion in McDonald's corporate world.[9] The company tries to produce managers "with ketchup in their veins," a common McDonald's phrase for people who love their work, take pride in it, and are extraordinarily hardworking, competitive, and loyal to McDonald's. A line I heard frequently at Hamburger U. was, "We take hamburgers very seriously here." Nothing I saw called this fixity of purpose into doubt.

Ensuring uniformity of service and products in its far-flung empire is a

major challenge for McDonald's. In each McDonald's store, in regional training centers, and at Hamburger University, crew people, managers, and franchisees learn that there is a McDonald's way to handle virtually every detail
of the business, and that doing things differently means doing things wrong.
Training begins in the stores, where crew people are instructed using materials provided by the corporation, and where managers prepare for more advanced training. Management trainees and managers seeking promotion
work with their store managers to learn materials in manuals and workbooks
provided by the corporation. When they have completed the manual for the
appropriate level, they are eligible for courses taught in regional training centers and at Hamburger University: the Basic Operations Course, the Intermediate Operations Course, the Applied Equipment Course, and, finally, the
Advanced Operations Course, taught only at Hamburger University. Altogether, the full training program requires approximately six hundred to one
thousand hours of work. It is required of everyone who wishes to own a
McDonald's store, and it is strongly recommended for all store managers. By
the time trainees get to Hamburger University for the Advanced Operations
Course, they have already put in considerable time working in a McDonald's
store—two to three and a half years, on average—and have acquired much
detailed knowledge about McDonald's workings.

Hamburger University sometimes offers special programs and seminars
in addition to the regular training courses. For example, a group of McDonald's office workers attended Hamburger University during my visit; a training manager told me that they had been brought in to get "a little shot of
ketchup and mustard." [10]

The zeal and competence of franchisees and managers are of special
concern to McDonald's, since they are the people responsible for daily
enforcement of corporate standards. Their training therefore focuses as much
on building commitment and motivation as on extending knowledge of
company procedures. In teaching management skills, McDonald's also works
on the personalities of its managers, encouraging both rigid adherence to
routines and, somewhat paradoxically, personal flexibility. Flexibility is presented as a virtue both because the company wants to minimize resistance to
adopting McDonald's ways of doing things and to frequent revision of procedures, and because managers must provide whatever responsiveness to
special circumstances the system has, since crew people are allowed virtually no discretion. Hamburger University therefore provides a large dose of
personal-growth cheerleading along with more prosaic skills training.

. . .

The curriculum of the Advanced Operating Course includes inculcation
with pride in McDonald's. Sessions are devoted to McDonald's history and
McDonald's dedication to ever-improving QSC. Lectures are sprinkled with
statistics attesting to McDonald's phenomenal success. Students hear the

story of Ray Kroc's rise to wealth and prominence, based on his strength of character and willingness to work hard, and are assigned his autobiography, *Grinding It Out* (Kroc with Anderson 1977). Kroc is quoted frequently in lectures, and students are encouraged to model themselves on him. They are told repeatedly that they have all proven themselves "winners" by getting as far as they have at McDonald's. The theme throughout is, "We're the best in the world, we know exactly what we're doing, but our success depends on the best efforts of every one of you." [11]

About 3,500 students from all over the world attend classes at Hamburger University each year, most of them taking the Advanced Operations Course (Rosenthal 1989). Those who complete the course receive diplomas proclaiming them Doctors of Hamburgerology. As late as 1978 or 1979, a training manager told me, most classes included only one or two women, but women now comprise 40–60 percent of the students, and women and minorities now make up 54 percent of McDonald's franchisees (Bertagnoli 1989, p. 33). In my homeroom, however, the proportion of women was much smaller, and there was just a handful of minority students.

The course lasts two weeks and is extremely rigorous. Class time is about evenly divided between work in the labs and lectures on store operations and personnel management. In the labs, trainees learn the mechanics of ensuring that McDonald's food is of consistent quality and its stores in good working order. They learn to check the equipment and maintain it properly so that fries cook at precisely the right temperature, shakes are mixed to just the right consistency, and ice cubes are uniform. "Taste of Quality" labs reinforce McDonald's standards for food quality. For instance, in a Condiments Lab, trainees are taught exactly how to store vegetables and sauces, what the shelf lives of these products are, and how they should look and taste. Samples of "McDonald's quality" Big Mac Special Sauce are contrasted with samples that have been left too long unrefrigerated and should be discarded. The importance of serving only food that meets McDonald's standards is constantly emphasized and, a trainer pointed out, "McDonald's has standards for everything, down to the width of the pickle slices."

· · ·

The training at Hamburger University combines a sense of fun with dead seriousness about keeping McDonald's on top in the hamburger business through relentless quality control and effective management of workers and customers. It is up to the owners and managers of individual McDonald's stores to make that happen.

· · ·

Learning the Job

As a manager at Hamburger University explained to me, the crew training process is how McDonald's standardization is maintained, how the company ensures that Big Macs are the same everywhere in the world. The McDonald's central administration supplies franchisees with videotapes and other materials for use in training workers to meet the company's exacting specifications. The company produces a separate videotape for each job in the store, and it encourages franchisees to keep their tape libraries up-to-date as product specifications change. The Hamburger University professor who taught the Advanced Operating Course session on training said that, to keep current, franchisees should be buying 10 or 12 tapes a year. For each work station in the store McDonald's also has a "Station Operation Checklist" (SOC), a short but highly detailed job description that lays out exactly how the job should be done: how much ketchup and mustard go on each kind of hamburger, in what sequence the products customers order are to be gathered, what arm motion is to be used in salting a batch of fries, and so on.

· · ·

The Routine

McDonald's had routinized the work of its crews so thoroughly that decision making had practically been eliminated from the jobs. As one window worker told me, "They've tried to break it down so that it's almost idiot-proof." Most of the workers agreed that there was little call for them to use their own judgment on the job, since there were rules about everything. If an unusual problem arose, the workers were supposed to turn it over to a manager.

Many of the noninteractive parts of the window workers' job had been made idiot-proof through automation.[12] The soda machines, for example, automatically dispensed the proper amount of beverage for regular, medium, and large cups. Computerized cash registers performed a variety of functions handled elsewhere by human waitresses, waiters, and cashiers, making some kinds of skill and knowledge unnecessary. As a customer gave an order, the window worker simply pressed the cash register button labeled with the name of the selected product. There was no need to write the orders down, because the buttons lit up to indicate which products had been selected. Nor was there any need to remember prices, because the prices were programmed into the machines. Like most new cash registers, these added the tax automatically and told workers how much change customers were owed, so the window crew did not need to know how to do those calculations. The cash registers also helped regulate some of the crew's interactive work by reminding them to try to increase the size of each sale. For example, when a customer ordered a Big Mac, large fries, and a regular Coke, the cash register buttons for cookies, hot apple pies, ice cream cones, and ice cream sundaes would light up, prompting the worker to suggest dessert. It took some skill to operate the relatively complicated cash register, as my difficulties during my first work shift made clear, but this organizationally specific skill could soon be acquired on the job.

In addition to doing much of the workers' thinking for them, the computerized cash registers made it possible for managers to monitor the crew members' work and the store's inventory very closely.[13] For example, if the number of Quarter Pounder with Cheese boxes gone did not match the number of Quarter Pounders with Cheese sold or accounted for as waste, managers might suspect that workers were giving away or taking food. Managers could easily tell which workers had brought in the most money during a given interval and who was doing the best job of persuading customers to buy a particular item. The computerized system could also complicate what would otherwise have been simple customer requests, however. For example, when a man who had not realized the benefit of ordering his son's food as a Happy Meal came back to the counter to ask whether his little boy could have one of the plastic beach pails the Happy Meals were served in, I had to ask a manager what to do, since fulfilling the request would produce a discrepancy between the inventory and the receipts.[14] Sometimes the extreme systematization can induce rather than prevent idiocy, as when a window worker says she cannot serve a cup of coffee that is half decaffeinated and half regular because she would not know how to ring up the sale.[15]

The interactive part of window work is routinized through the Six Steps of Window Service and also through rules aimed at standardizing attitudes and demeanors as well as words and actions. The window workers were taught that they represented McDonald's to the public and that their attitudes were therefore an important component of service quality. Crew people could be reprimanded for not smiling, and often were. The window workers were supposed to be cheerful and polite at all times, but they were also told to be themselves while on the job. McDonald's does not want its workers to seem like robots, so part of the emotion work asked of the window crew is that they act naturally. "Being yourself" in this situation meant behaving in a way that did not seem stilted. Although workers had some latitude to go beyond the script, the short, highly schematic routine obviously did not allow much room for genuine self-expression.

Workers were not the only ones constrained by McDonald's routines, of course. The cooperation of service recipients was crucial to the smooth functioning of the operation. In many kinds of interactive service work . . . constructing the compliance of service recipients is an important part of the service worker's job. The routines such workers use may be designed to maximize the control each worker has over customers. McDonald's window workers' routines were not intended to give them much leverage over customers' behavior, however. The window workers interacted only with people who had already decided to do business with McDonald's and who therefore did not need to be persuaded to take part in the service interaction. Furthermore, almost all customers were familiar enough with McDonald's routines to know how they were expected to behave. For instance, I never saw a customer who did not know that she or he was supposed to come up to the counter rather than sit down and wait to be served. This customer training was accomplished through advertising, spatial design, customer experience, and the example of other customers, making it unnecessary for the window crew to put much effort into getting customers to fit into their work routines.[16]

McDonald's ubiquitous advertising trains consumers at the same time that it tries to attract them to McDonald's. Television commercials demonstrate how the service system is supposed to work and familiarize customers with new products. Additional cues about expected customer behavior are provided by the design of the restaurants. For example, the entrances usually lead to the service counter, not to the dining area, making it unlikely that customers will fail to realize that they should get in line, and the placement of waste cans makes clear that customers are expected to throw out their own trash. Most important, the majority of customers have had years of experience with McDonald's, as well as with other fast-food restaurants that have similar arrangements. The company estimates that the average customer visits a McDonald's 20 times a year (Koepp 1978, p. 58), and it is not uncommon for a customer to come in several times per week. For many customers, then, ordering at McDonald's is as routine an interaction as it is for the window worker. Indeed, because employee turnover is so high, steady customers may be more familiar with the work routines than the workers serving them are. Customers who are new to McDonald's can take their cue from more experienced customers.[17]

Not surprisingly, then, most customers at the McDonald's I studied knew what was expected of them and tried to play their part well. They sorted themselves into lines and gazed up at the menu boards while waiting to be served. They usually gave their orders in the conventional sequence: burgers or other entrees, french fries or other side orders, drinks, and desserts. Hurried customers with savvy might order an item "only if it's in the bin," that is, ready to be served. Many customers prepared carefully so that they could give their orders promptly when they got to the counter. This preparation sometimes became apparent when a worker interrupted to ask, "What kind of dressing?" or "Cream and sugar?", flustering customers who could not deliver their orders as planned.

McDonald's routines, like those of other interactive service businesses, depend on the predictability of customers, but these businesses must not grind to a halt if customers are not completely cooperative. Some types of deviations from standard customer behavior are so common that they become routine themselves, and these can be handled through subroutines (Stinchcombe 1990, p. 39). McDonald's routines work most efficiently when all customers accept their products exactly as they are usually prepared; indeed, the whole business is based on this premise. Since, however, some people give special instructions for customized products, such as "no onions," the routine allows for these exceptions.[18] At the franchise I studied, workers could key the special requests into their cash registers, which automatically printed out "grill slips" with the instructions for the grill workers to follow. Under this system, the customer making the special order had to wait for it to be prepared, but the smooth flow of service for other customers was not interrupted. Another type of routine difficulty was customer dissatisfaction with food quality. Whenever a customer had a complaint about the food—cold fries, dried-out burger—window workers were authorized to supply a new product immediately without consulting a supervisor.[19]

These two kinds of difficulties—special orders and complaints about food—were the only irregularities window workers were authorized to handle. The subroutines increased the flexibility of the service system, but they did not increase the workers' discretion, since procedures were in place for dealing with both situations. All other kinds of demands fell outside the window crew's purview. If they were faced with a dispute about money, an extraordinary request, or a furious customer, workers were instructed to call a manager; the crew had no authority to handle such problems.

Given the almost complete regimentation of tasks and preemption of decision making, does McDonald's need the flexibility and thoughtfulness of human workers? As the declining supply of teenagers and legislated increases in the minimum wage drive up labor costs, it is not surprising that McDonald's is experimenting with electronic replacements. So far, the only robot in use handles behind-the-scenes work rather than customer interactions. ARCH (Automated Restaurant Crew Helper) works in a Minnesota McDonald's where it does all the frying and lets workers know when to prepare sandwich buns, when supplies are running low, and when fries are no longer fresh enough to sell. Other McDonald's stores (along with Arby's and Burger King units) are experimenting with a touch-screen computer system that lets customers order their meals themselves, further curtailing the role of the window worker. Although it requires increased customer socialization and cooperation, early reports are that the system cuts service time by 30 seconds and increases sales per window worker 10–20 percent (Chaudhry 1989, p. F61).

Overview

McDonald's pioneered the routinization of interactive service work and remains an exemplar of extreme standardization. Innovation is not discouraged at McDonald's; the company favors experimentation, at least among managers and franchisees. Ironically, though, "the object is to look for new, innovative ways to create an experience that is exactly the same no matter what McDonald's you walk into, no matter where it is in the world" (Rosenthal 1989, p. 12). Thus, when someone in the field comes up with a good idea—and such McDonald's success stories as the Egg McMuffin and the Big Mac were store-level inspirations (Koepp 1987, p. 60)—the corporation experiments, tests, and refines the idea and finally implements it in a uniform way systemwide. One distinctive feature of McDonald's-style routinization is that there, to a great extent, uniformity is a goal in itself.

. . .

McDonald's . . . does promise uniform products and consistent service, and to provide them the company has broken down virtually every task required to run a store into detailed routines with clear instructions and standards. For those routines to run smoothly, conditions must be relatively predictable, so McDonald's tries to control as many contingencies as possible, including the attitudes and behavior of workers, managers, and customers. The company uses a wide array of socialization and control techniques to ensure that these people are familiar with McDonald's procedures and willing to comply with them.

Most McDonald's work is organized as low-paying, low-status, part-time jobs that give workers little autonomy. Almost every decision about how to do crew people's tasks has been made in advance by the corporation, and many of the decisions have been built into the stores' technology. Why use human workers at all, if not to take advantage of the human capacity to respond to circumstances flexibly? McDonald's does want to provide at least a simulacrum of the human attributes of warmth, friendliness, and recognition. For that reason, not only workers' movements but also their words, demeanor, and attitudes are subject to managerial control.

Although predictability is McDonald's hallmark, not all factors can be controlled by management. One of the most serious irregularities that store management must deal with is fluctuation in the flow of customers, both expected and unexpected. Since personnel costs are the most manipulable variable affecting a store's profitability, managers want to match labor power to consumer demand as exactly as possible. They do so by paying all crew people by the hour, giving them highly irregular hours based on expected sales—sometimes including split shifts—and sending workers home early or keeping them late as conditions require. In other words, the costs of uneven demand are shifted to workers whenever possible. Since most McDonald's crew people cannot count on working a particular number of hours at precisely scheduled times, it is hard for them to make plans based on how much money they will earn or exactly what times they will be free. Workers are pressured to be flexible in order to maximize the organization's own flexibility in staffing levels. In contrast, of course, flexibility in the work process itself is minimized.

Routinization has not made the crew people's work easy. Their jobs, although highly structured and repetitive, are often demanding and stressful. Under these working conditions, the organization's limited commitment to workers, as reflected in job security, wages, and benefits, makes the task of maintaining worker motivation and discipline even more challenging. A variety of factors, many orchestrated by the corporation, keeps McDonald's crew people hard at work despite the limited rewards. Socialization into McDonald's norms, extremely close supervision (both human and electronic), individual and group incentives, peer pressure, and pressure from customers all play their part in getting workers to do things the McDonald's way.

Because franchisees and store-level managers are responsible for enforcing standardization throughout the McDonald's system, their socialization includes a more intensive focus on building commitment to and pride in the organization than does crew training. In fact, it is the corporate attempt at transforming these higher-level McDonald's people by making them more loyal, confident, flexible, and sensitive to others, as well as more knowledgeable about company procedures, that makes the extreme rigidity of the crew training workable. The crew people do not have to be trusted with decision-making authority, because all unusual problems are referred to managers. Their more extensive training gives them the knowledge and attitudes to make the kinds of decisions the corporation would approve. . . . In addition to thorough socialization, McDonald's managers and franchisees are subjected to close corporate oversight. Every aspect of their stores' operations is rated by corporate staff, and they are sanctioned accordingly.

Despite elaborate socialization and social controls, McDonald's stores do not, of course, carry out every corporate directive exactly as recommended. In the store I studied, managers did not always provide their workers with the mandated support and encouragement, crew trainers did not always follow the four-step training system, and window workers did not always carry out the Six Steps of Window Service with the required eye contact and smile. There were many kinds of pressures to deviate from corporate standards. Nonetheless, the benefits of standardization should not be underestimated. As every Durkheimian knows, clear rules and shared standards provide support and coherence as well as constraint. Although some aspects of the routines did strike the participants as overly constraining, undignified, or silly, the approved routines largely worked. In all of these examples of deviation, the routines would have produced more efficient and pleasant service, and those that apply to management and training would have benefited workers as well as customers.

Obtaining the cooperation of workers and managers is not enough to ensure the smooth functioning of McDonald's relatively inflexible routines. Customers must be routinized as well. Not only do customers have to understand the service routine and accept the limited range of choices the company offers, they also must be willing to do some kinds of work that are done for them in conventional restaurants, including carrying food to the table and throwing out their trash. Experience, advertising, the example set by other customers, and clear environmental cues familiarize customers with McDonald's routines, and most want to cooperate in order to speed service. For these reasons, McDonald's interactive service workers do not have to direct most customers, and window workers' routines are therefore not designed to give them power over customers.

NOTES

1. Suppliers, competitors, and other parties outside of the organization are also relevant actors, but organizational efforts to control their behavior will not be considered here (see Prus 1989).
2. The 1990s may bring unprecedented changes to McDonald's. Although its overseas business continues to thrive, domestic sales have been declining. To overcome the challenges to profitability presented by the economic recession, lower-priced competitors, and changes in consumer tastes, CEO Michael Quinlan has instituted experimental changes in the menu, in pricing strategy, and even in the degree of flexibility granted to franchisees (see *Advertising Age* 1991; Berg 1991; *McDonald's Annual Report* for 1990; Therrien 1991).
3. McDonald's restaurants are generally referred to as "stores" by McDonald's staff. The company's share of the domestic fast-food market has declined from 18.7 percent in 1985 to 16.6 percent in 1990 (Therrien 1991).
4. Information about McDonald's history comes primarily from Boas and Chain 1976; Kroc with Anderson 1977; Love 1986; Luxenberg 1985; and McDonald's training materials. Reiter's (1991) description of Burger King reveals numerous parallels in the operation of the two companies, although Burger King, unlike McDonald's, is a subsidiary of a multinational conglomerate.
5. In addition to paid advertising, McDonald's bolsters its public image with promotional and philanthropic activities such as an All-American High School Basketball Game, essay contests and scholarship programs for black and Hispanic students, and Ronald McDonald Houses where outpatient children and their families and the parents of hospitalized children can stay at minimal cost.
6. Conversely, details of the routines are designed with marketing in mind. The bags that hold the regular-size portions of french fries are shorter than the french fries are, so that when workers fill them with their regulation french-fry scoops, the servings seem generous, overflowing the packaging. The names of the serving sizes also are intended to give customers the impression that they are getting a lot for their money: French fries come in regular and large sizes, sodas in regular, medium, and large cups. I was quickly corrected during a work shift when I inadvertently referred to an order for a "small" drink.
7. Some commentators fall into the trap of assuming that workers' preferences are determinative of working conditions, a mistake they do not make when discussing higher-status workers such as faculty who must rely on a string of temporary appointments.
8. Actually, Kroc usually spoke of QSCV—quality, service, cleanliness, and value (see Kroc with Anderson 1977)—but QSC was the term used in most McDonald's training and motivational materials at the time of my research. The company cannot enforce "value" because antitrust restrictions prevent McDonald's from dictating prices to its franchisees (Love 1986, p. 145). Nevertheless, recent materials return to the original four-part pledge of QSC & V (see, e.g., *McDonald's Annual Report* for 1989, p. i).
9. Branches of Hamburger University now operate in London, Munich, and Tokyo (*McDonald's Annual Report* for 1989, p. 28). Burger King University is similar in many respects (Reiter 1991).

10. The effort to involve corporate employees in the central mission of the organization extends beyond such special programs. McDonald's prides itself on keeping its corporate focus firmly on store-level operations, and it wants all its employees to have a clear idea of what it takes to make a McDonald's restaurant work. Therefore, all McDonald's employees, from attorneys to data-entry clerks, spend time working in a McDonald's restaurant.

11. Biggart (1989, pp. 143–47) shows that both adulation of a charismatic founder and repeated characterization of participants as winners are common in direct-sales organizations. Like McDonald's, such organizations face the problem of motivating people who are widely dispersed geographically and who are not corporate employees.

12. The in-store processors similarly affected managers' work. A disaffected McDonald's manager told Garson, "There is no such thing as a McDonald's manager. The computer manages the store" (Garson 1988, p. 39).

13. Garson (1988) provides an extended discussion of this point.

14. The manager gave him the pail but had to ring it up on the machine as if he had given away a whole Happy Meal.

15. Thanks to Charles Bosk for this story.

16. Mills (1986) elaborates on "customer socialization." Environmental design as a factor in service provision is discussed by Wener (1985) and Normann (1984).

17. The importance of customer socialization becomes apparent when people with very different consumer experiences are introduced to a service system. When the first McDonald's opened in the Soviet Union in 1990, Moscow's citizens did not find the system immediately comprehensible. They had to be persuaded to get on the shortest lines at the counter, since they had learned from experience that desirable goods were available only where there are long lines (Goldman 1990).

18. Burger King's "Have it your way" campaign virtually forced McDonald's to allow such customized service.

19. The defective food or its container was put into a special waste bin. Each shift, one worker or manager had the unenviable task of counting the items in the waste bin so that the inventory could be reconciled with the cash intake.

REFERENCES

Advertising Age. 1990. "Adman of the Decade: McDonald's Fred Turner: Making All the Right Moves." (January 1): 6.

——. 1991. "100 Leading National Advertisers: McDonald's." (September 25): 49–50.

Berg, Eric N. May 12, 1991. "An American Icon Wrestles with a Troubled Future." *New York Times* sec. 3, pp. 1, 6.

Bertagnoli, Lisa. July 10, 1989. "McDonald's: Company of the Quarter Century." *Restaurants and Institutions* pp. 32–60.

Biggart, Nicole Woolsey. 1989. *Charismatic Capitalism: Direct Selling Organizations in America.* Chicago: University of Chicago Press, pp. 128, 143–47.

Boas, Max and Steve Chain. 1976. *Big Mac: The Unauthorized Story of McDonald's.* New York: New American Library, p. 19.

Chaudhry, Rajan. August 7, 1989. "Burger Giants Singed by Battle." *Nation's Restaurant News,* p. F61.

"Fortune Global Service 500: The 50 Largest Retailing Companies." *Fortune* (August 26, 1991), p. 179.

Garson, Barbara. 1988. *The Electronic Sweatshop: How Computers Are Transforming the*

Office of the Future into the Factory of the Past. New York: Simon and Schuster, p. 39.

Gibson, Richard and Robert Johnson. September 29, 1989. "Big Mac Plots Strategy to Regain Sizzle." *Wall Street Journal,* p. B1.

Goldman, Marshall. May 17, 1990. Presentation at colloquium on Reforming the Soviet Economy, University of Pennsylvania.

Greenberger, Ellen and Laurence Steinberg. 1986. *When Teenagers Work: The Psychological and Social Costs of Adolescent Employment.* New York: Basic Books.

Koepp, Stephen. April 13, 1987. "Big Mac Strikes Back." *Time,* p. 60.

Kroc, Ray with Robert Anderson. 1977. *Grinding It Out: The Making of McDonald's.* Chicago: Contemporary Books, p. 124.

Love, John F. 1986. *McDonald's: Behind the Arches.* New York: Bantam Books, p. 145.

Luxenberg, Stan. 1985. *Roadside Empires: How the Chains Franchised America.* New York: Viking.

McDonald's Annual Report. 1989. Oak Brook, Illinois, pp. i, 28, 29, 32.

———. 1990. Oak Brook, Illinois, pp. 1–2.

Mills, Peter K. 1986. *Managing Service Industries: Organizational Practices in a Post-Industrial Economy.* Cambridge, MA: Ballinger.

Normann, Richard. 1984. *Service Management: Strategy and Leadership in Service Businesses.* Chichester: Wiley.

Prus, Robert. 1989. *Pursuing Customers: An Ethnography of Marketing Activities.* Newbury Park, CA: Sage.

Reiter, Ester. 1991. *Making Fast Food: From the Frying Pan into the Fryer.* Montreal: McGill-Queen's University Press.

Rosenthal, Herman M. June 4, 1989. "Inside Big Mac's World." *Newsday,* p. 12.

Stinchcombe, Arthur L. 1990. *Information and Organizations.* Berkeley: University of California Press, p. 39.

Therrien, Lois. October 21, 1991. "McRisky." *Business Week,* pp. 114–22.

Wener, Richard E. 1985. "The Environmental Psychology of Service Encounters." Pp. 101–12 in *The Service Encounter: Managing Employee/Customer Interaction in Service Businesses,* edited by John A. Czepiel, Michael R. Solomon, and Carol F. Surprenant. Lexington, MA: Lexington Books.

Wildavsky, Ben. 1989. "McJobs: Inside America's Largest Youth Training Program." *Policy Review* 49:30–37.

42

SHADOW WORK

DAVID A. SNOW • LEON ANDERSON

This reading by David A. Snow and Leon Anderson provides an insider view into the economy of homelessness. Using nonparticipant observation and interviews, Snow and Anderson found that the homeless engage in different types of work in order to survive. In this selection, they describe the four broad types of work that the homeless do: selling and trading, soliciting donations, scavenging, and theft. What is intriguing about Snow and Anderson's study is that the authors not only describe these types of work in detail, but they also shatter our notions that homeless people are all alike, performing the same economic activities.

It's 8:30 on Sunday morning. There are only a few cars on the streets, and even fewer pedestrians, except near the Sally, where some homeless have begun to congregate to await the bus that will take them to the Central Assembly of God Church on the outskirts of town. As we walk toward this pick-up point, we hear some rustling in a large garbage dumpster and then see a head pop up. It's Gypsy, already at work scavenging for salvageable items: food, clothing, tin cans, and other throwaways he can use directly or sell on the streets or in pawn shops.

On another day, at noon on the Drag, we notice two long-haired hippie tramps panhandling passersby. "Hey, man, you got any spare change? Just a quarter?" they ask. It's Gimpy Dan and a sidekick trying to make ends meet. A bit further down the Drag, in front of the major campus bookstore, sits another homeless person playing a beat-up guitar and singing songs about Jesus. It's Banjo trying to coax passersby to toss some loose change into his guitar case. And just around the corner, by an open crafts area, we spot Rhyming Mike reciting his street poetry in exchange for a few nickels and dimes.

That evening, when we queue up for dinner at the Sally, we observe two rather infirm and weather-beaten men, both in their 50s or 60s, scouring an empty parking lot across the street for aluminum cans. One spots a Coke can, picks it up, and drops it into a plastic garbage bag held open by his partner. It is Indio and his friend JJ. The bag is bulging—they have had a productive day.

While we are still waiting in the dinner line we see two fellows in their mid-20s leave the queue and scurry across the street to talk to Bill-Bob and his redneck friends. They make a quick exchange and then sprint back to the dinner line. Grinning, they say they got a good deal: "A couple of joints for two bucks each." Across the street Bill-Bob is smiling too, probably because he has just added a dollar or two to his cash supply.

Later, stretched out in the winter warehouse, we hear the barely audible voice of a homeless entrepreneur. Walking through the cavernous room after lights-out, he whispers, just loud enough to be heard over the coughing and muffled conversations, "Joints! Joints! Joints for sale!"

In each of the preceding vignettes, we see one or more homeless persons at work. It is not work as traditionally conceived, to be sure. But it is work, for in each case attention and energy are riveted on the procurement of money or other material goods for personal use or exchange. Unlike wage labor, though, in these activities there is little to no regularized exchange of labor for money. Nor are the activities officially sanctioned or their time and place bureaucratically controlled.[1] Instead, they are compensatory subsistence strategies that are fashioned or pursued in the shadow of more conventional work because of exclusion from existing labor markets, because participation in those markets fails to provide a living wage, because public assistance is insufficient, or because such strategies provide a more reliable means of survival. We call these compensatory, non–wage labor subsistence strategies "shadow work."[2]

Besides being unofficial, unenumerated work existing outside the wage labor economy, shadow work is characterized further by its highly opportunistic and innovative nature. It involves, at the very minimum, the recognition and exploitation of whatever resources and unofficial markets happen to be available whenever a few dollars are needed. As Jacqueline Wiseman observed in her field study of skid-row alcoholics in the 1960s, "When the skid row man thinks of getting money, he . . . must show ingenuity in creating something out of nothing. Thus, he thinks in terms of objects, relationships, or short-term tasks that can be converted into enough cash to take care of current needs—liquor, food, shelter, incidentals."[3] The same is true of many of the homeless we came to know. They trade their personal possessions, sell their plasma, scavenge through the refuse of others in search of salable items, perform in prime space, and panhandle passersby. Seldom does any one homeless person engage in all of these activities consistently, but often, as need and opportunity arise, they combine various of these strategies with day labor and/or public assistance, or they develop individual repertoires of shadow work. The homeless we studied are not only people of needs, but, in the words of one observer of their contemporaries in another city, "grudging players in a rough theater of improvisation."[4]

In this [selection] we explore this characterization by examining the nature and range of shadow work pursued by the homeless in Austin. Four categories of such work were identified during the course of our field research: selling and trading, soliciting donations in public places, scavenging, and theft. We consider each variety in turn, noting, as well, the extent to which the different types of homeless engage in the various kinds of shadow work.

Selling and Trading

As in the domiciled world, so among the homeless, too, the sale and exchange of goods and services are central forms of shadow work. We observed three basic variants of sales work among the homeless in Austin: selling and trading junk and personal possessions, selling illegal goods and services, and selling plasma.

Selling and Trading Junk and Personal Possessions

Sale of junk and personal possessions is not uncommon among most social classes.[5] Among the working and middle classes, these exchanges take the form of weekend garage sales, and among the upper classes they manifest themselves as estate sales.[6] Among the homeless, however, sale of junk and personal possessions takes on a distinctive cast. For one thing, the proceeds are much more fundamental to their subsistence than is typically the case for other strata. If and when the homeless peddle personal items, it is not because they have no use for them or want to clean house, so to speak, but because they need cash. Additionally, the homeless usually have few personal possessions. Their sales thus vary according to what they have recently purchased, scavenged, received as a gift, or stolen. Whatever their source, the sales items most often consist of clothing such as jackets, belts, and shoes, watches and rings, calculators and cassette tapes, and cigarettes and beer.

The asking price for such goods is low, undoubtedly because the other homeless, who make up the primary market, have little money to spend. There are exceptions, though. One afternoon we observed a 28-year-old male trying to hawk a new pair of jeans his mother had sent him. As he sat on the sidewalk, propped up against a building in the middle of the city's downtown nightlife section, he would hold up the jeans as men walked by and yell out, "Man, they're brand new jeans and they're not hot!" They *were* new, too, with the labels still attached. He eventually sold them for $11.00 to a fellow who appeared to be a college student, an extraordinarily good price for a street sale. Sometimes an energetic peddler will attempt to sell his wares to the more affluent university market. For example, when Lance McCay was short of cash he would sell students his gifts from home or items he had purchased with his Social Security money, as when he sold his $400 briefcase for a mere $10 to a college student.

The sales price is usually considerably lower than even $10 or $11, though, not only because the homeless peddle primarily among each other, but also because the goods for sale are often cheap, recycled items in poor condition, items most people would regard as junk. One evening, for instance, we observed an elderly man going from group to group at the Salvation Army, trying to sell a rusty alarm clock he insisted would work even though no one could get in to run. On another occasion a young black man walked beside the Sally dinner line, hawking several old and well-worn *Playboy* magazines. "This is fine stuff," he told the men in line as he tantalizingly showed them the centerfold photos. "And only a buck apiece." He generated obvious interest, but it was Sunday evening, when few of the homeless have any loose change. Consequently, the *Playboy* hawker could find no buyers.

Among the few homeless who own vehicles, the selling or trading of auto parts is common. When times are difficult and work is scarce, they sell tires, batteries, or other parts, expecting, of course, to buy replacements in more prosperous times. Unfortunately, there are many more bad days than good, and homeless car owners frequently find themselves selling off one part after another. This creates problems for them, since a car that is not running cannot be used for transportation and is likely to get numerous parking tickets.

. . .

Pawn shops also provide a market for personal possessions, especially jewelry and tools. The amount a pawn shop will pay for an item is usually far below its value, but the possibility remains of redeeming the item. Just as with car parts, however, there is the risk of falling behind and not being able to catch up, as is illustrated in a comment by a former carpenter waiting for day labor at TEC [Texas Employment Commission] one morning:

> I could be getting better work than this if I just had my tools, but they're in the pawn shop downtown. I wouldn't let 'em give me no more than 30 bucks when I pawned 'em so I wouldn't have trouble getting 'em out. But work's been so slow I haven't even been able to get that much together yet.

Selling Illegal Goods and Services

An alternative form of selling pursued by some of the homeless is the sale of illegal goods and services, particularly drugs and sex. Not all the homeless are involved in this form of sales work, though. The recently dislocated, whose energies and hopes are still focused on wage labor, tend to shy away from such illicit activity, as do the mentally ill, who have neither the interactional skills nor the persistence to be much good at it. And the majority of both traditional tramps and traditional bums seem either too old, too rickety, or too inebriated to get involved competitively in either drug trafficking or prostitution. That leaves the regular straddlers, hippie tramps, and redneck bums, all of whom are involved in varying degrees in this illicit form of shadow work, particularly in drug dealing.

Drug Dealing   Although drug dealing can be readily observed among regular straddlers as well as hippie tramps and redneck bums, it is not as salient to the survival of the straddlers as it is for the other two types. For them, and particularly for the hippie tramps, drug dealing is more commonly a primary subsistence strategy. There are other differences between the groups. Regular straddlers deal drugs predominantly to other homeless individuals, and each deal usually involves only one to three joints of marijuana.[7] Sellers solicit customers in locations where the homeless gather in the downtown area. In the mornings there are usually several people at the Labor Corner and the Labor Pool selling joints at "two bucks apiece, three for five dollars." In the afternoons, individual sellers walk up and down the Sally dinner line soliciting buyers, and in the evenings it is common for sellers to walk along the rows of mats in the Sally's sleeping quarters, calling out in muffled tones,

"Joints! Joints!" The number of sales regular straddlers make on a given day is highly dependent on the amount of money being funneled into the street economy from day labor and other forms of shadow work. When the street economy is good, sales are brisk. But when the weather turns bad, curtailing day labor, and on the weekends, when day labor is scarce and the plasma centers are closed, few people have the money for joints.

A few regular straddlers whom we observed selling drugs seemed to engage in this economic activity almost exclusively. One of them, a stocky young man in his mid-20s who went by the name of Streeter, carried two cigarette cases filled with joints on his daily rounds of the major gathering spots for the homeless. One morning at the Labor Corner we saw him do a particularly good business, making a dozen transactions within half an hour. Except for occasional day labor or, during slow times, the sale of plasma, Streeter did not pursue any other work. . . .

Unlike Streeter . . . most regular straddlers who sell drugs do so infrequently and as a supplement to other economic activity. During one of his periods of manic employment, Ron Whitaker purchased an ounce of marijuana at a time, rolled it into thin joints, and sold enough to pay for the ounce. He could then smoke what was left for free. Many others on the streets spoke of this as a shrewd and frugal practice and engaged in it when they could. Since the economic fortunes of the homeless are dependent on external circumstances, however, often when times were good enough that one person was able to buy a quarter-ounce, others were able to do so as well. As a result, the market would diminish and price wars would develop as individuals undercut each other in an effort to earn back their investment.

The redneck bums also cater primarily to other homeless, but they tend to work together as a team rather than individually. Additionally, they are rumored to sell better-quality marijuana. And, unlike the straddlers, the redneck bums seem to have a steady supply. Sometimes when the straddlers are unable to score, the rednecks do a particularly brisk business, as can often be seen by the number of homeless darting back and forth between the Sally dinner line and the street corner where the rednecks hang out.

The drug trade of the hippie tramps is strikingly different from that of either the straddlers or the rednecks. Their turf, as we have said, is around the Drag, adjacent to the university campus. Partly as a consequence of having staked out this niche, the hippie tramps sell drugs predominantly to people outside their own group, especially to students from the university. The market around the Drag is considerably more affluent and stable than the homeless market, except during school breaks, when the students disappear. Sales are typically larger, too—in the quarter-ounce to ounce range for marijuana—and the variety of drugs sold is greater. We observed on a number of occasions the selling of psychedelic drugs and various forms of "speed." For example, one mid-afternoon as we were chatting with Gimpy Dan and several other hippie tramps on a side street off the Drag, two punk-looking college-aged women approached the gathering and asked where they "could get some acid." Gimpy told them he "could get them Red Star for $5.00 a hit." He had one of the women walk with him up the street for half a block while the other stayed with us. Apparently he needed to check with an associate on the availability of the acid. After he found the man and talked with him a bit, Gimpy and the woman returned. He told them he would have the acid in a while and instructed them to "get lost and come back and see me in half an hour." As they walked away, he assured them that Red Star acid is the best around. "Ask any of the tramps around here," he yelled to them, "and they'll tell you that Red Star is the best."

. . .

Prostitution   The second form of illicit sales work observed among the homeless is prostitution, both homosexual and heterosexual. That some of the homeless would engage in prostitution should be expected, considering their dire economic situation and the fact that prostitution has long been rec- ognized as an activity often pursued by individuals with limited economic prospects.[8]

Our observations indicate that homosexual prostitution is the more prominent, in large part simply because there are more homeless men than women. It is pursued more often by the younger homeless men. How wide- spread it is among the homeless is unclear, however. Three of our key informants openly admitted to engaging in prostitution, but many more homeless talked about having been approached by men who offered to pay them for sex. Furthermore, when dinner-line conversation among the homeless turned to "rolling queers," it seemed that everyone within earshot chipped in with one or more experiences of having robbed a gay man during a prostitution encounter. One Sunday evening, for instance, a lanky weather- beaten man in his mid-30s rambled on to an interested gathering about once having gone home with a gay man he had "drugged with three Quaaludes." "Then," he boasted, "I split with his Caddy, a stereo, and a new TV and sold them on the streets for twenty-five hundred bucks." Having the crowd's at- tention, he continued by recounting an episode with "this other dude who's an accountant here in town who used to give me 50 bucks to tie him up and fuck him. But once I got him tied up I'd just take the rest of his money and split." Another man, who appeared to be about five years younger despite having lost several front teeth, responded, "Let's go find that guy and offer to do a double on him." The younger man then proceeded with a story of his own:

> I went into this bar one time—it was a peter bar, but, hell, I didn't know it—and this guy offered me 50 bucks to go home with him. So we get there and he tells me he wants me to fuck him in the ass, and I told him "Man, I gotta be drunk to do that." So I kept mixing him doubles and me singles until he passed out. Then I swiped his car and took off down the freeway, only I was drunk on my ass and I kept bashing into the other

cars, so I pulled off and went to sleep. Next morning I woke up, man, that car was beat to shit.

We suspect that such talk about preying on gay men is not only highly embellished but offers the homeless a relatively safe way to discuss an activity that is fairly common, while still allowing them distance from the stigma of homosexuality. In these stories they can admit contact with homosexuals and even, obliquely, some sexual activity. But by focusing on predation as the central theme of such encounters, they can avoid identification with gays.[9]

. . .

We also observed a few instances of heterosexual prostitution among the homeless. They were all situations in which a single woman was managed by a man to whom she exhibited some degree of attachment. In one case a man in his early 20s did a brisk business for a couple of weeks arranging sex for $20 and up between his young girlfriend and men who were staying at the Salvation Army. A case of cheaper prostitution was witnessed one afternoon at the plasma center: A man was soliciting men to have sex with his wife in the back of their pick-up truck for $8 to $10—the amount received for a plasma donation.

Heterosexual prostitution appeared to be relatively rare, however, as a result of the paucity of women on the streets, the unwillingness of those who are there to engage in such activity, and the lack of much disposable cash among most homeless males. More common for homeless women was a sort of serial monogamous or polygamous prostitution in which a woman attached herself to one or more men in exchange for support. As one homeless male told us, "You wonder why there's not very many women living on the streets? It's because those women are living with men who aren't on the streets, you know. They've worked out some kind of arrangement, whether it's sex or whatever, where they can be living with some guy."

. . .

Selling Plasma

In a world of limited and irregular opportunities to make a few dollars, an outcropping of economic regularity stands out like a beacon on a dark night. The blood banks or plasma centers are unique in offering the homeless a sure opportunity to pick up a few dollars. Perhaps this certainty helps explain the upbeat ambience of the blood bank compared to the anxious gloom that pervades the day-labor spots. As with most things the homeless do, there is a trade-off to selling plasma—in this case, sitting for an hour and a half with a needle in the arm—but it is a trade-off that many find worthwhile, especially when their pockets are empty.

Austin has two plasma centers, both located nearly three miles north of the Sally, near the university campus. Some of the homeless check out the day-labor spots in the morning and then, if they do not land a job, go to Caritas for a sandwich and then to the main plasma center to "sell some blood." Others try to avoid the long wait to sell their plasma by foregoing the search for a job and getting to the doorstep by 8:00 A.M., when the center opens. Paid plasma donors are allowed to sell plasma twice a week. They are paid $8 for the first donation and $10 for the second. On Monday mornings, which is usually the busiest morning since the homeless have so few opportunities to make money on the weekends, at least 30 broke and homeless individuals will be sitting in front of the plasma center when the doors open. The "Plasmapheresis Informed Consent Form," which donors at the Austin Plasma Center must sign, explains the plasmapheresis procedure:

> The clue to this procedure is the word "plasma." In plasmapheresis you donate only your plasma, the straw-colored liquid portion of your blood which the body replaces much more rapidly than red blood cells. Your red blood cells, which, if donated, would take your body several weeks to replace, are returned to you. By giving only your plasma, you can safely donate as often as twice a week.
>
> The plasmapheresis requires removing 500–600 ml of whole blood, separating the red blood cells from the plasma, and returning the red cells to you. The procedure is repeated a second time through the same needle puncture. 600 ml is withdrawn from donors weighing 175 pounds or more; 500 ml from donors weighing less.

Posters at the plasma center focus on society's need for plasma and the beneficence of the donors, on the one hand, and on financial incentives for continued selling of plasma, on the other. One poster shows a man sitting in a plasma center while his blood is being extracted for plasmapheresis. The caption underneath the picture reads: "This man is a paid blood donor. He represents one-third of all the blood donors in America. We owe him a debt of gratitude." Another poster shows a smiling adolescent hemophiliac sitting on a bicycle, with the caption: "Hey Plasma Donor! Thanks!" These posters are slick, colorful, and professionally made. The signs promoting financial incentives, handmade by the plasma center staff, are less professional and more direct. One proclaims: "$ BONUSES! $25.00 Drawings at the end of the month. 2 Winners every month!" Another states: "$20 Bonus for the 7th donation in the month."

The income from regular plasma donation is an important means of subsistence for some of the homeless. At $18 per week plus the $20 bonus for the seventh donation of the month, a homeless individual can earn about $95 per month selling plasma. If calculated in terms of hourly wage, taking into account the long walk to the plasma center, the long wait there, and the hour and a half to two hours the process takes, the homeless individual earns little more than $2.50 per hour. Nonetheless, it is a guaranteed $2.50, as opposed to the uncertain money to be made from day labor. Some of the homeless plan their otherwise unpredictable weeks around their guaranteed plasma sales, as is illustrated in the following excerpt from a conversation overheard between two homeless males in their mid-20s as they waited in the plasma center to be called for their Monday morning donations:

> "Hey, tomorrow I'm going to the Labor Pool and get some work."
> "You got a car?"
> "No, you 'spose I'll just end up sitting around then?"
> "Yeah, I always do."
> "Well, I'm gonna try it. I need a $40 day bad. I can get my 10 bucks here on Wednesday if I don't get out tomorrow."

. . .

Soliciting Donations in Public Places

A somewhat different pattern emerges for the public solicitation of handouts through begging and panhandling.[10] Both strategies are used most frequently by outsiders, and particularly by traditional and hippie tramps and traditional bums, the groups with the longest spans of time on the streets. . . . Both involve fleeting attempts to persuade others to part with a sum of money, usually quite small, without providing anything tangible in return. As such, they are antithetical to the work ethic, which decrees that honorable subsistence involves the exchange of labor for pay or, at the very least, making do without handouts from others. As a consequence, begging and panhandling can engender considerable shame and embarrassment in individuals still imbued with the work ethic as conventionally understood, as are most recently dislocated and many regular straddlers. Tony Jones, who had been on the streets for only two to three weeks when we first met, told us, for example, "I got too much pride to beg. As long as I got my hands and feet, I'll be damned if I'll get on my knees and beg." And Ron Whitaker, who has been homeless somewhat longer, said that when he first hit the streets he "found panhandling downright embarrassing." He learned to swallow his pride, however, when his pockets were empty and he had exhausted his other options. As he put it, "You can't let pride get in your way. I used to and still do sometimes, but there are times you have to ask people for a couple of quarters because you ain't got a dime."[11]

Apparently the sense of shame that some homeless attach to begging and panhandling is minimal or nonexistent for the outsiders. Most have been on the streets too long or have drifted too far from the world of regular work and its underlying values to permit them to circumscribe survival activities. Moreover, as Ron Whitaker began to realize, the exigencies of street life have a way of withering prior constraints and understandings.

But even outsiders differ among themselves in how they elicit money from passing strangers: Some beg, others panhandle. The difference is behavioral and a matter of degree. Beggars humbly and passively solicit donations; panhandlers accost and importune. Partly as a consequence, beggars tend to be objects of pity, whereas panhandlers often engender fear or scorn or both.[12] Consistent with these distinctions, begging tends to predominate among the traditional bums, largely because of their physical degeneration. Gypsy Bill, who claimed to be particularly good at begging, informed us, "Sparing change is easier for me than it is for a lot of guys. I don't have to hassle anybody, 'cause they just look at me and feel sorry. I just sit on my bedroll on the sidewalk and when people come by they drop some change in my hat." In contrast, it was primarily hippie tramps and redneck bums who panhandled. It was not uncommon, for example, to see Bill-Bob and a fellow redneck bum accosting passersby either in the downtown area or in the vicinity of the plasma centers and following them for half a block or more, arguing with them if they refused the request for money. Traditional tramps and the mentally ill engaged in a greater mix of begging and panhandling activities than did traditional and redneck bums. The tack they took depended on such factors as degree of sobriety, interactional capabilities, or general state of mind. An example is provided by a mentally ill woman with a shaved head, who spent most days wandering barefoot along the Drag and whose soliciting style was highly dependent on her mood. Some days she would sit quietly soliciting donations with a sign, but at other times she would scream at and chase after those who refused her requests.

. . .

Scavenging

Scavenging, the third general form of shadow work, is a salvaging process that entails rummaging through discarded materials to find usable or salable items. Since its material base is the refuse of others, scavenging reflects the location of the homeless at the bottom of the social order. Many of the homeless, not surprisingly, hold scavenging in low regard, and they engage in it only as a last resort. We seldom observed scavenging among the recently dislocated, and only a few straddlers scavenged, and then only when other options were not available, such as on weekends when there was no prospect of day labor. One Sunday morning, for instance, Pat Manchester explained to us, "I couldn't sleep this morning, so I went out looking through dumpsters till I got enough cans to sell so I could buy a breakfast taco and some coffee." The traditional and hippie tramps and the redneck bums also scavenge only rarely, and it is clearly not a favored form of shadow work.

Traditional bums and the mentally ill, by contrast, tend to scavenge fairly regularly. It is the former's primary subsistence activity and the mentally ill's second most important means of survival, next to public assistance. Their patterns of scavenging are quite different, however. Traditional bums often work in a team, whereas the mentally ill engage in solitary scavenging that both reflects and reinforces their social isolation.

The most common items the homeless in Austin scavenge are aluminum beer and pop cans, which they then sell at the going rate. One 41-year-old traditional bum, known on the streets as Pushcart, makes almost daily rounds of the student-housing area that surrounds the university campus, pushing an expropriated grocery cart that he loads with aluminum cans he collects from dumpsters, parking lots and the side of the road. When asked why he engaged in this activity, Pushcart replied, "I've been in the Marines, man, and I've taken too many orders too long. Scrapping for cans, there's nobody telling me what to do. I'm my own boss, and when I want to take a break or call it a day, I can."

The price paid for aluminum varies. During the course of our research, it fluctuated between 14 and 21 cents per pound at the metal recycling companies and supermarkets in Austin.[13] Several 24-hour mechanical recycling stations are located in busy parts of Austin. These machines usually pay 5 to 8 cents per pound less for cans than supermarkets, but they are more accessible. On a good day, according to Pushcart, a diligent worker can collect $5 to $10 worth of cans.

Large apartment complexes, particularly those in which the relatively affluent and heavy-drinking student population resides, are a favorite hunting ground for aluminum cans. The traditional bum keeps an eye out for other items as well: clothes, magazines, broken radios, and the like. The recycling that results from this scavenging is graphically illustrated by the experiences recounted by Elbert, a 47-year-old self-proclaimed "burnt-out bum" who has spent the last two years living at a charity-supported rural facility for homeless substance abusers:

> When I was on the streets I knew where to find things and I knew how to fix them. I've put together good televisions out of parts I got from dumpsters. One time I sold the junk I found in just one dumpster for more than a hundred bucks. I made a living on stuff other people threw away. . . . If I was living in Calcutta with the beggars, I could get by better than most of them, 'cause I know what to do.

Similar sentiments were voiced by a 37-year-old traditional bum who was among the homeless who traveled to the Oregon community of Antelope when the Rajneeshee cult made their much-publicized recruiting sweep to gather voters for local elections. One night in the winter warehouse, after he had returned disillusioned, he rambled at length about the useful items to be garnered from student dumpsters:

> You wouldn't believe the stuff students throw away. I've found radios and clocks and clothes. Hell, everything I've got almost I found in dumpsters. I haven't bought a pair of shoes in a year and a half. A couple days

ago I found a $65 pair of running shoes in a dumpster. And shirts—you can find good shirts. And pants. One time I even found a pair of pants with five bucks in a pocket.

As was suggested earlier, traditional bums will frequently try to sell scavenged items to other homeless people. Indeed, the area around the Sally functions at times as a sort of scavenger's flea market. Traditional bums also resourcefully search through dumpsters for food. Gypsy Bill, who, as we mentioned before, considered himself "an expert dumpster diver," described the activity well:

When we had the camp at Bull Creek, some of the guys would go in to TEC every morning and try to get out on jobs. The ones who did would come back in the evening and buy beer for the rest of us. My job was camp cook, and part of that was dumpster-diving down at Safeway. There were these two brothers who would help me—they'd toss me into the dumpster and I'd start going through junk, looking around. Bread and fruit and meat—good meat, just outdated was all. I'd make supper from what I found: a stew, fried chicken, or something! Man, between them working and buying the beer and me dumpster-diving and cooking dinner, we could party every night.

When traditional bums locate a good dumpster, they tend to develop a pattern of regular usage. For instance, most afternoons about 10 bums were observed waiting patiently beside two dumpsters where a vending-machine company tossed its unsold burritos and sandwiches. Such patterns are occasionally broken when grocery stores and restaurants decide to "clean up the area" and take measures, such as chaining the dumpsters, to prevent dumpster-diving.[14]

We noted earlier that scavenging tends to be held in low repute by many of the homeless, largely because of the obdurate fact that it means rummaging through garbage. But we suspect that another reason more homeless do not scavenge on a regular basis is that most lack the skill to do it effectively. It is necessary not only to know where to look and when but also to have a sense of what to look for, that is, to have good judgment about its salability or edibility. This is what Gypsy meant when he called himself an "expert dumpster-diver," a "craftsman" at scavenging. Such know-how can be acquired only through firsthand experience over time, something the traditional bums have had plenty of, with 93 percent having been on the streets for more than two years.

Know-how is evident in the scavenging activities of the mentally ill, but they approach it in a more isolated or solitary manner than the traditional bums do. Jorge Herrera, for example, scavenges alone for food and change, making a regular circuit of convenience store and fast-food restaurant garbage cans and telephone booths. Similarly, we often observed a mentally ill woman in her mid-30s alone in fast-food restaurants in the university area, picking up bits of food that customers had left on the tables. The solitary survival activities of the homeless mentally ill reflect their isolation not only from each other but within the world of the homeless in general. Nonetheless, the subsistence of the homeless mentally ill in Austin, just as for the traditional bum, is contingent in part on their scavenging activities.

Theft

The final type of shadow work engaged in by some of the homeless is theft and related criminal activities such as burglary and fencing stolen goods.[15] Although theft is almost always performed surreptitiously, we did learn indirectly that it is fairly commonplace among some of the homeless. A few confessed to having stolen this or that, as when Tom Fisk told us about his theft of a motorcycle, for which he spent 37 days in jail, or when Pushcart admitted to stealing the scavenged cans of other homeless, but only when they are drunk and passed out in public. "I'll say, 'Hey, wake up! I'm gonna take your cans!' If he doesn't wake up, it's 'Sayonara.' Hey, it's happened to me. What goes around, comes around."

Some of the homeless would talk openly with each other about what they had stolen, on occasion even flaunting the stolen item. One afternoon in front of one of the plasma centers, for instance, a homeless woman who was only about 18 showed Nona a set of earrings she had stolen and then bragged about them until Nona refocused the discussion onto her own exploits at thievery. On other occasions, homeless people would show up inexplicably with new personal possessions, such as radios and tape recorders, or with goods they would try to sell at cut-rate prices. We met a 20-year-old man, who frequently sold joints around the Sally, one evening several blocks west of the Sally fencing what we took to be stolen goods:

> We were walking toward the Sally when a street acquaintance called to us from across Congress Avenue. We crossed over and he showed us a suitcase full of freshly washed, almost new jeans and asked if we would buy a pair. He sold six pairs for five bucks each while we were hanging around. He told us he had met a guy on the street who sold him the suitcase for 50 cents. "At least I'm making honest money," he said. "And I'm not selling dope either."

More direct evidence of theft comes from the tracking sample data [used in this study]. Of the 697 criminal offenses for which the homeless in our sample were arrested in Austin, fewer than a quarter of the arrests were for felonies.[16] But 62 percent of these felonies involved theft and another 27 percent burglary, usually for the purpose of theft. Thus, 89 percent of all felonies for which the homeless were arrested locally were theft-related. When this finding is considered in conjunction with the corroborating finding that the age-standardized arrest rates for burglary and theft per 1,000 homeless adult males are 1.5 and 1.3 times higher than the corresponding rates for non-homeless adult males, it seems clear that theft and related criminal activity constitute a fairly salient subsistence strategy for some of the homeless.[17] This finding is unsurprising, considering the meager funds at the disposal of most of the homeless and the fact that many begin each day penniless. After all, theft is one of the few means available to the homeless for procuring cig-arettes, coffee, beer, and snacks when their pockets are empty or nearly so. Moreover, opportunity for theft abounds, with convenience stores and gas stations on the corners of nearly every major intersection. Were it not for the vigilance of convenience-store proprietors and employees whenever the homeless are shopping or browsing in their stores, the incidence of theft among the homeless might be even higher.[18]

As with the other types of shadow work, theft is not chosen randomly by the homeless. Although the clandestine nature of theft made it impossible to discern fine-tuned variation across the types of homeless, several findings from the tracking data point to significant clustering and variation. . . . Since thefts constitute the plurality of felonies committed by the homeless and since the recently dislocated average less than six months on the streets, it seems likely that theft is engaged in more often by straddlers and outsiders who are not physically incapacitated.[19] For many of these individuals, theft functions as an adaptive strategy that, like other forms of shadow work, fa-cilitates survival in a world shorn of more conventional ways of making do.

Summary

. . . We have examined an array of non–wage labor subsistence strategies the homeless fashion because they are excluded from existing labor markets, be-cause participation in those markets fails to offer them a living wage, because institutionalized assistance proves inadequate, or because these unconven-tional strategies provide a more reliable means of survival on the streets. We have called these compensatory subsistence strategies shadow work because they are not traditionally counted as work and because they are pursued in the shadow of regular work—that is, on the sidewalks of urban America and in its back alleys and refuse receptacles. And . . . we have found here varia-tion in the extent to which the various types of homeless engage in the dif-ferent kinds of shadow work.

These observations . . . raise a number of issues that warrant discussion in order to illuminate further the subsistence activities of the homeless. The first concerns the mix of strategies employed by each type of homeless. Although it is clear that the set of subsistence strategies available to the homeless is limited, it is equally clear that each type of homeless has its own peculiar mix of strategies, such that we may speak of type-specific or person-alized repertoires of material subsistence. The existence of such repertoires suggests that some degree of selectivity is exercised with respect to the strategies pursued. Yet, the use of one strategy rather than another is not merely a matter of choice. No single strategy can ensure subsistence on the streets, and no matter how strongly one subsistence activity is preferred over another, there is no guarantee from one day to the next that it will still be a viable option. Day labor is not sufficiently abundant to ensure paid work day after day, and it is virtually nonexistent on weekends. Plasma centers, too, are closed on the weekends. And Sundays are particularly bad days for begging and panhandling, because few non-homeless pedestrians are on the streets.

Survival, then, is contingent on the opportunistic fashioning and utilization of a mix of strategies. The recently dislocated and straddlers may frown on scavenging, but, as Pat Manchester discovered when he turned to dumpster-diving in search of funds for breakfast one Sunday, necessity may leave them with little choice but to engage in some subsistence activity they hold in low regard.

These constraints and uncertainties notwithstanding, what is perhaps most noteworthy is that the different types of homeless do have preferred strategies and that they pursue those more regularly than the other strategies. Such selectivity suggests both that the homeless attempt to exercise some autonomy in their lives and that material survival on the streets is more than a random or chaotic affair. Like most spheres of life, it is patterned and ordered, not solely by the network of street institutions that structure the routines and options of the homeless, but also by the preferences and idiosyncrasies of the different types of homeless themselves.

A second and related issue is why outsiders do not pursue wage labor as persistently as the recently dislocated and even the regular straddlers. The traditional tramps are somewhat of an exception to this tendency, but even their mean score for wage labor is lower than that for both the recently dislocated and the straddlers. Thus, the general tendency is that the longer the homeless are on the streets and the more they drift into the world of the outsider, the less salient wage labor becomes as a mode of subsistence for them and the more prominent become one or more forms of shadow work.

. . .

Most of [the homeless] have little confidence that their actions today will yield a better tomorrow for them. As we have seen, the wage labor that awaits them, if they are lucky enough to secure any, typically involves jobs that lead only to the repetition of their current plight. With this negative articulation between their immediate present and their anticipated future, it is little wonder that many drift from the world of regular work to the world of shadow work. It is not so much because they are present-oriented—although they have good reason to be so, given that their daily survival commands all the resources they can muster. Rather, it is because the tomorrows they can realistically imagine are not ones that inspire either the investment of whatever limited resources they may have scrimped to save or the adoption of lines of action that go beyond the world of shadow work. For many of the homeless, then, the repeated failure of the world of wage labor to yield a fair return on the time and energy invested pushes them into the world of shadow work. Initially, shadow work is seen primarily as a stop-gap measure, as a kind of supplemental, temporary work. In time, however, as experience and familiarity with it increase, it can become a way of life.

NOTES

1. Although textual discussions of work do not always specify the criteria used to distinguish it from nonwork, three criteria can be culled from most such discussions: remuneration, regulation, and enumeration. Thus, work as conventionally conceived is an activity for which an individual is paid; time, place, and rate of pay are regulated; and it can be enumerated or counted by local, state, and federal governments. These criteria result in a rather "limited set of activities and roles that are deemed legitimate ways of making a living" (Miller 1981, p. 133). This narrow focus has begun to expand in recent years, however, with the growing recognition, due in part to the feminist movement, that non-occupational tasks such as housework and volunteer activities also constitute work, as do various illegal enterprises, such as prostitution, fencing, numbers running, and drug dealing, which are typically described as "deviant work." Still, the focus of most textual discussions of work is on jobs, occupations, and professions (Hodson and Sullivan 1990; Miller 1981; and Ritzer and Walczak 1986).

    Moreover, since so much of what we know about conventional work is based on government statistics, it is understandable that some students of work and labor processes emphasize state regulation as the key factor in their conceptualization (Lozano 1983; Portes and Walton 1981).

2. The concept of shadow work is borrowed from the philosopher, historian, and social critic Ivan Illich (1981). Illich uses the term for unpaid work that is a necessary requisite for and complement to productive and consumptive activity, such as housework, grocery shopping, and commuting. We use the term somewhat differently, to refer to unpaid subsistence activities. We do so for several reasons. For one thing, it resonates with the obdurate fact that the subsistence strategies engaged in by the homeless take place in the shadow of regular work. Additionally, it is consistent with the adaptive and behavioral thrust of our conceptualization of the subculture of street life. And, finally, we find *shadow work* preferable to a number of kindred terms. Some labor economists and students of informal sector activity in the Third World have used the term *nonmarket work* to encompass "all work not performed for wages, profits, or rents, including housework and even commuting work" (Uzzell, 1980, p. 42). But not all shadow work is nonmarket work. As we shall see shortly, some types of shadow work exist only within a market context, but the market is neither officially regulated nor sanctioned. Instead, it is an ephemeral one that exists outside the dominant economic system and thus constitutes part of the "shadow economy." . . .

3. Wiseman (1970, p. 27).

4. Hopper et al. (1985, p. 194). Although Hopper and his associates correctly argue that the makeshift activities we call shadow work figure prominently in the lifestyle and subsistence of the homeless, neither they nor other students of the homeless of the 1980s have examined these activities in a detailed and systematic fashion. To be sure, a handful of survey studies have asked the homeless about their income sources and have found that a number of activities we call shadow work (e.g., panhandling, selling cans, selling plasma) are engaged in by many of

the homeless (Baumann et al. 1985, pp. 124–26; Brown et al. 1983, pp. 44–46; Burt and Cohen 1989, p. 43; Robertson et al. 1985, pp. 53–54; and Rossi 1989, pp. 108–14). But substantial discussion of these findings is rare (for an exception, see Wiegand 1990).

Moreover, when the homeless are asked about their sources of income, the phrasing of the questions often elicits the most important sources, rather than how they interact or are used in combination. . . . In the August, 1984, street survey in Austin, the homeless were asked not only about income sources but also about their relative importance. Relatively few pointed to shadow work as their most important source of income (only 9 percent), but it was the second most frequently listed source of income for 53 percent of the 117 homeless respondents (Baumann et al. 1985, pp. 124–26).

A final confounding problem with the way income sources have been pursued by survey procedures is that the questions are typically followed by a fixed list of choices that rarely encompasses the full range of shadow work. Even if the responses are open-ended, it is likely that some of the criminal and more stigmatizing forms of shadow work will not be mentioned by all who have engaged in them. These considerations, then, give good reason to presume that shadow work is a more important means of subsistence among the homeless than some of the research would have us believe.

5. It is important to keep in mind that the distinction between junk and reasonably attractive personal possessions is largely subjective. . . . Thus, what is defined as junk and what as nonjunk is likely to vary not only from person to person but also from one situation to the next. To the homeless, what is seen as a worthy personal possession one day may be redefined as a salable item or a piece of junk the next day.

6. For an interesting and relevant discussion of garage sales, see Herrman and Soiffer (1984). They note that although the motives underlying garage sales can be quite varied, often they function as an adaptive survival strategy when times are difficult economically. For a recent analysis of estate sales and auctions, see Smith (1989).

7. We neither observed nor learned of more expensive drugs being sold by regular straddlers to homeless individuals. Some of the homeless might be interested in obtaining such drugs, but most lack the money to buy them. It is also important to note that our research was conducted in 1984 to 1986, before "crack," a relatively new and cheap form of cocaine, was available, at least on the streets of Austin.

8. Writing of sex and prostitution in the nineteenth century, Tannahill observes that "the girls who became prostitutes in [this] century usually did so because they needed the money. At one end of the scale there was the independent-minded career woman who knew that, without any capital other than herself, only prostitution and the stage offered the prospect of making a good living; at the other, the young widow or unmarried mother able to earn little but almost certain to be separated from her child if she applied for the parish relief that would save them both from starvation" (1980, pp. 357–58). Although the character of prostitution may have changed somewhat since the Victorian era, the economic impetus still remains prominent, as Miller's (1986) study of the survival strategies of underclass women in Milwaukee makes clear. Financial considerations also figure heavily in the process of entering male prostitution, but other contextual factors are operative, too, as research on male prostitution demonstrates (Calhoun 1988; Luckenbill 1985).

9. Such distancing techniques are not peculiar to the homeless but have also been observed among domiciled male prostitutes (Calhoun 1988; Reiss 1961).

10. This distinction is not commonplace in the literature, where *begging* and *panhandling* tend to be used interchangeably. However, we find it useful to distinguish between the two because our observations in Austin and Tucson indicate that solicitation of money in public places can be arrayed on a continuum, from quite passive gestures or postures intended to elicit sympathy to more aggressive, harassing overtures. . . .

11. In a recent study of panhandling in Tucson, consisting of field observations and interviews with 80 panhandlers, embarrassment was found to be a powerful impediment. As the study reported, "[T]he most consistent finding regarding how panhandlers felt about panhandling is that it doesn't come easily, and that it is not an enjoyable activity . . . it was repeatedly stated that panhandling is 'embarrassing' and that it takes 'courage and nerve'" (Costello et al. 1990, p. 31). . . .

12. Evidence of both fear and scorn surfaced during our observations of panhandling in Austin. Fear showed in the aversion of the targets' eyes, the hastening of their pace, and the expansion of the lateral distance between the panhandler and themselves. Scorn was also reflected at times in the angry and hostile comments of some passersby, such as "Get lost, you lazy bum."

13. Texas did not have a container law at the time of our research. For the homeless, this was both a blessing and a curse. The price paid for cans is much higher where there is a container law (typically 5 to 10 cents per can), but cans are not discarded as frequently in those states. . . . Recently the price of aluminum has increased nationwide, encouraging more people to save and collect cans and thus reducing the number of cans the homeless can scavenge.

14. Just as measures have been taken to curtail panhandling throughout the country, so scavenging has been targeted for control. In the fall of 1984, Fort Lauderdale passed an ordinance making it illegal to take garbage from a dumpster without the written permission of the owner. And one of the city's commissioners went so far as to suggest that rat poison be used as a topping for garbage to discourage scavenging (*Time*, March 11, 1985, p. 68). Similar ordinances have been considered in Santa Barbara, among other cities (*Los Angeles Times*, December 13, 1984).

15. As defined by the Federal Bureau of Investigation, theft involves "the unlawful taking, carrying, leading or riding away of property from the possession or constructive possession of another. Examples are thefts of bicycles or automobile accessories, shoplifting, pocket-picking, or the stealing of any property or article that is not taken by force and violence or by fraud." Burglary, in contrast, involves "the unlawful entry of a structure to commit a felony or a theft." (See any recent edition of the FBI's *Uniform Crime Reports in the United States*, Washington, DC: U.S. Government Printing Office.)

16. Two hundred and forty-eight of 767 homeless in the tracking sample were arrested in Austin on one or more occasions during the 27-month period between January 1, 1983, and March 31, 1985. The data extraction for this phase of the research was confined to this period because the Austin police department's individual records were not fully entered into the computer until January 1, 1983, and because we began this portion of the research in March, 1985. If any of the 767 tracking cases had an arrest contact with the Austin police during the period, a computer match was made and the relevant data became part of the pool of crime data on the homeless in Austin. For a more detailed discussion of these data, see Snow et al. (1989).

17. In order to place the arrest data on the homeless in a broader and more meaningful context, data were also compiled on the arrests for all domiciled adult males in Austin over the same 27-month period. Since domiciled adult males greatly outnumber the homeless, it was necessary to control for population size. We also

controlled for age. The resultant age-standardized arrest rate per 1,000 homeless and non-homeless for burglary was 44.45 and 28.35, respectively, and 125.56 and 95.62 for theft.

18. The comparatively high arrest rate for theft should not be read as indicative of heightened criminal tendencies among the homeless. Not only is the age-standardized arrest rate for crimes of violence (murder, rape, assault, robbery) among the homeless one-half that for the domiciled male population (11.98 compared to 23.59), but nearly 50 percent of all thefts are for shoplifting of cigarettes, small quantities of food and drink, and occasionally calculators and other such items that are then sold on the streets or in pawn shops. These additional findings suggest that the homeless are not so much serious and dangerous criminals as deprived individuals who sometimes turn to theft in the absence of the financial resources and discretionary income most citizens take for granted. In assessing arrest statistics on the homeless, it is also important to keep in mind that research on crime and the criminal-justice system suggests that the marginal are more likely to be subjected to police scrutiny. See, for example, Black (1976, p. 51).

19. This presumes, of course, that higher rates of arrest among the homeless with longer stretches of time on the streets are not merely a function of greater exposure to the police. Although we certainly acknowledge this as a possibility, we think that the greater frequency of arrest among the homeless who have been on the streets for more than six months results in part from the observed fact that some of them do engage in more criminal behavior because such behaviors—panhandling, begging, and theft—have become more salient aspects of their survival repertoires. These individuals are more likely than others to catch the attention of the police and to have higher arrest rates.

REFERENCES

Baumann, Donald J., Cheryl Beauvais, Charles Grigsby, and F. D. Schultz. 1985. *The Austin Homeless: Final Report Provided to the Hogg Foundation for Mental Health.* Austin: Hogg Foundation for Mental Health.

Black, Donald. 1976. *The Behavior of Law.* New York: Academic Press.

Brown, Carl, S. McFarlane, Ron Paredes, and Louisa Stark. 1983. *The Homeless of Phoenix: Who Are They? What Should Be Done?* Phoenix: Phoenix South Community Mental Health Center.

Burt, Martha R. and Barbara E. Cohen. 1989. *America's Homeless: Numbers, Characteristics, and Programs That Serve Them.* Washington, DC: Urban Institute Press.

Calhoun, Thomas C. 1988. "Theoretical Considerations on the Entrance and Stabilization of Male Street Prostitutes." Ph.D. dissertation, University of Kentucky.

Costello, Barbara, Joseph Heirling, Frank Hunsaker, and Terry McCulloch. 1990. "Panhandling in Tucson." Paper, Department of Sociology, University of Arizona.

Herrmann, Gretchen M. and Stephen M. Soiffer. 1984. "For Fun and Profit: An Analysis of the American Garage Sale." *Urban Life* 12:397–421.

Hodson, Randy and Teresa A. Sullivan. 1990. *The Social Organization of Work.* Belmont, CA: Wadsworth.

Hopper, Kim, Ezra Susser, and Sarah Conover. 1985. "Economics of Makeshift: Deindustrialization and Homelessness in New York City." *Urban Anthropology* 14:183–236.

Illich, Ivan, 1981. *Shadow Work.* Boston: Marian Boyars.

Los Angeles Times. 1984. "Santa Barbara—A Lid on Hobos' Food?" December 13.

Lozano, Beverly. 1983. "Informal Sector Workers: Walking Out the System's Front Door?" *International Journal of Urban and Regional Research* 7:340–61.

Luckenbill, David F. 1985. "Entering Male Prostitution." *Urban Life* 14:131–53.

Miller, Eleanor M. 1986. *Street Women*. Philadelphia: Temple University Press.

Miller, Gale. 1981. *It's a Living: Work in Modern Society*. New York: St. Martin's Press.

Portes, Alejandro, and John Walton. 1981. *Labor, Class and the International System*. New York: Academic Press.

Reiss, Albert J., Jr. 1961. "The Social Integration of Queers and Peers." *Social Problems* 9:102–19.

Ritzer, George and David Walczak. 1986. *Working: Conflict and Change*. Englewood Cliffs, NJ: Prentice-Hall.

Robertson, Marjorie J., Richard Ropers, and Richard Boyer. 1985. *The Homeless of Los Angeles County: An Empirical Evaluation*. Document no. 4. Los Angeles: Basic Shelter Research Project, School of Public Health, University of California, Los Angeles.

Rossi, Peter. 1989. *Down and Out in America: The Origins of Homelessness*. Chicago: University of Chicago Press.

Smith, Charles W. 1989. *Auctions: The Social Construction of Value*. New York: Free Press.

Snow, David A., Susan G. Baker, and Leon Anderson. 1989. "Criminality among Homeless Men: An Empirical Assessment." *Social Problems* 36:532–49.

Tannahill, Reay. 1980. *Sex in History*. New York: Stein and Day.

Time. 1985. "Harassing the Homeless." March 11, p. 68.

Uzzell, J. Douglas. 1980. "Mixed Strategies and the Informal Sector: Three Facts of Reserved Labor." *Human Organization* 39:40–49.

Wiseman, Jacqueline. 1970. *Stations of the Lost: The Treatment of Skid Row Alcoholics*. Chicago: University of Chicago Press.

RELIGION

43

THE ELEMENTARY FORMS OF THE RELIGIOUS LIFE

EMILE DURKHEIM

The institution of religion is the topic of the following four selections. Sociologists have long studied how religion affects the social structure and the personal experience of individuals in society. Emile Durkheim (1858–1917), for example, often placed religion at the center of his social analyses. Durkheim was especially concerned with the meaning of religion and how it contributed to social cohesion. This selection is an excerpt from his definitive study of religion among the Australian aborigines, "The Elementary Forms of Religious Life." In his analysis of the functions of religion in society, Durkheim states that religious beliefs and rituals are real and reflect the societies in which they exist. Moreover, Durkheim argues for a separation between the knowledge of religion and the knowledge of science.

T he theorists who have undertaken to explain religion in rational terms have generally seen in it before all else a system of ideas, corresponding to some determined object. This object has been conceived in a multitude of ways: nature, the infinite, the unknowable, the ideal, etc.; but these differences matter but little. In any case, it was the conceptions and beliefs which were considered as the essential elements of religion. As for the rites, from this point of view they appear to be only an external translation, contingent and material, of these internal states which alone pass as having any intrinsic value. This conception is so commonly held that generally the disputes of which religion is the theme turn about the question whether it can conciliate itself with science or not, that is to say, whether or not there is a place beside our scientific knowledge for another form of thought which would be specifically religious.

But the believers, the men who lead the religious life and have a direct sensation of what it really is, object to this way of regarding it, saying that it does not correspond to their daily experience. In fact, they feel that the real function of religion is not to make us think, to enrich our knowledge, nor to add to the conceptions which we owe to science others of another origin and another character, but rather, it is to make us act, to aid us to live. The believer who has communicated with his god is not merely a man who sees new truths of which the unbeliever is ignorant; he is a man who is *stronger.* He feels within him more force, either to endure the trials of existence, or to conquer them. It is as though he were raised above the miseries of the world, because he is raised above his condition as a mere man; he believes that he is saved from evil, under whatever form he may conceive this evil. The first article in every creed is the belief in salvation by faith. But it is hard to see how a mere idea could have this efficacy. An idea is in reality only a part of ourselves; then how could it confer upon us powers superior to those which we have of our own nature? Howsoever rich it might be in affective virtues, it could add nothing to our natural vitality; for it could only release the motive powers which are within us, neither creating them nor increasing them. From the mere fact that we consider an object worthy of being loved and sought after, it does not follow that we feel ourselves stronger afterwards; it is also necessary that this object set free energies superior to these which we ordinarily have at our command and also that we have some means of making these enter into us and unite themselves to our interior lives. Now for that, it is not enough that we think of them; it is also indispensable that we place ourselves within their sphere of action, and that we set ourselves where we may best feel their influence; in a word, it is necessary that we act, and that we repeat the acts thus necessary every time we feel the need of renewing their effects. From this point of view, it is readily seen how that group of regularly repeated acts which form the cult get their importance. In fact, whoever has really practised a religion knows very well that it is the cult which gives rise to these impressions of joy, of interior peace, of serenity, of enthusiasm which are, for the believer, an experimental proof of his beliefs. The cult is not simply a system of signs by which the faith is outwardly translated; it is a collection of the means by which this is created and recreated periodically. Whether it consists in material acts or mental operations, it is always this which is efficacious.

Our entire study rests upon this postulate that the unanimous sentiment of the believers of all times cannot be purely illusory. Together with a recent apologist of the faith[1] we admit that these religious beliefs rest upon a specific experience whose demonstrative value is, in one sense, not one bit inferior to that of scientific experiments, though different from them. We, too, think that "a tree is known by its fruits," and that fertility is the best proof of what the roots are worth. But from the fact that a "religious experience," if we choose to call it this, does exist and that it has a certain foundation—and, by the way, is there any experience which has none?—it does not follow that the reality which is its foundation conforms objectively to the idea which believers have of it. The very fact that the fashion in which it has been conceived has varied infinitely in different times is enough to prove that none of these conceptions express it adequately. If a scientist states it as an axiom that the sensations of heat and light which we feel correspond to some objective cause, he does not conclude that this is what it appears to the senses to be. Likewise, even if the impressions which the faithful feel are not imaginary, still they are in no way privileged intuitions; there is no reason for believing that they inform us better upon the nature of their object than do ordinary sensations upon the nature of bodies and their properties. In order to discover what this object consists of, we must submit them to an examination and elaboration analogous to that which has substituted for the sensuous idea of the world another which is scientific and conceptual.

This is precisely what we have tried to do, and we have seen that this reality, which mythologies have represented under so many different forms, but which is the universal and eternal objective cause of these sensations *sui generis* out of which religious experience is made, is society. We have shown what moral forces it develops and how it awakens this sentiment of a refuge, of a shield and of a guardian support which attaches the believer to his cult. It is that which raises him outside himself; it is even that which made him. For that which makes a man is the totality of the intellectual property which constitutes civilization, and civilization is the work of society. Thus is explained the preponderating role of the cult in all religions, whichever they may be. This is because society cannot make its influence felt unless it is in action, and it is not in action unless the individuals who compose it are assembled together and act in common. It is by common action that it takes consciousness of itself and realizes its position; it is before all else an active cooperation. The collective ideas and sentiments are even possible only owing to these exterior movements which symbolize them, as we have established. Then it is action which dominates the religious life, because of the mere fact that it is society which is its source. . . .

Religious forces are therefore human forces, moral forces. It is true that since collective sentiments can become conscious of themselves only by fixing themselves upon external objects, they have not been able to take form without adopting some of their characteristics from other things: They have thus acquired a sort of physical nature; in this way they have come to mix themselves with the life of the material world, and then have considered themselves capable of explaining what passes there. But when they are considered only from this point of view and in this role, only their most superficial aspect is seen. In reality, the essential elements of which these collective sentiments are made have been borrowed by the understanding. It ordinarily seems that they should have a human character only when they are conceived under human forms;[2] but even the most impersonal and the most anonymous are nothing else than objectified sentiments. . . .

Some reply that men have a natural faculty for idealizing, that is to say, of substituting for the real world another different one, to which they transport themselves by thought. But that is merely changing the terms of the problem; it is not resolving it or even advancing it. This systematic idealization is an essential characteristic of religions. Explaining them by an innate power of idealization is simply replacing one word by another which is the equivalent of the first; it is as if they said that men have made religions because they have a religious nature. Animals know only one world, the one which they perceive by experience, internal as well as external. Men alone have the faculty of conceiving the ideal, of adding something to the real. Now where does this singular privilege come from? Before making it an initial fact or a mysterious virtue which escapes science, we must be sure that it does not depend upon empirically determinable conditions.

The explanation of religion which we have proposed has precisely this advantage, that it gives an answer to this question. For our definition of the sacred is that it is something added to and above the real: Now the ideal answers to this same definition; we cannot explain one without explaining the other. In fact, we have seen that if collective life awakens religious thought on reaching a certain degree of intensity, it is because it brings about a state of effervescence which changes the conditions of psychic activity. Vital energies are overexcited, passions more active, sensations stronger; there are even some which are produced only at this moment. A man does not recognize himself; he feels himself transformed and consequently he transforms the environment which surrounds him. In order to account for the very particular impressions which he receives, he attributes to the things with which he is in most direct contact properties which they have not, exceptional powers and virtues which the objects of everyday experience do not possess. In a word, above the real world where his profane life passes he has placed another which, in one sense, does not exist except in thought, but to which he attributes a higher sort of dignity than to the first. Thus, from a double point of view it is an ideal world.

The formation of the ideal world is therefore not an irreducible fact which escapes science; it depends upon conditions which observation can touch; it is a natural product of social life. For a society to become conscious of itself and maintain at the necessary degree of intensity the sentiments which it thus attains, it must assemble and concentrate itself. Now this concentration brings about an exaltation of the mental life which takes form in a group of ideal conceptions where is portrayed the new life thus awakened; they correspond to this new set of psychical forces which is added to those which we have at our disposition for the daily tasks of existence. A society can neither create itself nor recreate itself without at the same time creating an ideal. This creation is not a sort of work of supererogation for it, by which it would complete itself, being already formed; it is the act by which it is periodically made and remade. Therefore when some oppose the ideal society to the real society, like two antagonists which would lead us in opposite directions, they materialize and oppose abstractions. The ideal society is not outside of the real society; it is a part of it. Far from being divided between them as between two poles which mutually repel each other, we cannot hold to one without holding to the other. For a society is not made up merely of the mass of individuals who compose it, the ground which they occupy, the things which they use and the movements which they perform, but above all is the idea which it forms of itself. It is undoubtedly true that it hesitates over the manner in which it ought to conceive itself; it feels itself drawn in divergent directions. But these conflicts which break forth are not between the ideal and reality, but between two different ideals, that of yesterday and that of today, that which has the authority of tradition and that which has the hope of the future. There is surely a place for investigating whence these ideals evolve; but whatever solution may be given to this problem, it still remains that all passes in the world of the ideal.

Thus the collective ideal which religion expresses is far from being due to a vague innate power of the individual, but it is rather at the school of collective life that the individual has learned to idealize. It is in assimilating the ideals elaborated by society that he has become capable of conceiving the ideal. It is society which, by leading him within its sphere of action, has made him acquire the need of raising himself above the world of experience and has at the same time furnished him with the means of conceiving another. For society has constructed this new world in constructing itself, since it is society which this expresses. This both with the individual and in the group, the faculty of idealizing has nothing mysterious about it. It is not a sort of luxury which a man could get along without, but a condition of his very existence. He could not be a social being, that is to say, he could not be a man, if he had not acquired it. It is true that in incarnating themselves in individuals, collective ideals tend to individualize themselves. Each understands them after his own fashion and marks them with his own stamp; he suppresses certain elements and adds others. Thus the personal ideal disengages itself from the social ideal in proportion as the individual personality develops itself and becomes an autonomous source of action. But if we wish to understand this aptitude, so singular in appearance, of living outside of reality, it is enough to connect it with the social conditions upon which it depends.

Therefore it is necessary to avoid seeing in this theory of religion a simple restatement of historical materialism: That would be misunderstanding our thought to an extreme degree. In showing that religion is something essentially social, we do not mean to say that it confines itself to translating into another language the material forms of society and its immediate vital necessities. It is true that we take it as evident that social life depends upon its material foundation and bears its mark, just as the mental life of an individual depends upon his nervous system and in fact his whole organism. But collective consciousness is something more than a mere epiphenomenon of its morphological basis, just as individual consciousness is something more than a simple efflorescence of the nervous system. In order that the former may appear, a synthesis *sui generis* of particular consciousnesses is required. Now this synthesis has the effect of disengaging a whole world of sentiments, ideas, and images which, once born, obey laws all their own. They attract each other, repel each other, unite, divide themselves, and multiply, though these combinations are not commanded and necessitated by the condition of the underlying reality. The life thus brought into being even enjoys so great an independence that it sometimes indulges in manifestations with no purpose or utility of any sort, for the mere pleasure of affirming itself. We have shown that this is often precisely the case with ritual activity and mythological thought.[3] . . .

That is what the conflict between science and religion really amounts to. It is said that science denies religion in principle. But religion exists; it is a system of given facts; in a word, it is a reality. How could science deny this reality? Also, insofar as religion is action, and insofar as it is a means of making men live, science could not take its place, for even if this expresses life, it does not create it; it may well seek to explain the faith, but by that very act it presupposes it. Thus there is no conflict except upon one limited point. Of the two functions which religion originally fulfilled, there is one, and only one, which tends to escape it more and more: That is its speculative function. That which science refuses to grant to religion is not its right to exist, but its right to dogmatize upon the nature of things and the special competence which it claims for itself for knowing man and the world. As a matter of fact, it does not know itself. It does not even know what it is made of, nor to what need it answers. It is itself a subject for science, so far is it from being able to make the law for science! And from another point of view, since there is no proper subject for religious speculation outside that reality to which scientific reflection is applied, it is evident that this former cannot play the same role in the future that it has played in the past.

However, it seems destined to transform itself rather than to disappear. . . .

NOTES

1. James, William. 1902. *The Varieties of Religious Experience*. New York: Longmans, Green.
2. It is for this reason that Frazer and even Preuss set impersonal religious forces outside of, or at least on the threshold of religion, to attach them to magic.

3. On this same question, see our article, "Representations individuelles et representations collectives." In *Revue du Metaphysique*, May, 1898.

44

TOWARD THE YEAR 2000
Reconstructions of Religious Space

WADE CLARK ROOF

Sociologists and other social thinkers have argued that the institution of religion is either a force for conservatism or a force for revolutionary change. In
this reading, Wade Clark Roof continues this tradition by investigating how
the institution of religion has been undergoing radical modifications. Roof is
particularly concerned with how baby boomers (individuals born between
1946 and 1964) are reconstructing the institution of religion given the rise of
racial-ethnic diversity in the inner cities, the shifts within the institution of
the family, and the growth of new forms of spirituality. Roof describes what
these specific transformations might look like by the year 2000.

Already in the early 1990s there is a mounting awareness of living in
the last days—the last days of a century and, even more, of a millen-
nium. And year by year, as the decade unfolds, we will no doubt feel
even more of a gravitational pull toward the year 2000. Even if that benchmark does not result in millennial madness, some great outburst of religious
energies, it most certainly will be a time of considerable reflection and re-
assessment for Americans. Questions such as "Who are we?" and "Where are
we headed?" will be standard fare for commentators as they assess the country demographically, politically, economically, globally, and, most assuredly,
in a deeper religious and spiritual sense as well.

Still seven years before that benchmark, I am not going to offer any premature general assessment; however, I take this opportunity to describe what
I believe to be some important trends helping to shape the American future.
Over the past five years I have had an unusual opportunity afforded me by
the Lilly Endowment, Inc., to explore religious trends broadly of the postwar
baby-boom generation. With the help of my research assistants, I have talked
to hundreds of young Americans over the telephone, visited dozens of them
in their homes, conducted group interviews in churches and synagogues,
gone to New Age festivals and seminaries, sat through countless church services, observed and informally interviewed people wherever I could—on
airplanes, in classes, at bars, in ticket lines at the movies.[1] Based on all of this,

I have some general observations about what is happening in the 1990s, best described by a simple rubric: reconstructions of religious space.

Sidney E. Mead once wrote that if we are to understand religion in America, we must understand that it took shape in relation to a people's movement through space and that space has overshadowed time in creating the ideals most cherished by the American mind and spirit.[2] Mead spoke, of course, about white settlers for whom there was never enough time to spare but for whom there was a plentiful supply of space. Vast physical spaces invited people to pack up and move, to keep on the go; however, there were also two other types of space: social space and inner space. Those settling the continent had largely broken the binding ties of habit, custom, and tradition, and thus they set out to create new social space, opening up possibilities for what we would later call social mobility. And inner space and experience— the psychological realm William James called "the sphere of felicity"—beckoned those who like Emerson and others dared to journey inward, to make spiritual movement. Space for Americans, at least for the dominant cultural groups, has meant freedom to move, whether physically, socially, or inwardly. This being so deeply embedded in the American experience, the year 2000—whatever else it may mean—is likely to present us with reconstructions of space, in the many senses of that term.

The term I use—*reconstruction*—suggests that I prefer to move beyond the customary arguments on the decline of religion among sociologists, in favor of what I take to be a more insightful, more nuanced interpretation of religion in America. My approach is in keeping with a newer sociology-of-religion paradigm gradually emerging that is more historically informed and that privileges themes of voluntarism and innovation, the continuing vitality of American religious culture, and supply-side rather than exclusively demand-side explanations of change.[3] It presupposes the viability of religion as an energizing force despite changing forms rather than secular assumptions of shrinking plausibilities. Hence in this article I look for embryonic and holistic forms of religion, often unstable and sporadic but that appear to be filling in spaces opened up by broad-scaled changes in what is increasingly called a post-modern world. The focus especially is on cultural and psychological themes, which provides, I think, clues of the shape of the religious in the years ahead.

The New Religious Pluralism

Let us begin with something quite simple, yet quite complex: the country's new religious pluralism. By "new" pluralism, I do not mean simply a declining Protestant population, a growing Catholic population, and fairly stable Jewish and religiously unaffiliated populations, although these are all interesting and important trends of religious analysis. Nor am I referring to the declining old-line Protestant hegemony over the culture or the fast-growing evangelical and fundamentalist faiths or even the more amorphous New Age spiritualities that have attracted so much attention in recent times—all significant trends as well bearing upon the country's future religious makeup. What I have in mind is something far more simple: the changing mix of peoples and cultures in this country that began to emerge in the 1960s. A new religious and ethnic demography began to appear about that time that seems to have permanently altered the nation's religious landscape. Its full impact, in fact, is just now beginning to become apparent in many American cities; indeed, it took the Los Angeles riots of 1992 to jolt many of us into an awareness of this new style of pluralism.

Let me cite the case of San Jose, California, a city not all that unusual on the West Coast. In the early 1960s, it was a city predominantly of whites, of Catholics and WASPs, plus a sprinkling of African Americans and Latinos. But two decades later the demographic mix had changed dramatically with a massive influx of young immigrants from Laos, Vietnam, Mexico, El Salvador, Nicaragua, Colombia, Sri Lanka, the Philippines, India, and the Pacific Islands. By then, the Hispanic and Asian populations were sizable, as were the many differing ethnic traditions of Christianity and of Buddhism and Hinduism. The local telephone directory tells much of the story: It takes 14 pages to list the Vietnamese surname Nguyen but only 8 pages for Smith.[4] Alternatively, consider Boston, Massachusetts, on the other side of the continent. The 1990 census showed this city to be a major center for refugees and immigrants, not Irish and Italians as was once the case but Salvadorans, Brazilians, Haitians, Guatemalans, Cambodians, and Cape Verdians. From 1980 to 1990, the rate of increase in immigrants to the city was staggering; there were an estimated 100,000 undocumented immigrants in 1990 alone, mostly people of color, Asians, and Hispanics.[5] Boston is a repository for the Atlantic Rim as cities in California are for the Pacific Rim.

It may well be that by the year 2000, as historians look back on the American Century, the Immigration Reform Act of 1965 will be remembered as the twin and equal of the Civil Rights Act of 1964. The Civil Rights Act sought to institutionalize equality—to redefine, if you will, the historical social space of blacks and whites—while passage of the immigration act opened the gates to a massive population movement that, slowly, is reshaping American culture. In 1965, legislators expected neither Latin American immigration on the scale we have come to know nor, much less, Asian immigration to play so vital a part in the country's future. Impoverished conditions in so much of Africa and in South America, combined with the disruptions of war in South Asia, the rumbles of war in Central America, and, of course, a global network of multinational corporations, created a backdrop that, once the legislation passed, led to massive population shifts. Stated differently, what happened was a significant fast-forwarding in the globalization of American life: the bringing together of many differing peoples and cultures into a new, reconstructed space, sustained, of course, by a changing political and economic world order. It has created a new global ethnic mix for America, new alignments of religion and ethnicity, and, as Jack Miles points out, a "new American dilemma" of young blacks and browns pitted against one another in fierce competition for dead-end jobs.[6]

What does all this mean for religion? For one thing, it means that these new residents of America's inner cities—most of whom are poor and unskilled—have been thrust together in a common fate. A reconstructed space opens up possibilities of greater exposure to religions and cultures that are qualitatively different from the earlier mixes of immigrants in the cities—far more diverse culturally, ethnically, and religiously. Even members of the same tradition—for example, Muslims—discover in today's urban centers just how diverse they are and worry about ethnic and nationality divisions threatening their unity as they move toward becoming the second-largest faith in the country. But it also means something more: This new global context encourages new-style, multiethnic religious communities in places like San Jose and Boston where groups of differing backgrounds gather—for example, Catholics to celebrate the Eucharist in a variety of languages—and then discover each other's holidays, festivals, saints, heroes, and day-to-day problems. Inner-city Catholic schools are increasingly multicultural, multiracial, and multireligious, open not just to Catholics but also to Protestants, Muslims, Hindus, and sectarian faiths of many varieties. The schools and parishes hold workshops in language training, ethnic history, and child care and health and, in a nod to this new pluralism, conduct what they call "discussions" on other religions. Boundaries are being redefined, often in ways signifying that social and religious space is becoming more complex, as we saw during the Los Angeles riots when Vietnamese American Buddhists responded to attacks on their stores differently from the way Vietnamese American Catholics did. Faith and social location seem to have meshed together in new ways, reshaping once again American-style pluralism.

The result is not just greater exposure to a multicultural and multireligious world but also, some say, greater religious vitality. Casual observation suggests that multiethnic parishes are among the most alive within American Catholicism today; an example is St. Brigid's parish in the riot-torn South Central area of Los Angeles. Here, one can find Southern Baptist hymns and African music; red, black, and green African American freedom flags hanging over the altar; and a portrait of Dr. Martin Luther King, Jr., under the stained-glass windows. The choir dresses with African *kufi* hats, as do many in the congregation. People of color from many nationality backgrounds come together, creating what C. Eric Lincoln and Lawrence Mamiya call a "black sacred cosmos," a shared world of meaning and belonging.[7] When asked if this is a Catholic church, the pastor replies, "This is just as Catholic as Rome, but we're allowed to use the culture of the people."[8]

Using "the culture of the people" is not new, of course, to African Americans and other minorities, but what is striking is the openness and forthrightness about these new solidarities today. Similar accounts can be told about the emerging *mestizo* cultures in Hispanic parishes. Those religious communities that are most vibrant allow for separate groups to have what religion in America has always provided: "free social space," as Sara Evans and Harry Boyte say in their intriguing analysis of the sources of democratic change in America.[9] Religion continues to bring people together and to mobilize group action. At the hands of innovative religious leaders—for example, the Reverend Cecil Murray of the First African Methodist Episcopal Church in Los Angeles—old religious structures still have power, solidifying religious as well as political and economic philosophies—for example, the Reverend Murray's plan for "trickle-up" urban development—and channel energies in the direction of gaining control over community institutions. Yet at the same time, this refuge of free association and group organizing now occurs in a larger space of multicultural tolerance and respect for one another's traditions. Today, in inner cities across the country, groups are experimenting to find ways of working together and reshaping the alignments of ethnicity and religion. There are both continuity and change, a good example of religion's structural adaptability, and also new visions of unity forged out of the racial and ethnic regroupings created by a new world order. In such times of regrouping, there is more than simply cultural blending; there is also what Timothy Smith describes as a "theologizing experience."[10]

It should also be noted, however, that there can be religious anomalies in a global world. An example is that within old-line, white Anglo-Saxon Protestantism—the aging WASP institutions—there is a pattern of new recruits who are immigrants from the Third World countries. As one might expect, the styles of faith and practice for these two constituencies are strikingly different despite their often having a common denominational heritage. People whose families were converted by missionaries one, two, or possibly three generations ago in places like Korea and China have migrated to this country; they decide to affiliate with a religious institution and often seek out the same faith traditions that they left behind. What they find here typically is a pale form of faith compared to the missionary-style evangelical religion they remember from their childhood; often they create an all-ethnic United Church of Christ or Presbyterian congregation that stands out as really different from other congregations in the same tradition. There is more than a little irony here, considering that what little growth there is within liberal Protestantism in the late twentieth century is now coming from this more conservative offspring of the nineteenth-century missionary movement. In this instance of a reconstructed social and religious space, as Barbara Brown Zikmund points out, "more and more members of mainline liberal Protestant denominations literally do not understand the liberal traditions of their church."[11]

New Patterns of Family and Religion

Next we turn to a different type of reconstructed space: the changing linkages between family and religion. Here I rely more heavily on the larger constituency of white, mostly middle-class baby boomers, that sector of the generation that has been at the center of gender, family, and lifestyle changes that have engulfed this country since mid-century.

This is a generation with many firsts—the first generation to grow up on television, the first generation to be identified as a mass-marketing audience by modern advertising, the first generation to grow up with the birth-control pill. Growing up in the era of postwar affluence and optimism, they had high hopes and expectations, but they also experienced wars, assassinations, long gas lines, racial injustice, environmental destruction, and the threat of nuclear annihilation. Demography and history thus combined to shape a generation who as young adults still today are very self-conscious and aware of how they differ from their parents' generation. The 1992 presidential election offered a vivid confrontation between these two generational cultures: Bush, the aging Cold War warrior against the youthful Clinton, who throughout the campaign was hounded by charges of dodging the draft during Vietnam; wife Barbara, the homemaker, mother, and grandmother, and Hillary, the career woman with her own opinions; and a campaign rhetoric saturated with themes of patriotism, use of drugs, views on abortion, and, of course, "family values."

It is not surprising that family values have surfaced in today's cultural wars. The massive changes in family life since mid-century, more so than in any other realm, continue to arouse the religious Right and to mobilize groups seeking to restore a Norman Rockwell America. Cultural changes evoke strong anxieties, especially when they touch upon such intimate realms as sexuality and family arrangements. My purpose here is not to describe these family changes; the situation of singles living alone, cohabiting singles, single parents, childless couples, blended families, gay and lesbian couples, and all sorts of extended-family arrangements is well known. No one watching television today is likely to mistake *Murphy Brown* or *Different Strokes* for reruns of *Ozzie and Harriet*. And without question, the implications for organized religion and for religious socialization within the family are substantial.

In the older, white bourgeois Protestant family that came to be the normative nuclear family, religious and family symbolism were closely intertwined—indeed, one might say families created religious space. The family was an extension of the church, the place where faith and practice were lived out. Grace at meals, family prayers, and family celebrations all helped to pass along the tradition. The mainline churches relied heavily on intact families with children to replenish them. Penny Long Marler's research shows that, among other demographic changes, declines in nuclear family units have contributed most to the decline in Protestant church membership since 1950, leading her to conclude that "as the family goes, so goes the church." [12]

Today, the family-religion connection is radically altered in a time when almost one-half of all boomer marriages fail, when 75 percent of boomer women are in the paid labor force, and when many second marriages blend together children of differing religious backgrounds. We would expect considerable erosion in the norms surrounding the family-religion connection, but the extent of the changes is perhaps greater than realized. In our young-adult survey, the question was asked, "Is it important to you to attend church/synagogue as a family, or should family members make individual choices about religion?" The point of the question was to see how far contemporary norms of individualism had invaded the family sphere, traditionally a stronghold of shared religious worlds. Our findings show a young-adult population only slightly more inclined to the family-oriented norms: 55 percent indicating a desire for families to have a shared faith, 45 percent saying members within families should make their own choices. Among conservative Protestants, family togetherness as a theme is more pronounced, yet, even here, a third of born-again boomer Christians endorse the individualistic response. Two factors more than any others influence this type of individualism: work and family type. Full-time working women emphasize individual choice. So also do the divorced and separated and, not surprisingly, those without children.

But there is also another side to these changes. While the individualistic types are the least committed to traditional faith and practice, it should not be overlooked that they are the ones leading the way in creating new religious space within families. Historically, people on the margins of religious institutions—and women especially—have been innovators. Today, there are signs of a deep ferment once again. Such people start support groups, organize new programs for children, and look for more creative ways to do things; if the established religious institutions cannot accommodate them, they often turn elsewhere. They are the lay equivalents to entrepreneurial religious leaders, drawing off the same supply-side spirituality that Americans have long been known for and that encourages expressive spirituality and pragmatic and changing religious forms.

Even among interfaith and blended families, where traditional religious socialization is greatly eroded, there are new developments. One is synagogues that are now setting up forums to deal openly with interfaith marriages. A topic often deemed taboo in Jewish circles has emerged as an opportunity, especially in synagogues with large boomer constituencies, for exploring new, enriched religious styles. Another example is the trend for grandparents in all the faiths to take more active roles in helping to socialize the children. My research suggests that the grandparent connection is far more important than has been suggested in the past: even when grandparents are physically removed and cannot assume direct responsibilities, there appears to be a growing respect for the types of religious and spiritual styles they represent, on the part of both boomer parents and their children. When checked into further, this often means an appreciation for simplicity, integrity, commitment, and living in accordance with one's beliefs—all primitive religious and spiritual values in keeping with currents flowing today toward holistic, experiential, and often syncretistic meaning systems.

The changed worlds of work and family have created new opportunities for the infusion of religious and spiritual values. Career women with families especially quest after new religious formulations. Juggling the demands of work while keeping marriages going and raising children, many women do not fit into the older gender-based groups as found in the religious establishment, which were created in an earlier time—hence so many new women's support groups. These groups empower and envision, renew and revise, or reconstruct significant spaces in women's lives. This reconstructing is occurring across religious sectors—in evangelical Protestant churches, in mainline Protestant and Catholic churches, and outside the established religions altogether.

This reconstruction is not limited to women. An integral part of such reconstruction is the creation of new family rituals. Manuals are available in the self-help section of bookstores to assist families in resacralizing family experiences, whether enriching marriages, building bonds between mothers and daughters and fathers and sons, celebrating a family's happy moments, or dealing with its crises. Close analysis of this literature reveals frequent reference to space—"finding space," "sharing space," "creating space," all, of course, implying psychological reconstructions. Moreover, this literature is replete with resources from various religious traditions to assist people to enhance their lives and their relationships. Put simply, as boomers have been remaking family life, so have they been redefining religious space in the family.

These reconstructions of family and religion show up in unexpected places and even in paradoxical ways. In her study of Orthodox Jews, for example, Lynn Davidman tells of young, boomer-age women—career women in New York City who have achieved considerable success in their jobs—who are attracted to a faith that to radical feminists would seem very stifling. Inquiring further, she discovers that a major reason is that they are looking for a private sphere in which they do not have to be "out there" asserting themselves. Wanting to be married and to have families, these women, Davidman says, find the "clear delineation of separate roles for men and women . . . a welcome contrast to the blurring and confusion about these roles in secular society." [13] They want clarity in gender definitions, though not necessarily all the old sexist meanings: The women turning to Orthodox Judaism still wanted men who would help with the child care! Definitions of Orthodox Judaism are undergoing redefinition, and so too are the spaces between the genders and between parents and children.

Similar observations are made about working-class women who turn to evangelicalism. Judith Stacey and Susan Gerard write that such women's "turn to evangelicalism represents . . . a strategy that refuses to forfeit, and even builds upon, the feminist critique of men and the 'traditional' family" and provides them with "effective strategies for reshaping husbands in their own image." [14] To say that evangelicalism and feminism do not mix is to spin fiction contrary to the "brave new families" that Stacey observes. In both of these contexts—career-minded Jewish women and working-class evangelical women, very different religiously and socially—we see evidence of a new balance that blends elements of contemporary feminism and individualism with a more traditional conception of gender roles.

New Forms of Spirituality

Finally, we look more generally at religious and spiritual trends today. Again I draw from the experiences of a generation of young adults, for whom space—both physical and psychological—figures prominently now and for whom it was prominent in the past: They were crowded into classrooms growing up; they were aware that colleges and universities expanded to accommodate them; they have known since childhood that market researchers play to their consumer tastes and the pollsters to their opinions. Now, with many of them facing mid-life, their quests and concerns are very much before the whole society.

To start with, it is not so much that this generation is less religious than their parents, although on some indicators that may well be the case. Far more important is how they are religious. For sure, this is a religiously diverse generation: One-third have remained fairly loyal to the faiths in which they grew up; among the two-thirds who dropped out as youths, about 40 percent of them are involved again in some kind of religious group, but the majority of the dropouts have no meaningful, ongoing connection with a church, synagogue, temple, or mosque. Better put, what they have are revised interpretations about religion, more along the line of looking to religious institutions to provide services in times of personal or family need. Even those most estranged from religious institutions still look to them for what the French call *rites de passage* at times of birth, marriage, and death, or as some wag in this country puts it, at times of "hatching, matching, and dispatching."

Several themes are important for grasping boomer religious styles, all interpretable as a result of the reduced institutional space. Perhaps the most striking is that of choice. Canadian sociologist Reginald Bibby's apt phrase "religion a la carte" summarizes the highly selective way boomers involve themselves in religion.[15] Especially, educated, middle-class boomers, from all religious backgrounds—Protestant, Catholic, Jewish, Muslim—look upon religion much the same way they look upon choice of lifestyle and consumption patterns. One rejects a fixed menu and picks and chooses among religious alternatives. Personal growth is at the basis of such choice: One participates in a congregation or cultivates a New Age spirituality, or does both as is not so uncommon, much for the same reason as one is involved in a 12-step recovery group—"if it helps you," as we heard repeatedly in our interviews with boomers. Choice and growth are articulated less among evangelical boomers, of which there are many, yet, even here, one uncovers evidence of the fusion of psychology and faith as well as the trend toward "menu diversification," or the increased options made available for styles of religious involvement in megachurches.

A second theme is the high degree of faith exploration. Boomers grew up exposed to the world religions; they remember the Beatles' turning East. As they move in and out of religious involvement, they check out various religious and spiritual possibilities and construct, or reconstruct, their own personal form of spirituality, drawing from a variety of sources. When we asked our interviewees if they should explore the teachings of various religions or stick to a particular faith tradition, less than a third said stick to one tradition. Sixty percent said one should explore other possibilities. Consequently, it should come as no real surprise that multilayered meaning systems are commonplace—that is, pastiche styles of belief and practice, combining elements from such diverse sources as Eastern meditation, Native American spirituality, psychotherapy, ecology, feminism, Jungian psychology, as well as more traditional Judeo-Christian beliefs.

But there is more than just greater choice and faith exploration—themes conjuring up notions of fads and fashions in a consumer religious economy. One senses a strong reaction to modernity's highly differentiated world, which bifurcates body and spirit, public and private, institution and life. The craving for holism spills over into renewed appreciation for connections with all of life—with the environment, with animals, with people both globally and locally. There is renewal of power as found in relations over against that of dominance and destruction, in earthborn rather than skyborne energy. There are spiritual rediscoveries, such as appreciation of the body and its ties with nature—for example, "women's mysteries" as related to monthly cycles. Among men, too, at least some men, there is an awareness of breaking out of old notions of manhood and exploring new aspects of their identity. There is a profound searching, but not so much that of navel gazing, as was often alleged in the past, as a quest for balance—between self and others, between self-fulfillment and social responsibilities. Especially among the older members of this generation, one finds a discernible "ethic of commitment," as pollster Daniel Yankelovich termed it some years ago.[16]

In the culture at large, questions of faith and spirit seem to have gone public: Television programs, novels, magazine stories, and newspaper articles now give serious attention to the spiritual and religious questions of a generation that grew up suspicious of the faith and morality handed down to them by their elders. Popular culture is saturated with spiritual concerns but with a distinctive 1960s and 1970s twist. "The religious search that seems to be emerging," writes Craig Dykstra, "is not a nostalgic revisiting of a safe, comfortable, sentimental religiousness. . . . Rather the search is for a truer, healthier suspiciousness, one that can smoke out deceit, oppression, violence, and evil . . . and tell it for what it is." Then Dykstra goes on to identify what I believe is a powerful existential force behind this generation's spiritual quests. He writes, "To support the suspiciousness, there must be something that is not suspiciousness itself, something that is not so ultimately suspicious it must finally suspect itself." [17] For many, what is beyond suspiciousness is called God; for others it is a Higher Power, a Life-Force, or some other symbolic expression of ultimacy and significance.

This attention to spirituality is not limited to the United States. In many European societies, the young adults are the carriers of a postmodern spirituality. Political scientist Ronald Inglehart documents a "culture shift" toward postmaterialist values of peace, egalitarianism, environmentalism, and quality of life in a dozen or more advanced industrial societies during the post–World War II years.[18] Cross-cultural research that my collaborators and I have undertaken shows a heightened interest in spirituality and faith exploration despite declines in institutional religion, and both are closely related to this shift in values.[19] In fact, the real impact of the postwar generation on religion may yet lie ahead. In the United States, especially, there is reason to expect continuing spiritual vitality. Between now and the year 2000, year by year, the thirtysomething population turns into the fortysomething population. Boomer demography thus assures a large supply of young adults passing through mid-life transitions well into the next century. If developmental psychologists are correct about identifying these years as the peak time of reflection and realignment of loyalties, then we can expect a heightened religious and spiritual ferment for some years to come.

. . .

We have barely begun to see where all this new religious freedom might lead. One thing I think we will see is new emergent forms of community, perhaps of many differing kinds. It is simply not true, for example, that boomers are not interested in community or commitment: They were galvanized in youth into strong social solidarities and passionate concerns and are still capable of them. What is true is that existing social institutions do not always give expression to their concerns. Hence they often turn to small groups and interaction rituals—both within and outside of organized religion. As one person told us: "It's not that they are anti-commitment . . . rather they are weighing what commitment means." I sense this reaching out to commit, a yearning for connections and the importance of sacred and expressive values. The yearning comes through in many ways: in the concern about family and for deeper personal relationships; in the questioning of instrumental values in favor of a closer relationship to the land, the mountains, and the oceans; in quests of simple values such as harmony, peace, and a holistic conception of life; in untapped idealism and reverential thinking as expressed in the ideal of community. When Bill Clinton calls for a "new covenant," for example, he gives voice to that ideal of community.

Conclusion

Given what I have described here about reconstructions of groups, institutions, and lives, I am not as concerned as Robert Bellah and his associates are in their book *Habits of the Heart* and its sequel, *The Good Society*, about the corrosive effects of individualism on religious belonging.[20] Their analysis suggests a sort of parallelism, almost a zero-sum game, as if individualism is the antithesis of institutional commitment. I think a more fruitful approach would be to recognize more nuanced patterns of individuals and institutions and to acknowledge that social rituals and institutions are social constructions—if these constructions mediate self-transcendence, people find meaning with them, and if they do not, then people turn to other institutions or modalities. There are many reasons why rituals and institutions may or may not be satisfying for people, but a fundamental one concerns whether they affirm and extend the self. Clearly, as we approach the year 2000, not only is there a good deal of weighing what commitment means but also a sorting out of institutions and forms to give expression to people's deepest commitments.

NOTES

1. I was funded by the Lilly Endowment, Inc., for a study of the baby-boom generation, born after World War II. The book reporting this research is *A Generation of Seekers: The Spiritual Journeys of the Baby Boom Generation* (San Francisco: Harper San Francisco, 1993).

2. Sidney E. Mead, *The Lively Experiment: The Shaping of Christianity in America* (New York: Harper & Row, 1963), chap. 1.

3. See R. Stephen Warner, "Work in Progress toward a New Paradigm for the Sociological Study of Religion in the United States," *American Journal of Sociology*, vol. 99 (March 1993).

4. See *Los Angeles Times*, August 1, 1992.

5. See *Boston Globe*, February 18, 1991.

6. Jack Miles, "Immigration and the New American Dilemma," *Atlantic*, vol. 220 (October 1992).

7. C. Eric Lincoln and Lawrence H. Mamiya, *The Black Church in the African American Experience* (Durham, NC: Duke University Press, 1990).

8. *Los Angeles Times*, February 23, 1992.

9. Sara M. Evans and Harry C. Boyte, *Free Spaces: The Sources of Democratic Change in America* (New York: Harper & Row, 1986).

10. Timothy L. Smith, "Religion and Ethnicity in America," *American Historical Review* 83 (December 1978): 1175.

11. Barbara Brown Zikmund, "Liberal Protestantism and the Language of Faith," in *Liberal Protestantism*, ed. Robert S. Michaelsen and Wade Clark Roof (New York: Pilgrim Press, 1986), p. 189.

12. Penny Long Marler, "Lost in the Fifties: The Changing Family and the Nostalgic

Church," in *Work, Family and Religion: New Patterns among Institutions,* ed. Nancy Ammerman and Wade Clark Roof (forthcoming).

13. Lynn Davidman, "Women's Search for Family and Roots: A Jewish Religious Solution to a Modern Dilemma," in *In Gods We Trust,* ed. Thomas Robbins and Dick Anthony (New Brunswick, NJ: Transaction, 1990), p. 392.

14. Judith Stacey and Susan E. Gerard, "'We Are Not Doormats': The Influence of Feminism on Contemporary Evangelicals in the United States," in *Uncertain Terms: Negotiating Gender in American Culture,* ed. Faye Ginsburg and Anna L. Tsing (Boston: Beacon Press, 1990), pp. 112–13.

15. Reginald W. Bibby, *Fragmented Gods* (Toronto: Irwin, 1987).

16. Daniel Yankelovich, *New Rules: Searching for Self-Fulfillment in a World Turned Upside Down* (New York: Random House, 1981).

17. Craig Dykstra, [Editorial], *Theology Today* 46 (July 1989): 127.

18. Ronald Inglehart, *Culture Shift in Advanced Society* (Princeton, NJ: Princeton University Press, 1990).

19. Wade Clark Roof, Jackson W. Carroll, and David A. Roozen, *The Post-War Generation and Religious Establishment: Cross-Cultural Perspectives* (forthcoming).

20. Robert N. Bellah et al., *Habits of the Heart: Individualism and Commitment in American Life* (Berkeley: University of California Press, 1985); Robert N. Bellah, et al., *The Good Society* (New York: Alfred A. Knopf, 1991).

45

THE ANTI-ABORTION MOVEMENT AND THE RISE OF THE RELIGIOUS RIGHT

DALLAS A. BLANCHARD

Dallas Blanchard is interested in the social change characteristics of religion, especially the history and growth of religious fundamentalism in the United States. In this reading, Blanchard examines how religious fundamentalism has impacted other current social issues, especially the debates concerning abortion and the influence of the Moral Majority on American politics.

For the nearly three decades in which the anti-abortion movement has been active, a variety of individuals and organizations have influenced both the form and the intensity of its protest. This [reading] looks at some of the determining factors in movement participation, particularly at what have become perhaps the most important influences in the 1980s and early 1990s—religious and cultural fundamentalism.

Why and How People Join the Anti-Abortion Movement

Researchers have posited a variety of explanations for what motivates people to join the anti-abortion movement. As with any other social movement, the anti-abortion movement has within it various subgroups, or organizations, each of which attracts different kinds of participants and expects different levels of participation. It might in fact be more appropriate to speak of anti-abortion *movements*.

Those opposing abortion are not unified. Some organizations have a single-issue orientation, opposing abortion alone, while others take what they consider to be a "pro-life" stance on many issues, opposing abortion as well as euthanasia, capital punishment, and the use of nuclear and chemical arms. The importance of abortion varies among the latter groups. There are also paper organizations, having virtually no real membership beyond a single organizer and perhaps several persons willing to lend their names to a letterhead. These are usually front groups for other organizations, designed to address topical issues; Defenders of the Defenders of Life, for instance, served the sole purpose of issuing press releases in defense of persons being tried for arsons and bombings. Some organizations arise and die, wax and wane over time as the climate surrounding an issue—in this case, abortion—changes. The rise, demise, and multiplication of various movement organizations can indicate the overall state of the movement: from growing public support and strength to desperation arising from a lack of support. Organizations also differ on goals, tactics, and strategies. The result of all of this differentiation is that various organizations may distance themselves from one another, depending on the disparities between their missions and their means of fulfilling those missions.

Just as the organizations within a movement differ, so do individuals vary in their motivations for joining it. Some anti-abortion activists are clearly anti-feminist, while others act out of communitarian, familistic, or even feminist concerns. Some are motivated by personal history, while others act on the basis of philosophical principle. A combination of factors in an individual's life history and social background contributes to the decision to join the movement in general and to participate in one organization in particular.

Researchers have identified a number of pathways for joining the anti-abortion movement. Luker, in her 1984 study of the early California movement, found that activists in the initial stages of the movement found their way to it through professional associations. The earliest opponents of abortion liberalization were primarily physicians and attorneys who disagreed with their professional associations' endorsement of abortion reform. It is my hypothesis that membership in organizations that concentrate on the education of the public or religious constituencies and on political lobbying is orchestrated primarily through professional networks. With the passage of the California reform bill and the increase in abortion rates several years later, many recruits to the movement fell into the category Luker refers to as "self-selected"; that is, they were not recruited through existing networks but sought out or sometimes formed organizations through which to express their opposition.

Himmelstein (1984), in summarizing the research on the anti-abortion movement available in the 10 years following *Roe v. Wade,* concluded that religious networks were the primary source of recruitment. Religious networks appear to be more crucial in the recruitment of persons into high-profile and/or violence prone groups (Blanchard and Prewitt 1992)—of which Operation Rescue is an example—than into the earlier, milder activist groups (although such networks are generally important throughout the movement). Such networks were also important, apparently, in recruitment into local Right to Life Committees, sponsored by the National Right to Life Committee and the Catholic church. The National Right to Life Committee, for example, is 72 percent Roman Catholic (Granberg 1981). It appears that the earliest anti-abortion organizations were essentially Catholic and dependent on church networks for their members; the recruitment of Protestants later on has also been dependent on religious networks (Cuneo 1989; Maxwell 1992).

Other avenues for participation in the anti-abortion movement opened up through association with other issues. Feminists for Life, for example, was founded by women involved in the feminist movement. Sojourners, a socially conscious evangelical group concerned with issues such as poverty and racism, has an anti-abortion position. Some anti-nuclear and anti-death penalty groups have also been the basis for the organization for anti-abortion efforts.

Clearly, preexisting networks and organizational memberships are crucial in initial enlistment into the movement. Hall (1993) maintains that individual mobilization into a social movement requires the conditions of attitudinal, network, and biographical availability. My conclusions regarding the anti-abortion movement support this contention. Indeed, biographical availability—the interaction of social class, occupation, familial status, sex, and age—is particularly related to the type of organization with which and the level of activism at which an individual will engage.

General social movement theory places the motivation to join the anti-abortion movement into four basic categories: status defense; anti-feminism; moral commitment; and cultural fundamentalism, or defense.

The earliest explanation for the movement was that participants were members of the working class attempting to shore up, or defend, their declining social status. Clarke, in his 1987 study of English anti-abortionists, finds this explanation to be inadequate, as do Wood and Hughes in their 1984 investigation of an anti-pornography movement group.

Petchesky (1984) concludes that the movement is basically anti-feminist—against the changing status of women. From this position, the primary goal of the movement is to "keep women in their place" and, in particular, to make them suffer for sexual "libertinism." Statements by some anti-abortion activists support this theory. Cuneo (1989), for example, finds what he calls "sexual puritans" on the fringe of the anti-abortion movement in Toronto. Abortion opponent and long-time right-wing activist Phyllis Schlaffley states this position: "It's very healthy for a young girl to be deterred from promiscuity by fear of contracting a painful, incurable disease, or cervical cancer, or sterility, or the likelihood of giving birth to a dead, blind or brain-damaged baby (even ten years later when she may be happily married)" (Planned Parenthood pamphlet, no title, n.d. [1990]).

Judie Brown, president of the American Life League, offers this judgment in "The Human Life Amendment" (n.d.):

> The woman who is raped has a right to resist her attacker. But the pre-born child is an innocent non-aggressor who should not be killed because of the crime of the father. More to the point, since a woman has a right to resist the rapist, she also has the right to resist his sperm. . . . However, once the innocent third party to a rape, the preborn child, is conceived, he should not be killed. . . . Incest is a voluntary act on the woman's part. If it were not, it would be rape. And to kill a child because of the identity of his father is no more proper in the case of incest than it is in the case of rape. (p. 18)

A number of researchers have concluded that sexual moralism is the strongest predictor of anti-abortion attitudes.

The theory of moral commitment proposes that movement participants are motivated by concern for the human status of the fetus. It is probably as close as any explanation comes to "pure altruism." Although there is a growing body of research on altruism, researchers on the abortion issue have tended to ignore this as a possible draw to the movement, while movement participants almost exclusively claim this position: that since the fetus is incapable of defending itself, they must act on its behalf.

In examining and categorizing the motivations of participants in the anti-abortion movement in Toronto, Cuneo (1989, pp. 85ff) found only one category—civil rights—that might be considered altruistic. The people in this category tend to be nonreligious and embarrassed by the activities of religious activists; they feel that fetuses have a right to exist but cannot speak for themselves. Cuneo's other primary categories of motivation are characterized by concerns related to the "traditional" family, the status of women in the family, and religion. He also finds an activist fringe composed of what he calls religious seekers; sexual therapeutics, "plagued by guilt and fear of female sexual power" (p. 115); and punitive puritans, who want to punish women for sexual transgressions. All of Cuneo's categories of participant, with the exception of the civil rights category, seek to maintain traditional male/female hierarchies and statuses. If we can generalize Cuneo's Toronto sample to the U.S. anti-abortion movement, I conclude that the majority, but by no means all, of those involved in the movement act out of self-interest, particularly out of defense of a cultural fundamentalist position.

The theory of cultural fundamentalism, or defense, proposes that the anti-abortion movement is largely an expression of the desire to return to what its proponents perceive to be "traditional culture." This theory incorporates elements of the status defense and anti-feminist theories.

It is important to note that a number of researchers at different points in time (Cuneo 1989; Ginsburg 1990; Luker 1984; Maxwell 1991, 1992) have indicated that (1) there have been changes over time in who gets recruited into the movement and why, (2) different motivations tend to bring different kinds of people into different types of activism, and (3) even particular movement organizations draw different kinds of people with quite different motivations. At this point in the history of the anti-abortion movement, the dominant motivation, particularly in the more activist organizations such as Operation Rescue, appears to be cultural fundamentalism. Closely informing cultural fundamentalism are the tenets of religious fundamentalism, usually associated with certain Protestant denominations but also evident in the Catholic and Mormon faiths. It is to the topics of religious and cultural fundamentalism as they relate to the anti-abortion movement that . . . we now turn.

Religious and Cultural Fundamentalism Defined

Cultural fundamentalism is in large part a protest against cultural change: against the rising status of women; against the greater acceptance of "deviant" lifestyles such as homosexuality; against the loss of prayer and Bible reading in the schools; and against the increase in sexual openness and freedom. Wood and Hughes (1984) describe cultural fundamentalism as "adherence to traditional norms, respect for family and religious authority, asceticism and control of impulse. Above all, it is an unflinching and thoroughgoing moralistic outlook on the world; moralism provides a common orientation and common discourse for concerns with the use of alcohol and pornography, the rights for homosexuals, 'pro-family' and 'decency' issues" (p. 89). The theologies of Protestants and Catholics active in the anti-abortion movement—many of whom could also be termed fundamentalists—reflect these concerns.

Protestant fundamentalism arose in the 1880s as a response to the use by Protestant scholars of the relatively new linguistic techniques of text and form criticism in their study of the Bible. These scholars determined that the Pentateuch was a compilation of at least five separate documents written from differing religious perspectives. Similar techniques applied to the New Testament questioned the traditionally assigned authorship of many of its books. The "mainline" denominations of the time (Episcopalian, Congregational, Methodist, Unitarian, and some Presbyterian) began to teach these new insights in their seminaries. With these approaches tended to go a general acceptance of other new and expanding scientific findings, such as evolution.

By 1900 the urbanization and industrialization of the United States were well under way, with their attendant social dislocations. One response to this upheaval was the Social Gospel movement, which strove to enact humanitarian laws regulating such things as child labor, unions, old-age benefits, and guaranteed living wages. With the Social Gospel movement and the acceptance of new scientific discoveries tended to go an optimism about the perfectibility of human nature and society.

Fundamentalism solidified its positions in opposition to these trends as well as in response to social change and the loss of the religious consensus, which came with the influx of European Jewish and Catholic immigrants to America. While fundamentalism was a growing movement prior to 1900, its trumpet was significantly sounded with the publication in 1910 of the first volume of a 12-volume series titled *The Fundamentals.* Prior to the 1920s and 1930s, it was primarily a movement of the North; growth in the South came mostly after 1950.

There are divisions within Protestant fundamentalism, but there is a general common basis of belief. Customary beliefs include a personal experience of salvation; verbal inspiration and literal interpretation of scriptures as worded in the King James Bible; the divinity of Jesus; the literal, physical resurrection of Jesus; special creation of the world in six days, as opposed to the theory of evolution; the virgin birth of Jesus; and the substitutionary atonement (Jesus' death on the cross as a substitution for each of the "saved"). The heart of Protestant fundamentalism is the literal interpretation of the Bible; secondary to this is the belief in substitutionary atonement.

Fundamentalists have also shown a strong tendency toward separatism—separation from the secular world as much as possible and separation from "apostates" (liberals and nonfundamentalist denominations). They are also united in their views on "traditional" family issues: opposing abortion, divorce, the Equal Rights Amendment, and civil rights for homosexuals. While their separatism was expressed prior to the 1970s in extreme hostilities toward Roman Catholicism, fundamentalists and Catholics share a large set of family values, which has led to their pragmatic cooperation in the anti-abortion movement.

Another tie between some Protestant fundamentalists and some Catholics lies in the Charismatic Renewal Movement. This movement, which coalesced in the 1920s, emphasized glossolalia (speaking in tongues) and faith healing. Charismatics were denied admission to the World's Christian Fundamental Association in 1928 because of these emphases. By the 1960s charismaticism began spreading to some mainline denominations and Catholic churches. While Presbyterians, United Methodists, Disciples of Christ, Episcopalians, and Lutherans sometimes reluctantly accepted this new charismatic movement, Southern Baptists and Churches of Christ adamantly opposed it, especially the speaking in tongues. But the Catholic charismatics have tended to be quite conservative both theologically and socially, giving them ideological ties with the charismatic Protestant fundamentalists and fostering cooperation between the two in interdenominational charismatic conferences, a prelude to cooperation in the anti-abortion movement.

There is also a Catholic "fundamentalism," which may or may not be charismatic and which centers on church dogma rather than biblical literalism, the Protestant a priori dogma. Catholic fundamentalists accept virtually unquestioningly the teachings of the church. They share with Protestant fundamentalists the assumption that dogma precedes and supersedes analytical reason, while in liberal Catholic and Protestant thought and in the nation's law reason supersedes dogma. Similar to Catholic fundamentalism is the Mormon faith (or the Church of Jesus Christ of Latter Day Saints), which also takes church dogma at face value.

There are at least six basic commonalities to what can be called Protestant, Catholic, and Mormon fundamentalisms: (1) an attitude of certitude—that one may know the final truth, which includes antagonism to ambiguity; (2) an external source for that certitude—the Bible or church dogma; (3) a belief system that is at root dualistic; (4) an ethic based on the "traditional" family; (5) a justification for violence; and therefore, (6) a rejection of modernism (secularization).

Taking those six commonalities point by point:

1. The certitude of fundamentalism rests on dependence on an external authority. That attitude correlates with authoritarianism which includes obedience to an external authority, and, on that basis, the willingness to assert authority over others.
2. While the Protestant fundamentalists accept their particular interpretation of the King James Version of the Bible as the authoritative source, Mormon and Catholic fundamentalists tend to view church dogma as authoritative.
3. The dualism of Catholics, Protestants, and Mormons includes those of body/soul, body/mind, physical/spiritual. More basically, they see a distinction between God and Satan, the forces of good and evil. In the fundamentalist worldview, Satan is limited and finite; he can be in only one place at one time. He has servants, however, demons who are constantly working his will, trying to deceive believers. A most important gift of the Spirit is the ability to distinguish between the activities of God and those of Satan and his demons.
4. The "traditional" family in the fundamentalist view of things has the father as head of the household, making the basic decisions, with the wife and children subject to his wishes. Obedience is stressed for both wives and children. Physical punishment is generally approved for use against both wives and children.

   This "traditional" family with the father as breadwinner and the mother as homemaker, together rearing a large family, is really not all that traditional. It arose on the family farm, prior to 1900, where large numbers of children were an economic asset. Even then, women were essential in the work of the farm. . . . in the urban environment, the "traditional" family structure was an option primarily for the middle and upper classes, and they limited their family size even prior to the development of efficient birth control methods. Throughout human history women have usually been breadwinners themselves, and the "traditional" family structure was not an option.

5. The justification for violence lies in the substitutionary theory of the atonement theology of both Protestant and Catholics. In this theory, the justice of God demands punishment for human sin. This God also supervises a literal hell, the images of which come more from Dante's *Inferno* than from the pages of the Bible. Fundamentalism, then, worships a violent God and offers a rationale for human violence (such as Old Testament demands for death when adultery, murder, and other sins are committed). The fundamentalist mindset espouses physical punishment of children, the death penalty, and the use of nuclear weapons; fundamentalists are more frequently wife abusers, committers of incest, and child abusers (Brinkerhoff and Pupri 1988).

6. Modernism entails a general acceptance of ambiguity, contingency, probability (versus certitude), and a unitary view of the universe; that is, the view that there is no separation between body and soul, physical and spiritual, body and mind (when the body dies, the self is thought to die with it). Rejection of modernism and postmodernism is inherent in the rejection of a unitary worldview in favor of a dualistic worldview. The classic fundamentalist position embraces a return to religion as the central social institution, with education, the family, economics, and politics serving religious ends, fashioned after the social structure characteristic of medieval times.

Also characteristic of Catholic, Protestant, and Mormon fundamentalists are a belief in individualism (which supports a naive capitalism); pietism; a chauvinistic Americanism (among some fundamentalists) that sees the United States as the New Israel and its inhabitants as God's new chosen people; and a general opposition to intellectualism, modern science, the tenets of the Social Gospel, and communism. . . . Amid this complex of beliefs and alongside the opposition to evolution, interestingly, is an underlying espousal of social Darwinism, the "survival of the fittest" ethos that presumes American society to be truly civilized, the pinnacle of social progress. This nineteenth-century American neocolonialism dominates the contemporary political views held by the religious right. It is also inherent in their belief in individualism and opposition to social welfare programs.

Particular personality characteristics also correlate with the fundamentalist syndrome: authoritarianism, self-righteousness, prejudice against minorities, moral absolutism (a refusal to compromise on perceived moral issues), and anti-analytical, anti-critical thinking. Many fundamentalists refuse to accept ambiguity as a given in moral decision making and tend to arrive at simplistic solutions to complex problems. For example, many hold that the solution to changes in the contemporary family can be answered by fathers' reasserting their primacy, by forcing their children and wives into blind obedience. Or, they say, premarital sex can be prevented by promoting abstinence. One popular spokesman, Tim LaHaye (1980), asserts that the antidote to sexual desire, especially on the part of teenagers, lies in censoring reading materials. Strict parental discipline automatically engenders self-discipline in children, he asserts. The implication is that enforced other-directedness by parents produces inner-directed children, while the evidence indicates that they are more likely to exchange parental authoritarianism for that of another parental figure. To develop inner direction under such circumstances requires, as a first step, rebellion against and rejection of parental authority—the opposite of parental intent.

One aspect of fundamentalism, particularly the Protestant variety, is its insistence on the subservient role of women. The wife is expected to be subject to the direction of her husband, children to their father. While Luker (1984) found that anti-abortionists in California supported this position and that proponents of choice generally favored equal status for women, recent research has shown that reasons for involvement in the anti-abortion movement vary by denomination. That is, some Catholics tend to be involved in the movement more from a "right to life" position, while Protestants and other Catholics are more concerned with sexual morality. The broader right to life position is consistent with the official Catholic position against the death penalty and nuclear arms, while Protestant fundamentalists generally support the death penalty and a strong military. Thus, Protestant fundamentalists, and some Catholic activists, appear to be more concerned with premarital sexual behavior than with the life of the fetus.

Protestants and Catholics (especially traditional, ethnic Catholics), however, are both concerned with the "proper," or subordinate, role of women and the dominant role of men. Wives should obey their husbands, and unmarried women should refrain from sexual intercourse. Abortion, for the Protestants in particular, is an indication of sexual licentiousness. Therefore, the total abolition of abortion would be a strong deterrent to such behavior, helping to reestablish traditional morality in women. Contemporary, more liberal views of sexual morality cast the virgin female as deviant. The male virgin has long been regarded as deviant. The fundamentalist ethic appears to accept this traditional double standard with its relative silence on male virginity.

Another aspect of this gender role ethic lies in the home-related roles of females. Women are expected to remain at home, to bear children, and to care for them, while also serving the needs of their husbands. Again, this is also related to social class and the social role expectations of the lower and working classes, who tend to expect women to "stay in their place."

Luker's (1984) research reveals that some women in the anti-abortion movement are motivated by a concern for maintaining their ability to rely on men (husbands) to support their social roles as mothers, while pro-choice women tend to want to maintain their independent status. Some of the men involved in anti-abortion violence are clearly acting out of a desire to maintain the dependent status of women and the dominant roles of men. Some of those violent males reveal an inability to establish "normal" relationships with women, which indicates that their violence may arise from a basic insecurity with the performance of normal male roles in relationships with women. This does not mean that these men do not have relationships with women. Indeed, it is in the context of relationships with women that dominance-related tendencies become more manifest. It is likely that insecurity-driven behaviors are characteristic of violent males generally, but psychiatric data are not available to confirm this, even for the population in question.

The Complex of Fundamentalist Issues

The values and beliefs inherent to religious and cultural fundamentalism are expressed in a number of issues other than abortion. Those issues bear some discussion here, particularly as they relate to the abortion question.

1. *Contraception.* Fundamentalists, Catholic, Protestant, and Mormon, generally oppose the use of contraceptives since they limit family size and the intentions of God in sexuality. They especially oppose sex education in the schools and the availability of contraceptives to minors without the approval of their parents. This is because control of women and sexuality are intertwined. If a girl has knowledge of birth control, she is potentially freed of the threat of pregnancy if she becomes sexually active. This frees her from parental control and discovery of illegitimate sexual intercourse.
2. *Prenatal testing, pregnancies from rape or incest, or those endangering a woman's life.* Since every pregnancy is divinely intended, opposition to prenatal testing arises from its use to abort severely defective fetuses and, in some cases, for sex selection. Abortion is wrong regardless of the origins of the pregnancy or the consequences of it.
3. *In vitro fertilization, artificial fertilization, surrogate motherhood.* These are opposed because they interfere with the "natural" fertilization process and because they may mean the destruction of some fertilized embryos.
4. *Homosexuality.* Homophobia is characteristic of fundamentalism, because homosexual behavior is viewed as being "unnatural" and is prohibited in the Bible.

5. *Uses of fetal tissue.* The uses of fetal tissue in research and in the treatment of medical conditions such as Parkinson's disease is opposed, because it is thought to encourage abortion.

6. *Foreign relations issues.* Fundamentalists generally support aid to Israel and military funding (Diamond 1989). Indeed, as previously mentioned, they commonly view the United States as the New Israel. Protestant fundamentalists tend to be pre-millenialists, who maintain that biblical prophecies ordain that the reestablishment of the State of Israel will precede the Second Coming of Christ. Thus, they support aid to Israel to hasten the Second Coming, which actually, then, has an element of anti-Semitism to it, since Jews will not be among the saved.

7. *Euthanasia.* So-called right to life groups have frequently intervened in cases where relatives have sought to remove a patient from life-support systems. Most see a connection with abortion in that both abortion and the removal of life support interfere with God's decision as to when life should begin and end.

The most radical expression of cultural fundamentalism is that of Christian Reconstructionism, to which Randall Terry, former director of Operation Rescue, subscribes. The adherents of Christian Reconstructionism, while a distinct minority, have some congregations of up to 12,000 members and count among their number Methodists, Presbyterians, Lutherans, Baptists, Catholics, and former Jews. They are unabashed theocratists. They believe every area of life—law, politics, the arts, education, medicine, the media, business, and especially morality—should be governed in accordance with the tenets of Christian Reconstructionism. Some, such as Gary North, a prominent reconstructionist and son-in-law of Rousas John Rushdoony, considered the father of reconstructionism, would deny religious liberty—the freedom of religious expression—to "the enemies of God," whom the reconstructionists, of course, would identify.

The reconstructionists want to establish a "God-centered government," a Kingdom of God on Earth, instituting the Old Testament as the Law of the Land. The goal of reconstructionism is to reestablish biblical, Jerusalemic society. Their program is quite specific. Those criminals which the Old Testament condemned to death would be executed, including homosexuals, sodomites, rapists, adulterers, and "incorrigible" youths. Jails would become primarily holding tanks for those awaiting execution or assignment as servants indentured to those whom they wronged as one form of restitution. The media would be censored extensively to reflect the views of the church. Public education and welfare would be abolished (only those who work should eat), and taxes would be limited to the tithe, 10 percent of income, regardless of income level, most of it paid to the church. Property, Social Security, and inheritance taxes would be eliminated. Church elders would serve as judges in courts overseeing moral issues, while "civil" courts would handle other issues. The country would return to the gold standard. Debts, including, for example, 30-year mortgages, would be limited to six years. In short, Christian Reconstructionists see democracy as being opposed to Christianity, as placing the rule of man above the rule of God. They also believe that "true" Christianity has its earthly rewards. They see it as the road to economic prosperity, with God blessing the faithful.

REFERENCES

Editor's Note: The original chapter from which this selection was taken has extensive footnotes and references that could not be listed in their entirety here. For more explanation and documentation of sources, please see Dallas A. Blanchard. 1994. *The Anti-Abortion Movement and the Rise of the Religious Right: From Polite to Fiery Protest.* New York: Twayne Publishers.

Blanchard, Dallas A. and Terry J. Prewitt. 1993. *Religious Violence and Abortion: The Gideon Project.* Gainesville: University Press of Florida.
Brinkerhoff, Merlin B. and Eugene Pupri. 1988. "Religious Involvement and Spousal Abuse: The Canadian Case." Paper presented at the Society of the Scientific Study of Religion.
Clarke, Alan. 1987. "Collective Action against Abortion Represents a Display of, and Concern for, Cultural Values, Rather than an Expression of Status Discontent." *British Journal of Sociology* 38:235–53.
Cuneo, Michael. 1989. *Catholics against the Church: Anti-Abortion Protest in Toronto, 1969–1985.* Toronto: University of Toronto Press.
Diamond, Sara. 1989. *Spiritual Warfare: The Politics of the Christian Right.* Boston: South End Press.
Ginsburg, Faye. 1990. *Contested Lives: The Abortion Debate in an American Community.* Berkeley: University of California Press.
Granberg, Donald. 1978. "Pro-Life or Reflection of Conservative Ideology? An Analysis of Opposition to Legalized Abortion." *Sociology and Social Research* 62:421–23.
———. 1981. "The Abortion Activists." *Family Planning Perspectives* 18:158–61.
Hall, Charles. 1993. "Social Networks and Availability Factors: Mobilizing Adherents for Social Movement Participation" (Ph.D. dissertation, Purdue University).
Himmelstein, Jerome L. 1984. "The Social Basis of Anti-Feminism: Religious Networks and Culture." *Journal for the Scientific Study of Religion* 25:1–25.
LaHaye, Tim. 1980. *The Battle for the Mind.* Old Tappan, NJ: Fleming H. Revell Co.
Luker, Kristin. 1984. *Abortion and the Politics of Motherhood.* Berkeley: University of California Press.
Maxwell, Carol. 1991. "Where's the Land of Happy?: Individual Meanings in Pro-Life Direct Action." Paper presented at the Society for the Scientific Study of Religion.
———. 1992. "Denomination, Meaning, and Persistence: Difference in Individual Motivation to Obstruct Abortion Practice." Paper presented at the Society for the Scientific Study of Religion.
Petchesky, Rosalind P. 1984. *Abortion and Woman's Choice: The State, Sexuality, and Reproductive Freedom.* New York: Longman.
Planned Parenthood Federation of America. 1990. Public Affairs Action Letter. (No title, no date).
Wood, M. and M. Hughes. 1984. "The Moral Basis of Moral Reform: Status Discontent vs. Culture and Socialization as Explanations of Anti-Pornography Social Movement Adherence." *American Sociological Review* 44:86–99.

46

MIAMI'S LITTLE HAVANA
Yard Shrines, Cult Religion, and Landscape

JAMES R. CURTIS

In addition to being an agent of social change and a defender of the status quo, the institution of religion provides many people with a profound sense of identity and membership in a social group. The local congregation is typically a cohesive social organization in many communities. In this selection, James R. Curtis investigates one local religious community that uniquely combines Cuban culture, Catholicism, and the Afro-Caribbean religion, Santeria. Curtis shows that religious identities often involve complex combinations of belief systems, rituals, and regional geographies.

In the summer of 1978 a brief article entitled "Neighbors Irate over Family's Shrine" appeared in *The Miami Herald*.[1] The story told of a group of residents in the predominantly non-Latin city of South Miami who feared that a newly-erected, seven-foot shrine in the front yard of a Cuban neighbor would lower property values. City officials called in to investigate found that the shrine was located too close to the front property line, and thus was in violation of municipal building and zoning laws. Confused and saddened by the turmoil created the Cuban family stated that the shrine had been built (at a cost of $1,500) in gratitude to Santa Barbara "for answering all of our prayers."

More than an isolated human interest story, the above incident is perhaps symbolic of the bicultural social adjustments, and urban landscape transformations, which have taken place and are continuing to occur in the greater Miami area as a result of Cuban in-migration. In the short span of only 20 years, beginning in 1959, the Cuban population of Dade County has ballooned from about 20,000 to a current estimate of 430,000.[2] Counting the 94,000 non-Cuban Latins residing in the county—mostly Puerto Ricans, Mexicans and Central and South Americans—Latins constitute approximately 35 per cent of the county's population, as compared to only 5 percent in 1960.[3] Moreover, Latins have settled in distinct residential concentrations, thereby greatly accentuating the "Latinization" of selected locales.[4] The city of Miami, for example, is almost 56 percent Latin (207,000 out of 370,000); Hialeah, with a population of 133,000, is over 65 percent Latin, most of whom are Cuban. The impact of such sudden and fundamental change in the pattern of ethnicity has profoundly altered both material and nonmaterial elements of culture in the region. Nowhere are these transformations better manifested than in Little Havana, a four-square-mile enclave of Cuban culture located a scant mile southwest of downtown Miami.

Often referred to as "a city (or "nation") within a city," Little Havana is the nucleus, the core, of Cuban life in Miami. Once a healthy middle-class Anglo neighborhood, dating from the immediate post–World War I era, by the mid-1950s it had deteriorated and was declining in population as urban growth and increased mobility opened up newer housing areas for the middle-class in the outlying suburbs.[5] For the newly arriving Cuban refugees this area was preferred in respect to having available and affordable housing units and vacant shops for potential business endeavors.[6] It was also served by public transportation and near the central business district where social services and employment opportunities were most abundant. The neighborhood was reborn as "Little Havana" almost literally overnight. Although its function as the principal receptor area has declined in recent years as the Cuban population has grown in numbers and affluence,[7] and has since spread out to other settlement areas, Little Havana remains in spirit, if not in landscape, the traditional Cuban quarter.

In most important respect, Little Havana is a self-contained community which has evolved, by design, to suit the needs and tastes of its residents, and in so doing has embellished the landscape with a pronounced Cuban flavor. Along West Flagler and Southwest Eighth Streets (the latter know locally as *"Calle Ocho"*), the two principal commercial strips which cut through the district, a full complement of goods and services is offered which cater to the Cuban population. If so desired, a Cuban who lives in Little Havana and speaks only Spanish, could shop, dine out, be medically cared for, attend churches, schools, shows and theaters, die, and be buried without a word of English being uttered.

The commercial landscape of Little Havana reflects in both vivid and subtle ways this impress of Cuban culture. From the older stucco buildings of Spanish and art deco styles, and from the small shopping plazas which have been built of late, neon store signs flash *"Joyeria," "Ferreteria," "Muebleria," "Farmacia," "Mercado," "Zapateria,"* and so on. One frequently encounters small groups of three and four gathered at the countless vest-pocket, open-air coffee counters to sip the syrupy-dark, bittersweet *cafe cubano* and consume fresh *pasteles* (pastry).

The newsstands and bookstores in the district display a plethora of Spanish-language books, magazines, and newspapers, including *El Miami Herald* with a circulation in excess of 50,000. The acrid smell of cured tobacco wafts from the 30 or so small cigar factories located in the area where old men (*tabaqueros*) patiently roll cigars *a mano* (by hand).[8] At Antonio Maceo Mini Park, on *Calle Ocho*, men play continuous games of dominoes on permanently fixed tables and benches designed specifically for that purpose. Fresh fruits and vegetables are sold in open-air markets and stands which dot the district. The sweet smell of simmering garlic hangs heavy over the hundred-plus restaurants featuring Cuban and Spanish cuisine, ranging from elegant supper clubs with valet parking to four-stool cafes.

The life and vitality of these places, however, stand in stark contrast to the somberness surrounding the Cuban Memorial Plaza, where flowers and wreaths are faithfully placed at the base of the Bay of Pigs monument in memory of loved ones who fell during that ill-fated invasion. To be sure, the landscape of Little Havana conveys a strong feeling of pre-revolutionary Cuba, but the sense of a people in exile remains pervasive. The existence of nearly one hundred officially recognized "municipalities in exile," which function as social and quasi-political organizations composed of former residents of particular municipalities in Cuba, attests to their vitality.[9] Many of these groups, in fact, have converted houses and other buildings in Little Havana into meeting halls where lectures, concerts and dances are periodically held, and where informational and historical newsletters are published.

Thus, as befitting a people caught inextricably between two cultures, Little Havana is not an isolated community devoid of contact and consequence with the surrounding society and environment. Rather, in culture and landscape, it is a mixture of both Cuban and American influences. Cuban and American flags, for example, proudly bedeck the streets of Little Havana during national holidays of both countries. Cuban (grocery) shoppers may patronize the neighborhood Winn Dixie or Pantry Pride supermarkets, and then walk to the back parking lot of these stores and barter with itinerant Cuban peddlers selling fresh fish, poultry, fruit, and vegetables. Teenagers sip on *batidos* (exotic fruit milkshakes) from Cuban ice cream shops and eat *grandes macs* from the local McDonald's. In language as well, especially among the younger Cubans, one now hears a curious mixture of Spanish and English ("Spanglish," as it is known).[10] Signs on some store windows, for example, announce "*Gran* Sale." Young people may be heard shouting to one another, "*Tenga un* nice day."

Although the housing area of Little Havana has been significantly upgraded and changed as a consequence of the Cuban tenure, the residential landscape is not nearly as "Latinized" as the commercial strips in the district. In fact, a quick drive through the area would probably leave the impression that it is largely indistinguishable from neighboring Anglo residential areas. Yet, upon closer inspection, differences unfold. Fences, for example, now enclose many front yards, and wrought iron and tile have been added to some houses for decorative purposes. Even these characteristically Hispanic features, however, remain relatively minor in comparison to what one might expect to find in most Latin communities. If anything, one is impressed more by how little these embellishments reflect the fundamental replacement of culture groups which has occurred in the area. This observation, however, is somewhat misleading, for it fails to include the single most conspicuous landscape element which clearly distinguishes Little Havana from non-Cuban residential areas.

Yard Shrines

If the Cuban family in the story recounted at the beginning of this article had lived in Little Havana, it would not have aroused the resentment, or even stirred the curiosity, of neighbors over the construction of its yard shrine. City officials would not have been brought in to search for some minor infraction of local building or zoning laws to force its removal. More commonplace than exceptional, there are literally hundreds of yard shrines gracing the cultural landscape of Little Havana.[11]

The shrines may be found anywhere in the yard area—front, back, or along the sides—although the front yard, especially near the sidewalk, appears to be a favored location. Regardless of placement, however, the front of the shrine always faces the street. Since these are personal shrines, built to suit the religious needs and preferences of individuals, no two are exactly alike; diversity is the standard. In size, the shrines range from about two to ten feet in height, and two to six feet in width. Most are rectangular in shape, although octagonal and circular structures are not uncommon. The most frequently used building materials include brick, cement, stone, and glass; wood is rarely, if ever, used except for trimming. Exterior walls, though, are often stuccoed or tiled. A single cross may adorn the top of a shrine, and use of latticework and other forms of ornamentation are occasionally found, but in general the degree of exterior embellishment is more austere than ornate.

Regardless of size, materials used, or shape, the interiors of the shrines remain visible through either sealed glass side panels or a single glass door enclosing the front of the sanctuary. Pedestaled inside, usually on an elevated platform or altar, stands a single statue. At the base of the statue, and occasionally on a small stairwell leading to the base, one finds an utterly baffling array of items, including, for example, fresh-cut or artificial flowers, candles, crucifixes, jars of leaves, bowls of water, beads, stones, miniature figures of men or animals, and other assorted paraphernalia.

The statues themselves are of Catholic saints, the Madonna and Jesus, each identifiable (at least to the knowing eye) by sex, colors, adornment, and particular symbols, such as a cup, a cane, or a cross. By far, the three saints which are enshrined most commonly in Little Havana are, in order, Santa Barbara, Our Lady of Charity (patron saint of Cuba), and Saint Lazarus. Other saints, particularly Saint Francis of Assisi, Saint Christopher, and Saint Peter are also found, but with much less frequency. Likewise, shrines built in honor of the Madonna and Jesus are not nearly as numerous as those erected to the main three saints.

Santa Barbara is most often portrayed as a young woman dressed in a white tunic with a red mantle bordered with gold trimming. She wears a golden crown and holds a golden goblet in her right hand and a golden sword in her left. Our Lady of Charity is similarly represented as a young woman dressed in a white tunic. Her cloak, however, is either blue or white. She holds a child in her left arm. At her feet, seated or kneeling in a boat, are two or three small male figures looking reverently upward. Saint Lazarus is usually depicted as a bent and crippled man of middle age, with open wounds and sores, supported with the aid of crutches. Two or three small dog figures often stand at his feet. This particular portrayal of Lazarus is not the image officially recognized or sanctioned by the Church; it has evolved from Cuban tradition.

Sacred elements in the landscape often convey much less religious context from which they spring than observation alone would suggest. The religious beliefs which inspire the construction of yard shrines in Little Havana are illustrative of this contention. Considering, for example, that a vast majority of Cubans are Roman Catholics, and that most of the shrines are built in apparent homage to saints, one might logically suspect that these shrines are erected by followers of the Catholic faith. This assumption, however, is neither entirely correct nor incorrect. In truth, many of the shrines are built by Catholics, but perhaps an equal number, if not more, are erected by followers of a fascinating, syncretic Afro-Cuban cult religion called *Santeria*.

Santeria: An Afro-Cuban Religion

The history of the West Indies is rich in examples of the spontaneous melding of European and African culture traits and complexes. This process of transculturation—in which different cultural elements are jumbled, mixed, and fused—played an important role in the shaping of present cultural patterns in the region, particularly in the nonmaterial aspects of culture such as language, music, and religion. More notable examples of religious syncretism in the New World in which elements of Catholicism were combined with ancient African tribal beliefs and practices include *Vodun* (i.e., voodoo) in Haiti, *Xango* in Trinidad, and *Santeria* in Cuba.[12]

Santeria, like other syncretic Afro-Christian folk religions, combines an elaborate ensemble of ritual, magical, medical, and theological beliefs to form a total magico-religious world view. The *Santeria* religion evolved among descendants of the Yoruba slaves who had been brought to Cuba from Nigeria beginning in the sixteenth century, but particularly in the first half of the nineteenth century.[13] These descendants—known in Cuba as the *Lucumi*—learned from oral history the tribal religion of their ancestral home. It was a complex polytheistic religion involving a pantheon of gods and goddesses called *orishas*.[14] It was also colorful in its mythology. In many respects it was extraordinarily reminiscent of ancient Greek mythology.[15] The African religion was rather quickly altered, however, as the Cuban *Lucumis* fell increasingly under the sway of the Spanish culture.[16] Exposure to the Catholic religion, particularly its veneration of numerous saints, greatly influenced the nature of the emergent folk religion.[17] In time, the Yoruba deities came to be identified with the images of Catholic saints.[18] The *orishas* then became *santos* (saints), and their worship became known as *Santeria*—literally the worship of saints. Thus, to the *santero* (i.e., the practitioner of *Santeria*), a shrine may be built to house a statue in the image of a Catholic saint, but the saint is actually representative of a Yoruba god. It is exceedingly difficult to determine accurately, based solely on appearance, whether a yard shrine in Little Havana actually belongs to a Catholic or a follower of *Santeria.* In general, however, yard shrines built by practitioners of *Santeria* are more likely to contain nontraditional religious items such as bowls of water, stones, and jars of leaves.

The followers of *Santeria* believe in a supreme god called *Olodumare, Olofi,* or *Olorún.* He is thought to be a distant, lofty figure. Contact with this supreme deity is attainable only through the *orishals* who serve as intermediaries.[19] Thus, worship of god-saints serves as the focus for formal and informal devotional practices; there are no subcults or special rites exclusively in honor of *Olodumare.*

The saints—who are known both by their Catholic names and their Yoruba appellations—are associated with specific colors, particular symbols or "weapons," such as thunder, fire, or swords, and are considered to have the same supernatural powers ascribed to the African deities.[20] Each is believed to possess specific attributes, which in total govern all aspects of human life and natural phenomena. A *santero* might seek to invoke the power, for example, of *Babalu-Aye* (associated with Saint Lazarus), god of illness and disease, to cure a particular ailment, or *Orúnmila* (associated with Saint Francis of Assisi), god of wisdom and divination, to bestow knowledge. Others, purportedly, can assure success in a job, ward off an evil spirit, bring back a former lover, and so on.

The numerous deities, however, are not all venerated equally; some are more favored than others, often leading to the formation of a special subcult devoted to a particular god-saint. In Cuba, as in Miami now *Changó* (associated with Saint Barbara), god of fire, thunder, and lightning, is the most popular of all the *orishas.*[21] *Changó* represents a curious form of syncretism involving a change of sex from the male Yoruba god to the female Catholic saint. *Oshún* (associated with Our Lady of Charity, patron saint of Cuba), god of love, marriage, and gold, and *Babalu-Aye* are also extremely popular in Miami. Seven of the most revered and powerful *orishas* are often worshipped collectively. This group is known among *santeros* as the "Seven African Powers." The *orishas* which make up this septet, their associated Catholic images, colors, human aspects controlled, and weapons are shown in Table 46.1.

The ritual and devotional activities of *santeros* are confined, in most cases, to private residences. The more important functions, such as an initiation into the cult, a funeral, or a consultation in which some form of divination is sought is presided over by a high "priest" of the religion, called a

TABLE 46.1　The Seven African Powers

Orisha	Catholic Image	Colors	Human Aspect Controlled	Weapons or Symbols
Changó	Santa Barbara	red/white	passion, enemies	thunder, sword, cup
Elegguá	Holy Guardian Angel	red/black	messages	iron nails, small iron rooster
Obatalá	Our Lady of Mercy	white	peace, purity	all white substances
Oggún	Saint Peter	green/black	war, employment	iron, knives, steel
Orúnmila	Saint Francis of Assisi	green/yellow	divination	Table of Ifa (a divination board)
Oshún	Our Lady of Charity	yellow/red/green	love, marriage, gold	mirror, seashells, pumpkins
Yemayá	Our Lady of Regla	blue/white	maternity, womenhood	canoe, seashells, fans

Source: Migene Gonzalez-Wippler, *Santeria: African Magic in Latin America* (New York: Julian Press), 1973.

babaloa.[22] Lesser orders of priesthood attend to the more mundane rites and rituals. The rituals themselves are primitive, bizzare affairs, often involving the consumption of beverages concocted from exotic herbs and roots, the use of incense, oils, and foreign perfumes, drumming, dancing, trance inducement, and animal sacrifices.[23] Many of the liturgical practices including phraseology used in prayers and incantations, as well as various paraphernalia needed for ritualistic purposes, are also borrowed from Catholicism. A *Santeria* priest might even suggest to a follower that he or she attend a Catholic mass; in many cases simply to obtain holy water or even a piece of the consecrated host for use in a subsequent ritual.[24]

The Expansion of Santeria

As surprising as it may seem, *Santeria* today is neither a predominantly rural nor a lower socioeconomic class phenomenon. Indeed, authorities on the religion confirm that *Santeria* has permeated all racial groups and socioeconomic classes in Cuba, and now in the Cuban community in exile.[25] With the Cuban immigration to the United States, *Santeria* is known to be thriving in the larger cities where Cuban refugees have settled, including New York, Los Angeles, Detroit, Chicago, and particularly Miami. A precise determination of the numbers of adherents to *Santeria* in Miami is virtually impossible to ascertain, since they do not build public churches or publish membership records. It is believed, however, that their numbers run into the thousands. One rough indication is provide by anthropologist William Bascom who estimated in 1969 that there were at least 83 *babaloas*, or high priests, practicing in Miami.[26] This may be compared to Havana, which is the stronghold of *Santeria* with tens of thousands of followers, where Bascom estimated the number of *babaloas* at about 200 just prior to the Cuban Revolution.[27] Perhaps a better indicator is the existence in Miami of over 12 *botanicas*, which are retail supply outlets catering to the *Santeria* trade.

By all scholarly accounts, *Santeria* is becoming increasingly popular among certain segments of the Cuban exile community. The reason most commonly cited for this kindling of interest is the fear of some Cuban refugees of losing their cultural identity through acculturation to the American way of life.[28] Such a conversion would perhaps represent an attempt to maintain linkage to a more stable past in the face of rapidly changing values and lifestyles. Disenchantment with the Catholic faith is another factor also frequently mentioned as contributing to the apparent expansion of *Santeria* in the United States. In this respect, the Catholic church's questioning of the historical validity of certain saints who were popular in Cuba (such as Saint Lazarus and Saint Christopher), the elimination of many rituals practiced in Cuba, and just the size and institutionalized nature of the Catholic religion have reportedly prompted some Cuban-Americans to seek out alternative religious affiliation, including *Santeria*.[29] Furthermore, the adaptive nature of the *Santeria* religion itself has apparently contributed to its expansion. Mercedes Sandoval, for example, concludes: "Its intrinsic flexibility, eclecticism and heterogeneity have been advantages in helping ensure functional, dogmatic and ritual changes which enable it to meet the different needs of its many followers."[30] Evidently one of the more important and attractive aspects of *Santeria* for the Cuban community in Miami is its function as a mental health care system.[31]

In the process of change and modification as practiced in the United States, however, many African chants and dances, the use of certain herbs and roots and other medicinal and ritualistic elements have been abandoned. One of the more interesting adaptations, for example, involves a change in the Oil of the Seven African Powers, used in the worship of those deities. The "oil" is now available in *botanicas* in Miami as an aerosol spray. Directions on the side of the container read as follows: "Repeat as necessary. Make your petition. Make the sign of the cross. Air freshener, deodorizer."

Perhaps the apparent expansion of interest in *Santeria* among certain members of the Cuban exile community is only a transitional phenomenon which will subside, or die out completely, as the process of acculturation speeds ahead; [this] occurred, for example, in Italian American cult religions.[32] At the present time, however, as one follower of *Santeria* said, "When we hear thunder in Miami, we know that *Changó* is in exile."[33] Regardless of the future of this particular religious cult, the yard shrines and other contributions to the cultural landscape associated with the Cuban sector reflect the growing social diversity of this rapidly changing cosmopolitan city.

NOTES

1. Sam Jacobs, "Neighbors Irate over Family's Shrine," *The Miami Herald* (July 2, 1978), section A, p. 23.

2. Strategy Research Corporation, "Latin Market Survey," Miami, Florida, 1977, p. 78; Metropolitan Dade County Office of the County Manager, "Profile of the Latin Population in the Metropolitan Dade County Area," Miami, Florida, 1976.

3. Strategy Research Corporation, p. 78.

4. Metropolitan Dade County Planning Department, "Ethnic Breakdown by Census Tract," Miami, Florida, 1975.

5. Metropolitan Dade County Office of the City Manager, "Impact of the Community Development Program on Private Involvement in the Commercial Rehabilitation of the 'Little Havana' Neighborhood," Miami, Florida, 1978, p. 2.

6. Kimball D. Woodbury, "The Spatial Diffusion of the Cuban Community in Dade County, Florida" (unpublished M.A. thesis, University of Florida, Department of Geography, 1978) p. 33.

7. F. Pierce Eichelberger, "The Cubans in Miami: Residential Movements and Ethnic Group Differentiation" (unpublished M.A. thesis, University of Cincinnati, Department of Geography, 1974), p. 83.

8. William D. Montalbano, "Vanishing Hands," *The Miami Herald* (Feb. 4, 1979), Tropic section, pp. 19–21.

9. Ileana Oroza, "The Traditionalist," *The Miami Herald* (July 4, 1978), section A, p. 16.

10. John Dorschner, "Growing up Spanglish in Miami," *The Miami Herald* (Sept. 11, 1977), Tropic section, pp. 6–13.

11. Matthew Creelman, "Count Your Built-In Blessings," *The Miami Herald* (July 21, 1979), Section D, p. 3.

12. George E. Simpson, *Religious Cults of the Caribbean: Trinidad, Jamaica, and Haiti* (Rio Piedras, Puerto Rico: Institute of Caribbean Studies, 1970), p. 11.

13. Migene Gonzalez-Wippler, *Santeria: African Magic in Latin America* (New York: Julian Press, 1973), p. 1.

14. D. E. Baldwin, *The Yoruba of Southwest Nigeria* (Boston: G. K. Hall, 1976).

15. J. O. Lucas, *The Religions of the Yorubas* (Lagos: C.M.S. Bookshop, 1942).

16. William Bascom, "The Yoruba in Cuba," *Nigeria*, 37 (1951).

17. William Bascom, "The Focus of Cuban Santeria," *Southwestern Journal of Anthropology*, 6 (Spring, 1950): 64–68.

18. Gonzalez-Wippler, p. 3; Melville J. Herskovits, "African Gods and Catholic Saints in New World Negro Belief," *American Anthropologist*, 39 (Oct–Dec., 1937): 635–43.

19. Isabel Mercedes Castellanos, "The Use of Language in Afro-Cuban Religion" (unpublished Ph.D. dissertation, Georgetown University, Dept. of Languages and Linguistics, 1976), pp. 31–33.

20. Gonzalez-Wippler, p. 16.

21. Mercedes C. Sandoval, "Santeria as a Mental Health Care System: An Historical

Overview," *Social Science and Medicine,* 13B (April, 1979): 139; William R. Bascom, *Shango in the New World* (Austin, Texas: Univ. of Texas Press, 1972), pp. 13–15.

22. Castellanos, "The Use of Language in Afro-Cuban Religion," p. 35.
23. Mercedes C. Sandoval, *La Religion Afro-Cubana* (Madrid, Spain: Playor, S.A., 1975); Lydia Cabrera, *El Monte* (Miami: Ediciones, C.R., 1971); Ellen Hampton, "Drums Beating and Animals Shrieking Frightening Southwest Dade Residents," *The Miami Herald* (Nov. 25, 1979), section B, p. 19.
24. Gonzalez-Wippler, p. 4.
25. Sandoval, *La Religion Afro-Cubana,* pp. 270–72; Castellanos, pp. 163–64.
26. Bascom, *Shango in the New World,* p. 20.
27. *Ibid.*
28. Castellanos, p. 164.
29. Sandoval, *La Religion Afro-Cubana,* p. 272.
30. Sandoval, "Santeria as a Mental Health Care System," p. 137.
31. *Ibid.,* pp. 137–51; Clarrisa S. Scott, "Health and Healing Practices among Five Ethnic Groups in Miami, Florida," *Public Health Reports,* 89 (Nov.–Dec., 1974): 526–27.
32. Rudolph J. Vecoli, "Cult and Occult in Italian-American Culture: The Persistence of a Religious Heritage," in *Immigrants and Religion in Urban Culture,* ed. Randall M. Miller and Thomas D. Marzik (Philadelphia: Temple University Press, 1977), pp. 25–47.
33. Sandoval, *La Religion Afro-Cubana,* p. 274.

EDUCATION

47

EDUCATION AND THE STRUGGLE AGAINST RACE, CLASS, AND GENDER INEQUALITY

ROSLYN ARLIN MICKELSON

STEPHEN SAMUEL SMITH

College students often describe everything outside of school as the "real world": real life supposedly doesn't begin until after graduation. However, nothing could be further from the truth. Few social institutions mold the social environment as faithfully as schools do. Moreover, by design, education is a conservative institution because its purpose is to preserve, *not* to transform, culture. Thus, the institution of education reinforces social inequality by teaching the dominant culture's values and an ethnocentric view of history. The following reading by Roslyn Arlin Mickelson and Stephen Samuel Smith, the first of four on education, examines how the social institution of education has replicated social hierarchies that perpetuate social inequality. They illustrate how race, social class, and gender bias permeate the institution of education.

Introduction

For the past 35 years, policy makers have claimed that federal education policies seek, among other things, to further equality among the races, between the sexes, and, to a much lesser extent, among social classes.[1] In this respect, educational policy makers have shared one of the assumptions that has long been part of the putative dominant ideology: a "good education" is *the* meal ticket. It will unlock the door to economic opportunity and thus enable disadvantaged groups or individuals to improve their lot dramatically. According to the dominant ideology, the United States is basically a meritocracy in which hard work and individual effort are rewarded, especially in financial terms. Related to this central belief are a series of culturally enshrined misconceptions about poverty and wealth. The central one is that poverty and wealth are the result of individual inadequacies or strengths rather than the results of the distributive mechanisms of the capitalist economy. A second misconception is the belief that everyone is the master of her or his own fate.[2] The dominant ideology assumes that American society is open and competitive, a place where an individual's status depends on talent and motivation, not inherited position. To compete, everyone must have access to education free of the fetters of family background or ascriptive factors like gender and race.[3] Since the middle of this century the reform policies of the federal government have been designed, at least officially, to enhance individuals' opportunities to acquire education.

We begin this essay by discussing the major educational doctrines and policies of the past 35 years that claim to have been aimed at promoting equality through greater equality of educational opportunity. This discussion includes the success and failures of programs such as school desegregation, compensatory education, Title IX, and job training. We then focus on the barriers such programs face in actually promoting equality. Here our point is that inequality is so deeply rooted in the structure and operation of the U.S. political economy that, at best, educational reforms can play only a limited role in ameliorating such inequality. Considerable evidence indicates that the educational system helps legitimate, if not actually reproduce, significant aspects of social inequality.

First, let us distinguish among equality, equality of opportunity, and equality of educational opportunity. The term *equality* has been the subject of extensive scholarly and political debate, much of which is beyond the scope of this essay. Most Americans reject equality of life conditions as a goal, because it would require a fundamental transformation of our basic economic and political institutions, a scenario most are unwilling to accept.[4] In the words of one observer, "So long as we live in a democratic capitalist society—that is, so long as we maintain the formal promise of political and social equality while encouraging the practice of economic inequality—we need the idea of equal opportunity to bridge that otherwise unacceptable contradiction."[5] The distinction between equality of opportunity and equality of outcome is important. Through this country's history, equality has most typically been understood in the former way. Rather than a call for the equal distribution of money, property, or many other social goods, the concern over equality has been with equal opportunity in pursuit of these goods. As Ralph Waldo Emerson put it: "The genius of our country has worked out our true policy—opportunity. Opportunity of civil rights, of education, of personal power, and not less of wealth; doors wide open."[6] To use a current metaphor: If life is a game, the playing field must be level; if life is a race, the starting line must be in the same place for everyone. For the playing field to be level, many believe education is crucial, giving individuals the wherewithal to compete in the allegedly meritocratic system. Thus equality of opportunity hinges on equality of educational opportunity.[7]

The Spotty Record of Federal Educational Reforms

In the past 35 years a series of educational reforms initiated at the national level has been introduced into local school systems. All of the reforms aimed to move education closer to the ideal of equality of educational opportunity. Here we discuss several of these reforms and how the evolution of the concept of equality of educational opportunity, spurred on by the Coleman Report, shaped many of these reforms during the past two decades. Given the importance of race and racism in American social history, many of the federal education policies during this period attempted to redress the most egregious forms of inequality based on race.

School Desegregation

Although American society has long claimed to be based on freedom, justice, and equality of opportunity, the history of race relations has long suggested the opposite. Perhaps the most influential early discussion of this disparity was Gunnar Myrdal's *An American Dilemma,* published in 1944, which vividly exposed the contradictions between the ethos of freedom, justice, equality of opportunity, and the actual experiences of African Americans in the United States.[8] Segregated schools presented observers like Myrdal with direct evidence of the shallowness of American claims to equality for all.

The school desegregation movement, whose first phase culminated in the 1954 *Brown* decision outlawing de jure segregation in schools, was the first orchestrated attempt in U.S. history to directly address inequality of educational opportunity.[9] The links among desegregation, equality of educational opportunity, and the larger issue of equality of opportunity are very clear from the history of the desegregation movement. The NAACP strategically chose school segregation to be the camel's nose under the tent of Jim Crow society.[10] That one of the nation's foremost civil rights organizations saw the attack on segregated schools as the opening salvo in the battle against society-wide inequality indicates the pivotal role of education in the American belief system in promoting equality of opportunity.

Has desegregation succeeded? This is really two questions: First, have desegregation efforts integrated public schools? Second, have desegregation efforts enhanced students' educational opportunities? Since 1954 progress toward integrated education has been limited at best. As Hochschild notes, racial isolation has only diminished; it has not gone away. In 1968, 77 percent of African American students were in schools with student bodies composed of predominantly nonwhite youths. By 1984, 64 percent of African Americans were in such schools. Moreover, 70.5 percent of Hispanic students attend predominantly minority schools.[11] Furthermore, integrated schools are often resegregated at the classroom level by tracking or ability grouping. Since 1954 racial isolation has declined everywhere but the Northeast. Ironically, today the greatest degree of racial segregation occurs in the Northeast and the least is in the South.[12] The answer to the first question, then, is that desegregation policies have had only a limited effect on overall school integration.

Has desegregation helped to equalize educational outcomes nationwide? As Hochschild points out, a better question might be which desegregation programs under which circumstances accomplish which goals.[13] Where desegregation has succeeded, its effects have been for the most part positive.[14] Evidence from desegregation research suggests that, overall, minority and majority children benefit academically and socially from well-run programs. The city in which we live, Charlotte, North Carolina, is an example of one such success story.[15] Despite these limited but positive outcomes, in the last decade of the twentieth century, most American children attend schools segregated by race, ethnicity, and class. Consequently, 35 years of official federal interventions aimed at achieving equality of educational opportunity through school desegregation have not achieved that goal; children from different race and class backgrounds continue to receive significantly segregated and largely unequal educations.[16]

The Coleman Report

Based largely on the massive data introduced in the 1954 *Brown* desegregation case, which showed that resources in black and white schools were grossly unequal, Congress mandated in 1964 a national study of the "lack of availability of equality of educational opportunity for individuals due to race, color, religion, or national origin in public schools." The authors of the study, James Coleman and his associates, expected to find glaring disparities in educational resources available to African American and white students and that these differences would explain the substantial achievement differences between white and minority students.[17]

Instead, the Coleman Report, released in 1966, produced some very unexpected findings. The researchers found that 12 years after *Brown*, most Americans still attended segregated schools but that the characteristics of black and white schools (such as facilities, books, labs, teacher experience, and expenditures) were surprisingly similar. Apparently, segregated Southern districts upgraded black educational facilities in the wake of the *Brown* decisions. More importantly, Coleman and his colleagues found that school resources had relatively little to do with variations in students' school performance. Instead, they found that family background influenced school achievement more than any other factor, including school characteristics.[18]

The effects of the last finding were dramatic. It deflected attention from how schools operate and instead focused public policy upon poor and minority children and their families as the ultimate sources of unequal school outcomes. Numerous observers concluded that schools were not primarily to blame for black-white educational differences, overlooking another Coleman Report finding that could implicate schools in inequality of educational outcomes. The overlooked finding showed that African American and white achievement differences increased with every year of schooling. That is, the achievement gap between black and white first graders was much smaller than the gap between twelfth graders. This finding suggests that at best schools reinforce the disadvantages of race and class and at worst are themselves a major source of educational inequality.

Although published a quarter of a century ago, the Coleman Report remains one of the most important and controversial pieces of social research ever completed. One of its many lasting results was a redefinition of the concept of equality of educational opportunity because it made clear that greater inputs into schools were not associated with greater student achievement. No longer were financial inputs a satisfactory measure of equality of opportunity. Only to the extent that academic outcomes of achievement (how well a student performs in school) and attainment (how many years of education a student acquires) are equal can claims be advanced about the putative extent of equality of educational opportunity.[19]

Compensatory Education

A second lasting outcome of the Coleman Report was widespread support for compensatory education. Policy makers interpreted the finding that family background explains more of the variance in students' achievement than any other factor as evidence of "cultural deprivation" among poor and minority families. This notion was consistent with Oscar Lewis' then-popular thesis on the culture of poverty.[20] Such an interpretation of the Coleman Report gave impetus to an education movement to compensate for the alleged cultural deficiencies of non-middle-class, nonwhite families so that when so-called disadvantaged children came to school they could compete without the handicap of their background.

Compensatory education refers to the many programs that began with the passage of the Elementary and Secondary Education Act in 1965. These programs target children who are both poor and underachieving and provide them with developmental preschool or a variety of individualized programs in math, reading, and language arts once they are in elementary school. The following are included under the compensatory education rubric:

▼ Early childhood education such as Head Start
▼ Follow Through, where Head Start children, now in elementary school, continue to receive special programs
▼ Bilingual education
▼ Chapter 1 (formerly called Title I), which provides language arts and math programs plus food, medicine, and clothing to needy children in primary schools
▼ Guidance and counseling in secondary schools
▼ Higher education programs designed to identify potential college students in high schools and special admissions, transition, and retention programs for qualified students going to college[21]

Compensatory education has a controversial history. Initially, critics from the left charged that the underlying premise of compensatory education, that poor and minority families were deficient relative to middle-class white families, was racist and elitist. Compensatory education's most famous critic on the right was Arthur Jensen. His 1969 article on IQ and scholastic achievement argued that compensatory education was a waste of time and money because the lower African American achievement scores indicated that blacks were less intelligent than whites.[22] This criticism of compensatory education miscast the debate over poverty and education into one about race and education because it ignored the fact that many compensatory education students were white and most African American children at the time did not participate in the programs.

Despite attacks like Jensen's and an initial absence of evidence that the programs accomplished any of their goals, the compensatory education movement survived the past 20 years. Recent research has begun to demonstrate both the cognitive and social benefits from compensatory education,[23] although the achievement gaps between minority and white and between working- and middle-class children remain. No doubt this is true in part because today only 18 percent of income-eligible students participate in the most famous and successful program, Head Start.[24] While the recent evidence regarding the effects of these programs continues to be positive, we must conclude that compensatory education, like integrated education, has not brought about equality of school outcomes.

Human Capital Theory and Job Training Programs

The notion that "good" education is *the* meal ticket has received theoretical exposition in human capital theory, which views education as a capital investment in human beings. Theodore Schultz, a University of Chicago economist, originally put forth this theory. He argued that "earnings, especially those of minority groups, reflect . . . inadequate investment in their health and education."[25] The social policies developed to remedy shortages in human capital among minority and working-class youth included job training programs like the Comprehensive Education and Training Act (CETA) and its successor, the Job Training and Partnership Act (JTPA). A central problem with both programs is that graduates have few if any jobs once the training is over.[26] The failure of both programs to eradicate inequality stems from the faulty premise that individual, not structural, factors are at the heart of poverty. The poor often have a great deal of skills and education. What they lack is available, well-paying jobs in which to invest their skills.[27] We elaborate on this crucial point later in this article.

These criticisms apply as well to more conventional high school vocational education programs. Vocational students tend to be disproportionately working class and minorities, and the courses are highly segregated by gender. Vocational education classes in high school and community colleges are frequently tailored to local businesses' labor force requirements. Too often they train students in obsolete, narrow skills that are virtually useless once the student graduates from the educational program. Much of the recent corporate interest in school reform stems from the results of these processes.[28] The track record of job training programs (CETA and JTPA) and secondary school vocational education programs indicate human capital–based educational reforms do not, and cannot, narrow race, class, and gender differences in equality of educational opportunity in this society.

Title IX

Title IX is the primary federal law prohibiting sex discrimination in education. It states, "No person in the United States shall, on the basis of sex, be excluded from participation in, be denied benefit of, or be subjected to discrimination under any program or activity receiving Federal financial assistance." Until its passage in 1972, gender inequality in educational opportunity received minimal legislative attention. Title IX covers admissions quotas by sex, different courses, and athletic programs. It requires [that] existing school programs be examined for gender-based discrimination and mandates equal treatment of all students in courses, financial aid, counseling services, and employment.[29]

Although Title IX was passed in 1972, it lacked implementing regulations until 1975. Nor was it ever accompanied by substantial federal or state financial assistance. Title IX was potentially damaged in February 1984, when the Supreme Court ruled in *Grove City College* v. *Bell* that coverage of Title IX was limited to programs and activities, rather than entire institutions, receiving federal money.[30] The effects of this ruling remain unclear.[31]

Sexism in education persists despite laws prohibiting it. Even though female achievement and attainment levels are comparable to those of males, many sexist practices remain an integral part of schooling at all levels. For example, curricular materials from kindergarten to college reveal a preponderance of male characters. In addition, male and female characters usually reflect traditional gender roles and behaviors. Although the gap is narrowing, women who graduate from high school are frequently less well prepared in college-level math and science than men are and consequently cannot enroll in math, science, engineering, or computer science courses in the same frequencies as men.[32] Vocational education at the high school and college level remains highly sex segregated. Administrators are overwhelmingly male although most teachers are female. Women in academia face barriers to promotion and continue to earn less than their male colleagues.[33]

Recent civil rights legislation fails to address any of these problems. Like the laws and policies aimed at eliminating race differences in school processes and outcomes, those aiming to eliminate gender differences in educational opportunities have, at best, only narrowed differences. Educational opportunity in the United States remains highly unequal for people of different gender, race, ethnic, and class backgrounds.

Equality of Educational Opportunity and Equality of Income

The educational reforms intended to lessen inequality were designed primarily to give all students access to better playgrounds, computers, books, teachers, and athletic facilities. Greater equality in the distribution of these resources was seen as a means to better equip minorities, women, and to a lesser extent, working-class whites to improve their chances in life once they become adults. Equality of educational opportunity, as noted earlier, was viewed as a means of promoting equality of opportunity.

Whatever increase in the equality of educational opportunity has resulted from the reforms discussed earlier, it has not led to a significantly greater equality of life-chances, at least as measured by income, one of the most telling and broadest gauges of equality in the United States. Much of a person's social standing depends on income because in a capitalist society income is related to all other forms of inequality. Although this measure does not address the social class basis of inequality, income is one useful and clear measure of inequality in this society.[34] In addition, the disjunction between the greater equality of educational opportunity and lack of a corresponding increase in the equality of incomes can be explained by the nature of the U.S. political economy. The main cause of income inequality is the structure and operation of U.S. capitalism, which have scarcely been affected by the educational reforms discussed earlier.

Several years after the publication of the landmark Coleman Report, Jencks and his associates reanalyzed the data on which it was based to explore the conventional wisdom that a "good education" was how disadvantaged individuals and groups could improve their economic situation. Their findings were published in a now famous book, *Inequality* (1972). Among its conclusions was the following:

> The evidence suggests that equalizing educational opportunity [achievement and attainment] would do very little to make adults more equal. . . . The experience of the past 25 years suggests that even fairly substantial reductions in the range of educational attainments do not appreciably reduce economic inequality among adults.[35]

Almost 20 years of educational reforms have elapsed since those remarks were made. Sadly, the evidence in support of that conclusion is stronger now than it was in 1972. Current statistics on educational and income attainment show that race and gender differences in educational achievement continue to narrow and differences in attainment have all but disappeared.[36] Nevertheless, race and gender differences in income remain stable over time (see Figures 47.1 and 47.2).

While race differences in educational attainment have virtually disappeared, and women attain slightly more education than men, both minorities and women remain "less equal" than men—that is, on average they earn significantly less income than white males with comparable educational credentials (see Figure 47.2). Equality of educational opportunity, indicated by years of attainment, simply has not produced anything resembling equality of income.

The greater equality of educational opportunity has not led to a corresponding increase in the equality of incomes because educational reforms do not create more good-paying jobs, affect sex-segregated and racially segmented occupational structures, or limit the mobility of capital either between regions of the country or between the United States and other countries. For example, no matter how good an education white working-class or minority youth may receive, it does nothing to alter the fact that thousands of relatively good-paying manufacturing jobs have left Northern inner cities for Northern suburbs, the Sunbelt, or foreign countries.[37] Perhaps service jobs are left in the wake of such capital flight or have been created in its place, but they pay less than manufacturing jobs. An economy in which McDonald's employs more people than USX Corporation (the former industrial giant U.S. Steel Corporation) is one in which the economic opportunities for minority and working-class youth are limited. Without changes in the structure

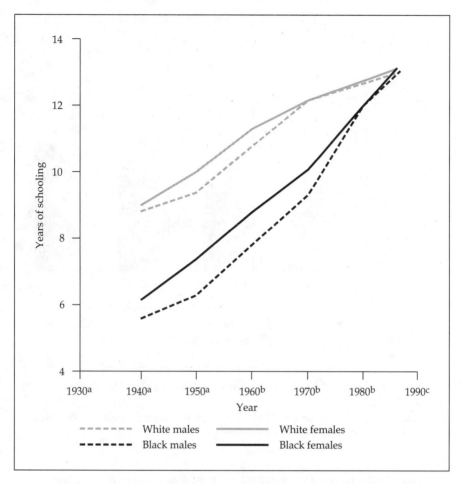

FIGURE 47.1   Median Educational Attainment by Sex and Race, 1940–1987

[a]*Source:* Series H 395–406 Historical Statistics of U.S. Colonial Times to 1957. U.S. Dept. of Commerce. Bureau of the Census. Washington, DC: U.S. Government Printing Office.

[b]*Source:* U.S. Census of Population 1960, 1970, 1980; Current Population Reports Series P-20 N. 403, U.S. Dept. of Commerce. Bureau of the Census. Washington, DC: U.S. Government Printing Office.

[c]*Source:* Current Population Reports Series P-20 N. 428. U.S. Dept. of Commerce. Bureau of the Census. Washington, DC: U.S. Government Printing Office.

and operation of the capitalist economy, educational reforms may enable some members of disadvantaged groups to improve their situation, but they cannot markedly improve the social and economic position of these groups in their entirety. This is the primary reason that educational reforms do little to affect the gross social inequalities that inspired them in the first place.

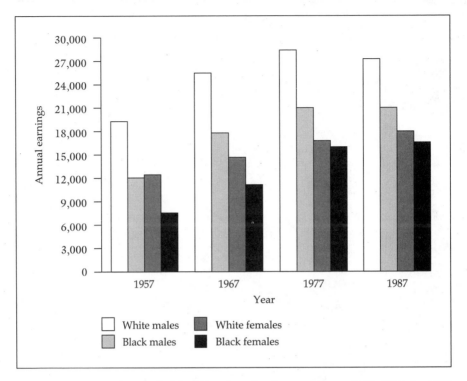

FIGURE 47.2   Median Individual Earnings by Sex and Race, 1957–1987, in 1987 Constant Dollars

Source: Current Population Series P-60 N. 162. U.S. Dept. of Commerce. Bureau of the Census. Washington, DC: U.S. Government Printing Office.

Beyond Attainment: The Persistence of Educational Inequality

Educational reforms have not led to greater equality for several additional reasons. Many aspects of school processes and curricular content are deeply connected to race, class, and gender inequality. But gross measures of educational outputs, such as median years of schooling completed, mask these indicators of inequality. The data in Figure 47.1 indicate that today African Americans as a group have attained essentially as much education as have whites as a group; the same is true for women compared to men. But aggregate data like these obscure gross differences in attainment within race and gender groups. These within-group differences are primarily linked to class and region. For example, in the 1980s children of black farmers averaged 8.65 years of educational attainment; children of black professionals averaged 13.97 years of schooling.[38] Similar differences by class exist for whites. Within-group differences demonstrate the extent to which educational opportunity remains inequitable. Despite significant within-group differences, the comparable median levels of educational attainment by race and gender can illustrate our theoretical point regarding the structural inability of increases in education to reduce income inequality. Were we to compare income by race and by gender for different levels of educational attainment, our argument would be even stronger. For any level of educational attainment, blacks earn less than whites with comparable levels of education and women earn less than men with similar credentials. Furthermore, the disparities in returns to education increase as levels of educational attainment increase.[39]

Another example of persistent inequality of educational opportunity is credential inflation. Even though women, minorities, and members of the working class now obtain higher levels of education than they did before, the most privileged in society gain even higher levels of education. At the same time, the educational requirements for the best jobs (those with the highest salaries, benefits, agreeable working conditions, autonomy, responsibility) are growing so that only those with the most education from the best schools are eligible for the best jobs. Because the more privileged are almost always in a better position to gain these desirable educational credentials, members of the working class, women, and minorities are still at a competitive disadvantage. Due to credential inflation, previous educational requirements for good jobs, now within the reach of many dispossessed groups, are inadequate and insufficient in today's labor market.[40]

Although gaps in educational attainment between males and females and between minorities and whites have narrowed (see Figure 47.1), not all educational experiences are alike. Four years of public high school in Beverly Hills are quite different from four years in an inner-city school.[41] Dreeben and Gamoran examined race differences in learning to read among first-grade children in the Chicago area. They concluded that the explanation for why nonblacks learned more than blacks rests, in part, in features of teacher instructional practices, which differ by school. Black children in their sample who attended minority schools were provided with less time in basal instruction—the core activity of primary school reading—and covered fewer new vocabulary words than did black and white children in either integrated or all white schools. The authors concluded, "Blacks learned less than nonblacks . . . mainly because of the instructional inadequacies prevailing in all-black schools."[42]

One additional aspect of these differences is what sociologists of education call the hidden curriculum, which refers to two separate but related processes. The first is that the content and process of education differ for children according to their race, gender, and class. The second is that these differences help reproduce the inequalities based on race, gender, and class that characterize U.S. society.

One aspect of the hidden curriculum is the formal curriculum's ideological content. Anyon's work on U.S. history texts demonstrates that children from more privileged backgrounds are more likely to be exposed to rich, sophisticated, and complex materials than are their working-class counter-parts.[43] Another aspect of the hidden curriculum concerns the social organi-zation of the school and the classroom. Some hidden curriculum theorists suggest that tracking, ability grouping, and conventional teacher-centered classroom interactions contribute to the reproduction of the social rela-tions of production at the workplace. This perspective derives from the work of Bowles and Gintis; their seminal work, *Schooling in Capitalist America,* proposes that there is a correspondence among the social relations of the workplace, the home, and the school.[44] Lower-track classrooms are dispro-portionately filled with working-class and minority students. Students in lower tracks are more likely than those in higher tracks to be assigned repet-itive exercises at a very low level of cognitive challenge. Lower-track stu-dents are likely to work individually and to lack classroom experience with problem solving or other independent, creative activities.[45] Such activities are more conducive to preparing students for working-class jobs than for professional and managerial positions. Many proponents of the correspon-dence principle argue that educational experiences from preschool to high school differentially prepare students for their ultimate positions in the workforce, and a student's placement in various school programs is based primarily on her or his race and class origin.[46] The correspondence principle has sometimes been applied in too deterministic and mechanical a fashion.[47] Nonetheless, in certain cases, it is a compelling contribution to explanations of how and why school processes and outcomes are so markedly affected by the race, gender, and class of students. . . .

Conclusion

In this [reading] we have argued that educational reforms cannot eliminate inequality. But education remains important to any struggle to reduce in-equality. Moreover, it is more than a meal ticket; it is intrinsically worth-while. Desegregation, compensatory education, Title IX, and bilingual education all facilitate cognitive growth and promote important nonsexist, nonracist attitudes and practices; they make schools a more humane place for adults and children. Furthermore, education, even reformist liberal edu-cation, contains the seeds of individual and social transformation. Those of us committed to the struggle against inequality cannot be paralyzed by the structural barriers that make it impossible for education to eliminate in-equality. We must look upon the schools as arenas of struggle. To do other-wise would be to concede what must be contested in every way.

NOTES

1. This essay draws on an article by Roslyn Arlin Mickelson that appeared as "Edu-cation and the Struggle against Race, Class, and Gender Inequality," *Humanity and Society* 11, no. 4 (1987): 440–64. The authors thank Kevin Hawk for his technical as-sistance in the preparation of the graphs.

2. R. H. deLone, *Small Futures* (New York: Harcourt Brace Jovanovich, 1979). Ascertaining whether a set of beliefs constitutes the dominant ideology in a particular society or social formation involves a host of difficult theoretical and empirical questions. For this reason we use the term *putative dominant ideology*. For discussions of these questions, see Nicholas Abercrombie et al., *The Dominant Ideology Thesis* (London: George Allen & Unwin, 1980); James C. Scott, *Weapons of the Weak* (New Haven: Yale University Press, 1985); Stephen Samuel Smith, "Political Acquiescence and Beliefs about State Coercion" (Ph.D. dissertation, Stanford University, 1990).

3. Whether racism and sexism are epiphenomena is too large an issue to address in this article. We take the position that the logic of capitalism breeds sexism and racism, but that both have a quasi-independent cultural history and are therefore important social phenomena in their own right. See C. A. MacKinnon, "Feminism, Marxism, Method, and the State: An Agenda for Theory," in N. O. Keohane et al. (eds.), *Feminist Theory* (Chicago: University of Chicago Press, 1981).

4. Kevin Dougherty, "After the Fall: Research on School Effects Since the Coleman Report," *Harvard Educational Review* 51, no. 2 (1981): 301–308.

5. Jennifer L. Hochschild, "The Double-Edged Sword of Equal Educational Opportunity." Paper presented at the meeting of the American Education Research Association, Washington, DC, April 22, 1987.

6. Douglas Rae, *Equalities* (Cambridge, MA: Harvard University Press, 1981), p. 64.

7. C. J. Hurn, *The Limits and Possibilities of Schooling* (Boston: Allyn & Bacon, 1978).

8. G. Myrdal, *An American Dilemma: The Negro Problem and Modern Democracy* (New York: Harper & Row, 1944).

9. R. Kluger, *Simple Justice* (New York: Knopf, 1975).

10. Ibid.

11. E. B. Fiske, "Integration Lags in Public Schools," *New York Times,* July 26, 1987, pp. 1, 24–25.

12. J. L. Hochschild, *The New American Dilemma* (New Haven: Yale University Press, 1984).

13. Ibid.

14. Jomills H. Braddock II, Robert L. Crain, and James M. McPartland, "A Long-Term View of School Desegregation: Some Recent Studies of Graduates as Adults," in Jeanne H. Ballantine (ed.), *Schools and Society* (Mountain View, CA: Mayfield, 1989), pp. 303–13; Robert L. Crain et al., *Making Desegregation Work* (Cambridge, MA: Ballinger, 1982); Hochschild, *New American Dilemma;* Charles V. Willie, *Desegregation Plans That Work* (Westport, CT: Greenwood Press, 1984).

15. Frye Gaillard, *The Dream Long Deferred* (Chapel Hill: University of North Carolina Press, 1989).

16. Fiske, "Integration Lags."

17. J. Karabel and A. H. Halsey, *Power and Ideology in Education* (New York: Oxford University Press, 1977), p. 20.

18. J. S. Coleman et al., *Equality of Educational Opportunity* (Washington, DC: U.S. Government Printing Office, 1966); Karabel and Halsey, *Power and Ideology.*

19. B. Heyns, "Educational Effects: Issues in Conceptualization and Measurement," in J. C. Richardson (ed.), *Handbook of Theory and Research for the Sociology of Education* (New York: Greenwood Press, 1986).

20. O. Lewis, "The Culture of Poverty," *Scientific American* (October 1966), pp. 19–25.

21. J. H. Ballantine, *The Sociology of Education* (Englewood Cliffs, NJ: Prentice-Hall, 1983).

22. A. F. Jensen, "How Much Can We Boost IQ and Scholastic Achievement?" *Harvard Educational Review* 39 (Winter 1969): 1–123. The genetic model of human intelligence Jensen used to substantiate his claims of African Americans' alleged lower levels of intelligence was the work of the late Sir Cyril Burt. In the mid-1970s, however, scientists exposed Burt's work as a major scientific fraud because he had fabricated his data on the IQs of separated identical twins as well as the existence of the two women who supposedly assisted him during his research. Stephen J. Gould's *The Mismeasure of Man* (New York: Norton, 1981) is a masterful exposé of Burt's fakery as well as the scientific and moral bankruptcy of the sexist, classist, and racist underpinnings of much of the intelligence testing movement.

23. J. F. Berrueta-Clement et al., *Changed Lives: The Effects of the Perry Preschool Project on Youths Through Age 19* (Ypsilanti, MI: The High/Scope Press, 1985); L. F. Carter, "The Sustaining Effects of Compensatory and Elementary Education," *Educational Researcher* 13, no. 7 (1984): 3–11.

24. Ronald Henkoff, "Now Everyone Loves Head Start," *Fortune,* Special Issue on Saving Our Schools (Spring 1990), pp. 35–43.

25. T. Schultz, "Investment in Human Capital," *American Economic Review* (March 1961), pp. 1–17; Karabel and Halsey, *Power and Ideology,* pp. 313–24.

26. Wilford Wilms, personal communication (1984); Paul Weckstein, personal interview (Washington, DC, March 8, 1990).

27. B. Bluestone, "Economic Policy and the Fate of the Poor," *Social Policy,* no. 2 (1972): 30–31.

28. Carol A. Ray and Roslyn A. Mickelson, "Corporate Leaders, Resistant Youth, and School Reform in Sunbelt City: The Political Economy of Education," *Social Problems* 37, no. 2 (1990): 178–90.

29. Ballantine, *Sociology of Education;* S. S. Klein, *Handbook for Achieving Sex Equity in Education* (Baltimore: Johns Hopkins University Press, 1985).

30. Klein, *Handbook,* pp. 94–95.

31. Title IX is not the only federal law attempting to achieve gender equity in education through legislative reforms. Other federal programs that target sexism in education include Title IV of the 1964 Civil Rights Act, the Women's Educational Equity Act of 1974 and 1978, an amendment to the 1976 Vocational Education Act, the law authorizing the National Institute of Education, and the laws creating the National Science Foundation and the U.S. Commission on Civil Rights. Klein, *Handbook;* R. Salomone, *Equality of Education under the Law* (New York: St. Martin's Press, 1986).

32. Elizabeth Fennema and Gilah C. Leder, *Mathematics and Gender* (New York: Teachers College Press, 1990); Klein, *Handbook;* Cornelius Riordan, *Girls and Boys in School: Together or Separate* (New York: Teachers College Press, 1990).

33. L. McMillen, "Women Professors Pressing to Close Salary Gap: Some Colleges Adjust Pay, Others Face Lawsuits," *Chronicle of Higher Education* 33, (1987), p. 1.

34. To be sure, income does not measure class-based inequality, but there is a positive correlation between income and class. Income has the additional advantage of being easily quantifiable. Were we to use another measure of inequality—wealth— the disjuncture between it and increases in educational attainment would appear even larger. The distribution of wealth in U.S. society has remained fairly stable since the Depression, with the richest 10 percent of the population owning about 65 percent of the total wealth. Since the Reagan administration's regressive fiscal and monetary policies have been in effect, the wealth of this country has been further redistributed upward at the expense of the working and middle classes.

35. C. Jencks et al., *Inequality* (New York: Harper & Row, 1972), p. 11.

36. Ira Shor, *Culture Wars* (Boston: Routledge & Kegan Paul, 1986).

37. Lois Weis, *Working Class without Work: High School Students in a Deindustrialized Economy* (New York: Routledge, 1990); William J. Wilson, *The Truly Disadvantaged* (Chicago: University of Chicago Press, 1988).

38. Hochschild, *New American Dilemma*, pp. 14–16.

39. Reynolds Farley, *Blacks and Whites: Narrowing the Gap?* (Cambridge, MA: Harvard University Press, 1984).

40. R. Collins, *Credential Society* (New York: Academic Press, 1979); R. B. Freeman, *The Over-Educated American* (New York: Academic Press, 1976).

41. Jean Anyon, "Social Class and the Hidden Curriculum of Work," *Journal of Education* 162, no. 1 (1980): 67–92; Jean Anyon, "Social Class and School Knowledge," *Curriculum Inquiry*, no. 10 (1981): 3–42; Roslyn Mickelson, "The Secondary School's Role in Social Stratification: A Comparison of Beverly Hills High School and Morningside High School," *Journal of Education* 162, no. 4 (1980): 83–112.

42. Robert Dreeben and Adam Gamoran, "Race, Instruction, and Learning," *American Sociological Review* 51, no. 5 (1986): 660–69.

43. Anyon, "Social Class and the Hidden Curriculum"; "Social Class and School Knowledge."

44. S. Bowles and H. Gintis, *Schooling in Capitalist America: Educational Reform and the Contradictions of Economic Life* (New York: Basic Books, 1976).

45. Jeannie Oakes, *Keeping Track* (New Haven, CT: Yale University Press, 1985).

46. Ibid.; S. Lubeck, *Sandbox Society* (Philadelphia: Falmer Press, 1985); Mickelson, "Secondary School's Role"; R. A. Mickelson, "The Case of the Missing Brackets: Teachers and Social Reproduction," *Journal of Education* 169, no. 2 (1987): 78–88.

47. M. Apple and L. Weis (eds.), *Ideology and Practice in Schooling* (Philadelphia: Temple University Press, 1983); H. Giroux, *Theory and Resistance in Education* (Boston: Bergin and Garvey, 1983).

48

CIVILIZE THEM WITH A STICK

MARY CROW DOG • RICHARD ERDOES

Few students are aware of our nation's policies toward Native Americans, which included the separation of Indian children from their families and cultures so that these children could be "civilized" into the dominant society. Consequently, thousands of Native American children were forced to leave the reservation to attend boarding schools, day schools, or schools in converted Army posts. These total institutions used tactics similar to those used by the military to resocialize the young Native Americans. In the following selection, Mary Crow Dog and Richard Erdoes reveal how the institution of education can be an agent of social control whose purpose is to assimilate racial-ethnic populations, such as Native Americans, into the dominate culture.

. . . Gathered from the cabin, the wickiup, and the tepee,
partly by cajolery and partly by threats;
partly by bribery and partly by force,
they are induced to leave their kindred
to enter these schools and take upon themselves
the outward appearance of civilized life.
—ANNUAL REPORT OF THE DEPARTMENT OF INTERIOR, 1901

It is almost impossible to explain to a sympathetic white person what a typical old Indian boarding school was like; how it affected the Indian child suddenly dumped into it like a small creature from another world, helpless, defenseless, bewildered, trying desperately and instinctively to survive and sometimes not surviving at all. I think such children were like the victims of Nazi concentration camps trying to tell average, middle-class Americans what their experience had been like. Even now, when these schools are much improved, when the buildings are new, all gleaming steel and glass, the food tolerable, the teachers well trained and well intentioned, even trained in child psychology—unfortunately the psychology of white children, which is different from ours—the shock to the child upon arrival is still tremendous. Some just seem to shrivel up, don't speak for days on end, and have an empty look in their eyes. I know of an 11-year-old on another reservation who hanged herself, and in our school, while I was there, a girl jumped out of the window, trying to kill herself to escape an unbearable situation. That first shock is always there.

Although the old tiyospaye has been destroyed, in the traditional Sioux families, especially in those where there is no drinking, the child is never left alone. It is always surrounded by relatives, carried around, enveloped in warmth. It is treated with the respect due to any human being, even a small one. It is seldom forced to do anything against its will, seldom screamed at, and never beaten. That much, at least, is left of the old family group among full-bloods. And then suddenly a bus or car arrives, full of strangers, usually white strangers, who yank the child out of the arms of those who love it, taking it screaming to the boarding school. The only word I can think of for what is done to these children is kidnapping.

Even now, in a good school, there is impersonality instead of close human contact; a sterile, cold atmosphere, an unfamiliar routine, language problems, and above all the maza-skan-skan, that damn clock—white man's time as opposed to Indian time, which is natural time. Like eating when you are hungry and sleeping when you are tired, not when that damn clock says you must. But I was not taken to one of the better, modern schools. I was taken to the old-fashioned mission school at St. Francis, run by the nuns and

Catholic fathers, built sometime around the turn of the century and not improved a bit when I arrived, not improved as far as the buildings, the food, the teachers, or their methods were concerned.

In the old days, nature was our people's only school and they needed no other. Girls had their toy tipis and dolls, boys their toy bows and arrows. Both rode and swam and played the rough Indian games together. Kids watched their peers and elders and naturally grew from children into adults. Life in the tipi circle was harmonious—until the whiskey peddlers arrived with their wagons and barrels of "Injun whiskey." I often wished I could have grown up in the old, before-whiskey days.

Oddly enough, we owed our unspeakable boarding schools to the do-gooders, the white Indian-lovers. The schools were intended as an alternative to the outright extermination seriously advocated by generals Sherman and Sheridan, as well as by most settlers and prospectors overrunning our land. "You don't have to kill those poor benighted heathen," the do-gooders said, "in order to solve the Indian Problem. Just give us a chance to turn them into useful farmhands, laborers, and chambermaids who will break their backs for you at low wages." In that way the boarding schools were born. The kids were taken away from their villages and pueblos, in their blankets and moccasins, kept completely isolated from their families—sometimes for as long as ten years—suddenly coming back, their short hair slick with pomade, their necks raw from stiff, high collars, their thick jackets always short in the sleeves and pinching under the arms, their tight patent leather shoes giving them corns, the girls in starched white blouses and clumsy, high-buttoned boots—caricatures of white people. When they found out—and they found out quickly—that they were neither wanted by whites nor by Indians, they got good and drunk, many of them staying drunk for the rest of their lives. I still have a poster I found among my grandfather's stuff, given to him by the missionaries to tack up on his wall. It reads:

1. Let Jesus save you.
2. Come out of your blanket, cut your hair, and dress like a white man.
3. Have a Christian family with one wife for life only.
4. Live in a house like your white brother. Work hard and wash often.
5. Learn the value of a hard-earned dollar. Do not waste your money on giveaways. Be punctual.
6. Believe that property and wealth are signs of divine approval.
7. Keep away from saloons and strong spirits.
8. Speak the language of your white brother. Send your children to school to do likewise.
9. Go to church often and regularly.
10. Do not go to Indian dances or to the medicine men.

The people who were stuck upon "solving the Indian Problem" by making us into whites retreated from this position only step by step in the wake of Indian protests.

The mission school at St. Francis was a curse for our family for generations. My grandmother went there, then my mother, then my sisters and I. At one time or other every one of us tried to run away. Grandma told me once about the bad times she had experienced at St. Francis. In those days they let students go home only for one week every year. Two days were used up for transportation, which meant spending just five days out of 365 with her family. And that was an improvement. Before grandma's time, on many reservations they did not let the students go home at all until they had finished school. Anybody who disobeyed the nuns was severely punished. The building in which my grandmother stayed had three floors, for girls only. Way up in the attic were little cells, about five by five by ten feet. One time she was in church and instead of praying she was playing jacks. As punishment they took her to one of those little cubicles where she stayed in darkness because the windows had been boarded up. They left her there for a whole week with only bread and water for nourishment. After she came out she promptly ran away, together with three other girls. They were found and brought back. The nuns stripped them naked and whipped them. They used a horse buggy whip on my grandmother. Then she was put back into the attic—for two weeks.

My mother had much the same experiences but never wanted to talk about them, and then there I was, in the same place. The school is now run by the BIA—the Bureau of Indian Affairs—but only since about 15 years ago. When I was there, during the 1960s, it was still run by the Church. The Jesuit fathers ran the boys' wing and the Sisters of the Sacred Heart ran us—with the help of the strap. Nothing had changed since my grandmother's days. I have been told recently that even in the '70s they were still beating children at that school. All I got out of school was being taught how to pray. I learned quickly that I would be beaten if I failed in my devotions or, God forbid, prayed the wrong way, especially prayed in Indian to Wakan Tanka, the Indian Creator.

The girls' wing was built like an F and was run like a penal institution. Every morning at five o'clock the sisters would come into our large dormitory to wake us up, and immediately we had to kneel down at the sides of our beds and recite the prayers. At six o'clock we were herded into the church for more of the same. I did not take kindly to the discipline and to marching by the clock, left-right, left-right. I was never one to like being forced to do something. I do something because I feel like doing it. I felt this way always, as far as I can remember, and my sister Barbara felt the same way. An old medicine man once told me: "Us Lakotas are not like dogs who can be trained, who can be beaten and keep on wagging their tails, licking the hand that whipped them. We are like cats, little cats, big cats, wildcats, bobcats, mountain lions. It doesn't matter what kind, but cats who can't be tamed, who scratch if you step on their tails." But I was only a kitten and my claws were still small.

Barbara was still in the school when I arrived and during my first year or two she could still protect me a little bit. When Barb was a seventh grader she ran away together with five other girls, early in the morning before sunrise. They brought them back in the evening. The girls had to wait for two hours in front of the mother superior's office. They were hungry and cold, frozen through. It was wintertime and they had been running the whole day without food, trying to make good their escape. The mother superior asked each girl, "Would you do this again?" She told them that as punishment they would not be allowed to visit home for a month and that she'd keep them busy on work details until the skin on their knees and elbows had worn off. At the end of her speech she told each girl, "Get up from this chair and lean over it." She then lifted the girls' skirts and pulled down their underpants. Not little girls either, but teenagers. She had a leather strap about a foot long and four inches wide fastened to a stick, and beat the girls, one after another, until they cried. Barb did not give her that satisfaction but just clenched her teeth. There was one girl, Barb told me, the nun kept on beating and beating until her arm got tired.

I did not escape my share of the strap. Once, when I was 13 years old, I refused to go to Mass. I did not want to go to church because I did not feel well. A nun grabbed me by the hair, dragged me upstairs, made me stoop over, pulled my dress up (we were not allowed at the time to wear jeans), pulled my panties down, and gave me what they called "swats"—25 swats with a board around which Scotch tape had been wound. She hurt me badly.

My classroom was right next to the principal's office and almost every day I could hear him swatting the boys. Beating was the common punishment for not doing one's homework, or for being late to school. It had such a bad effect upon me that I hated and mistrusted every white person on sight, because I met only one kind. It was not until much later that I met sincere white people I could relate to and be friends with. Racism breeds racism in reverse.

The routine at St. Francis was dreary. Six A.M., kneeling in church for an hour or so; seven o'clock, breakfast; eight o'clock, scrub the floor, peel spuds, make classes. We had to mop the dining room twice every day and scrub the tables. If you were caught taking a rest, doodling on the bench with a fingernail or knife, or just rapping, the nun would come up with a dish towel and just slap it across your face, saying, "You're not supposed to be talking, you're supposed to be working!" Monday mornings we had cornmeal mush, Tuesday oatmeal, Wednesday rice and raisins, Thursday cornflakes, and Friday all the leftovers mixed together or sometimes fish. Frequently the food had bugs or rocks in it. We were eating hot dogs that were weeks old, while the nuns were dining on ham, whipped potatoes, sweet peas, and cranberry sauce. In winter our dorm was icy cold while the nuns' rooms were always warm.

I have seen little girls arrive at the school, first graders, just fresh from home and totally unprepared for what awaited them, little girls with pretty braids, and the first thing the nuns did was chop their hair off and tie up what was left behind their ears. Next they would dump the children into tubs of alcohol, a sort of rubbing alcohol, "to get the germs off." Many of the nuns were German immigrants, some from Bavaria, so that we sometimes speculated whether Bavaria was some sort of Dracula country inhabited by monsters. For the sake of objectivity I ought to mention that two of the German fathers were great linguists and that the only Lakota-English dictionaries and grammars which are worth anything were put together by them.

At night some of the girls would huddle in bed together for comfort and reassurance. Then the nun in charge of the dorm would come in and say, "What are the two of you doing in bed together? I smell evil in this room. You girls are evil incarnate. You are sinning. You are going to hell and burn forever. You can act that way in the devil's frying pan." She would get them out of bed in the middle of the night, making them kneel and pray until morning. We had not the slightest idea what it was all about. At home we slept two and three in a bed for animal warmth and a feeling of security.

The nuns and the girls in the two top grades were constantly battling it out physically with fists, nails, and hair-pulling. I myself was growing from a kitten into an undersized cat. My claws were getting bigger and were itching for action. About 1969 or 1970 a strange young white girl appeared on the reservation. She looked about 18 or 20 years old. She was pretty and had long, blond hair down to her waist, patched jeans, boots, and a backpack. She was different from any other white person we had met before. I think her name was Wise. I do not know how she managed to overcome our reluctance and distrust, getting us into a corner, making us listen to her, asking us how we were treated. She told us that she was from New York. She was the first real hippie or Yippie we had come across. She told us of people called the Black Panthers, Young Lords, and Weathermen. She said, "Black people are getting it on. Indians are getting it on in St. Paul and California. How about you?" She also said, "Why don't you put out an underground paper, mimeograph it. It's easy. Tell it like it is. Let it all hang out." She spoke a strange lingo but we caught on fast.

Charlene Left Hand Bull and Gina One Star were two full-blood girls I used to hang out with. We did everything together. They were willing to join me in a Sioux uprising. We put together a newspaper which we called the *Red Panther.* In it we wrote how bad the school was, what kind of slop we had to eat—slimy, rotten, blackened potatoes for two weeks—the way we were beaten. I think I was the one who wrote the worst article about our principal of the moment, Father Keeler. I put all my anger and venom into it. I called him a goddam wasičun son of a bitch. I wrote that he knew nothing about Indians and should go back to where he came from, teaching white children whom he could relate to. I wrote that we knew which priests slept with which nuns and that all they ever could think about was filling their bellies and buying a new car. It was the kind of writing which foamed at the mouth, but which also lifted a great deal of weight from one's soul.

On Saint Patrick's Day, when everybody was at the big powwow, we distributed our newspapers. We put them on windshields and bulletin boards, in desks and pews, in dorms and toilets. But someone saw us and snitched on us. The shit hit the fan. The three of us were taken before a board meeting. Our parents, in my case my mother, had to come. They were told that ours was a most serious matter, the worst thing that had ever happened in the school's long history. One of the nuns told my mother, "Your daughter really needs to be talked to." "What's wrong with my daughter?" my mother asked. She was given one of our *Red Panther* newspapers. The nun pointed out its name to her and then my piece, waiting for mom's reaction. After a while she asked, "Well, what have you got to say to this? What do you think?"

My mother said, "Well, when I went to school here, some years back, I was treated a lot worse than these kids are. I really can't see how they can have any complaints, because we was treated a lot stricter. We could not even wear skirts halfway up our knees. These girls have it made. But you should forgive them because they are young. And it's supposed to be a free country, free speech and all that. I don't believe what they done is wrong." So all I got out of it was scrubbing six flights of stairs on my hands and knees, every day. And no boy-side privileges.

The boys and girls were still pretty much separated. The only time one could meet a member of the opposite sex was during free time, between 4 and 5:30, in the study hall or on benches or the volleyball court outside, and that was strictly supervised. One day Charlene and I went over to the boys' side. We were on the ball team and they had to let us practice. We played three extra minutes, only three minutes more than we were supposed to. Here was the nuns' opportunity for revenge. We got 25 swats. I told Charlene, "We are getting too old to have our bare asses whipped that way. We are old enough to have babies. Enough of this shit. Next time we fight back." Charlene only said, "Hoka-hay!"

. . .

In a school like this there is always a lot of favoritism. At St. Francis it was strongly tinged with racism. Girls who were near-white, who came from what the nuns called "nice families," got preferential treatment. They waited on the faculty and got to eat ham or eggs and bacon in the morning. They got the easy jobs while the skins, who did not have the right kind of background—myself among them—always wound up in the laundry room sorting out 10-bushel baskets of dirty boys' socks every day. Or we wound up scrubbing the floors and doing all the dishes. The school therefore fostered fights and antagonism between whites and breeds, and between breeds and skins. At one time Charlene and I had to iron all the robes and vestments the priests wore when saying Mass. We had to fold them up and put them into a chest in the back of the church. In a corner, looking over our shoulders, was a statue of the crucified Savior, all bloody and beaten up. Charlene looked up and said, "Look at that poor Indian. The pigs sure worked him over." That was the closest I ever came to seeing Jesus.

I was held up as a bad example and didn't mind. I was old enough to have a boyfriend and promptly got one. At the school we had an hour and a half for ourselves. Between the boys' and the girls' wings were some benches where one could sit. My boyfriend and I used to go there just to hold hands and talk. The nuns were very uptight about any boy-girl stuff. They had an exaggerated fear of anything having even the faintest connection with sex. One day in religion class, an all-girl class, Sister Bernard singled me out for some remarks, pointing me out as a bad example, an example that should be shown. She said that I was too free with my body. That I was holding hands which meant that I was not a good example to follow. She also said that I wore unchaste dresses, skirts which were too short, too suggestive, shorter than regulations permitted, and for that I would be punished. She dressed me down before the whole class, carrying on and on about my unchastity.

. . .

We got a new priest in English. During one of his first classes he asked one of the boys a certain question. The boy was shy. He spoke poor English, but he had the right answer. The priest told him, "You did not say it right. Correct yourself. Say it over again." The boy got flustered and stammered. He could hardly get out a word. But the priest kept after him: "Didn't you hear? I told you to do the whole thing over. Get it right this time." He kept on and on.

I stood up and said, "Father, don't be doing that. If you go into an Indian's home and try to talk Indian, they might laugh at you and say, 'Do it over correctly. Get it right this time!'"

He shouted at me, "Mary, you stay after class. Sit down right now!"

I stayed after class, until after the bell. He told me, "Get over here!" He grabbed me by the arm, pushing me against the blackboard, shouting, "Why are you always mocking us? You have no reason to do this."

I said, "Sure I do. You were making fun of him. You embarrassed him. He needs strengthening, not weakening. You hurt him. I did not hurt you."

He twisted my arm and pushed real hard. I turned around and hit him in the face, giving him a bloody nose. After that I ran out of the room, slamming the door behind me. He and I went to Sister Bernard's office. I told her, "Today I quit school. I'm not taking any more of this, none of this shit anymore. None of this treatment. Better give me my diploma. I can't waste any more time on you people."

Sister Bernard looked at me for a long, long time. She said, "All right, Mary Ellen, go home today. Come back in a few days and get your diploma." And that was that. Oddly enough, that priest turned out okay. He taught a class in grammar, orthography, composition, things like that. I think he wanted more respect in class. He was still young and unsure of himself. But I was in there too long. I didn't feel like hearing it. Later he became a good friend of the Indians, a personal friend of myself and my husband. He stood up for us during Wounded Knee and after. He stood up to his superiors, stuck his neck way out, became a real people's priest. He even learned our language. He died prematurely of cancer. It is not only the good Indians who die young, but the good whites, too. It is the timid ones who know how to take care of themselves who grow old. I am still grateful to that priest for what he did for us later and for the quarrel he picked with me—or did I pick it with him?—because it ended a situation which had become unendurable for me. The day of my fight with him was my last day in school.

49

PREPARING FOR POWER
Cultural Capital and Curricula in America's Elite Boarding Schools

PETER W. COOKSON, JR.
CAROLINE HODGES PERSELL

In addition to teaching individuals life skills, such as reading, writing, and critical thinking, another important function of education is to help select the future employment of students. Thus, education tracks and trains people for certain jobs. Many jobs in society are based on *credentialing* or the requirement of certain educational degrees in order to be hired and promoted. Schools also provide the valued *cultural capital* of the middle and upper classes. This knowledge of cultural background, norms, and skills of the upper classes enables students to obtain higher socioeconomic statuses. This reading by Peter W. Cookson, Jr., and Caroline Hodges Persell examines the cultural capital students gain in elite boarding schools.

Borrowing from the British, early American headmasters and teachers advocated a boarding school curriculum that was classical, conservative, and disciplined. It wasn't until the latter part of the nineteenth century that such "soft" subjects as English, history, and mathematics were given a place beside Latin, Greek, rhetoric, and logic in the syllabus. It was the early schoolmasters' belief that young minds, especially boys' minds, if left to their own devices, were undisciplined, even anarchic. The only reliable antidote to mental flabbiness was a rigorous, regular regime of mental calisthenics. A boy who could not flawlessly recite long Latin passages was required to increase his mental workouts. Classical languages were to the mind what cold showers were to the body: tonics against waywardness.

Girls, with some exceptions, were not thought of as needing much mental preparation for their future roles as wives and mothers. Their heads were best left uncluttered by thought; too much book learning could give a girl ideas about independence. Besides, the great majority of them were not going on to college, where even more classical languages were required.

As an intellectual status symbol, the classical curriculum helped distinguish gentlemen from virtually everyone else and thus defined the difference between an "educated" man and an untutored one, as well as the difference between high culture and popular culture. Such a division is critical to exclude nonmembers from groups seeking status. For a long time a classical curriculum was the only path to admission to a university, as Harvard and many others required candidates to demonstrate proficiency in Latin and Greek (Levine 1980). Thus, the curriculum of boarding schools has long served both social and practical functions.

Culture, much like real estate or stocks, can be considered a form of capital. As the French scholars Pierre Bourdieu and Jean-Claude Passeron (1977) have indicated, the accumulation of cultural capital can be used to reinforce class differences. Cultural capital is socially created: What constitutes the "best in western civilization" is not arrived at by happenstance, nor was it decided upon by public election. The more deeply embedded the values, the more likely they will be perceived as value free and universal.

Thus curriculum is the nursery of culture and the classical curriculum is the cradle of high culture. The definition of what is a classical course of study has evolved, of course, since the nineteenth century. Greek and Latin are no longer required subjects in most schools—electives abound. But the disciplined and trained mind is still the major objective of the boarding school curriculum.

> The Groton curriculum is predicated on the belief that certain qualities of mind are of major importance: precise and articulate communication; the ability to compute accurately and to reason quantitatively; a grasp of scientific approaches to problem-solving; an understanding of the cultural, social, scientific, and political background of Western civilization; and the ability to reason carefully and logically and to think imaginatively and sensitively. Consequently the School puts considerable emphasis on language, mathematics, science, history, and the arts. (*Groton School* 1981–82, p. 15)

The contrast between the relatively lean curricula of many public schools and the abundant courses offered by boarding schools is apparent. In catalogues of the boarding school's academic requirements, courses are usually grouped by subject matter, and at the larger schools course listings and descriptions can go on for several dozen pages. Far from sounding dreary, the courses described in most catalogues are designed to whet the intellectual appetite. Elective subjects in particular have intriguing titles such as "Hemingway: The Man and His Work," "Varieties of the Poetic Experience," "Effecting Political Change," "Rendezvous with Armageddon," and for those with a scientific bent, "Vertebrate Zoology" and "Mammalian Anatomy and Physiology."

Boarding school students are urged to read deeply and widely. A term course on modern American literature may include works from as many as 10 authors, ranging from William Faulkner to Jack Kerouac. Almost all schools offer a course in Shakespeare in which six or seven plays will be read.

In history, original works are far more likely to be assigned than excerpts from a textbook. A course on the presidency at one school included the following required readings: Rossiter, *The American Presidency*; Hofstadter, *The American Political Tradition*; Hargrove, *Presidential Leadership*; Schlesinger, *A Thousand Days*; Kearns, *Lyndon Johnson and the American Dream*; and White, *Breach of Faith*. Courses often use a college-level text, such as Garraty's *The American Nation* or Palmer's *A History of the Modern World*. Economic history is taught as well—in one school we observed a discussion of the interplay between politics and the depression of 1837—and the idea that there are multiple viewpoints in history is stressed. It is little wonder that many prep school graduates find their first year of college relatively easy.

An advanced-placement English class uses a collection of *The Canterbury Tales* by Geoffrey Chaucer that includes the original middle English on the left page and a modern English translation on the right. An advanced third-year French course includes three or four novels as well as two books of grammar and readings. Even social science courses require a great deal of reading. In a course called "An Introduction to Human Behavior" students are assigned 11 texts including works from B. F. Skinner, Sigmund Freud, Erich Fromm, Jean Piaget, and Rollo May.

Diploma requirements usually include: four years of English, three years of math, three years in one foreign language, two years of history or social science, two years of laboratory science, and one year of art. Many schools require a year of philosophy or religion and also may have such noncredit diploma requirements as four years of physical education, a library skills course, introduction to computers, and a seminar on human sexuality. On average, American public high school seniors take one year less English and math, and more than a year less foreign language than boarding school students (Coleman, Hoffer, and Kilgore 1982, p. 90). Moreover, in the past two decades there has been a historical decline in the number of academic subjects taken by students in the public schools (Adelman 1983).

Because success on the Scholastic Aptitude Test is so critical for admission to a selective college, it is not uncommon for schools to offer English review classes that are specifically designed to help students prepare for the tests. Most schools also offer tutorials and remedial opportunities for students who are weak in a particular subject. For foreign students there is often a course in English as a second language.

As the arts will be part of the future roles of boarding school students, the music, art, and theater programs at many schools are enriching, with special courses such as "The Sound and Sense of Music," "Advanced Drawing," and "The Creative Eye in Film." Student art work is usually on display, and almost every school will produce several full-length plays each year, for example, *Arsenic and Old Lace, A Thurber Carnival, Dracula,* and *The Mousetrap.*

Music is a cherished tradition in many boarding schools, in keeping with their British ancestry. The long-standing "Songs" at Harrow, made famous because Winston Churchill liked to return to them for solace during World War II, are a remarkable display of school solidarity. All 750 boys participate, wearing identical morning coats with tails. Every seat is filled in the circular, sharply tiered replica of Shakespeare's Globe Theater as the boys rise in unison, their voices resonating in the rotunda.

The belief that a well-rounded education includes some "hands-on" experience and travel runs deep in the prep view of learning. Virtually every boarding school provides opportunities for their students to study and work off campus. As volunteers, Taft students, for instance, can "tutor on a one-to-one basis in inner-city schools in Waterbury, act as teachers' helpers in Waterbury Public Schools and work with retarded children at Southbury Training School." They can also work in convalescent homes, hospitals, and day-care centers, and act as "apprentices to veterinarians and help with Girl Scout troops" (*Taft* 1981–82, p. 21). At the Ethel Walker School in Connecticut, girls can go on whale watches, trips to the theater, or work in the office of a local politician. The Madeira School in Virginia has a co-curriculum program requiring students to spend every Wednesday participating in volunteer or internship situations.

Generally speaking, the schools that take the position that manual labor and firsthand experience are good for the soul as well as the mind and body, are more progressive in orientation than other schools. At the Putney School every student has to take a tour of duty at the cow barn, starting at 5:30 A.M. In their own words, "Putney's work program is ambitious. We grow much of our own food, mill our own lumber, pick up our own trash, and have a large part in building our buildings. . . . Stoves won't heat until wood is cut and split" (*The Putney School* 1982, p. 3).

Various styles of student-built structures dot the campus of the Colorado Rocky Mountain School, and at the tiny Midland School in California, there is no service staff, except for one cook. When the water pump breaks, faculty and students fix it, and when buildings are to be built, faculty and students pitch in. "We choose to live simply, to distinguish between our needs and our wants, to do without many of the comforts which often obscure the significant things in life" (*Midland School* 1983, p. 1). The creed of self-reliance is reenacted every day at Midland. When a trustee offered to buy the school a swimming pool, he was turned down. Lounging around a pool is not part of the Midland philosophy.

Travel is very much part of the prep way of life and is continued right through the school year. Not only are semesters or a year abroad (usually in France or Spain) offered, but at some of the smaller schools, everyone goes on an extensive field trip. Every March at the Verde Valley School in Arizona the students travel to "Hopi, Navajo and Zuni reservations, to small villages in northern Mexico, to isolated Spanish-American communities in northern New Mexico and to ethnic neighborhoods of Southwestern cities. They live with native families, attend and teach in schools, work on ranches, and participate in the lives of the host families and their communities" (*Verde Valley School* 1982–83, p. 9). Not all boarding schools, of course, place such a high value on rubbing shoulders with the outside world. At most of the academies, entrepreneurial, and girls' schools the emphasis is on service rather than sharing.

While boarding schools may vary in their general philosophy, the actual curricula do not widely differ. The pressures exerted on prep schools to get their students into good colleges means that virtually all students must study the same core subjects. Although not quick to embrace educational innovation, many boarding schools have added computers to their curricula. This has no doubt been encouraged by announcements by a number of Ivy League and other elite colleges that they want their future applicants to be "computer literate." While people at most boarding schools, or anywhere else for that matter, are not quite sure what is meant by computer literate, they are trying to provide well-equipped computer rooms and teachers who can move their students toward computer proficiency.

For students who have particular interests that cannot be met by the formal curriculum, almost all schools offer independent study, which gives students and teachers at boarding schools a great deal of intellectual flexibility. At Groton, for example, independent study can cover a diverse set of topics including listening to the works of Wagner, conducting a scientific experiment, or studying a special aspect of history.

The boarding school curriculum offers students an abundant buffet of regular course work, electives, volunteer opportunities, travel, and independent study, from which to choose a course of study. By encouraging students to treat academic work as an exciting challenge rather than just a job to be done, the prep schools not only pass on culture but increase their students' competitive edge in the scramble for admission to selective colleges.

The Importance of Sports

Even the most diligent student cannot sit in classrooms all day, and because the prep philosophy emphasizes the whole person, boarding schools offer an impressive array of extracurricular activities, the most important of which is athletics. At progressive schools, the competitive nature of sport is deemphasized. The "afternoon out-of-door program" at Putney, for example, allows for a wide variety of outdoor activities that are noncompetitive; in fact, "skiing is the ideal sport for Putney as one may ski chiefly to enjoy himself, the air, the snow" (*The Putney School* 1982, p. 15).

Putney's sense that sport should be part of a communion with nature is not shared by most other schools, however. At most prep schools sport is about competition, and even more important, about winning. An athletically powerful prep school will field varsity, junior varsity, and third-string teams in most major sports. A typical coed or boys' school will offer football, soccer, cross-country, water polo, ice hockey, swimming, squash, basketball, wrestling, winter track, gymnastics, tennis, golf, baseball, track, and lacrosse. For the faint-hearted there are alternative activities such as modern dance, cycling, tai chi, yoga, ballet, and for the hopelessly unathletic, a "fitness" class. A truly traditional prep school will also have crew like their English forebears at Eton and Harrow. Certain schools have retained such British games as "Fives," but most stop short of the mayhem masquerading as a game called rugby.

Prep teams compete with college freshmen teams, other prep teams, and occasionally with public schools, although public school competitors are picked with care. Not only is there the possible problem of humiliation on the field, there is the even more explosive problem of fraternization in the stands when prep meets townie. Some schools, known as "jock" schools, act essentially as farm teams for Ivy League colleges, consistently providing them with athletes who have been polished by the prep experience. Many prep schools take public high school graduates for a postgraduate year, as a way of adding some size and weight to their football teams.

Prep girls also love sports; they participate as much as the boys, often in the same sports, and with as much vigor. A girls' field hockey game between Exeter and Andover is as intense as when the varsity football teams clash. Horseback riding at girls' schools is still popular; a number of the girls go on to ride in the show or hunt circuit. Unlike many of the girls in public schools, the boarding-school girl is discouraged from being a spectator. Loafing is considered to be almost as bad for girls as it is for boys.

During the school year the halls of nearly all prep schools are decorated with either bulletins of sporting outcomes or posters urging victory in some upcoming game. Pep rallies are common, as are assemblies when awards are given and competitive spirit is eulogized. Often the whole school will be bussed to an opponent's campus if the game is considered to be crucial or if the rivalry is long-standing.

Alumni return to see games, and there are frequent contests between alumni and varsity teams. Because preps retain the love of fitness and sports, it is not uncommon for the old warriors to give the young warriors a thrashing. Similarly, the prep life also invariably includes ritual competitions between, say, the girls' field hockey team and a pick-up faculty team.

Nowhere is the spirit of victory more pronounced than on the ice of the hockey rink. Few public schools can afford a hockey rink so prep schools can attract the best players without much competition. Some prep schools import a few Canadians each year to fill out the roster. Speed, strength, endurance, and fearlessness are the qualities that produce winning hockey and more than one freshman team from an Ivy League college has found itself out-skated by a prep team. Whatever else may be, in Holden Caulfield's term, "phony" about prep schools, sports are for real. This emphasis on sport is not without its critics. At the Harrow School in London, the new headmaster, who was an all-England rugby player, has begun a program to reward artistic and musical prowess as well as athletic and academic skills.

The athletic facilities at prep schools are impressive, and at the larger schools, lavish. Acres and acres of playing fields, scores of tennis courts, one or more gyms, a hockey rink, a golf course, swimming pools, squash courts, workout rooms—all can be found on many prep school campuses. Generally, the facilities are extremely well maintained. The equipment most preps use is the best, as are the uniforms. One boy described how "when your gym clothes get dirty, you simply turn them in at the locker room for a fresh set." The cost of all this, of course, is extraordinary, but considered necessary, because excellence in sport is part of the definition of a gentleman or gentlewoman.

The pressure for athletic success is intense on many campuses, and a student's, as well as a school's, social standing can ride on the narrow margin between victory and defeat. Perhaps because of this, schools generally take great pains to play schools of their own size and social eliteness. A study of who plays whom among prep schools reveals that schools will travel great distances, at considerable expense, to play other prep schools whose students and traditions are similar to their own.

Extracurriculars and Preparation for Life

Not all prep school extracurricular activities require sweating, however. Like public school students, preps can work on the school newspaper or yearbook, help to organize a dance, or be part of a blood donor drive, and are much more likely than their public school counterparts to be involved in such activities. For example, one in three boarding school students is involved in student government compared to one in five public school students, and two in five are involved in the school newspaper or yearbook compared to one in five. This evidence is consistent with other research. Coleman, Hoffer, and Kilgore (1982) found that private school students participate more in extracurricular activities than do public school students. The fact that more boarding school students than public school students are involved in activities provides additional opportunities for them to practice their verbal, interpersonal, and leadership skills.

The catalogue of clubs at prep schools is nearly endless. The opportunity for students to develop special nonacademic interests is one of the qualities of life at prep schools that distinguishes them from many public schools. Special interest clubs for chess, sailing, bowling, or gun clubs are popular at boys' schools. One elite boys' school has a "war games" club. As the boys at this school are feverishly calculating their country's next strategic arms move, the girls in a Connecticut school are attending a meeting of Amnesty International. Girls, in general, tend to spend their off hours studying the gentler arts such as gourmet cooking and art history. One girls' school has a club with a permanent service mission to the governor's office.

At some schools students can learn printing, metalwork, or woodworking. The shop for the latter at Groton is amply equipped and much of the work turned out by the students is of professional quality. The less traditional schools offer clubs for vegetarian cooking, weaving, quilting, folk music, and—in subtle juxtaposition to the Connecticut girls' school—international cooking. At western schools, the horse still reigns supreme and many students spend endless hours riding, training, cleaning, and loving their own horse, or a horse they have leased from the school.

With the prep emphasis on music, choirs, glee clubs, madrigals, chamber music groups, as well as informal ensembles are all given places to practice. Most schools also have individual practice rooms, and like athletic teams, many prep musicians travel to other schools for concerts and performances.

Some schools offer a five-week "Winterim," during which students and faculty propose and organize a variety of off- and on-campus activities and studies. Such a program breaks the monotony of the usual class routine in the middle of winter, a season teachers repeatedly told us was the worst time at boarding school. It also enables students and faculty to explore new areas or interests in a safe way, that is, without grades.

In prep schools there is a perceived need for students to exercise authority as apprentice leaders early in their educational careers. The tradition of delegating real authority to students has British roots, where head boys and prefects have real power within the public schools. Head boys can discipline other boys by setting punishments and are treated by headmaster and housemasters alike as a part of the administration. In the United States, student power is generally more limited, although at the progressive schools students can be quite involved in the administrative decision-making process.

Virtually all prep schools have a student government. The formal structure of government usually includes a student body president, vice president, treasurer, secretary, class presidents, and dorm prefects, representatives, or "whips," as they are called at one school. Clubs also have presidents and there are always committees to be headed. Some schools have student-faculty senates and in schools like Wooster, in Connecticut, students are expected to play a major part in the disciplinary system. An ambitious student can obtain a great deal of experience in committee work, developing transferable skills for later leadership positions in finance, law, management, or politics.

The office of student body president or head prefect is used by the administration primarily as an extension of the official school culture, and most of the students who fill these offices are quite good at advancing the school's best public relations face. A successful student body president, like a good head, is artful in developing an easy leadership style, which is useful because he or she is in a structural political dilemma. Elected by the students but responsible to the school administration, the student politician is a classic go-between, always running the danger of being seen as "selling out" by students and as "uncooperative" by the administration. Occasionally students rebel against too much pandering to the administration and elect a rebel leader, who makes it his or her business to be a thorn in the side of the administration. A number of heads and deans of students watch elections closely, because if elections go "badly" it could mean a difficult year for them.

The actual content of real power varies by school. At some, authority is more apparent than real; at others, student power can affect important school decisions. At Putney, the "Big Committee" is composed of the school director, student leaders, and teachers. The powers of the Big Committee are laid out in the school's constitution, and students at Putney have real input into the decision-making process. At the Thacher School in California, the Student Leadership Council, which is composed of the school chairman, presidents of the three lower classes, and head prefects, is not only responsible for student activities and events, but also grants funds to groups who petition for special allocations. The power of the purse is learned early in the life of a prep school student. At the Westtown School in Pennsylvania, the student council arrives at decisions not by voting yea or nay, "but by following the Quaker custom of arriving at a 'sense of the meeting'" (*Westtown School* 1982–83, p. 25).

Not all students, of course, participate in school politics; it may well be that many of the students most admired by their peers never run, or never would run, for a political position. The guerrilla leaders who emerge and flourish in the student underlife—or counterculture—may have far greater real power than the "superschoolies" that tend to get elected to public office.

In most coeducational schools boys tend to monopolize positions of power. The highest offices are generally held by boys; girls are found in the vice presidential and secretarial positions. Politics can be important to prep families and we suspect that a number of prep boys arrive at boarding school with a good supply of political ambition. One of the reasons advanced in support of all-girls' schools is that girls can gain important leadership experience there.

Some schools try to capture what they see as the best aspects of single-sex and coed schools. They do this by having boys and girls elect distinct school leaders, by having certain customs, places, and events that they share only with members of their own sex, and by having classes, certain other activities, and social events be coeducational. These schools, often called co-ordinate schools, see themselves as offering the chance to form strong single-sex bonds, to build self-confidence in adolescents, and to provide experience in working and relating to members of both sexes. Girls at coed schools more generally are likely to say they think in 10 years they will find the social skills they learned to be the most valuable part of their boarding-school experience.

Learning by Example

Part of the social learning students obtain is exposure to significant public personalities. Virtually all the schools have guest speaker programs in which well-known people can be seen and heard. Some of the speakers that have appeared at Miss Porter's School in the last several years include Alex Haley, author; Russell Baker, humorist; Arthur Miller, playwright; and Dick Gregory, comedian. At the boys' schools there is a tendency to invite men who are successful in politics and journalism. Recent speakers at the Hill School include James A. Baker III, Secretary of the Treasury (Hill class of 1948); James Reston, columnist; Frank Borman, astronaut and president of Eastern Airlines; and William Proxmire, United States senator (Hill class of 1934).

Inviting successful alumni to return for talks is one of the ways boarding schools can pass on a sense of the school's efficacy. Throughout the year panels, assemblies, and forums are organized for these occasions. Often the alumni speakers will also have informal sessions with students, visit classrooms, and stay for lunch, tea, or supper.

In keeping with cultural environments of prep schools, especially the select 16 schools, professional musicians, actors, and dancers are regularly invited to perform. Art and sculpture exhibits are common and some schools, such as Andover and Exeter, have permanent art galleries. The art at prep schools is generally either original works by artists such as Toulouse-Lautrec, Matisse, or Daumier, or the work of established contemporary artists such as Frank Stella, who graduated from Andover. At a large school there may be so much cultural activity that it is unnecessary to leave campus for any kind of high cultural event.

Those who come to elite boarding schools to talk or perform are the makers of culture. For adolescents seeking to be the best, these successful individuals give them a sense of importance and empowerment. All around them are the symbols of their special importance—in Groton's main hallway hangs a personal letter from Ronald Reagen to the headmaster, reminding the students that Groton "boasts a former President of the United States and some of America's finest statesmen." Five or six books a year will be published by a school's alumni; Exeter in particular has many alumni authors,

including James Agee, Nathaniel G. Benchley, John Knowles, Dwight Mac-
donald, Jr., Arthur M. Schlesinger, Jr., Sloan Wilson, and Gore Vidal. Roger L.
Stevens, Alan Jay Lerner, and Edward Albee are all Choate-Rosemary Hall
alumni, adding luster to a theater program that trains many professional actresses and actors. A student at an elite school is part of a world where success is expected, and celebrity and power are part of the unfolding of life.
Not every school is as culturally rich as the elite eastern prep schools, but in
the main, most schools work hard to develop an appreciation for high culture. At the Orme School in Arizona, a week is set aside each year in which
the whole school participates in looking at art, watching art being made, and
making art.

Nowhere is the drive for athletic, cultural, and academic excellence more
apparent than in the awards, honors, and prizes that are given to outstanding teams or students at the end of each year. Sporting trophies are often
large silver cups with the names of annual champions engraved on several
sides. At some schools the triumphs have come with enough regularity to
warrant building several hundred yards of glass casing to hold the dozens of
medals, trophies, and other mementos that are the victors' spoils. Pictures of
past winning teams, looking directly into the camera, seem frozen in time.

Academic prizes tend to be slightly less flashy but no less important.
Much like British schoolmasters, American schoolmasters believe in rewarding excellence, so most schools give a number of cultural, service, and academic prizes at the end of each year. There is usually at least one prize in
each academic discipline, as well as prizes for overall achievement and effort. There are service prizes for dedicated volunteers, as well as debating
and creative writing prizes. Almost all schools have cum laude and other
honor societies.

Sitting through a graduation ceremony at a boarding school can be an
endurance test—some schools give so many prizes that one could fly from
New York to Boston and back in the time it takes to go from the classics prize
to the prize for the best woodworking or weaving project. But of course, the
greatest prize of all is graduation, and more than a few schools chisel, paint,
etch, or carve the names of the graduates into wood, stone, or metal to im-
mortalize their passage from the total institution into the world.

REFERENCES

Adleman, Clifford. 1983. "Devalutaion, Diffusion and the College Connection: A
  Study of High School Transcripts, 1964–1981. "Washington, DC: National Com-
  mission on Excellence in Education.
Bourdieu, Pierre and Jean-Claude Passeron. 1977. *Reproduction: In Education, Society,
  and Culture.* Beverly Hills, CA: Sage.
Coleman, James S., Thomas Hoffer, and Sally Kilgore. 1982. *High School Achievement.*
  New York: Basic Books, p. 90.
Levine, Steven B. 1980. "The Rise of American Boarding Schools and the Develop-
  ment of a National Upper Class." *Social Problems* 28:63–94.

50

KICKING BACK AT "RAGING HIGH"

WAYNE S. WOODEN

As an effective socializing agent, the institution of education should help us develop self-confidence and teach us how to get along with others. Unfortunately, many students slip through the school system without ever being acknowledged as unique human beings. Instead, students find their identities through the social groups to which they belong in school. This reading by Wayne S. Wooden examines the social cliques in four high schools. These cliques reflect the social hierarchies that form in every high school based on race, gender, and other social characteristics. Membership in these social cliques not only modifies the everyday life of the students at school but also has an enormous impact on the self-esteem of individuals.

"Truancy Soaring: Why Go to Class When Mall Beckons?"

On a typical day last month, nearly one of every three Sacramento County high school students—more than 10,000—missed one or more academic classes.

The problem is reaching crisis proportions at some schools, where nearly half the students skip class each day, *The Sacramento Bee* learned by examining attendance records in the county's five largest school districts.

"It's easy enough—you just walk out," said Rachel, a 15-year-old sophomore at McClatchy High School. "They have hall monitors, but if you skip every day, you know what you're doing. It's easy to get away with it."

Rachel said most of her classmates skip about 10 periods a week. Typically, they forge their parents' signatures on notes to get back into class, she said.[1]

. . .

According to material collected by a gang prevention and intervention project located in Southern California, Turning Point, the major key to resolving the "social ills" of our junior high and high school campuses is to focus on how to improve and bolster each student's self-esteem.

. . .

Students who hold themselves in low self-esteem frequently resort to antisocial and delinquent behavior. When such behaviors are expressed within the school context, as they often are, they can take many forms. On the personal level, these frustrated students frequently engage in acts of truancy; experience despondency or depression; resort to drug and/or alcohol abuse; attempt or commit suicide; show disrespect for their parents, teachers, and authorities; become disruptive and inattentive in class; and/or fail to perform up to their academic potential.

. . .

Social Cliques and Youth Culture

The modern high school campus is frequently the locale where teenagers are most critically judged and evaluated by their peers. It is in high school that students establish a social hierarchy. One's position within this hierarchy plays a major role in shaping one's self-esteem. Popular students who are placed high in the status hierarchy frequently express high self-esteem, while less popular students who are placed lower on the scale often express lower self-esteem.

The positioning of one's *clique*, or social group, relative to the other cliques and students on campus also affects self-esteem. Not fitting in with any clique is bound to produce unpleasant experiences. Being identified with a less popular clique is apt to negatively affect a youngster who may have a fragile ego.

Several researchers have looked at the impact of cliques on adolescent behavior. Cliques—defined as small, exclusive groups made up of three or more individuals who share similar interests and strong loyalties toward one another—provide their members with a refuge from the pressures of home and school.[2]

As early as age eight, same sex, close-knit groups or cliques take shape. During the teens, almost all of both sexes become involved in cliques. A clique's members are usually of similar social status, although someone of a different background may be included if they share attributes such as attractiveness, personality traits, or athletic prowess that are highly valued by that particular clique.[3]

All adolescent groups, including cliques, constitute the so-called peer or *youth culture,* which presumably possesses a distinct social identity. One observer views the youth culture as not always explicitly anti-adult, but as belligerently nonadult. This peer culture is usually independent of the larger society and has its own distinctive values and behaviors.[4]

Youth culture in general serves several functions. It helps the adolescent define her or his values and behaviors. Most youths today do not follow in the footsteps of their parents. They face an array of alternatives concerning career choices, moral codes, and lifestyles. As a result, they find refuge in their own culture until they have developed their own identity. They use their peer group to sort themselves out.

One sociologist sees cultural differences in this pattern, with adolescent peer groups assuming more importance in some societies than in others. Such groups are most important in nations, like the United States, where the family unit fails to adequately meet youths' social needs due, in part, to parents and other family members having their own set of priorities.[5]

Although not all sociologists are in agreement about whether there is such a thing as a "common" youth culture, most observers of contemporary youths would concur that there are distinctive youth styles that differentiate the various peer groups. They would also concur that youth cultures share values that distinguish them from adult culture. As one observer of youth cultures noted, "(They) can be defined only in terms of distinctive life styles which are to a great extent self-generated and autonomous."[6]

Several people have commented on the various factors that encourage the growth of youth cultures. One has argued that the affluence of Western society accounts for these distinctive youth styles:

> Only a wealthy society can afford a large leisure class of teenagers not yet in the labor force but already consumers on a large scale. What adolescents earn, besides what they succeed in wresting from their elders, they spend chiefly on themselves, for such items as records, cars, travel, clothes, cosmetics, and recreational paraphernalia. Meanwhile, this same affluence demands, for its support, a high level of training which itself prolongs the transitional period to adulthood.[7]

Up to age 12, and after age 19, parents generally have more influence on their offspring than peers. But from ages 12 through 18, what peers say often matters more than what parents say.

Not all teenagers participate equally in the youth culture. In fact, the vast majority of youths are basically "conformist-oriented," to apply one of the five cultural adaptations observed by Robert K. Merton.[8] Such youths shy away from assuming a "total identity" or "master status" of any particular youth style—whether that be an identity of a punk rocker, a heavy metaler, or a racist skinhead. Instead, conformists opt to be just the typical, average teenager who, although affiliating with the general youth culture because of their age, choose not to affiliate with any one distinctive youth culture.

The other adaptations according to Merton include innovators, ritualists, retreatists, and rebels. Such a typology is useful in examining the array of youth styles that will be discussed in this [reading]. In fact, punk rockers, for instance, can be categorized as innovators in that from their perspective they see themselves as trying to change and improve their social environment. On the other hand, others might categorize their behavior as one of the other three groups: ritualists in that they mimic the behavior and dress of other youths like themselves; retreatists because many have seemed to drop out of society; or rebels in that some espouse anarchy and civil disobedience.

. . .

Clique Structures in Four Suburban High Schools

Patusa High School was located in a small-town, middle-American, rural setting. For the purposes of this study, I decided to examine the teenage clique structures of several suburban high schools located in the Southern California area. Of particular interest in this analysis would be the following five issues:

1. Were the teenage status hierarchies similar in each of these Southern California high schools, including the terminologies used to distinguish one social clique from the other?
2. Were the status hierarchies in the Southern California schools similar to those found in Patusa High School, or were there differences in the rank ordering of the different youth groups because of differences in geographic region or locale?
3. What was the demeanor of some of those youths at the top of the clique structure in terms of how they handled their special status, and how they treated some female students?
4. How did those students who were part of less-popular cliques feel about their position, and how were they treated by the other cliques in their school?
5. And could the various youth cultures found in these Southern California suburban high schools be grouped according to the four subcultures observed by Trow and Clark in their study of collegiate subcultures?

Of the many studies of local high schools submitted to me by my students, four "typical" suburban high schools were selected for comparative analysis with the Patusa study. With the assistance of several of my university students who had attended these particular high schools as recently as three years preceding the analysis, the clique structures and status hierarchies of the four high schools were examined. The study analyzed the senior yearbooks of each of these four schools. For purposes of discussion, each graduating senior was classified into his or her respective social clique and group.

All four of the high schools examined shared similar characteristics. They were large, cosmopolitan, and located in the suburban areas that served as "feeder schools" to California State Polytechnic University (Cal Poly) in Pomona. The students who attended these high schools were predominantly Caucasian and from middle- to upper-middle-class socioeconomic backgrounds. As part of the research, each of the four schools was visited, and the clique structure was discussed with representatives of the school administration such as senior counselors who commented on, and validated, the findings.

Similarity of Status Hierarchies

As the summary table, "Southern California High School Clique Structures," depicts, the status hierarchy of cliques was generally similar in each of the four high schools analyzed, although the students in the schools often used different names or terminology to distinguish one social clique from the other. Each group is listed in *descending* order of popularity [see Table 50.1].

High School Case Study 1

Jocks   The jocks at this school consisted of boys who actively participated in many of the sports on campus. They strutted the campus in letterman jackets to prove to all other students their athletic ability. Most were self-centered and egotistical. At parties jocks could be seen participating in beer-drinking contests and smoking marijuana. They had no problems finding dates, and they tended to choose cheerleaders as their girlfriends. For jocks, high school was fun—a positive part of life, increasing their self-image.

Cheerleaders   The cheerleaders were attractive, school spirited, and popular. They were constantly being elected homecoming and prom queens. Unlike the jocks, the cheerleaders acknowledged other students who were not as popular, wanting to be everyone's idol and friend. They had high self-esteem and confidence.

Tweakies   The tweakies were boys who had an extremely "laid back" attitude toward school. They often skipped class to go to the beach, and they consumed alcohol whenever they had the chance. Surfboards and girls were more important than school. They had their own slang, including words such as "bogus" (terrible), "righteous" (out of sight, the best), "gnarly" (cool), and "sweet" (perfect). They wore baggy clothing and sandals.

TABLE 50.1   Southern California High School Clique Structures

1	2	3	4
Jocks	Jocks	Jocks	Jocks
Cheerleaders	Socs	Partiers	Surfers
Tweakies	Cheerleaders	Cheerleaders/ Barbie dolls	Trendies/Preppies
Trendies	Death rockers	Preppies	Punks/Metalers
Drama freaks	Cha-Chas	Burners	Death rockers/ Dance clubbers
Bandos	Brains	Band members	
Smacks	Metal heads	Geeks/Nerds	Cholos
Dirtbags	Asians	Brains	Brains
Sluts			
Punks			
Loners			

Trendies   The trendies were desperate to fit in and spent their time shopping for the latest trends in clothing. They constantly changed their looks in hopes of finding a style that would make them popular. To be labeled a "trendie" was not good. It meant that you were "hard-up" for friends and would do anything, other than be yourself, to become popular.

Drama Freaks   The drama freaks were students who were completely engrossed in acting. Constantly practicing for upcoming plays and musicals, they were viewed by others as an extremely loud and obnoxious group. The majority of students considered "drama freaks" to be fake. They dressed in high fashion, and the girls wore brightly colored makeup. Many of them were excellent actors, but they could never draw a distinct line between fantasy and reality.

Bandos   The bandos were similar to the drama freaks, but instead of being centered on acting, they were centered on band. Students viewed them as "nerds" and thought of them as "uncool." Bandos spent the majority of their time practicing their instruments and were never seen at any of the weekend parties. They were very conservative in dress.

Smacks   The smacks were students who had extremely high GPAs. They were overly friendly to all teachers and always had their hands up in class. They spent many hours studying while their peers were shopping, partying, or playing sports. Only those students who were not popular were labeled smacks. A few students in the popular cliques who received high grades were not labeled as smacks.

Dirtbags   The dirtbags came from middle-class families, but they were considered the "lowlifes" of the campus. They roamed around school constantly brushing long hair out of their eyes. They were always skipping school to smoke marijuana or party at a friend's house. Many of the dirtbags were enrolled in remedial level classes, and many were held back from graduating or dropped out because of failing grades. Their typical dress consisted of heavy-metal-band T-shirts and jeans.

Sluts   Some girls were labeled sluts because of their provocative clothing, such as tight jeans, high heels, and no undergarments. They usually had bleached hair and wore a lot of makeup. They were popular merely for sexual purposes. They loved to party and had sex with many fellow male students.

Punks   The punks dressed in torn jeans, combat boots, and wore Mohawks. They were harmless, merely making a statement of their individuality. Many of them were intelligent and enrolled in honors classes. They could be found on the outskirts of campus. Fellow students did not see them as a threat and respected their uniqueness.

Loners   The loners had no peer group to socialize with, and they were always in a corner eating lunch or studying. Everyone tended to ignore them, and the loners avoided contact with any of the cliques. They were very introverted and never talked in the classroom.

High School Case Study 2

Jocks   Similar to the status hierarchy of high school 1, the jocks in this second high school were also the most popular students. The jocks were bonded together by their sport and Friday night parties. They always ended the week with a huge party and five kegs of beer. The jocks were very cocky and obnoxious. They were not very successful with grades. In this high school there were no African American or Asian jocks; they were mainly Anglo with some Hispanics.

Socs   The socs were rich, white students and the metal heads' worst enemy. The typical "soc" always wore the latest fashion—Guess jeans, a Gennera shirt, and Reebok tennis shoes—and their hair was always neat and clean with a salon look. The soc community was very exclusive.

Cheerleaders   The cheerleaders were usually part of the soc clique. They were involved in student government and many were scholastically intelligent. They did use drugs but often tried to hide their addiction from parents and teachers.

Death Rockers   The death rockers were bonded together by music, which was generally an alternative Hollywood underground type, bordering on punk rock. Their clique was entirely open and nondiscriminatory. They wore black clothing, black makeup, and dyed black hair. Their appearance challenged, "Like me for who I am, not for where I live or what I wear." They were seldom athletic or extracurricular, but they were very scholastic.

Cha-chas   The cha-chas were mostly Hispanic and wore "GQ"-type outfits. The boys styled their hair in pompadours and the girls teased theirs to resemble a lion's mane. They drove lowered mini-trucks with huge speakers that created incredible bass sounds, listening mainly to rap music. The only sport they played was soccer. Most cha-chas dropped out of school or failed to earn enough credits to graduate.

Brains   This group was bound by the classes they took: math, biology, chemistry, physics, computer programming, and honors courses. They never were invited to any parties and had a reputation for never touching any alcohol or drugs. They did not thrive on fashion and had no set dress code nor hairstyle. They ate lunch in the cafeteria and studied in the library when finished. Tennis was the only sport that a brain would consider playing. They belonged to the science club and the California Scholastic Federation.

Metal Heads   They were the students who idolized Van Halen, bonded in their clique by hard rock music from the 1970s, and heavy metal music from the 1980s. Their dress consisted of old Levi jeans, concert T-shirts, cowboy boots, and long hair. They never denied the use of drugs, and often flaunted it. They did not participate in sports and were not involved in student government. The metal heads did not usually excel scholastically, and the only thing they could see as a profession was stardom in the music industry.

Asians This clique included groups of Vietnamese, Chinese, and Filipinos. Anybody who could not speak their language was automatically rejected by them. They rarely spoke English except to teachers. Asians excelled in math and computer classes, but lacked the verbal ability to excel in the English and social science classes. Because they were different, the jocks and socs ridiculed them no end.

High School Case Study 3

Jocks They were the most predominant clique, and they ran the school. They always knew what was going on and were always at the center of attention. Underclassmen stayed away from jocks because they had the power and ability to force them to do what they wanted. Jocks wore their letterman jackets to remind everyone of their status. They also sometimes received preferential treatment from teachers after intervention by their coach.

Partiers The partiers were mostly in the average track, able to party without sacrificing their grades enough to avoid being placed into any remedial classes. The partiers included a group called the "Lunch Club" who met at lunchtime on every Thursday to drink heavily at the home of a student whose parents were working. To be accepted into this group you needed to play an assortment of drinking games that usually made you sick. They frequented parties during the weekend and always brought alcohol into the football games.

Cheerleaders or Barbie Dolls They were the girls that all the guys desired. When they were not in their cheerleading uniforms, they wore all the fashionable clothes. They partied and hung out with the athletes. If you were seen with a cheerleader, you were perceived to be popular.

Preppies The preppies arrived at school in flashy new sports cars that their parents bought for them soon after they turned 16. They wore plaid pants or shorts, along with an Izod or Polo shirt, penny loafers, and matching argyle socks.

Burners Often placed into the remedial track, burners appeared to be stoned most of the time. This group included the rocker crowd, along with some punkers. Their territory was the school-provided smoking area and a park across the street from school called "Toke" Grove, instead of Oak Grove, because of the constant drug activity there.

Band Members On the surface they were perceived as squares who enjoyed playing music, until sporting events when their playing abilities focused positive attention on them. In actuality, they were the most rowdy group. They had privileges others did not have such as being in parades or going to special events, but they often partied and got into trouble more often than any other group.

Geeks or Nerds   These students were not accepted into any group, so they formed their own. They were often the target of many practical jokes. Geeks retaliated by throwing soda, water balloons, or rotten fruit off the third floor onto targets in the quad below. They were avid members of the Science Fiction Club, and they were also among the few people who actually ate lunch in the cafeteria.

Brains   These were the people who threw the GPA of every class off the scale. Brains usually spent their lunch in one of the labs or in the library working on their homework. They preferred not to socialize with anyone.

High School Case Study 4

Jocks   They were the most influential group on this campus as well. Unfortunately, there were numerous instances in which jocks beat up people at parties or in public places for no apparent reason. The assaults were committed gang-style, with three or four jocks beating up on one person. A few of them were convicted and sent to jail or juvenile hall. It was later learned that their aggressive behavior had been caused by steroid use.

However, most of the jocks were not like this; they were nice "All-American" boys who dated cheerleaders—but were not especially intelligent. Another group of jocks were labeled the "502 Crew." This group prided themselves on their drinking ability. Still another group of jocks, the "TKE" (Tappa Kegga Encinitas), were the rivals of the "502 Crew."

Surfers   They were the second largest group on campus. Surfers tended to keep to themselves merely because their lifestyle was so different. They had their own lingo and a laid-back attitude—"Smoke some pot, drink some beer, kick back, eat some Mexican food, and catch a wave." They were hardly ever at school because they were at the beach.

Trendies or Preppies   These were the mainstream kids. They were the homecoming and prom queens, the associated student body officers, and the student leaders. On the surface, they were every parent's dream. But, they were just as into drugs as everyone else.

Punks and Metalers   They were the devils and did whatever they wanted, not caring who knew. They got wasted before, during, and after school. They sold drugs on campus, and they were often kicked out of their classes and put on detention. In reality, they were not any worse than anyone else. They just chose not to hide their beliefs and attitudes or drug use.

Death Rockers or Dance Clubbers   They were known as the "wall people" because they hung out at the wall in the center of campus. They had a "holier than thou" attitude that turned people off. They were too soft-core for the punks, yet too strange for the mainstream kids. Everyone usually ignored them or teased them.

Cholos No one really knew much about the cholos because there were so few of them at school. Being a white, middle-class suburban high school, these lower-class Mexican Americans did not fit in here. They had their gangs and every once in a while they fought rival gangs. Usually, the only sign of their existence was some occasional graffiti written on the outside school walls or in the bathrooms.

Brains While they occasionally drank, they were the only group on campus who did not do drugs. They were not respected for their high intelligence and grades because they felt that they were superior to everyone else and they formed an elite. Usually, brains are considered nerds and ostracized, but these people ostracized everyone else. They were the most isolated group because they felt they had no need to socialize with others.

Beyond these four "typical" high school clique structures, our study turned up even more groups, often with derogatory names. Some of these other high school cliques included

- ▾ *Black cockroaches:* kids that wore all black such as the death rockers
- ▾ *BAs:* students of Native American ancestry or "bows and arrows"
- ▾ *Shanks:* girlfriends of the heavy metal groups
- ▾ *Motorheads:* guys who drove old Mustangs or Camaros
- ▾ *Water jockeys:* swimmers and water polo players
- ▾ *Kickers:* cowboys and sons of cowboys
- ▾ *The tuna barge:* fast girls
- ▾ *Daddy's girls:* spoiled rich girls
- ▾ *Puppy power:* those freshmen and sophomore males who were popular partly due to being good in sports
- ▾ *The shadows:* students who were into death rock
- ▾ *Disco biscuits:* youths who liked to party and drink and did not care for school at all
- ▾ *Dog squad:* girls on the drill team that wanted to be cheerleaders but were less attractive and less coordinated, and came from lower socioeconomic backgrounds

Finally, one of my students, looking at the entire clique structure at her high school, summed up the various groups in this fashion: "The first clique was the trendy, the second was the 'worker bees,' the third was intelligent, and the last was simply lost."

Implications of the Findings

As the clique summaries indicate, the teenage status hierarchies in these four Southern California suburban high schools were generally similar. However, each high school—apart from the categories for jocks, cheerleaders, and brains—used different terminology to describe the other cliques on campus. Furthermore, in two of the high schools (1 and 3), the terms used to refer to some of the less popular cliques were downright cruel. In the first school, derogatory terms included "smacks," "dirtbags," and "sluts"; and in the third high school, the derogatory terms used were "burners," "geeks," or "nerds."

In most instances, the top clique comprised the jocks, followed closely by either the cheerleaders or the wealthier students who were part of either the socs or the partiers' cliques. The clique structure of Patusa High School, however, also grouped the brains—along with the athletes and student politicos—into the top clique, or youth elites. By contrast, the brains in the Southern California cliques were much lower on the hierarchy. In fact, in two of the four schools, the brains were the *least* popular of the student groupings.

Perhaps the greatest difference, however, between the Southern California schools and Patusa High School was the placement of the religious group. Whereas the religious youths played a major role in the rural, midwestern high school, religious youths were less of a visible, collective group on these suburban, West Coast, public high school campuses.

More similar in status hierarchical placement was the middle-to-lower range positioning of the fashionable freaks (or their equivalents) in the two regions. Likewise, the greasers (and their equivalents) held comparable lower status in both geographical sections (and time periods) of the country.

Of particular interest to this [reading] . . . are these latter two groups at the bottom of the suburban high school clique hierarchies: those fashionable freaks who engaged in the popular youth cultures of the day (such as punkers and metalers), and the modern equivalent of the greasers or teen rebels: taggers, racist skinheads, stoners, and satanists. But, first, let us examine the rowdy and immoral behavior of some of those youths at the top of the high school clique hierarchy: the jocks.

The Leaders of the Pack

As our analysis denotes, there is no doubt that the high school athlete—particularly those males who letter in such prestigious sports as football and basketball—are given special privileges at high school. But what happens when such status goes to their heads and they begin to act indifferently and insensitively toward others in their school and community?

This issue reached national debate with the shocking case of the Spur Posse that unfolded in spring 1993 at Lakewood High School in Southern California, a suburban community located just 30 miles from Cal Poly, Pomona. The nation's news media were quick to focus on this alarming incident. . . .

Perhaps one of the leads from the *Los Angeles Times* best delineates the scope of the problem—"A Stain Spreads in Suburbia: Issues of teen promiscuity, forced sex and parental neglect rock Lakewood, once a bastion of morality. Many see the town and its unrepentant Spur Posse as symbols of a declining America."[9] This comment from an article in *Newsweek* further laments the problem: "Mixed Messages: California's 'Spur Posse' scandal underscores the varying signals society sends teens about sex."[10]

As the *Los Angeles Times* article pointed out:

> All of a sudden, in a glaring media spotlight, Lakewood stands as a reluctant symbol of declining America. Sex sprees, violence and turmoil were about the last things many residents might have expected in the mostly white middle-class community—the prototype of the modern California suburb when it was laid out on nine square miles of sugar beet fields in the early 1950s. What the founders created—a verdant sprawl of parks, ball diamonds and quiet streets—seemed all but immune to today's spreading plague of gang warfare. If any city could make the claim, Lakewood remained Norman Rockwell's America, a family place, as solid a bastion of traditional ethical values as might be found.
>
> But no more. The innocence has given way to hard questions and self-searching. Residents talk fearfully, and some escort their teen-agers to school because of recent street fights and alleged threats of retribution—all involving mostly white youths raised without financial hardship, the products of fine schools. Issues of promiscuity, forced sex and parental neglect are out in the open.[11]

What concerned this community (and the country as a whole) was the disclosure that a clique called the "Spur Posse," most of them top athletes at the local high school, told investigators that they had kept tally or scores of the number of young girls they had bedded. Founded in 1989 as a sort of high school fraternity, many juveniles of the Spur Posse, which counted 20 to 30 boys as members and was named for the San Antonio Spurs professional basketball team, brashly claimed they had sex with as many as 60 girls.

It appears as if one of their main activities was "hooking up," or having sex, with as many girls as possible. Furthermore, because of their local hero status as athletes, the boys took turns having sex with the same girls and later boasted about their conquests, labeling some of the girls as "sluts" for "putting out" for them and their friends.

Eight members of this high school boys' clique were arrested on charges of lewd conduct, unlawful intercourse, and rape allegedly involving seven girls from 10 to 16 years of age. Other charges filed by the authorities included burglary, assault, intimidation of witnesses, and other crimes.

But what also shocked the community was the staunch support these athletes received from other students who denounced the Spurs' accusers as "whores" and "promiscuous girls who got what they asked for." Furthermore, many of the parents of those accused were equally unrepentant. The "boys will be boys" attitude of some of the parents was particularly bothersome. One father *boasted* to reporters about the virility of his three sons, one of whom had been a founder of the Spur Posse.

Teenage sex without responsibility—and without precaution in this time of AIDS and other sexually transmitted diseases—is serious business and foolhardy, to say the least. But in truth, the most striking thing about the Spur Posse, as one reporter noted, was that these juveniles' actions appeared to be more about "scoring" than about sex, about conquest rather than intimacy. Sex, like the athletic field, had become yet another arena in which these teenagers competed.[12]

Such alarming behavior is not just found in Southern California. In October 1993, in Rockville, Maryland, a 16-year-old son of a Washington-area school superintendent was one of five juveniles charged with rape in connection with a gang named the Chronics whose objective was also to have sex with as many girls as possible.[13]

Sex, and sexual promiscuity, has become another fact of adolescent life. And over the past few decades, the age of initial sexual experience has been declining. According to a 1990 survey by the Centers for Disease Control and Prevention, 7 out of 10 high school seniors and over half (54 percent) of ninth through twelfth graders have had intercourse at least once.[14]

The extraordinary attention given the Spur Posse, according to one commentator in the Los Angeles area, was partly due to the increased interest in sexual harassment on campus. Citing figures from a recent magazine survey which found that almost 90 percent of 2,002 high school-age girls had been sexually harassed, he notes that the Lakewood High School incident has been but another case in which girls continue to submit to sexual aggression when they do not want to. And if these girls complain afterward, they are told they wanted it and are mocked by unsympathetic peers.[15]

Sadly, the community of Lakewood was left with many unanswered questions in the wake of the sex scandal and all of the negative publicity that it generated. But as our previous discussion of four other Southern California suburban high schools pointed out, Lakewood High is obviously not alone in these matters.

The Byrds

One student in one of the other schools examined for this study spoke about the top group at her high school, a group known as "The Byrds," of which she was a member.

> The group consisted of approximately twelve guys and eight girls. "The Byrds" were established when we were juniors by four of my guy friends. When I look back now at what The Byrds stood for, it really sickens me. Only the guys could be a "Byrd." It was formed by them, but as they got more and more recognition, the name just became applied to the rest of the group.

The guys in my clique were all drop-dead beautiful. I guess you could say that they were the big men on campus. They were desired by every girl. Well, of course, they knew it, and The Byrds were born.

They were like a nonviolent gang. They had a full initiation ceremony to become a Byrd, and the quest was sex. It was by no means forced sex, and they did not keep tabs either. To become a Byrd, a guy must first be accepted by the rest of the guys. Then the "pledge" would have to find a girl that was willing to have sex with him. The actual initiation ceremony consisted of a Byrd and a pledge having sexual intercourse with two girls at the same time, in the same room. They called this "going side by side." This, of course, was the one aspect of our group that the other girls and I were not proud of. We thought they were so disrespectful.

The girls in the clique were never used in the initiations. We were like their sisters, and were completely off limits to any kind of activities like that. Our clique was special. We were like one big family. We differed from the other cliques in school because ours was not based on superficial friendships and egoism. We looked out for one another and took care of each other. We loved to drive into Los Angeles and the club scene. That was our way of life outside of campus. We were always aware of the latest trends and fashions and were one of the first to sport them at school.

Obviously, the behavior exhibited by certain males of the Lakewood Spur Posse and The Byrds is reprehensible. With the prestige that comes with being a star athlete or a popular student should come the responsibility of setting a good example, of showing respect and restraint. If not their parents, then teachers and other persons in authority have their task cut out for them: to instill in these youngsters some rules of conduct and some good common sense.

Comments by Students Who Have Been Ostracized

Another issue raised in our analysis of the four suburban high school clique structures was the impact on the student of being placed in a less prestigious position or social clique. What pressures were placed on the student to be selected or accepted into, and remain within, a particular social clique?

As the following statements of students who were ostracized by their high school peers indicate, being taunted and experiencing ridicule and discrimination were not pleasant experiences.

One male Asian student recalls his high school days, and explains why he chose to become a punk rocker.

Like many other Vietnamese teenagers, I began to question my identity. Although I had made some American friends in school, they did not treat me the same as others. I was often made fun of because of my slanted eyes and my accent. Feeling left out from everybody, I started to go out frequently and was introduced to other Vietnamese teenagers who were having the same problem. A community of Oriental punkers was formed, and they fought and stole as a daily practice. I joined these teenagers and became a punker. Being one of them gave me a sense of belonging and security. It gave me an identity. In school and at home I paid little attention to anybody.

One of the so-named fashionable freaks in high school recalls her experience.

We were shunned and made fun of. We were called freaks. We were different and not well liked. We were harassed. We had food thrown at us and we were spit upon. The attackers were primarily the jocks. We were treated worse as a group than as individuals. An example of this is how I was treated by my former "friends."

When I was with my fashionable freak friends, my former friends and other cliques ignored me, but if I were alone they would talk to me as if I was still their friend. This angered me and I eventually cut off all ties with those type of people. I think the reason we were treated so badly is because people were jealous and envious of our individuality and they felt threatened by us because we were different.

A female student recalls the process of becoming a member of the punk social clique during high school, as well as the attending consequences this decision had for her.

Being new in school was hard, and I started to hang around with the "weird" kids. I had always been a straight "A" student, but suddenly grades became unimportant to me. I began to slowly get into more and more trouble. I had no curfew and stayed out all night. I met a lot of new people who introduced me to crystal, coke, acid, and other various drugs. I ditched all of my classes, and for the first time in life, I began failing in school.

I had also turned punk and my appearance was strange. I wore all black, including my makeup. My hair was short in some places, long in others, and ranged from white to orange to pink to black. I wore chains, crosses, and skulls. After getting arrested for possession of cocaine, I soon became tired of the whole punk scene—tired of people laughing at the way I looked, staring at me, and making fun of me.

Another Cal Poly college student remembers his high school experience, and his heavy involvement with drugs and alcohol.

Upon entering high school, I was exposed to many new people. In order to maintain my status of being a leader and high achiever, I strived to be the biggest drug addict on campus. All that was required of me to be in this drug group was to experiment with different drugs. It is just amazing what one will do in such a group situation. One example is drinking tequila every day for a couple of months in order to be with your friends.

Another example is burglarizing houses, including neighbors and family friends, in order to obtain money and alcohol to party with. I know that these decisions would never have been made by myself, but with the help of "friends," the answer didn't seem to be very hard to come by.

During the time span from freshman to junior year in high school, I had become a complete idiot. My education assumed the lowest space on my priority list, and selling drugs and having a good time were at the top.

One college student recalls his rambunctious high school days as a "stoner."

Like many presumptuous teenagers, I was thoroughly convinced that I knew what life was all about, and anyone who didn't see reality as I did was a fool. I was basically a loner, ostracized by my peers; but I did have a handful of friends, most were in one faction of the "stoner" clique.

Stoners (at my school) cultivated the reputation of being wild, self-destructive, party animals. Our motto was SFB—shoot for a buzz. Most of us would snort some coke or drop acid on occasion, but for the most part, pot was the drug of choice, followed closely by beer. Stoners were, in my judgment, second in the social hierarchy.

Although the occasional drug bust would occur, a good percentage of us—myself included—would get stoned nearly every day. What was taking place in the parking lots and in the field by the gym was common knowledge. I remember one particularly brash incident: Two students actually lit up a joint while a film was being shown by a substitute teacher. As I recall, the only penalty they suffered was not being able to finish the whole cigarette.

Another college student recalls his high school days and the "punk phase" he went through in this way, as he describes a typical high school punk party scene.

The people gathered were of various ages and interests. Several people, for the most part fellow high school students, were present who didn't display punk dress or hairstyle. Although not directly associated with the punk movement, they seemed to enjoy the social aspects of punk music or had friends who were punkers. The true high school punks made up the largest part of the crowd. Appearing in similar style and dress, they constituted the most visible and active of all present.

Many people, especially high schoolers, embrace the social, stylistic, and musical aspects of the punk culture without abandoning traditional forms of livelihood. They gain financial support from their families and in most cases continue their education and pursue a career. They seem to find in punk an identification with a cause, a quality which may be lacking in their lives. They seem to find refuge in the adoption of a style of dress and taste which provides an identity and enables them to stand out. This type of punk—which I was—is apt to look back at their affiliation with the movement as their "punk phase."

Still another college senior majoring in psychology examines what punk has meant to him.

> I was a "hard-core" punker throughout high school. I was the typical stereotype of a punker. I became a punker for individualistic reasons. I wanted to form my own identity and be different. Now that I am in college I have "grown up" after being a punk. In many of my thoughts and ideals, I still think along those terms. Instead of exploiting myself externally, I have tried to internalize my youthful rebellion and transform it into positive and helpful actions. I think that's one reason why I want to counsel people.

And, finally, one college student summed up her experience in high school and its relentless pressure to conform.

> Would I relive my high school years if I could? No, thanks! I really had a hard time in high school. The courses were interesting, but the peer pressure was just too much. High school in America is not really about academics. It's pretty much learning social skills. How someone interacts in a social setting is the main focus of secondary education. I feel this needs no further explanation because any high school graduate probably understands my point of view.

The Clustering of High School Cliques

There were similarities between the high school youth cultures in our study and those uncovered by Trow and Clark in their collegiate study. That is, as the following summary depicts, high school cliques in Southern California—based on this small sample of four suburban high schools—could be grouped or clustered in ways comparable to the four distinctive groups of collegiate, vocational, academic, and nonconformist subcultures found to exist among college students.

The first group is the *collegiate* student. These high school cliques would include the jocks, cheerleaders, socs, partiers, surfers, tweakies (laid back), and Barbie dolls. These students attend high school not just for academic reasons—most do plan to or hope to attend college—but for athletic and social reasons as well. Their activities give them popularity. This group also includes those "wannabes" or "poseurs" who try to gain popularity by associating with the more popular students.

The second category is the *vocational* student. They include the cholos, cha-chas, dirtbags, burners, beaners (Mexicans), rap groups, and sluts. In high school . . . these students are frequently tracked into the non-college preparatory vocational classes such as woodshop, auto mechanics, and other vocational and agricultural programs for males; and typing, homemaking skills, and general secretarial programs for females. Vocational students also include those from traditional ethnic backgrounds who dress according to their (sub)culture's expectations. This group would include many of the ethnic gang members as well (although few gang members were present in the more affluent high schools analyzed for this study), and females who have reputations for being sexually active and available.

The third group found in high school are the *academic* students. These include a wide variety of high school cliques, including the brains, geeks or nerds, ugly pets, smacks, drama freaks, and bandos. The academic group affiliate strongly with the high school in terms of academics as well as specialized group activities or interests. These students generally excelled in some aspect of school life, but were not in the mainstream, popular high school cliques. These students would eventually go on to college, often getting admitted to prestigious public and private universities because of their top scholastic records.

Finally, the *nonconformists* were present in high school but they differed from the nonconformists of the college setting in important ways. In high school, the nonconformists, located often near the bottom of the school hierarchy, include the punk rockers, heavy metalers, death rockers, loners, and skinheads.

Although many of the punk rockers and heavy metalers in high school could be compared to the radicals, intellectuals, and alienated students of college, other high school youths in the nonconformist category would not be college bound. These include the more delinquent punkers, metalers, taggers, skinheads, stoners, and satanists. Furthermore, often their exploits as teenagers, both in and out of high school, would eventually bring them to the attention of the authorities and the juvenile justice system.

NOTES

1. Jim Sanders and Patrick Hoge, "Truancy Soaring: Why Go to Class When Mall Beckons?" *The Sacramento Bee* (June 11, 1989), p. A-1.
2. D. C. Dunphy, "The Social Structure of Urban Adolescent Peer Groups," *Sociometry* 26 (1963): 230–46.
3. Ibid.
4. Ibid.
5. Peter L. Berger, *Invitation to Sociology: A Humanistic Perspective* (Garden City, NY: Doubleday / Anchor, 1963).
6. Ibid., p. 396.
7. R. E. Grinder, "Distinctiveness and Thrust in the American Youth Culture," *Journal of Social Issues,* 25 no. 2 (1969): pp. 7–19.
8. Robert K. Merton, *Social Theory and Social Structure* (New York: Free Press, 1957).
9. David Ferrell and Somini Sengupta, "A Stain Spreads in Suburbia," *Los Angeles Times* (April 6, 1993), p. A-1.
10. David Gelman and Patrick Rogers, "Mixed Signals: California's 'Spur Posse' Scandal," *Newsweek* (April 12, 1993), pp. 28–29.

11. Ferrell and Sengupta, "A Stain Spreads."

12. Gelman and Rogers, "Mixed Signals."

13. "School Chief's Son in Sex Scandal," *Arizona Republic* (October 30, 1993), p. A–21.

14. Gelman and Rogers, "Mixed Signals," p. 28.

15. Robin Abcarian, "Spur Posse Case—the Same Old (Sad) Story," *Los Angeles Times* (April 7, 1993), p. E–1.

THE FAMILY

51

THE AMERICAN FAMILY
Its Relations to Personality
and to the Social Structure

TALCOTT PARSONS

This work by Talcott Parsons is the first of four about the social institution of the family. In recent years, we have heard a great deal of public debate about the family being in crisis. Many conservative and liberal politicians, in addition to other social critics, have argued that the American family is dying or in moral decline. A major rebuttal to this assertion, and one that is clearly argued from a sociologist's point of view, is that the family is not dying; it is changing. In this excerpt from Talcott Parsons' classic 1955 essay on the family, Parsons argues that the family is changing because its functions in society are changing. As these functions change, the family takes on new forms.

The American family has, in the past generation or more, been undergoing a profound process of change. There has been much difference of opinion among social scientists, as well as among others concerned, as to the interpretation of these changes. Some have cited facts such as the very high rates of divorce, the changes in the older sex morality, and until fairly recently, the decline in birth rates, as evidence of a trend to disorganization in the absolute sense. Such considerations as these have in turn often been linked with what has sometimes been called the "loss of function" of the family.[1] This refers to the fact that so many needs, [such] as . . . clothing, which formerly were met by family members working in the home, are now met by outside agencies. Thus clothing is now usually bought ready-made;

there is much less food processing in the household, there is a great deal of commercial recreation outside the home, etc.

That changes of a major character have been going on seems to be beyond doubt. That some of them have involved disorganization of a serious character is clear. But we know that major structural change in social systems always involve strain and disorganization, so the question of evaluating symptoms of disorganization, of which we can regard the high divorce rates as one, involves the question of how much is a general trend to disorganization as such, how much is what may be called the "disorganization of transition."

. . .

The transition from a high birth rate–high death rate population economy of most of history to one where low death rates have to be balanced by substantially lower birth rates than before is one of the profoundest adjustments human societies have ever had to make, going as it does to the deepest roots of motivation. In processes of such magnitude it is not unusual for there to be swings of great amplitude to levels which are incompatible with longer-run stability.

. . .

There is a further bit of evidence which may be of significance. The family after all is a residential unit in our society. If the family were breaking up, one would think that this would be associated with a decline of the importance of the "family home" as the preferred place to live in the population. Recent trends of development seem to indicate that far from family homes being "on their way out" there has, in recent years, been an impressive confirmation that even more than before this is the preferred residential pattern.

. . .

We are going to argue both that there are certain very important elements of constancy in the structure and in the functional significance of the family on a human cultural level, and that these elements of constancy are by no means wholly or even mainly a reflection of its biological composition. But this view is, in our opinion, by no means incompatible with an emphasis, in other respects, on certain important elements of variation in the family. The set of these latter elements on which we wish now to focus attention is that concerned with the level of structural differentiation in the society.

It is a striking fact of sociological discussion that there has been no settled agreement on either of two fundamental problems. One is the problem of the structural and functional relations between nuclear family on the one hand, and the other elements of the kinship complex in the same society. Structural analysis of kinship is, we feel, just reaching a point where the importance of clear discriminations in this field is coming to be appreciated. Second, there has been no clear conception of what are important "functions of the family." Procreation and child care are always included, as is some reference to sexual relations, but in addition there are frequent references to "economic" functions, religious functions and various others.

There has been little attempt to work out the implications of the suggestion that there are certain "root functions" which must be found wherever there is a family or kinship system at all, while other functions may be present or not according to the *kind* of family or kinship system under consideration, and its place in the structure of the rest of the society.

The aspect of this problem in which we are particularly interested concerns its relations to the problem of structural differentiation in societies. It is well known that in any "primitive" societies there is a sense in which kinship "dominates" the social structure; there are few concrete structures in which participation is independent of kinship status. In comparative perspective it is clear that in the more "advanced" societies a far greater part is played by non-kinship structures. States, churches, the larger business firms, universities and professional associations cannot be treated as mere "extensions" of the kinship system.

The process by which non-kinship units become of prime importance in a social structure, inevitably entails "loss of function" on the part of some or even all of the kinship units. In the processes of social evolution there have been many stages by which this process has gone on, and many different directions in which it has worked out.

Our suggestion is, in this perspective, that what has recently been happening to the American family constitutes part of one of these stages of a process of differentiation. This process has involved a further step in the reduction of the importance in our society of kinship units other than the nuclear family. It has also resulted in the transfer of a variety of functions from the nuclear family to other structures of the society, notably the occupationally organized sectors of it. This means that the family has become *a more specialized agency than before,* probably more specialized than it has been in any previously known society. This represents a decline of *certain* features which traditionally have been associated with families; but whether it represents a "decline of the family" in a more general sense is another matter; we think not. We think the trend of the evidence points to the beginning of the relative stabilization of a *new* type of family structure in a new relation to a general social structure, one in which the family is more specialized than before, but not in any general sense less important, because the society is dependent *more* exclusively on it for the performance of *certain* of its vital functions.

. . .

The Principal Functions of the Nuclear Family

Within this broad setting of the structure of the society, what can we say about the functions of the family, that is, the isolated nuclear family? There are, we think, two main types of considerations. The first is that the "loss of function," both in our own recent history and as seen in broader comparative perspective, means that the family has become, on the "macroscopic" levels, almost completely functionless. It does not itself, except here and there, engage in much economic production; it is not a significant unit in the political power system; it is not a major direct agency of integration of the larger society. Its individual members participate in all these functions, but they do so "as individuals" not in their roles as family members.[2]

The most important implication of this view is that the functions of the family in a highly differentiated society are not to be interpreted as functions directly on behalf of the society, but on behalf of personality. If, as some psychologists seem to assume, the essentials of human personality were determined biologically, independently of involvement in social systems, there would be no need for families, since reproduction as such does not require family organization. It is because the *human* personality is not "born" but must be "made" through the socialization process that in the first instance families are necesary. They are "factories" which produce human personalities. But at the same time even once produced, it cannot be assumed that the human personality would remain stable in the respects which are vital to social functioning, if there were not mechanisms of stabilization which were organically integrated with the socialization process. We therefore suggest that the basic and irreducible functions of the family are two: first, the primary socialization of children so that they can truly become members of the society into which they have been born; second, the stabilization of the adult personalities of the population of the society. It is the combination of these two functional imperatives, which explains why, in the "normal" case it is both true that *every adult* is a member of a nuclear family and that every child must begin his process of socialization in a nuclear family. It will be one of the most important theses of our subsequent analysis that these two circumstances are most intimately interconnected. Their connection goes back to the fact that it is control of the residua of the process of socialization which constitutes the primary focus of the problem of stabilization of the adult personality.

. . .

A primary function and characteristic of the family is that it should be a social group in which in the earliest stages the child can "invest" *all* of his emotional resources, to which he can become overwhelmingly "committed" or on which he can become fully "dependent." But, at the same time, in the nature of the socialization process, this dependency must be temporary rather than permanent. Therefore, it is very important that the socializing agents should not themselves be *too* completely immersed in their family ties. It is a condition equally important with facilitating dependency that a family should, in due course, help in emancipating the child from his dependency on the family. *Hence the family must be a differentiated subsystem of a society, not itself a "little society" or anything too closely approaching it.* More specifically this means that the adult members must have roles other than their familial roles which occupy strategically important places in their own personalities. In our own society the most important of these other roles, though by no means the only one, is the occupational role of the father.

The second primary function of the family, along with socialization of children, concerns regulation of balances in the personalities of the adult members of both sexes. It is clear that this function is concentrated on the marriage relation as such. From this point of view a particularly significant aspect of the isolation of the nuclear family in our society is again the sharp discrimination in status which it emphasizes between family members and nonmembers. In particular, then, spouses are thrown upon each other, and their ties with members of their own families of orientation, notably parents and adult siblings, are correspondingly weakened. In its negative aspect as a source of strain, the consequence of this may be stated as the fact that the family of procreation, and in particular the marriage pair, are in a "structurally unsupported" situation. Neither party has any other adult kin on whom they have a right to "lean for support" in a sense closely comparable to the position of the spouse.

. . .

We suggest then that children are important to adults because it is important to the latter to express what are essentially the "childish" elements of their own personalities. There can be no better way of doing this than living with and interacting on their own level with *real* children. But at the same time it is essential that this should not be an unregulated acting out, a mere opportunity for regressive indulgence. The fact that it takes place in the parental role, with all its responsibilities, not least of which is the necessity to renounce earlier modes of indulgence as the child grows older, is, as seen in this connection, of the first importance. . . . The general thesis . . . is that the family and, in a particularly visible and trenchant way, the modern isolated family, incorporates an intricate set of interactive mechanisms whereby these two essential functions for personality are interlocked and interwoven.

NOTES

1. Emphasized particularly by W. F. Ogburn. See, for instance, Chapter 13, "The Family and Its Functions," *Recent Social Trends in the U.S.,* Report of President's Research Committee on Social Trends, 1933.

2. In terms of our technical analytical scheme we interpret this to mean that the family belongs in the "latency" or "pattern-maintenance–tension-management" subsystem as seen in functional terms. See Chapter 5, Section 8 of Talcott Parsons, Robert F. Bales, and E. A. Shils, *Working Papers in Theory of Action* (Glencoe, IL: The Free Press, 1953).

52

LOVE AND PROPERTY

RANDALL COLLINS

Here Randall Collins examines how families are constructed around different types of property relationships. His analysis shows that as the power dynamics change within the larger society, the social institution of the family also has changed to accommodate the civil rights of women and children. Thus, the vast power of the family, as an institution, has declined over time.

For a very long time the family and the relation between the sexes was one of the most taken-for-granted aspects of society. The obvious view has been that men and women have certain natural functions. Man's place is at work and in the public realm. Woman's place is at home, minding the kitchen and the children. The family is a natural division of labor between sexes. Man is the breadwinner and defender, woman the homemaker and childrearer.

In the twentieth century women left the household in large numbers, but even then for a long time it was taken for granted that women at work would be subservient to men: They could work as a secretary, a nurse, a waitress, or a stewardess, serving a male boss or a male customer. A woman might be a school teacher of small children, but not a college professor, except in an all-female college. Even in the public realm, women were expected to carry over the same role that they had in the home, taking care of men and children.

This view has now come under attack. Once again, vigorous movement for sexual liberation is under way, and has begun to put pressure against some of the most obvious instances of job discrimination against women. At the same time, it is clear that the feminist movement has a long way to go in achieving its goal of equality between the sexes. Some women have begun to make it into the higher realms of the professions, business, and politics. But the vast majority of working women are still trapped in sex-typed occupations like secretarial work and nursing, which are not only relatively low-paying, but offer no chances of promotion into the higher, male-dominated spheres of their bosses. The family, too, remains largely traditional in its operation, as women are left with most of the household and childrearing responsibilities, even if they also have a job.

What is likely to happen in the future? The obvious view offers little guidance. On the one hand, if the old division of labor between the sexes were absolutely natural, then no change would be possible at all. The fact that *some* change has occurred is inexplicable on this traditional view. A reactionary movement has cropped up in some quarters in response to women's liberation. This movement tries to push women back in the confines of the family and to reestablish all the old traditional sexual attitudes. But the very existence of the profamily, antifeminist movement is itself a sign that something has gone wrong with the traditional arrangement of things. If the old-fashioned family were so natural, it would not be necessary to force people back into it.

On the other hand, there is a growing feeling that the family itself may be on the way out. The birth rate has fallen off, so that there are fewer children, and the divorce rate has climbed to a very high level. How does this fit into the picture? Is it a sign of social disorganization and approaching doom, as the traditionalists would have it? Or is it somehow connected with the movement toward women's liberation?

Here sociological theory has an important nonobvious contribution to make. But once again, we must be selective. A good deal of traditional sociology has only embellished a version of the obvious view, seeing the family and traditional sex roles as perfectly functional units in modern society. But there is another, much more sophisticated view of things. A branch of the sociological tradition as far back as Friedrich Engels in the late nineteenth century has helped us to understand that the family and sexual relations are not just natural but exist as part of a system of stratification. The theory of sexual stratification is right now in the process of being developed, and there is a good deal of discussion over just how it works. But certain basic, and nonobvious, points can be made.

The guiding idea that I will follow here is that family relations are relations of property. This property is of several kinds: (1) property rights over human bodies, which we might call *erotic property;* (2) property rights regarding children—let us call this *generational property;* (3) property rights over goods held by the family—call this *household property.*

The family is made up of these three kinds of property. The way in which they mesh with the world of work, I contend, is a major determinant of sexual job discrimination. Once we can understand these forms of property, it becomes important to see that they are not static. Property systems, including sexual ones, are not natural and immutable forever. They are produced by certain social circumstances, and they change with those circumstances. If we understand these conditions, we can predict the rise and fall of various kinds of sexual stratification. The current type of family structure, and of sexual domination, has not existed forever, and it will not continue indefinitely into the future. If we wish to know how far women's liberation can proceed, and what conditions can make it possible, it is to a theory such as this that we must turn.

Erotic Property

How can people be property? Except for slavery, which hardly exists anymore, people cannot be bought and sold. Human beings have no monetary value; we regard ourselves as beyond money. People are not things; they are ends in themselves. Hence, it would seem that people are not property, at least not in the modern world.

The mistake, though, is to think of property as a thing, and especially as a thing that can be bought and sold for money. Property is not actually the thing itself, a physical object. Property is a social relationship, *a way in which people act toward things.* What does it mean, for instance, that a piece of land "belongs" to someone? It means that person can use it, live on it, go on it when he or she likes, and that other people must stay off unless they are given permission. If they don't, the owner can call the police or go to court to keep others off. Property is a relationship among people regarding things; it is some kind of enforceable agreement as to who can or cannot do what with certain things, and who will back others up in enforcing these actions. It is the society, that makes something property, and not some inviolable relationship between one individual and the soil.

. . .

If property is a social relationship, then, rather than the thing itself, it makes sense to look at love and sex as forms of property. The key aspect of property is the right of possession, the right to keep someone else from possessing it, and the willingness of society to back up those rights. The very core of a marriage is property in just that sense.

. . .

What makes people married? It is not primarily the marriage vow, nor the civil or religious ceremony. A couple who live together and have sexual intercourse exclusively with each other are for all intents and purposes married. If this goes on for several years, in many places they are thereby legally married, as a "common law" marriage. On the other hand, a couple who are legally married but never have sexual intercourse is said not to have "consummated" the marriage. This is grounds for legal annulment, since the implicit terms of the marriage contract are not put into effect. In our society, marriage is a contract for exclusive rights to sexual access between two people. Socially speaking, they are exchanging their bodies as sexual property to each other.

This sexual property is the key to the family structure; it is the hinge on which everything else turns. Marriages are created by establishing the sexual tie. The old traditions of the wedding night and the honeymoon point directly to this fact. The more traditional the marriage, the more ceremony there was surrounding the first act of sexual intercourse. This went on whether or not people censored the fact that they were establishing a form of erotic property. Traditionally, before the legal reforms of recent decades, the only way one could get divorced was by proving adultery. This has been true virtually up to the present day in conservative, Catholic-dominated countries such as Italy. Why is adultery so crucial? Because it is a breaking of the central property right, exclusive sexual access.

Similarly, in traditional societies, heavy emphasis was placed upon the bride being a virgin at marriage. The husband's property rights over her body would have been sullied if she had had intercourse with another man. That these same societies tended not to regard male virginity at marriage as very important implies that the property system was much more one of males owning women's bodies than vice versa. I will come back to this.

The erotic property system is especially visible when we look at the points at which it is violated. There has long been a sort of unwritten law, which condoned spouses taking violent action when their sexual property was abused. A judge or jury usually would not convict a man of murder for killing his wife's lover, or even his wife, when he discovered her having an adulterous affair. Presumably, this should apply in reverse, too, but instances of wives getting away with killing their husbands or their lovers seem to have been less common—an example of sexist bias here, even in the right to kill. The notable thing is that such a killing is not usually regarded as a murder, and the killer is allowed to go free or given a light sentence. The custom of allowing a completely unpunished killing to take place in these circumstances has declined somewhat in contemporary times. Why this is so also reveals something about the sexual property system.

The practice of adultery-killing was strongest in places where marriage was regarded as most inviolate and divorces were least common. Why should this be so? Because this traditional marriage system meant that a woman would have only one sexual partner in her lifetime; her body was the exclusive sexual property of her husband. Such arrangements have usually had a rather sexist tone in that men were more likely to be allowed to have extramarital affairs or access to prostitutes; so, although a marriage was in principle unbreakable, the man had more opportunities for compensating for erotic and emotional incompatibility. With the rise of the divorce rate, though, in many communities it is generally expected that most people will have more than one marriage, and hence more than one sexual partner in their lifetime. For this reason, sexual property is no longer taken as such an absolute, something that if tarnished once is forever gone. This is not to say that sexual property no longer exists. But it has shifted into a different modality: one might say, from absolute long-term property to a series of short-term property arrangements. People still get angry about adultery, but the result is more likely to be a divorce instead of a violent death.

. . .

All of this discussion seems to imply that marriage is simply a matter of sex, and that there is no affection, no love, involved. But this is certainly not so. Erotic relations are the key to the marriage contract, both legally and in the unwritten laws of customary belief. But this is by no means exclusive of emotional ties. In fact, the emotional ties now usually go along with the sexual ones. Love and sex, from a sociological viewpoint, are part of the same complex. At least this is so in the modern marriage system, which places a great deal of emphasis on an ideal expression of love. One might even refer to modern marriage as a ritual-love system of erotic property. In a certain sense, the erotic relations are deeper, and go back further. Marriage in traditional societies (as we shall see) placed little or no importance upon love, and concentrated instead on the control of erotic property and the other forms of property exchange involved in the main alliance. Modern marriage, though, has shifted into a form in which love is a crucial element in establishing a sexual tie.

. . .

The comparative study of jealousy gives a neat illustration of the social basis of emotions. Whom one feels jealous toward is relative to how sexual property is arranged. In our society, where erotically exclusive male-female pairs are the predominant form of sexual exchange, each partner is jealous of anyone who threatens to impose on the affections, or the genitals, of their partner. In polyandrous societies, however, the situation is quite different. This is a type of system, found for example in some of the mountain tribes of India and Tibet, in which a woman has several husbands. Usually it is a group of brothers who have the same wife. They are not jealous of each other, and all are expected to have a share in the woman's body and attentions. This does not mean such people are so broad-minded as to be incapable of jealousy. On the contrary, they can be quite jealous of outsiders who are not part of the polyandrous situation. Similarly, Eskimo men frequently share their wives, on a temporary basis, with visitors who come their way on long hunting expeditions. At the same time, Eskimo societies have had a very high incidence of fights and murders, often over possession of a woman. It makes a tremendous difference whether a guest is invited to share a woman (implicitly in return for some later reciprocity) or if he simply helps himself. Property, in short, is not given up when it is given away. In fact, the giving of a gift (in this case, a loan of a woman's body) reaffirms the sense of property, precisely because it makes clear to everyone involved that someone is doing something with *their* property and that they expect it to be received in a proper way.

These kinds of polyandrous or wife-lending situations actually are rather rare on the world scene. Somewhat more common are marriage systems in which a man has several wives. Such polygynous systems are especially prominent in tribal Africa. There, again, we find jealousy turned in quite different directions than in our own society. The various co-wives are usually not jealous of one another, although they may be jealous of outside women who are not part of the family situation. There is usually a chief wife, who has certain rights and powers over the other wives. In such a situation, a woman contemplating marriage may be more concerned about whether she will be moving into a family in which she gets on well with the co-wives than with how well she likes the husband himself.

This kind of anthropological comparison lets us see that the emotions we usually associate with sexual relations are variable, but not at all random. Just how much affection there is, and how much jealousy, and at whom it is directed, depends on the typical structure of sexual property relations. In our own society, erotic relationships are heavily imbued with romance, and emotions of affection and love are a crucial part of this. I am not saying that people fall in love because they feel they are supposed to. It is true that our popular culture tends to make people expect that this will happen, but the widespread experience of love is by no means simply the result of indoctrination by the media. Rather, it follows naturally from the type of negotiating that people must do in order to find a sexual partner in a situation of free individual bargaining.

. . .

Erotic property and its counterpart, feelings of love and jealousy, are not the only sort of property relationships in a marriage. Moreover, their intensity does not stay at the peak hit when the relation bond was first being established. After a while, the excitement is gone, along with the anxiety and the contrasting joy. As a couple lives on into a marriage, the intensity of affection falls off and so does the frequency of sexual intercourse. They spend less time with one another and more time with other people. Hence the conditions for a strong ritual bond between them are weakened. But even as the intensity of erotic love falls, other ties frequently come in to take its place. I turn now to some of the others.

Generational Property

In an important respect, children are property too. Parents have certain rights over them, and they act to defend those rights in the same way as they protect other kinds of property. Children are not, however, sexual property. All societies are very strict about this. The incest taboo within the nuclear family is virtually universal; sexual intercourse between parents and children, or among siblings, and sometimes among other relatives, too, is regarded with particularly strong revulsion. The incest taboo ought to be considered part of the generational property system; it is one of the principle *negative* rules as to what people *cannot* do with their generational property. (There are equivalent negative rules about physical property, too; zoning ordinances forbidding certain kinds of modifications of your house or land are instances of this.)

The incest taboo cannot simply be taken for granted, though. It is not a natural or instinctual revulsion; if so, no one would ever commit incest, whereas in fact the incest taboo is violated to a surprising extent. Rather, it is enforced above all from *outside* the family, by other people who look upon incest as improper and prosecute it as illegal. Why outsiders do this has largely to do with the general system of sexual bargaining that takes place in that society. People expect the children of other families to be available as sexual partners to outsiders, not to be monopolized within the family. It is possible to demonstrate this because different societies vary as to just what they count as incest, and these variations are tied to the kind of marriage system that prevails.

In some societies, like our own only a few generations ago, marriage with cousins was prohibited as incestuous, and people were expected to marry further afield. In many tribal societies, on the other hand, certain cousins are expected to marry each other whenever possible. This is because there is a system of regular alliances among families, and the continuous intermarriages of cousins (especially what are called "cross-cousins") is what keeps the families tied together generation by generation. Such examples, incidentally, prove that the reason for the incest taboo is not because people are concerned about possible genetic defects from inbreeding; societies practicing regular cousin marriage are obviously following the opposite of such a policy. Moreover, these same societies have incest rules that are in some respects much more extreme than our own; they prohibit large categories of people from marrying because they belong to the wrong lineage, even though we would consider them not very closely related biologically at all.

The reasons for the incest taboo are not biological but are part of the larger system of sexual property exchange. In our own society, wholesale alliances of families are no longer important, and our incest taboos have shrunk to the bare minimum that will still require children to leave their own family to find sexual partners in the larger marriage market.

The incest taboo, then, is a negative rule of the generational property system. It regulates what parents cannot do with their children, as well as what children are not allowed to do with each other. The positive aspects of generational property include a number of things. Parents have a certain physical property right over their children: the power to keep them in their houses, send them to school, and whatever else they wish to do with them. Parents have rights to direct their children's behavior in many respects: to determine how they dress; what religious training they are to be given, if any; whom they should associate with; and many other things. These rights are not necessarily very much enforced these days. We have come a long way from the Roman family in which the father could punish his children any way he wished, and even put them to death.

In general, the recent trend is toward reducing parents' control over children. Much of this follows from the loss of parental control over a crucial aspect of generational property, the power to determine whom their children would marry. (A vestige of this still existed just a few years ago, in the formality of a man asking his bride-to-be's father for her hand in marriage; and it is still common for the father to "give his daughter away" at the wedding ceremony.) Obviously, control over children's marriages extended generational property past the immediate offspring to control in shaping subsequent generations of lineage. As family lineages have declined in importance, generational property has been shrinking, down to what applies only within the nuclear family during children's earlier years.

Generational property also has an economic aspect. Legally, children's incomes are the property of their parents, until they reach their majority. Again, this is a form of generational property that is not very much enforced these days. If anything, the opposite claim of children upon parents' income is much more prominent. But this only serves to tell us what changes have been happening in the recent family system. Not so long ago—and still today, in some very traditional families, such as where the whole family runs a store or a farm—children were expected to help support the family, either by working without pay in the family business or by going out and getting a job, and bringing their earnings back home.

Just as the erotic property system has been changing, the generational property system has been changing as well, and in a somewhat parallel direction. Another striking similarity between these two kinds of family property, though, is that both of them have a very prominent emotional side. And as in erotic property where spouses claim the right to each other's affections, parents have a right over their children's affection. Moreover, at the same time that the emotional relations among adults have become more central in the modern marriage, the affectional relations with children have come to displace the traditional emphasis on children as part of the farm economy or agents for carrying on the family name.

Again, we can see the strength of these emotional claims at the point where they are threatened by being broken. In contemporary divorces, usually the main point of contention is custody of the children. Parents fight over who will have physical possession, as well as over visitation rights. What is especially characteristic of the current situation is that both parents frequently are concerned to maintain maximal control over their children. It is no longer automatically assumed that children belong primarily to their mother. Fathers now want possession of their children much more than in the past. In effect, a certain aspect of generational property has become much more prominent, while other aspects decline. Emotional rights over children's affection has become central as the old economic and lineage concerns have declined. The situation has even given rise to a new species of "crime"— kidnappings in which one of the ex-spouses defies a court order giving custody to the other spouse and takes the children anyway. The fact that such cases are actually prosecuted, and are treated with so much emotion, shows how important emotional property rights over children have become.

Generational property, of course, cuts both ways. Parents have property rights over their children, but the reverse is also true. Children have a claim to a place in their parents' home, part of their income, and a certain amount of care. These rights, moreover, have apparently expanded in current society. Legally, these property obligations of parents to their kids come to an end at age 18, but there is considerable informal pressure to extend them beyond this point, as in paying for college expenses. The most important part of children's property claims upon their parents, however, used to be their inheritance. When much of the economy was run by family businesses, especially farms, this aspect of generational property was overwhelmingly important. It held the family together very tightly across the generations, but not necessarily in a way that was very affectionate.

Although the "obvious," conventional belief of today is that the family is nowhere nearly as tightly knit now as in the past, it is probably true that today's families place much more emphasis on emotional relations between parents and children, as well as between spouses, than traditional ones did. The traditional family was held together because people had no choice: It was an economic unit, and people had to stick with it or risk starvation. This made for some rather cold-blooded attitudes toward family loyalty. Such families were strong but not usually very nice to live in. Today's families, for the most part, have relatively little material inheritance to pass on. People find jobs on their own and inherit little more than a few pieces of family furniture. Only among wealthy families has the old inheritance pattern remained important. For most other people there is little else left but the emotional ties. To be sure, these do not appear automatically. Many modern families do break up, whereas traditional ones probably would have stayed together even in the absence of affection just because the economic situation demanded it. But those modern families that do stay together do so more for emotional reasons than for external ones. In this respect, families are probably more strongly bonded than ever before.

Household Property

It is not true, though, that the family is no longer an economic unit. It is just not a permanent economic unit based on the intergenerational transmission of property. From a certain point of view, it is an ongoing business, engaged in running a household. The business is by no means permanent; it can break apart much more easily than in the past. But while it exists, it is a cooperative enterprise for preparing food, doing cleaning, providing lodging, and caring for children. From an economic viewpoint, the family is a combination of hotel, restaurant, laundry, and baby-sitting agency.

In a traditional household, a great deal of the work would likely have been done by servants. Of course, only the higher social classes would have servants. A truly rich household would have a large number of them, but even a modest middle-class family would have at least a maid or a cook. What about the lower classes? To a fair degree, many of them had no household of their own: They were servants in someone else's household. This meant that family life was very skewed around social class patterns. It was largely the higher social classes who could afford to get married and set up a household of their own. Many of the working class men and women, living and working in someone else's house, would never have the opportunity to have families of their own.

One of the big changes in the modern family is the disappearance of this kind of large servant-based household. It is not that the upper class no longer exists, but its lifestyle has certainly become less dramatic and less grand; and the servant class has gradually faded away, certainly to a tiny fraction of what it once was.

Much of the servant class consisted of women who did the household chores in some else's house. What remains of the servant class today is even more exclusively female; the butler and the valet have more or less disappeared, while the maid still comes to many upper-middle-class homes today. For the most part, domestic labor has now fallen into the hands of wives. Insofar as the household is a place where work is done, it is primarily women who do it.

Officially and legally, the property of the household is now jointly held between husband and wife. In a divorce settlement, they have equal claims upon the goods accrued during their marriage; and if one spouse dies without a will, the other automatically inherits. But this is only taking the property as things. What about the things as they are actually used? A house, dishes, food, clothes—none of these are actually really usable just on their own. It takes a certain amount of labor to put them into operation. The house has to be kept clean, the clothes ironed, the beds made, the food bought and prepared and put on the table. In a common household economy, the husband may put in his labor outside the household and bring home money, which he invests in these various household materials. They are generally "raw goods," and the wife puts in her labor in converting them into consumable products. Moreover, this pattern tends to hold even if the wife also works outside the household: She still takes care of the home and the children, cooking breakfast before she goes to work, cooking dinner when she comes back in the evening.

For this reason, the household economy can be described as one of sex-based domination. Property is officially equal, but only if one ignores the actual labor that turns it into usable, consumable goods. In the traditional case, where the husband alone is working and bringing in money to invest in the household, we have a household economy very much like a capitalist-owned factory. The husband provides the raw capital; the wife is the worker who has nothing to trade but her labor. Like any other worker, she is forced by the pressures of staying alive on the labor market to sell her labor to somone who can afford to buy it; only in this case she sells it (or rather barters it) in a household rather than a factory. But her labor is essential; the husband/capitalist cannot transform his raw materials into usable goods without it.

Of course, we can think of various differences between the two situations: the factory worker does not end up inheriting the factory; and the worker does not usually have sexual intercourse with the owner, bear his children, share his social status, or express any love and affection for him. Leaving these things aside, though, recent Marxist-oriented feminist writers have argued that the household really is a capitalist institution. It is not only capitalist in its inner workings but is part of the larger capitalist system of the society. What women's work in the home does for the larger capitalist economy is to *reproduce the labor force.* All the cooking, cleaning, shopping, child care, and even the emotional affection given to husbands serves to keep the extra-familial male labor force ready to go to work the next day. Labor is a crucial aspect of the capitalist economy, but the capitalists themselves do not see to its everyday maintenance. This is left to the hidden economy of the household, where women do this essential work of keeping the capitalist sytem going.

The inference that is sometimes drawn from this is that women do not have a distinctive grievance vis-à-vis men; their grievance is really with the capitalist system. It may be true that the male working class is overtly more sexist in the way it treats women than the male middle or upper class is, but the overall picture throughout the society is one in which women do the household work for the sake of the capitalist system in general. It follows that women's real ally should be the working class (which they are really a part of); if they joined together in overthrowing capitalism, presumably women's subjugation in household labor would disappear too.

Short of some long-term revolution, at any rate, this sort of argument has various implications for reforming the system of household labor. It has been argued that wives should be paid salaries for their work, that there should be a minimum wage, and that they should be eligible for social security benefits. Alternatively, household labor should be socialized. Child care can be taken over by a collective, extrafamilial child-care center. Similarly, cleaning, laundry, food preparation can all be shifted to outside workers instead of being done by the wife in the home.

Interestingly enough, the latter pattern does seem to be emerging already. By and large it is not emerging in a socialized form, although public child-care facilities are becoming more common. Much of the rest is provided by private business: fast food chains, prepared foods, cleaning services, and the like. To a considerable extent women now are in the paid labor force themselves, and they make use of other people to help take care of their children and their household economy. This is only partial, to be sure; as long as women are not paid as much as men for their outside work, the family is less likely to be able to afford to completely make up these family services with paid outside labor. Full-scale sexual equality in the future might well bring about this transformation of the household.

53

FAMILIES WE CHOOSE
Lesbians, Gays, Kinship

KATH WESTON

Some scholars argue that to really understand the current debate about family, we need to examine the changing definitions of family. For example, many people define "family" only in terms of marriage and blood ties. If we delineate family based on only these two criteria, think of all the people this definition leaves out, including adopted and foster children, cohabiting couples, gay and lesbian couples, and friends who are often closer than blood relatives. In the following selection, Kath Weston challenges us to examine our heterosexist and narrow definitions of family. Weston suggests that "family" is not defined by biological links and nuptial arrangements but by individuals spending time together and forming a primary group.

Friendship is an upstart category, for it to usurp the place of kinship or even intrude upon it is an impertinence.

—ELSIE CLEWS PARSONS

Every Thursday night in the cityscape that framed my experience of "the field," my lover and I had dinner with Liz Andrews. The three of us juggled work schedules, basketball practice, and open-ended interviews around this weekly event. Occasionally these gatherings meant candlelight dinners, but more often Thursday found us savoring our repast in front of the TV. The first few weeks of gourmet meals gave way to everyday fare with a special touch, like avocado in the salad or Italian sausage in the spaghetti sauce.

Responsibility for planning, preparing, and subsidizing the meals rotated along with their location, which alternated between Liz's home and the apartment I shared with my lover. At only one point did this egalitarian division of labor and resources become the subject of conscious evaluation. Liz offered to pay a proportionately greater share of a high-ticket meal, reasoning that she had the largest income. In the ensuing discussion, reluctance to complicate "power dynamics" in the group resolved the issue in favor of maintaining equal contributions.

After supper we might play cards, trade anecdotes about mutual acquaintances, describe recent encounters with heterosexism, discuss world politics or the opening of a new lesbian strip show, exchange recipes, explain how we would reorganize the Forty-Niner offensive lineup, or propose strategies for handling the rising cost of living in San Francisco. Or we might continue watching television, taking advantage of commercial breaks to debate the perennial enigma: "What *do* heterosexual women see in Tom Selleck, anyway?" While we grew comfortable with argument and with differences in our class backgrounds, age, and experiences, we tended to assume a degree of mutual comprehension as white women who all identified ourselves as lesbians.

After a few months of these dinners we began to apply the terms "family" and "extended family" to one another. Our remarks found a curious counterpart in a series of comments on changes in the behavior of Liz's cat. Once an unsociable creature that took to hiding and growling from the other room when strangers invaded her realm, now she watched silently from beneath the telephone table and even ventured forth to greet her visitors. Not that she does that for everyone, Liz reminded us: Clearly we were being taken into an inner circle.

In retrospect, the incipient trust and solidarity imaged in this depiction of a world viewed through cat's eyes appears as one of several elements that combined to make Thursdays feel like family occasions. The centrality of the meal—sharing food on a regular basis in a domestic setting—certainly contributed to our growing sense of relatedness. In the United States, where the household is the normative unit of routinized consumption, many family relationships are also commensal relationships. Although we occupied separate households, we interpreted the option of independent residence as a feature distinguishing gay families from straight, one that qualified "our" kind of family as a creative innovation. In truth, this contrast may have been a bit overdrawn. Moving to the same neighborhood had prompted the routinization of the weekly dinner meetings, and I personally enjoyed walking over to Liz's apartment when it was her turn to cook. These evening strolls underlined the spatial contiguity of our households while allowing me to avoid the seemingly interminable search for a parking space in San Francisco.

Efforts to encourage a low-key atmosphere framed our interactions during supper as everyday experience rather than a guest-host relationship. It was not uncommon for any one of us to leave immediately following the meal if we were tired or had other things to do. Conversation, while often lively, seldom felt obligatory. Also facilitating the developing family feeling was a sense of time depth that arose after the arrangement had endured several months, a dimension augmented by a 10-year friendship between Liz and myself.

On some occasions other people joined our core group for activities, events, and even Thursday night get-togethers. Once Liz asked two gay male friends to dinner, and another time—with somewhat more anticipation and formality—the group extended an invitation to Liz's parents. When her parents arrived a guest-host relationship prevailed, but Liz, my lover, and I became the collective hosts, preparing and serving the food and making sure that her parents were entertained. One could imagine other possible alignments: for example, Liz and her parents busy in her kitchen while my lover and I waited to be served. The differentiation of activities and space presented a graphic juxtaposition of the family Liz was creating with the family in which she had been raised. By introducing my lover and me to her parents in the context of a Thursday night meal, Liz hoped to bridge these two domains.

About the time that the three of us began to classify ourselves as family, we also began to provide one another with material assistance that went beyond cooking and cleaning up the dinner dishes. When one of us left on vacation, another volunteered to pick up the mail. After Liz injured her foot and decided to stay at her parents' house, I fed the cat. On street cleaning days Liz and my lover moved each other's vehicles. Liz offered me the use of her apartment for interviews or studying while she was at work. "Emotional support" accompanied this sort of assistance, exemplified by midweek phone calls to discuss problems that could not wait until Thursday. Our joint activities began to expand beyond the kitchen and living room, extending to the beach, the bars, political events, restaurants, a tour of Liz's workplace, and Giants games at Candlestick Park.

Faced with the task of analyzing this type of self-described family relationship among lesbians and gay men, my inclination while yet in the field was to treat it as an instance of what anthropologists in the past have termed *fictive kin.* The concept of fictive kin lost credibility with the advent of symbolic anthropology and the realization that all kinship is in some sense fictional—that is, meaningfully constituted rather than "out there" in a positivist sense. Viewed in this light, genes and blood appear as symbols implicated in one culturally specific way of demarcating and calculating relationships. . . . Although the category fictive kin has fallen from grace in the social sciences, it retains intuitive validity for many people in the United States when applied to chosen families. From coverage in the popular press to child custody suits and legislative initiatives, phrases such as "pretended family relations" and "so-called family" are recurrently applied to lesbian or gay couples, parents, and families of friends.

The very concept of a substitute or surrogate family suffers from a functionalism that assumes people intrinsically *need* families (whether for psychological support or material assistance). Commentators who dispute the legitimacy of gay families typically set up a hierarchical relationship in which biogenetic ties constitute a primary domain upon which fictive kin relations are metaphorically predicated. Within this secondary domain, relationships are said to be "like" family, that is, similar to and probably imitative of the relations presumed to actually comprise kinship. When anthropologists have discussed the institutionalization of "going for sisters" (or brothers, or cousins) among urban blacks in the United States, for example, they have emphasized that such relationships can be "just as real" as blood ties to the persons involved. . . . While framed as a defense of participants' perspectives, this type of argument implicitly takes blood relations as its point of departure. Insofar as analysis becomes circumscribed by the unvoiced question that asks how authentic these "fictive" relations are, it makes little difference that authenticity refers back to a privileged and apparently unified symbolic system rather than an empirically observable universe.

Theoretically I have adopted a very different approach by treating gay kinship ideologies as historical *transformations* rather than derivatives of other sorts of kinship relations. . . .

. . .

Gay families do not occupy a subsidiary domain that passively reflects or imitates the primary tenets of a coherent "American kinship system." The historical construction of an ideological contrast between chosen (gay) families and blood (straight) family has not left biologistic and procreative conceptions of kinship untouched. But if coming out has supplied gay families with a specific content (the organizing principle of choice) by exposing the selective aspects of blood relations, it remains to be shown how choice became allied with kinship and gay identity to produce a discourse on families we choose.

Building Gay Families

The sign at the 1987 Gay and Lesbian March on Washington read: "Love makes a family—nothing more, nothing less." From the stage, speakers arguing for domestic partner benefits and gay people's right to parent repeatedly invoked love as both the necessary *and the sufficient* criterion for defining kinship. Grounding kinship in love deemphasized distinctions between erotic and nonerotic relations while bringing friends, lovers, and children together under a single concept. As such, love offered a symbol well suited to carry the nuances of identity and unity so central to kinship in the United States, yet circumvent the procreative assumption embedded in symbols like heterosexual intercourse and blood ties.

It has become almost a truism that "family" can mean very different things when complicated (as it always is) by class, race, ethnicity, and gender. . . . In her studies of kinship among Japanese-Americans, Sylvia Yanagisako (1978, 1985) has demonstrated how the unit used to calculate relatedness ("families" or "persons") may change, and additional meanings adhere to symbols like love, based on variable definitions of context that invoke racial or cultural identities. Determining who is a relative in a context that an individual perceives as "Japanese" may draw on different meanings and categories than determining relationship in a context defined as "American."

In speaking broadly of "gay families," my objective is not to focus on that most impoverished level of analysis, the least common denominator, or to describe symbolic contrasts in pristine seclusion from social relations. Neither do I mean to imply an absence of differences among lesbians and gay men, or that gay families are constructed in isolation from identities of gender, race, or class. Rather, I have situated chosen families in the specific context of an ideological opposition between families defined as straight and gay—families identified with biology and choice, respectively. On the one hand, this highly generalized opposition oversimplifies the complexities of kinship organization by ignoring other identities while presenting its own categories as timeless and fundamental. On the other hand, the same discourse complicates understandings of kinship in the United States by pairing categories previously believed to be at variance ("gay" and "family").

The families I saw gay men and lesbians creating in the Bay Area tended to have extremely fluid boundaries, not unlike kinship organization among sectors of the African American, American Indian, and white working class. David Schneider and Raymond Smith (1978, p. 42) have characterized this type of organization as one that can "create kinship ties out of relationships which are originally ties of friendship." Listen for a moment to Toni Williams' account of the people she called kin:

> In my family, all of us kids are godparents to each others' kids, okay? So we're very connected that way. But when I go to have a kid, I'm not gonna have my sisters as godparents. I'm gonna have people that are around me, that are gay. That are straight. I don't have that many straight friends, but certainly I would integrate them in my life. They would help me. They would babysit my child, or . . . like my kitty, I'm not calling up my family and saying, "Hey, Mom, can you watch my cat?" No, I call on my inner family—my community, or whatever—to help me with my life. . . .

What Toni portrayed was an ego-centered calculus of relations that pictured family members as a cluster surrounding a single individual, rather than taking couples or groups as units of affiliation. This meant that even the most nuclear of couples would construct theoretically distinguishable families, although an area of overlapping membership generally developed. At the same time, chosen families were not restricted to person-to-person ties. Individuals occasionally added entire groups with preexisting, multiplex connections among members. In one such case, a woman reported incorporating a "circle" of her new lover's gay family into her own kinship universe.

In the Bay Area, families we choose resembled networks in the sense that they could cross household lines, and both were based on ties that radiated outward from individuals like spokes on a wheel. However, gay families differed from networks to the extent that they quite consciously incorporated symbolic demonstrations of love, shared history, material or emotional assistance, and other signs of enduring solidarity. Although many gay families included friends, not just any friend would do.[1]

Fluid boundaries and varied membership meant no neatly replicable units, no defined cycles of expansion and contraction, no patterns of dispersal. What might have represented a nightmare to an anthropologist in search of mappable family structures appeared to most participants in a highly positive light as the product of unfettered creativity. The subjective agency implicit in gay kinship surfaced in the very labels developed to describe it: "families *we* choose," "families *we* create." In the language of significant others, significance rested in the eye of the beholder. Participants tended to depict their chosen families as thoroughly individualistic affairs, insofar as each and every ego was left to be the chooser. Paradoxically, the very notion of idiosyncratic choice—originally conceived in opposition to biogenetic givens—lent structural coherence to what people presented as unique renditions of family.

. . .

"Choice" is an individualistic and, if you will, bourgeois notion that focuses on the subjective power of an "I" to formulate relationships to people and things, untrammeled by worldly constraints. Yet as Karl Marx (1963, p. 15) pointed out in an often quoted passage from *The 18th Brumaire,* "Men [sic] make their own history, but they do not make it just as they please; they do not make it under circumstances chosen by themselves, but under circumstances directly encountered, given and transmitted from the past." Only after coming out to blood relatives emerged as a historical possibility could the element of selection in kinship become isolated in gay experience and subsequently elevated to a constitutive feature of gay families.

Despite the ideological characterization of gay families as freely chosen, in practice the particular choices made yielded families that were far from randomly selected, much less demographically representative. When I asked people who said they had gay families to list the individuals they included under that rubric, their lists were primarily, though not exclusively, composed of other lesbians and gay men. Not surprisingly, the majority of people listed tended to come from the same gender, class, race, and age cohort as the respondent.

Both men and women consistently counted lovers as family, often placing their partners at the head of a list of relatives. A few believed a lover, or a lover plus children, would be essential in order to have a gay family, but the vast majority felt that all gay men and lesbians, including those who are single, can create families of their own. The partner of someone already considered family might or might not be included as kin. "Yeah, they're part of the family, but they're like in-laws," laughed one man. "You know, you love them, and yet there isn't that same closeness."

Former lovers presented a particularly interesting case. Their inclusion in families we choose was far from automatic, but most people hoped to stay connected to ex-lovers as friends and family (cf. Becker 1988; Clunis and Green 1988).[2] When former lovers remained estranged, the surprise voiced by friends underscored the power of this ideal. "It's been 10 years since you two broke up!" one man exclaimed to another. "Hasn't he gotten over it yet?" Of course, when a breakup involved hard feelings or a property dispute, such continuity was not always realizable. After an initial period of separation, many ex-lovers did in fact reestablish contact, while others continued to strive for this type of reintegration. As Diane Kunin put it, "After you break up, a lot of people sort of become as if they were parents and sisters, and relate to your new lover as if *they* were the in-law." I also learned of several men who had renewed ties after a former lover developed AIDS or ARC (AIDS-Related Complex). This emphasis on making a transition from lover to friend while remaining within the bounds of gay families contrasted with heterosexual partners in the Bay Area, for whom separation or divorce often meant permanent rupture of a kinship tie.

. . .

A lover's biological or adoptive relatives might or might not be classified as kin, contingent upon their "rejecting" or "accepting" attitudes. Gina Pellegrini, for example, found refuge at a lover's house after her parents kicked her out of her own home as an adolescent. She was out to her lover's mother before her own parents, and still considered this woman family. Jorge Quintana claimed that his mother adored his ex-lover and vice versa, although Jorge had broken up with this man many years earlier. . . . Jerry Freitag and his partner Kurt had made a point of introducing their parents to one another. "My mother and his mother talk on the phone every once in a while and write letters and stuff. Like my grandmother just died. Kurt's mother was one of the first people to call my mom." For Charlyne Harris, however, calling her ex-lover's mother "family" would have been out of the question. "Her mother didn't like me. Number one, she didn't want her to be *in* a lesbian relationship; number two, she knew that I was black. So I didn't have a lot of good things to say about her mother. . . . Pam told me, 'She can't even say your name!'"

In addition to friendships and relationships with lovers or ex-lovers, chosen family might also embrace ties to children or people who shared a residence. *Gay Community News* published a series of letters from gay male prisoners who had united to form "the Del-Ray Family" (only to be separated by the warden). Back in San Francisco, Rose Ellis told me about the apartment she has shared with several friends. One woman in particular, she said, was "like a big sister to me." When this woman died of cancer, the household split up, and "that kind of broke the family thing." In other circumstances, however, hardship drew people together across household lines. Groups organized to assist individuals who were chronically or terminally ill often incorporated love and persisted through time, characteristics some participants took as signs of kinship. . . .

The relative absence of institutionalization or rituals associated with these emergent gay families sometimes raised problems of definition and mutuality: I may count you as a member of my family, but do you number me in yours? In this context offers of assistance, commitment to "working through" conflicts, and a common history measured by months or years, all became confirming signs of kinship. By symbolically testifying to the presence of intangibles such as solidarity and love, these demonstrations operated to persuade and to concretize, to move a relationship toward reciprocity while seeking recognition for a kin tie.

Like their heterosexual counterparts, most gay men and lesbians insisted that family members are people who are "there for you," people you can count on emotionally and materially. "They take care of me," said one man, "I take care of them." According to Rayna Rapp (1982) the "middle class" in the United States tends to share affective support but not material resources within friendships. In the Bay Area, however, lesbians and gay men from all classes and class backgrounds, regularly rendered both sorts of assistance to one another. Many considered this an important way of demarcating friend from family. Diane Kunin, a writer, described family as people who will care for you when you're sick, get you out of jail, help you fix a flat tire, or drive you to the airport. . . .

Overall, the interface between property relations and kinship relations among lesbians and gay men who called one another family seemed consistent with such relations elsewhere in the society, with the exception of a somewhat greater expectation for financial independence and self-sufficiency on the part of each member of a couple. Individuals distributed their own earnings and resources; where pooling occurred, it usually involved an agreement with a lover or a limited common fund with housemates. Some households divided bills evenly, while others negotiated splits proportionate to income. A person might support a lover for a period of time, but this was not the rule for either men or women. Putting a partner through school or taking time off from wage work for childrearing represented the type of short-term arrangements most commonly associated with substantial financial support.

Across household lines, material aid was less likely to take the form of direct monetary contributions, unless a dependent child was involved. Services exchanged between members of different households who considered themselves kin included everything from walking a dog to preparing meals, running errands, and fixing cars. Lending tools, supplies, videotapes, clothes, books, and almost anything else imaginable was commonplace in some relationships. Many people had extended loans to gay or straight kin at some time. Some had given money to relatives confronted with the high cost of medical care in the United States, and a few from working-class backgrounds reported contributing to the support of biological or adoptive relatives (either their own or a lover's).

Another frequently cited criterion for separating "just plain" friends from friends who were also family was a shared past. In this case, the years a relationship had persisted could become a measure of closeness, reflecting the presumption that common experiences would lead to common understandings. Jenny Chin explained it this way:

> I have, not blood family, but other kind of family. And I think it really takes a lot to get to that point. Like years. Like five years, 10 years, or whatever. I think that we're gonna have to do that to survive. That's just a fact of life. Because the whole fact of being gay, you're estranged from your own family. At a certain level, pretty basic level. Unless you're lucky. There are some exceptions.
>
> So to survive, you have to have support networks and all that kind of stuff. And if you're settled enough, I think you do get into a . . . those people become family. If you kind of settle in together. And your work, and your lives, and your house, and your kids or whatever become very intertwined.

While people sometimes depicted the creation of ties to chosen kin as a search for relationships that could carry the burden of family, there are many conceivable ways to move furniture, solicit advice, reminisce, share affections, or find baby-sitters for your children. All can be accomplished by calling on relationships understood to be something other than family, or by purchasing services if a person has the necessary funds. But allied to the emphasis on survival in Jenny's account was the notion of a cooperative history that emerged as she bent her litany of years to the task of establishing rather than assuming a solidarity that endures.

Relationships that had weathered conflict, like relationships sustained over miles but especially over time, also testified to attachment. Allusions to disagreements, quarrels, and annoyance were often accompanied by laughter. Charlyne Harris named five lesbians she counted as kin "because if they don't see me within a certain amount of time [they check up on me], and they're always in my business! Sometimes they get mad, too. They're like sisters. I know they care a lot." Another woman chuckled, "I never see these family, so you can tell they're family!" Still others mentioned, as a sign of kinship, hearing from people only when they wanted something. Through reversal and inversion, an ironic humor underscored meanings of intimacy and solidarity carried by the notion of family in the United States (cf. Pratt 1977).

. . .

Substitute for Biological Family?

Far from viewing families we choose as imitations or derivatives of family ties created elsewhere in their society, many lesbians and gay men alluded to the difficulty and excitement of constructing kinship in the *absence* of what they called "models." Others, however, echoed the viewpoint—popular in this society at large—that chosen families offer substitutes for blood ties lost through outright rejection or the distance introduced into relationships by remaining in the closet.[3] "There will always be an empty place where the blood family should be," one man told me. "But Tim and I fill for each other some of the emptiness of blood family that aren't there." In Louise Romero's opinion,

> A lot of lesbians . . . I think they're just looking for stuff—maybe the same stuff I am. Like my family ties, before coming out, there was a lot of closeness. I could share stuff with my sisters. You used to talk all your deep dark secrets. You can't any more 'cause they think you're weird. Which is true in my case—they really do. . . . I think a lot of women look for that, and you need that.

This theory has a certain appeal, not only because it speaks to the strong impact of coming out on lesbian and gay notions of kinship, but also because it is consistent with the elaboration of chosen families in conceptual opposition to biological family. On a practical level, most of the services that chosen kin provide for one another might otherwise be performed by relatives calculated according to blood, adoption, or marriage.

Although gay families are families a person creates in adult life, this theory portrays them primarily as *replacements* for, rather than chronological successors to, the families in which individuals came to adulthood. If chosen families simply represent some form of compensation for rejection by heterosexual relatives, however, gay families should logically focus on the establishment of intergenerational relationships. (Remember that the loss of parents, as opposed to other categories of relatives, was the main concern in deciding whether or not to reveal a gay or lesbian identity to straight family.) But when lesbians and gay men in the Bay Area applied kinship terminology to their chosen families, they usually placed themselves in the relationship of sisters and brothers to one another, regardless of their respective ages. In cases where gay families included children, adults who were chosen kin but not co-parents to a child sometimes characterized themselves as aunts or uncles.

As with any generalization, this one admits exceptions. Margie Jamison, active in organizing a Christian ministry to lesbians and gay men, described her work with PWAs (persons with AIDS) while tears streamed down her face. "When I have held them in my arms and they were dying, it's like my sons. Like my sons." In this case the intergenerational kinship terminology invoked Margie's pastoral role as well as her experience raising two sons from a previous heterosexual marriage. However, the characterization of most ties to chosen kin as peer relationships brings families we choose closer to so-called fictive kin relations found elsewhere in the United States than to even a moderately faithful reconstruction of the families in which lesbian- and gay-identified individuals grew up.

Equally significant, the minority of gay people who had been disowned were not the only ones who participated in the elaboration of gay kinship. Many who classified relations with their biological or adoptive relatives as cordial to excellent employed the opposition between gay and straight family. Among those whose relations with their straight families had gradually improved over the years, ties to chosen kin generally had not diminished in importance. If laying claim to a gay family in no way depends upon a break with one's family of origin, the theory of chosen family as a surrogate for kinship lost dissolves. A satisfactory explanation for the historical emergence of gay families requires an understanding of the changing relation of friendship to sexual identity among the large numbers of gay people who flocked to urban areas after the second world war.

Friends and Lovers

"That's the way one builds a good life: a set of friends." At 64, Harold Sanders had no hesitation about indulging his passion for aphorisms, the turn of phrase stretched backward to gather in experiences of a lifetime. His statement reflected a conviction very widely shared by lesbians and gay men of all ages. People from diverse backgrounds depicted themselves as the beneficiaries of better friendships than heterosexuals, or made a case for the greater significance and respect they believed gay people accord to friendship.[4] Most likely such comments reflected a mixture of observation and self-congratulation, but they also drew attention to the connection many lesbians and gay men made between friendship and sexual identity (as well as race or ethnicity). The same individuals tended to portray heterosexuals as people who place family and friends in an exclusive, even antagonistic, relationship. As a child growing up in a Chinese American family, said Jenny Chin,

> I had a lot drilled into me about your friends are just your friends. *Just* friends. Very minimalizing and discounting [of] friendships. Because family was supposed to be all-important. Everything was done to pre-

serve the family unit. Even if people were killing each other; even if people had 20-year-old grudges and hadn't spoken.

In contrast, discussions of gay families pictured kinship as an *extension* of friendship, rather than viewing the two as competitors or assimilating friendships to biogenetic relationships regarded as somehow more fundamental. It was not unusual for a gay man or lesbian to speak of another as family in one breath and friend in the next. Yet the solidarity implicit in such statements has not always been a taken-for-granted feature of gay lives. According to John D'Emilio (1983), recognition of the possibility of establishing nonerotic ties among homosexuals constituted a key historical development that paved the way for the emergence of lesbian and gay "community"—and, I might add, for the later appearance of the ideological opposition between biological family and families we choose.

NOTES

1. Cf. Riley (1988), who found in a small study of 11 lesbians in New York City that those friends characterized as family were "intimate" rather than "social" friends.
2. In practice this generalization may hold more for lesbians than for gay men, although many gay men also shared the ideal of transforming the formerly erotic tie to an ex-lover into an enduring nonerotic bond.
3. The notion of a substitute family can also be criticized as functionalist in that it assumes all people have a need for family. Social scientists have applied theories of surrogate family to many marginalized groups in the United States. See, for example, Vigil (1988) on barrio gangs in Southern California.
4. Cf. Hooker (1965) on the importance placed on friendship by gay men of an earlier era.

REFERENCES

Becker, Carol S. 1988. *Unbroken Ties: Lesbian Ex-Lovers*. Boston: Alyson.

Clunis, D. Merilee and G. Dorsey Green. 1988. *Lesbian Couples*. Seattle: Seal Press.

D'Emilio, John. 1983. *Sexual Politics, Sexual Communities: The Making of a Homosexual Minority in the United States, 1940–1970*. Chicago: University of Chicago Press.

Hooker, Evelyn. 1965. "Male Homosexuals and Their 'Worlds.'" Pp. 83–107 in *Sexual Inversion*, edited by Judd Marmor. New York: Basic Books.

Marx, Karl. 1963. *The 18th Brumaire of Louis Bonaparte*. New York: International Publishers, p. 15.

Pratt, Mary Louise. 1977. *Toward a Speech Act Theory of Literary Discourse*. Bloomington: Indiana University Press.

Rapp, Rayna. 1982. "Family and Class in Contemporary America: Notes toward an Understanding of Ideology." Pp. 168–187 in *Rethinking the Family*, edited by Barrie Thorne with Marilyn Yalom. New York: Longman.

Riley, Claire. 1988. "American Kinship: A Lesbian Account." *Feminist Studies* 8:75–94.

Schneider, David and Raymond Smith. 1978. *Class Differences in American Kinship*. Ann Arbor: University of Michigan Press, p. 42.

Vigil, James Diego. 1988. *Barrio Gangs: Street Life and Identity in Southern California*. Austin: University of Texas Press.

Yanagisako, Sylvia. 1978. "Variance in American Kinship: Implications for Cultural Analysis." *American Ethnologist* 5:15–29.
————. 1985. *Transforming the Past: Tradition and Kinship among Japanese Americans.* Stanford: Stanford University Press.

54

THE MEANING OF MOTHERHOOD
IN BLACK CULTURE

PATRICIA HILL COLLINS

In this selection, Patricia Hill Collins observes how motherhood is socially constructed within the black community. Collins states that black children often are raised by othermothers, grandmothers, and extended kin relations. These racial-ethnic differences in family formation patterns and parenting challenge the dominant culture's stereotype of the nuclear family. Moreover, Collins' research illustrates that the family, regardless of its membership or structure, is, like Talcott Parsons argued, an institution that primarily socializes children and stabilizes adults.

Bloodmothers, Othermothers, and Women-Centered Networks

In African American communities, the boundaries distinguishing biological mothers of children from other women who care for children are often fluid and changing. Biological mothers or bloodmothers are expected to care for their children. But African and African American communities have also recognized that vesting one person with full responsibility for mothering a child may not be wise or possible. As a result, "othermothers," women who assist bloodmothers by sharing mothering responsibilities, traditionally have been central to the institution of Black motherhood.[1]

The centrality of women in African American extended families is well known.[2] Organized, resilient, women-centered networks of bloodmothers and othermothers are key in understanding this centrality: Grandmothers, sisters, aunts, or cousins acted as othermothers by taking on child care responsibilities for each other's children. When needed, temporary child-care arrangements turned into long-term care or informal adoption.[3]

In African American communities, these women-centered networks of community-based child care often extend beyond the boundaries of biologically related extended families to support "fictive kin."[4] Civil rights activist Ella Baker describes how informal adoption by othermothers functioned in the Southern, rural community of her childhood:

> My aunt who had thirteen children of her own raised three more. She had become a midwife, and a child was born who was covered with sores. Nobody was particularly wanting the child, so she took the child and raised him . . . and another mother decided she didn't want to be bothered with two children. So my aunt took one and raised him . . . they were part of the family.[5]

Even when relationships were not between kin or fictive kin, African American community norms were such that neighbors cared for each other's children. In the following passage, Sara Brooks, a Southern domestic worker, describes the importance of the community-based child care that a neighbor offered her daughter. In doing so, she also shows how the African American cultural value placed on cooperative child care found institutional support in the adverse conditions under which so many Black women mothered.

> She kept Vivian and she didn't charge me nothin either. You see, people used to look after each other, but now it's not that way. I reckon it's because we all was poor, and I guess they put theirself in the place of the person that they was helpin.[6]

Othermothers were key not only in supporting children but also in supporting bloodmothers who, for whatever reason, were ill-prepared or had little desire to care for their children. Given the pressures from the larger political economy, the emphasis placed on community-based child care and the respect given to othermothers who assume the responsibilities of child care have served a critical function in African American communities. Children orphaned by sale or death of their parents under slavery; children conceived through rape; children of young mothers; children born into extreme poverty; or children, who for other reasons have been rejected by their bloodmothers, have all been supported by othermothers who, like Ella Baker's aunt, took in additional children, even when they had enough of their own.

Providing as Part of Mothering

The work done by African American women in providing the economic resources essential to Black family well-being affects motherhood in a contradictory fashion. On the one hand, African American women have long integrated their activities as economic providers into their mothering relationships. In contrast to the cult of true womanhood where work is defined as being in opposition to and incompatible with motherhood, work for Black women has been an important and valued dimension of Afro-centric definitions of Black motherhood. On the other hand, African American women's experiences as mothers under oppression were such that the type and purpose of work Black women were forced to do greatly impacted on the type of mothering relationships bloodmothers and othermothers had with Black children.

While slavery both disrupted West African family patterns and exposed enslaved Africans to the gender ideologies and practices of slaveowners, it simultaneously made it impossible, had they wanted to do so, for enslaved Africans to implement slaveowner's ideologies. Thus, the separate spheres of providing as a male domain and affective nurturing as a female domain did not develop within African American families.[7] Providing for Black children's physical survival and attending to their affective, emotional needs continued as interdependent dimensions of an Afrocentric ideology of motherhood. However, by changing the conditions under which Black women worked and the purpose of the work itself, slavery introduced the problem of how best to continue traditional Afrocentric values under oppressive conditions. Institutions of community-based child care, informal adoption, greater reliance on othermothers, all emerge as adaptations to the exigencies of combining exploitative work with nurturing children.

In spite of the change in political status brought on by emancipation, the majority of African American women remained exploited agricultural workers. However, their placement in southern political economies allowed them to combine child care with field labor. Sara Brooks describes how strong the links between providing and caring for others were for her:

> When I was about nine I was nursin my sister Sally—I'm about seven or eight years older than Sally. And when I would put her to sleep, instead of me goin somewhere and sit down and play, I'd get my little old hoe and get out there and work right in the field around the house.[8]

Black women's shift from southern agriculture to domestic work in southern and northern towns and cities represented a change in the type of work done, but not in the meaning of work to women and their families. Whether they wanted to or not, the majority of African American women had to work and could not afford the luxury of motherhood as a noneconomically productive, female "occupation."

Community Othermothers and Social Activism

Black women's experiences as othermothers have provided a foundation for Black women's social activism. Black women's feelings of responsibility for nurturing the children in their own extended family network have stimulated a more generalized ethic of care where Black women feel accountable to all the Black community's children.

This notion of Black women as community othermothers for all Black children traditionally allowed Black women to treat biologically unrelated children as if they were members of their own families. For example, sociologist Karen Fields describes how her grandmother, Mamie Garvin Fields, draws on her power as a community othermother when dealing with unfamiliar children.

> She will say to a child on the street who looks up to no good, picking out a name at random, "Aren't you Miz Pinckney's boy?" in that same reproving tone. If the reply is, "No, *ma'am*, my mother is Miz Gadsden," whatever threat there was dissipates.[9]

The use of family language in referring to members of the Black community also illustrates this dimension of Black motherhood. For example, Mamie Garvin Fields describes how she became active in surveying the poor housing conditions of Black people in Charleston.

> I was one of the volunteers they got to make a survey of the places where we were paying extortious rents for indescribable property. I said "we," although it wasn't Bob and me. We had our own home, and so did many of the Federated Women. Yet we still felt like it really was "we" living in those terrible places, and it was up to us to do something about them.[10]

To take another example, while describing her increasingly successful efforts to teach a boy who had given other teachers problems, my daughter's kindergarten teacher stated, "You know how it can be—the majority of the children in the learning disabled classes are *our children*. I know he didn't belong there, so I volunteered to take him." In these statements, both women invoke the language of family to describe the ties that bind them as Black women to their responsibilities to other members of the Black community as family.

Sociologist Cheryl Gilkes suggests that community othermother relationships are sometimes behind Black women's decisions to become community activists.[11] Gilkes notes that many of the Black women community activists in her study became involved in community organizing in response to the needs of their own children and of those in their communities. The following comment is typical of how many of the Black women in Gilkes' study relate to Black children: "There were a lot of summer programs springing up for kids, but they were exclusive . . . and I found that most of *our kids* (emphasis mine) were excluded."[12] For many women, what began as the daily expression of their obligations as community othermothers, as was the case for the kindergarten teacher, developed into full-fledged roles as community leaders.

NOTES

1. The terms used in this section appear in Rosalie Riegle Troester, "Turbulence and Tenderness: Mothers, Daughters, and Othermothers" in Paule Marshall's *Brown Girl, Brownstones," SAGE: A Scholarly Journal on Black Women* 1 (Fall 1984): 13–16.
2. See Tanner's discussion of matrifocality, 1974; see also Carrie Allen McCray, "The Black Woman and Family Roles," in *The Black Woman,* ed. LaFrances Rogers-Rose

(Beverly Hills, CA: Sage, 1980), pp. 67–78; Elmer Martin and Joanne Mitchell Martin, *The Black Extended Family* (Chicago: University of Chicago, 1978); Joyce Aschenbrenner, *Lifelines, Black Families in Chicago* (Prospect Heights, IL: Waveland, 1975); and Carol B. Stack, *All Our Kin* (New York: Harper & Row, 1974).

3. Martin and Martin, *The Black Extended Family;* Stack, *All Our Kin;* and Virginia Young, "Family and Childhood in a Southern Negro Community," *American Anthropologist* 72 (1970): 269–88.

4. Stack, *All Our Kin.*

5. Ellen Cantarow, *Moving the Mountain: Women Working for Social Change* (Old Westbury, NY: Feminist Press, 1980), p. 59.

6. Thordis Simonsen, ed., *You May Plow Here, The Narrative of Sara Brooks* (New York: Touchstone, 1986), p. 81.

7. Deborah White, *Arn't I a Woman? Female Slaves in the Plantation South* (New York: Norton, 1984); Bonnie Thornton Dill, "Our Mothers' Grief: Racial Ethnic Women and the Maintenance of Families," Research Paper 4, Center for Research on Women (Memphis, TN: Memphis State University, 1986); Leith Mullings, "Uneven Development: Class, Race and Gender in the United States before 1900," in *Women's Work, Development and the Division of Labor by Gender,* eds. Eleanor Leacock and Helen Safa (South Hadley, MA: Bergin & Garvey, 1986), pp. 41–57.

8. Simonsen, *You May Plow Here,* p. 86.

9. Mamie Garvin Fields and Karen Fields, *Lemon Swamp and Other Places: A Carolina Memoir* (New York: Free Press, 1983), p. xvii.

10. Ibid, p. 195.

11. Cheryl Gilkes, "'Holding Back the Ocean with a Broom,' Black Women and Community Work," in Rogers-Rose, *The Black Woman,* pp. 217–31; "Going Up for the Oppressed: The Career Mobility of Black Women Community Workers," *Journal of Social Issues* 39 (1983): 115–39.

12. Gilkes, "'Holding Back,'" p. 219.

PART VIII
Social Change

55

THE McDONALDIZATION OF SOCIETY

GEORGE RITZER

In this reading, the first of four to focus on social change, George Ritzer examines the larger consequences of having an organization, such as McDonald's, in society. Ritzer argues that societies are being transformed by a process he labels "McDonaldization," in which the principles of the fast-food restaurant have come to influence other aspects of the social structure, such as the family, politics, education, travel, and leisure. Ritzer also summarizes the societal costs and benefits of this widespread social change.

A wide-ranging process of *rationalization* is occurring across American society and is having an increasingly powerful impact in many other parts of the world. It encompasses such disparate phenomena as fast-food restaurants, TV dinners, packaged tours, industrial robots, plea bargaining, and open-heart surgery on an assembly-line basis. As widespread and as important as these developments are, it is clear that we have barely begun a process that promises even more extraordinary changes (e.g., genetic engineering) in the years to come. We can think of rationalization as a historical process and rationality as the end result of that development. As a historical process, rationalization has distinctive roots in the western world. Writing in the late nineteenth and early twentieth centuries, the great German sociologist Max Weber saw his society as the center of the ongoing process of rationalization and the bureaucracy as its paradigm case. The model of rationalization, at least in contemporary America, is no longer the bureaucracy, but might be better though of as the fast-food restaurant. As a result, our concern here is with what might be termed the "McDonaldization of Society." While the fast-food restaurant is not the ultimate expression of rationality, it is the current exemplar for future developments in rationalization.

A society characterized by rationality is one which emphasizes *efficiency, predictability, calculability, substitution of nonhuman for human technology, and control over uncertainty*. In discussing the various dimensions of rationalization, we will be little concerned with the gains already made, and yet to be realized, by greater rationalization. These advantages are widely discussed in schools and in the mass media. In fact, we are in danger of being seduced by the innumerable advantages already offered, and promised in the future, by rationalization. The glitter of these accomplishments and promises has served to distract most people from the grave dangers posed by progressive rationalization. In other words, we are ultimately concerned here with the irrational consequences that often flow from rational systems. Thus, the second major theme of this essay might be termed "the irrationality of rationality." . . .

Efficiency

The process of rationalization leads to a society in which a great deal of emphasis is placed on finding the best or optimum means to any given end. Whatever a group of people define as an end, and everything they so define, is to be pursued by attempting to find the best means to achieve the end. Thus, in the Germany of Weber's day, the bureaucracy was seen as the most efficient means of handling a wide array of administrative tasks. Somewhat later, the Nazis came to develop the concentration camp, its ovens, and other devices as the optimum method of collecting and murdering millions of Jews and other people. The efficiency that Weber described in turn-of-the-century Germany, and which later came to characterize many Nazi activities, has become a basic principle of life in virtually every sector of a rational society.

The modern American family, often with two wage earners, has little time to prepare elaborate meals. For the relatively few who still cook such meals, there is likely to be great reliance on cookbooks that make cooking from scratch much more efficient. However, such cooking is relatively rare today. Most families take as their objective quickly and easily prepared meals. To this end, much use is made of prepackaged meals and frozen TV dinners.

For many modern families, the TV dinner is no longer efficient enough. To many people, eating out, particularly in a fast-food restaurant, is a far more efficient way of obtaining their meals. Fast-food restaurants capitalize on this by being organized so that diners are fed as efficiently as possible. They offer a limited, simple menu that can be cooked and served in an assembly-line fashion. The latest development in fast-food restaurants, the addition of drive-through windows, constitutes an effort to increase still further the efficiency of the dining experience. The family now can simply drive through, pick up its order, and eat it while driving to the next, undoubtedly efficiently organized, activity. The success of the fast-food restaurant has come full circle with frozen food manufacturers now touting products for the home modeled after those served in fast-food restaurants.

Increasingly, efficiently organized food production and distribution systems lie at the base of the ability of people to eat their food efficiently at home, in the fast-food restaurant, or in their cars. Farms, groves, ranches, slaughterhouses, warehouses, transportation systems, and retailers are all oriented toward increasing efficiency. A notable example is chicken production where they are mass-bred, force-fed (often with many chemicals), slaughtered on an assembly line, iced or fast frozen, and shipped to all parts of the country. Some may argue that such chickens do not taste as good as the fresh-killed, local variety, but their complaints are likely to be drowned in a flood of mass-produced chickens. Then there is bacon which is more efficiently shipped, stored, and sold when it is preserved by sodium nitrate, a chemical which is unfortunately thought by many to be carcinogenic. Whatever one may say about the quality or the danger of the products, the fact remains that they are all shaped by the drive for efficiency. . . .

One of the most interesting and important aspects of efficiency is that it often comes to be not a means but an end in itself. This "displacement of goals" is a major problem in a rationalizing society. We have, for example, the bureaucrats who slavishly follow the rules even though their inflexibility negatively affects the organization's ability to achieve its goals. Then there are the bureaucrats who are so concerned with efficiency that they lose sight of the ultimate goals the means are designed to achieve. A good example was the Nazi concentration camp officers who, in devoting so much attention to maximizing the efficiency of the camps' operation, lost sight of the fact that the ultimate purpose of the camps was the murder of millions of people.

Predictability

A second component of rationalization involves the effort to ensure predictability from one place to another. In a rational society, people want to know what to expect when they enter a given setting or acquire some sort of commodity. They neither want nor expect surprises. They want to know that if they journey to another locale, the setting they enter or the commodity they buy will be essentially the same as the setting they entered or product they purchased earlier. Furthermore, people want to be sure that what they encounter is much like what they encountered at earlier times. In order to ensure predictability over time and place a rational society must emphasize such things as discipline, order, systemization, formalization, routine, consistency, and methodical operation.

One of the attractions of TV dinners for modern families is that they are highly predictable. The TV dinner composed of fried chicken, mashed potatoes, green peas, and peach cobbler is exactly the same from one time to another and one city to another. Home cooking from scratch is, conversely, a notoriously unpredictable enterprise with little assurance that dishes will taste the same time after time. However, the cookbook cannot eliminate all unpredictability. There are often simply too many ingredients and other variables involved. Thus the cookbook dish is far less predictable than the TV dinner or a wide array of other prepared dishes.

Fast-food restaurants rank very high on the dimension of predictability.

In order to help ensure consistency, the fast-food restaurant offers only a limited menu. Predictable end products are made possible by the use of similar raw materials, technologies, and preparation and serving techniques. Not only the food is predictable; the physical structures, the logo, the "ambience," and even the personnel are as well.

The food that is shipped to our homes and our fast-food restaurants is itself affected by the process of increasing predictability. Thus our favorite white bread is indistinguishable from one place to another. In fact, food producers have made great efforts to ensure such predictability.

On packaged tours travelers can be fairly sure that the people they travel with will be much like themselves. The planes, buses, hotel accommodations, restaurants, and at least the way in which the sites are visited are very similar from one location to another. Many people go on packaged tours *because* they are far more predictable than travel undertaken on an individual basis.

Amusement parks used to be highly unpredictable affairs. People could never be sure, from one park to another, precisely what sorts of rides, events, foods, visitors, and employees they would encounter. All of that has changed in the era of the theme parks inspired by Disneyland. Such parks seek to ensure predictability in various ways. For example, a specific type of young person is hired in these parks, and they are all trained in much the same way, so that they have a robot-like predictability.

Other leisure-time activities have grown similarly predictable. Camping in the wild is loaded with uncertainties—bugs, bears, rain, cold, and the like. To make camping more predictable, organized grounds have sprung up around the country. Gone are many of the elements of unpredictability replaced by RVs, paved-over parking lots, sanitized campsites, fences and enclosed camp centers that provide laundry and food services, recreational activities, television, and video games. Sporting events, too, have in a variety of ways been made more predictable. The use of artificial turf in baseball makes for a more predictable bounce of a ball. . . .

Calculability or Quantity Rather than Quality

It could easily be argued that the emphasis on quantifiable measures, on things that can be counted, is *the* most defining characteristic of a rational society. Quality is notoriously difficult to evaluate. How do we assess the quality of a hamburger, or a physician, or a student? Instead of even trying, in an increasing number of cases, a rational society seeks to develop a series of quantifiable measures that it takes as surrogates for quality. This urge to quantify has given great impetus to the development of the computer and has, in turn, been spurred by the widespread use and increasing sophistication of the computer.

The fact is that many aspects of modern rational society, especially as far as calculable issues are concerned, are made possible and more widespread by the computer. We need not belabor the ability of the computer to handle large numbers of virtually anything, but somewhat less obvious is the use of the computer to give the illusion of personal attention in a world made increasingly impersonal in large part because of the computer's capacity to turn virtually everything into quantifiable dimensions. We have all now had many experiences where we open a letter personally addressed to us only to find a computer letter. We are aware that the names and addresses of millions of people have been stored on tape and that with the aid of a number of word processors a form letter has been sent to every name on the list. Although the computer is able to give a sense of personal attention, most people are nothing more than an item on a huge mailing list.

Our main concern here, though, is not with the computer, but with the emphasis on quantity rather than quality that it has helped foster. One of the most obvious examples in the university is the emphasis given to grades and cumulative grade point averages. With less and less contact between professor and student, there is little real effort to assess the quality of what students know, let alone the quality of their overall abilities. Instead, the sole measure of the quality of most college students is their grade in a given course and their grade point averages. Another blatant example is the emphasis on a variety of uniform exams such as SATs and GREs in which the essence of an applicant is reduced to a few simple scores and percentiles.

Within the educational institution, the importance of grades is well known, but somewhat less known is the way quantifiable factors have become an essential part of the process of evaluating college professors. For example, teaching ability is very hard to evaluate. Administrators have difficulty assessing teaching quality and thus substitute quantitative scores. Of course each score involves qualitative judgments, but this is conveniently ignored. Student opinion polls are taken and the scores are summed, averaged, and compared. Those who score well are deemed good teachers while those who don't are seen as poor teachers. There are many problems involved in relying on these scores such as the fact that easy teachers in "gut" courses may well obtain high ratings while rigorous teachers of difficult courses are likely to score poorly. . . .

In the workworld we find many examples of the effort to substitute quantity for quality. Scientific management was heavily oriented to turning everything work-related into quantifiable dimensions. Instead of relying on the "rule of thumb" of the operator, scientific management sought to develop precise measures of how much work was to be done by each and every motion of the worker. Everything that could be was reduced to numbers and all these numbers were then analyzable using a variety of mathematical formulae. The assembly line is similarly oriented to a variety of quantifiable dimensions such as optimizing the speed of the line, minimizing time for each task, lowering the price of the finished product, increasing sales and ultimately increasing profits. The divisional system pioneered by General Motors and thought to be one of the major reasons for its past success was oriented to the reduction of the performance of each division to a few, bottom-line numbers. By monitoring and comparing these numbers, General Motors was able to exercise control over the results without getting involved in the day-to-day activities of each division. . . .

Thus, the third dimension of rationalization, calculability or the emphasis on quantity rather than quality, has wide applicability to the social world. It is truly central, if not the central, component of a rationalizing society. To return to our favorite example, it is the case that McDonald's expends far more effort telling us how many billions of hamburgers it has sold than it does in telling us about the quality of those burgers. Relatedly, it touts the size of its product (the "Big Mac") more than the quality of the product (it is not the "Good Mac"). The bottom line in many settings is the number of customers processed, the speed with which they are processed, and the profits produced. Quality is secondary, if indeed there is any concern at all for it.

Substitution of Nonhuman Technology

In spite of Herculean efforts, there are important limits to the ability to rationalize what human beings think and do. Seemingly no matter what one does, people still retain at least the ultimate capacity to think and act in a variety of unanticipated ways. Thus, in spite of great efforts to make human behavior more efficient, more predictable, more calculable, people continue to act in unforeseen ways. People continue to make home-cooked meals from scratch, to camp in tents in the wild, to eat in old-fashioned diners, and to sabotage the assembly lines. Because of these realities, there is great interest among those who foster increasing rationality in using rational technologies to limit individual independence and ultimately to replace human beings with machines and other technologies that lack the ability to think and act in unpredictable ways.

McDonald's does not yet have robots to serve us food, but it does have teenagers whose ability to act autonomously is almost completely eliminated by techniques, procedures, routines, and machines. There are numerous examples of this including rules which prescribe all the things a counterperson should do in dealing with a customer as well as a large variety of technologies which determine the actions of workers such as drink dispensers which shut themselves off when the cup is full; buzzers, lights, and bells which indicate when food (e.g., french fries) is done; and cash registers which have the prices of each item programmed in. One of the latest attempts to constrain individual action is Denny's use of pre-measured packages of dehydrated food that are "cooked" simply by putting them under the hot water tap. Because of such tools and machines, as well as the elaborate rules dictating worker behavior, people often feel like they are dealing with human robots when they relate to the personnel of a fast-food restaurant. When human robots are found, mechanical robots cannot be far behind. Once people are reduced to a few robot-like actions, it is a relatively easy step to replace them with mechanical robots. Thus Burgerworld is reportedly opening a prototypical restaurant in which mechanical robots serve the food.

Much of the recent history of work, especially manual work, is a history of efforts to replace human technology with nonhuman technology. Scientific management was oriented to the development of an elaborate and rigid set of rules about how jobs were to be done. The workers were to blindly and obediently follow those rules and not to do the work the way they saw fit. The various skills needed to perform a task were carefully delineated and broken down into a series of routine steps that could be taught to all workers. The skills, in other words, were built into the routines rather than belonging to skilled craftspersons. Similar points can be made about the assembly line which is basically a set of nonhuman technologies that have the needed steps and skills built into them. The human worker is reduced to performing a limited number of simple, repetitive operations. However, the control of this technology over the individual worker is so great and omnipresent that individual workers have reacted negatively manifesting such things as tardiness, absenteeism, turnover, and even sabotage. We are now witnessing a new stage in this technological development with automated processes now totally replacing many workers with robots. With the coming of robots we have reached the ultimate stage in the replacement of humans with nonhuman technology.

Even religion and religious crusades have not been unaffected by the spread of nonhuman technologies. The growth of large religious organizations, the use of Madison Avenue techniques, and even drive-in churches all reflect the incursion of modern technology. But it is in the electronic church, religion through the TV screens, that replacement of human by non-human technology in religion is most visible and has its most important manifestation. . . .

Control

This leads us to the fifth major dimension of rationalization—control. Rational systems are oriented toward, and structured to expedite, control in a variety of senses. At the most general level, we can say that rational systems are set up to allow for greater control over the uncertainties of life—birth, death, food production and distribution, housing, religious salvation, and many, many others. More specifically, rational systems are oriented to gaining greater control over the major source of uncertainty in social life—other people. Among other things, this means control over subordinates by superiors and control of clients and customers by workers.

There are many examples of rationalization oriented toward gaining greater control over the uncertainties of life. The burgeoning of the genetic engineering movement can be seen as being aimed at gaining better control over the production of life itself. Similarly, amniocentesis can be seen as a technique which will allow the parents to determine the kind of child they will have. The efforts to rationalize food production and distribution can be seen as being aimed at gaining greater control over the problems of hunger and starvation. A steady and regular supply of food can make life itself more certain for large numbers of people who today live under the threat of death from starvation.

At a more specific level, the rationalization of food preparation and serving at McDonald's gives it great control over its employees. The automobile assembly line has a similar impact. In fact, the vast majority of the structures of a rational society exert extraordinary control over the people who labor in them. But because of the limits that still exist on the degree of control that rational structures can exercise over individuals, many rationalizing employers are driven to seek to more fully rationalize their operations and totally eliminate the worker. The result is an automated, robot-like technology over which, barring some *2001* rebellion, there is almost total control.

In addition to control over employees, rational systems are also interested in controlling the customer/clients they serve. For example, the fast-food restaurant with its counter, the absence of waiters and waitresses, the limited seating, and the drive-through windows all tend to lead customers to do certain things and not to do others.

Irrationality of Rationality

Although not an inherent part of rationalization, the *irrationality of rationality* is a seemingly inevitable byproduct of the process. We can think of the irrationality of rationality in several ways. At the most general level it can simply be seen as an overarching label for all the negative effects of rationalization. More specifically, it can be seen as the opposite of rationality, at least in some of its senses. For example, there are the inefficiencies and unpredictabilities that are often produced by seemingly rational systems. Thus, although bureaucracies are constructed to bring about greater efficiency in organizational work, the fact is that there are notorious inefficiencies such as the "red tape" associated with the operation of most bureaucracies. Or, take the example of the arms race in which a focus on quantifiable aspects of nuclear weapons may well have made the occurrence of nuclear war more, rather than less, unpredictable.

Of greatest importance, however, is the variety of negative effects that rational systems have on the individuals who live, work, and are served by them. We might say that *rational systems are not reasonable systems*. As we've already discussed, rationality brings with it great dehumanization as people are reduced to acting like robots. Among the dehumanizing aspects of a rational society are large lecture classes, computer letters, pray TV, work on the automobile assembly line, and dining at a fast-food restaurant. Rationalization also tends to bring with it disenchantment leaving much of our lives without any mystery or excitement. Production by a hand craftsman is far more mysterious than an assembly-line technology where each worker does a single, very limited operation. Camping in an RV tends to suffer in comparison to the joys to be derived from camping in the wild. Overall a fully rational society would be a very bleak and uninteresting place.

Conclusions

Rationalization, with McDonald's as the paradigm case, is occurring throughout America, and, increasingly, other societies. In virtually every sector of society more and more emphasis is placed on efficiency, predictability, calculability, replacement of human by nonhuman technology, and control over uncertainty. Although progressive rationalization has brought with it innumerable advantages, it has also created a number of problems, the various irrationalities of rationality, which threaten to accelerate in the years to come. These problems, and their acceleration should not be taken as a case for the return to a less rational form of society. Such a return is not only impossible but also undesirable. What is needed is not a less rational society, but greater control over the process of rationalization involving, among other things, efforts to ameliorate its irrational consequences.

56

THE QUEST FOR ENVIRONMENTAL EQUITY
Mobilizing the African American Community
for Social Change

ROBERT D. BULLARD • BEVERLY H. WRIGHT

This selection is a study of social change written by two sociologists, Robert D. Bullard and Beverly H. Wright. In their research, Bullard and Wright combine analyses of environmental racism, social movement organizations, and social justice issues. Their investigation reveals why African American communities are more active and militant in grassroots environmental movements than in mainstream groups. Moreover, to illustrate their argument, Bullard and Wright present case studies of five African American communities that were involved in environmental disputes.

Much research has been devoted to analyzing environmental movements in the United States. Despite this wide coverage, there is a dearth of material on the convergence of environmentalism and social justice advocacy. Nearly two decades ago, Gale (1972) compared the civil rights movement and the environmental movement. The modern

environmental movement has its roots in the civil rights and antiwar movements of the late sixties (Humphrey and Buttel 1982). Student activists who
broke away from the civil rights and antiwar movements formed the core of
the environmental movement in the early 1970s.

There is a substantial body of literature on grass-roots environmental
groups (Freudenberg 1984; Freudenberg and Steinsapir 1990; Gottlieb and
Ingram 1988). However, little research has been conducted on African American, Latino, and Native American grassroots environmental groups such
as the Gulf Coast Tenants Organization (New Orleans), Mothers of East Los
Angeles, Concerned Citizens of South Central Los Angeles, Southwest Organizing Project (Albuquerque), Toxic Avengers of Brooklyn, West Harlem
Environmental Action, or Native Americans for a Clean Environment (Oklahoma). A special issue of *Environmental Action* highlighted the fact that the
time is long overdue for the nation to move "beyond white environmentalism" (Truax 1990).

This paper analyzes environmental activism within five African American communities in the South. The issues that are addressed include (1) factors that shape environmental mobilization, (2) the level of convergence
between environmental justice and social equity goals, (3) the source of environmental leadership, and (4) types of dispute resolution strategies used.

The Environmental Justice Movement

The civil rights movement has its roots in the southern United States. Southern racism deprived blacks of "political rights, economic opportunity, social
justice, and human dignity" (Bloom 1987, p. 18). However, racism is by no
means limited to any one region of the country. The environmental justice
movement for African Americans is centered in the South, a region where
marked ecological disparities exist between black and white communities.
Many of these disparities were institutionalized by laws and public policies
during the "Jim Crow" era. African American communities systematically
became the "dumping grounds" (Bullard 1990, p. 43) for all kinds of locally
unwanted land uses (LULUs).

The literature is replete with studies documenting the disproportionate
environmental burden borne by African Americans (Bullard 1990; Bullard
and Wright 1986, 1987a; Commission for Racial Justice [United Church of
Christ] 1987; Gianessi, Peskin, and Wolff 1979; Jordon 1980; Kazis and Grossman 1983; Kruvant 1975; McCaull 1975; U.S. General Accounting Office
1983). These ecological disparities were highlighted in the 1983 Urban Environment Conference whose theme was "taking back our health." The conference was held in New Orleans and was one of the first national forums that
brought together Third World people in this country and progressive whites
to talk about environmental justice and coalition building. This broad-based
group of civil rights activists, organized labor leaders, and grass-roots envi-

ronmental activists formed a loose alliance (Urban Environment Conference, Inc. 1985, p. 29). Cooperative action between social justice and environmental groups was seen as one of the best strategies to weaken the hold of "job blackmail"—the threat of job loss or plant closure—on the working class and communities of color (Kazis and Grossman, 1983).

A growing number of African American grass-roots environmental groups and their leaders have begun to adopt confrontational strategies (e.g., protests, neighborhood demonstrations, picketing, political pressure, and litigation) similar to those used in earlier civil rights disputes. These activists advocate a brand of environmentalism that attempts to address disparate impact and equity issues. Documentation of civil rights violations has strengthened the move to make environmental quality a basic right of all individuals (Bullard and Wright 1987a, 1987b).

Social justice advocate Reverend Ben Chavis defines many of the ecological inequities within the African American community as direct results of "environmental racism." The privileges of whites (access to a clean environment) are created and institutionalized at the expense of people of color (Commission for Racial Justice 1987, p. x). Thus the practice of targeting urban ghettos or rural blackbelt communities for noxious facilities (i.e., hazardous waste landfills, incinerators, paper mills, garbage dumps, and other polluting industries) is seen as another expression of institutional racism.

The U.S. General Accounting Office (1983) observed a strong relationship between the locations of off-site hazardous waste landfills and the racial and socioeconomic status of surrounding communities. The GAO looked at eight southern states that comprised the federal Environmental Protection Agency's (EPA's) Region IV (Alabama, Florida, Georgia, Kentucky, Mississippi, North Carolina, South Carolina, and Tennessee). The government study identified four off-site hazardous waste landfills in the region. African Americans made up a majority of the population in three of the four communities where the off-site hazardous waste landfills are located. The fourth site is located in a community where 38 percent of the population is African American. In 1990, only two off-site hazardous waste landfills were operating in Region IV, and both of these sites are located in African American communities. African Americans, who make up only 20 percent of the region's population, continue to shoulder a heavier toxic waste burden than any other group in the region.

The Commission for Racial Justice's (1987) ground-breaking report *Toxic Wastes and Race* clearly shows that African American communities and other communities of color bear a heavier burden than society at large in the disposal of the nation's hazardous waste. Race was the most potent variable in predicting the location of uncontrolled (abandoned) and commercial toxic waste sites in the United States.

The nation's total hazardous waste disposal capacity was 127,989 acre-feet in 1987 (Commission for Racial Justice, 1987). In 1987, three of the nation's largest commercial hazardous waste sites were located in African American or Latino communities. These three sites—Chemical Waste Management site in Emelle, Alabama (black); Rollins Environmental Services in Scotlandville, Louisiana (black); and Chemical Waste Management site in Kettleman City, California (Latino)—accounted for 51,070 acre-feet of the disposal capacity, or 40 percent of the nation's total hazardous waste disposal capacity in 1987 (Commission for Racial Justice 1987).

The first national protest by African Americans against environmental racism came in 1982 after the mostly black Warren County, North Carolina, was selected as the burial site for 32,000 cubic yards of soil contaminated with highly toxic polychlorinated biphenyls, or PCBs. The soil was illegally dumped along the roadways in 14 North Carolina counties in 1978. African American civil rights activists, political leaders, and local residents marched in protest demonstrations against the construction of the PCB landfill in their community. More than 400 demonstrators were jailed. Although the protests were unsuccessful in halting the landfill construction, they marked the first time that blacks mobilized a nationally broad-based group to protest environmental inequities and the first time that demonstrators had been sent to jail for protesting against a hazardous waste landfill (Bullard and Wright 1986; Geiser and Waneck 1983, pp. 13–17).

. . .

Case Studies from the Southern United States

The African American community is bombarded with all kinds of environmental stressors. Our goal was to select varied noxious facilities—municipal landfill, hazardous waste landfill and incinerator, and lead smelter facilities—and then gauge public opposition to these facilities. On the surface, municipal landfills may seem nonthreatening because they receive household garbage. However, sanitary landfills routinely accept household waste—some of which is highly toxic—and many receive illegally dumped hazardous waste. The threat (whether real or perceived) of living next to a toxic waste dump and incinerator has been well publicized. Similarly, the ill-effects of lead poisoning have been known since the Roman era.

The heightened militancy among African Americans on environmental issues served as a backdrop for studying a special brand of environmentalism. This analysis centered on five African American communities that were involved in environmental disputes during 1979–1987: Houston's Northwood Manor neighborhood (Texas), the West Dallas neighborhood (Texas), Institute (West Virginia), Alsen (Louisiana), and Emelle (Alabama). Although the communities have different histories, they share the common action of challenging the notion that social justice and environmental concern are incompatible goals.

The analysis is based on in-depth interviews conducted with a total of 15 opinion leaders who were identified through the "reputational" approach and who were active in the local environmental disputes. The interviews were conducted in the summer of 1988 and were supplemented with archival documents and newspaper articles, editorials, and feature stories on the disputes. The data addressed the following: (1) issue crystallization (e.g., each opinion leader was asked how he or she defined the local dispute), (2) citizen opposition tactics used, (3) type of leadership that spearheaded the citizen opposition, (4) methods used to resolve the dispute, and (5) outcome of the dispute.

Houston, Texas

Houston in the 1970s was dubbed the "golden buckle" of the Sunbelt. In 1982 it became the nation's fourth largest city, with 1.7 million inhabitants. Houston is the only major U.S. city that does not have zoning, a policy that has contributed to haphazard and irrational land-use planning and infrastructure chaos (Babcock 1982; Bullard 1984, 1987; Feagin 1985, 1987). Discriminatory facility-siting decisions allowed the city's black neighborhoods to become the "dumping grounds" for Houston's municipal garbage (Bullard 1983). From the late 1920s to the late 1970s, more than three-fourths of the city's solid waste sites (incinerators and landfills) were located in black neighborhoods, although African Americans made up only one-fourth of Houston's population.

In 1979 residents of the city's Northwood Manor neighborhood (where African Americans made up more than 84 percent of the total residents) chose to challenge the Browning-Ferris Industries' (one of the world's largest waste disposal firms) selection of their area for a garbage dump. Residents from this middle-income suburban neighborhood (some 83 percent of the residents own their homes) mobilized soon after they discovered the construction was not an expansion of their subdivision but a municipal landfill.

Dallas, Texas

Dallas is the nation's seventh largest city, with a population of 904,078 in 1980. African Americans represent 29.4 percent of the city's population. The African American population remains segregated: eight of every ten blacks live in mostly black neighborhoods. West Dallas is just one of these segregated enclaves, and African Americans make up 85 percent of the neighborhood residents. This low-income neighborhood dates back to the turn of the century. For more than five decades, residents were bombarded with toxic emissions from the nearby RSR Corp. lead smelter facility (Dallas Alliance Environmental Task Force 1983). The smelter routinely pumped more than 269 tons of lead particles each year into the air. After repeated violations and citations, residents from West Dallas in 1981 mobilized to close the plant and get the lead-tainted soil removed from their neighborhood.

Institute, West Virginia

Institute is located in the Kanawha River Valley just six miles west of Charleston, the state capital. It is an unincorporated community where African Americans represent more than 90 percent of the population. The community dates back to 1891 when the state legislature selected the site for West Virginia Colored Institute (later renamed West Virginia State College). The community is also home to the Union Carbide chemical plant that was the prototype for the company's plant in Bhopal, India. The Institute plant was the only plant in the United States that manufactured the same deadly methyl isocyanate (MIC) responsible for the 1984 Bhopal disaster. A leak on August 11, 1985 at the Union Carbide Institute plant sent more than 135 local residents to the hospital. This accident heightened an already uneasy relationship that had existed for years between Union Carbide and Institute residents. People were concerned that another Bhopal incident would happen in Institute (Franklin, 1986; Slaughter, 1985). Institute residents organized themselves into a group called People Concerned about MIC to combat this toxic threat.

Alsen, Louisiana

Alsen is an unincorporated community located on the Mississippi River several miles north of Baton Rouge, Louisiana's state capital. African Americans make up 98.9 percent of this community, which lies at the beginning of the 85-mile industrial corridor where one-quarter of the nation's petrochemicals are produced. This corridor has been described as a "massive human experiment" and a "national sacrifice zone" (Brown 1987, pp. 152–161). The nation's fourth largest hazardous waste landfill is located adjacent to the Alsen community. The landfill opened in the late seventies. The site represented 11.3 percent of the nation's remaining hazardous waste landfill capacity in 1986 (Commission for Racial Justice 1987). Between 1980 and 1985, Rollins, the company operating the site, was cited for more than 100 state and federal toxic emission violations but did not pay any penalties. The community began organizing in late 1981 against the Rollins hazardous waste facility.

Emelle, Alabama

This Sumter County community is located in the heart of west Alabama's economically impoverished "blackbelt." African Americans make up more than 90 percent of the rural community's 626 residents. Emelle is home to Chemical Waste Management's "Cadillac" of hazardous waste landfills, the nation's largest hazardous waste dump (Gunter and Williams 1986, p. 19).

The site covers more than 2,400 acres and represented nearly one-fourth of the nation's hazardous waste landfill capacity in 1986. The Emelle landfill opened in 1978 and is one of two hazardous waste landfills located in EPA's Region IV (i.e., the eight states in the southeastern United States). The landfill receives some of the most toxic waste in the country, including waste from cleaned-up "Superfund" sites. Public opposition began after residents discovered the new job-generating industry was not a brick factory (as was rumored) but a toxic waste dump. The initial protest against the facility, led by members of the Minority Peoples' Council, was over worker safety rather than risks to the larger community.

Environmental Conflict Resolution

The environmental disputes explored in this analysis were seen by grassroots leaders as based on unfair treatment and as an expression of racial discrimination. These activists saw their communities sharing a disparate burden and degree of risk associated with the industrial plants. The noxious facility siting disputes were linked to earlier civil rights disputes that centered on racial disparities. Residents in Houston and Dallas, the neighborhoods in the two large cities studied, were able to inject their environmental disputes into the local political elections. Of the five communities studied, Emelle, which is a community heavily dependent upon the millions of industrial dollars pumped into the local economy annually, gave the strongest endorsement of jobs over the environment. However, even residents from this rural community were not willing to sit silent and watch their area turned into a toxic wasteland.

The opposition strategies varied somewhat across the communities. However, several common strategies were used by residents in the affected communities. For example, all five communities used protest demonstrations, petitions, and press lobbying to publicize their plight. Three of the communities (West Dallas, Alsen, and Houston's Northwood Manor neighborhood) were successful in enlisting the assistance of government agencies in their efforts to redress their environmental problem. The West Dallas community was the only one to actually convince the city and state to join them in litigation against the industrial polluter. Houston's city council, after intense pressure from the African American community, passed a resolution opposing the controversial municipal sanitary landfill. Alsen residents convinced state environmental officials to take action against Rollins over its toxic emissions. These same three communities also filed class-action lawsuits against the industrial firms.

Who spearheaded the local opposition against the polluting industries? There is clear evidence that indigenous social action groups and their leaders held the most important and visible roles in mobilizing the opposition to industrial polluters. African American church leaders, community improvement workers, and civil rights activists planned and initiated most of the local opposition strategies. Mainstream environmental leaders and other "outside elites" played only a minor role in mobilizing citizen opposition in these communities. The West Dallas community was able to get a government-sanctioned citizen group, the Dallas Alliance Environmental Task Force, to work on the local lead pollution problem. Institute's People Concerned about MIC was initiated by a white professor from West Virginia State College and included a broad cross-section of the community. In Emelle, African American civil rights activists (e.g., Minority People's Council) and white environmentalists (e.g., Alabamians for a Clean Environment) have forged a loose alliance to work on the local hazardous waste problem. This is not a small point, given the history of race relations in Alabama's blackbelt.

How were the environmental disputes resolved? The disputes in the West Dallas, Alsen, and Houston neighborhoods were resolved by governmental decisions and adjudication. Bargaining and negotiation were the chief tools used to address (though not resolve) the ongoing environmental disputes in Emelle and Institute. Only West Dallas was able to force the polluting industry to completely shut down (but not dismantle and clean up the site), whereas capacity reductions were placed on the industries in Alsen, Houston, and Institute.

Litigation brought by citizens from West Dallas and Alsen resulted in out-of-court settlement agreements in favor of the plaintiffs and fines paid to governmental regulatory agencies for pollution and safety violations. In 1985 the West Dallas plaintiffs (370 children who lived in the nearby public housing project and 40 property owners) won a $20 million settlement against RSR Corp. The Alsen plaintiffs agreed to settle their dispute for an undisclosed amount (it is reported that Rollins awarded each Alsen plaintiff an average of $3,000). Government officials also fined the Institute and Emelle facilities for pollution and safety violations. Citizens in Alsen and Institute were able to extract some concessions from the firms, mainly in the form of technical modifications in the plant operations, updated safety and pollution monitoring systems, and reduced emission levels.

The federal court in 1984 ruled against the Houston plaintiffs (five years after the suit was brought and the site opened), and the landfill was built. The Northwood Manor residents, however, were able to force the city and state to modify their requirements for siting solid waste facilities. The Houston city council passed ordinances that (1) prohibited city-owned solid waste trucks from dumping at the controversial landfill and (2) regulated the distance that future landfills could be placed near public facilities (e.g., schools, parks, and recreation playgrounds). This was not a small concession given the fact that the city has long resisted any more to institute land-use zoning. The Texas Department of Health, which is the state permit agency for municipal landfills, also modified its regulations requiring waste disposal applicants to include socioeconomic information on census tracts contiguous to the proposed sites.

Conclusion

In their search for operating space, industries such as waste disposal and treatment facilities, heavy metals operations, and chemical plants found minority communities to be logical choices for their expansion. These communities and their leaders were seen as having a Third World view of development—that is, any development is better than no development at all. Moreover, many residents in these communities were suspicious of environmentalists, a sentiment that aligned them with the pro-growth advocates.

African Americans have begun to challenge the legitimacy of environment–jobs trade-offs. They are now asking whether the costs borne by their communities are imposed to spare the larger community. Can environmental inequities (resulting from industrial facility siting decisions) be compensated? What are "acceptable" risks? Concern about inequity—the inherent imbalance between localized costs and dispersed benefits—appears to be the driving force around which African American communities are organizing.

A great deal of overlap exists between the leadership of African American social action groups, neighborhood associations, and community-based grass-roots environmental groups that are formed to challenge local environmental problems. Preexisting institutions and their leaders play a pivotal role in the organization, planning, and mobilization stages of the opposition activities.

The Not in My Backyard (NIMBY) syndrome has trickled down to nearly all communities, including African Americans in the suburbs, impoverished ghettos, and rural blackbelt. Few residents want garbage dumps, landfills, incinerators, or other polluting industries in their backyards. The price of siting noxious facilities has skyrocketed in recent years as a result of more stringent federal regulations and the growing militancy among communities of the poor, of the working class, and of color.

African Americans and other people of color are still underrepresented in the mainstream environmental organizations at all levels. This picture must change if the U.S. national environmental movement is to provide leadership in the global environmental movement, i.e., the Third World, where most of the world's population is located. On the other hand, by embracing environmental justice issues, grass-roots environmental groups have been able to make progress toward alliances with African American communities around the toxics issue.

Changing demographics point to a more racially diverse nation. It is time for the environmental movement to diversify and reach out to the "other"

United States. This does not mean the Big Ten should swallow up grass-roots efforts. The 1990s offer some challenging opportunities for the environmental movement in the United States to embrace social justice and redistributive policies. African Americans and other people of color must be empowered through their own organizations to address the problems in their communities. Some positive signs indicate that the larger environmental and social justice community is beginning to take the first steps toward reducing the artificial barriers that have kept them apart.

REFERENCES

Authors' Note: Research for this paper was supported by a grant from Resources for the Future Small Grants Program.

Babcock, Richard. 1982. "Houston: Unzoned, Unfettered, and Most Unrepentent." *Planning* 48:21–23.
Bloom, Jack. 1987. *Class, Race and the Civil Rights Movement.* Bloomington: Indiana University Press.
Brown, Michael H. 1987. *The Toxic Cloud: The Poisoning of America's Air.* New York: Harper & Row.
Bullard, Robert D. 1983. "Solid Waste Sites and the Black Houston Community." *Sociological Inquiry* 53:273–88.
———. 1984. "Endangered Environs: The Price of Unplanned Growth in Boomtown Houston." *California Sociologist* 7:84–102.
———. 1990. *Dumping in Dixie: Race, Class, and Environmental Quality.* Boulder, CO: Westview.
Bullard, Robert D. and Beverly H. Wright. 1986. "The Politics of Pollution: Implications for the Black Community." *Phylon* 47:71–78.
———. 1987a. "Blacks and the Environment." *Humboldt Journal of Social Relations* 14:165–84.
———. 1987b. "Environmentalism and the Politics of Equity: Emergent Trends in the Black Community." *Mid-American Review of Sociology* 12:21–37.
Commission for Racial Justice. 1987. *Toxic Wastes and Race: A National Report on the Racial and Socioeconomic Characteristics of Communities with Hazardous Wastes Sites.* New York: United Church of Christ.
Dallas Alliance Environmental Task Force. 1983, June 29. *Final Report.* Dallas, Texas: Author.
Feagin, Joe R. 1985. "The Global Context of Metropolitan Growth: Houston and the Oil Industry." *American Journal of Sociology* 90:1204–30.
———. 1987. *Free Enterprise City: Houston in Political and Economic Perspective.* New Brunswick, NJ: Rutgers University Press.
Franklin, Ben A. 1986. "In the Shadow of the Valley." *Sierra* 71:38–43.
Freudenberg, Nicholas. 1984. "Citizen Action for Environmental Health: Report of a Survey of Community Organizations." *American Journal of Public Health* 74:444–48.
Freudenberg, N. and C. Steinsapir. 1990. February 15–20. "The Grass Roots Environmental Movement: Not in Our Backyards." Paper presented at the annual meeting of the American Association for the Advancement of Science, New Orleans.
Gale, Richard P. 1972. "From Sit-in to Hike-in: A Comparison of the Civil Rights and Environmental Movements." Pp. 280–305 in *Social Behavior, Natural Resources, and the Environment,* eds. W. R. Burch, N. H. Cheek, and L. Taylor. New York: Harper & Row.
———. 1983. "The Environmental Movement and the Left: Antagonists or Allies?" *Sociological Inquiry* 53:179–99.

Geiser, Ken and Gerry Waneck. 1983. "PCBs and Warren County." *Science for the People* 15:13–17.

Gianessi, L. P., H. M. Peskin, and E. Wolff. 1979, May. "The Distributional Effect of Uniform Air Pollution Policy in the U.S." *Quarterly Journal of Economics* 93:281–301.

Gottlieb, Robert and Helen Ingram. 1988. "The New Environmentalists." *The Progressive* 52:14–15.

Gunter, Booth and Mike Williams. 1986. "The Cadillac of Dumps." *Sierra* 71:9–22.

Humphrey, Craig R. and Frederick R. Buttel. 1982. *Environment, Energy and Society.* Belmont, CA: Wadsworth.

Jordon, Vernon. 1980. "Sins of Omission." *Environmental Action* 11:26–30.

Kazis, Richard and Richard Grossman. 1983. *Fear at Work: Job Blackmail, Labor, and the Environment.* New York: The Pilgrim Press.

Kruvant, W. J. 1975. "People, Energy and Pollution." Pp. 125–67 in *The American Energy Consumer,* eds. D. Newman and D. Dawn. Cambridge, MA: Ballinger.

McCaull, Julian. 1975. "Discriminatory Air Pollution: If the Poor Don't Breathe." *Environment* 19:26–32.

Slaughter, Jane. 1985. "Valley of the Shadow of Death." *The Progressive* 49:50.

Truax, Hawley. 1990. "Beyond White Environmentalism: Minorities and the Environment." *Environmental Action* 21:19–30.

U.S. General Accounting Office. 1983. *Siting of Hazardous Waste Landfills and their Correlation with Racial and Economic Status of Surrounding Communities.* Washington, DC: Government Printing Office.

Urban Environment Conference, Inc. 1985. *Taking Back our Health: An Institute on Surviving the Threat to Minority Communities.* Washington, DC: Urban Environment Inc.

57

THE DYNAMICS OF RUMOR-PANICS ABOUT SATANIC CULTS

JEFFREY S. VICTOR

Jeffrey S. Victor is interested in social change caused by collective behavior, such as rumors and panics. In this selection, Victor argues that rumors usually escalate in response to other socioeconomic stresses in society, and he documents this argument by showing how satanic cult rumors began and were spread across the country. Victor also explains the content and interpretation of satanic cult stories.

Perhaps no other form of crime in history has been a better index to social disruption and change, for outbreaks of witchcraft mania have generally taken place in societies which are experiencing a shift of religious focus—societies, we would say, confronting a relocation of boundaries.

—KAI ERIKSON, *WAYWARD PURITANS* (1966, P. 153)

Satanic cult rumors are best understood as a cultural metaphor. They do indeed have truth in them, but not a literal truth. Bizarre stories of animal sacrifice, child kidnapping, ritual torture, infanticide, blood drinking, and cannibalism must be interpreted symbolically, in terms of culturally inherited symbolic meanings. The origin of these stories can be found in the collectively shared anxieties from which they arise. Although they may not be deliberately created by any group, certain groups are more likely to believe the stories and actively disseminate them.

Satanic cult stories arise as a response to widespread socioeconomic stresses, particularly those affecting parenting and family relationships. These social stresses are products of the rapid social change and social disorganization that began during the 1960s, and that caused a deep cultural crisis of values and authority.[1] The satanic cult legend says, in symbolic form, that our moral values are threatened by evil forces beyond our control, and that we have lost faith in our authorities to deal with the threat.

Theoretical Background

Persistent Rumors

A rumor is a story told in conversations between people, containing assertions of truth that cannot be confirmed by incontrovertible evidence at the time and are widely regarded as being literally true, or at least plausible. Usually communicated by word of mouth, rumors also may be disseminated by the mass media. Rumors are usually short-lived, locally situated, and specific in content. Rumor stories may or may not be true, in the sense that they may be verified eventually by legal or scientific methods; truth is not the central issue in defining rumors. A story is a rumor if it is a collectively created and shared perception of reality, without any manifestly obvious evidence to substantiate it (Rosnow 1980).

Rumors usually arise when something unusual or unexpected happens. According to Shibutani (1966), rumors originate as a substitute for "hard news." He suggests that rumors are a collaborative attempt to find an explanation for an ambiguous and disturbing set of events. They usually arise when people do not trust "official" sources of news. When people lose faith in their authorities, they will regard bizarre and frightening rumors as plausible because it seems dangerous to disregard them.

A rumor persists when it offers a plausible explanation for people's shared anxieties (Rosnow 1980; Rosnow and Kimmel 1979). Several different conditions give rumors plausibility. Rumors gain credibility when they offer specific details about an anxiety-provoking situation. They grow through a "snowball" process, as more and more people contribute supportive details to the collective story. The most crucial supportive "evidence" comes from eye-witness testimonials. There will always be people who volunteer eye-witness accounts that seem to verify even the most bizarre rumor stories.

They do so to satisfy a variety of personal motives: to obtain attention and prestige, express their own fantastic fears, attack some group they hate, as a prank, or give expression to some mental delusion.

Satanic Cult Rumor-Panics

On rare occasions, fear-provoking rumor stories give rise to panics in crowds or even in whole communities. The classic case is the "War of the Worlds" panic in the region around New York City in 1939. Although there have been several studies of communitywide panics, there is no standardized definition or criterion that can be used to identify a panic. This study uses the following definition: a rumor-panic is a collective reaction to rumors about immediately threatening circumstances. A rumor-panic in a community is identified by the existence of widely occurring, fear-provoked behavior, indicated by numerous incidents of extraordinary fight–flight reaction. This collective behavior may include protective behavior, such as the widespread buying of guns, or preventing children from being in public places. It may also include aggressive behavior, such as group attacks on people perceived to be sources of threat, or destruction of property. It may also include agitated information seeking for "news" about the threat, and intensified surveillance of the community by authorities.

Rumor-panics in response to satanic cult stories do not arise from purely local events (Victor 1989). The process begins when widespread economic insecurity and family problems give rise to tension and frustrations felt by a great many people in a community. Next, an ambiguous local event, such as a teenage suicide, vandalism of a cemetery, or the appearance of mysterious graffiti on walls, becomes a concrete focus of attention for community anxiety and gossip. Satanic cult stories, coming from mass media and folklore sources, provide a plausible explanation for the ambiguity of unfocused anxieties and unclear events. These stories become incorporated into local gossip as persistent rumors. Satanic cult rumors gain credibility, as rumors usually do, through the process of consensual validation of reality. People come to believe the rumors because they are repeated so often; "everyone" they talk to says that the rumors are true. The similarity of rumor stories from location to location suggests that rumors that give rise to rumor-panics are one manifestation of a contemporary legend-making process in American society.

Research Methods

I conducted a community study of a rumor-panic in southwestern New York and northwestern Pennsylvania (Victor 1989) immediately after it occurred on May 13, 1988, using several methods to collect data. (1) I interviewed local authorities, including police detectives, newspaper reporters, school administrators, clergymen, and the directors of the youth bureau [and] the animal protection society. (2) Students in one of my courses conducted and recorded interviews with a sample of 50 local people in three categories: teenagers, parents, and authority figures such as teachers and ministers. (3) One student, a Methodist minister, taped interviews with 10 local ministers of fundamentalist churches. (4) Another student conducted and recorded interviews with 30 local high school students from three different teenage subcultures: "punks," "preppies," and religious activists.

In addition to this case study, I have collected data from several other sources. (1) I located newspaper reports about other satanic cult rumor-panics as well as teenage satanism, satanic ritualistic crimes, and ritual sexual abuse of children, through the *Newsbank* microfiche collection. (2) I observed a police seminar on satanic cult crime, a church revival concerning satanism in popular music, and a psychiatric seminar about the ritual sexual abuse of children by satanic cults. (3) I collected audiotapes of antisatanist speeches presented on Christian radio programs and in churches, and gathered an extensive collection of antisatanist publications, books, magazine articles, and pamphlets—most published by Christian religious presses or volunteer crime-fighting organizations. (4) I collected transcripts of national television talk-show programs about satanism, including the episodes of *Geraldo, Oprah Winfrey, Sally Jesse Raphael,* and *Phil Donahue.*

Community Panics in Response to Satanic Cult Rumors in Rural Areas of the United States

My search of small-town newspaper articles located reports of 31 satanic cult rumor-panics in locations across the United States, between 1984 and 1989. I also found reports of similar rumor-panics in Canada. In no case was anything found that resembled a "satanic cult"; none of the panics involved an organized group committing crimes and justifying them with a "satanic" ideology. The 31 cases probably do not include all rumor-panics in the United States because my research source, *Newsbank,* reprints articles from only about 200 American newspapers.

This series of communitywide rumor-panics is a unique social phenomenon. There have been many examples of locally situated rumor-panics and, indeed, examples of rumors that swept the nation. However, as far as I know, there has been no other series of community rumor-panics across the country, with recurrences over several years. Curiously, this phenomenon has not been reported in the national press.

Behavioral Indicators of Collective Panic

The western New York rumor-panic I investigated featured many behavioral indicators of collective panic, including protective, aggressive, and information-seeking behavior (Victor 1989). A great many parents, for example, kept their children home from school, for fear that they might be kidnapped by "the cult." Over 100 cars showed up at a rumored ritual site in a wooded area, where they were stopped by police barricades. Some of the cars contained weapons—clubs, knives, and hunting guns. At a warehouse rumored to be another ritual meeting place, about $4,000 of damage was done to musical equipment and interior walls. The police, school officials, and youth bureau were inundated with hundreds of telephone calls reporting bizarre incidents. Several teenagers of an unconventional "punk" appearance were labeled "satanist" and received threatening telephone calls. These counter-cultural kids were merely scapegoat targets for community tensions, due to their publicly visible, "strange" hair and clothing style.

Indicators of behavior driven by fear were reported in newspapers throughout the 250-mile-wide region. School officials from small towns and centralized rural school districts reported hundreds of school children absent, as fearful parents kept their children home. Police departments received an avalanche of telephone calls from people who reported having seen mutilated animals, satanic symbols, hit lists of planned victims, and even human corpses. Town meetings were held in many locations; enraged parents demanded "action" from police and school authorities. Prayer meetings were held in some rural fundamentalist churches to pray for help in fighting Satan's influence. Sunday school instruction was given at some churches to warn children about the danger of playing with the occult. In addition, some churches invited religious satan-hunters from out of town to speak.

The newspaper articles about satanic cult rumor-panics in other locations reported similar collective behavior. I used reports of this kind of behavior as my criterion for including a location on my list of rumor-panics. I did not include locations where satanic cult rumors were merely reported to be circulating, without provoking widespread panic-driven behavior in a community or region. I did not include, for example, locations where newspaper articles reported rumors about supposed teenage satanists, or satanic ritual abuse at child-care centers.

What Are the Underlying Causes of These Rumor-Panics?

Theories of collective behavior suggest that rumors and panics arise from shared sources of social stress; underlying conditions cause widespread anxiety and frustration (Miller 1985). Clues to these sources of social stress may be found in socioeconomic conditions in locations where rumor-panics have occurred, and in the symbolic content of the rumors themselves.

Rural and Small Town Locations

In every case except one (Kansas City, Missouri), the 31 rumor-panics occurred in rural areas and small towns rather than large cities. Rumor-panics that took place near large cities, such as Pittsburgh, Pennsylvania, or Richmond, Virginia, did not penetrate into the urban area.

My own research confirms this anomaly. The rumor-panic I studied in depth covered a huge, 250-mile-wide area of farmlands and small towns across southwestern New York and northwestern Pennsylvania. However, it did not occur in Erie, Pennsylvania, the region's largest city with about 120,000 people. People in small towns near Erie became very agitated about dangerous satanic cults, but people in Erie had not even heard the rumors (*Erie Time-News* May 12, 1988).

Interpretation   The rural location of these rumor-panics calls for an explanation. One hypothesis is that underlying socioeconomic stresses, and the resultant cultural crisis in traditional values, are particularly acute in rural and small town areas (Victor 1989). There is good evidence for greatly increased economic stress on unskilled, poorly educated parents, due to the rapid loss of well-paid blue-collar jobs in small-town America (O'Hare 1988; Porter 1989). One major study, for example, reported that "the poverty rate for the 54 million Americans who live in rural areas has climbed to 18 percent—50 percent higher than in urban areas. By 1986, one out of every five young rural families was living below the poverty line" (O'Hare 1988). There is also evidence that problems in raising children, such as alcohol and drug abuse, juvenile crime, depression, and child abuse, have increased proportionately more in rural areas than in urban and suburban areas (Helge 1990). A complementary hypothesis is that the communication networks that transmit the legend, especially among fundamentalist Protestants, are stronger in rural and small-town areas.

The Content of the Rumor Stories

The newspaper reports of the 31 rumor-panics reveal that rumor stories from across the country feature surprisingly similar content. About 75 percent of the stories mention animal mutilations; about 65 percent describe the kidnapping and ritual sacrifice of children. Many of the kidnapping stories take the form of predictions, but others claim that such crimes had already taken place and were concealed from public knowledge. Interestingly, about 40 percent of these kidnapping stories specifically mention blond, blue-eyed children or virgins—cultural symbols of innocence and purity.

Other rumor motifs are less common. About 20 percent of the rumors made claims that satanists had committed murder or mass murders (without specific mention of children). Ritual sexual abuse of children by a satanic cult appeared in only about 5 percent of the rumors. Other crimes mentioned only once each included the sacrifice of human fetuses, ritual torture, sexual orgies, and teenage suicide due to satanism.

In the western New York rumor-panic, many people claimed to have seen things that did not exist or to have knowledge of events that did not occur. The police and humane society received hundreds of reports about cats (and sometimes dogs) having been sacrificed by the satanic cult. Cats, for example, were "seen" hanging from light poles in downtown Jamestown. Many high school students "found" black roses and death threats in their lockers. Many people reported "seeing" red satanic graffiti painted on walls in the downtown warehouse area, near a site of rumored ritual meetings.

However, the most fear-provoking rumor was "the satanic cult was planning to kidnap and sacrifice a blond, blue-eyed virgin." This rumor surfaced only about two weeks before the panic reached its peak intensity—on Friday the 13th, May, 1988. It served to heighten tensions that had been growing since mid-winter, as one fear-provoking rumor built upon another (Victor 1989).

Interpretation Stories about the kidnapping and ritual sacrifice of children are at the core of these satanic cult rumors. Historical comparison shows that this motif derives from the ancient blood ritual myth, which commonly recurs during periods of cultural crisis, when people are frustrated and anxious about changing cultural values.

Many parents worry about threats to the safety and well-being of children, such as those from drug abuse, teenage pregnancy, teenage suicide, sexual molestation, and kidnapping. Many traditionalist people are morally appalled by the existence of widely available pornography, the acceptance of premarital sex, the tolerance of homosexuals, the easy availability of abortion, and other manifestations of what they consider moral decadence and threats to secure family life. (Intellectuals may regard these concerns as misplaced. Nevertheless, they are powerful themes for masses of Americans, as evidenced by popular campaign issues in national elections.) A good deal of research shows widespread feelings of powerlessness among Americans and an increasing "crisis of confidence" in institutions and authorities of American society to change things for the better (Lipset and Schneider 1983; Harris 1987).

How Do Rumor-Panics Begin?

Before a rumor-panic begins, some kind of "triggering event" acts as a catalyst to release growing social tensions. This triggering event is not the "cause" of the panic behavior, even though people may consciously point to it as the cause of their fear. However, fear is actually a response to the collective definition of social reality embedded in the rumor stories (Shibutani 1966).

Possible Triggering Events The newspaper articles about the rumor-panics reported as important antecedent events whatever each reporter considered to be possible "causes" of the rumors. The reporters no doubt overlooked some antecedent events that may have functioned as triggering events. It was sometimes not possible for me to determine from the newspaper accounts whether the reported events had precipitated the panic or only provoked rumors long before the panic erupted.

The newspaper reports indicate that some antecedent events commonly precede community panics. These include the sighting of so-called satanic graffiti (mentioned in 39% of cases), cemetery vandalism (23%), or some violent, local crime, such as a murder or suicide (45%). Other antecedent events mentioned less frequently included a local church meeting or police conference concerning the dangers of satanism (16%), a mass media presentation about the dangers of satanism (13%), conflict between local youth groups involving accusations of satanism (13%), or discovery of mutilated animals (6%).

In the rumor-panic that I studied, the symbolic significance of Friday the 13th functioned as a "trigger" to release tensions that had been building for months over the region. However, other local events reported in the press triggered the preceding rumor process; different communities focused on different events—a teenage suicide, the discovery of "satanic" graffiti, or conflict between teenage cliques (Victor 1989).

In Jamestown, the rumor process started with the appearance of the new "punk" counterculture of high school students and private rock music parties attended by those youths at a warehouse rented for the purpose of band practice. Although these events were not particularly dramatic, they did give rise to anxiety-provoking gossip about supposed teenage drug use and sex orgies. Over several months, this gossip gradually transformed the countercultural teenagers into symbols of satanic cult rumor stories. One catalyst for this transformation was a *Geraldo* talk show about satanic cult influences upon teenagers (*Geraldo* November 19, 1987). Another was a national news item about a teenager who killed his mother and himself, supposedly due to the influence of satanism (*Jamestown Post-Journal* January 12, 1988). The existence of a local "satanic cult" gradually became a taken-for-granted reality in the community, through the process of consensual validation, as the rumor stories were repeated by many different people.

The acceptance of this socially constructed "reality" was by no means uniform; a great many people remained skeptical of all the rumors. (Most importantly, the local police, except for one or two officers, remained skeptical.) The key factor relevant to the acceptance of the rumor stories appeared to be participation in a communication network that constantly repeated the stories. Once the process of consensual validation gave the stories credibility, many people seemed to have a strong need to believe them.

Interpretation   It appears that antecedent to a satanic cult rumor-panic, there is usually one or more ambiguous local events that, in people's collective imagination, evoke the symbolic themes of the emerging satanic cult legend. Thus, the legend is collectively used to provide an explanation for some event of widespread local concern, for which there exists no other ready explanation (Shibutani 1966).

How Do the Rumors Spread?

Rumors spread through communication networks that are receptive to them, and not through other networks in which people remain skeptical or disinterested (Rogers and Kincaid 1981). In receptive communication networks, some people actively promote rumor stories, like propagandists. My survey of the news articles indicates that, in many cases, so-called experts in identifying satanic cult ritual crime contributed to the fears generated by satanic cult rumors. Newspaper articles report that experts' claims about the supposed dangers of satanic cults lent credibility to bizarre rumor stories. In about 33 percent of the rumor cases, police "experts" in satanic cult crime were active in promoting such claims, while about 25 percent of the cases featured claims about satanism by religious satan-hunters.

> In April, 1985, a local Deputy Sheriff in rural Union County, Ohio, claimed to know of five secret "cells" of satanists, with at least 1,500 members. (*Columbus Dispatch* April 14, 1985)

> In May, 1989, police satan hunters at a state-wide conference in New Hampshire said that there are over two million members of satanic cults in the United States, organized into "criminal cartels." According to these crime "experts," many unsolved kidnappings and serial murders in our country are committed by highly secret satanic cults. (*Boston Globe* May 28, 1989)

> In Jamestown, fundamentalist churches functioned as an important communication network for dissemination of satanic cult rumor stories in sermons, church meetings about the rumors, prayer sessions, speeches by invited out-of-town satan-hunters, and church newsletters. Several fundamentalist ministers, responding to the growing fears of their parishioners, were particularly active in claims-making about the supposed satanic cult. These activities aggravated the rumor-panic (Victor 1989).

Interpretation   Satanic cult rumors are spread by the mass media, but in local communities, the stories are disseminated as a "political cause." Certain groups in American society are more receptive to satanic cult rumors and more likely to disseminate them actively. These groups include small-town police and traditionally religious people.

Macrosociological Interpretations: The Contemporary Legend-Making Process

My thesis is that satanic cult stories arise in Western societies during periods of cultural crisis as part of a historically recurring cultural pattern involving the spread of subversion myths and a search for scapegoats to blame for social problems. This pattern links the motifs of ancient legends to currently popular explanations for social problems.

Contemporary Legends

The scholarly study of contemporary legends by folklorists began attracting notice in the 1970s. The concept of a contemporary legend (or urban legend) provides a new intellectual tool for understanding forms of collective behavior, previously discussed in terms of persistent rumors transmitted both orally and through the mass media (Ellis 1990). Jan Harold Brunvand's first collection of "urban legends," *The Vanishing Hitchhiker* (1981), brought this concept to the attention of scholars in other disciplines, as well as the general public. Brunvand defined urban legends as a "subclass of folk narratives . . . that—unlike fairy tales—are believed, or at least believable, and that—unlike myths—are set in the recent past and involve normal human beings rather than ancient gods or demigods." In his brief survey of attempts to clarify the concept, Ellis notes that contemporary legends deal with events that are alleged to have "just happened," or with threats that have recently emerged. These stories (1) are presented as being "news" freshly arisen from the storyteller's social setting, (2) deal with some kind of perceived emergency or social problem which urgently needs attention, and (3) express attempts to gain social control over an ambiguous situation and are, therefore, "fundamentally political acts" (Ellis 1990).

It is most useful to conceptualize a contemporary legend as an interactive process of collective behavior, rather than a fixed and unchanging narrative. The collective behavior consists primarily of collaborative creation and communication of persistent rumor stories, in ever-changing variation. A contemporary legend is, therefore, always emergent out of interaction and is never finished.

The Link between Legends and Rumors

There is no clear-cut distinction between persistent rumors and contemporary legends (Mullens 1972). Both are products of people's collaborative storytelling, attempts to deal with anxiety-provoking, ambiguous situations. Mullens, for example, notes that although rumors are usually brief propositions without any long narrative about people and events, many contemporary legends are short stories about incidents alleged to have occurred recently. In discussing the connection between rumors and legends, Mullens (1972) points out that persistent rumors sometimes become incorporated into popular folklore, to be passed on from generation to generation. However, the connection most important for this study is that the themes and symbolism of legends are sometimes used by people to construct the content of rumor stories. In other words, traditional legends offer ready-made scripts, which people can use to create stories offering plausible explanations for unfamiliar, threatening circumstances.

The scripts of traditional legends learned early in life structure our preconceptions about human nature and the nature of things supernatural. Legends are not only "out there" in our shared culture. They are also "in us," psychologically. They are the exemplars and paradigms by which we live (Keen 1988). A person does not need to know all the details of a rumor built on a traditional legend to fill in the details. A good imagination will suffice.

For this reason, it is usually not possible to trace the origin of a contemporary legend to any specific event; its origin may lie in ancient sources.

Origin of the Satanic Cult Legend

Satanic cult rumor stories derive from an ancient myth, usually referred to as the "blood ritual myth," which tells of children kidnapped and murdered by a secret conspiracy of evil strangers, who use the children's blood and body parts in religious rituals (Hsia 1988; Ridley 1987). This myth endures because it offers universal appeal to the latent fears of parents everywhere. Variations of the myth commonly are elaborated with symbols of mysterious evil: graveyard robberies and mutilated corpses, secret meetings of people engaged in secret rituals, strange incantations and symbols, and people clothed in black robes making ritual animal sacrifices and sometimes eating human body parts in cannibalistic rites. These are all omens that indicate that purity and innocence are endangered by powerful agents of absolute evil.

The evil internal enemy in blood ritual subversion stories is usually some widely despised group. Such groups function as scapegoats for anxieties caused by widespread social stresses. In ancient Rome, subversion stories claimed that Christians were kidnapping Roman children for secret ritual sacrifices (Ellis 1985). The murder of innocent children was a symbol of Christianity's absolute evil, for only total evil preys upon total innocence. Later, during the Middle Ages, similar stories claimed that Christian children were being kidnapped by Jews for use in secret, religious ritual sacrifices. When this myth is used in antisemitic attacks, it is known as the "blood libel" (Hsia 1988). In France, just before the French Revolution, similar stories accused aristocrats of kidnapping poor children to use their blood in medical baths.

Today, the blood ritual myth is constantly being reworked in popular culture entertainment. Many horror novels and movies use the theme of kidnapping and murder for a variety of unsavory purposes, such as ritual sacrifices (*The Believers*) or use of body parts (*Coma*). Similarly, some fairy tales depict children kidnapped, usually by witches or monsters, who may cook or eat them. Thus, popular culture keeps alive and makes familiar an ancient story's mythology. The point is that satanic cult stories are being fabricated out of these same cultural materials.

The satanic cult legend combines the blood ritual myth with another ancient subversion myth, which concerns Satan's rebellion against God and his struggle to subvert the souls of men and women, thereby destroying God's moral order. This particular combination of myths has a long history. It was frequently used in scapegoating attacks on Jews, lepers, and people accused of being heretics or witches (Cohn 1975; Tractenberg, 1983; Moore 1987). The power of this combination is that it offers both secular and sacred symbols, thus appealing to both secular professionals and religious traditionalists. The presumed satanists can be regarded as either dangerous social deviants, agents of supernatural evil, or both. The danger of such powerful subversion mythology lies in its demand to find scapegoats; inevitably, real, living scapegoats will be found.

Mythology of the Satanic Cult Legend

American society went through a very disruptive period of rapid social change during the 1960s and early 1970s. Those changes challenged traditional American cultural assumptions and values about such central issues as family roles and the meaning of work. Many people still find it difficult to adjust to those massive changes. In this context, we can recognize the satanic cult legend as an attempt to restore an idealized society to past greatness and moral purity, an attempt to locate and blame an evil enemy, a scapegoat, for the subversion of dominant cultural values.

The blood ritual myth and similar subversion myths usually arise at times when a society is undergoing a deep cultural crisis of values, following rapid social changes that cause disorganization and widespread social stress (Levack 1987; Schoeneman 1975). Indeed, subversion myths and their resulting witch hunts can be taken as indicators of cultural crisis (Erikson 1966). These stories function as a collective metaphor to express a group or society's anxieties about its future. They say, in symbolic form, that our future (our children) is threatened by mysterious forces that we cannot fully comprehend or control.

The satanic cult legend's meaning can be found in the cultural symbolism of its metaphor (Victor 1989). Particular satanic cult claims, rumors, and stories contribute to the process of collaborative storytelling. However, the overall metaphor says that very powerful, secretive, evil forces threaten the legitimate moral order. The threat derives from "heresy" against sacred, traditional values, which were once the solid foundation of our stable way of life. The evil enemy's values are opposite everything we cherish. Their power may derive from mysterious occult sources or "hidden" connections within the power elite in our society. The enemy's evil image functions, just as in times of war, to confirm our society's essential goodness.

This metaphor may be a projection of people's loss of faith in the ability of our society's institutions and authorities to solve threatening social problems. Satan symbolizes a loss of faith in legitimate moral authority. People who are most likely to take this symbol seriously are those who feel that loss of faith most intensely. The satanic cult legend is an expression of people's shared feelings of powerlessness to change our society for the better.

The Function of the Satanic Legend

Satanic cult rumors function as "improvised news" to provide an explanation for ambiguous sources of shared social stress. These stories provide fantasy scapegoats to blame for widespread feelings of frustration, anger, and powerlessness. The selective location of satanic cult rumor-panics in rural areas and small towns may be due to the greater socioeconomic stress and cultural crisis in values experienced there. Economic stress upon unskilled, poorly educated, working-class parents and the problems of parenting children may have increased proportionately more in rural areas than in urban and suburban areas.

The Dissemination of Satanic Cult Stories

Finally, we must ask: Whose purposes are being served by the spread of satanic cult stories? Subversion myths commonly serve vested interests of particular social groups.

Communication networks that actively disseminate satanic cult rumors are likely to be stronger in rural and small town areas. Satanic cult stories are disseminated by local police "experts" in ritualistic crime, and by religious traditionalists (sociopolitically conservative Protestants and Catholics), whose ideological preconceptions make them receptive to satanic cult stories.[2]

Satanic cult stories serve to justify and support the power and prestige of radical-right Christians. Their ideology professes that American social problems are largely due to a loss of faith in God and a loss of patriotism in America, which is God's chosen land. Conservative Christian publications about satanism target "New Age" enthusiasts and neopagans as satanists, accusing such people of either committing or encouraging ritualistic crime (Carlson et al. 1989).

However, I suggest that these groups are only proxy targets, much like Communists were proxy targets used to attack American liberals during the 1950s "Red Scare." The real targets are liberal, modernist Protestants and Catholics. Satanic cult stories are ideological weapons in a conflict among Christians, traditionalists versus modernists. This internal conflict in American society fosters the propagation of satanic cult stories. Historical research provides evidence that "witch hunts" for scapegoats are most common in regions and societies where internal conflict is greatest (Levack 1987; Moore 1987). Therefore, we can predict that satanic cult rumors and claims will arise in regions experiencing the greatest conflict between traditionalist and modernist Christians. As Coser notes, "the inner enemy . . . may be simply invented, in order to bring about through a common hostility toward him the social solidarity which the group so badly needs" (Coser 1956, p. 107).

NOTES

Author's Note: I would like to express my appreciation to several people who helped me to put together information and interpretations presented in this chapter. Bill Ellis and Phillips Stevens offered me many insights about contemporary legends, provided me with many sources of information, and gave a critical reading to an initial draft of this material. Robert Hicks, Debbie Nathan, and Sherrill Mulhern kindly shared their own research with me and sent me an abundance of research sources.

Some material appeared in my article in *Western Folklore* (1990). I want to thank the editor of that journal, Pack Carnes, for permission to include that material in this chapter.

1. Research evidence of this value crisis in Western societies comes from Inglehart (1990), who finds cross-cultural evidence of a value shift toward greater individual autonomy, innovation, and self-expression, and a tendency to challenge rather than accept authority. These values challenge traditionalist value priorities of obedience to authority and unquestioning acceptance of the wisdom of the past; they particularly threaten traditionalist (but not modernist) Christian preconceptions.

2. This does not mean that all traditionalist Christians automatically accept satanic cult stories as "fact." Also, other groups with quite different ideologies may be receptive to satanic cult conspiracy stories. For example, in recent years feminists have become dedicated to uncovering the "hidden victims" of child sexual abuse and incest.

REFERENCES

Boston Globe. 1989. "Cult Scare Seen as Overrated." (May 28).

Brunvand, Jan Harold. 1981. *The Vanishing Hitchhiker: American Urban Legends and Their Meanings.* New York: W. W. Norton.

Carlson, Shawn and Gerald Larue with G. O'Sullivan, A. Masche, and D. Frew. 1989. *Satanism in America.* El Cerrito, CA: Gaia Press.

Cohn, Norman. 1975. *Europe's Inner Demons: An Enquiry Inspired by the Great Witch-Hunt.* New York: New American Library.

Columbus Dispatch (Ohio). 1985. "No Bodies Found Yet in Cult Probe." (June 21), "Satanic Murders: A Great Story That Wasn't There." (June 23).

Coser, Lewis. 1956. *The Functions of Social Conflict.* New York: Free Press.

Ellis, Bill. 1985. "De Legendis Urbis: Modern Legends in Ancient Rome." *Journal of American Folklore* 96:200–208.

————. 1990. "Introduction: Special Issue: Contemporary Legends in Emergence" *Western Folklore* 49:1–10.

Erie Times-News (Pa.) 1988. "Reports of Satanism Prove Unfounded"; "Far-Reaching Rumors Trigger Fear, Anxiety." (May 12).

Erikson, Kai T. 1966. *Wayward Puritans: A Study in the Sociology of Deviance.* New York: John Wiley.

Geraldo. 1987. "Satanic Cults and Children" (Nov. 19). Transcript from *Journal Graphics,* Inc., New York.

Harris, Louis. 1987. *Inside America.* New York: Random House.

Helge, Doris. 1990. "National Study Regarding Rural, Suburban and Urban At-Risk Students." Bellingham, WA: National Rural Development Institute, Western Washington University. Research report.

Hsia, R. Po-Chia. 1988. *The Myth of Ritual Murder: Jews and Magic in Reformation Germany.* New Haven: Yale University Press.

Inglehart, Ronald. 1990. *Culture Shift in Advanced Industrial Society.* Princeton, NJ: Princeton University Press.

Jamestown Post-Journal. 1988. "Boy Scout Kills Mom, Then Himself." (January 16).

Keen, Sam. 1988. "The Stories We Live By." *Psychology Today* (December): 43–47.

Levack, Brian P. 1987. *The Witch-Hunt in Early Modern Europe.* New York: Longman.

Lipset, Seymour M. and William Schneider. 1983. *The Confidence Gap: Business, Labor and Government in the Public Mind.* New York: Free Press.

Miller, David. 1985. *Introduction to Collective Behavior.* Belmont, CA: Wadsworth.

Moore, R. I. 1987. *The Formation of a Persecuting Society: Power and Deviance in Western Europe, 950–1250.* New York: Basil Blackwell.

Mullens, Patrick B. 1972. "Modern Legend and Rumor Theory." *Journal of the American Folklore Institute* 9:95–109.

O'Hare, William P. 1988. *The Rise of Poverty in Rural America*. Washington, D.C.: Population Reference Bureau (July).

Porter, Kathryn H. 1989. *Poverty in Rural America: A National Overview*. Washington D.C.: Center on Budget and Policy Priorities.

Ridley, Florence H. 1987. "A Tale Told Too Often." *Journal of American Folklore* 26: 153–56.

Rogers, Everett M. and D. Lawrence Kincaid. 1981. *Communication Networks*. New York: Free Press.

Rosnow, Ralph L. 1980. "The Psychology of Rumor Reconsidered." *Psychological Bulletin* 87:578–91.

Rosnow, Ralph L. and Allan J. Kimmel. 1979. "Lives of a Rumor." *Psychology Today* (June): 88–92.

Schoeneman, Thomas J. 1975. "The Witch Hunt as a Culture Change Phenomenon." *Ethos* 3:529–54.

Shibutani, Tamotsu. 1966. *Improvised News: A Sociological Study of Rumors*. Indianapolis: Bobbs-Merrill.

Tractenberg, Joshua. 1983. *The Devil and the Jews*. New Haven: Yale University Press, [1943].

Victor, Jeffrey S. 1989. "A Rumor-Panic About a Dangerous Satanic Cult in Western New York." *New York Folklore* 15:23–49.

———. 1990. "Satanic Cult Rumors as Contemporary Legend." *Western Folklore* 49: 51–81.

58

SIXTY MILLION ON THE MOVE

ALAN B. SIMMONS

This last reading is by a Canadian sociologist, Alan B. Simmons. Simmons analyzes another aspect of social change, that which is related to demographic shifts within the population, particularly the global impact of international migration patterns. The increasing population growth in less developed countries not only has affected national and international migration, but also significantly has impacted the environment and the international division of labor.

The modern scientific community takes pride in providing answers to world problems, yet, paradoxically, it often makes a greater contribution by the perspicacity with which it continues to ask questions. The premature proposal of simple solutions to difficult problems often does no more than reveal ignorance.

The complex emerging patterns of international migration are a case in point. Efforts by Europe, North America, and other developed regions to shut the door on the rising tide of migrants from the Third World are not only questionable on ethical grounds but may also turn out to be impractical as well. Many migrants will find ways around all but the most costly, vigorous, and harsh control systems. This is because the very logic of social and economic change tends to create new avenues and opportunities for migrants. Just how this works is only now beginning to be understood.

Equally misguided is the argument that coordinated international development efforts and economic growth in the countries of out-migration will soon lead to a reduction in South-to-North migration. There is a considerable body of historical evidence to contradict this argument. After a long period of economic growth in the South, pressures promoting current migration trends are indeed likely to ease or stop, but in the short to medium term—over 20 to 30 years or even longer—development efforts will probably tend to increase South-North migration. This is because the mechanization and increased efficiency required to boost productivity will mean that large numbers of workers will lose their jobs. As unemployment rises, so too will the numbers of people seeking refuge elsewhere. The process may run over several decades, since even in the best possible circumstances development is gradual.

It is estimated that some 60 million people in the world are currently "on the move." This figure includes people displaced by war, civil strife, political repression, environmental catastrophe, the threat of starvation, economic hardship or the desire to better their circumstances. Some 16 million of these people are political refugees within the definition of the United Nations Charter, that is, they are individuals seeking asylum from a well-founded fear of persecution.

Potential migrants are heavily concentrated in the poor regions of the South—in the previously colonial nations of Africa, Asia, the Caribbean and Latin America, and in the southern regions of the Soviet Union. They not only move to neighbouring countries within their own regions, but, more and more, they are seeking to move to industrially advanced regions such as Europe, North America, and Australia.

The northern nations (and some migrant-receiving nations in the South) are reacting with alarm. In the North, this alarm has been fed by graphic images in the press of Haitian, Albanian, and Sri Lankan "boat people" arriving in Florida, Italy, and Canada. Some leaders are calling for the expulsion of unwelcome migrants, while others are calling for increased efforts to solve the economic problems in the sending regions so that migrant flows will be stopped at source. In some countries pressure is mounting to stop virtually all immigration.

The concerns underlying these attitudes are complex, ranging from fear that migrants will steal jobs or be a burden on social services, to xenophobia and even racism.

The "Globalization" of Trade

There is a tendency to blame current South-to-North migration on development failures in the South and indeed, the 1980s, the "Decade of Development," were marked by economic stagnation and declining levels of real per capita income in Africa, the Caribbean, and Latin America. The decade will also be viewed historically as a period of dramatic shift toward "globalization" of markets and a related global coordination of national economic policies.

Key trends, which are still under way, include globalization of production (final assembly based on parts manufactured in various parts of the world); globalization of consumer markets (goods assembled in one nation are sold in many others); the spread of "structural adjustment" programmes (to favour export-oriented development); the rise of international trading blocs (Europe, the North American Free Trade Agreement, the Southern Cone trading bloc in Latin America, etc.). Clearly globalization is not an accident. It is the result of deliberate policies promoted by the developed nations, by major international institutions, and by many less-developed countries that have taken their lead from one of the major players.

One of the principal effects of globalization has been to differentiate more sharply between the "winners" and the "losers" in economic development. Globalization and the policies supporting it have, for example, worked to benefit the fast-growing economies of the Pacific Rim (the Republic of Korea, Hong Kong, Taiwan, Singapore, Malaysia, and Thailand) because they combined political stability, progressive policies on education, low wages, and other elements to attract investors and promote exports. Mexico may gain in the near future from globalization due to the size of its labour force, industrial infrastructure, and access to the United States.

Other regions have clearly been losers in the new global trade and development game. Africa, for example, has such poorly developed economic infrastructures and such underdeveloped labour force skills that even its very low wages and geographic proximity to Europe did not attract many new investors in the 1980s. Development aid has been insufficient to fill this gap. Foreign direct investment in Africa actually declined over the 1980s, as it did in most countries of Latin America.

Third World countries that have experienced economic growth in recent decades have also generally experienced long periods of high unemployment and significant out-migration, although there are some exceptions. Puerto Rico since the 1950s, Mexico in the 1960s and 1970s, and Korea in the 1970s and 1980s, all experienced rather spectacular economic growth, while at the same time losing large numbers of workers and their families through international migration. High rates of natural population growth and the impact of mechanization in agriculture and industry created far more workers in these countries than could be absorbed in the local economy. In the late 1970s, on the other hand, Malaysia's economic growth was so fast that it actually suffered from labour shortages. This, however, was an exceptional case and cannot be taken as a general model.

Over the 1980s, a much larger number of countries lost ground economically, and rising unemployment and falling real incomes in these nations generated political crises and rising pressure for emigration. We have no crystal ball to indicate which countries will be tomorrow's winners and losers in the global development game. What does seem clear is that development in the new era of globalization will be inherently uneven and will inevitably continue to generate large pressures for international migration. The places of origin of the migrants will shift as global circumstances change.

The Environmental Impact

Poor nations with limited capital and technology are obliged to seek economic growth through export of those products they can produce cheaply and, when wood and minerals are key exports, control over the negative environmental impacts of forestry and mining tends to become lax. Similarly, the drive to be competitive lowers the state's revenues for environmental programmes, so that deforestation, brought about as poor people seek fuel or new land to cultivate or as entrepreneurs turn jungle into grazing land for cattle, continues unabated.

Environmental degradation is but one element in the interconnected web of forces tending to generate new patterns of South-to-North movement. High unemployment, the rise of an underground economy in illicit drugs, animal skins, or ivory, and international migration are all linked in this web.

The developed nations are also involved. Not only do the wealthy nations promote structural adjustment and export-driven trade policies in Third World countries (through their central role in the International Monetary Fund and other international financial institutions), but the logic of internal development patterns in countries of the North creates opportunities for migrants from the South.

An International Division of Labour

Globalization of production has reinforced an international division of labour in which scientific, technological, design, finance, management and control jobs are concentrated in the North, while labour-intensive and manual manufacturing jobs are concentrated in the South. Economic growth in the North leads to an expanding demand for low-cost service and support activities in the developed countries themselves. These are jobs which workers in the developed countries do not want, or will not take at the prevailing wage level—in building, cleaning, gardening, garbage collection, etc. This situation lends itself to the subcontracting of services to smaller companies which in turn may hire foreign-born workers, including illegal immigrants.

The demand for drugs and other illicit international commodities arises mainly in the North. This has led to a globalization of underground commerce, creating further employment opportunities in both the exporting and importing countries. Illicit commercial opportunities in the importing countries favor migrants since they are well placed to work across languages and to link vendors in their home countries with buyers in their new countries of residence.

A further effect of the globalization of trade and international commerce has been to bring about a dramatic fall in travel and communications costs. Information flows across international boundaries have increased enormously and have given rise to an unprecedented level of information in the South about informal job niches and economic opportunities in the North. This, together with the globalization of consumer products and advertising, has generated a rising demand for income and purchasing power, all of which fuels motivation of potential migrants in poor countries.

An additional level of complexity arises in some major migrant-receiving regions in the North, where the presence of large ethnic communities changes the politics of immigration. Families and ethnic groups originating in Third World countries press the state to open the door to ethnic kin. These pressures are most evident in the multi-ethnic receiving countries—the United States, Canada, and Australia.

A Changing Social and Economic World

The conclusion that current trends in South-North migration are part of a global system of changing social and economic relationships, favoured and promoted by the North, will not please those who see the current migration crisis as a process that can be stopped by stiff migration controls or by short-term development programmes.

Solutions to the current crisis must include a longer-term perspective. It must be recognized that, although international development efforts will probably reduce migration in the longer term, these same efforts will almost certainly increase pressures for South-to-North migration in the short to intermediate term.

The overall international system, and the way in which the economies of the northern countries function within it, imply at least moderate levels of international migration. Levels that are too low will be opposed internally as well as externally and will work against economic development and cooperation in the international system.

It is difficult to imagine how economic growth can take place in the South without extensive and rising trade, technical exchange, and cooperation with the North. Similarly, it is difficult to imagine how the North can achieve greater security without fair and just cooperation with the South. This mutuality of interest in the new global context will require legitimate procedures to permit the short- and long-term movement of rather substantial numbers of people from South to North as new international institutions and arrangements are forged and strains arising from uneven international development are compassionately dealt with. To imagine otherwise is to go back to a state of greater isolation of nations, conflict between states and international chaos.

Credits

ELIJAH ANDERSON, "The Code of the Streets" from *The Code of the Streets*. Originally in *The Atlantic Monthly* 273, no. 5 (May 1994): 81–94. Copyright © 1994 by Elijah Anderson. Reprinted with the permission of W. W. Norton & Company, Inc.

JOHN WARD ANDERSON and MOLLY MOORE, "The Burden of Womanhood," *The Washington Post National Weekly Edition* (March 22–28, 1993): 6–7. Copyright © 1993 by The Washington Post. Reprinted with the permission of the publishers.

RICHARD J. BARNET and JOHN CAVANAGH, "The New Division of Labor and the Global Job Crisis" from *Global Dreams: Imperial Corporations and the New World Order*, pp. 13–22. Copyright © 1994 by Richard J. Barnet and John Cavanagh. Reprinted with the permission of Simon & Schuster.

DALLAS A. BLANCHARD, "The Anti-Abortion Movement and the Rise of the Religious Right" from *The Anti-Abortion Movement and the Rise of the Religious Right: From Polite to Fiery Protest*, pp. 37–50. Copyright © 1994 by Twayne Publishers. Reprinted with the permission of the publishers.

KATHLEEN BLEE, "Women of the Klan" from *Women of the Klan: Racism and Gender in the 1920s*, pp. 27–41. Copyright © 1991 by The Regents of the University of California. Reprinted with the permission of the University of California Press.

ROBERT D. BULLARD and BEVERLY H. WRIGHT, "The Quest for Environmental Equity: Mobilizing the African-American Community for Social Change" from *American Environmentalism: The U.S. Environmental Movement, 1970–1990*, pp. 39–49. Originally presented at the annual meeting of the American Sociological Association, San Francisco, August 9–13, 1989. Copyright © 1992 by Taylor & Francis, Inc. Reprinted with the permission of the publishers.

KATHY CHARMAZ, "Disclosing Illness" from *Good Days, Bad Days: The Self in Chronic Illness and Time*, pp. 107–119. Copyright © 1991 by Kathleen C. Charmaz. Reprinted with the permission of Rutgers University Press.

DAN CLAWSON, ALAN NEUSTADTL, and DENISE SCOTT, "Money Talks: Corporate PACS and Political Influence" from *Money Talks: Corporate PACS and Political Influence*, pp. 1–14. Copyright © 1992 by Dan Clawson, Alan Neustadtl, and Denise Scott. Reprinted with the permission of BasicBooks, A Division of HarperCollins Publishers, Inc.

PATRICIA HILL COLLINS, "Black Women and Motherhood" from *Black Feminist Thought: Knowledge, Consciousness, and the Politics of Empowerment*, pp. 119–132. Copyright © 1990 by Unwin Hyman, Inc. Reprinted with the permission of the author and publishers.

RANDALL COLLINS, "Love and Property" from *Sociological Insight: An Introduction to Non-Obvious Sociology, Second Edition*, pp. 119–124, 125, 126–128, 131–139. Copyright © 1982, 1992 by Oxford University Press, Inc. Reprinted with the permission of the publishers.

PETER W. COOKSON, JR. and CAROLINE HODGES PERSELL, "Culture Capital: Curricula and Teachers" from *Preparing for Power: America's Elite Boarding Schools*, pp. 73–84. Copyright © 1985 by Peter W. Cookson, Jr. and Caroline Hodges Persell. Reprinted with the permission of BasicBooks, A Division of HarperCollins Publishers, Inc.

MARY CROW DOG and RICHARD ERDOES, "Civilize Them With a Stick" from *Lakota Woman*, pp. 28–37, 38–39, and 40–41. Copyright © 1990 by Mary Crow Dog and Richard Erdoes. Reprinted with the permission of Grove Weidenfeld.